Mr. Environment

The Willard Munger Story

Mark Munger

Duluth, Minnesota

Cloquet River Press
5353 Knudsen Road
Duluth, Minnesota 55803
cloquetriverpress@yahoo.com
www.cloquetriverpress.com
(218) 721-3213

Mr. Environment: the Willard Munger story

This story is nonfiction, based upon the author's research,
interviews, perceptions, and opinions. References to people, events, places, or
situations are colored by the views of eyewitnesses interviewed by the author, by the
historical record, by newspaper accounts of actual events, or by other source materials.

Edited by Scribendi.
Cover design concept by René Munger.
Interior design and layout by Tony Dierckins.

First Edition, 2009
09 10 11 12 13 • 5 4 3 2 1

Library of Congress Control Number: 2008905192
ISBN: 978-0-9792175-2-4

Printed in the United States of America

Dedicated to the farmers and laborers of Minnesota.
— M. M.

Contents

Part Three: Citizen Legislator

Appendix

Acknowledgments

Trying to capture the life of a man as multi-faceted and long-lived as Willard Munger, a man whose public life spanned 43 years of elected office over five decades, and whose involvement in politics began during the Roaring '20s is not a task that a part-time journalist easily undertakes. Completing the task would have been impossible but for the kind aid and assistance given to me by the surviving family members of the Munger, Zuehlsdorf and Winter families; Harry Munger, Jr., Kenneth Clamby, Will Munger, Jr., Patsy Munger-Lehr, Mary Holo and Helen Trueblood, all of whom knew and loved Willard in personal and varying ways. Each of these relatives contributed insights of and stories about Willard's early days in Otter Tail County and his involvement with both the Nonpartisan League and the Farmer-Labor Party. Without their contributions, any discussion regarding the roots of Willard's political ideology and philosophy would be sketchy at best. For their contributions to this work, I thank them and I hope that I have relayed their perceptions and memories accurately.

Old newspaper articles regarding Willard's upbringing in Friberg Township were graciously assembled by the staff of the Otter Tail County Historical Society in Fergus Falls, Minnesota. Similarly, the staff of the Minnesota Historical Society provided materials from their archives and allowed my unfettered use of an oral history compiled from interviews with Willard. Both organizations play vital and continuing roles in the preservation and dissemination of Minnesota history and are to be applauded for the work they do in this regard.

The *Minneapolis Star Tribune* and the *Duluth Herald* and *News Tribune* graciously allowed me to use excerpts from articles and editorials originally published in their newspapers. Without these contemporaneous perspectives, this work would be far less lush and detailed. In addition, the varied and exemplary writing styles of the newspaper writers and editors whose work I've included gives the book a breadth and depth that one writer, working alone, could not possibly achieve.

Many of the newspaper pieces referenced in this biography were obtained from the microfilm archives of the Duluth Public Library. The library staff assisted me in locating newspaper articles, city directories, maps and other documents. Again, the writing of this book would have been impossible but for the library's kind assistance.

Those who sat patiently, either on the other end of a telephone, or met with me in their homes or at local eateries while I stumbled through questions concerning Willard's life and legacy, provided immeasurable detail to this story. Each interviewee put flesh upon the bare bones of Willard's life. Each interviewee, whether public official or FOW (Friend of Willard), added humorous anecdotes and snippets of reality to the book. In no particular order, the following folks contributed their time and thoughts to this biography:

Walter F. Mondale, Arne Carlson, Dave Battaglia, Harry Munger, Jr., Patsy Munger-Lehr, Will Munger, Jr., Mike Jaros, Rod Searle, Dave Bishop, Heidi Lindberg, Gary Glass, Grant Merritt, Kenny Clamby, Mary Holo, Helen Trueblood, Dave Zentner, Tom Rukavina, Gerald Heaney, Larry Yetka, Al Netland, Ann Glumac, Betty Goihl, and Jackie Rosholt.

In addition, I would like to thank the kind souls who read the original manuscript of this work and provided comments, criticism and thoughtful critique to assist the author in weaning Willard's story down to manageable size. Again, without denoting significance to order, the following spent hours poring over the unedited version of this book:

Harry Munger, Jr., Jen Claseman, Mark Rubin, Dick Pemberton, John Helland, Ann Glumac, Dr. Dick Hudelson, Dr. Craig Grau, Chuck Dayton, Bill Durbin, Ann Perry-Moore, Ron McVean, Mike Jaros, Al Netland, Renata Skube, and Randy McCarty.

Thanks as well to distant relation and Zuehlsdorf descendent, Elma Zuehlsdorf Wittman for researching and providing the genealogy of Albert Zuehlsdorf.

This has been an exhausting, rewarding, frustrating and somewhat daunting project. Most of the writing of this book took place between 5 A.M. to 7 A.M. over a period of four years. Nearly every evening was taken up with editing, collating photographs and conducting interviews. Throughout all of this, my wife René, my strongest supporter, artistic collaborator, and critic, and my sons, Jack, Chris, Dylan and Matt, have remained supportive and understanding while I immersed myself in another person's life. I cannot thank them enough. Thanks also to Harry Munger, Gerald Anderson, Mike Jaros, Patsy Munger-Lehr and Will Munger, Jr. for assisting in the financing of this book.

Most importantly, I want to thank my father, Harry Munger, Jr., and my cousins Patsy Munger-Lehr and Will Munger, Jr. for entrusting Willard's remarkable story to me. I hope I got it right.

— Mark Munger
Duluth, Minnesota
January 20, 2009

As long as I live, I'll hear waterfalls and birds and winds sing. I'll interpret the rocks, learn the language of flood, storm and the avalanche. I'll acquaint myself with the glaciers and the wild gardens, and get as near to the heart of the world as I can.

Only by going alone in silence, without baggage, can one truly get into the heart of the wilderness. All other travel is mere dust and hotels and baggage and clatter.

The world's big, and I want to have a good look at it before it gets dark.

The grand show is eternal. It is always sunrise somewhere; the dew is never all dried at once; a shower is forever falling; vapor is ever rising. Eternal sunrise, eternal sunset, eternal dawn and gloaming, on sea and continents and islands, each in its turn, as the round earth rolls.

— John Muir
(excerpted from *The Mountains of California*)

Former Minnesota Governor Rudy Perpich with author Mark Munger and his uncle, Minnesota State Representative Willard Marcus Munger.

Willard & Me

When I began this project four years ago, my first thought was that I was undertaking the impossible. By writing Willard's biography, I was seeking to reduce the life of one of Minnesota's most beloved legislators, a man who served in the Minnesota House of Representatives for over four decades, to mere words, sentences, paragraphs and chapters. Chronicling Willard's impressive career seemed daunting enough. But as I started to review the archives of old newspaper articles housed at the Duluth Public Library concerning Willard's life and career in Duluth, and as I began rummaging through Willard's Personal Collection of photographs, newspaper articles, letters, speech notes and the like in the basement of his home on Indian Point, a greater fear began to assail me. How could I, a family member, distance myself from "Uncle Willard" sufficiently so as to gauge his life with a neutral eye? The more I thought about the project that loomed before me, the less I felt equipped, as a writer, as a historian, and as a human being, to tackle Willard's story. In the end, after talking to Willard's children and learning that no one else had stepped forward to write about Willard's life, I gave in to the muse and started work.

The volume you are holding is the result of, as I've said, four years of research, interviewing and writing. Whether the book measures up to the man, I'll leave to you, the reader, to decide. However, what I have tried to do in putting Willard's story together is to avoid inserting myself as a character in the narrative despite the familial ties between me, the writer, and Willard, the subject. I have tried to stay out of the way and let the records, letters, articles, interviews, photographs and Willard's own words tell his story. But, being that he was my uncle, I feel somewhat cheated in not being part of the parade of anecdotes and stories that appear in this book. This essay, then, is my bow to vanity.

Most of my early memories of Willard center around Christmas Eve dinners in the community room of the motel, where all the Munger kin gathered for roast turkey and Willard's famous giblet dressing. Willard and my dad would argue every Christmas about the dressing; whether there was enough sage or too much salt or whatever. They would also argue politics. Christmas Eve at the motel was a carnival of political bickering, familial love, loud voices, and children darting in and out of piles of carefully wrapped packages.

Then there were the famous victory parties held in the same community room of the Willard Motel. Every year, from the completion of the motel until Willard's last campaign; Willard, his friends, colleagues and supporters would gather in the basement of the motel to watch election returns on TV and celebrate another Munger victory. I missed Willard's last election night party, the one held in November of 1998, not because I wasn't interested in my uncle's success but because I was at the Blackwood's Restaurant in Proctor awaiting the results of my own campaign. Willard and I were on the ballot together that year; he for his last campaign for the House and me, for my first judicial race.

Many Saturday mornings I wandered out to the motel coffee shop to eat Willard's famous pancakes and listen to politics. I was there on any number of occasions when Governor Perpich stopped in for breakfast. What others have said about the two men is true: Rudy and Willard were down to earth. They were from common stock. They never forgot where they came from. There was no pretense about either of them and they refused to tolerate pretense from anyone around them.

Though Willard wasn't overly demonstrative with his affection, he liked kids. I remember Willard asking us to push the big wart on his forehead. We'd push the ugly thing—Willard would make a weird noise—and quarters would pop into our outstretched palms as if the wart was somehow connected to Willard's pocket full of change. He was always asking what you wanted to eat, and if you sat long enough on a stool at the lunch counter in the coffee shop, you'd soon have a four-egg Denver sandwich, a cheeseburger, a malt, or at the very least, a piece of homemade apple pie with ice cream in front of you. He stocked Nesbit's orange and grape soda and Dad's root beer in bottles. He never charged us for the pop and he rarely charged anyone he knew who drifted into the place on a Saturday morning for breakfast.

I went to work for Willard when I was in high school, both at the motel, managing the place at night while he was in St. Paul with Frances during legislative sessions, and as a laborer at his property on Indian Point. He was a fair boss but disorganized. One day, Willard told me and Ray Baker, the other kid working with me on the Point, to move a pile of railroad ties. We hauled several hundred ties from one place to another. Willard wandered down from the motel to check on us. He was furious. He wanted to know why the hell we'd moved his ties! It was always like that. He'd have me start painting a motel unit and then come and holler about the lawn that hadn't been mowed, never stopping to realize I couldn't be in two places at once. He paid me ten bucks a night to manage the motel when he was in St. Paul and he sent his mother (my grandmother) Elsie Munger over after Angie the cook had gone home just to make sure Karen (my girlfriend at the time) and I weren't "up to anything" in the living quarters behind the coffee shop where I stayed.

Willard was a gifted man when it came to woodworking. Like so many of his close friends and relatives, my wife and I are the proud owners of several beautiful black walnut picture frames that Willard painstakingly made for us. My two oldest sons received wooden cars crafted by their great uncle; elegant models crafted from Rod Searle's black walnut. Willard was working on a wooden truck for my third son when he got sick. I'm sure my fourth boy would have received his own black walnut vehicle at some point had Willard been able to beat the cancer that claimed him.

The picnics Willard held for the LCMR have been profiled by others. But what Al Netland said is absolutely true. The mixture of folks who made their way to Willard and Frances's home on Indian Point for those events was as eclectic a group of people as any one politician could assemble. Folks as well-known as Paul Wellstone and as obscure as long-time Munger friend, Oren Olson broke bread together on those sunny summer afternoons in the shade of Willard's implausible walnut trees. And Willard loved them all with equal fervor. It didn't matter who you were or what your title happened to be. Willard wanted you there. And he wanted to hear what you had to say.

Two stories come to mind. Both involve Willard and Rudy Perpich. When the recreational trail between Duluth and Carlton was going to be renamed the "Willard Munger Trail," Willard asked my dad to be part of the festivities. For whatever reason, my dad couldn't attend. So I did. When Willard saw me at the dedication, his eyes sparkled. I knew it meant a lot to him that I'd left whatever legal work I was doing to attend the celebration. My uncle put his arm around me and said, "Governor, this is my nephew. He's my lawyer. You know why he's my lawyer?" Rudy shook his head "No." "Well, I'll tell you," Willard said. "My brother Harry thinks that he's the best lawyer in the Munger family. But my brother is wrong. I've got the best lawyer in the Munger family working for me!"

The second story took place a few years later. Someone in the DFL Party got the bright idea that I'd be a natural to run against State Senator Jim Gustafson (IR-Duluth) in an upcoming election. Well, it's pretty flattering to be in your late 20s and have the governor (Rudy again) and the Senate Majority Leader (Roger Moe) calling you at home, waking you up to urge you to run for office. My wife René and I were asked to drive down to a DFL Senate Caucus event where a guy by the name of Garrison Keillor was the featured entertainment. Having been a fan of Garrison's Prairie Home Morning Show, and seeing no downside to accepting free drinks and food from a bunch of DFLers, we attended the gathering, where Garrison stood off by himself in the corner, broodily towering over everyone else, and Roger Moe badgered me about making a decision. I told Moe that I'd "sleep on it."

Since I'd been around politics my whole life, I figured that I was more or less being asked to be a sacrificial lamb for the DFL. I knew Jim Gustafson. I liked Jim Gustafson. Hell, I'd even voted for him! So I sort of knew the lay of the land. But I wanted to make sure my instincts were right. As soon as I got back to Duluth, I called Willard and asked to see him. He told me to come on out. When I got to the motel, Willard made me breakfast and I told him why I was there. He sat down, pulled hard on his cup of coffee, and considered me with those blue eyes of his.

"So they want you to run against Gustafson, do they?"

"Yep."

"You're thinking about it?"

"Yep."

There was a long pause.

"Mark, let me ask you something: Do you want your first run for office to be your last?"

Willard pretty much told me what I'd already figured out. The Party was playing me for a fool. Willard's counsel gave me the ability to say "no."

There's not much more I can tell you that others haven't already related. Willard Munger wasn't a perfect man. He could be thorny and cranky and down-right ornery. But he had a great laugh and he loved people. He treated everyone, regardless of color or creed or gender or age or circumstance exactly as he expected to be treated.

He taught me that.

And I miss him.

— Mark Munger
Duluth, Minnesota
January 20. 2009

High Ideals & Principles

I first met Willard Munger during the 1948 Democratic-Farmer-Labor (DFL) state convention. I was a young college student attending my first major political gathering and Willard was already a veteran of partisan politics, having run and lost his first race for the state legislature as a Farmer-Labor Party candidate back in 1934.

Over the years, Willard and I became personal friends, a friendship fueled, I think, in part because we shared a common background, coming as we did from rural Minnesota and from Minnesota's Progressive tradition. My own childhood, growing up in Ceylon, Heron Lake, and Elmore, Minnesota, all small farming communities located near the Minnesota-Iowa border, was spent surrounded by geography much different from where Willard hailed from. Elmore sits in platter-flat southern Minnesota, the best farm land anywhere, but where the only appreciable surface water is limited to slow, meandering streams and rivers, and where forest is only a rumor.

In contrast, Willard grew up surrounded by the hardwood forests and lakes and potholes of Otter Tail County in northwestern Minnesota, the rugged and somewhat inhospitable landscape described in Herbert Krause's "Pockerbrush" stories. It seems a certainty that the geography that nurtured Willard's childhood (along with the walks and lectures Willard endured from his paternal grandfather) prepared Willard Munger for his life as Minnesota's foremost conservation advocate.

What is most remarkable about Willard's journey as a legislator and environmentalist is that he accomplished what he did with a high school education, a limited mastery of public speaking, and a rumpled personal appearance. But behind this seemingly inept facade beat the heart of an astute politician, a true believer in government's ability to make life better for ordinary folks, and a man of high ideals and principles.

Regrettably, in this day and age when personal attack ads foretell the beginning of yet another campaign season, Willard Munger might seem to be an anachronism. But he isn't. His legacy, his most important gift to all of us in public service, from township supervisors to aspirants to the presidency, isn't the countless environmental laws he sponsored and helped enact, as important as they are, but his example of basic honesty and courage.

No greater praise can be given a man or woman in any occupation, and certainly no greater platitude can be used to describe an elected official, than this simple beatitude:

Willard Munger was a man of his word. What he said, he meant. You could bet your life, and the lives of your grandchildren on a promise made by Willard Munger.

Willard was my friend, my colleague and my political mentor. I will always cherish the time I spent with him at political conventions, in the coffee shop of the Willard Motel, and in his brother's Duluth home talking about issues of concern to Minnesotans.

Enjoy this in-depth look into the life of one of Minnesota's most underappreciated politicians, a man who was truly "Mr. Environment."

— Walter F. Mondale
Minneapolis, December, 2008

Willard Munger and Walter Mondale in a 1964 campaign brochure photo.

Part One:

Pockerbrush Boy

Father had an eighty, more than half in timber standing on the root, the rest under plow except for a few patches blanket-sized and tough with sod for grass, and the hay bottoms along the rice lake. Land so young the brown shells of roots forked up with the share and stumps lifted gray butts in the wheat; heavy with clay, most of it, like the high field south, burning to rock under July suns. Clearings on lower ground were better and the ten-acre piece by the meadow wallowed in thick wet loam.

The trees marched in from the ridges off south, miles of them, with here a cleared space and there a slash on the bark to show where a farm's end might be. Far back where second growth leaved in fainter green than older wood, loops of wire lost in the kinnikinnicks told of work begun by men, fox-hearted and with eyes elsewhere than on home-building, and timber was thick and solid and the windfalls of no account. Only the creek and the willows bordering it stopped the elms and basswood from climbing over the hog fence and taking root in our barnyards.

— Herbert Krause
(from *Wind Without Rain*)

CHAPTER 1

Beginnings

Few people alive today have heard of, much less read, author Herbert Krause's literary gems, *Wind Without Rain* and *The Thresher*, novels set in the hardscrabble farmland of northwestern Minnesota. Herbert Krause and Willard Munger shared a common place of upbringing (Friberg Township in Otter Tail County, Minnesota) a place Krause labeled "Pockerbrush" in his fiction. Though Krause was born eight years before Munger, the men co-existed for a time in the same rural family-farm-dominated landscape; their ancestors sharing a common faith (the rigidity of Missouri Synod Lutheranism) and a legacy of emigration from Germany. But though the author and the politician shared Germanic roots, it was Munger's other side, his paternal side, which weighed most heavily in his upbringing.

Willard Munger was born in a log cabin (built by his paternal grandfather, Lyman Robert Munger) on January 20, 1911. Willard's parents, Harry and Elsie Munger, lived in that cabin and farmed a 40 acre parcel of Lyman Munger's 160 acre homestead in Friberg Township. Willard was the second child in a family that included older brother Robert, younger brother Barney, younger sister Elsie, and the youngest Munger, brother Harry Munger, Jr. Though Grandpa Lyman Munger was ambitious in many ways, he wasn't much of a farmer. The same cannot be said of Willard's maternal grandfather, Albert Zuehlsdorf.

Albert Zuehlsdorf married Bertha Zahn in 1877 in Germany and immigrated with Bertha and their three oldest children, Ida, Elizabeth and Reinhold to the United States in 1882. Four other Zuehlsdorf children were born in the United States: Fred, Martha, Elsie (Willard's mother) and Linda. As was often the case in the late 19th century, three other pregnancies ended in miscarriage.

Albert Zuehlsdorf settled his family in Aurdal Township in Otter Tail County. The family's life there was described in Albert's obituary:

> Albert Zuehlsdorf, one of the pioneer citizens of Aurdal Community, died…
> from pneumonia…(He] was born in Germany and was 78 years of age…His
> marriage took place there…his bride being Miss Bertha Zahn, and they came
> to this country fifty-two years ago, arriving in Fergus Falls in October 1882.
> Mr. Zuehlsdorf located immediately in the town of Aurdal…He was an in-
> dustrious, hardworking man, and acquired four farms there, two of which he
> retained up until the time of his death…
>
> (*Fergus Falls Daily Journal*, undated.)

Albert Zuehlsdorf's real-life story is mirrored in Herbert Krause's fiction.

In *Wind Without Rain*, the harsh reality experienced by Otter Tail County
farmers is transformed by Krause's prose into a first-rate immigrant tragedy. The
driven nature of farmer Vildvogel and the tenuous existence depicted in the book
recount the struggle engaged in by Albert Zuehlsdorf as he sought to build a family
farm in his adopted home; though Zuehlsdorf's striving never became an all-en-
compassing obsession, like the greed which took hold of Johnny Black, Krause's
protagonist in *The Thresher*.

It is also significant that the Munger children (unlike the characters in Krause's
work) were spared the sternness of Missouri Synod Lutheranism:

> "Friberg Township was made up of a variety of different nationalities," Wil-
> lard Munger later recalled. "I went to the Norwegian Lutheran Church up in
> the northern part of the district even though I am not Norwegian."
>
> (*Oral History of Willard Munger*, November 23, 24, 1987 and June 10, 1988.
> Interviewer Margaret Robertson, Minnesota Historical Society, p. 40.)

Willard Munger's parents, Harry and Elsie Munger, lived their lives on the edge of
poverty, eventually leaving Lyman Munger's farm after experiencing tragedy. Willard's younger brother Barney died of scarlet fever while in his teens, an event that
was rarely, if ever, discussed by the family. "I was a replacement of sorts for Barney,"
Harry, Jr., recalls. "I was born when both my parents were up there in age."

Other family members recall the differences between the three oldest Munger
boys.

"Barney babysat me," Munger cousin Kenneth Clamby recalls. "One day,
when I was little and visiting Grandpa Lyman's place, Barney was supposed to be
watching me. I snuck off to find a place to take a nap. Barney found me sleeping in
the horse stall with the draft horses," Clamby says with a smile. "And I spent a lot of
time fishing with Robert. He loved to fish. I went to Mule Lake once or twice with

Willard but Willard wasn't much of a fisherman. He was too serious for a little kid like me. He wasn't all that much fun to be around. He never hunted much and he didn't trap. He was more interested in making things easier for the working class, trying to give them a leg up."

Cousin Mary Holo recalls that Barney "was the one everyone loved." And Robert was "a ladies' man." "Willard," Holo continues, "was the one we always asked about politics. He knew where all the bodies were buried. He was always very serious."

It must have been an immense blow to Willard (whose Christian faith was tenuous throughout his life) to witness Barney's death.

> The whole community has been shocked at the sudden death of Barney D. Munger, the youngest son of Mr. and Mrs. H.L. Munger of the township of Friberg.
>
> Barney took sick Tuesday evening with scarlet fever...In the afternoon he called his mother to his bedside and asked her to look after his setting hen... She returned in a few minutes and asked how he was...Barney answered, "O, I feel fine." With those words, he dropped into a state of coma and never regained consciousness...
>
> Barney would have been 13 years old this coming 5th of September. He was a boy of quick mind and action, a kind, friendly chap to old and young and who always spoke well of others.
>
> Everybody knew Barney. He greeted all with a most loving smile which will be missed by all his friends.
>
> He was an active boy in farm work; he raised pigs and chickens and put by money himself to help toward his high school education...
>
> His grandpa [Lyman Munger] was his standby in all his activities that he planned on his farm for his education. His great uncle, Will Armstrong, also enjoyed his cheerful company...
>
> — Mrs. Hanna J. Kempfer
> (*Fergus Falls Daily Journal,* June 6, 1925.)

Willard Munger often reflected on the contrasts between his two grandfathers.

> "I was raised in a kettle of stew," state Rep. Willard Munger, a DFLer from Duluth said years later. "I had two grandfathers and one was entirely opposite from the other."
>
> Willard, who often accompanied his father on his trips to organize farmers, said his grandfather Munger was a Norman Thomas socialist who home-steaded 160 acres of land north of Fergus Falls at the turn of the century. He

was a well-read scholar whose love of books and nature was greater than any affection he may have had for farming.

His grandfather on his mother's side was a sound farmer who had little time for politics or philosophers.

"He used to say to me, 'Willard, why do you hang around with your grandfather Munger so much? You know all he does is sit at home and read those books and preach to you all day long. You go out and look at his barn door. He props it up with a post; he doesn't even put hinges on. But he sits there and reads those damned books. I think he would like me to divide up my farm with him because of that Socialist idea he has.'"

(*The Fargo Forum*, October 3, 1999;
"Minnesota Produces Two Vice Presidents" by John Sundvor.)

Willard Munger was born at a time when man was still learning to fly and when the primary mode of transportation was by horse and buggy. The Rural Electrification Administration (the federal program that would bring electricity to family farms across America) was still two decades away. And though public education was available in Friberg Township in the form of rural country schools, Munger's parents never completed elementary school.

"Dad only had a 4th – 5th grade education," Harry Munger, Jr. recalls, "and Mom only had a 5th – 6th grade education in a German- speaking (Missouri Synod) school."

Kenneth Clamby concurs, indicating that his mother and Willard's mother "stopped going to German school in Friberg Township after 4th grade because Grandpa Zuehlsdorf made them herd cattle."

Willard Munger's first educational experience came at School No. 229 in Friberg Township. The one-room school boasted 40 kids and a single teacher for grades one through eight.

"I went to Fergus Falls High School when we moved to town, (in 1928)," Willard recalled. He eventually graduated (in 1932) from Washington High School in Fergus Falls.

"[W]hen I was young, I had some health problems. I had an operation for a ruptured appendix which kept me out of school for about a year. Then I had another operation that kept me out of school for another year. So I didn't go to high school until our folks moved to town, and I was older than the rest of them when I graduated…"

(*Oral History of Willard Munger*, ibid, p. 40.)

Though Munger desired to further his education (taking extension courses, public speaking and political science through the University of Minnesota when he lived in Otter Tail County; and attending night classes in maritime drafting after he moved to Duluth) he never obtained a college degree. Of the four Munger children who survived to adulthood, only Harry, Jr. went to college, ultimately graduating from the St. Paul College of Law with a juris doctorate degree.

> "The kind of education I got in that rural school affected my life…We had one teacher…the school board would never hire a teacher for a second term because she might ask for an increase in salary," Willard recalled. "This teacher had grades one to eight…It was impossible for her to teach everything so she'd skip grammar…This was a handicap for me when I went to high school, and I still make grammatical errors when I talk. That's because of the basics that were missing…"
>
> (*Oral History of Willard Munger*, ibid, p. 40.)

Though Munger's schooling may not have given him all the tools he needed for a life in politics, growing up a Pockerbrush Boy had other advantages.

> "I raised a lot of beans one year on the farm," Willard recalled. "I didn't like to thresh beans out by hitting them with a stick. So I went up in the granary and got a lot of my grandpa's good oak…I made myself a kind of little woodworking shop in an old building that we had on the farm. Believe it or not, I built myself a bean thresher that I ran with one of those little gasoline engines. It really worked. I had a fan on it, the shakers on it, and the things to knock down the beans. I lent it to a neighbor. I always wanted to get that thing back, but I never can remember who borrowed it. But it really worked, and everybody in the neighborhood was bragging about that bean thresher."
>
> (*Oral History of Willard Munger*, ibid, p. 59.)

Mary Holo recalls the bean thresher and other projects that Munger busied himself with as a young man.

"The old farm, Grandpa Lyman's place on the north shore of McCoy Lake, was right next to where we lived. We had a place down in the hollow, on Long Branch Creek, and Willard was always doing something constructive. He was sober and business-like about whatever he did. I was six years old," Mary recalls, "when we moved from our place up to the old farm. The remnants of the bean threshing machine were still there in the old blacksmith's shop. There was also a summer kitchen with a screen porch for cooking attached to the old house. Willard built that porch himself. He also built a kids' tree house down by the granary."

Mary Holo's mother, Margaret Munger Miller, once reminded Willard that not all his projects were as successful as the bean thresher.

> "I have an aunt about ninety-three years old," Willard recalled. "My father's sister. She's in a nursing home, and I hadn't seen her for many years...So last summer I said, 'I'm going to drive down and see her...' I walked in and said, 'Aunt Margaret, you don't know who I am, do you?' [She said] 'Why sure I know who you are. You're Willard. I remember when you built your first boat. It sank, didn't it?'
>
> (*Oral History of Willard Munger*, ibid, pp. 58 – 59.)

Though Munger's formal education was limited, he took full advantage of the political advice offered to him by his paternal grandfather.

> "My grandfather {Lyman Munger] was a great environmentalist. He used to take me on fishing trips through the woods, through the wetlands. I remember his favorite fishing lake was a lake called Mule Lake...To get to the lake, we'd have to take about a full mile walk. That took us through the swamp, through the wetlands, and through a variety of different environmental conditions. I remember when we would go through that swamp, we'd stop and look at the pink lady slippers, which are the most beautiful things you ever could look at in a swamp. It was so dark and dreary in there, and then you'd see these beautiful, big, pink lady slippers. That left an awful big impression on me because ten years later, they drained the swamp and the lady slippers died. All the vegetation died and it reverted back to more or less a wasteful piece of land.
>
> "Then we would go on to that lake there through the wetlands. We would see the ducks and the geese get up out of the wetlands like blackbirds. They would fly around and settle back down...Then we would go into Mule Lake. My grandfather would cut us off an ironwood pole, tie a string on it, and fish. Sitting there in silence, we used to talk about the environment. He would tell me, 'Now, when you grow up, you better do something to keep this in perpetuity for yourself and your children, and for you grandchildren. The only way you can do it is to do it by political action.'
>
> "He used to preach to me how important it was to become involved in politics. He would point to the huge black stumps. He said, 'They stand as monuments to the greed of the past. There used to be virgin forests here. Now it's nothing but brush land. It will be that way for the next hundred years because of man's greed and exploitation'...I guess because of my boyhood training and my grandfather's environmental and Socialist philosophy, it stayed with me. Grandpa Munger took me hunting, berry picking, fishing.

Talked about the great things of nature. How important it was to preserve the rivers, keep them clean."

(*Oral History of Willard Munger*, ibid, pp. 17 – 18.)

Harry Munger, Jr. recalls that, despite Grandpa Lyman's influence, Willard never became an avid outdoorsman.

"Willard's a lot like Fritz [Walter] Mondale when it comes to hunting. Neither one can shoot straight. It's a good thing that trait doesn't carry over into their politics," Harry muses. "My brother wasn't much of a sportsman. He and I and Martha [Willard's first wife] and my first wife Barbara were out on Big Winnie duck hunting. He'd never duck hunted as a kid but I had. So I was operating the outboard motor in a small open boat. The four of us set out. It was foggier than hell. I kept puttering around, trying to find an opening out to the lake where we could drop our decoys. Willard kept saying 'Do you know where the hell you're going?' I said 'I certainly do.' After an hour or so of chugging around with no clue where we were, we ended up back at the boat landing where we'd started. Just as we touched shore, a flock of geese kicked up and nearly took Willard's head off. He never got off a shot!

"I was the fisherman. Willard was the politician. My older brother Bob was a fisherman too, particularly trout. There was a creek, a trout stream, that ran out of Long Lake and it was full of brookies that Bob liked to fish. I don't remember Willard ever trout fishing like Bob did."

Though Grandpa Munger taught Willard much about resource conservation, environmental foresight had not been Lyman Munger's earlier legacy.

Lyman Robert Munger was born in East Rushford, Allegheny County, New York, on August 16th, 1850. He came to Minneapolis in 1873 and then worked in the Rosemount area as a field hand, binding wheat by hand in the summer, and working for Dan Day on the Prairie River near Grand Rapids on a lumber crew during the winter. He worked from 1874 – 1875 as a sled tender for G.S. Hanson on the Prairie River and Hanson Brook. During the summer for those two years, he drove logs on the Mississippi. Indians allegedly killed two of his crew while working on the Prairie River. He then went to Winnipeg, Manitoba during the summer of 1876, traveling to Winnipeg by steam boat on the Red River. Sleeping on the boat, he recalled being awakened by the squeaking of the Red River carts being drawn along the bank by a single ox. He ran a crew clearing the right-of-way for the Canadian Pacific west of Winnipeg.

Lyman Munger then returned to the States, locating in the Perham area, again employed by G.S. Hanson in a camp and driving logs through the Toad River, Ottertail Lake and into Fergus Falls via the Ottertail River. The logs arrived in Fergus on July 1, 1876 and were cut at the George B. Wright Mill. He was the foreman on a four-man crew working the Ottertail for four years. In 1878, Munger and Wm. Holmes bought the east half of Sec. 35, Salt Springs [state land] in Buse Township. In 1879, Mr. Knowles was hired to break apart the land and the first wheat crop was harvested in 1880. Munger then worked as foreman under G.S. Hanson again and took a tie drive out of the Red Eye River down the Crow Wing River to Motley. Hanson and Munger continued to work in partnership and lumbered at Lake Franklin and Lake Lizzie, cutting hardwood timber. These logs were driven down the Pelican River to Pelican Rapids. In 1882, the partnership bought the George B. Wright sawmill machinery and moved it to Pelican Rapids to saw their logs. Munger used some of the wood to build his home in Buse.

During the year 1887 – 88, Munger also ran a lumber camp for the Blake Brothers on Harley Lake. The following year, he ran a camp for Holmes and Van Ness on the Pine River. He worked the St. Paul boom for G.S. Hanson in 1889 as well. 1889 – 90 saw Lyman working for G.S. Prairie in Morrison County. Logs were hauled to the Mississippi River and he worked the job for two winters. The fall of 1890 saw Munger running a lumber camp at Fort Ripley for Lincoln Brothers.

Aside from his work in the logging profession, Lyman Munger also farmed, homesteading 160 acres of land in Sec. 17, Friberg Township. He remained on this land until his death on January 13, 1934. He was greatly interested in politics and progressive movements, and served as the treasurer for School District 31 in Buse, and Clerk of District 229, Friberg, for 15 years. He was a charter member of the Populist Party in Buse…He was also a member of the Masonic fraternity.

(Interview with Mrs. L.R. Munger, November 14, 1939.)

Much has been written about the connection between Lyman Munger's grassroots environmentalism and his grandson's seemingly inexhaustible interest in protecting the natural world. The story previously described, of Munger and his grandfather making the trek from the Munger farm to Mule Lake, has been retold countless times and is often cited as a precursor of Willard Munger's political involvement. In essence, Munger recounted that he was advised to get into politics by his paternal grandfather. But what sort of politics would a young man from Pockerbrush embrace?

CHAPTER 2

Influences

Some might say that Willard Munger was an accidental Democrat in that he was not born into the politics of the Minnesota Democratic Party. From the time of Munger's birth in 1911 until he ran for office in Otter Tail County in the early 1930s, the Democrats in Minnesota were shut out of state politics, losing every gubernatorial race between 1909 and 1930 to the Republicans, with the exception of an eight-month period when Democrat Winfield Scott Hammond was the state's 18th governor in 1915 (Hammond died in office of ptomaine poisoning and was replaced by Republican Lieutenant Governor J.A.A. Burnquist: It was an era when the lieutenant governor and governor could be elected from different parties). During two decades of Republican dominance, Munger's political philosophy and outlook were formed by forces outside mainstream politics.

> "My father was an organizer for the Nonpartisan League," Willard recounted. "And A.C. Townley was the founder of the League…The Nonpartisan League had its inception in about 1915 and lasted all the way up into the '20s. In 1918, because of the war, it began declining in power. The Farmer-Labor Party more or less was the aftermath of the Nonpartisan League."
>
> (*Oral History of Willard Munger*, ibid, p. 15.)

Willard Munger's childhood occurred during an era of tycoons and stock market speculation. It was also a time of day-to-day struggles for folks living and working on family farms. A.C. Townley's message, one of grassroots agrarian control of the essential elements of the farm market; the granaries, the railroads and the banks, touched a nerve with many despondent farmers.

> "The Nonpartisan League in North Dakota at one time was absolutely powerful under A.C. Townley's leadership," Willard recalled. "They had complete control of the legislature and they passed many legislative bills that were designed to help the farmer. As an example, they created the state-owned

flour mill, the state-owned bank, and the state-owned elevators—a lot of things that were directly related to the farm economy of North Dakota."

(*Oral History of Willard Munger,* ibid, pp. 15 – 16.)

During an interview for "Album" on Duluth's PBS affiliate in 1993 with Julie Kellner, Munger emphasized that his affiliation with the Nonpartisan League began at an early age.

"I grew up in politics," Willard recalled during the interview. "I had my first fight when I was seven years old. It was during a Nonpartisan League (NPL) campaign. I wore a button to school at a time when there were a lot of anti-NPL feelings. The parents of other kids told their kids to rip off any NPL buttons they saw. I wouldn't let the kids do that so I got into my first fight."

Arthur C. (A.C.) Townley was a political genius and the head of the North Dakota Nonpartisan movement. He was born in Minnesota, graduated from Alexandria High School, and taught school in Minnesota before moving to Beach, North Dakota where he farmed with his brother. Townley went bankrupt and became a Socialist. He originated the idea of having Socialists infiltrate the Republican Party of North Dakota. In February of 1915, Townley founded the Nonpartisan League (NPL) to run ordinary farmers as candidates within the Republican Party in local and state races. In 1916, NPL candidates won most of the seats in the North Dakota Legislature. This victory allowed the NPL to initiate changes in the social order; their 1917 legislative program included better schools, roads, civil service, minimum wage legislation, nonpartisan ballots, and state-owned utilities.

After the NPL's success in North Dakota, Townley sought to expand the movement. The problem in neighboring Minnesota was that the old line Socialists didn't want to be pragmatic. In addition, Minnesota was not strictly an agrarian economy like North Dakota. There was a pronounced urban and rural split in Minnesota's population, exacerbated by the growing size of the Twin Cities of Minneapolis and St. Paul. In addition, the Russian Revolution had occurred. With the United States' intervention on the side of the Whites against the Reds, patriotic fever caused a backlash against the Socialists and Communists in the U.S.A. But despite this backlash, there were signs that Minnesota was ready for change.

In the 1912 elections (in a state that had been dominated by the Republicans since 1861), William Taft (the endorsed Republican candidate for president) won only

19% of the popular vote while Progressive Teddy Roosevelt won the state handily, pulling in 38% of the vote to Democrat Woodrow Wilson's 32%. Socialist candidate Eugene Debs also garnered an impressive 8%.

Despite this trend towards Progressivism, after war was declared in 1917 the pacifists within the NPL were silenced by the Public Safety Commission at the direction of Republican Governor J.A.A. Burnquist. As a result, the Republicans retained all of the major state offices in the 1918 election. Though many NPLers realized that they would not be able to foster change through the existing political parties, Townley refused to admit defeat and continued to press for NPL infiltration of the Republican Party. This split between Townley's faction of the NPL (which was strong in rural areas) and more Left-leaning NPLers (located in Minnesota's cities) fostered a Republican landslide in 1920.

> "The point I am trying to make is I got my political education from my dad as a Nonpartisan Leaguer. Then all through the '20s until Olson [Governor Floyd B. Olson] came to power in 1930, I was active in campaigns just as a kid. When I was in high school, of course, I became extremely active. I ran around with Townley an awful lot..." Willard recalled. "I guess there are three people in my life who had a lot of influence on me as far as politics and the environment are concerned. One was A.C. Townley. One was Floyd B. Olson. And one was my grandfather (Lyman Munger).
>
> "You know, I grew up in an environment with kind of a Socialist background. My grandfather was a Norman Thomas Socialist, a Eugene Debs Socialist. Of course, when Roosevelt [FDR] came to power, he put them all out of business because he adopted their programs."
>
> (*Oral History of Willard Munger,* ibid, p. 16.)

Though Willard rarely cited his father as a political influence, Harry Munger, Sr. was also a force in Otter Tail County politics during the early 20th century. In an article from the *Fergus Falls Daily Journal* shortly after the kidnapping of famed aviator Charles Lindbergh, Jr.'s infant son, Harry, Sr. recounted his connection to the Lindbergh family. The aviator's father, Charles Lindbergh, Sr. had served as a Republican Congressman from the 6th District in Minnesota from 1907 to 1917. He ran for Senate in 1918 as a Progressive, and for governor as a Farmer-Laborite in 1924, the year he died.

> "I knew Charles Lindbergh when he was like any other gangling, unknown boy," said Game Warden Harry Munger while discussing the Lindbergh kidnapping today.

When Charles A. Lindbergh, Sr., ran for United States Senator in 1918 and later when he was a candidate for governor, Mr. Munger accompanied him on his campaign trips through the Ninth Congressional District. Charles A. Lindbergh, Jr., was the driver of Lindbergh's rather dilapidated car.

"There was nothing about young Lindbergh to set him off from the ordinary young man," said Mr. Munger. "He had little to say, and when stops were made the young man usually went off somewhere by himself."

Mr. Munger recalls, however, that there seemed to be a deep affection between the father and the son, though neither of them expressed this feeling in words.

"Young Charles drove the old car very carefully over some of the treacherous roads of that time and seemed to be much more interested in the mechanism of the car than in his father's politics."

(*Fergus Falls Daily Journal*, March 11, 1932.)

While this passage seems innocuous, it does illustrate Harry Munger, Sr.'s importance in the world of third-party politics. Though Charles Lindbergh, Sr. failed in his bids for higher office, he was an instrumental founder of the Farmer-Labor movement. And while Harry Munger, Sr. wasn't a politician himself, his immersion in the world of third-party politics heightened his son's affinity for the Nonpartisan League and the Farmer-Labor Party.

In addition, behind Willard Munger's political education loomed the persona of another political giant; Theodore Roosevelt. After his ascendency to the presidency in 1901 (following President William McKinley's assassination) the former vice president moved further and further to the Left, alienating the traditional Republican base that had helped elect McKinley. Roosevelt, like A.C. Townley and the Socialists admired by Lyman Munger, saw the need to take on the Eastern money interests through "trust busting" and to promote social change, including universal suffrage for women. Roosevelt's leftward shift led to his loss of the Republican nomination in 1908 to William Taft. Taft's presidential administration retreated from Roosevelt's progressive, reformist values which prompted Roosevelt to run for president in 1912. Though he won 9 of 12 primaries (fellow Progressive Robert Lafollette of Wisconsin won two; Taft won a single primary) Roosevelt was unable to capture the nomination at the Republican National Convention. Disgruntled, Roosevelt formed the Progressive Party, otherwise known as the Bull Moose Party (Roosevelt claiming he was ready for the rigors of a presidential campaign—"I'm as fit as a bull moose!") for the general election and finished second, knocking Taft out of contention but swinging the election to Democrat Woodrow Wilson.

Roosevelt, like Lafollette in Wisconsin and A.C. Townley in North Dakota was, despite wearing the Republican label, a reformer. An avid hunter and out-doorsman, Roosevelt was also the first conservationist president, setting aside vast tracts of federal land as national parks, monuments and forests. And, despite his participation in the Spanish-American War, Roosevelt was interested in calming world tensions. He received the Nobel Peace Prize in 1906 (the first president to do so) for his efforts in ending the Russo-Japanese War. Roosevelt's influence on re-formist political groups cannot be overstated. The fact that a third-party candidate could come within a whisker's breath of capturing the White House proved mighty attractive to Progressives and Liberals of all stripes.

During the 1920s, Willard Munger battled physical maladies, the loss of his be-loved younger brother Barney, and moved with his family from his grandfather's log cabin to a house in Fergus Falls. The move took place in 1928, just ahead of the Crash in October of 1929, the event that plunged the United States into the Great Depression.

"Dad went to work selling Woodman Insurance," Harry Munger, Jr. recalls. "But he only had a 4th-5th grade education so he wasn't much good at it. He also went to work soliciting memberships in the Nonpartisan League. He'd pretty much given up farming. He wasn't much good at that either."

Harry, Jr. also remembers A. C. Townley coming to their house in town to talk strategy with Harry, Sr. "A.C. Townley was a big, powerful-looking man," Harry Jr. recalls. "He always gave me a nickel for an ice cream cone when he came to visit. Then after Floyd B. Olson was elected governor in 1930, Dad was appointed game warden, becoming the Senior Game Warden of the region in 1931."

That appointment didn't deter Harry, Sr.'s political involvement as he con-tinued to travel around Otter Tail County soliciting memberships in the Farmer-Labor Clubs (local affiliates of the state-wide Farmer Labor Association). "Times were very, very tough," Harry Jr. relates. "Even with Dad working as a warden, we got help from relatives out on the farm in the form of donated food. Our parents also had a big garden in town, nearly an acre. Money was very tight," Harry, Jr. reminisces. "Many of the relative kids on both sides came to live with us in town to complete their educations at Fergus Falls High School. Our house had three upstairs bedrooms and an outhouse. While it was wired for electricity, it barely had power. We used pennies in the fuse box as fuses. It didn't have a cement floor in the basement; only dirt."

The Farmer-Labor Association of Minnesota drafted and adopted its constitution on March 20, 1925. The constitution was amended at various times but its essence is preserved in the following excerpt from the original document.

> **Article I. Name and Purpose.**
>
> Section 1. The name of the organization shall be the Farmer-Labor Association. Its purpose shall be to unite the members of all farmer, labor, and other kindred organizations and unorganized elements which support independent political action by economic groups, into political association; and to carry on an extensive program of education and organization incidental to participation in the political campaigns of the Farmer-Labor movement...
>
> (Willard Munger Personal Collection.)

During the late 1920s, Willard Munger resumed his education (which had been delayed due to illness) and continued his political involvement.

> "I was a real activist...All the way through high school...I was nicknamed 'A.C.' I thought the world of Townley. I really did. I saw him as the most powerful man in the world...," Willard recalled. "During the Depression years, the Norman Thomas Socialist party was quite strong in Minnesota... We had a Socialist mayor in Minneapolis and one in St. Paul...Getting back to Townley again, (he) was arrested during WWI as being Pro-German, disloyal and all that. That's what brought the defeat of the Nonpartisan League. Everybody was hysterical as far as patriotism was concerned. If you didn't believe a certain way, if you even were a mild Socialist or even thought in that direction—you were disloyal—you were not a good patriotic American...So [Townley] was jailed..."
>
> (*Oral History of Willard Munger,* ibid, pp. 20 – 21.)

Munger's memory of the situation is accurate. Though Townley continued to press for the organization of rural Minnesotans under the NPL banner, his efforts were lost amidst a swirl of activity by the Farmer-Laborites. With the decline of Townley's power and the ineffectiveness of the Nonpartisan League to galvanize itself into something more than an agrarian movement; with the Republican Party in Minnesota remaining aligned with the conservative, non-progressive wing of the National

Party; and with the Democrats in Minnesota unable to garner any serious support, two disparate groups, the farmers and the labor unions began to form alliances.

Both the farmers and the industrial workers in Minnesota shared a similar fate during the post-war period. In rural Minnesota, years of successive drought and bad harvests caused small family farms to face foreclosure at an unprecedented rate. Jobs were scarce and wages were low in Minnesota's cities due to the influx of men coming back from the Great War. The result was a melding of disenfranchised farmers and workers into the Farmer-Labor Party, which became the Farmer-Labor Federation, ultimately becoming the Farmer-Labor Association (FL).

Furthering the prospects for change was the fact that Townley, having become a millstone to reform due to his arrest and detention as a pro-German organizer during the war, resigned as the president of the Nonpartisan League. The Democrats, seeing no opportunity for success in the 1922 elections, approached the FL with a proposition: They would forego a candidate to the United States Senate and back the candidacy of Henrik Shipstead, the FL candidate, in hopes of capturing the seat.

Shipstead, a Glenwood, Minnesota dentist, proclaimed that he was going to establish a "new deal" for Minnesota farmers (the phrase would be co-opted by Democrat Franklin Delano Roosevelt a few years later). Shipstead (who pledged that he would work for the "little men and women") aligned himself with Progressives of every political stripe (including the remaining Bull Moosers) and won. Shipstead's election fueled other successes, including FL victories in two of Minnesota's nine congressional districts and in one state-wide office (Clerk of the Minnesota Supreme Court).

Adopting Shipstead's moderate reform agenda, Magnus Johnson defeated Republican Governor Jake Preus in the special election in 1923 for Minnesota's other U.S. Senate seat. Though rising FL star Floyd B. Olson's 1924 gubernatorial bid fell short, the FLers claimed three of the nine Minnesota Congressional seats; and with the advent of universal suffrage, new women voters helped elect FL candidate Myrtle Cain to the Minnesota House of Representatives in 1922.

Willard Munger's freshman report card from Washington High School in Fergus Falls included final grades of 77 in English, 84 in general science, 93 in joinery, 86 in mechanical drawing, 75 in algebra, and 82 in physical training. His sophomore work during the 1929 to 1930 session (when he concentrated on "scientific" course work) wasn't as strong. Munger's highest grade for the year was an 82 in biology, with his other grades being a 75 in 2nd year English, an 80 in geometry, and a 77 in modern history. Though not stellar, his performance allowed him to graduate from high school in June of 1932.

> "[I] went to high school and graduated right into the midst of the Great Depression. When I got out...there was no work to be found, so I finally went to work for the Standard Oil Company managing one of their stations," Willard recalled. "I was just barely able to buy food. That's about all it amounted to."
>
> (*Oral History of Willard Munger,* ibid, p. 41.)

Munger's recollection of the economics of running the service station is borne out by his financial records. A ledger from September of 1933 shows Munger drawing a base salary of $70.00 and a commission of $145.67 for a total gross monthly wage of $215.67 at the gas station. His salary was reduced by various amounts, including advances, cash shortages, and personal fuel purchased on credit, in the amount of $67.97, making Munger's take-home pay for the month $147.70. Presuming a 40-hour-work-week (which doesn't take into account nighttime or Saturday hours) Munger made less than a dollar an hour. This reality is also reflected in the young man's bank account at the Fergus Falls National Bank and Trust Co. His checking account balance as of October 18, 1933 was exactly 18 cents!

The economic hard times prompted Munger to remain active in Townley's agrarian movement even after the Nonpartisan League ceased to be a factor.

> "[A]fter I got out of high school, I became active in the farm organization known as the Farm Holiday Association. The Farm Holiday Association was organized to protect farmers from losing their farms. It organized the farmers," Willard remembered. "When the banks would advertise a foreclosure sale, the farmers would all get together and go to the sale. When the banker came out to hold the...sale, they kept the bidding down. As an example, they would bid ten cents for a cow, five cents for a pig, and so forth. Anybody who wanted to take advantage of that would be surrounded and squeezed a little bit...so his bidding would stop in one heck of a quick hurry. My job, especially when Townley was conducting the meetings, was to pass around the hat and collect enough money to pay off the bank. So, for example, if the bank had a $10,000 mortgage, we'd settle with the bank for about a $150 or...less..."
>
> (*Oral History of Willard Munger,* ibid, p. 41.)

Willard Munger was, above all else, a pragmatist. This is not to say he was someone whose views changed to suit public opinion. Hypocrisy and flip-flopping on issues were traits Willard Munger avoided over the entirety of his long political career. Munger's political pragmatism likely developed as he watched Townley's reformist agenda fail to gain momentum in Minnesota. By witnessing Townley's downfall, Willard Munger learned the importance of compromise in one's political strategy, if not in one's ideals.

It is also probable that Munger's common-sense approach to politics was influenced by observing men and women of all political stripes and backgrounds hash out the principles and ideals of the Farmer-Labor Association during the FL meetings and conventions he attended.

With his first political challenge looming, Willard Munger was young, optimistic and ready to espouse carefully-honed Liberal principles, principles learned at the knee of his grandfather, his father, his mentor, and a powerful orator who would captivate the state and the nation with his third-party win in the 1930 Minnesota gubernatorial race.

CHAPTER 3

The Farmer-Laborites

Following his graduation from high school, Willard Munger continued to work at the Standard Oil station in Fergus Falls. He also increased his involvement with the Farm Holiday movement: Farm Holiday adherents not only used peer pressure to stop farm auctions and foreclosures; they relied upon farm strikes to protest low farm prices. Violence broke out in Minnesota surrounding these strikes, which caused newly elected Farmer-Laborite Governor Floyd B. Olson to disassociate himself from the movement.

The Farm Holiday Association was actually an offshoot of the Farmers' Union, a cooperative association that owned grain elevators and mills throughout the Midwest. The Association garnered its first public attention on September 9, 1931 when, at a governor's convention being held in Iowa, Farm Holiday supporters threatened to call a sixteen-state strike unless their demands were met. The demands included:

- A floor on farm commodity prices;

- A moratorium on farm foreclosures and repossessions; and

- The refinancing of farm loans at affordable interest rates.

Though Floyd B. Olson had been elected Minnesota's governor in 1930 as a Farmer-Laborite, he didn't approve of the Farm Holiday Association's tactics. While supporting the farmers' *right* to strike, Olson never supported *the strikes* themselves. Though Olson's opposition to the strikes didn't cost him subsequent elections, his use of force (to drive off picketers and disburse camps of disgruntled farmers) did cost him votes. (*The Political Career of Floyd B. Olson* by George H. Mayer; University of Minnesota Press, 1951.)

To say that Willard Munger idolized the handsome and dashing Depression-era governor would be an understatement. As Townley's inability to adjust to changes in Minnesota's political landscape became apparent, Munger realized that Floyd B. Olson had the tools to become a factor on the national political stage. Olson also possessed a compelling personal history. Olson had been a longshoreman (and briefly, a member of the International Workers of the World) while living in Seattle, Washington before returning to Minnesota and enrolling in night law school. After obtaining his juris doctorate in 1915, Olson worked as an Assistant County Attorney in Hennepin County. Olson was one of the Committee of 48 who drafted Robert Lafollette, Sr. (the Progressive Senator from Wisconsin) to run as a third-party candidate for president in 1920. Tabbed to replace a corrupt Hennepin County Attorney by the Hennepin County Board, Olson ran successfully for county attorney in 1922 and 1926. Building a reputation as tough on crime and as a reformer (Olson battled the Ku Klux Klan and fought for labor rights) Olson sought the support of the Democrats for a Congressional bid. When he wasn't endorsed by the Democrats, Olson switched his allegiance to the newly formed Farmer-Labor Federation (the name was later changed to Farmer-Labor Association to end rumors that the group was Communist) and became the fledgling party's candidate for governor in 1924, narrowly losing that race to Republican Theodore Christianson.

Olson ran again for governor in 1930. Using an "All Party" strategy to attract supporters away from the Democrats, the Republicans and the Socialists, Olson managed to appeal to the progressive elements of all three to win. In his first term as governor, Olson proposed progressive legislation regarding the establishment of the St. Lawrence Seaway (to benefit the Port of Duluth), standardization of the state budget, improvement of inland waterways, protection for investors, farm reform, tax reduction, opposition to anti-labor legislation, appointment to state employment by merit and opposition to railroad mergers.

Olson's surprising victory in 1930 (assisted in large part by Henrik Shipstead's reluctant endorsement of Olson—Shipstead was wary of Olson being "too liberal") gave the new governor a mandate for change, though the exact extent of his power to bring about change was problematic.

> Undoubtedly, Olson had received a great mandate from the people. But it was not clear what this mandate entitled him to do. During the campaign, he had been all things to all men. He had spoken words of encouragement to radicals and conservatives alike. He had insisted that farmers, laborers and independent businessmen possessed similar interests…Those who voted for

him did so primarily to express protest against depression rather than to endorse his doctrine of intergroup solidarity.

(*The Political Career of Floyd B. Olson*, ibid, pp. 55 – 56.)

In addition to Olson's opposition to the Farm Holiday movement, a position that put him directly at odds with young Willard Munger's personal views, the two men's philosophies clashed on another matter; political patronage.

Due to the patronage system that was in place when Olson took office in 1931, the hiring and firing of state employees was an issue that Olson needed to address immediately upon taking office. Olson attempted to make a gradual switch to a more merit-based system of public employment. Rather than replace all the Democrats and Republicans holding state jobs (from commissioners of the major departments to the janitors sweeping the halls of the Capitol) with FL loyalists, Olson replaced only *some* of the commissioners and department heads with his followers and allowed them to use discretion as to whether or not employees with other political affiliations should be retained. This progressive approach immediately angered Olson's FL supporters who viewed their victory in November of 1930 as a mandate for rewarding loyal FLers with state jobs.

The issue of political patronage affected the Munger family. At the time of Olson's election in 1930, game warden jobs located throughout the state were expected to be snatched up by FL loyalists who had supported the new governor. Caving in to party pressure, Olson ultimately fired all the game wardens in Minnesota and replaced them with FL applicants. The Izaak Walton League (its members were predominantly Republican) protested and claimed Olson was "playing politics with wildlife." In a sad turn of events, one of the discharged wardens, a veteran of WWI, became so upset over the loss of his job that he committed suicide, prompting the American Legion to allege that Olson had violated Minnesota's Veterans' Preference laws. The furor eventually died down and Olson's appointment of Harry Munger, Sr. as a game warden in Otter Tail County stuck for the better part of a decade.

"I suppose I'll have to go back to the first time I met Floyd B. Olson. My father, like I told you, was very active in organizing the Nonpartisan League—he was one of their top organizers. I think it was 1924 when my father took me to the *Fergus Falls Free Press*, their Farmer-Labor newspaper, to meet Floyd B. Olson. He was running for governor," Willard recounts, "on the Farmer-Labor ticket and got beat...He had a wonderful speaking ability," Willard continued. "I don't think there's anybody I've ever met who even comes close...A lot of people say Hubert Humphrey was a great orator, but there is no comparison…When Hubert talked, you always used to think of a trip hammer. He talked so fast that you didn't remember everything he said…Floyd B. Olson, on the other hand, was just exactly the opposite. He had a really deep booming voice, and he talked with such strong conviction that you listened carefully and remembered every single word he said."

(*Oral History of Willard Munger,* ibid, p. 50.)

Though Olson frowned upon some of the tactics Munger and the other Farm Holiday members employed, Olson was pragmatic and understood the frustrations of the rural citizenry.

"[H]e wasn't as radical as his talk," Willard recalled. "[H]e could analyze the situation, he could analyze people. He knew what to say at the right time and he said it so eloquently that people never forgot what he said. He ran on the Farmer-Labor ticket, but his real strength was in the ability to take disgruntled Republicans, disgruntled Democrats—and there were a lot of them at the time of the Depression—and put together a so-called All Party Committee…He ran on the Farmer-Labor ticket but he wasn't as radical as the Farmer-Labor Party was…"

(*Oral History of Willard Munger,* ibid, p. 51.)

Even though Olson wasn't supportive of the Farm Holiday movement, he didn't turn a blind eye towards Minnesota's farmers.

When a farm was to be auctioned off at a sheriff's sale, agents notified all farmers in the township when the sale would take place…[S]ilent men would filter into the county courthouse, filling it so full that the sheriff was unable to get through…Finally, a Farm Holiday spokesman would urge the sheriff to phone the governor for a postponement…[H]e usually acted on this advice and found that Olson would grant the necessary permission…

(*The Political Career of Floyd B. Olson,* ibid, p. 124.)

Olson did more than simply postpone foreclosures: He supported federal legislation to impose a moratorium on farm repossessions. And when violence continued to break out due to confrontations between farmers and law enforcement at foreclosure sales, Olson issued a proclamation halting foreclosures in Minnesota. (*Minneapolis Star Tribune,* October 21, 1979.)

Olson also weighed in, though somewhat reluctantly, on a major conservation issue. The Minnesota and Ontario Paper Co. wanted to develop hydroelectric power by establishing dams in the Rainy Lake watershed on the Minnesota border with Ontario, Canada. The dams would have raised the water level of Rainy and other border lakes by varying levels, from five to eighty feet. The Izaak Walton League established the Quetico-Superior Council to fight the proposal. At the same time, Minnesota Power, an electrical utility in Duluth, sought to establish the Gabbro Lake Project which would have had a similar adverse impact on other northeastern Minnesota lakes. Olson supported the Shipstead-Nolan Act, the forerunner of the Boundary Waters Canoe Area Wilderness. The federal act was buttressed by state legislation barring further damming of border area lakes and rivers.

Olson also supported efforts to create new state forests for recreation, hunting, and timber management during his first term as governor. Olson's conservation positions doubtlessly caused Willard Munger to become more deeply involved in the Farmer-Labor Club of Otter Tail County. Still, there was friction between Olson and former Nonpartisan Leaguers.

> "It [the All Party machine] was a powerful vehicle for him to use, but it caused a lot of problems after the elections. Those were the days of the spoils system and jobs were given out, to a great extent, based upon your party affiliations. The problem was that when it came to the top jobs, the All Party machine had the people with the best education and the most experience in business. So they got the top jobs. The Farmer-Laborites had to pick themselves up and that created a very big fight," Willard recalled. "Townley said to me, 'We've got to organize a committee that's going to force the governor into recognizing the Farmer-Laborites. There's just as many intelligent Farmer-Laborites as there are in this All Party group. ' So we organized," Willard continued, "...what we called the Committee of One Hundred. A.I. Johnson was chairman of that committee. He was a legislator and later became the first DFL Speaker of the House when I was first elected [in 1954]. The Committee of One Hundred, led by Townley and...Johnson met with Governor Olson, and I came along. We didn't get a very good reception because Olson despised Townley."
>
> (*Oral History of Willard Munger*, ibid, p. 51.)

The meeting was also an attempt by the group to make the new governor realize his personal life wasn't helping his reputation.

> Floyd...proved to be personable and provocative. As governor, he was a strong drinker and womanizer. Munger said he and a delegation of other *Farmer-Labor Leaders* urged Olson to tone down his extra-curricular activities...
>
> ("Minnesota Produces Two Vice Presidents," ibid.)

After Olson's success in 1930, Townley gave up his attempts to formulate his own political power structure.

> Among the candidates for congress was Arthur C. Townley, "czar" of North Dakota politics during heyday of the Nonpartisan League, whose will made or broke public officials. He filed for a Farmer-Labor nomination, sharing a place on the party primary ticket with 31 other party satellites.
>
> (*Fergus Falls Daily Journal*, May 12, 1932.)

Though both Townley and Olson campaigned under the FL banner, there was little love between the two men.

> "You know, there wasn't any real competition there," Willard remembered. "[B]ut I suppose Olson looked back on Townley's ability to organize and realized that there was potential there for political competition...There was no friendship between the two of them at all...[But] we [the Committee of One Hundred] did succeed in raising so much fuss about it [the patronage issue] that Olson did finally concede. After the election of 1932 [which Olson won], he [Olson] found out that all the holdovers he had allowed to stay in were disloyal to him. They went out and worked for all the Republican candidates. Even some of the fellows working on the highways—the maintenance people—would have their posters with them. They [the Committee of One Hundred] worked out an agreement with the Farmer-Labor committee when I.C. ["Dutch"] Strout was secretary that the smaller jobs would have to be approved by the county committees...
>
> "That's where I came into the picture—not only as chairman of the county organization, but also as secretary of the Farmer-Labor Club [of Fergus Falls], the biggest in the county. From then on, most of the jobs were delegated through the committee structure. I have letters dealing with that...[but] I am reluctant to turn them over to the historical society because there are some sad stories in those appointments and dismissals. But if you look at it, the Farmer-Laborites were walking the streets with no jobs trying to change the system and seeing people holding onto jobs who were perpetuating the system that put them out on the street...
>
> "Olson...felt a little bit obligated to keep the old holdovers. He was elected in 1930, and thought that by keeping them on until the 1932 election, they would all be working their heads off for him. It turned out just exactly the opposite. They all went out against him because everybody thought he was just a one-term governor—that all they had to do was defeat him the second time and their jobs would be secured. The holdovers worked harder against Olson in '32 than they

did in 1930. In 1930, they didn't pay much attention to the election because no
one thought a Farmer-Laborite could beat the Republican Party...."

(*Oral History of Willard Munger,* ibid, pp. 51 – 52.)

In reality, there was little difference between Townley and Olson when it came
to political ideology. Townley's 1932 campaign for Congress included a brochure
entitled "The Real Cause of Hard Times: Starvation in a Time of Plenty," which
outlined his platform.

> Who commands that you pay interest? Your religion condemns it-your God
> forbids it. Only man made law-during the last 300 years-permits interest-
> money lender made law. MAN MADE LAW CAN BE REMADE. The
> money lenders' law can be repealed....LET THE NATIONAL CONGRESS
> DECLARE A TEMPORARY MORATORIUM FOR ONE TO FIVE
> YEARS-NO INTEREST AND NO FORECLOSURES...
>
> How foolish for 120 million people, after they labor and produce all the
> good things they need to live on, to permit a few friends (?) to fix a price on
> their own product for an amount twice as much as they get for producing the
> stuff, and then to borrow the difference of these benefactors (?) so they can
> eat the food and wear the clothes they made for themselves? The day comes
> when monopoly and money must be servants of all the people-if the people
> are to live. And the day is here, now...

> (From the pamphlet "The Real Cause of Hard Times: Starvation in the Midst of
> Plenty "by A.C. Townley; Willard Munger Personal Collection.)

The reformist ideals announced in Townley's political literature echoed the 1934
FL platform.

> The preamble of the Farmer-Labor platform embodies two distinct programs;
> one of which can be attained by voluntary action and without legislative pro-
> cedure-a "cooperative organization"; the other which may be enacted when
> the people adopt it by referendum vote—"public ownership. "
>
> Sweden, Norway, and Denmark have been scarcely affected by the world-
> wide collapse of the existing order of economics because each has closely
> approached a cooperative commonwealth. In these nations, industries deal-
> ing with necessities are owned by the people through cooperative societies.
> Transportation, communication, and power utilities are state owned...
>
> The Farmer-Labor Party is opposed to state ownership and operation of
> small businesses...It seeks to protect small businesses from destructive com-
> petition of monopolistic institutions...

> (1934 Farmer-Labor Platform; Willard Munger Personal Collection.)

Unfortunately, Floyd B. Olson was unaware of the exact contents of the 1934 FL platform, which were far more radical than Olson's own views. Historians generally consider Olson to have been a compromiser; someone who tried to bring Minnesota to prosperity by charting a course between Progressivism and Socialism. Though he supported limited governmental control of some industries (utilities for example) Olson sought to use governmental restrictions rather than state ownership to control industry. He was more attuned to cooperativism and less inclined to collectiveism. (www.geocities.com/CapitolHill/Senate/8713/politics.)

Willard Munger recounted Olson's surprise at learning the contents of the 1934 Farmer-Labor platform.

> "It was 1934, during the height of the Depression, with the Farm Holiday Association stopping the farm sales. There was a lot of unrest and a lot of people out of work. The Farmer-Labor convention, to which I was a delegate, met in St. Paul. I was also a member of the credentials committee. Sigmund Slonim of Duluth was chairman of the platform committee. The discussion at the time was about the really socialistic planks in the platform. The real left wing group—the Socialists—had control of the convention…Olson had to go to Washington to meet with Roosevelt. Sig Slonim happened to be a real close friend of mine. Olson came in and handed Sig some papers—I remember it as if it were yesterday—and said 'Sigmund, this is the platform I'd like to have…' Sigmund took the papers and stuck them in his inside pocket and thanked the governor.
>
> "While [Olson] was in Washington…we adopted the most radical, Socialistic platform that's ever been adopted…It called for public ownership of… everything. It came out of the platform committee with Sigmund's own approval and passed the convention by a slight margin. When…Olson came out of Roosevelt's office, the reporters said, 'Governor, do you support the Farmer-Labor platform as adopted?' Thinking it was the one he gave Sigmund, he said, 'Gentlemen, I support it one hundred percent.' He spent all the rest of the campaign [explaining]…the platform, but he never refuted it…"

> (*Oral History of Willard Munger,* ibid, pp. 52 – 53.)

Floyd B. Olson constantly battled radical elements in his All Party coalition, including those that leaned even further to the Left than the 1934 platform.

> "During the…convention…I was on the credentials committee," Willard recalled. "The Dunne brothers were there. They had led the big Teamsters strike in Minneapolis…They were both Trotskyites…The Commies had a

small following. They were small but they were awful noisy. Don't confuse
the Commies (or the Trotskyites) with the Socialists because they were bitter
enemies. The Commies say that all the Socialists do is prolong the agony—
that they are staving off the revolution....

"[We] had a bitter, bitter fight. Of course, most of the members of the
credentials committee were afraid of these Trotskyites, so there was a tie
vote. I voted to seat the Trotskyites, and they were eventually seated...I have
a picture in my files...The credentials committee was [depicted]... sitting
with the Trotskyites. I'm in that picture. Funny somebody in my [later cam-
paigns] didn't use it [against me]. But they never did..."

(*Oral History of Willard Munger,* ibid, p. 54.)

Olson's popularity compelled the Republicans to seek an alliance with an unlikely
bedfellow.

We believe that the issue in the coming state campaign is between Socialism
and Capitalism and that those who believe in individualism should fight side
by side whether they be Republicans or Democrats. We recommend to our
delegates to the coming state Republican convention at Minneapolis, that an
effort be made to ensure cooperation between the Republican and Democratic parties in the coming state campaign.

(*Fergus Falls Daily Journal,* April 9, 1934.)

Liberal, Socialist or Progressive, whatever label one wishes to put on the four two-
year terms FL governors served during the Great Depression (it wasn't until 1964
that the governor's term was extended to four years), it's clear that the period from
1930 through 1938 (six years of Olson's rule and two of his successor, Elmer Benson) marked a big change in the political philosophy of most Minnesotans.

Why does Minnesota spend so much? We can begin with those blasted winters, devourers of heating and snow removal budgets. Add our tendency to
live slow and die old, thus outlasting our life savings and falling back on state
subsidized Medicaid payments. Our high graduation rate means more students stay in school, and this requires more teachers and more spending...

Don't forget the Minnesota tradition since statehood of "do something"
government. Or the Depression-era rise of the liberal Farmer-Labor Party,
which permanently altered the state's political climate....Minnesota's political leaders never hesitated to reach for the pocketbook in response to perceived problems, from bailing out farmers victimized by locust plagues in the

late 1800s to getting into the day-care business in the 1980s. Minnesota was one of the first states to extend voting rights to blacks [1868] and along with Wisconsin and New York, the first to install a highly progressive income tax [1933]…

"We do things a little differently here," said Russell Fridley, recently retired director of the Minnesota Historical Society…

"As long as I sit in the governor's chair, there is not going to be any misery in this state if I can humanly prevent it," [Floyd B.] Olson once said…

(*Minneapolis Star Tribune*, January 29, 1988.)

However instrumental the 1934 FL platform was in forming Minnesota's Liberal political tradition, Olson and other moderates within the Party were worried that the platform might derail Olson's re-election bid. Consequently, Olson did all he could to marginalize the document.

No State Ownership of Stores, Small Businesses, Nor of Private Property

To clarify the intent and purpose of the Farmer-Labor platform, and to state those purposes free from the mass of misinformation and deliberate misrepresentation of Capitalist newspapers and Capitalist politicians, the State Committee of the Farmer-Labor Association of Minnesota has prepared an analysis. It sets forth clearly what parts of the platform can be enacted by the state legislature, what parts must go to the people on referendum, and what portions are recommendations to the national government…

(*Farmer-Labor Leader*, May 15, 1934.)

CHAPTER 4

The Gold Net

Willard Munger was a handsome young man, with piercing blue eyes, a quick smile, an understated sense of humor and a lean profile. Serious and political, there is little evidence that he spent much time pursuing the opposite sex. But shortly after his graduation from high school, Munger met a young woman who captured his attention. Her name was Gina Volden. The only surviving evidence of their connection is a single letter.

August 5, 1932

Dearest Willard:

Sorry dear that I didn't write to you before. I do admit it was not nice of me not to go over and see you before I left…I stayed for the State Fair at Fargo the Monday before I had to go back. Took the train from there to the Cities and just couldn't stop off at Fergus because I had to work Tuesday night.

Last night I got the Photo. And you know I could hardly sleep all night thinking of you and how nice to get it…

I'll have a picture taken so I can send you one too. Wonder if it would thrill you getting mine as it did me when I got yours. After the nurse had handed me the parcel I still expected a letter. Thinking she had it and just wanting me to ask. Was surprised when I received the FL Leader. Read it all through and think it's a fine paper. Now I only wish more people were interested in politics.

This is the third day I've spent in bed with a bad cold…Funny time to have a cold, eh? Will get up in the morning and work in the evening. It's so hard writing in bed so you must excuse my writing. Have ear phones on, this is just what I heard on the radio: "Oh gosh, we only walked. Oh gosh, we only talked. But in the satisfaction of holding my honey's hand…" It brings back fond memories of when we last were together. Wonder when I'll see you again.

When I get off duty every morning I go out swimming with about five or six other girls. I sure do love to dive and swim. Believe I could almost live in the water. I look dark as any Indian you'd see. Just as bad as my patients who take sun all day for their TB infected bones.

I take steam inhalations for the cold. It sure does its stuff.

What are you doing now days? Do you still paint? Are you going to school this fall?

Hope to hear from you soon. With a heart full of love and oceans of hugs and kisses.

Gina Volden

In 1932, the simple act of giving a person of the opposite gender your graduation picture was a sincere gesture. But apparently distance and time cooled whatever affections had heated up under the hot Otter Tail County summer sun. There is no record that Willard Munger and Gina Volden ever reconnected.

Willard Munger's sister Elsie had a friend by the name of Martha Winter. Eventually little Martha Winter's comings and goings around the Munger house caught Willard's eye.

"Dad always loved Mom," Willard's daughter, Patsy Munger-Lehr recalls. "It was a love like you see in old movies. He couldn't keep his hands off her. As a young woman, I found that embarrassing. But he really loved her. She was his lady slipper (the Minnesota state flower) and he kept a picture of a lady slipper with her photo in his wallet."

Helen Trueblood (Martha's sister) remembers that Willard pursued his one true love with determination. "Willard really wanted to date Martha," Trueblood recalls. "He wanted to go steady. Martha had lots of friends because she was smart and good looking. She eventually scorned all others to date Willard…It was a love story for their whole lives."

Willard's son, Willard ("Will") Munger, Jr. agrees.

"I never remember my parents fighting," Will says. "Their marriage was solid. That they would ever split up wasn't a thought. Dad had great respect for Mom."

State Representative Mike Jaros (DFL-Duluth) adds that, long after Martha's death and Willard's remarriage to Francis Herou in 1964, Willard remained devoted to his first wife. "He always talked about Martha. She was his high school sweetheart, his one great love."

Former legislative committee administrator, Ann Glumac, recalls being told years later by Munger that the reason he returned to high school after graduation to take post-graduate courses (including a class in shorthand) was "to see Martha."

At the beginning of their courtship, Willard and Martha wrote to each other constantly. Willard preserved the couple's correspondence in an old cigar box. The box remained in Willard's possession until his death. The letters begin with Martha Winter recounting a dance the two attended shortly before Willard's twenty-second birthday.

> January 8, 1933
>
> Dear Willard,
>
> You asked me to write and I think I should have after last nite. Say, you know I feel so darn blue. I don't know why. I did have a good time but I feel as tho I hurt your feelings…Well, Willard, you know there's a streak of devilry in me and when I get going, I am the berries. Sometimes I'm as shy as can be, but I sure can get full of the dickens…You know why I think you were hurt? Because you went in the other room and played cards. You never came out and danced with me…
>
> Say, can you feature this: I never got a scolding for being out late. Gee, I could have jumped over the moon. All my dad said was: "Did you have an accident?" I said no…I told them about the party and the Dueno boys and they [my parents] asked me how many dances I gave you…My dad said "Yes, it's just like you to dance more with the good for nothings than a fellow who knows something…" Boy I'm glad he likes you…Remember what I told you last nite? Well always remember that and then you'll know what I really think in my heart…
>
> Bye, all my love,
>
> Martha B. Winter

The young man apparently learned his lesson.

> January 9, 1933
>
> Dear Martha,
>
> I sure am sorry, Martha, to treat you the way I did by playing cards in the other room…I must admit that I did have a reason for going in the other room. It was partly a test which I thought I would try out. The following reasons are:
>
> First, I was tired and didn't feel like dancing.
>
> Second, someone hurt my feelings by telling me that I was jealous of you…
>
> Third, I never danced much and am not an expert…
>
> Fourth, and most important was the test which I was going to experiment to see whether you really cared for me as you have said…
>
> Martha, I wish you wouldn't take me to be a deadbeat because I don't act up like some of the boys…I don't believe in getting drunk just to be cute. I have

higher ideals ahead of me than that and I'm sure you'll agree with me if I were to go to these parties and get tite, it would have its after-affects later on. Of course, if a person hasn't anything to look forward to, I don't suppose it makes any diff. I had drinks offered to me four or five times but I refused them all. It takes a strong will power to refuse when they are offered by your friends. I haven't anything against anyone who takes a drink of beer. I'm not that narrow...

He had for months been working on a secret formula from which were to be made strings: Strings to weave a most priceless net that he hoped would never tarnish. The formula consisted of alloys of Love, Character, and Kindness, all as pure as could be found. This was the secret formula which he hoped would produce a string for a net that would never tarnish...

When the day had drawn to a close and the messenger was fast asleep in his nest, then out to her house he would go to receive the secret, which she had promised to him on the first day of spring. I shall remember it, Martha...

Willard M. Munger

Willard's apology came close to reoffending Martha.

January 10, 1933

Dear Willard,

I feel somewhat better now since I've read your letter. I surely did think I have made you angry at me. I know that I acted like I had a drink. I never would have acted that way if you would have stayed in the room and danced.

I've got to tell you something. You said that it was a test. Well, don't experiment anymore, Willard, because I don't always react the same way. Another thing. I thought you were up to something...I was just angry enough to make a date with some other guy...

This morning Elsie asked me if I had made a date with Vernie. He asked me but I didn't. I wouldn't make a date with him when I like and maybe could go [if he wants me] with the best boy in the county. I wouldn't miss a Saturday nite with you for anything...

Willard why do you think I don't know who I like the best? I like to flirt and tease boys but I don't do that with you...

Say, I wonder if you're just trying to make me care a lot for you and then laugh...No wonder romance is heaven...

I have to quit now so goodbye...

Martha B. Winter

P.S. Send more strings of gold for weaving.

In his next letter, Willard vowed to stay away from experiments.

January 11, 1933

My Dear Martha,

[M]artha, I'm going to promise you that I'm not going to experiment anymore, especially with such delicate substance as love. I'd be like the old professor who was experimenting with a new gas he had just discovered. He wasn't quite satisfied with it—he wanted to see would it really explode and finally held a match to it, and all he had left of his discovery was a bang! And a lost formula. That's what just about happened to me Saturday night, only I didn't know who held the secret formula. Now I do. Oh what a formula I discovered. Einstein and a dozen more like him could work until they are gray headed and I know they could never discover a better one for me. I shall keep it in a vault of Love, Kindness and Character. Don't you think it ought to be safe there? As long as I have made my great discovery, I might as well retire...

Martha, don't you ever wonder what a good time we have, and at the same time, think of the thousands of fine young boys and girls who are deprived of an education and all chance of becoming something...? It's no fault of their own, but rather an unsound economic order, which has been made and manipulated by a few exploiters who have endeavored to concentrate wealth from the great class of working people into the control of a few monied groups until they have about wrecked the country, destroyed the happiness of millions of hard working American people, and have decreased the moral standard of society...When you think of a country which is the richest in the world and has too much of everything and yet, millions are on the verge of starvation, then there must be something radically wrong with our economic order...

Willard Munger

Martha's ardor was not deterred by her suitor's political lecture.

January 15, 1933

My Dearest Willard,

How can I write what my heart tells me? Willard I'm in hell and it's the darn right truth. I don't know whatever came over me. The bad luck started Friday. I nearly cried Friday nite. Saturday in the daytime was a thrilling day. I couldn't wait till the evening when I was sure I would see you. The bottom fell out of everything when you called up...

My ma says it serves me right to suffer. My pa says the same. I am not getting any sympathy...

Willard, don't give up weaving…Only a few tears are getting in and I only wanted happiness and pleasure. Tears make things lots sweeter and more dear. I value that net above anything else in the world.

I talked to Lilly tonight and she told me how you felt last nite. I just can't write how evil I feel…I feel like a devil for making you feel hurt. I don't want to hurt you for anything in the world. If only I was home when you called the second time…

Your love,

Martha Winter

Martha's contrition made an impression on Willard.

January 16, 1933

My Dear Martha,

Don't feel bad for what you did Sat. night. I shall forgive you and forget all about it…

Friday night was a big nite for me. We held a Farmer-Labor meeting to organize a Fergus Falls Farmer-Labor Club. What do you suppose happened? I was nominated for secretary and then a lawyer from Fergus Falls was nominated to run against me. We were both told to leave the room because they didn't want us present while they voted. I felt that I had no chance against a lawyer, but when the votes were counted, I had everyone but three. This means a lot to me, Martha. Some time when I get you all to myself I'm going to tell you all about it…

As Ever…,

Willard Munger

Martha spent a good deal of her time accompanying her mother to church and using her musical talents to serve her Missouri Synod Lutheran faith.

January 18, 1933

My Dear Willard,

I've just got home from choir practice. I didn't know whether I would get time to answer your wonderful note or not…

Boy was I glad to get your letter. Willard, you are so good, I could ___ you. I guess I'm just beginning to really know you.

You know what I did after choir practice? I fell down those steps leading to the sidewalk. I didn't get hurt…Aldo Seam was right behind me. I could have got up but I thought how much nicer to let Aldo do it. I bet you think I'm the limit. You know why I fell? Well Elma asked me a question about you and I got so nervous, I never saw the steps! That's the truth. Ray and

Alfred laughed over me falling. I guess it was funny because I fell just like a snowflake—so soft like.

I'm so glad you were elected secretary…Gee, I know you'd win out if you were nominated for an office…Say, pretty soon you'll get so high that you won't know a little unkind girl named Martha…

Your love,
Martha Winter

Willard's reply included a discussion of Mr. Idtse; a teacher and the high school principal.

January 19, 1933
My Dear Martha,

I'm sorry that I won't be able to write a nice long note like you told me to because we just had a house full of company…It's way past 12 o'clock now, but I just had to write…Mr. Idtse was up here tonight…so if he looks tired tomorrow, you'll know the reason why.

Say, Martha, today when I was reading your note, the second period, Mr. Idtse came up to me from the back of the room & before I saw him, he was talking to me. He took me by surprise. I didn't have time to cover up so I just left it lay as if it was alright. He just had a smile and never said a word about it. If that would have been some woman teacher, she would have had me into Mr. Idtse's office before I could wink an eye!…

Look into the Fergus Falls Journal when you get home and see some of the resolutions that were made at our last meeting. We are going to have a meeting Friday night and I wish you could be there. I haven't made out my reports yet of the last meeting but will have to do that tomorrow. I believe I have to let you type them out. Ha ha.

Willard Munger

The discourse between the two young love birds wasn't limited to a burgeoning romance. Martha Winter possessed a keen intellect. Her grades were superior to Willard's. Her report card for sixth grade (1927) boasted a high of 99 in spelling and a low of 93 in writing and geography. That Martha was interested in political issues shouldn't be surprising given her mental acuity.

January 19, 1933
Dear Willard,

[I] read about your meeting in the paper. I don't agree with that first resolution about abolishing capital punishment. Anyone who is capable of a very bad crime certainly should be put out of this world. A man like that is a menace to society. He influences others to do bad things. The state is wasting money on reforming murderers and the like. That certainly is a debatable subject so I won't say any more...

Martha

Willard cautioned Martha about using alcohol or tobacco.

January 30, 1933

Dear Martha,

[S]ay, Martha, you said that you would like to hear more about weaving than about politics. That sounds good to me also. The reason I spend my time on politics and such is partly on account of you. Remember what I said last Saturday night about it. I have a future to look ahead to. I wish I could include the net in that, but I haven't anything to say about that...

What Mr. Idtse said in the general assembly ought to be a lesson to some of the smokers. It always will pay to lead a good clean life even though it isn't so popular nowadays, but those kind of popular people soon fade away. I'm so glad, Martha, that you lead such a clean life-that's why everyone likes you; they know you'll amount to something. I'm so glad that you don't believe in smoking or drinking. I'll bet there isn't many girls in school that don't. You're an exception and that's why I think so much of you. Haven't I a reason to be proud of you?

Willard Munger

Martha's next letter reminded Willard of "that Promise."

February 1, 1933

Dear Willard,

[S]ay, I'm just teasing you when I call you "Scotch." You ought to know better. I like you for what you are regardless of how much I tease you...

Oh yes, about that Promise. Don't mention it any more cause I'll tell you when the right time comes. It's something I've never said before. You'll know that it is the promise by that...

It's wonderful to be young, isn't it big boy? Gosh, I wish I could always be young. I believe the net weaver is getting more than he thinks wound up in the meshes.

I don't laugh over you and your interest in politics. I won't tell you what I think, but it is favorable to you...

Martha

During his courtship of Martha Winter, Willard Munger remained active in the Farm Holiday Association. In a very real sense, Munger was dividing his loyalties. Acknowledging that the Farmer-Labor Party was likely the means of winning elected office, Munger accepted leadership positions within the FL Party but refused to disassociate himself from A.C. Townley. When Townley gave a speech at Washington High School, Munger was in attendance and was not pleased by what transpired.

> February 2, 1933
>
> Well, I suppose you think I am a fine girl after last nite. I will admit that I did act foolishly. Are you angry at me? You were last nite and you can't deny it either. I felt crazy last nite and I sure did act it too. It wouldn't have been so bad but with Ray and Les there, I just couldn't be sour and sober as a judge.
>
> Somebody told me that you didn't care if you did give me a black look. Did you have a good time after the meeting? I went home and to bed when I tried to sleep and dreamed ugly dreams. I always do when I know I have been mean.
>
> Heck, I'm mad at myself. I can't say why exactly. I know one thing and that is you are peeved...
>
> You think Townley is a perfect man or something the way you talk. He is good all right, but we all have bad spots and plenty of them. The parts of his speech that I heard were good and he is a good speaker. Even I'll admit that. My dad thinks a lot of him. Why, I don't know or can't understand. I never have read much about him, I guess.
>
> I think I'm going to leave for a different place pretty soon. If I can get the cash, I'm going. If I don't go, I'm going to the dogs. Darn it anyway. I feel so blame blue that I think I'll sit down and cry...
>
> Your pal,
>
> Mart

Willard attempted to explain his actions.

> February 2, 1933
>
> Dear Martha,
>
> [M]artha, don't think for a minute that I was angry at you because how could anyone get angry at a little angel like you? Why it's just impossible. I didn't like the way some of those kids acted and I still believe the same. Anyone that doesn't have any respect for a speaker should at least have enough respect for himself...You don't know how disturbing it is for a speaker when there is someone annoying him. Put yourself in his place and see how you would like it. If that was during a campaign speech and someone would annoy a speaker the

opponents would surely capitalize on it very readily...I know because I've had that same experience before. Of course, they wouldn't pay so much attention to kids. The reasons I looked over there the way I did was because I thought those kids would take a hint and stop, but I guess they were too dumb. I think a lot of Mr. Townley and I can't afford to have him change his mind about me on account of a few kids. I'm not an old man or don't care to be yet, but I do think there is a place for everything. I like to have fun but I don't believe in annoying anyone who is talking even though I would dislike it. It is his meeting and he has the absolute right to say what he thinks...What would you say if I went to your church and annoyed your minister every time he said something?...

Martha, you must realize if I would act like a kid how long would I last with Townley? I must protect myself first, and have my good time stuff later. Townley is a Big Man and I am proud to be associated with him...

Your Pal,

Willard

Though their relationship was but a few months old, Willard was nostalgic and a bit apologetic in his next letter.

February 9, 1933

My Dear Martha,

[S]ay, Martha, this has been the most lonesome week that I have ever spent; I don't really know how much I miss you until I'm departed from you for a while. Today I went to my treasure box and got out all the letters which you have written to me. It sure was inspiring to read them; you can't imagine how much they mean to me. I found the first one that you wrote to me-the one about the way I treated you the night of the Junior-Senior Banquet.

I'm going to keep my letters which I got from you locked up in a little box so when I become an old bachelor...sitting lonely in my house with a storm raging from the north and the temperature like it is today. Then...I shall go to my treasure box and take out your letters and read them. They will refresh me, I'm sure...they will remind me of my good old school days and also of a beautiful little girl that I thought so much of-the only one I ever loved. I will not only remember her beauty but her fine personality and those wonderful words which she told me...

The couple continued building a relationship.

February 19, 1933, (3 o'clock)

Dear Willard,

[H]ave you done your shorthand test? I haven't done a thing. Guess I'll find myself in a pretty corner if I don't get over my laziness soon. I can't study. Other thoughts are better to concentrate on.

I didn't tell you that compliment that I heard from Ferber last nite. Well, he said that he thought the party was pretty wild and that he didn't see any good girls there but one. He said he didn't care to dance with any other than me, and that I was the only girl that he cared for at the whole dance. Can you beat that? That's an American-German for you...

Say, isn't it a dreary Sunday? I don't like such sorry weather...I used to go skating, sleighing and skiing but I haven't gone out for any of that stuff once this year. I wonder if I'm getting old or what...

Gee, I stuck a hole through that celluloid glass in our heater. I bet I'll get a scolding for that. I do such things like that when my thoughts wander...I get thoughtless of other things around me.

I wish it were summertime...Wouldn't that be wonderful? Gee, I better not think of it, 'cause summer is too far away.

Some of those men and women certainly were full of wild oats last nite. You could tell they were married by their actions.

Last nite when I looked at all the people on the floor, I thought what saps they are compared to you. That's true...

Martha.

Willard reminded Martha to stay true to her values.

February 23, 1933

Dear Martha,

[S]ay. Martha, don't think for a minute that I think that you are sour because you didn't like the kind of dance I took you to...You don't have to achieve any education, or have any plans...but you must refrain from doing what the crowd does.

Gee, Martha, I sure wish I could have been out to your place Wednesday & helped you build that snowman. I'm coming out some day and then we'll build a good one; if the snow isn't all gone by that time...

Willard

Martha voiced concern that Willard was burning the midnight oil to his detriment.

February 27, 1933

Dear Willard,

My ink is gone and I have no pen so that means I have to write in pencil or not at all...

Say, I would rather have stayed up at your place last nite but I promised the kids I'd come to their party so I didn't want to break it. Guess who was my supper partner? It was Hafner. Gee, but he gets quite talkative. Say, we ate in the bedroom on the sewing machine 'cause another couple was close by. He sat on one side and I sat on the other side. He always is so quiet but he was getting full of the dickens when I ate with him. I wished it would have been somebody else. Guess who.

Ernie was so nosey that it wasn't even funny. Gee, those kids were going to operate on Lulla Fralsming. She had a toothache [we had all-nite suckers]. They had butcher knives, curling irons, forks, can openers, and everything. At first Lulla joked with them but then she got scared when it came down to brass tacks. One of the girls got her sucker stuck in the throat. She had a lot of rouge on and the tears running down her face looked red...

I would have taken you kids along to the party but they made a resolution or something to that effect, that we'd have to have the consent of the committee, and at our choir parties, only members of the choir are allowed...

How do you feel? You look tired...

Martha

P.S. Write a note. Now don't disappoint me...How is that typed letter I wrote for you? Are you going to throw it in the wastebasket?

Willard's position as an officer of the Fergus Falls Farmer-Labor Club was referenced in his next letter. He also had some advice for Martha as a novice automobile driver.

My Dear Martha,

I'm sorry that I didn't answer your most wonderful letter last night, but I'm sure you will forgive me if I tell you the reasons why. I had to go downtown on account of some of those job seekers that want the recommendation of the Club. The seven executive members decide their fate and it was my duty to be present. I didn't get back until late. I really intended to write when I got home, but Walter Kalling was there and it was just about impossible to write when he was present...

Gee, Martha, I didn't know you could drive so well; it seems as though you can do just about anything. You better be careful or you'll be running over someone and I wouldn't want anything like that to happen to you. Ha ha. Don't take my advice too seriously, but only remember a lot of funny things can happen. I get a great kick out of your driving. You're a wonderful driver-for a girl. A lot of boys can't drive half that good. That Ford is a famous car to me. I'd rather see that car coming down the street than any other. I guess it's because of the driver...

Willard

Willard's subsequent correspondence recounted his grandmother's first impression of Martha.

March 13, 1933

My Dearest Martha,

[M]artha, I've got to tell you something funny. Last Sunday my grandmother said she wanted to go to church in Fergus. I told her she should go to your church because there was a pretty girl that always sang in the choir and I wanted to know what she thought of her singing. Say, Martha, I just about died laughing when she got back. She asked, in English-German: "Is that your girl, my oh, my oh! But dat's a pretty girl. Where did you find her?"

I said: "No, she's not mine but I wish she was."

Grandma said: "I like the looks of that girl. She must be an awful nice girl because I know her mother and she came from the old country, Germany."

She didn't like it that you didn't come last night, she wanted to talk with you, she said. This morning she said: "Martha has gotten mad at you, no? Villard why for you look so down-hearted? Didn't you be nice to her?"

If you would have heard the questions that she asked you would have died laughing, I believe...

Bye bye.

Willard

P.S. Please write soon if you still love me. A Happy Birthday!

Martha reminded Willard that he "wasn't the only rooster in the hen house."

March 16, 1933

Dear Willard,

[I] feel just like raising the dickens. Boy how, I would like to skip school this afternoon. I'd surely go to some exciting place.

This morning I was so tired that I could hardly get out of bed. My mother says lazy on your birthday, you'll be lazy for the rest of the year, but I don't think so.

You should have been with us kids last nite. We had bushels of fun. That little Tailor sat in the hall looking straight at me for about ten minutes. He would smile and you know what I did? I smiled right back. I did some undercover flirting. You want to know the result? Well, he asked Bill how the roads were out to our place. Gosh, I could have died laughing. He is the berries...

Many thanks for the beautiful card.

I'll type those other letters tonight and then you can get them tomorrow morning. Is that O.K.? Am I too slow? If I am, tell me & give me a boost.

Say, it's exactly eleven thirty, you know what happened then. Well, after eleven thirty, I was existing in this world exactly 18 years ago. That's what my authorities tell me. Sure don't seem very long to me...

Mart

Willard continued to tease Martha about her driving.

March 16, 1933 (11 o'clock P.M.)

Dear Martha,

[T]hat letter you typed for me was just grand. I didn't think you would do it so nice for me. I was so proud of your typing that I even showed it to my folks and the rest that were present with the remark: "Boy that girl is a wonder-she surely knows how to do things right. Why there isn't another in the country that could do it as good." I guess I'll have to hire you some day but I suppose you'll want such outrageous prices that no one can afford to hire you but some rich fellow and that won't be me...

You're eighteen years old, are you? I bet you think you're some pumpkin now. It's a wonder you'll speak to a fellow like me. I bet you feel like a person that's just been pardoned from a long prison term, don't you? Eighteen! Why just think of it. You're your own boss. You can regulate your own gas now...

I sometimes tease you about your driving but I don't mean it. You're a wonderful driver for a girl...

I wish you could have been up to the courthouse yesterday. Gosh, but I had fun. I don't believe I've ever had so many questions asked before in my life. They were mostly all Republicans and they sure tried to get me tangled up but they didn't get far. There must have been fifty men or more. That's what I call real fun-not as much fun as being with you, though. I believe I made a lot of new friends because I didn't get angry at all like some did...One fellow took me to his car and gave me a lot of literature. Perhaps he thinks he can change my opinion but I'm not like a weather-cock that turns which way the wind blows the strongest.

Tell your father and brother that there will be a Farmer-Labor meeting Friday night. Why don't you come along with them?...

Are you going to keep that promise that you told me about...

Willard…
  Happy Birthday and many more.

When the young politician was summoned by A.C. Townley to a meeting in St. Paul, he kept in touch with Martha by sending her a postcard. The note on the back of the card was brief.

March 22, 1933
  Dear Martha,
  Have been having a good time down here. Met Townley as soon as I got here.
  I wish you were here.
  Willard

Upon his return to Fergus Falls, Willard had a discussion with an FL Club member that boiled over into a confrontation.

March 23, 1933
  My Dearest Martha,
  I am awfully sorry that I didn't write to you before…Martha, those letters of yours were just wonderful. It made me happy that you'd write such wonderful letters to me. I had some of those letters along with me to St. Paul…and when I was alone I would read them over and think of you…
  Yesterday, one of the district men of Standard Oil Company called up and said I should go along with him in the afternoon and that's one of the reasons why I wasn't to school. He wanted to find out what kind of fellow I was, I guess. He sure used me fine. I don't think he found any fault with me.
  Say, Martha, I sure wish you could have been along with me to St. Paul. I had a peach of a time at the Capitol. I got acquainted with a lot of representatives from different parts of the state. It was the best education I believe that I could get in a short time. There was one thing missing down there and that was you. Gosh, but I get lonely without you, Martha. I guess that's because I love you so much.
  Say, Martha, you're one of the finest girls that I've ever met. The whole week that I spent in St. Paul and Minneapolis I never saw one that could be compared to you and that's saying quite a bit because I saw and talked to lots of them. You should see the way some of those girls smoked. They haven't any respect for themselves or anyone else. I don't believe. When I see girls like those down there and think of you, it just makes me happy to think that I am fortunate in having a girl that is so much better than those kind…

You should have heard the balling out I got the other day at the station. A man came in and wanted to know if my name was Willard Munger and I said "yes." He wanted a job on the highway and was mad because he didn't get on. He told me at first that the ones that I had picked out were no good and that he was much better fitted for the job. When I got through talking to him, he wasn't quite so smart. Yesterday, he came back again and he was just like pie. That isn't the first time that I have caught hail Columbia over that but I guess I'll have to get used to it. You can't please everyone in this old world...

Willard

Though Martha Winter had turned 18, she was still a junior in high school and had to abide by her parents' rules.

Dear Willard,

Well, since you've told me that you're going to write, I think that I will too. You know that it really is your turn.

I've stayed home every nite this week, went to bed about 9:30 & 10 o'clock.

Well, I was just starting this when you called...You could have come out but when I looked at the time, I saw it was nearly ten o'clock so I decided that it was rather late. My folks wouldn't have liked it. Not so late on a school night. It would have been O.K. if it was 8:00 or 8:30.

I'm writing this upstairs and it's rather cold. My mother thought I was going to bed, I guess...

Mart

One of the hallmarks of Willard Munger's personality was his compassion for the downtrodden. The following letter reveals that Munger's generosity was a trait he developed early in life.

April 6, 1933

My Dearest Martha,

[I] sure didn't like to come out & get you in that old wreck because I know it wasn't good enough for you. There is nothing that's too good for you, Martha. We can go for a nice ride some summer night now, can't we, dear? And then, I'll think of summer, that wonderful season, bringing with it the sweet flowers and many things—a promise that's dearer than all. Martha, I'm not going to forget "the promise" and I hope you don't either. I'm going to ask Old Father Time if it isn't possible for him to speed up things a bit & see if he can't roll summer around a little sooner. Don't you think it could be possible, Martha?...

Tell your father that there will not be any meeting of the Farmer-Labor Club Friday night because there is going to be a meeting in New York Mills and I'm supposed to go there but I don't think I can. Mr. Townley wrote a letter stating that I should be there…

Say, Martha, a young boy came into the oil station tonight and didn't have any money or any place to sleep so I took him home with me…I have too much of a heart to let anybody sleep out in the cold. I am writing this standing up because I have used all the chairs to make a bed for him so please excuse this writing. We have a house full of company and none of the rest will share their bed so I'm going to sleep down here with him. One don't realize what a home means until he gets out in the world among strangers with no money and nothing to eat. He is only about 16 years old and says that he lives on a farm but wanted to find work. I believe what he says because I gave him a good cross-examination before I took him home…

Gee, Martha, I think an awful lot of you…I got lonesome the other day over at the oil station and I read over your last note and just as I took out my pocket book to look at your little picture that I carry, a car came into the driveway and I left it on the desk. A fellow came in and this is what he said: "Where in the world did you find a good looking girl like that?" I said: "And she's just as good as she looks."

Willard

Between Willard's letter of April 6 and Martha's next correspondence (April 18, 1933), Willard was promoted to the position of station manager with Standard Oil.

Dear Manager,

[W]ell, to tell the truth, I don't know what to write that would be appropriate for a manager. This cut and dried stuff don't seem to fit…

Say, wasn't it just grand out? Boy, I could walk ten miles on a day like today. I bet you're busy…

This world is funny. People can't do what they want to. If I had my wish, I wouldn't be in school today. Maybe next week I'd be in school but I'd like to go out camping this week. Guess a bug has bitten me trying to make me go places. I wish that I was a boy then I'd catch on a freight train and be a hobo…

Mart

Martha urged her parents to become customers of a certain service station in town.

Dear Willard,

[W]asn't that a pretty good joke Sunday when that fellow put 10 cents worth of gas in his car? He said he thought it was full but I told him he better fill, 'cause I might make him take me someplace else. I know him real well, and then he is a German & you can fool a lot with them. He said he felt rather cheap about a dime's worth of gas, so I told him to go back there again when he needed a whole lot. He said he would.

Say, it takes me to get customers. Boy, I sure did talk my folks into going to your station. I convinced my mother and then she & I convinced my dad. 'Course Bill will never be convinced. I had his arguments to go against always. It don't make any diff to my folks where they trade just so the car runs...

You know, I hate to look back in the northeast corner of the assembly. It makes me feel lonesome, sort 'o lost feeling. Ever feel like that? Course, you're more grown up than I am. Yesterday I didn't do a single thing during fourth hour. Just sat thinking...I suppose you'll be forgetting how to read shorthand pretty soon. I do hope you won't forget all of the things in this high school.

Doesn't life seem just wonderful when everything is O.K.? When everything harmonizes. Gee, I feel just like spring today. Guess, it's because you called me up. I had to laugh last nite. When I got home about 4 o'clock, my dad had to go downtown. So I told them they had to get gas. My mother said, "Well, you better get it from Munger." They needed kerosene too. We always get our kerosene from Tolin, but I told them Standard has kerosene too. They wanted to know how much Standard asked per gallon. So mother says I should better call up. So you see, that's how you got a call from me & also a sale...

Say, I haven't ate all those bon bons yet. In fact, I only ate one and a half. I gave my sis and mother part of them. Gee, I gained about five pounds in April, so I'm quitting eating candy and cake. That's what I say, but I bake a cake every night after school and then eat about four pieces. No wonder I'm gaining...

Bye, Willy.

Mart.

Martha's next note recounts a ride she took into town to visit Willard at the service station.

Dear Willard,

Say, I was down to your station yesterday after school but you weren't there so I didn't leave my note there either. I didn't care to leave it with those two fellows you had there...

Sal, or whatever his name is, told me you were down at the River Inn yesterday. Said you wouldn't be back till 5 or six so I went home and took my note with me...

Make your man work down there. He just monkeys around. Better not tell him I said that because it's hard to start on a job if you don't know much about it...

Well, I'm going to sign off. Bye.

Mart

Martha's immaturity comes through clearly in her next letter.

April 22, 1933

Dear Willard,

[W]hy didn't you call up earlier, instead of letting me think all kinds of things? You surely knew about 9 o'clock that you couldn't get your work done...

When the clock struck ten last nite, I flew off the handle and went to bed, I just couldn't stay up anymore and have Bill tease me about going out, without crying, so I went to bed...My folks get lot of kick out of it. To them, it's the first time I ever stayed home for any boy... And I get plenty of teasing...My mother told me I had not better stay home for any man and I'm going to believe like that too...

I know you couldn't come out last nite. I guess you won't come out very much anymore. Work comes before pleasure. I realize that it's hard for anyone to start right out on the job like you did and you are a swell manager. I'm sure the company thinks the same...

Mart

P.S. Got those letters from Elsie this morning. I'll type them tonight.

The rift caused by Willard's insensitivity continued for a time.

May 8, 1933

Dear Willard,

[B]illy, if you just want to hurt me, well, you're doing it and plenty of it too...

Yesterday, you acted so blame frozen up and cold toward me that I really felt like crying...You are so hurtful at times. Well, I suppose you think I'm just another fool. Maybe, I am but if I am, I do hope that I won't be a fool much longer...

My gosh, but I feel blue...Well, I guess the law of compensations will even things up. It always does. For every hurt, there is a joy so I ought to have a joy coming and a lot of them too 'cause I've been feeling blue for a long while...

I'm going to quit before I make a bigger fool of myself...

It's no use asking you to write or call either so I won't anymore.

Willard, you understand why I sometimes doubt your love, why I sometimes think you're just fooling around? At times like last nite...I have to finish this in pencil as my pen is dry.

Well, I think I'll quit...bell has rung. So bye...

Mart

A week later, Martha was her cheery old self.

Dear Willard,

I have just about three minutes to write...Don't you wish we could have a real hike and picnic? Gee, I think such stuff is fun, but it was too dark last nite. About 6 – 7 o'clock is better for such stuff, the picnics, you know.

How is Clayton this morning...?

I'll sign off now.

Mart

After Martha's short note of May 15th, correspondence between the two young love-birds essentially ends, though on August 2, 1933 while in St. Paul on FL business, Willard found the time to send Martha a postcard.

Dearest Martha,

Just about ready to go to bed but had to send you a card first. I have been over to the Capitol until 10:00 P.M. and am going back in the morning.

Willard

Martha's next note to Willard was sent months later.

November 1, 1933

This note is going to be short. Say, remember what I told you last nite? Well, I didn't go to any dance. I was just kidding you. You know I like to do that sometimes...

From your love,

Martha

Finally, on November 22, 1933, Martha made a bold and clairvoyant prediction.

Willard Munger

Fergus Falls, Minnesota

I am going to marry you...

Because you promised me.

Sworn before me this 22nd day of November 1933.

Martha.

CHAPTER 5

The Party Man

Willard Munger joined the Nonpartisan League as a high school student because he believed in A.C. Townley. When Floyd B. Olson was elected governor in 1930, Munger recognized that Townley's agrarian movement couldn't achieve the same level of success in Minnesota it had in North Dakota. This recognition prompted Munger's involvement in the Fergus Falls Farmer-Labor (FL) Club. By early 1934, Willard Munger was on the cusp of running for political office as an FL candidate when the unexpected happened: Lyman Robert Munger died on January 13, 1934.

Lyman Munger's death ended the political discourse between the old man and his grandson. And though Willard's father, Harry Munger, Sr. was also active in third-party politics, it was Lyman Munger who had primarily formed Willard's Liberal political outlook and his love of the natural world.

In the period immediately following his grandfather's death, Willard Munger maintained his connection to A.C. Townley despite a growing affinity for the political acumen of the new governor.

> "It was finally decided that we ought to go to Washington and call upon the president of the United States to initiate a moratorium…," Munger recalled. "Townley suggested that because I had worked so diligently passing the hat around and raising the money for all those meetings that I should be selected as one of the delegates…Then they passed around the hat for me and I got eighty-five dollars…"
>
> (*Oral History of Willard Munger,* ibid, p. 41.)

Munger also recalled that, unlike the state legislative races, where FL candidates were unable to wrest control of the Minnesota Legislature from the Conservatives, the FL made significant inroads in Congress, capturing five of Minnesota's nine Congressional seats in the 1932 election.

"I think there were about five of them altogether. So we spent quite a bit of time with our Congressmen there, and we did present our case. The president, Franklin D. Roosevelt, finally issued an order for a moratorium on all farm sales, which was in effect for one or two years. So we did accomplish something. I think if it hadn't been for that moratorium, it would have eventually led to violence."

(*Oral History of Willard Munger,* ibid, p. 42.)

Munger's 1934 trip to Washington proved to be a rare opportunity for the young politician. In a series of postcards and letters he sent to his beloved Martha (then in her senior year in high school) Munger shared some of the new-found insights he gained while traveling through America.

> *[Photo oil postcard of State Street, Chicago]*
> February 22, 1934
> My Dearest Martha,
> Just arrived in Chicago at 12:00 A.M. Wednesday and everything is fine.
> I'm sure having a good time…
> Willard

One can only imagine Munger's wide-eyed excitement as his train pulled into downtown Chicago. So far as is known, Munger's 1934 trip to Washington was the first time the young politician had traveled outside the state of Minnesota.

The next day, Willard mailed a second postcard to Martha.

> *[Photo oil of Penn Station, Pittsburgh, Pennsylvania]*
> February 23
> My Dearest Martha,
> Just got through taking a bath and am ready to go to bed. Haven't had any sleep since I left home. Met General Coxey on the train and had a long talk with him. In 7th Street Hotel, Pittsburgh, right now.
> Your sweetheart,
> Willard

The reference to "General Coxey" is to Jacob Sechier Coxey. During the Panic of 1893 Coxey led an "army" of unemployed men on a march to Washington; D.C. Coxey, who worked as an engineer in Massillon, Ohio, left Massillon on Easter Sunday, 1893 with 100 men, believing his "army" would swell to a mass of 100,000 unemployed men. In reality, by the time Coxey arrived in Washington, D.C. (where he was promptly arrested for trespassing on the White House lawn) Coxey's contingent numbered only 500.

While the march of Coxey's Army didn't achieve its stated goal of uniting the unemployed in protest, it did spawn a modest political career for Jacob Coxey. He was twice elected mayor of Massillon and was an unsuccessful candidate for the presidency in 1932 and 1934, making Coxey a man of somewhat mythical reputation when he sat next to young Willard Munger on the train in 1934.

Upon arriving at the Capitol Park Hotel in Washington, D.C. on February 23, 1934, Willard penned a lengthy letter to Martha.

My Dearest Martha,

Arrived in Washington, D.C., 2:30 P.M. today in good condition. It sure has been a fine trip all the way. I have seen so many new things that I can't stand to tell you about it in this letter so will wait until I get home. I would start to tell you about my trip in this letter…I have a room on the 7th story and it sure seems funny to be up so high. The hotel is just a block from the Capitol & it sure gives us a wonderful view of the city. The city has a population of over 500,000.

We met Mr. Townley at the hotel tonight and he states everything is coming along fine so far. He went down before we did. We are going over to the Capitol tomorrow. There are 12 of us; six from N.D. and six from Minn.

Say, Sweetheart, I will not be back for about two weeks-that is from the time I started-I am going to New York before I come home.

How is my little darling getting along without being able to see her sweetheart for such a long time? I sure have been thinking a lot about you since I left. I wish you were here tonight to give me a kiss. It sure is lonesome without you, honey. I never thought you would miss a person so much but I sure found out.

Suppose you are having a lot of fun when I'm gone. Have a lot of fun but don't forget about your little "Willy" in Washington, D.C. because he soon will be back to put his arms around you.

It's getting late and so will have to stop for tonight but will write again tomorrow.

I am writing this letter on the bed so please excuse it, won't you dear?

From Your Loving Sweetheart,

Willard

Willard next wrote on February 25, 1934, confirming the couple's intention to marry, and promising to take Martha to Washington, D.C. (a promise he never fulfilled). In the letter, Willard also expressed an interest in the Soviet Union and Communism, though there is no evidence that he ever seriously considered joining the Far Left.

My Dearest Martha:

Gee it sure seems lonesome to be away from you for such a long time; I sure wished you could be here this afternoon. I have a swell place in the hotel. It's just across the street from the Capitol.

I'll bet you'll be happy when I tell you what I did this forenoon. I went to church! The people in the churches are more friendly than they are back home. They made us acquainted with a lot of people in the church.

It sure is a bad day out today. It has been snowing all day. Everything is covered white. This is the most snow that they have had for quite a long time. We were going on a sightseeing trip but the weather made it impossible to do so.

On our way back from church, we stopped at Washington's Monument and went up to the top. This monument is 568 feet high and we could have seen the whole city of Washington, D.C. if it hadn't been snowing. There is a lot of wonderful things to see. I'm sure going to take you out here when we get married.

We are invited out tonight for dinner at Congressman Shoemaker's home. He's that Congressman that you have heard so much about.

After we left Chicago, General Coxey got on the bus and I had a long talk with him. He told me all about his march to Washington in 1894 with 5,000 men. He started in Massillon, Ohio. It took him 35 days to make the trip. He believes about the same in politics as I do. He is 80 years old and sure is spry for a man of his age.

I also met a motion picture manager who had just gotten back from three years in Europe and I sure got a lot of interesting facts from him in regards to Russia. He made extensive visits to Russia and learned a lot about the country that I was interested in knowing. He said the same thing about conditions in Russia as was told by the man from Duluth who spoke in the M. church in Fergus Falls some time ago. He said at the present time Russia is further advanced than any country in Europe. Conditions over there are the best of any country he visited on his whole trip. There is no unemployed at all and everyone seems to be happy.

I haven't heard a word from home since I left and I don't know whether everything is O.K. or not. If you would have written me before I would have gotten it before because I am going to be here until next Wed. but by the time you get this letter, it will be too late because I will be gone before your letter gets back.

On my way back, I'm going to New York City or when I leave here; New York City is not on my way back. It only cost a few more dollars to go to New York so I thought it would be worth it.

I'm writing this letter in the hotel lobby with the radio playing some soft music and the snow is falling softly outside. Gee, this makes me lonesome for you, my dear little sweetheart. I wish you could really know how much I really think of you, Martha. I think you are the most wonderful girl in the whole world. Your beautiful smile seems to be with me all the time. I can't help but remember that sweet kiss you gave me at the railroad station just before I left. No other girls here in Washington, D.C. mean a thing to me even though there are a lot of them here.

Don't you get a little lonesome without me, dear? I believe you do. If you don't get another letter from me tomorrow or the next day, don't feel hurt because I will be busy.

It is getting about time for me to go up to my room and get ready for dinner and so will have to quit for the time being.

Your Loving Sweetheart,

Willard

The "Congressman Shoemaker" Willard referenced was Francis Henry Shoemaker, a farmer from Renville, Minnesota, who was a charter member of the Farmer-Labor Association. Born in 1889, Shoemaker assisted in organizing the Farmer-Laborites in Chicago in 1924 and was the editor of numerous Liberal newspapers. He was elected to Congress in 1932 but did not seek re-election in 1934, preferring to run for the United States Senate. His bid for a Senate seat failed, and though he ran again several times for Congress as an independent, he never won another election.

Munger followed up his long letter with a series of postcards.

[Photo oil postcard of the United States Capitol at night]

February 27, 1934

My Dearest Martha,

I was very busy today. Had our meeting with Mr. Townley and things look good...

Willard M.

[Photo oil postcard of U.S. Government Printing Office]

February 28, 1934

Dear Sweetheart,

Leaving for New York in the morning. Gee, I wish I would get a letter from you. I haven't heard a word from anyone yet...

Willard

[Photo oil postcard of Japanese cherry blossoms]

February 28, 1934

My Dear Sweetheart,

I have been with Congressman Shoemaker all day and have learned a lot of new things. He gave us a high class dinner in the Capitol and boy did I ever get sick!

I feel much better tonight.

Willard

When interviewed later in life about his infamous trip to Washington, one of the highlights Munger recalled was witnessing Populist Senator Huey Long of Louisiana debate Socialist (and Lyman Munger's political hero) Norman Thomas in New York City.

"[W]hen we were in Washington, I ran out of money because I used my last two and a half dollars to go out and listen to a debate between Norman Thomas and Huey Long…Norman Thomas just wiped the ground with him," Willard related in his oral history. "That was the most interesting debate I have ever attended. You know, Huey Long was quite an orator in his own right. He was a demagogue, but he was quite an orator…That was the high point of my trip. "

(*Oral History of Willard Munger,* ibid, p. 42.)

Munger's memory was a bit off. The impression one is left with is that the debate between Long and Thomas took place in Washington, D.C. The event actually took place in New York City as confirmed by Munger's next letter home.

March 1, 1934

Hotel Imperial New York, New York

My Dear Darling,

Just arrived in our room in the Hotel Imperial, New York City and is it a city! It's just like being in a large forest. The walls go way up into the air on all sides and it sure makes a person feel small. Our hotel is just about two blocks from the Empire State Building which is over 102 stories high. Our hotel is 16 stories high and it looks like a little ant hill compared to the Empire State.

Tomorrow morning we are going up in it and look the town over; it cost 50 cents to go up. I am sending a post card with picture.

After we leave the Empire Building, I am going out to Ellis Island and Governor's Island & watch the boats come in. From there I'm going to visit the slums —that is where the poor people live. I want to find out some facts in regards to these districts.

In the evening, it will be a great event for me. Mr. Norman Thomas and Huey Long are going to debate on the subject of public ownership and I sure am going to take that in. After the debate we are leaving for Niagara Falls and from there-home. This will take us home Tuesday.

There sure has been a lot of snow out here. It is piled up along the road.

After we left Washington going towards New York, the people are not as friendly as they are back home. I wouldn't trade Minnesota for all of these eastern states put together.

Martha, this trip sure has been worth a lot for me. You can tell them there that I will have plenty to tell them regarding politics. I have talked with a lot of big men, both Dem. & Rep. and am bringing home a lot of material for the convention.

Say, Martha, I haven't talked to a single girl except one since I left home and that was a Russian girl who sat down beside me on the bus. She told me some interesting things about Russia; it isn't so what the papers say about that country. I was glad to get the information because it will help in proving it.

Say, Martha, I'm going to tell you something and I want you to believe it because it's true and comes from the bottom of my heart and that is: I haven't seen a girl on our whole trip that could be compared to my little sweetheart back in Fergus Falls. All these girls do out here is paint their faces and smoke.

Gee, Martha, I never really knew a person could love a girl as much as I do you. I think about you all the time. I am really home sick for you. I wish you could be up here on the 7th floor in Room 734 with me tonight.

I know you won't go out with other fellows when I'm gone because I know you love me too much for that so I'm not thinking about that. You know I won't.

It's getting late & I must quit.

Your Sweetheart,

Willard

Imagining what it was like for Willard Munger, a twenty-three year old gas station manager from Fergus Falls, Minnesota, to encounter New York City in all its glory, with the recently completed Empire State Building dominating its skyline, is difficult. But even as he was likely awed by man-made wonders, Munger kept his eyes and ears open in terms of learning all he could about the socio-economic structure of the United States. He took time to see Ellis Island, the place where immigrants like his maternal grandparents arrived from the Old Country; to visit the slums; to see two noted political giants debate social policy; and to listen to the story of an ordinary Russian girl on a city bus. Munger was not some everyday tourist from the heartland on his first visit to the Big Apple. There was a purpose, an educational component to Willard Munger's journey that he would never forget.

The debate witnessed by Munger was a debate between two of the most intriguing politicians of the early part of the 20th century. Huey Long has been called the South's answer to Floyd B. Olson. Whereas Olson's Progressive politics arose out of agricultural malaise, Long's politics grew out of a strong Populist tradition fueled by his opposition to the Great War. A lawyer by training, Long won a seat on the Louisiana Railroad Commission before running unsuccessfully for governor in 1924. Revamping his campaign platform to include free textbooks for school children and a call for public works, Long won the governorship in 1928, which fueled the beginnings of a massive political machine. Calling himself "Kingfish" (after a popular radio character of the day) Huey Long went on to win a seat in the United States Senate in 1930. He ultimately broke with FDR over the New Deal, claiming that things weren't progressing fast enough to cure the economic ills of the South. Long announced that he would challenge FDR for the presidency in 1936 but he was assassinated in 1935, a year after Munger watched him debate Norman Thomas.

Norman Thomas came from a vastly different political heritage. The son of a minister, Thomas was born in Ohio in 1884. He was a student of Woodrow Wilson's at Princeton and became convinced (while doing social work in New York City) that Socialism could affect positive change. Like Long, Thomas opposed WWI. He was one of the founders (along with Upton Sinclair and Elizabeth Gurley Flynn) of the American Civil Liberties Union. He was associate editor of *The Nation*, joined the Socialist Party, and, upon the death of Eugene Debs, became that party's perennial candidate for president. Thomas opposed Communism, initially opposed the United States' involvement in WWII and continued his opposition to American intervention in places like Vietnam, protesting that conflict up until his death in 1968.

These were the men, one an idealistic Socialist, the other, a pragmatic, dishonest Populist, who mesmerized young Willard Munger during their colorful debate in New York City in March of 1934. In his only written account of the debate, Willard's recollection was cursory.

> *[Photo oil postcard of Statute of Liberty; New York, New York]*
> March 3, 1934
> Dear Sweetheart,
> Just got back…and ready to leave on the bus within 20 minutes. Gee it was a wonderful debate!
> Willard

CHAPTER 6

Candidate Munger

When Willard Munger returned to Fergus Falls from Washington, D.C., it is likely that his political will was bolstered by his lengthy sojourn. He'd seen the nation's Capitol in the throes of great political unrest. He'd met Senators, Congressmen, cabinet members, a former militant protester and watched a debate between two nationally renowned politicians. More importantly, the political education Munger received during the trip was not written on a blank slate: It was applied to a template prepared by past associations.

As previously described, Munger's early political indoctrination came at the knee of his grandfather during their meanders through Pockerbrush. But there was more to Lyman Munger's lesson plan for his grandson than home-spun wisdom. Despite being of limited education, Lyman Munger was a curious man who imparted his thirst for knowledge upon young Willard.

"Grandpa Munger," recalls Munger cousin Mary Holo, "was always reading. Despite having a very limited education, having gone to work when he was 13 years old, Lyman was a well-read man. He owned the only *Encyclopedia Britannica* in Otter Tail County, which teachers often borrowed to look up information. And he took more than one newspaper to keep up on politics," Holo remembers. "When he worked as a logger, while the other men would play cards during breaks, Grandpa would read Shakespeare!"

Willard Munger's Personal Collection is replete with evidence that he too was a constant learner; a perpetual student of the human condition. His collection of newspapers, magazines and redacted articles from the 1930s is a compendium of political thought and discourse.

As an example, his Personal Collection includes a copy of the *Minnesota Voice* from October, 1932 in which the *Voice* (a conservative publication) railed against the dangers of continuing Governor Floyd B. Olson's "political machine."

Other articles of note saved by the young politician included a piece from the *American Guardian,* a Leftist publication from Oklahoma dated February 5, 1932, which included a call for the formation of a national third-party movement.

> In anticipation of the stormiest election since 1912, a four-year presidential plan issued by the League for Independent Political Action headed by Dr. John Dewey, makes an open bid for a united third party. It seeks to combine the organized minority parties and leaderless progressive groups in the two old parties...Dr. John Dewey, chairman of the League, declares "We are in the midst of a tragic breakdown of industry, employment and finance with all the attendant suffering. The Republican and Democratic parties cannot meet the emergency for they are the tools and servants of the forces and the men who have promoted the very policies which have, to large measure, brought about the crisis..."

The article went on to disclose that Norman Thomas was a possible choice for president, though his candidacy was not supported by the Progressives, who felt Thomas was too "Bolshevik" for broad support.

The following piece, an editorial by Republican U.S. Senator Thomas Schall of Minnesota, confirms that Munger read and analyzed what the opposition had to say.

> One of the chief causes of the destruction of credit of the American Farmer and producer was brought about by the Federal Reserve Bank and its operations in deflating the American Farmer...I have introduced a bill...which, if passed, will permit the Federal Reserve Bank to discount first liens on improved farm lands and I hope it may be given attention that it will remedy discrimination against the farmer.
>
> The farmer's collateral is excluded and farm mortgages are not allowed to be used as a basis of credit. On the other hand, industry, the banks, the railroad companies and the trust companies have been taken care of by the Federal Reserve Bank. The withdrawal of credit will ruin any business; the refusal to finance agriculture...is directly responsible for much of the condition that afflicts farmers today.
>
> (*Farmers Union Herald,* April, 1932.)

Missing in the Senator's proposed solution to the farm crisis was what to do about farms already in foreclosure. Fortunately, Senator Schall, who had been blinded in an accident involving an electric cigar lighter in 1907, wasn't the subject of unkind barbs for being "blind" to the plight of rural Minnesotans. Schall's solution, to free up additional credit for farmers, wasn't of much use to farmers already in jeopardy of losing their farms due to their inability to pay existing debts.

Though deeply engrossed in politics, Munger still harbored the dream of furthering his education. In the early 1930s, he started work on a wooden scale model stagecoach, the completion of which would have made him eligible for an engineering scholarship. Harry Munger, Jr. recalls the project.

"[W]hen Willard was in high school, he tried for a scholarship making a model of a horse drawn coach. But due to the Depression, he didn't have the money to finish it and he never got the scholarship, never went to college."

The unfinished stagecoach remains in a suitcase in daughter Patsy Munger-Lehr's basement, a testament to a man with immense talent but little time to accomplish everything he wanted to do.

Willard Munger remained deeply engaged in Farmer-Laborite politics throughout early 1934.

> A.C. Townley was endorsed as a candidate for Congress...A crowd of about 250 people, about 150 of them delegates, crowded into the Creamery Hall...
>
> Three were nominated for chairman: Willard Munger, Max Kronemann and Louis Ward Martin. Mr. Munger was elected. Chairman Munger announced that A.C. Townley would file as a candidate for Congress...provided he received the endorsement of the Farmer-Labor Party of Otter Tail County.
>
> Judge Henry Nycklemoe of this city has already filed as a candidate for the position...
>
> (*Fergus Falls Daily Journal*, March 12, 1934.)

For Willard Munger, Townley's candidacy was a triumph of sorts in that Townley, though personally at odds with Governor Olson, was willing to work within the framework of the FL Party to achieve power. Even still, Townley's run for Congress generated conflict within the FL Party.

> Unanimously endorsed by Progressive-minded men and women, Judge Henry Nycklemoe, candidate for Congress in the 9th District on the Farmer-Labor ticket has the endorsement of the All-Party Progressive Association consisting of Farmer-Laborites and all Progressives...

Nycklemoe was born on a farm in Otter Tail County. He worked his way through school. He is a graduate of St. Olaf College and University Law School....Nycklemoe is a practicing attorney in Fergus Falls, elected Municipal Judge in 1928, re-elected in 1932 by a large majority and recently endorsed for Federal Judge by the Farmer-Labor Party...

(Henry Nycklemoe For Congress Flyer, 1934; Willard Munger Personal Collection.)

As chairman of the Ottertail County FL Association, Munger was drawn into the dispute between Townley and Nycklemoe.

Socialist Platform Endorsed: Farmer-Labor Party Candidates Named

As church bells throughout the county pealed forth their solemn invitation to attend services Sunday forenoon, many cars from all corners of the county were en-route to Ottertail village to attend the annual county convention of the Farmer-Labor Party...County Chairman Willard Munger called the convention to order. He said the meeting was of vital importance this year, and expressed his happiness over the good turnout.

Munger outlined briefly the aims of the party, touching on the fact that many of its members had been staunch supporters of the Nonpartisan League.

He asked for complete harmony and warned candidates who might lose out in the balloting to pledge their support to those who were successful. He said it would be poor policy to go out and start a small party of their own, as was recently done in Fergus Falls. "The so-called All Progressive Party is sponsored by a few Republicans and Democrats who know that the only way to defeat the Farmer-Labor Party is to get into the party," he said...Mr. Munger said this kind of work was apparent at the convention at Erskine...at which A.C. Townley lost the party's endorsement..."There are only about four Farmer-Labor members who have joined the All-Progressive Party..." No representative of Judge Nycklemoe's newly-formed progressive club were present at the meeting...

Peter Sande of Maine got the floor and stated that for many years he had fought for Socialism. He has hesitated in joining the Farmer-Labor Party, he said, but now that it had stolen the entire Socialist platform, he was ready to join. "I wish to warn you, however, you will now be classed as atheists, free-lovers, etc..." he said.

Mr. Martin [Lewis Ward Martin, temporary chairman] replied: "We have not stolen the Socialist platform...we merely took it because it wasn't being used..."

The final ballot resulted in the endorsement of the following [for the Minnesota House]:

Mrs. Kraywinkle: 74 votes

Martin Olson: 70 votes

Martin Schmidt: 67 votes

Willard Munger: 59 votes…

T. H. Johnson [state senate candidate] is engaged in business in the city, and is a former member of the House.

Mrs. Kraywinkle is a well-known resident of this city and has frequently written on political topics.

Willard Munger is the son of Game Warden Harry Munger and graduated from Fergus Falls High School last year. He is in charge of the Standard Oil Co. station at the intersection of Mill and Cavour.

Mr. Schmidt operates a plumbing and heating shop at Perham.

Mr. Olson is a farmer…

A stray dog had found his way into the hall but was not particularly noticed until Rev. Flint of Underwood was chosen as temporary secretary. As Rev. Flint ascended the rostrum, he was given a vigorous hand…The stray dog joined in with some vigorous barking. Naturally this brought out some humorous comments which were lost in laughter. When the laughter subsided, Anton Veason, the fiery orator from St. Olaf, remarked: "He's only a Republican howling about our platform!…"

(*Fergus Falls Daily Journal,* April 9, 1934.)

Another article details A.C. Townley's fate.

The famous A.C. Townley climbed up the hill…almost to victory, but the Farmer-Labor Party set him aside and turned to Senator R.T. Buckler of Crookston as its candidate for Congress in the Ninth District. Townley got much attention at the recent state convention, winning such titles as "father of the party" because it grew out of the Nonpartisan League. On that history, he and his cohorts waged a powerful fight…but he failed by the narrowest of margins. It took six ballots to settle the issue, and in the end, Buckler won, 311 to 278…

Townley won his first victory when the convention refused to seat a delegation from Otter Tail County which was supporting Henry Nycklemoe of Fergus Falls for Congress. Nycklemoe has filed and announced he will stay in the race for the Farmer-Labor nomination…All through the balloting, Townley had led by a threatening margin. All through the balloting the whispered conferences around the edges insisted that Townley must be beaten. And at the last, enough of the scattered vote swung to Buckler to get him by and the convention could call it a day.

Townley had pledged, along with the other candidates, his support to the winner. "I don't think anyone can accuse me of supporting a Republican," he said in his only appearance…

(Fergus Falls Daily Journal, April 9, 1934.)

Though Munger initially supported Townley's candidacy, Munger's support ended when Townley backtracked on his word. Throughout his political career, Willard Munger championed the sort of politics where a man's word is his bond. Townley's decision (to challenge the endorsed candidate in the primary) was the end of Munger's involvement in Townley's campaign.

Townley Forgets Recent Pledge: Wants to Run for Congress

Progressives in the 9th Congressional District were surprised to learn this week that A.C. Townley is refusing to abide by the Erskine Convention and his pledge to delegates…and wants to run for Congress. The Townley movement for Congress is being engineered by a small group of men living at Detroit Lakes and Fergus Falls…

It is hoped that Governor Floyd B. Olson will become aware of the split in the party this group is causing in this section of the state and properly relegate them to the sidelines…

Who are these men who are killing the party from within? What are their records?

(Country Press, April 20, 1934.)

Munger quit his job with Standard Oil to run for the legislature. It was a precarious decision, especially given that he and Martha were secretly engaged to be married. It was a whirlwind of emotion and excitement that caught the young man from Friberg Township during the late winter, spring and early summer of 1934, having journeyed to Washington to meet with Congressmen and cabinet members; having witnessed a debate between two infamous national politicians; having presided over a raucous political convention; and having quit his job and found himself on the threshold of marriage. Yet another level of complexity was added to Munger's life when he was selected to be a leader in a national third-party movement.

April 25, 1934

Dear Mr. Munger:

You have been elected as a member of our State Committee of forty. We shall meet at least once a month with the members of the National Committee to consider not only state but national action…

We hope very much that you will accept membership…Kindly notify us of your action on the enclosed postal card. Every good wish.

Sincerely,

Howard Y. Williams

As Munger began his first campaign for the Minnesota Legislature, he sustained another personal setback. His maternal grandfather, Albert Zuehlsdorf, (the "good farmer" according to Munger's description of the man) passed away on April 20, 1934. Albert Zuehlsdorf's conservative tendencies mirrored the political leanings of most Otter Tail County residents, and the fact that his grandson was running as a Liberal in an extremely Republican district was not lost upon young Willard.

> "I don't suppose I could have gotten elected in Fergus Falls, because Fergus Falls is a real conservative area," Willard recalled. "You talked about the environment down there—back in 1934, they figured that those lakes would never deteriorate…If anyone talked about the environment, they would have been considered fit for Fergus Falls (State) Hospital…a mental institution."
>
> (*Oral History of Willard Munger,* ibid, p. 23)

Munger's comment is echoed by his cousins, Kenneth Clamby and Mary Holo. According to Mrs. Holo, her mother (Willard's paternal aunt), Margaret Miller, often sent political letters to the *Fergus Falls Daily Journal.*

"The old editors of the paper would turn over in their grave if they could see some of the positions the editors take in the paper today," Holo says. "It's not such a Republican paper anymore. Letters my mother wrote about issues in an upcoming election would appear after the election to ensure that the Liberal voice wasn't heard. It's not that way anymore."

Ken Clamby agrees that Munger's electoral chances in Pockerbrush country were grim.

"I was only 13 years old in 1934 but I handed out flyers for Willard," Clamby recounts. "Willard was always a politician. He'd argue with anyone about anything. But he was clever and he treated folks right. It made sense that Willard left here for Duluth. He wasn't going to get elected, even with the hard times, as a Farmer-Laborite in Otter Tail County."

Not only was Munger facing an uphill battle as a reform-minded Liberal in an extremely conservative district, he was also up against one of the area's most beloved politicians. Her name was Hannah Kempfer. Some say she was a Republican. Others say she was an Independent. Whatever her true ideology, everyone in Otter Tail County knew Mrs. Kempfer.

CHAPTER 7

Hannah Kempfer

Born on December 22, 1880, Hannah Kempfer was the product of a romance between an English sea captain and a young stewardess serving aboard the captain's ship. After a tumultuous voyage from England to Norway (which convinced Hannah's mother that a steamship was no place to raise a child) Hannah was left in the care of the Jensen family. The Jensens ultimately adopted Hannah, immigrated to the United States in 1888 after the passage of the Homestead Act, and claimed a 160 acre parcel in Erhard's Grove Township in Otter Tail County. With the Crash of '93, times were hard and young Hannah was forced to find a job. She worked summers in town as a maid and returned to the farm in the fall for school. She attended Tonseth Lutheran Church; the same church attended by the Munger family. At age 17, she took and passed the teacher's exam. She was placed at School No. 229 in Friberg Township; the school where Lyman Munger served as clerk of the school board and where the four oldest Munger children received their primary educations.

Hannah Kempfer was an inspiration to her students. One boy, Barney Kempfer, asked how she came to be a teacher. She gave him some advice and he enrolled in college in Fergus Falls, eventually becoming a teacher himself. Through her friendship with Barney Kempfer, Hannah Jensen met Kempfer's brother, Charles. (*Hannah Kempfer, An Immigrant Girl* by Linda Frances Lein; Anika Publications, 2002). After her marriage to Charles Kempfer, Hannah moved to School No. 187, a school immediately adjacent to the Kempfer homestead, and it was there she came into contact with Margaret Munger Miller, the younger sister of Harry Munger, Sr.

> I first remember her when she visited my mother [Mary Emily Munger, Lyman Munger's wife] and asked us to come to her last day of school program…I remember my parents saying that Miss Jensen had a splendid program…My mother said "She is a natural born teacher and I wish we could send our little girl to school where she teaches…"

I was not able to start school with Hannah Jensen as she taught school too far away for a few years. In the meantime, Hannah Jensen had married Charles Kempfer, and she lived on the Kempfer farm and taught the home school, old District 187. Our home was only about two miles from this school, so my parents got permission to send me to this school.

Mrs. Kempfer was a thorough and diligent teacher...although she was not a generous marker...I went to school with Mrs. Kempfer as long as she taught nearby, and after I became a teacher myself I taught for two years in old 187, her home school, and boarded with her. She was always interested in helping others get an education...

("Former Pupil Tells About How Hannah Kept School" by Mrs. Arthur Miller, *Fergus Falls Daily Journal*, February 14, 1966.)

One of the innovations Hannah Jensen (as she was known before her marriage) installed in her schools was hot lunch.

It was characteristic of her that on her first day as teacher, she decided to give the children a hot lunch every noon—an unheard of practice at the time... [S]he bought a twenty-quart kettle and collected supplies. The next morning she kept the kettle boiling during lessons and made dumplings for the midday soup. Afterwards, some of the children brought meat and vegetables from their homes and various farmers in the vicinity contributed. Her school became known as the Hot Soup School. Other teachers in other parts of the country learned of what she was doing and followed her example.

("Beyond Herself" by Peter Gray, *Fergus Falls Daily Journal*, February 14, 1966.)

Though Hannah and Charles Kempfer deeply desired children, they never had a family of their own. Mrs. Kempfer continued teaching through the 1927 school year. She also became involved in civic affairs, helping to establish a farmer's club for children and assisting in the creation of the Otter Tail County Fair. With the passage of women's suffrage in 1919, Mrs. Kempfer was a natural choice to run for the legislature and in conservative Otter Tail County, Mrs. Kempfer's affiliation with important Republicans was an asset. Even though Minnesota Legislative races were nonpartisan contests (from 1913 – 1974), party labels still held sway with the voters.

Mrs. Kempfer was approached to run for office by Conservative Elmer E. Adams, the owner of the *Fergus Falls Daily Journal*. Adams' support of Kempfer was no small matter as Adams had been a member of the University of Minnesota Board of Regents, served in the Minnesota House of Representatives for seven non-consecutive terms and ran for the state senate (unsuccessfully) in the 1922 election. He beat noted Republican boss, Roy Dunn for a state senate seat in 1930, ran unsuccessfully for Congress as a Republican candidate in 1932, and was re-elected to the state senate in 1938. (*Otter Tail Record*, Otter Tail County Historical Society, Fall, 1984.)

In a letter to Adams dated February 7, 1922, Mrs. Kempfer made it clear that, while she considered herself an Independent, in the end, she was more Republican than not.

> I thank you very much for your interest and consideration of me in even thinking me able to fill such an office...I would prefer being independent. I never belonged to any party but can see the good and bad in all of them, and if I must accept party affiliations, I prefer the Republicans.... I hope to see you sometime and talk the matter over...
>
> (*Hannah Kempfer, An Immigrant Girl*, ibid, p. 120.)

Kempfer's true political allegiance is made clear in a review of the positions she took on various bills during the 1933 session. The *Farmer-Labor Leader* tracked the voting records of state legislators, including Mrs. Kempfer. While it is true that Kempfer was not as conservative as Elmer E. Adams (who scored a "zero" rating as adjudged by the editors of the *Leader* for his votes in the 1933 session: Adams supported none of the bills deemed to be of critical importance to the FL, including restraints on child labor), Mrs. Kempfer managed only a 29% favorable rating (she supported child labor restrictions and a graduated income tax but no other Progressive measures).

Because Mrs. Kempfer never knew her birth parents, she became active in establishing laws that conveyed inheritance rights upon illegitimate children. Kempfer also supported social welfare and resource conservation laws. As chairman of the House Committee on Game and Fish, Mrs. Kempfer worked to establish the first mandatory fee for fishing licenses, the proceeds of which were used for the re-stocking of fish in Minnesota's lakes, rivers and streams. For a brief moment (in 1925), Kempfer was also the first woman to hold the Speaker's Chair in the Minnesota House. (*Fergus Falls Daily Journal*, March 10, 1991) By the time Hannah Kempfer faced Willard Munger and others in the 1934 primary election, she had served five terms in the Minnesota House.

During her nine non-consecutive terms in the House, Mrs. Kempfer rejected all political endorsements, including endorsements from both Conservatives and

Liberals, preferring to be known as an Independent. After her primary victory in 1922, she wrote to the leaders of the Nonpartisan League, rejecting their support.

> I would rather stand for the principle of representing all of the people of Otter Tail County and be defeated than be elected under circumstances that oblige me to vote according to the dictation of any party or individuals…My guiding principle will be "equal opportunity for all with special privileges for none…"
>
> (*Pelican Rapids Press,* Excerpted from the
> *Minnesota Session Weekly,* dated May 5, 1999.)

A few years before Willard Munger's mythical journey to Washington, D.C., Mrs. Kempfer made a similar odyssey of her own. Though Mrs. Kempfer professed her political independence, she was clearly a Conservative as witnessed by her solid support of President Hoover.

> Mrs. Hannah Kempfer returned Friday from Washington, D.C., where she attended the Child Welfare Conference called by President Hoover…President Hoover took time from his many duties to address the conference and he and Mrs. Hoover held a reception for the delegates…
>
> Mrs. Kempfer returns from Washington thoroughly convinced that President Hoover is the best man who could have been selected for the presidency of this nation in these trying times…
>
> (*Fergus Falls Daily Journal,* November 29, 1930.)

However, as indicated in a speech given to high school students in Fergus Falls during her 1932 campaign, Kempfer could be pragmatic when the need arose.

> I want to assure you that I am not asking you people to support me because I am a woman; by no means. I am asking you to support me because I think I can hold my own in ability and understanding with those of men…
>
> I have not come to talk about the economy. I have practiced economy in my every vote in legislative sessions. I have never felt I should vote for any bonds, and new indebtedness, because such cannot be done in the private home when there is no means to pay with and should not be done in the public House of Minnesota…
>
> We talk about cutting salaries. There are stories out there about a 26% cut. I cannot say I am in favor of that. The man who works for $50 a month cannot stand such a cut, but a man working for $10,000…can afford a cut and it will not hurt him in the least…
>
> (*Fergus Falls Daily Journal,* October 27, 1932.)

As the story was retold by Willard Munger, he lost his first bid for public office by 34 votes to Hannah Kempfer. While it is true that Munger lost his first run for the House of Representatives in 1934, it is not literally correct to claim he lost the election *to* Mrs. Kempfer. Munger actually finished in ninth place, one spot shy of making it out of the primary and into the general election. His vote total, 2,327, was less than half of the 5,453 votes Mrs. Kempfer received (*Fergus Falls Daily Journal*, June 22, 1934.) Mrs. Kempfer finished third in the primary behind Conservatives Leonard Erickson and Roy Dunn, and ahead of William Ost, another Conservative. All four were later elected to serve in the 1935 Minnesota Legislature. T.H. Johnson, the FL candidate for state senator, was the only bright spot in the FL stable. Johnson survived the nonpartisan primary and eventually defeated Senator Elmer E. Adams in the general election.

One can only imagine the disappointment young Willard Munger felt when the results of the primary election became known. FL vote counters at polling places throughout the district would have alerted Munger to the fact that he was close to breaking through to the primary. Only the final vote tally, likely completed the day after polling closed, confirmed that Munger's dream of "being a big man" would have to wait.

With the primary election behind him (and Martha having graduated high school) Willard and his beloved "lady slipper" put their "promise" into action. The young lovers unceremoniously left town, leaving handwritten elopement notes behind.

> It was announced in the newspaper, from reliable contributors, that Miss Martha B. Winter, daughter of Mr. and Mrs. Ernest F. Winter, of Buse Township, and Mr. Willard M. Munger, son of Chief Deputy Game Warden and Mrs. Harry L. Munger of Fergus Falls, were quietly married a few days prior to the announcement. The wedding was done at an altar with a pastor of the church of the bride's denomination in a county seat of an adjacent state. The groom was attended by one of his fraternity. The bride was attended by an intimate acquaintance and that acquaintance's mother. Their ceremony took place at noon and was followed by a formal dinner at a fine hotel in the city where the wedding took place.
>
> It is understood that the union has the blessing of both parties' parents. Mr. Munger, though only 23 years of age, made an excellent showing in his recent campaign for the legislature; he is the chairman of the Farmer-Labor Association of the County; is energetic and ambitious and Martha is a young woman of ideal domestic virtues. The couple left on an extended honeymoon

to the northern part of the state and will begin residence in Fergus Falls after October 1.

(*Fergus Fall Daily Journal*, undated.)

The mystery of *where* the two were married was solved during the researching of this book. Kenneth Clamby recalls being told (by his mother) that the couple traveled to South Dakota to get married. This claim was verified by obtaining a copy of the couple's marriage certificate. Willard and Martha were married in Milbank, South Dakota on July 19, 1934.

CHAPTER 8

The Operative

At age 23, Willard Munger found himself living with his new wife in his in-law's farmhouse in Buse Township south of Fergus Falls. Bills and receipts from that timeframe indicate he was not above doing odd jobs, such as painting houses and commercial buildings to make ends meet. During the summer of 1934, Munger secured an appointment on a crew working for the United States Bureau of Public Roads doing a survey of Minnesota's roadways. This position would later require him to deflect criticism from Rep. Kempfer that he had been out "politick-ing" while employed by the government.

Once the primary was over, Munger became involved in Governor Floyd B. Olson's re-election effort. Attempts to smear Olson surfaced almost immediately during the 1934 contest.

> July 16, 1934
>> Dear Mr. Munger,
>> [W]ith reference to the "Birkeland Pamphlet," I am enclosing for your information a copy of a letter which the governor has sent to all those people who have written us on this matter…I believe that the letter we have been using is very effective in answering the Birkeland charges.
>> Sincerely,
>> Vince A. Day
>> Secretary to the Governor

The "Birkeland Pamphlet" was an attempt by Conservatives to cast doubt on Olson's work as Hennepin County Attorney. In 1925, Reverend K.B. Birkeland had been found dead in a Minneapolis apartment. The coroner was unable to establish a cause of death. There were rumors that a Mrs. Hodge (a suspected prostitute) had a hand in Birkeland's demise but efforts to extradite her back to Minnesota were unsuccessful. Without Mrs. Hodge's testimony, the grand jury was unable to reach a conclusion as to the cause of Birkeland's death. During the '34 election, Conservatives dragged the unsolved case back to the forefront of public scrutiny by contacting the dead man's father, who alleged that Olson had been derelict in performing his duties. The Republican Party repeated the distraught father's allegations in a letter to Lutheran congregations (Birkeland was a Lutheran pastor) throughout Minnesota. The letter Mr. Day referenced was a form letter prepared by Governor Olson in response to these allegations. In part, the letter read:

> I was interested in your recent letter concerning the distribution of the Birkeland pamphlet. I learned some weeks ago that this was being distributed among the Lutheran ministers of this state…I have always felt very sorry for Mr. Birkeland…His mental anguish has undoubtedly prevailed over his good judgment in setting out certain facts…
>
> This whole affair was taken before the…Grand Jury. After thorough consideration…these Grand Juries were definitely convinced that Reverend Birkeland was not murdered…

(Willard Munger Personal Collection.)

Tracking Willard Munger's relationship with Floyd B. Olson through Munger's personal correspondence makes it clear that, while the young man began his relationship with the governor as a wide-eyed admirer, Munger's steady work on behalf of the FL cause forged a friendship between the two men. With the legislature under the control of the Conservatives, and assorted maladies and disasters affecting his reign as chief executive, there's little doubt Olson needed all the friends he could muster. During the campaign, Munger (and other FL operatives) had to contend with the Birkeland pamphlet, as well as the public's reaction to the governor's handling of the 1934 Truckers' Strike.

On May 16, 1934, truck drivers in Minneapolis shut down the delivery of bread, milk, ice and other commodities in protest of long hours and low wages. The strike caused Governor Olson headaches with the third leg of his All Party coalition (small businesses) because Olson's response to the strike appeared to be sympathetic to labor. Matters became worse when a negotiated end to the walkout fell apart and a second, more intense boycott began in July. Minneapolis Chief of Police Mike Johanna pledged to protect delivery trucks with police. Tragedy struck on July 20, 1934 when police officers escorting a decoy truck discharged shotguns into a crowd of strikers, killing 2 and wounding 67. Twenty-five of the victims were shot in the back trying to run from the melee. In response, Governor Olson proclaimed martial law and, in a move never repeated in the annals of jurisprudence, Olson successfully represented the governor's office in federal court where he blocked an injunction against his imposition of martial law. Olson's victory in court prompted FDR to send mediators to the state. Mediation failed and Roosevelt himself came to Minnesota to broker a settlement. President Roosevelt convinced the banks propping up the businessmen during the strike to withdraw their financial support, resulting in a quick end to the dispute. Though the episode began as a major distraction for Floyd B. Olson's re-election campaign, by the time FDR left the state in late August of 1934, Olson's stature had increased substantially with Minnesota voters. (*Floyd. B. Olson: Minnesota's Greatest Liberal Governor*, ibid, p. 98.)

The 1934 campaign was also complicated by A.C. Townley's defection. Townley was so enraged by Olson's refusal to exclusively appoint FL loyalists to government jobs, he ran for governor on his own party label, a fact that caused Willard Munger personal angst as he traveled northwestern Minnesota in support of Olson's candidacy.

In addition, Munger's work for the federal government (on the road survey crew) took him away from his new bride.

> August 1, 1934
>
> My Dear Little Martha,
>
> I am leaving this morning for Marshall County; finished Red Lake yesterday. Send mail to Thief River Falls. I went into the post office this morning to get a letter from my sweetheart but there wasn't any. Please write to me to let me know how you are. I think about you all the time.
>
> I wish you could be along. It seems so lonesome without you.
>
> Tell your dad to be ready next Sunday. We'll have a fine time camping out, you & me.
>
> Your Loving Husband,
> Willard

The "Munger Family Legend" is that Willard and Martha lived in a canvas tent after they were married. There is a grain of truth to this myth in that the young couple *did* spend their honeymoon camping out in northern Minnesota and spent additional time together under canvas while Willard conducted road surveys.

> August 2, 1934
>
> My Dear Little Wife,
>
> I haven't heard a word from you since I left and I'm sure worried about you. I can't hardly wait until next Saturday when I'll see you. I sure wish you

were along. You have to drive 25 or 30 miles before you see a farm home. We
went over to Beltrami County to where George Armstrong is staying to have
the car fixed. I'm going to take you along Monday & show you things that
you have never seen before. We stayed in the county where the Great Fire of
'31 went through.

I've got to go to work.

Your Loving Husband,

Willard

During the 1934 campaign, Townley sought to fracture the All Party coalition Olson had used to change the face of Minnesota politics. Governor Olson picked up
his pen in response.

Mr. Townley believes in the political theory of gaining control of the dominant political party of the state. He has said nothing since the time he so bitterly opposed the formation of a third party to indicate he has changed from
his original theory. That he unsuccessfully sought political office through the
votes of the Farmer-Labor Party is no indication he has changed his mind.

The evidence is conclusive that he organized the Benson meeting; that he
dominated it; that he caused these communications and resolutions to be
drawn; that he did not permit anyone opposed to his designs to even speak;
and that his underlying motive was to become a candidate for governor...

I am glad that Mr. Townley has withdrawn from the Farmer-Labor Party
and severed even his claimed affiliation therewith. I sincerely hope you will
not be misled into a course of action, which knowing you as I do, I believe
you would continue to regret in the future...

(*Minneapolis Star,* September 7, 1934.)

If there was any question as to which horse Willard Munger was backing, the following letter puts such uncertainty to rest.

September 27, 1934

Dear Mr. Munger,

I appreciate your recent letter concerning Mr. Townley's activities at the
present time. I am glad to know where you stand in the matter and want to
thank you for your words of commendation and encouragement.

Sincerely yours,

Floyd B. Olson

Governor

Olson also had to weather a storm caused by his resignation as the Federal Relief Administrator for Minnesota. Olson quit the position in protest over policy but his resignation was used by Conservatives as a basis to claim corruption, a charge that was quickly dispelled.

> Relief Administrator Harry L. Hopkins, asked to comment on the resignation of Governor Floyd B. Olson as Minnesota Relief Administrator, said that "political activities in the state have never bothered me." Hopkins said emphatically that he had not asked for Olson's resignation. "I was never dissatisfied with the Minnesota relief set-up at any time and I am well satisfied with it now."
>
> (*Minneapolis Star*, October 19, 1934.)

Willard Munger made his support of Olson widely known.

> As county chairman of the Otter Tail County Farmer-Labor Association, I wish to state that I am 100% in back of Governor Olson for re-election and for the principles set forth in the Farmer-Labor platform.
>   Willard Munger
>
> (*Fergus Falls Daily Journal*, 1934.)

There was also public discussion of Olson's involvement in the Minneapolis truckers' strike in the *Journal*.

> Editor of the Journal:
>   I wish to take this means of thanking Mrs. Fred Homan for what she is saying for me. I do not want to be so dead as that no one can find fault with me. Criticism is good and proves at least that I am trying to...do something. I do not blame her for standing up for the industrial workers. She has worked with them and for them. I agree with her that they need protection. If I should be re-elected, I will do as I have done in the past—work for their rights—rights that they are entitled to have. My heart's interest at present and has always been in my fellow men and associates, the farmer and small business people whom I know and work with, and whose condition I am well aware of. I am as much interested in this class of people as Mrs. Homan is in her workers. If people want to oppose me for not believing in Governor Olson's platform, they have a right to do so, just as I have a right to believe otherwise.
>   I have never been a rubber stamp for Mr. Adams, Governor Olson or anyone else. Mr. Adams and the *Journal* have said some kind things about my work, but he has never asked me to vote for a bill or against a bill since I have been in public service...

I try to study all sides of a question and listen to both sides, then know enough to decide for myself what seems right to me to do. I am aware that I do make mistakes. I admit that. I believe that everyone feels his ideas are the right ideas. I make it a practice to listen to them and because I differ, I am not angry with either my friends or my enemies.

I am wishing every candidate the best of luck. The voters are going to be the choosers, and I am willing to abide by their decision without any fault-finding.

Sincerely yours,

Hannah Kempfer

(*Fergus Falls Daily Journal*, October 26, 1934.)

As the 1934 campaign came down to the wire, Willard Munger communicated with FL congressional candidate, C.A. Ryan from Jenkins, Minnesota. The men discussed the military build-up of Nazi Germany and the perpetuation of war, which both men abhorred. Munger and Ryan became acquainted during the 1934 Farm Holiday train trip to Washington, D.C.

Dear friend Willard,

I have sent material to Mr. Jaren for broadcasting of it and with the request that it be broadcast at 6:15 P.M. Wednesday evening…Hope it does some good. Don't you know of someone there who would have the station broadcast it again? It would help.

With kindest personal regards, I am

Your friend,

C.A. Ryan

The material Ryan referenced was read to the public over the airwaves before the election.

An unparalleled situation exists here in the state of Minnesota. Never before in the history of the United States has the people of any state in our Union thrown off the yoke and shackles of a capitalistic system that was so completely depriving them of their right to "life, liberty and the pursuit of happiness." Here in Minnesota, we have the unprecedented action of the people of a great state rising en masse and giving battle to the Wall Street gangster-led political machines…and had it not been for the great foresight and leadership of that great humanitarian and statesman, Franklin Delano Roosevelt, this country in all probability would be in the throes of a revolutionary war…

The Farmer-Labor Party platform which was approved and adopted…is one of the most outstanding political documents that has ever been written…It is a notice served on the exploiters of this state that the people of Minnesota refuse to be further exploited and that they are determined to finish the job of scrapping the old political machines and to drive all political gangsters from this state.

To the platform and policy of the Farmer-Labor Party, the World Peace Association gives its complete endorsement…

C.A. Ryan
Secretary-Treasurer
World Peace Association
Jenkins, Minnesota

Munger responded after the election.

December 5, 1934
Dear Mr. Ryan:
I am very sorry I didn't get time to write to you before. Your broadcast came over the radio, 6:00 P.M., November 5, the night before the election and it sure was good.

I have talked to many people in regards to that broadcast and everyone thought it was wonderful. They requested copies of the speech. I gave out all I had…

By the returns of the election, we still need to do a lot more educational work.

If you have any more copies of that speech…please send some down as I have many requests for copies…

Thanking you for your fine cooperation, I am
Very truly yours,
Willard M. Munger
County Chairman

The 1934 election maintained Floyd B. Olson in office but spelled trouble for the governor's All Party coalition. Though the impact of Townley's gubernatorial candidacy was insignificant (he garnered only 4,454 votes state-wide), Townley's defection was the tip of the iceberg in terms of Olson's problems.

The election of 1934 foreshadowed the final disintegration of the unstable farmer-worker alliance. Olson's survival in this, his last and hardest election, was primarily due to the steady leftward drift of urban sentiment and his tremendous personal prestige.

(*Floyd B. Olson: Minnesota's Greatest Liberal Govern*, ibid, p. 251.)

Years later, Willard Munger reflected upon the secret of Floyd B. Olson's success.

> "Olson took the middle of the road with the All-Party support," Willard remembered. "He had a powerful machine, plus his speaking ability…He was not only a good speaker, but he was a brilliant person. He had a way with him that would sweep anyone off their feet, even if they were Republican. He had a lot of Republican support. Yes, he initiated a lot of reforms. He was not a hypocrite. He generally carried out what promises he made regarding reform. There's no question about it. He got along pretty good with the moderate Republicans. You see, a lot of Republicans lost their businesses and were down and out, just like everybody else during the Depression. Minnesota never did have many Democrats. It was mostly a Republican state. Townley was partly responsible for that, because his whole concept of the Nonpartisan League was to move into the party that was the strongest. He wanted to capture the primary and get legislation passed that way. So he used the Republican Party, and by using the Republican Party, he built up a following that stayed with it. Olson was smart enough to capture that following through the All-Party organization."

> *(Oral History of Willard Munger*, ibid, pp. 54 – 55.)

The only FL candidate to prevail in Otter Tail County in 1934 was T.H. Johnson who was elected to the state senate. All four House seats in District 50 went to the Conservatives, making Willard's loss in the primary seem paltry when one considered the extent to which the Republicans controlled the legislature state-wide. Still, returning Floyd B. Olson to St. Paul for a third term was something Willard Munger and the other FL politicos had worked hard to achieve and Munger was rightly proud of that accomplishment.

> November 9, 1934
>
> Dear Mr. Day:
>
> We are having a Farmer-Labor Victory Banquet for those who helped work in the campaign, celebrating the re-election of Governor Floyd B. Olson and the defeat of Elmer E. Adams on Wednesday, November 14 in the Kaddatz Hotel at 7:30 P.M.
>
> If it is possible for you to be here, I would like to have you come to represent the governor. If you cannot come, please send some other good speaker.
>
> Please let me know in advance who is coming.
>
> Thanking you for your fine cooperation, I am
>
> Very truly yours,
>
> Willard M. Munger

The defection of Judge Henry Nycklemoe and other FL loyalists from the Party remained an issue that needed addressing.

> November 16, 1934
>
> Dear Mr. Day:
>
> At the last regular meeting of the Fergus Falls Farmer-Labor Club...the following resolution was passed unanimously:
>
> Be it resolved that for the best interests of the Farmer-Labor Club, that Mr. Henry Nycklemoe, Mr. A.T. Van Dyke, and Mr. Max Kronemann be read out of the Farmer-Labor Association of Fergus Falls...
>
> Very truly yours,
>
> Willard M. Munger
>
> Secretary, Fergus Falls Farmer-Labor Club

T.H. Johnson's election to the senate (and the ousting of *Daily Journal* editor and owner, Elmer E. Adams from that office) remained precariously uncertain. Johnson's margin of victory, 178 votes, was viewed as tenuous.

> December 4, 1934
>
> Dear Mr. Day:
>
> The rumor around Fergus Falls...is that Adams will try to throw the thing into the senate on some charges of misconduct or corrupt practice...I want therefore...to make proper arrangements through the office of the governor...I will have the assistance of attorneys...wholly and actively for Johnson; for I take it that the method of procedure in the senate will be quite different, in its setting, from that which is in court...I would not be so well acquainted with that end...
>
> And since there is a possibility that it may be brought to the senate, I want now, to have the governor fully aware and informed of things so that, if necessary, preparatory steps may proceed in the Capitol, while the case proceeds in the District Court of Otter Tail County...
>
> Respectfully,
>
> Lewis Ward Martin

Despite the controversy, Johnson's election was eventually confirmed and he was sworn in as a Minnesota State Senator.

Munger's activities on behalf of the FL continued. However, not all of his entreaties to Governor Olson or Olson's staff regarding patronage were successful (or even aimed in the right direction). As an example, Munger sent an application to Governor Olson on behalf of Yalmer Karvonen, a Finnish-American FLer from New York Mills, advising that Karvonen would be a good choice for postmaster of New York Mills. Of course, the office Munger referenced was a federal, not state, position, a distinction Olson made in his response to the young operative. Olson, ever the politician, didn't simply ignore the request, as misdirected as it was. He sent the request on to Mr. Joe Wolf, the National Democratic Committeeman from Minnesota, calling upon Olson's close ties with FDR and the Democrats nationally to assist Mr. Karvonen in finding work.

Munger also continued to correspond with peace activist C.A. Ryan.

> December 11, 1934
>
> Dear friend Munger:
>
> Your fine letter of December 5 received and very much appreciated...Am sorry I have only a few copies of my printed letter left...
>
> I have thought ever since coming back from Fergus Falls that those fine folks I met while with you, I mean your folk and your wife's, should have some representation in our World Peace organization and I am therefore sending you under separate cover a Certificate of Appointment as a Special Representative of this organization...
>
> The main thing for which our peace organization works is for the establishment of Democratic World Government with an International Congress as the highest legislative body...Ours is a fighting peace organization, not a pussy-footing bunch of molly coddlers and we are going to keep pounding away until we assume control of the affairs of the entire world and free this earth from the curse of war...
>
> Yours for a better world order,
>
> C.A. Ryan

Throughout the 1930s, Ryan unsuccessfully pursued election to Congress. His campaigns were primarily protests against militarism.

> In these crucial times, when the specter of war is again knocking at our door, we need courageous men in Congress—men not afraid to meet the forces of munitions makers and the war lord. Perhaps no man in America has contributed so much to the cause of world peace as Carl Ryan of Jenkins...His efforts in this field have won him praise from the Department of State and the International Red Cross...He will give the Sixth Congressional District the kind of representation it has not had since the days of Charles A. Lindbergh, Sr....After the voluntary retirement of the late Charles A. Lindbergh

from Congress, this district fell into the hands of a reactionary Republican machine...(Ryan's] election would retire from Congress the present incumbent who has consistently supported the program of Big Business in Washington.

(1938 Ryan Election Pamphlet, Willard Munger Personal Collection.)

At the time Ryan's letter to Munger was written, the Axis powers were rattling their swords and the League of Nations, President Woodrow Wilson's brilliantly conceived but fatally flawed vision of a unified world government (he was unable to convince the U.S. Senate to ratify the underlying agreement and thus, the U.S. never joined the League) was utterly incapable of dissuading Hitler, Mussolini, Stalin or Tojo from their expansionist intentions. A current of pacifism runs through all of Willard Munger's personal correspondence and it is clear, from Munger's later push to replace "The Star Spangled Banner" with "America the Beautiful" as the national anthem and his opposition to the Vietnam War, that Willard Munger's pacifist leanings remained strong throughout his life.

Munger continued to call Governor Olson's attention to those FLers who had remained loyal to the governor. In two letters to Olson dated January 7, 1935 and January 9, 1935, Munger listed 37 folks worthy of thanks from the governor in Otter Tail County (including his grandmother, Mary Emily Munger). Munger also sought to explain Olson's poor showing in Otter Tail County.

> January 7, 1935...
>
> I presume that you feel like I do, very much disappointed with the results from Otter Tail County. But under the circumstances, we couldn't expect much else. The *Fergus Falls Daily Journal*, which has a circulation of around 10,000, stooped to every low political trickery that is known and refused to print any of our articles in its columns...There is one outstanding achievement that we did accomplish and that is the defeat of Senator Elmer E. Adams, and the election of Hon. T.H. Johnson.
>
> Everything looked fairly well until the last two weeks when the churches put their nose in the campaign. As you probably know, Otter Tail County is very strong Lutheran Country and when they mixed in, it was impossible to do anything with them. You didn't receive the All Party vote that you got two years ago either. I am willing to assume some of the responsibility for Otter Tail County with the exception of the city of Fergus Falls, which was managed absolutely by Mr. Henry Nycklemoe during the campaign...
>
> Willard Munger

Munger's reflections to Olson continued.

> January 9, 1935...
>
> You probably know one of your bitterest enemies in the state is former Senator Elmer E. Adams of Fergus Falls, who is president of the *Fergus Falls Daily Journal,* which continually attacked you day after day before the election.
>
> The reason I am writing you this letter is to inform you who was one of the men most instrumental in defeating Mr. Adams and electing Mr. T.H. Johnson. I believe that it belongs to Mr. Lewis Ward Martin of Fergus Falls. I know this to be a fact because I arranged the meetings and Mr. Martin was one of the men that I could always depend on...
>
> I believe anyone who goes out and makes self sacrifices like he did should be given some consideration with the administration. People up here would appreciate it very much if you would give Mr. Martin a position in the legal department...
>
> Willard Munger

Often times (as noted above with respect to Munger's letter concerning Mr. Karvonen) Munger's patronage entreaties were misguided in that he confused federal with state positions, or directed his letters to the wrong department.

> I am aware of the fine work that Mr. L.W. Martin has done for the Farmer-Labor Party during the past few years and particularly in the campaign last fall...
>
> In your letter, you suggest that he be placed in the legal department. I presume your reference is to the Attorney General's Office. I have no jurisdiction over appointments made to that office and suggest you and Mr. Martin take that matter up personally with Mr. Harry Peterson, the Attorney General...
>
> Floyd B. Olson
> Governor

In dealing with patronage requests, there was also the reality that the Republicans controlled the Minnesota Legislature, which limited how much patronage Olson and his cabinet could spread around. In response to Munger's request to appoint Oran Bjorklund of Henning as a senate page, Lieutenant Governor Hjalmar Petersen, former legislator from Askov and owner of the Askov newspaper, noted that he lacked the power to do so.

January 10, 1935

You, of course, noted in the newspapers, that the Conservatives gained the organization of the Senate as well as the House, so they stripped me, as Presiding Officer of the Senate, of committee assignments. Their organization also gets the patronage. All I got was my secretary and stenographer. The Conservative Senators even took away the pages...

I appreciate your good wishes for success in my new office and if you happen to be in the Capitol city during the legislative session, I shall be glad to have you call for a handshake and to get personally acquainted.

Sincerely,

Hjalmar Petersen

Lieutenant Governor

Not only did Conservative control of the legislature make it difficult to secure patronage positions; it also spelled doom for reform.

January 13, 1935

My dear boy!

Well, both Houses are organized by the Conservatives, so we do not have much show. All we can do is to fight as hard as we possibly can and, of course, we will do so...

I hope that four years from now we will control both Houses regardless of who is elected. I do hope you and your nice little wife are both doing well and are very happy.

Sincerely yours,

T.H. Johnson

Senator

In addition to the roadblocks detailed above, there seemed to be no standard method for recommending patronage appointments, a procedural defect which caused frustration for both job seekers and the FL operatives supplying the names of potential employees to St. Paul.

Mr. Willard Munger

Chairman

Otter Tail County FL Association

Fergus Falls, Minnesota

January 10, 1935

Dear Mr. Munger,

There has been considerable discussion by members of the State Central Committee and others relative to the so-called "extra-preferred" and "preferred" list of candidates for positions...

In addition, county committees have apparently ignored their "preferred" lists and have urged appointments of recently endorsed candidates, so in effect, they have ignored their own preferred lists and in some instances, have acted so as to lead the undersigned to believe that said endorsed preferred list has been repudiated. The object of this letter is to ascertain whether this is true. I am attaching a form which I wish you would fill out and return to me so that my records may be more complete. I would appreciate it very much if this could be done as expeditiously as possible.

Thanking you in advance for your cooperation,

I am

Very truly yours,

Joseph A. Poirer

Special Assistant Attorney General

The ethical and political world that Willard Munger operated in as a party official in Depression-era Otter Tail County bears little resemblance to the power one would have in a similar position today. The world of patronage politics (which ended with the election of Republican Harold Stassen in 1938) was a nasty world, where the merits of a man's resume mattered far less than his political outlook.

If Willard Munger's work for the Farmer-Labor Association and his hero, Floyd B. Olson was exhausting and fulfilling, it was by no means capable of providing for his expanding family. With his wife expecting the couple's first child and his job as a road survey worker ended, Munger applied for a position with the federal government as an agricultural census enumerator.

Enumerators were to be paid per completed farm report, with an expected per diem rate of $4 to $5 per day. Munger passed the required written examination and was mailed his oath of office on February 1, 1935. Willard Munger's connection to the All-Party wing of the FL movement served him in good stead as he was supported in his job application by the Democratic Party of Otter Tail County.

January 30, 1935

Dear Sir:

The Otter Tail County Democratic Committee has recommended you to Mr. Clifford Bouvette, Supervisor of the Census, as one of the enumerators to be appointed in this county...

Your name had been selected from a group of fully one thousand applicants in this county, and in making the selection, we have done so considering your fitness and ability for the position.

I trust that you will merit the confidence reposed in you.

Yours very truly,

M.J. Daly, Jr.

Chairman

Otter Tail County Democratic Committee

Munger's supervisor in the enumerator position, Mr. Bouvette, explained (in a letter confirming Munger's successful application for the job) that Munger would be paid fifty cents per completed schedule and that there were 118 schedules to be completed for Friberg Township, the territory Munger was assigned. This resulted, when all the schedules were completed and returned, in a payment of $59.00 for the work. After completing his assignment, Munger's voucher for payment was sent to the Milwaukee Census Office. When the much-needed paycheck wasn't received, inquiries were made. A series of letters between Munger and his supervisors ensued, with Mr. Bouvette offering his apologies (and no check). Eventually, after a long delay, Munger finally received his pay.

Throughout his early political work with the third-party movement in Minnesota, Willard Munger continued to remain interested in Huey Long. The following is an article about Long that Munger clipped and saved.

> Why the noise against Huey P. Long? Many people naturally wonder why the large newspapers are giving Sen. Huey P. Long so much unfavorable publicity. It is largely because he is fighting entrenched wealth. That is a sin he cannot tolerate...Senator Long is a former Methodist minister who has gone in for a bit of evangelical work among the special privileged group. He perhaps thinks that the Christian religion applied to human society in actual practice would demonstrate that the philosophy of the lowly Nazarene is workable.
>
> (*Northern Minnesota Leader*, January 31, 1935.)

The same publication made note of Floyd B. Olson's Socialist leanings.

Governor Olson Stands Pat

Governor Olson believes that our social order should function so that there would be fewer debts and plenty of the worldly goods for all who are willing to do useful work. He is the friend of the farmer and worker. Never once has anyone had reason to doubt his sincerity to the principles which he expounds. Everyone knows where he stands on the great economic problems that confront the nation. Nor does he make any excuses for his beliefs.

(*Northern Minnesota Leader*, January 31, 1935.)

Munger wasn't shy about apprising Governor Olson of the barbs and rhetorical stones being flung in the governor's direction by Rep. Hannah Kempfer. What is intriguing about Munger's continued frustration with Kempfer's politics is the fact that, looking back to the connection between Kempfer and his own family (Munger's beloved brother Barney had been named after Kempfer's brother-in-law; Munger's aunt Margaret Munger Miller had been a student of Kempfer's; and Hannah Kempfer, according to recollections of cousin Kenneth Clamby, often gave Clamby rides into town) there should have been affection, not animosity between Munger and Kempfer. But there was something about Hannah Kempfer's politics that raised Munger's ire.

Maybe, as Mary Holo recounts, it had to do with hypocrisy. After all, Kempfer had been hand-picked to run for office by the leading Conservative in the county, Elmer E. Adams, the man who controlled the editorial page of the *Fergus Falls Daily Journal*, all the while claiming she was an Independent. Holo's recollection of Mrs. Kempfer and Holo's mother, Margaret Miller, "having it out" in School No. 229 after Mrs. Miller became a teacher seems to support the theory that it was Kempfer's failure to do what she said she'd do that likely irked Willard Munger.

"Hannah could tell a falsehood, no question about that," Mary Holo recalls. "We went to the same church with the Kempfers. My mother decided she'd had enough and called a meeting of the other women. It was held at the old school. My mother didn't have a problem confronting Hannah."

It was only natural then, that when Mrs. Kempfer raised a ruckus about Governor Olson's performance, Willard Munger, the loyal foot soldier, entered the debate on behalf of his general.

> January 28, 1935
>
> Dear Governor Olson:
>
> I am sending you a clipping from the *Fergus Falls Daily Journal* in regards to Rep. Hannah Kempfer's statement on the floor of the House that there were politics in relief, because she was asked to resign from the Otter Tail County Relief Committee.
>
> I am also sending you a copy of an article that I wrote in answer to her charges...
>
> Willard Munger

Munger's rebuke of Kemper's allegations was forceful and succinct.

Attacks Mrs. Kempfer

[M]rs. Kempfer had been successful in having three or four of her good friends and one relative placed in Fergus Falls on public payrolls and I can name more if necessary. That's a better deal than the Farmer-Laborites could get under a Republican administration.

Mrs. Kempfer, while on the Otter Tail County Relief Committee was very active in passing out a great number of Birkeland pamphlets, an immoral pamphlet. If necessary, I can give you the names of the ones that she passed it out to.

Now let's be fair. Who has been playing politics with relief? Has it been Governor Olson or Mrs. Kempfer?

Willard Munger

Olson's response was short and personal.

February 2, 1935

Dear Friend Will:

I thank you for sending me the clipping from the Fergus Falls Journal in regard to Hannah Kempfer's statement about politics in the relief administration.

I enjoyed your excellent reply...

Sincerely yours,

Floyd B. Olson

Governor

As Munger attempted to protect Olson's political backside, the Farm Holiday Association remained active in Minnesota.

February 4, 1935

Mr. Gilbert Brattland

Dear Mr. Brattland:

Here in Roseau County, we are coming along fine and next Friday the 8th in Roseau at 10:00 A.M., we have a big meeting by the Farm Holiday Association and the Farmers' Union together. We expect to have Kittson County boys over and would like to have you with us. Come, let us get together and do something and get action.

Hoping to see you,

Yours truly,

Joe Batling

County Chair

CC: Willard Munger

The federal farm foreclosure moratorium, a product of the 1934 Farm Holiday train trip to Washington, D.C., became the subject of litigation.

> Mr. Latimer...spoke on the Moratorium Bill at the recent Mid-West Legislative Conference.
>
> Mr. Latimer first pointed out the difference between our present and former moratoria. He outlined the history of these bills, emphasizing the fact that in former depressions the farmer or the owner of a small home could not be aided by the law. The Supreme Court of the United States always held that it was unconstitutional for him to keep his home, since to do so, he must violate a contract. This depression, however, has witnessed a rise of the moratoria to respectability; they have been granted to banks and insurance companies. In spite of that, some of the big financiers and their lawyers and politicians try to prove that a moratorium to a big company is that obscure thing, "constitutional," while moratoria to the still bigger mass of small property owners is that equally puzzling thing, "unconstitutional." Happily, five out of nine judges on the Supreme Court disagreed with them and held consistency in the granting of moratoria...
>
> (*Farmer-Labor Progressive*, February, 1935.)

In the same edition of the *Progressive*, the long-dreamed of resurrection of a viable national third-party was discussed. Not since Fighting Bob Lafollette and Teddy Roosevelt bolted the Republican Party had a serious national third-party effort emerged. With the advent of alternative political movements in the Midwest, it seemed that a new party, unaffiliated with the Democrats or the Republicans, was close to becoming a reality.

> **New National Political Party Will Be Launched in Spring**
>
> The new party is to come from the grass roots. In the discussion as to who should call the national conference to launch the new movement, the delegates showed their preference for rank and file organizations rather than national leaders.
>
> By unanimous decision of the Farmer-Labor Party of Minnesota, of Iowa, the Farmer-Labor Political Federations of Michigan, North Dakota, South Dakota, Montana and Kansas in conjunction with such other groups as have the fundamental purpose to create a new economic order based on representative government for and by those who toil, and that believe that the economic interests of the workers on the farms and in the factories, offices, stores and professions should be the prime motive of such new party were

asked to join in calling for a National Conference to launch the new political party...

Floyd B. Olson was first to hint of the need for a new national party when he stated "The people want a new deal, but more than that, they want a new deck..."

(Farmer-Labor Progressive, February 1935.)

Minnesota Congressman Henry G. Tiegan echoed Olson's sentiments:

A Farmer-Labor party is founded upon the organized masses. A Farmer-Labor party is built by getting organized progressive farm groups, labor unions, cooperatives, liberal organizations, organized unemployed, and political clubs that are composed of workers, farmers, professionals, and small merchants, by getting all these to associate themselves together to give expression to the economic needs they have in common.

(Unknown source; Willard Munger Personal Collection.)

The rhetoric of the leaders of the new third-party movement seemed perilously close to endorsing an all-out Socialistic or Communistic platform. At the time, the prospect of the U.S.A. falling into revolution and experiencing social and political upheaval similar to what had transformed the Russian Empire into the U.S.S.R. loomed large in the thoughts of many Americans. The prospect of a bloody end to the American experiment in representative democracy was frightening. Olson knew better than to let the more Socialistic members of his coalition run rampant over his All-Party course of moderate social and political change, and the *Minnesota Leader* did what it could to dispel such fears.

F-L Opens Fight on Communists, Fascists

With the campaign hysteria over and all but forgotten, a series of learned lectures in St. Paul the past week left Minnesota's "red-baited" Farmer-Labor Party, with its Cooperative Commonwealth program, marching down the middle of the political road bearing the banner of the true champion of democracy...

Governor Olson summed up the situation...

"There is nothing in common between the Communists and the Farmer-Laborites. The final, enduring champions of Democracy, whether the attack upon it be Fascist or Communist, will be members of left-wing political movements such as the Farmer-Labor movement..."

(Minnesota Leader, February 16, 1935.)

Willard Munger shared the view of many Farmer-Laborites, that it was time, in 1934 and 1935, for their party and its leader, Floyd B. Olson, to emerge from FDR's shadow. According to the "mouthpiece" of the FL movement, the *Minnesota Leader*, officials within the Farmer-Labor Party believed that it was time for their movement to be thrust into the national political spotlight.

> The National Farmer's Holiday Association this week attacked the New Deal and called for the founding of a national "farmer and labor" third party, but reaffirmed its allegiance to representative government and threw an alleged Communist group out of its convention...
>
> The third-party resolution asserted that, "It is the opinion of the Farm Holiday Association that a national political party expressing the desires of farmers and laborers should be formed at once..."
>
> (*Minnesota Leader*, May 4, 1935.)

Riots and violence caused by the burgeoning hardships of the Great Depression continued to plague the Midwest.

> **Police Bombing Women and Children Fires Fargo Strikers**
>
> Sentencing of 16 of the 60 Fargo strikers indicted for the "crime" of "riot" has failed to halt the strike and it is being carried on with renewed vigor and more intense feeling...
>
> Meanwhile, coal moves on the streets of Fargo only in rigs guarded by deputized men, mostly farmers who have not joined farmers' organizations.
>
> The intensity of feeling has been fueled not only by the sentencing of the 16 strikers to from two to six months in jail, but the gas-bombing of the Union Hall where the strikers, their wives and children were routed from a dance by a tear-bomb attack bearing detachment of police and deputies. Ninety-five union men were lined up on the sidewalk and marched to jail.
>
> Public feeling over the raids ran higher even than the indignation that marked the I.W.W. raids during and after the World War—raids for which Fargo became known throughout the nation.
>
> (*Minnesota Leader*, March 2, 1935.)

Despite his popularity and the perceived need for change, many third-party adherents were wary of Senator Huey Long's hold on the Progressive mindset of the nation. In an article in the *Farmer-Labor Progressive* from March, 1935, Wisconsin Congressman Thomas Amlie, one of the main advocates for a national third-party, decried Long's standing with the public.

Developments of the past few weeks in Washington have speeded up tremen-
dously the trend for a new political party on a national scale....As issue after
issue has come up and been settled with the Administration deciding in favor
of the powerful economic groups and against the interests of the agricultural
producers, the consumers, and labor, the liberals and progressive forces are
being pushed closer together...

One man in Washington has made good political capital out of the growing popular demand for a share of the potential plenty.

He is Senator Huey Long of Louisiana...

Senator Long is making rapid progress, especially among people of the
middle classes. If he attains a national following and gets into power, the
people are doomed to another disappointment because he cannot live up to
his promises...

Congressman Thomas Amlie, Wisconsin

(Unknown source; Willard Munger Personal Collection.)

Citizens began to rise up in the face of the slowness of governmental reaction to
their economic woes.

More than 5,000 persons participated in a parade to the Capitol. They represented some 60 organizations, including farmers and working men, who had
just concluded a three-day conference in St. Paul...

It was an orderly crowd; there was an entire absence of rowdyism. The
speaking was clear and earnest and during the afternoon, spectators heard
some spellbinders that would make a lot of Senators sound like rank ama-
teurs...

(*Minnesota Leader*, March 16, 1935.)

Munger saved articles from many sources, including clippings from Lieutenant
Governor Hjalmar Petersen's newspaper, the Askov American, regarding the political turmoil of the times. One issue that would remain volatile from the 1930s into
the 1960s was the issue of a state-wide sales tax. Willard Munger opposed the sales
tax, a regressive form of taxation, from his indoctrination in politics until the sales
tax was finally enacted into Minnesota law in 1967.

A sharp conflict of ideas on the reform of the state's taxing system is apparent
as the legislature prepares to "go to bat" on this important subject.

The Farmer-Labor Administration, believing that the fairest tax is that on net
income, is supporting a bill now before the legislature which would increase the

maximum net income tax in the higher brackets to 15 percent…Representing an opposing school of thought are those who want some form of sales tax…

(*Askov American*, March 28, 1935.)

The issue continued to resonate until the end of the 1935 legislative session.

Sales Tax Held Prize for Profit

Heading squarely into a veto by a governor whose motives are at wide variance with the element of business profit, the reactionary "octopus" tax bill was passed by the state senate this week…

The legislative conservatives call it an omnibus tax bill. It carries a heavy load of taxation, a variety of taxes, from the net income tax to the sales tax…

The sales tax is supported by the group which has continually and consistently sought to reduce salaries, to minimize relief allowances, to blacken the Farmer-Labor administration because it had the courage and the foresight to propose a cooperative, non-profit commonwealth. Those who support the sales tax do so because their motive is to make money…

(*Minnesota Leader*, April 20, 1935.)

It has always been a puzzle as to just what Willard Munger was in terms of his politics. Calling him a Liberal doesn't seem broad enough in scope. He certainly wasn't a Progressive, for as that term originally evolved, it meant a person of the Republican Party seeking progressive and modern change to the existing and established societal structure. Perhaps, as his long-time colleague and friend, State Rep. Mike Jaros (DFL-Duluth) says, "Maybe Willard was a Socialist. I know he hated being called a Democrat," Jaros recalls. "He would always say, 'I'm not a damn Democrat, I'm a Farmer-Laborite.'"

But whatever Munger's political philosophy was during his formative years, be it Norman Thomas Socialist or Floyd B. Olson All-Party Pragmatist, he was constantly searching for answers to the political questions of the day. Regardless of the label one might pin on young Willard in the years leading up to his first run for political office, one thing is for certain: Munger wasn't one to have his reputation tarnished by unfounded accusations. Take, for example, his blistering response to Mrs. Kempfer's assertion that he had been lining his pockets with taxpayer money while campaigning.

February 19, 1935
Hon. Mrs. Kempfer:

I have been informed by certain individuals that you have told them I received $700.00 while working for the Minnesota Highway Department. This is a mistake on your part and I request that you refrain from making like statements in the future.

The work that you talked about was not with the Minnesota Highway Department, but with the United States Bureau of the Public Roads; under supervision of A.W. Bartlett, who was supervisor of the Road Use Survey, of the United States Bureau of Public Roads...

If need be, I'll publish these letters from the United States Bureau of Public Roads and let the public know the truth.

While I had this job, I was not campaigning, as you stated, because I was sent up to work along the Canadian border. We may differ in our political thought but we should at least try and be fair in regards to the livelihood of others.

Very truly yours,

Willard M. Munger

As the winter of 1934-35 waned, Willard stayed attuned to issues of interest to him.

Hon. Wright Patman

United States House of Representatives

March 9, 1935

Hon. Wright Patman:

I heard your wonderful radio talk on the Soldier's Bonus and want to take this opportunity of extending my heartiest congratulations to you for the stand you took in regards to the big financiers in this country who are trying to kill your bill...

I am sure you can count on three Farmer-Labor Congressmen and our U.S. Senator from Minnesota to support your bill...

Very truly yours,

Willard M. Munger

Otter Tail County Chair

> (*Editor's Note: Wright Patman was a Democratic Congressman from Texas who served from 1928 until his death in 1976.*)

Munger also continued to assist would-be state employees applying for patronage jobs. Having been advised by Governor Olson that appointment of attorney Lewis Ward Martin to the "legal staff" would have to be scrutinized by the attorney general, Munger sought to have Martin appointed to the Industrial Commission. Once again, Olson re-directed Munger's effort.

I am referring this matter to the Industrial Commission and I am sure your recommendation and Mr. Martin's application will receive careful consideration...

(Letter from Olson to Munger; March 13, 1935.)

The movement to create and promote a national third-party began to take shape and Willard Munger was right in the thick of the new group's organizing efforts.

National Organization of the Farmer-Labor Political Federation and League
For Independent Action
Howard Williams, National Organizer
April 4, 1935
To Executive Committee Members:
Our April meeting will be held next Tuesday, April 9th, at 12:15pm, luncheon in the famous dining room of the Capitol Cooperative Café...
The agenda will include:

1. Report by National Organizer on recent month's organizing and speaking trips to East Coast;

2. Report of April 6th Exploratory Conference of Progressives called by us at Washington to discuss national party;

3. Report of State Conference of Iowa FL Party;

4. Discussion of call and agenda of our National Conference in Chicago tentatively set for June 1st and 2nd;

5. Question as to our attitude and cooperation with Senator Huey Long, Father Coughlin and Townsend groups...
Sincerely yours,
Howard Williams
National Organizer
P.S. At our March meeting, you were elected a member of the State Committee...We are most anxious to have you serve. Will you inform us on the enclosed parcel postal whether you will accept the election?

However flattered Munger was to be included in this venture, there was a practical limit to his ability to contribute financially to the organization's success.

Dear Mr. Williams:
I am returning the pledge card in this letter...All I can afford at the present time will be 25 cents a month. I would like to pledge more but financial circumstances will not allow it...

Thanking you in advance, I am

Very truly yours,

Willard M. Munger

County Chairman

As the summer of 1935 approached, Willard remained unemployed. In addition, he and Martha had just added a daughter to their family. The couple's first child, who was supposed to be named "Marilyn," was born March 17, 1935.

"The nurse who brought me to my mother after I was born named me," Patsy Munger-Lehr recalls. "I was born on St. Patrick's Day and when the nurse brought me to Mom, she said 'Here's Patricia' and the name stuck."

To say that the Mungers were in dire straits would not be an exaggeration. Despite the fact that Willard Munger had the power of the pen to seek a patronage position for himself, he resisted that temptation for a very long time. He did, however, continue on with his efforts to weed out undesirables from the Party's ranks, to deal with Mrs. Kempfer's slings and arrows, and to seek jobs for other FL loyalists.

Mr. A.B. Harris

April 21, 1935

Dear Mr. Harris:

Last week when I was in to see you, you perhaps remember that I talked to you regarding the Otter Tail County relief set-up which I told you was nothing as much as a relief set-up as a Republican machine.

I'm writing this letter to find out whether or not Mr. Prince is going to stay or be removed as Relief Administrator...

If we could have a man as administrator like Mr. Kingstedt, the present drought relief manager, we would get a 50% break at least, and it's a sure thing that the personnel of the relief set-up wouldn't be going out and knocking the administration as they have done...

Thanking you very much, I am

Very truly yours,

Willard M. Munger

Otter Tail County Chairman

Munger also tried to garner support for the governor's tax plan.

I immediately got busy and secured the Henning Commercial Club, Perham Commercial Club, and Wadena Club to send in resolutions asking the senate to support the bill...

It will be impossible for the Farm Holiday Assn. to raise any money at present...because they have had a little trouble here...A couple of their leaders were thrown in jail as a result of a foreclosure sale and they are busy raising money to pay their fines at the present time...

(Letter dated April 24, 1935 from Munger to Gilbert Brattland, former Thief River Falls FL operative working for Governor Olson.)

A name that would become intimately associated with the Farmer-Labor Party during the 1936 and 1938 elections surfaces for the first time in Munger's letters. That name is I.C. "Dutch" Strout.

May 22, 1935

Dear Governor Olson:

At the last regular meeting of the Fergus Falls Farmer-Labor Club...the following resolution...was passed...

"Be it resolved that the Fergus Falls Farmer-Labor Club go on record as favoring the reappointment of Mr. I.C. Strout as Budget Commissioner and Director of Personnel."

Mr. I.C. Strout, while acting as director of personnel, has cooperated 100% with our organization...

Mr. Strout has the support and cooperation of every Farmer-Laborer in the county.

Willard M. Munger

Secretary

Fergus Falls Farmer-Labor Club

With the bills mounting, a new mouth to feed, and no prospects for employment, Willard Munger bit the bullet and sought Olson's assistance.

May 21, 1935

Dear Mr. Dell:

This will acknowledge your recent letter in which you recommend Mr. Willard Munger for appointment as steward at the State Hospital, Fergus Falls. I am glad to take this up with the State Board of Control...

Floyd B. Olson

Governor

Willard Munger's precociousness regarding politics was clearly the result of his father's activities with the Nonpartisan League and the politcal indoctrination Willard experienced at the knee of his grandfather. His mother's family, the Zuehlsdorf side of the equation, wasn't politically active. However, Kenneth Clamby recalls, that when Willard was down and out, and politics wasn't feeding his new family, Munger approached Kenneth's father, farmer Peter Clamby, for help.

"Willard showed up one day," Kenneth recalls, "out at our farm, the farm that used to be Max Zuehlsdorf's place, out in Aurdal Township. Willard shows up one day in the summer and says, 'Uncle Pete, I need to borrow some money. I've got to get to Duluth to fill out an exam to be a special inspector.' My father borrowed him the money and Willard took me with him to Duluth. I can't remember who drove but we camped out somewhere north of Duluth, on the North Shore of Lake Superior. I slept in the car and Willard and another guy slept out under the stars. About midnight, the two of them came running back to the car all wide-eyed and awake. Seems they'd slept right next to a railroad line and when the train came through, it scared the begeebers out of them!"

While Munger waited to hear back regarding his application for a position with the Railroad and Warehouse Commission in Duluth as a state grain inspector, he continued to monitor the progress of the national third-party movement.

June is the Month set for Conference, Chicago is the Place

June is the month set for the national conference at Chicago for the purpose of launching a united new party based on a program of plentiful production for use.

This was the decision of a conference of twenty-five progressive Senators, Congressmen, trade union, farm, and socialist leaders held at Washington. The conference was called by Congressman Thomas R. Amlie of Wisconsin, National Chairman of the Farmer-Labor Political Federation, and Congressman Ernest Lundeen of Minnesota...

(*Farmer-Labor Progressive*, May 1935.)

A run for the presidency by Governor Olson seemed plausible. One can only imagine the excitement that was building in the breasts of young FL supporters like Willard Munger at the prospect of Olson taking a shot at the highest office in the land.

June 26, 1935

To Members of the State and National Committee:

We are asking the delegates to the Chicago Conference to meet with us. The following items will be discussed:

1. Instructions to Chicago delegates as to the advisability of national ticket for 1936 election, suggestions as to national organization and platform;

2. How to promote rural electrification;

3. Report on progress of Mid-West Youth Congress;

4. What can we do to help in capturing the Minnesota Legislature in 1936?

Howard Williams

National Organizer

Farmer-Labor Political Federation

Munger did not attend the convention in Chicago and ultimately, the national third-party movement died on the vine; the disparate branches of protest politics unable to form a cohesive, unified force. Despite the best, or worst, intentions of third-party adherents, FDR was re-elected to three additional terms as president, garnering the support of many Farmer-Laborites who refused to back a more radical candidate on the national level.

Within Minnesota, a scandal involving United States Senator Thomas Schall, a Republican and a serious critic of Floyd Olson and FDR, was brewing. One of Schall's operatives, a former FL newspaper man by the name of Walter W. Liggett, was arrested on charges of kidnapping and abduction of a 17-year-old girl from Austin, Minnesota. Liggett was found by police hiding in Schall's Minneapolis residence.

Liggett, F-L Traitor, Jailed in Schall Home

Walter W. Liggett, arch-assailant of Governor Olson and mountebank "liberal" writer who turned traitor to the Farmer-Labor cause to become the hireling propagandist of a reactionary political plunderbund, was arrested this week in the Minneapolis home of United States Senator Thomas D. Schall.

Liggett, publisher of political scandal sheets designed to undermine the Farmer-Labor Party, and most recently the alleged paid ally of reactionary Senator Schall, was jailed on charges of abduction made by a 17-year-old Austin girl…

The complaint alleges that Liggett and Frank Ellis, Austin labor organizer, brought two Austin girls to Minneapolis on March 22, 1935, and lodged them in a hotel. Ellis, who figured in the packing plant strike, was convicted of a statutory charge in Faribault…

Liggett has been one of the chief scandalmongers among the opponents of Governor Floyd B. Olson, though pretending to be a "liberal" himself, and last spring published a magazine article filled with obvious untruths and scandalous statements concerning the governor and the Farmer-labor administration…

(*Minnesota Leader*, June 29, 1935.)

Thomas Schall (who had defeated FL favorite Magnus Johnson) was considered a thorn in the side of both Floyd B. Olson and Franklin Delano Roosevelt. Though Schall's power in the Senate was on the ascendency when the above-article was clipped from the *Leader* by young Willard Munger, that rise was short lived. Schall was to die in a car accident within the year, giving Olson the opportunity to appoint FLer Elmer Benson to the United States Senate in Schall's stead.

Munger clipped another article from the *Leader* regarding his friend and mentor, I.C. "Dutch" Strout.

I.C. Strout Favored as Organizer

The State Central Committee of the Farmer-Labor Association has mapped out a new course through the sometimes rough patronage seas this week and launched the most sweeping statewide Farmer-Labor organization and membership drive ever undertaken in its history.

The committee set in motion a program seeking to build the Association to 150,000-200,000 members, open its doors to all true Liberals as active workers, and expand its membership "to the point where there can be no question as to its representing the vote and sentiment of the Farmer-Labor Party."

As immediate steps toward the new goal, the Central Committee:

Instructed the State Executive Committee to interview I.C. Strout, now state budget and personnel director, and work out details of the program in anticipation of employing him as full-time salaried organizer...

It adopted a report of its patronage committee which briefly outlined patronage problems. The report asserted that a check of state employees revealed instances where persons who had been appointed with indorsements of local and county committees and indorsements of individual *Farmer-Labor Leaders* without such indorsements being on file in the office of the personnel director...

(*Minnesota Leader*, August 24, 1935.)

Things within the Party were indeed grim. Governor Olson was once again up to his elbows in problems.

Olson Ends Riot, Locks Iron Plant

A growing demand that Thomas E. Latimer resign as mayor of Minneapolis and that the Farmer-Labor movement protect its own future progress by purging itself of leaders who lack decision and discernment, was the result of the strike riot in Minneapolis in which two persons were killed and 30 wounded...

Further violence was averted only when the state's Farmer-Labor governor, Floyd B. Olson, stepped in, turned out the "scabs" housed in the Flour City iron plant, and put a padlock on the door...

(*Minnesota Leader*, September 21, 1935.)

Even as Floyd Olson struggled to remain in power, he made certain Munger's loyalty was rewarded. Willard's patronage appointment as a state grain inspector was finally approved and in late 1935, the Munger family left Fergus Falls for Duluth. In many ways, Willard Munger was entering a world he knew very little about. But the promise of steady work and a more receptive audience for his Liberal ideals drew Munger east, across the state, to the shores of the Big Lake.

Pockerbrush Boy:
A Pictorial

Robert Munger (left) and Willard Munger (right) circa 1913.

Barney Munger, Willard Munger and Robert Munger, circa 1920.

Willard's high school graduation photograph, 1932.

Willard posing with car, 1936.

Martha Winter circa 1934.

Martha and Patsy, 1935.

Willard and Martha, 1936 Benson Campaign.

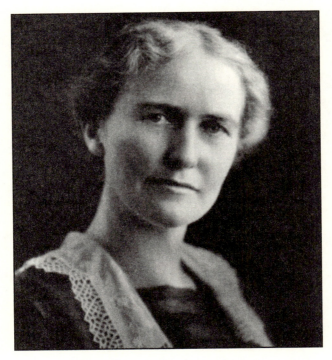

Hannah Kempfer, 1934.

Part Two:

Entrepreneur

Chapter 1

The Skipper is Gone

The grain inspection position Willard Munger accepted in Duluth was the third of a series of patronage jobs that he worked after leaving Standard Oil. Munger had been briefly employed (during the spring and summer of 1934) by the federal government doing a survey of the roads of northwestern Minnesota. In 1935, after he'd been out of work for a considerable period of time, Munger again worked temporarily for the federal government conducting a farm census in Friberg Township. Finally, he moved his young family to Duluth to accept another patronage job; inspecting grain being stored and shipped from Duluth's inland port.

It was fortuitous for the young Farmer-Laborite that the surname "Munger" was already familiar in Depression-era Duluth. Lumber baron Roger Munger and his brother, artist Gilbert Munger, had been well-known members of Duluth society during the late 1800s. A myriad of public buildings, roads and the like were named in honor of the famous Munger brothers, many of which (including the majestic Munger Terrace Apartments in downtown Duluth) remain in existence today.

Though Willard Munger did not know it at the time, he shared a common (if distant) heritage with the more famous "Duluth Mungers." Both families trace their origins back to Surrey, England and to immigrants Nicholas and Sarah Munger. The sons of Nicholas and Sarah, Samuel (born in 1662 or 1665) and John (born April 28, 1660) in New Haven, Connecticut form the respective ancestral branches of the two lines of the Munger family which came together in Duluth in 1935: Samuel being the patriarch of Willard's bloodline, and John being the patriarch of the line shared by Roger and Gilbert. Until the writing of this text, the "Otter Tail Mungers" had no knowledge that they shared a common ancestry with the "Duluth Mungers." In fact, the "Otter Tail Mungers," though flattered at the suggestion of a connection, always demurred when asked if they were related to the "Duluth

Mungers." Tangential as it may be, there is indeed a familial link. Willard Munger didn't know this when he moved to Duluth in 1935 and never learned of it before his death in 1999, though it is likely that Munger's well-known surname was advantageous to a young man interested in Duluth politics.

In 1935, Duluth, Minnesota was a swirling sea of protest politics set against a solid landscape of staunch conservativism rooted in family fortunes accumulated during the bully days of iron ore mining, timber harvesting, lumber milling, grain trading and manufacturing. At the time Willard and Martha Munger arrived in the bustling city, labor unrest was broiling in Duluth, as it was in most major municipalities in the Midwest.

> **Laundry Strikers to "Stick to their Guns"**
>
> Two striking men, employees of Duluth Linen Supply, Inc. were beaten, one so seriously he required medical attention...
>
> Four of the strikebreakers and the wife of one of them were arrested and two of them bound over to district court on second degree assault charges.
>
> Ben Ostrov, one of the striking employees, was beaten over the head with a blackjack in the hand of Ed Derwin. He was severely gashed over the right temple...
>
> (*Labor World*, October 16, 1935.)

Though he lived across the state from his old stomping grounds, Munger retained the chairmanship of the Otter Tail County FL Association and remained in contact with his associates from northwestern Minnesota.

> Mr. Willard Munger
>   225 E 2nd Street
>   Duluth, Minnesota
>   December 6, 1935
>   My Dear Willard:
>   [I]have been quite busy running around the District but it so happens I have not had an opportunity to visit Fergus Falls. I hope to get down there though before I run to Washington and will surely contact our mutual friend George Miller.
>   I certainly want to congratulate you on your aggressiveness in going to night school after working all day. I appreciate you keeping me advised of the situation from time to time in the past and hope you will continue to write me occasionally.

Whenever you think I can be of any service to you, please feel free in writing me.

With kindest regards and best wishes, I am,

Sincerely yours,

R.T. Buckler

Rich T. Buckler was first elected to Congress in 1934 and served from 1935 to 1943 from the old Ninth District (Minnesota, as previously discussed, briefly had not only nine, but ten Congressional Districts. The Tenth existed from 1915 to 1933. The Ninth, which included Otter Tail County, existed from 1903 to 1963). Buckler replaced FL Congressman Francis Shoemaker and was in turn replaced in 1943 by Harold Hagen, another FLer. Congressman Buckler was a farmer, former school board member and state senator who returned to farming after declining to run for another term in 1942. He died in Crookston, Minnesota in 1950.

Buckler was one of five of the nine Minnesota Congressmen in the 75th Congress (1937 to 1939) who were members of the Farmer-Labor Party (the others were Henry Tiegan, 3rd; Dewey Johnson, 5th; Paul John Kvale, 7th; and John Bernard, 8th). The 75th Congress marked the second and last time a majority of Minnesota's Congressional delegation came from the FL. (The other session to boast such a majority was the 73rd Congress, with Henry Ahrens, 1st; Magnus Johnson, 5th; Paul John Kvale, 7th; Ernest Lundeen, 8th; and Francis Shoemaker, 9th).

It was indeed a heady time for the FLers. In addition to capturing the majority of seats in the Minnesota Congressional delegation, the Party also managed, during three separate terms of Congress, to break Republican domination over Minnesota's two U.S. Senate seats.

The Republican Party had held Minnesota's two United States Senate seats almost exclusively since Minnesota achieved statehood in 1858. Though Democrats captured both Senate seats in 1857, they lost them in the next election. From that point on, Republicans from Minnesota sat in the U.S. Senate for every term of Congress with the exception of the 56th Congress in 1899, when Democrat Charles A. Towne was *appointed* to fill the seat vacated by Republican Cushman K. Davis's death. Towne lost his bid for election to the seat in 1901 to Republican Moses E. Clapp. It was not until FL Senator Henrik Shipstead was elected in 1923 that one of Minnesota's two U.S. Senate seats was wrested from Republican control.

The FL Party scored another victory in 1923 when Magnus Johnson was elected to serve out the unexpired term of Republican Senator Knut Nelson who died in office. Thus, from 1923 to 1925, Minnesota was represented in the U.S. Senate by two FL Senators. This scenario was repeated again in 1935 when Elmer Benson was *appointed* to serve out the unexpired term of Republican Senator Thomas D. Schall. Floyd B. Olson was running to replace Benson in the U.S. Senate, with Benson running for governor, when Olson died in August of 1936, prompting Congressman Ernest Lundeen to enter the race, which he won. Thus, the FL Party had men occupying both U.S. Senate seats for a third time (1937 – 1939). But the 75th Congress was the last term of Congress that would see the FL Party control both U.S. Senate seats.

Eventually, Henrik Shipstead, a man who leaned towards the Progressive side of the FL coalition, would bolt the FL Party in 1941 and be elected to an additional six year stint in the Senate as a Republican, leaving only Buckler and later, Harold Hagen, as FL stalwarts in Washington. But, at the time Rich Buckler was writing to Willard Munger in December of 1935, the FL Party, though troubled by internal dissension, appeared to be on the ascendency.

The move to Duluth didn't cure all of the Munger family's economic woes. The following is an excerpt from a letter Willard Munger sent in response to being dunned for medical bills related to his daughter's birth.

> I am surprised that you would turn this bill over to the collection agency without first sending me a bill. I considered you a higher type than this. I've always paid my bills and this is the first time anyone has ever done anything like this to me...

As dire as his purse might have been, Munger continued to work hard for the FL Party.

> Mr. Henry Moenkedick
>   Chairman
>   Perham, Minnesota Farmer-Labor Club
>   February 10, 1936
>   Dear Mr. Moenkedick:
>   I would like to send out the calls for the Farmer-Labor County Convention March 8, 1936, as this is the time I have a chance to get off and I want to attend the convention by all means as I rightfully should...
>   Tell the boys hello for me.
>   As ever,
>   Your friend,
>   Willard M. Munger

Munger's letters from this period are devoid of the environmental zeal that would later define his legislative career. While it is not for this writer to doubt the story Munger told later in life (where he claimed that his conservation ethic was instilled in him by his paternal grandfather during their sojourns to Mule Lake) there are no references to conservation-related issues in Munger's early correspondence.

What *is* interesting is that Munger's nemesis, Rep. Hannah Kempfer did, prior to Munger ever publically taking up the mantle of environmentalism, weigh in on conservation issues.

> Hannah wanted it [the chairmanship of the Committee of Game and Fish in the House] because of her determination to secure a fishing license law which would take care, financially, of the propagation of fish and the stocking of lakes and rivers with fry and would also cover the salaries connected with the work…

> (*Hannah Kempfer, An Immigrant Girl*, ibid, p. 138.)

Kempfer's interest in conservation can also be gleaned from a letter she wrote to Minnesota naturalist Carlos Avery in 1928.

> I find we have two kinds of sportsmen to deal with—one that poses as a conservationist, for the purpose of gaining the permission of killing all he can and who is always interested in getting special privileges to this end. And then, we have the real sportsman, who believes in real conservation for the purpose of going out to enjoy the companionship and to gain the truth, the health and love of all fellow creatures, whose homes may be anywhere and everywhere, as man will but let them…

> (*Hannah Kempfer, An Immigrant Girl*, ibid, p. 142.)

Munger never acknowledged Mrs. Kempfer's conservation ethic. And, other than some subtle references supporting conservation initiatives contained in Gov. Floyd B. Olson's speeches, or articles referencing Olson's sponsorship of state forests and parks, or news clippings revealing Olson's support for the Shipstead-Nolan Act preserved in Willard Munger's Personal Collection, there is little evidence to support Munger's later assertion that his political aspirations in Otter Tail County were based upon environmentalism. What *is* clear is that, shortly after coming to Duluth, Willard Munger came into direct contact with the St. Louis River, the watercourse that drains much of St. Louis County before emptying into Lake Superior.

In 1935, the St. Louis River was an environmental mess. Decades of dumping industrial and municipal waste into the river had left the once pristine estuary a cauldron of poison. Within a year of arriving in Duluth, Munger would open a service station and small grocery store within a stone's throw of the Minnesota bank of the St. Louis River. Munger's close physical proximity to the river likely caused him to recognize the environmental destruction of what had once been a wild and scenic river.

"I was born in Duluth on March 16, 1939," Will Munger, Jr. recalls. "As a kid, maybe six or seven years old, my parents would tell me, 'you stay off that river now'. But of course, I was a kid. I'd go down there with other kids and look at it. I was afraid of it. You could see the pollution. There was floating garbage everywhere. I was afraid to put my feet in the water."

In December of 1935, Governor Floyd B. Olson experienced severe stomach pain and was examined at the Mayo Clinic in Rochester, Minnesota. To complicate matters, Olson's illness surfaced amidst a conflict between the governor and the Conservative majorities in both houses of the Minnesota Legislature.

Olson, who understood he had little to lose in facing off with the Republicans, pushed his party's Far Left agenda even though he didn't personally believe in what it stood for. And the legislature pushed back; by reducing Olson's control over patronage positions; and by launching investigations into alleged abuses of power by the FL and by the governor.

> The three battles over relief, highway appropriations and taxation [the debate between sales and income taxation] overshadowed a dozen smaller tilts in which Olson lashed back at the legislature…He even vetoed a nonpolitical bill ratifying the local tax agreement between the city of Hibbing and the Oliver Mining Company because he doubted that the latter would act in good faith…
>
> (*Floyd B. Olson: Minnesota's Greatest Liberal Govern*, ibid, p. 272.)

In the midst of this political skirmishing, Olson, who had made it clear he wanted out of state politics (he'd declared his candidacy for the U.S. Senate), was seen at the Mayo on New Year's Eve. The examination did not portend good news: exploratory surgery revealed that Olson was suffering from cancer.

> The operation revealed a pancreatic cancer far advanced. Dr. William Mayo estimated that the governor would not live more than eight months.
>
> (*Floyd B. Olson: Minnesota's Greatest Liberal Govern*, ibid, p. 290.)

Willard Munger and other FL loyalists were not privy to the truth. The severity of the situation was concealed from even Olson himself: The governor was told that the "polyp" the surgeon had removed was likely benign, though it was suggested Olson undergo radiation therapy "just in case." Despite an inkling that "all was not right," Olson plunged ahead with his plans to run for the U.S. Senate seat occupied by Elmer Benson. And in early 1936, Senator Elmer Benson announced his own political intentions.

Sen. Benson in Race for Governor

United States Senator Elmer A. Benson on Tuesday announced his candidacy for indorsement for governor by the Farmer-Labor state convention...

"Governor Floyd B. Olson will definitely be the Farmer-Labor candidate for United States Senator. He will be indorsed unanimously for the seat I now hold by appointment. The voters of Minnesota will elect him overwhelmingly, and send him to Washington...

(Minnesota Leader, undated.)

Lieutenant Governor Hjalmar Petersen indicated that he would challenge Benson for the party's gubernatorial nomination. The backdrop of the conflict between Benson and Petersen had its genesis in the death of Republican U.S. Senator Thomas Schall in 1935. Floyd B. Olson resisted the temptation to resign as governor and have Lieutenant Governor Petersen step into the top position with the understanding that Petersen would appoint Olson to Schall's seat. Olson was a savvy politician. He understood that such chicanery would likely lead to voter backlash when he stood for re-election to the Senate. Olson appointed Banking Commissioner Elmer Benson to the Senate instead of seeking that plum for himself. But Olson's appointment of Benson was seen by FLers as a rejection of Petersen. It was widely believed that whomever Olson picked for the interim Senate seat would be the Party's endorsee for governor in 1936, a belief Petersen was well aware of when party darling Elmer Benson was chosen to replace Schall.

As the battle between Benson and Petersen loomed, Willard Munger took stock of Benson's efforts in the U.S. Senate.

Leads Fight for US Aid to Farmers

Minnesota's Farmer-Labor Senator, Elmer A. Benson, although a member for only three and a half months, led the fight this week in obtaining, against formidable odds, seed loan relief for some 23,000 Minnesota farmers who face desperate financial situations...

Through negotiations begun and carried through by Senator Benson, President Roosevelt abrogated an earlier veto order…and obtained recognition by the federal government of crop loan needs for Minnesota farmers who have failed to pay back last year's loans…

(*Minnesota Leader*, April 18, 1936.)

These accolades were repeated in a letter Munger sent to Benson.

I want to congratulate you, Elmer, on the splendid record you have made in the U.S. Senate fighting for Progressive legislation. I often say to people at meetings where I speak that you have done more towards building up the Progressive movement in the few months that you have been in the Senate than Shipstead has done in all the years he has been there, and I know that when you are elected governor of Minnesota, that same record is going to be carried on.

Thanking you for your fine cooperation in the past, I remain,

Your friend,

Willard Munger

Munger's interest in the leaders of the FL Party included clipping articles about Congressman Ernest Lundeen. Munger and Lundeen shared a pacifist bent and with storm clouds in Europe gathering at a frightening pace, Munger supported the FL Congressman's opposition to American involvement in another European conflict.

Lundeen to Speak at Peace Rally

Congressman Ernest Lundeen of Minnesota, who voted against United States participation in the last war [while serving as a Republican Congressman in 1917], will address the people in the new armory building in Minneapolis today following a peace parade through the loop district, according to a statement from the headquarters of the Minneapolis Peace Demonstration committee, representing more than 50 sponsoring organizations…

(*Minnesota Leader*, April 25, 1936.)

Ernest Lundeen joined the FL after having represented Minnesota's 5th District as a Republican Congressman. A veteran of the Spanish-American War, Lundeen was one of only fifty Congressmen to vote against America's involvement in WWI. He was defeated in 1918, then re-elected to the House in 1932 as an "At Large" Farmer-Labor candidate (the Minnesota Legislature failed to reapportion in 1932 and thus, all nine seats were elected "At Large") and again in 1934 from the 3rd

District. He would become a United States Senator in 1936, replacing interim Republican Senator Guy. V. Howard (who replaced Elmer Benson once Benson was elected governor in November of 1936). Lundeen served in the Senate until his own untimely death in an airplane accident on August 31, 1940. Ever the pacifist, Lundeen opposed any intervention by the U.S. in WWII, a position that led some to speculate that the "accident" which killed Lundeen was part of a plot to rid the Senate of a pro-German naysayer.

Decades later, Munger recalled the turmoil of the 1936 gubernatorial race.

> "Elmer Benson was a candidate for governor," Munger recalled. "Olson died in August. His lieutenant governor was Hjalmar Petersen but the party decided to pick Elmer Benson to run for the governorship…This created a lot of friction within the Farmer-Labor Party. I was asked to go out and campaign on behalf of Elmer Benson, which I did."
>
> (*Oral History of Willard Munger*, ibid, p. 42.)

In early 1936, Munger was a new father and a young husband. Despite these obligations, he agreed to take a leave of absence from his job to ensure Elmer Benson was elected governor.

> "To back up a little bit, at that time, I was working in the Railroad and Warehouse Commission here in Duluth as a grain inspector. I received that appointment from Knudt Wefald, who was one of the railroad and warehouse commissioners. At that time, the grain inspection was done by what used to be called the Railroad and Warehouse Commission, which had three members," Willard recalled. "I took a leave of absence from that job and spent about four or five months campaigning for Elmer Benson as the field representative for the whole Ninth Congressional District. Then I got in a little bit of a disagreement with Hjalmar Petersen because he opposed Benson for being chosen over him…We didn't have very good communication between us…The Executive Committee overlooked Hjalmar and nominated Benson as their candidate…That created a bitter, bitter, bitter fight."
>
> (*Oral History of Willard Munger*, ibid, pp. 42 – 43.)

Even party loyalists like Munger did not know the extent of Governor Olson's illness. According to the excellent biography of Floyd B. Olson, *Floyd B. Olson: Minnesota's Greatest Liberal Govern*, Olson was able to remain a candidate for the U.S. Senate during the 1936 campaign while making virtually no public appearances.

Olson managed to conceal the seriousness of his illness from the public until late spring. In an incredible display of true grit, he spoke for two hours and twelve minutes at the Farmer Labor convention, but thereafter, he lost ground rapidly. He spent most of the remaining months at Gull Lake, partly to hide his physical decline and partly because the solitude soothed his aching body. Occasionally he appeared in the Twin Cities or the communities around Gull Lake for a speech...

(*Floyd B. Olson: Minnesota's Greatest Liberal Govern*, ibid, p. 298.)

Olson's health prevented him from taking an active role in the election.

Toward the end of May, as the cancer grew into his esophagus, swallowing became exceedingly difficult, and he had to be fed intravenously...

Throughout June, he continued against increasing odds to play the role of governor and Senatorial candidate. Although he was literally a walking skeleton, he held a press conference after the primary, expressing pleasure at Benson's three-to-one victory...and talking optimistically about plans for a fall campaign...

(*Floyd B. Olson: Minnesota's Greatest Liberal Govern*, ibid, p. 299.)

In a letter to Congressman Buckler written two days before Floyd B. Olson's death, Munger reveals little insight into the governor's tenuous health.

August 20, 1936

Hon. R.T. Buckler

Crookston, Minnesota

Dear Mr. Buckler:

Well, it won't be long now until the political battle will be in full swing. I believe that this is going to be the dirtiest campaign that Minnesota will ever witness...With Gov. Olson handicapped, the reactionaries believe that this is their opportunity to recapture the state.

How does the political situation look in the Ninth...? Will Haugen of Pelican Rapids be a stronger opponent than Ole Sangeng? I understand that Martin Brandon is trying to capture a lot of the Farmer-Labor votes.

I am going to try to get three or four weeks of leave of absence so as to enable me to go out and do some campaign work in Otter Tail County and the Ninth...I've got a new car and can cover quite a bit of territory for the ticket as a whole.

If you have any more...documents on the T.V.A. project, I wish you would send them to me.

Be sure and call on me if there is anything I might be able to do for you between now and the election. I'll do all that I can in helping send you back to Congress...

Willard Munger

In reality, Olson's illness had not merely "handicapped" the governor; it had incapacitated him.

On June 25, he delivered the principal address at the Paul Bunyan celebration in Brainerd. Scarcely able to stand up, he gave a twenty-minute address...Four days later when he repeated the ordeal at Minnehaha Park in Minneapolis, he got through the speech but had to have help to reach his automobile...This was his last public appearance...

For a time, Olson's will to live actually seemed to heal his ailing body. On August 8 at his own insistence he was driven to Gull Lake [from the Mayo Clinic], stopping briefly in Minneapolis, where he held another optimistic press conference. But he had been at Gull Lake only a week when the cancer perforated the intestine, and it seemed unlikely that he would live long enough to get back to Rochester...

The death watch at Mayo Clinic lasted a week. As his life ebbed slowly away, Olson clung to old friends...

Halfway through the week, the governor was visibly cheered by the news that President Roosevelt would make a special trip to Rochester on August 31...But on Saturday, August 22, the struggle drew to a close...

(*Floyd B. Olson: Minnesota's Greatest Liberal Govern*, ibid, pp. 300 – 301.)

The press announced Olson's passing.

The Skipper is Gone by A.I. Harris

Floyd B. Olson is dead. It isn't true...only a dream. Fate couldn't be that way—to take one away when we need him so. We test ourselves to determine whether we are conscious. Yes, it is true. The shock is greater than any physical blow could possibly be. It makes one think...ponder...doubt.

It would have been a great thing for the Liberal and radical movement if Floyd B. Olson had left a political will. He didn't. He had hopes of beating a treacherous disease until the very last, even when his pain-tortured body was tossing in fever. His friends were too considerate of his feeling even to suggest a departing message. So were his doctors. They loved him too much...

(*Minnesota Leader*, August 29, 1936.)

The *Minneapolis Star Tribune* recounted the governor's last moments.

> Death ended a long illness from stomach cancer. He suffered a great deal of
> pain. Courageously fighting a hopeless fight, he seemed to be holding his
> own when the end came rapidly. His wife and daughter, Patricia, and many
> friends were near him when he died. To Maurice Rose, his chauffer and con-
> fidant, he smiled and whispered, "This has got us licked. But it might be for
> the best." He lapsed into a coma and death took him a short time later.
>
>   (*Minneapolis Star Tribune*, August 24, 1936.)

The Tribune estimated that 12,000 people crowded into the old Minneapolis Auditorium to attend the governor's funeral. Despite his obligations to home and
hearth, Willard Munger attended the service in Minneapolis where another 50,000
mourners filled the streets surrounding the auditorium and listened reverently to
the proceedings on loudspeakers.

With Olson gone, Hjalmar Petersen's supporters sought to wrest control of the FL
Party from Elmer Benson. As acting governor, Petersen tried to force the Party's
hand. But Benson refused to abandon his candidacy for governor. Willard Munger
stood firmly behind Benson's decision.

> Senator Elmer A. Benson
>   September 3, 1936
>   Dear Senator Benson:
>   You are to be congratulated on the stand that you took relative to the pro-
> posed changing of the state ticket. It was a noble act on your part to put the
> welfare of the Party above personal gain…
>   With you and Ernest Lundeen heading the state ticket, all factions within
> the Party are united and working together…
>   If it is at all possible, I would like to have a leave of absence the last three
> weeks or a month before the election so as to go out and campaign for you
> and the entire Farmer-Labor ticket…
>   Your friend,
>   Willard Munger

Benson was appreciative.

> Dear Friend:
>   Thank you very much for your letter…in which you commend me for the
> stand I took against any change in the state ticket.

In regard to the other matter [the leave of absence] of which you wrote, I hope to be able to let you know in a short while.

Sincerely yours,

Elmer A. Benson

Senator

Munger's financial woes continued. Money was so tight that by August, 1936, Munger was three months in arrears on his term life insurance premiums (despite the fact that the cost of the insurance was only a dollar a month). Regardless of his financial situation, Munger continued to support FLers in their quests for political office.

Mr. C.A. Ryan

Candidate for Congress

Jenkins, Minnesota

September 25, 1936

Dear Mr. Ryan:

Congratulations on your victory! I was indeed glad to see you win the primary. The people of the Sixth District used good judgment in selecting you their candidate for Congress. With all the War Lords preparing the nations for war, we will need men like you in Congress who will fight side by side with Ernest Lundeen in eliminating the causes of war.

How does it look for you? You don't want to leave any stones unturned. The old guards are going to spend thousands of dollars to defeat you and the whole Farmer-Labor Ticket. Money is like water to them.

At present, I am not in Fergus Falls as I have taken a job with the Railroad and Warehouse Commission and presently am located in Duluth. I am taking a leave of absence the last three weeks before the election to do some work. I hope to see you before the election...

Willard Munger

I.C. "Dutch" Strout was hired by the FL Party as a professional organizer and spent considerable effort exhorting Munger and other field representatives during the 1936 campaign.

It looks as though the territory in Hubbard County in and around LaPorte, as well as the territory in Cass County in and around Cass Lake has been given little or no attention.

Recently, we wired to Mr. H.V. Anderson, the Hubbard County Campaign Manager, and emphatically advised him of the necessity of his making a real county-wide distribution of whatever literature he receives...

On your next trip, be sure to check Hubbard and Cass Counties carefully for proper distribution…

(Letter of October 10, 1936, I.C. Strout to Willard Munger.)

Elmer A. Benson also rallied his "troops."

To All Farmer-Labor Party Supervisors
October 28, 1936
We are pledged to continue the great progress which our late beloved Governor Floyd B. Olson led with such courage, wisdom and strength. The most fitting monument we can erect to his memory will be to win a smashing victory…

While reactionaries have gathered to celebrate Governor Olson's death, which they hastened with their vicious attacks, we who have fought shoulder to shoulder with him resolved to carry on in the great work which he left unfinished…

Elmer A. Benson

Even young FLers got electioneering fever.

Tommy Benson is Wasting No Shots in Any Campaign

When Tommy Benson, 8-year-old son of Minnesota's Governor-elect goes out hunting votes, he doesn't believe in wasting any shots…

On one occasion, he rang a bell and a man came to the door.

"Won't you vote for my father for governor?" asked Tommy as he handed the man a Benson button.

"I'm sorry, sonny, but I can't. I'm a Republican," was the reply.

"All right then," said Tommy firmly, "give me back the button."

(*Minnesota Leader*, November 7, 1936.)

The results of the 1936 election were decisive. Elmer Benson bested Republican Martin A. Nelson by over 200,000 votes. Ernest Lundeen also rode the wave of Liberalism to victory, returning control of both United States Senate seats to the FL. FDR was re-elected to a second presidential term with ease (capturing every state of the Union but two). It was a heady time to be a Farmer-Laborite but, as Willard Munger would soon come to understand, the death of the Skipper would prove to be the Party's undoing.

Late 1936 and early 1937 saw Willard Munger continuing his work as a grain inspector for the Railroad and Warehouse Commission. Munger also remained active in the Farmer-Labor Party. With the death of Knudt Wefald (Munger's mentor on the Commission) Munger urged the Party to support Adolf Solem of Duluth as Wefald's replacement. Additionally, Munger continued his political organizing in the Ninth Congressional District under the supervision of I.C. "Dutch" Strout.

> November 11, 1936
> Dear Mr. Munger:
> You will recall that during the campaign you reported that the highway employees of Crow Wing County and in Otter Tail County were tearing down our posters.
> I believe you mentioned at the time some written instructions were issued by the Highway Department, and I would like to know if it would be possible for you to get a copy...
> Sincerely yours,
> I.C. Strout
> Sec-Treas. Farmer-Labor Association of Minnesota

Munger would later claim that he took a "four to five month" leave of absence from his job during the 1936 campaign. However, Munger's correspondence from the period indicates that he was off work for approximately a month. Whatever time frame Munger was actually away from his job, the financial impact of being without a paycheck took its toll.

> Mr. George Lund
> Chief Inspector
> November 26, 1936
> Dear George:
> [D]ue to the fact that I was off the payroll for the last month, I encumbered a number of financial obligations that is about impossible for me to meet with my present salary.
> If you thought it at all possible to transfer me to the inspection department the first of the month, I would highly appreciate it. I'm sure there is not a person here that would begrudge me the change. While at the elevator, I have spent my spare time working samples and I'm sure that I can handle the work in fine shape...
> Yours truly
> Willard M. Munger

C.A. Ryan was unsuccessful in his bid for the Sixth District Congressional seat. In his letter of condolence to Ryan, Munger also references his unpaid leave during the 1936 campaign.

The thing that made me feel bad after the election was to see you defeated but we'll send you to Congress two years from now...

If it is possible for you to come to Duluth in the near future, I'd like to have a talk with you in regards to your future campaign. Perhaps I could be of some assistance. We'll give Harold Knutson one of the worst trimmings he ever got two years from now...

I took it on the chin after all the work I done. George Lund, chief inspector of my department, didn't fulfill his promise and I never got a damn cent of salary for the month I took off.

(Letter from Munger to Ryan dated December 1, 1936.)

Willard Munger also requested "Dutch" Strout's assistance in getting Lund to pay him for the time he'd devoted to the 1936 election and clarified his allegation that highway workers loyal to Hjalmar Petersen had destroyed "Benson for Governor" signs during the campaign.

Your letter regarding the authorization of the highway boys to pull down the campaign posters was received and I have the following information...In Otter Tail County, Jack Kraywinkle told the boys to pull down the signs and the orders were given to him, I was told by Starry of Detroit Lakes...

I'm asking a special favor...and that is I would like to have you go to George Lund and Charlie Munn and ask them to transfer me to the inspection department. There hasn't been one Farmer-Laborite put in that department and they all are old holdovers...

Let me know how the fireworks are going. If there is anything that I can do to help you just let me know. You don't need to worry about me laying down on the job even if I do work for the R.R and Warehouse Commission.

Please let me know what results you have with Lund...

Willard Munger

Strout likely understood Willard's cryptic reference to "laying down on the job." The phrase confirmed that Munger wasn't about to change loyalties from Benson to Hjalmar Petersen (who was now Munger's boss, having been elected in 1936 as one of three Railroad and Warehouse Commissioners) simply to keep his job.

December 5, 1936

Dear Friend Willard:

Just sent a telegram and will explain a little further.

Dillon Peterson has been making meetings in many counties giving the certificates of meritorious award to the precinct captains. These meetings have been all arranged in advance…

Dillon was in today and we discussed the possibility of your coming over to his 1:30 P.M. meeting in Cloquet…then Dillon could give you all of the material for Cook County and you could go up there and represent the State Association in his place.

We appreciate that this is asking a lot, Willard…

Charles Munn has been in Fargo on some hearing for the past week. They expect him back today…Have been unable to get hold of George Lund either so far. Will certainly contact both at the very earliest chance, and do what I can for you.

Would like to drop in tonight and have a good chat with you fellows. There are many things that you ought to know. Of course, history is in the making right along. All in all, I feel we are still advancing in the direction we folks want to go and maybe we should be satisfied as long as we're not slipping back…

Dutch

Munger went to the meeting in Cloquet and made the long trip to Grand Marais.

I attended the meeting in Cloquet last Sunday and I am sure glad that I went. It was a splendid meeting. Dillon Peterson delivered a wonderful address. One of the finest speeches I have heard in a long while. He was right on point…

This man Henningson I found out is not so good. The people up there [Grand Marais] have found him out and you can see that he was not re-elected for chairman or delegate to central committee, although he was nominated. I have talked to a number of the boys up there and the information I got is not so good…

The mileage to Grand Marais and back was 220 miles. Round trip to Cloquet was 35 miles. Use your own judgment on this expense—if too much, cut it down…

Willard Munger

One facet of Farmer-Laborite control of state jobs was a requirement that employees holding their jobs through patronage were required to pay "dues" into an "educational association fund" (a slush fund for FL campaigns). Willard Munger was not immune from this requirement. In a letter to Dutch Strout dated December

14, 1936, Munger laments that, due to this obligation to pay "dues," he has limited resources to pledge additional money to the party.

> I'm only pledging myself a dollar a month as I am paying a $1.40 into our Duluth Grain Department Educational Association, which will be turned eventually over to you. This makes $2.50 a month that I am paying and that's about all that I can afford...
>
> How is the old battle coming? I hope to be able to see you Wednesday as I think I will be down. The Central Committee named me on the committee to go to bat for some appointments for some of the boys up here...
>
> Willard Munger

Even though Munger had been in Duluth for only a year, he managed to attain a position of prominence amongst Duluth FLers.

> Mr. Sermon
>> Secretary—St. Louis County
>> Farmer-Labor Association
>> December 31, 1936
>
> Dear Mr. Sermon:
>
> The following named persons have been duly elected as delegates to the regular annual convention to be held at the Moose Temple, 418 W. Superior St., Duluth, Minnesota on Sunday, December 27, 1936...
>
> Mr. Willard Munger, 2222 W 3rd St.
>
> Mr. H. M. Ojard, 1416 Jefferson St.
>
> These delegates were duly elected at the regular meeting of the Duluth Grain Employees Education Association...
>
> Very truly yours,
>
> Willard M. Munger
>
> Secretary

When Strout was slow to respond to his pleas, Munger lobbied Commissioner Charles Munn for a different job.

> Mr. Charles Munn
>> Railroad and Warehouse Commission
>> January 4, 1937
>
> Dear Mr. Munn:
>
> If it is possible for you to transfer me to the inspection department this month, I will highly appreciate it...

In consideration of my past association with the Farmer-Labor Movement, I feel that I am justified in asking for this small promotion. I have taken an active part in the campaigns of '30, '32, '34, and '36. During the last campaign, I took a leave of absence for one month without pay…and worked as District Manager of eight counties for the Farmer-Labor Association. During this time, I drove 9,000 miles and obligated myself to the extent of $300.00. This is a small amount of what I have spent in former campaigns at which time I was the chairman of Otter Tail County.

I did not enter this movement with the idea of obtaining a job nor do I begrudge a single cent I have ever spent in promoting the movement because I believe in the principles for which the movement stands; but I do believe that loyal members should be given consideration if they are qualified to handle the work…

Yours very truly,
Willard Munger

Munger also referenced his difficulties with Hjalmar Petersen in a letter to Governor Benson.

Although Hjalmar Petersen now has become my superior, he will not influence me in the least. I am now, as I have always been in the past, 100% for you because I know you represent the rank and file of the Farmer-Labor Movement and its principles. I absolutely disapprove of the methods used by Hjalmar Petersen while acting as governor, no political job will influence my way of thinking; it hasn't in the past and will not in the future.

During the coming session, I presume, the Conservatives in the legislature will cry about the 3% collected from state employees. I am sending you a letter sent out by the Republicans in the last campaign to collect money from old employees in the Railroad and Warehouse Commission, which I thought you perhaps might want to use…

(Letter from Munger to Benson, January 7, 1937.)

Despite the precarious nature of his position, Munger continued to advance the causes of others.

[M]r. Johnson is a high class man…He is a graduate of the University Agricultural School and is fitted for the line of work in your department. He and his folks are successful farmers.

The Johnson family has been pioneers in the progressive movement ever since the days of the Nonpartisan League and has contributed much time and money to the cause. They never asked any favor in the past. I don't know of any family in Otter Tail County that is more deserving in consideration...

(Letter from Munger to Charles Ommodt, Assistant Commissioner, Department of Agriculture, dated January 11, 1937. *Editor's Note: The letter was written on behalf of Elmer Johnson of Underwood, Minnesota.*)

CHAPTER 2

Intermission

Willard Munger continued to develop his own distinctive political philoso-phy. Consider, as an example of Munger's eclectic self-education, the fol-lowing excerpt from a Communist pamphlet Munger saved from the 1930s.

> The sweeping Farmer-Labor victory on November 3rd advanced the cause of progress and delivered a severe blow to the reactionary forces in Minnesota. This landslide was brought about, above all, by the growing unity within the Farmer-Labor Party. This unity expressed the determination of the common people to defeat reaction and improve their conditions...
>
> The common people have given the Farmer-Labor Party this great victory because they consider it their champion...
>
> In the course of daily economic and political struggles for better condi-tions and against fascism and war, and with assistance of the class-conscious Communist movement, the masses learn that capitalism is a decaying, robber system, that must be wiped out completely because it cannot fundamentally solve their problems...
>
> In truth, COMMUNISM IS 20TH CENTURY AMERICANISM. That is why the influence and prestige of the Communist Party are growing and why the most militant and intelligent fighters are gathering within its ranks...
>
> Join the Communist Party!
>
> (Willard Munger Personal Collection.)

There is no indication that Munger ever intended to throw his political zeal behind Marxism of any stripe. Though he had been instrumental in allowing the seating of Trotskyites as delegates during the 1934 FL Convention, Munger's position in that dispute was likely due to his innate sense of political fairness rather than any affinity for Communism. In similar fashion, Governor Olson broke bread with Earl Browder, the head of the American Communist Party, and allowed Communists to claim delegate seats during the 1936 FL Convention. Olson made these concessions, not because he believed in the tenets of Communism, but because he was pragmatic.

The bad blood between Elmer Benson and Hjalmar Petersen was not eliminated when Petersen won a seat on the Railroad and Warehouse Commission in 1936. Though Benson became Minnesota's second *elected* FL governor (Petersen had become the state's second FL governor by operation of law when Gov. Olson died in office) winning in convincing fashion (garnering 58% of the vote—a higher percentage than Olson ever achieved), the "shine was soon off the apple."

Unlike the gregarious and personable Olson, Benson was sternly countenanced and wholly unable to accept dissenting points of view, which made his appeal outside the FL problematic. Additionally, FDR's rising popularity gave Minnesota Democrats someone to attach their aspirations to. Since the early days of statehood, Minnesota's Democratic Party had essentially been a minority party. FDR's strong showing in the state gave Minnesota Democrats an expectation that other Democratic candidates could do well in upcoming contests. This optimism caused many Democratic supporters of Elmer Benson to migrate back to their own party after the 1936 election.

In addition, Hjalmar Petersen's supporters voiced strong opposition to Governor Benson being consecrated the FL Party's standard bearer.

> "I got in a little bit of a disagreement with Hjalmar Petersen because he opposed Benson for being chosen over him as a candidate for governor," Willard recalled. "We didn't have very good communication between us…"
>
> (*Oral History of Willard Munger*, ibid, p. 43.)

Though Petersen had the ability to make Munger's life difficult, Munger never wavered from his support of Elmer Benson.

> January 15, 1937
> Dear Willard:
> It was a great pleasure to receive your letter of congratulations on my inaugural address and to know that it met with your whole-hearted approval.
> These past days have been so full that I have been very slow thanking you, but I assure you that I greatly appreciate your message and your good wishes.
> Sincerely yours,
> Elmer Benson
> Governor

Benson and Munger shared a mutual philosophy, one dedicated to using political power to change the lives of ordinary people. At a time when few citizens had health insurance of any kind, Munger passed on a letter from Mr. Arthur Waugh (a private citizen) to Gov. Benson. Waugh's letter (dated January 23, 1937) proposed universal medical care for Minnesotans needing surgery.

Munger continued, in his role as the secretary of the Duluth Grain Department Employees Educational Association, to collect "dues" (the patronage tax) from fellow FL employees and send the money to St. Paul. Munger's letter to Dutch Strout dated January 27, 1937 indicates that the total assessment paid for the month by FL employees amounted to $8.40. Munger also continued to seek a job outside Hjalmar Petersen's sphere of influence.

> April 7, 1937
>
> Dear Congressman Buckler:
>
> I'm planning on taking the Federal Grain Inspection examination next month and I would like to have all the information that I could get pertaining to this Civil Service examination. Perhaps you could also send me a list of the latest bulletins pertaining to the different types of grain.
>
> If you have a picture of yourself handy there in your office, I'd like to have you autograph it and send it to me. My wife wants one to frame.
>
> After Congress adjourns, if you have occasion to come up this way, I'd very much like to have you come and see me, bring your wife along too.
>
> With kindest personal regards to you and your wife, I remain
>
> Your friend,
>
> Willard Munger

Having heard nothing from Benson or Strout regarding a transfer, Munger wrote to Commissioner of Agriculture Charles Ommodt on April 7, 1937.

> This is the first time I have ever asked for an appointment, but due to a misunderstanding politically, between the present leadership of the Railroad and Warehouse Commission and myself, I deem it obligatory that I leave this department...
>
> The foremost reason why I wish to work in your department is the fact that I consider you to be real Farmer-Laborite and a square shooter. Any consideration given me, I assure you, will be highly appreciated.
>
> Willard Munger

In the spring of 1937, Munger experienced the loss of his maternal grandmother, Bertha Zahn Zuehlsdorf, who died on May 6, 1937 at the age of 79. Bertha, who along with her husband Albert, helped build the Friberg German Lutheran (Missouri Synod) Church, was survived by seven children, nineteen grandchildren (including opera star Edna Weese), and nine great grandchildren. (*Fergus Falls Daily Journal*, May 7, 1937.)

Munger's efforts to secure a new job continued.

> May 19, 1937
> Dear Mr. Ommodt:
> At the regular meeting of the Otter Tail County Central Committee of the Farmer-Labor Association held in Henning on Monday, May 17th, 1937, the following resolution was duly considered and passed:
> Be it resolved: That this committee go on record as unanimously endorsing Willard Munger of Duluth, former chairman of the Otter Tail County Farmer-Labor Association, for a position with the Agriculture Department or any other department suitable.
> Mr. Munger has always been a hard worker in the movement and done a lot to build up the movement and is entitled to your consideration, and anything you may do will be highly appreciated by this committee.
> Very truly yours,
> W.W. Sherman
> Secretary
> CC: Governor Elmer A. Benson

A nearly identical letter was sent by the Eagle Lake FL Club to Ommodt.

The fact that Willard Munger was embroiled in an unpleasant situation in Duluth didn't stop him from seeking assistance for other FLers.

> Mr. Adolph Solem
> May 22, 1937
> Dear Adolph:
> [E]lmer is a real sincere governor and will do what's right.
> I took your situation up with Elmer and I told him the need of you getting out of the department you are in and he seemed to be very impressed with what I told him.
> There is an opening for an oil inspector in Duluth…He said you could have it if you want it. I believe, Adolph, you should take this. This is just the kind of job you want, not tied down, travel over your entire district, give you an opportunity to make wonderful contacts.

I wish you could please write to Elmer and make application for it. Do this right away...

Please keep this absolutely confidential...

Willard

Dutch Strout remained optimistic that Munger would be re-assigned.

May 27, 1937

Friend Willard:

Was very glad to get your letter and thanks much. However, had hoped you would get something definite from Benson. At any rate, he is with you and knows what you have done for the movement, especially last fall, and I feel sure in the end you will come out with a good berth...

Maybe I ought to make a play for Pearlove's job...Replacing a Jew with a Dutchman and with a man who already served on that commission...ought to look alright...

Regards, etc...

Sincerely yours,

Dutch Strout

The situation became serious when Hjalmar Petersen gave Munger a month off without pay and threatened to transfer Munger to a position in the Twin Cities as punishment for alleged insubordination.

Dear Carl:

At the present time I am in Fergus Falls enjoying one of Hjalmar Petersen's "payless vacations" for a month. That's what one gets for standing up for principles. I also had one month off during the campaign too without pay. The best of it all is that he is transferring me from Duluth to Minneapolis the 16th of this month, well knowing that with two months off without pay and spending $200.00 of my own money in the campaign besides, that it's impossible for me to move from one city to another. He knows that's a polite way of firing me as he knows I can't afford to move.

The reason why he is doing this is because I refused to go down the line with him... against Benson...They can't find anything wrong with my work, so therefore, they have no reason to fire me on that. There are plenty of single men in the department in Duluth he could transfer.

Now, if it isn't asking too much of you, Carl...I would like to have you write a letter to Charlie Ommodt and one to Elmer Benson urging them to appoint me in one of their departments, preferably the agriculture department. If I could work out of Duluth or in your district, I could do you a lot of good...

Willard Munger

(Letter to Carl Ryan.)

Not satisfied that his old friend could sway the powers that be, Munger wrote again to Commissioner of Agriculture Charles Ommodt.

June 7, 1937

Dear Mr. Ommodt:

If it is at all possible for you to place me in the 8th, 6th or 9th Congressional Districts, I would appreciate it very much as I have become very acquainted with these districts. In these districts, I believe I could be of most usefulness to you and your department. I would like to maintain my home in Duluth...

Willard Munger

As referenced in the following letter, Munger *was* transferred to Minneapolis for a brief period of time.

June 14, 1937

Dear Congressman Buckler:

I'm intending to go to work in Ommodt's department. Both Benson and Ommodt have promised me work but it is slow in coming. I hope to get back in the northern part of the state in the agricultural department, then I will be able to do you some good in the next election.

If it isn't too much of you, I would like to have you write a letter to Gov. Benson on behalf of I.C. Strout getting some department head job under the administration...If you would write an endorsement to Benson, I wish you would send a copy of it to Mr. Strout, the Spaulding Hotel, Duluth, Minn....I understand that Benson has promised him something...

Willard Munger

In the midst of his own crisis, Munger reminded Governor Benson of Mr. Solem's needs.

June 28, 1937

Dear Elmer:

The last time I was in your office I discussed with you the possibilities of Mr. Adolph Solem obtaining the oil inspection job in Duluth. He has just taken the examination for that position and I believe that he has passed the test...

Mr. Solem, I want to say this personally, belongs to that group of men in our movement who put the welfare of the movement ahead of individual gain. He has fought Hjalmar Petersen continuously despite the fact that he jeopardizes his own job by doing so...

Willard Munger

Munger's desperate entreaties caught Strout's attention.

Friend Willard:

Expect to go to the governor's office tomorrow...to see if we can't hurry that expense money for yourself and the others...

Have had talks with Solem [Adolph]. Bob Sermon, Mossberg, Joe Reinars, Sig Slonium, Johnny Bernard, and some of the other leaders...Solem is wanting some more dope on the oil inspector's job...

I'll speak to Benson...about hurrying your job with Ommodt. Wish you could be in some department with me, tho...

No doubt you have seen in the newspapers it is all the talk. Guess they are shivering around in St. Paul. Some of the boys are trying to talk me to take Pearlove's job if possible to get it.

There are three valid arguments in my favor that they mention, namely—1st it would be replacing a Jew with a Dutchman. 2nd I served 2 and 1/2 years on that same commission therefore there is no question about that part of it. 3rd-I am now working as a senior examiner right in the department and therefore qualified in the work and it would merely be promoting a man in the department...

[I]n the meantime, let me know what you think of going out and putting on a straight campaign for Pearlove's job...Haven't heard anything more about whether they are going to move Griffith or not either.

Best regards to yourself, wife, Dad, Mother, and George Miller, and all others there...

Dutch

Dutch Strout's intervention proved to be successful.

"So I quit the Railroad and Warehouse Commission and got a job as head of the marketing division for the Department of Agriculture," Willard later recalled, "with offices in Duluth. I then covered all of northern Minnesota. I had several people working under me...I loved that job...I loved working with the farmers and doing the inspection work on fruit and vegetables and potatoes and things like that...We'd inspect any fruit and vegetables that came in on car load lots...

to be sold at market here in Duluth...For instance, if a car load of strawberries came in from California and the price had gone down and the buyer said he was going to refuse the carload, the shipper would be at the mercy of the buyer in cases where the price went down. So he'd turn them down. Then the shipper would call for an inspection. If the inspection held up, if they were number one strawberries when they arrived here, he was obligated to accept the shipment. It was things like that that we were involved in...We also had the job of inspecting all fish that was shipped out of Duluth from Lake Superior."

(*Oral History of Willard Munger*, ibid, p. 43.)

With his new job secure, Munger plunged deeper into the world of Farmer-Laborite politics.

Festival Sunday Will Draw Thousands to Lincoln Park

Thousands of Duluth Liberals, trade unionists, and St. Louis County farmers will gather at Lincoln Park Sunday, July 25th, to participate in the third annual Duluth summer festival of the Farmer-labor Association. Governor Benson heads a speaking program of outstanding leaders in the Minnesota liberal movement, including Congressman John T. Bernard...

In charge of the event are: E.W. Mossberg, chairman; A.A. Sigler, vice chairman...They are being assisted by members of the general committee: Mmes. O.E. Thompson, Willard Munger...

Striking clerks at Duluth Woolworth stores will be guests of honor at the outing.

(*Minnesota Leader*, July 24, 1937.)

Munger also continued to be on the alert for evidence that Hjalmar Petersen's supporters were spreading disenchantment amongst state employees.

December 28, 1937

Dear Dutch:

Last night at the Southern St. Louis County Farmer-Labor Central Committee I presented and spoke in behalf of the Crow Wing resolution endorsing you for State Auditor and I am happy to state at this time that the resolution was adopted with only one dissenting vote...

If you see Gov. Benson or some of the other administration leaders you can tell them from me that Hjalmar Petersen has a number of paid workers up here in his behalf and that they better be on their toes...

Willard Munger

Munger's observations of skullduggery by Petersen's followers was, according to history, evidence of the growing tension within the FL movement between the Left and the more moderate center; between Benson and his Communist allies and Petersen and the old holdovers from the more conservative Nonpartisan League. Despite this conflict, Benson continued to advocate a "soak the rich" set of legislative reforms that became mired in the quicksand of a legislature he could not control. His proposal to provide social welfare to assist the impoverished of the state (through the setting of higher taxes and higher prices on commodities) couldn't find any steam within the Conservative-controlled legislature.

In addition, the uneasy alliance between the Liberals and the Communists within the Party began to splinter. When Thomas Latimer sought re-election as mayor of Minneapolis in 1937, the bond between the Liberals and the Far Left came unglued. Latimer was denied the FL endorsement when the Communists gained control of the Party in Minneapolis. This insurrection led to Latimer's loss in the primary and to the election of a Republican as mayor of Minnesota's largest city in the general election.

In northern St. Louis County, where iron miners strongly affiliated with the FL, the Party also enjoyed the support of other trade unions, most notably the American Federation of Labor (AFL). But when Finns, many of whom were Communists or radical Socialists, began claiming positions of power within the Party, the AFL defected. John Bernard's election to Congress from the 8th District in 1936 (a rousing defeat over Republican incumbent William Pittenger) led to Bernard proclaiming victory for "the Popular Front," a code phrase for Communism, which further alienated the AFL from the Farmer-Labor Party.

Heading into the 1938 campaign, Governor Benson faced serious opposition from union leaders regarding the ultra-radical orientation of the Farmer-Labor Party but there is little evidence that Elmer Benson realized just how damaging his reliance upon the Far Left would prove to be.

CHAPTER 3

Defeat

Willard Munger faced disloyalty in the Department of Agriculture similar to what he'd experienced working for the Railroad and Warehouse Commission. In his position as dairy and food inspector, Munger witnessed attempts by department employees to undermine Governor Benson's ideals and philosophy. In a letter to Commissioner Charles Ommodt dated January 5, 1938, Munger apprised his supervisor of his observations.

> A few weeks ago, Mr. Trovatten was up here lining up support for Hjalmar Petersen. I understand that a former employee in your department up here is his contact man. They had a meeting together here with some of the Conservatives within our ranks…I think Hjalmar Petersen has more men working under cover up here than we know of.

In an effort to restore party loyalty within the Railroad and Warehouse Commission, FLers in Duluth sought to have Adolph Solem endorsed as a candidate for commissioner.

> On Monday…the Farmer-Labor Central Committee of Duluth and Southern St. Louis County unanimously endorsed Adolph Solem as candidate for Railroad and Warehouse Commissioner with a further request that this communication with enclosed resolution be sent to the secretaries and chairmen of every county central committee, to be submitted for consideration at their next regular county Farmer-Labor endorsing convention.
>
> R.I. Sermon, Sec.
> January 10, 1938

In his personal life, Munger had, by 1938, experienced the deaths of three of his grandparents: Grandpa Lyman Munger in January of 1934; Grandpa Albert Zuehlsdorf in May of 1934; and Grandma Zuehlsdorf in May of 1937, leaving only the taciturn Mary Emily Armstrong Munger as a mentor and elder to Willard and his three surviving siblings. In a letter dated January 19, 1938, Grandma Munger wrote Willard on the eve of his birthday.

> Dear Willard, Martha, and Patsy:
>
> Well, Willard, tomorrow is your birthday, which makes you 27 years old. Your Aunt Margaret is sending you a chicken. Hope you get it all OK. We are all really well here but myself, I slipped on an icy floor and hurt my right side. I fell across a cream can. It was tough. Had the doctor out. He said I was lucky I did not break my hip. I am up now most of the time and do some sewing. I had good care. Margaret won't let me do anything. She is afraid I will get hurt again. Mary was home over the weekend. They had the Club Friday night. George Miller gave a good talk. They said they had a good crowd…
>
> Will close with Oceans of Love to you all.
>
> Grandma Munger

Willard Munger came to understand that the Farmer-Labor Party in Duluth relied heavily upon the *Labor* component of its membership; that the *Farmer* component of the Party was less politically significant in northeastern Minnesota than it had been in Otter Tail County. Through his Party connections, Munger became acquainted with union leaders, including Earl Bester, an officer in the steelworkers' local at the U.S. Steel plant in Duluth. But even Bester, a man of considerable importance and seniority with U.S. Steel, faced hardship during the Great Depression.

> February 14, 1938
>
> Dear Gov. Benson:
>
> In writing you this letter, I want to call your attention to one Mr. Earl Bester of Duluth who has been unanimously endorsed by the Farmer-Labor Central Body and many labor unions for employment with the state. He has a family to support and is very much in need of work.
>
> Mr. Bester is a loyal, sincere Farmer-Laborite, one who has spent a lot of time and money in behalf of labor and the progressive movement. Through his efforts…he has jeopardized his own job. He was one of those who organized the steel plant in West Duluth. The steel union, of which he is president, has over 2,200 paid up members. He was also elected chairman of the grievance committee. Through his efforts, the union has affiliated with the Farmer-Labor Central Committee…
>
> Due to Mr. Bester's prestige…Mr. Atwood and the Petersen forces have tried a number of times to line him up with them by offering him numerous positions…
>
> Willard Munger

Bester had his own interesting past.

> Bester was the son of an English immigrant who worked in the copper
> mines of Michigan's Upper Peninsula in the years before World War I. His
> father, a member of the Western Federation of Miners, was blacklisted after
> the failed strike of 1913. After serving in WWI, Earl Bester came to Duluth
> where he worked for U.S. Steel at the Mesabi Railway yards. Fired for refus-
> ing to scab during the strike, he was given a second chance and hired at the
> steel plant in Duluth in 1921 as a crane operator. Having been involved in
> the IWW, Bester had become a Socialist around 1920. At the steel plant,
> he became active in what remained of the AFL's Amalgamated Association
> of Iron, Steel and Tin Workers Union. The Amalgamated, which had been
> a powerful union late in the 19th century, had been badly beaten by the
> steel trust...Fingered by a labor spy in 1928, Bester...[was] fired, though
> two months later, he was hired back...Laid off as a result of the Depression,
> Bester was back to work in 1936, when he was recruited...to become...an
> organizer.
>
> (*By the Ore Docks*, Richard Hudelson and Carl Ross,
> University of Minnesota Press, 2006, p. 185.)

With another election cycle approaching, Munger geared up for the FL conventions being held in Minnesota's nine congressional districts. He also continued to
promote the candidacy of Adolph Solem to the Railroad and Warehouse Commission.

> Mr. Martin Odland
> Minneapolis, Minnesota
> March 9, 1938
> Dear Martin:
> I received your letter in regards to the Second District Convention in
> Mankato...and I have told Mr. Solem of it. Mr. Solem is planning on going
> and will no doubt see you there. I don't think that I will be able to go.
> A volunteer committee for Mr. Solem, of which I am secretary and trea-
> surer, is having a thousand letters printed for him in his behalf and I would
> be glad to send you some if you can use them.
> The Eighth Congressional District Convention held at Bovey last Sunday
> gave Solem the unanimous endorsement for RR Whse. Comm. As far as I
> can see, Solem is by far the strongest candidate now...
> Willard Munger

Solem's candidacy ended in defeat at the 1938 FL State Convention, a raucous and boisterous affair where Hjalmar Petersen went head-to-head with Elmer A. Benson for the Party's gubernatorial nomination.

> Cut the bonds which now tie Minnesota to an intolerable political machine by voting for Hjalmar Petersen for Governor-the only candidate running against Benson. The only candidate who can defeat the Benson rule is...Petersen...
>
> A vote for candidates on the Republican or Democratic tickets does not count against Benson. Success in defeating this machine can never come from scattered opposition votes among ten candidates where they do not count against existing rule.
>
> (Hjalmar Petersen 1938 campaign literature; Willard Munger's Personal Collection.)

Munger was a delegate to the 1938 FL Convention where Solem's bid fell short.

> Mr. Willard Munger
>
> Duluth, Minnesota
>
> March 30, 1938
>
> Dear Willard:
>
> It is possible that we may call on you if the campaign gets rather heavy along in October or the first week in November.
>
> May I congratulate you on your wonderful fight which you and your friends put up for that fine gentleman and scrapper, Mr. Adolph Solem. You and your friends and Mr. Solem should not have any regrets and you should be proud of the splendid battle you put up in face of heavy odds at the state convention...
>
> Harold Hagen
>
> Secretary to Congressman R.T. Buckler

The following letter references Solem's bitter defeat at the hands of Harold Atwood. The letter also questions the loyalty of Munger's friend and mentor, I.C. "Dutch" Strout, who was running for Clerk of the Minnesota Supreme Court.

> Dear Mr. Munger:
>
> Up so late waiting to hear from the convention I am shaky but I feel so badly about Mr. Solem losing...
>
> I had such hopes he would win over Atwood...
>
> Our party is surely rotten when a man who got their appointment like him can get by. I have about lost my faith in the human race.

So much so, I am wondering about Dutch Strout. Just what is up there? He hasn't contacted Doc nor our county chairman for a long time…

Now we know Dutch Strout was always OK but lately, we have begun to wonder about him…

I for one am not going to vote for the Republican nominee but I am NOT going to vote for Atwood. I will never have that on my conscience…

Munger remained loyal to Strout.

March 17, 1938

Dutch:

I suppose you know by this time that you were unanimously endorsed for Clerk of Supreme Court by the 8th Congressional District. Perhaps you don't approve of what I did at the convention, in regards to this endorsement. At first, I tried to get the endorsement committee to endorse you for auditor but I found too much support for Lyons and therefore, I got a unanimous endorsement for you for Clerk of the Supreme Court…

Willard

Munger's personal financial picture hadn't improved. He was still trying to satisfy old bills from his "time off" during the 1934 campaign.

Fergus Falls Paint Co.

May 14, 1938

I'm surprised to learn that you have turned this bill over to the collection agency without first sending me a statement. I have always paid my bills promptly and this is the first time I have ever had an account turned over to a collector…

Willard Munger

In truth, the paint company bill was not the first time Munger had dealt with a past-due obligation. The physician's invoice for Patsy's birth went through a similar collection process. Whether Munger was "fudging the truth" for purposes of highlighting his indignation at being dunned, or whether he had genuinely forgotten the prior episode involving the doctor's bill is unknown.

While Munger remained active in FL politics, he wasn't interested in repeating the exhausting work he had done on the Party's behalf in 1936.

"[W]hen Benson ran the next time, in 1938, Stassen filed on the Republican ticket and it became a very bitter campaign," Willard recalled. "I.C. Strout, the secretary of the Farmer-Labor Party said, 'We want you out into the field again. We're going to give you the Eighth Congressional District to work as a field representative.' I said 'I'm not going. I've still got debts from the last time I took a leave of absence.' They hadn't paid me in full. They were going to pay me my salary, see, because I didn't get any money from the state when I took a leave of absence. So I turned him down."

(*Oral History of Willard Munger*, ibid, pp. 43 – 44.)

Willard Munger was, in many ways, closer to Elmer A. Benson than he had been to Floyd B. Olson; a man Munger placed on an admiring but unrealistic pedestal. Munger had a solid and loyal appreciation for Benson's service to his country during the Great War, liked him as a man, but, either due to political savvy or the natural process of maturity, Munger was wary of Benson's chances in 1938. Still, Benson was not about to be denied the use of Munger's talents as a political organizer.

"A couple of hours later…Elmer Benson, called me up. He said, 'What is this I hear about you refusing to go out and campaign?' If you don't know Elmer Benson, he was really a hothead, see," Willard continued. "He was not very discreet in the choice of words he used.

I said, 'Yes, that's right. I'm not going out. I've got to look after my family a little bit. I've still got debts from the last campaign, and I just can't go out.'

He said, 'You're just like all the rest of those goddamn job holders, as soon as you get your own nest feathered, you don't care about anybody else.' That's the kind of language he used on me for about a half an hour. He wore me down.

Finally, I said, 'OK, I'll go out.'"

(*Oral History of Willard Munger*, ibid, p. 44.)

The position that Willard Munger reluctantly accepted was that of division supervisor for the 8th Congressional District. As such, Munger managed all of the district supervisors, who in turn, supervised the precinct captains throughout the district. At twenty-seven years old, and with another child on the way, Munger was working at the highest level in the FL Party outside St. Paul. And despite his reluctance in accepting the position, Munger worked hard for Benson and Strout.

Benson's 1938 re-election bid was personally difficult for Munger. Not only was Munger expected to "get up to speed" with respect to the nuances of politics in the 8th Congressional District (a political landscape Munger was newly acquainted with); he was also caught up in a series of disagreements with Benson's campaign manager (Dillon Peterson) regarding strategy.

August 18, 1938

    Mr. Peterson:

    I have a suggestion to make in regards to your set-up, which I feel will be a splendid way of keeping check on your seven division supervisors as to what they are really accomplishing. The plan I have in mind is that when you wrap your precinct literature that you have a self-addressed card attached to each precinct captain's literature with the name and address of the precinct captain on the card. There should be a place on this penny postal card for the precinct captain to sign his name and drop it in the mail box...

    This idea serves two distinct purposes namely, it will show your office who the active precinct captains are and also whether or not they receive their literature, and more importantly, it will make the precinct captains feel that a record in St. Paul is being kept of the work he is doing...

    I've drawn myself a diagram of the precinct captain set-up and am going to use it tonight in Aitkin at my first meeting...

    I haven't heard from you since I've been out, I don't know whether that's an indication I'm going to be fired or not, but until I hear further from you, I'm going to keep going.

    Willard Munger

Peterson took issue with Munger's suggestions.

    Supplies requested in Thursday's letter were given to Ed Anderson who was to meet you at Walker tonight. We have learned that you changed the plans entirely for that territory.

    Division supervisors are selected to assume charge of given territory. We try to pick individuals who can, and will, assume this responsibility. The division supervisors are expected to carry out the plan of the campaign...This is not a mileage contest but a political campaign. The least we could have expected in your sending Leppa to take care of the Walker meeting was a call to this office. This necessitated our calling Walker making arrangements for Ed Anderson, who had already left to meet Leppa. We also learned that Leppa is to make a meeting for you at Little Fork...Just when are you going to stop this flagrant abuse of authority and consult this office in matters of that kind?... Now, you are either going to work for us, or you can go back and work for your department. As for Little Fork, that is your meeting and we expect YOU to make it.

    In reference to the plan you suggest...Please forget your stuff and start doing our stuff—or else.

At the preliminary meeting you are to set the date for the first precinct captain meetings. We expect the division supervisor to make most of these meetings as he is the only one qualified to make them…Your work in Lake County and in Cook County was extremely poor. Finding out what you did in Cook County could have been done over the telephone for 1/3 of the expense. Our plan is for a precinct supervisor for every four or five of more precincts. We expect you to carry that plan out. If you can't sell it to the campaign manager and county officials, then go out and pick these supervisors yourself. We will expect you to work on our stuff this week and get your division in shape. Keep out of local squabbles, keep your feet on the ground, and do precinct captain work—THAT AND THAT ONLY.

Dillon Peterson

Precinct Captains Bureau Chair

The tone of Peterson's reply must have been quite a shock to Munger. One can sense frustration in Peterson's choice of words, likely the result of Peterson sensing that all was not going well in Greater Minnesota regarding the governor's re-election.

"So I went to work, and it was a really bitter campaign. When we got about two-thirds through it, I hadn't got my expenses because the Party was in debt," Willard remembered. "So I was on my own again, and I was borrowing money to go out and campaign…Finally, the representatives from each congressional district were called to a kind of roundtable discussion. I represented the Eighth Congressional District. Paul Rassenson, who was a village commissioner, was sitting at the head table, with Benson down at the other end. They asked all the field representatives for their evaluation of how it looked out in their areas. Everyone of course, said, 'Oh, it doesn't look bad. It's not as good as last time, but it looks pretty good.' A bunch of con artists, you know.

They came to me and I said, 'Governor, if the election were today, you'd get beat.'

He flew off the handle and got bitter. He said, 'I knew you'd say that. You didn't want to go out and campaign. I had to force you to go out and campaign. You talk like a goddamn Republican. Why don't you go back to Duluth where you belong? We don't need guys like you.' He went on like that, really bitter.

Finally, Paul Rassenson said, 'Governor, why don't you let Munger explain why he feels that way?'

I said, 'OK, I'll tell you why I feel that way. Two years ago when I went out campaigning, Elmer Benson stickers were on all the cars.'

We'd very seldom see a Republican sticker on the cars. Once in a while, you'd find them up north.

'But now I'm in a real Farmer-Labor District. I left St. Paul with a load of literature to go to International Falls, and I kept track of all the stickers that Benson had on cars and all the stickers that Stassen had on cars. Let me tell you, governor, the Stassen stickers were on old, dilapidated cars, about eight out of every ten. And that tells me you're in real trouble.'

So a heated argument continued for about ten minutes, and finally, the governor came to his senses. He said to me, 'Well, you better go back out in the field and do the best you can do…You better go out and carry on. But you talk like a loser and that bothers me.' So he gave me quite a lecture."

(*Oral History of Willard Munger*, ibid, p. 45.)

Willard Munger returned to the field. But Munger and the other FL activists supporting Benson were fighting a losing battle against a coalition of anti-Benson factions that had begun to coalesce the day Floyd B. Olson died. Olson himself had embraced support from the extreme Left. This upset businessmen who had formed an influential and important component of Olson's "All Party" coalition and it also caused ruptures within certain components of the labor movement, another key element to Olson's success. Hjalmar Petersen and the more conservative factions of the FL Party took advantage of these rifts by calling Benson's Leftist tendencies to the attention of the voters. The Republicans adopted this strategy and from the beginning of 1938 until the election in November, "Red-baiting" assaults on Benson and the other FL-endorsed candidates continued unabated.

One example of such propaganda (saved by Munger) is a handout printed exclusively in red ink. The pamphlet is an attack on FL Senator Ernest Lundeen.

Ernest Lundeen, with a group calling themselves "The First American Rank and File Labor Delegation to Soviet Russia" went to Moscow to attend the International Congress of "The Friends of Soviet Russia" in 1928…Ernest Lundeen was one of the official signers of [a] document urging union workmen of the United States to support and follow the lead of the Communists of Soviet Russia…

On February 25, 1936, Ernest Lundeen addressed a meeting of "The Friends of the Soviet Union" in Madison Square Garden in New York City. He began his speech by hailing the assemblage as "Tovarishi" the Russian word for comrades and said "it will not be long until everyone in this country understands that word."

(Willard Munger Personal Collection.)

The assaults upon Benson were equally severe and involved political chicanery of the highest degree. On August 7, 1937, Benson rode in an automobile in a Peace Parade in New York City. Mayor LaGuardia, the popular progressive Republican mayor of New York City, furnished the car Benson rode in. Other dignitaries, including three U.S. Senators, spoke at the event. Republican operatives, eager to portray Benson as a Communist, doctored a photograph of the motorcade so that it appeared Benson was riding in a car in a Communist parade; not the non-partisan Peace Parade he was actually participating in. The photograph surfaced shortly before the November election, essentially constituting an unpleasant, "October Surprise" that caught Benson off-guard. Despite the fact that Byrl Whitney of the Brotherhood of Railroad Trainmen defended Benson, the damage had been done. Whitney's attempt to undo the smear over WCCO radio's airwaves proved to be too little, too late.

The campaign of 1938 was decidedly nasty. The Red-baiting nature of the attacks upon Benson began in earnest in the spring and never let up until the final ballot was counted in November. In an attempt to thwart this assault, the FL Party, along with the Democrats (FDR was being slurred with the same murky undercurrent as his FL supporters), issued a variety of leaflets and pamphlets to the voters.

This attempt at educating Minnesota voters regarding "the truth" in the face of Stassen's unrelenting assault began with the issuance of a speaker's manual to all precinct captains in the FL organization. The document explained the FL platform and Benson's record in fairly simple and concrete terms, pointing out the following as key successes in the nearly 10-year history of FL rule in Minnesota:

- Passage of the Homestead Act exempting the first $4,000 of any farm or principle residence from property taxation;

- Aid to farmers suffering drought and the passage of mortgage foreclosure moratoriums on the state and national level;

- Passage of the Fair Trade Practices Act and Unfair Practices Act and the extension of Workers' Compensation, all of which were directed at assisting workers;

- Attempts to install a new and fairer system of income and property taxation, including the reduction of property taxes by 24%, which failed due to a Republican initiative to install a flat income tax.

(Paraphrased from 1938 Speaker's Manual; Willard Munger Personal Collection.)

As indicated, Stassen's camp wasn't content to simply attack Benson. Literature handed out throughout the state also claimed that FDR was "the most ruthless president the United States has ever known."

Amidst the disarray of Benson's 1938 campaign, one ray of sunshine entered Willard Munger's political life. It was during the '38 campaign that Munger met Homer Carr, a Liberal state senator from Proctor, Minnesota, who became one of Munger's political mentors in northeastern Minnesota. Carr's background (as depicted in his 1938 campaign literature) obviously touched a chord with Munger.

> I entered the service of the Great Northern Railway as a locomotive fire-man...leaving that service to enter the service of the Duluth, Missabe and Iron Range Railway July 1, 1910...I entered military service April 19, 1917 and was recommended for captain's commission by my colonel while serving in France...
>
> Elected to the House of Representatives...in 1932, I served...on the important committee of Education and Appropriations...Elected to the Senate...I became a member of the powerful Finance Committee...
>
> As a member of the Liberal bloc in the senate, which constitutes one-third of the senate membership, I was elected...chairman of the Special Session of 1936, when the Old Age and Unemployment Law was passed.
>
> (Willard Munger Personal Collection.)

In many ways, Homer Carr was the successor to another Proctorite, Congressman William Leighton Carss, one of the first FL politicians to gain office. A mechanical engineer by training, Carss settled in Proctor in 1893 where he worked for U.S. Steel as a locomotive engineer. He was elected as an FL Congressman from the 8th District in 1919, making him the earliest FL candidate to win office in Minnesota. Homer Carr was a product of Carss' early success in Proctor, a hotbed of Liberal, union-based politics originating from Proctor's sprawling Duluth, Missabe and Iron Range Railroad yard.

Benson tried to fight the image painted by the Conservatives; that he was, in a word, a Communist in Liberal clothing.

> Through the development of cooperatives, farmers and laborers can build economic machinery which, with progressive political parties, will protect them against the rise of Fascism and Communism...
>
> (1938 FL Party Platform, Willard Munger Personal Collection.)

Benson also stood squarely in opposition to the United States being dragged into another World War. As a veteran of the Great War, Benson knew first-hand the horrors of combat and did not want to see the U.S.A. commit its young men to fight in a war that was none of its business.

> Governor Benson was a soldier in the last war. After it was over, he became a leader in a veteran's organization, where he worked for the soldier's bonus, veteran's preference laws, AND PEACE...
>
> Addressing a student peace gathering, he said:
>
> "I speak as one who has been to war and lived through the days that followed the war. War is the great illusion of our civilization. Twenty years ago on Good Friday, the day dedicated to the world's apostle of peace, the world went to war... Twenty years after the war to end all wars, we live once more in a state of armed peace which is rapidly passing over into open warfare. Instead of democracy and a better world, people got military dictatorship, hunger, and more war.
>
> War, I repeat, is the great illusion. The only way out of this treadmill is to mobilize for peace as in the past we have mobilized for war."
>
> (1938 FL Platform; Willard Munger Personal Collection.)

As well-thought of as Benson's sentiments may have been by his most ardent followers, the Conservatives pressed their advantage.

Are We Awake to What is Happening in Minnesota?

> Is Communism Establishing a "Popular Front" in this State?
>
> The Farmer-Labor Party, in its platform in 1934, made the following declarations of its basic political policy:
>
> "Only complete re-organization of our social structure into a cooperative commonwealth will bring economic security and prevent a prolonged period of suffering...
>
> We, therefore, declare that capitalism has failed and immediate steps must be taken by the people to abolish capitalism in a peaceful and lawful manner and that a new sane and just society must be established..."
>
> That a "Popular Front" is being organized in America to function in 1940 is known to everyone. But many do not realize that the Minnesota Farmer-Labor Party is looked upon as the nucleus from which this coalition that is to change our form of government is to spring...
>
> It will do not do to say that the Communist Party's "Popular Front"—the Farmer-Labor Party above mentioned—is not identical with the Minnesota Farmer-Labor Party...
>
> (1938 Pamphlet; Willard Munger Personal Collection.)

A more difficult problem for the Party arose. As previously indicated, Benson's intra-party rival, Hjalmar Petersen, was not willing to let his defeat at the 1938 FL Convention go "gently into that good night." Petersen not only refused to back Benson, he threw his considerable weight behind the candidacy of Harold Stassen. After losing in a very close primary to Benson (218,235 votes to 202,205 votes), Petersen formed the "Independent Progressive Voters of Minnesota" and printed his views in The Independent Voters of America Newspaper, a vehicle of his own creation.

> Those of us who led the Petersen forces in the primary have bent every energy to reclaim and reconstruct the Farmer-Labor Party. Its present Communistic leaders have done nothing. Because we still believe in the justice for our cause, and the soundness of our progressive principles, we have advised and assisted in drafting the present Stassen platform and we know it is as liberal as the Farmer-Labor platform of 1930. We have demanded and received a pledge of Harold E. Stassen that he will be a governor of all the people. We appeal to all voters of all parties to rally to the cause and help elect Stassen governor.
>
> (Willard Munger Personal Collection.)

Despite his skepticism, Munger resumed his duties with the Benson campaign.

> "(I) went back out and campaigned, but I was convinced that we were going to lose because of the Stassen stickers on the old cars. If they had been on new cars, I wouldn't have thought much about it," Willard remembered.
>
> (*Oral History of Willard Munger*, ibid, p. 45.)

To make matters worse, Munger's own position within the Department of Agriculture had been called into question by men loyal to Hjalmar Petersen who demanded that a hearing be held to determine whether or not Munger was qualified to hold his job.

> October 7, 1938
>
> Dear Dutch:
>
> In receipt of your letter regarding the supervisor's meeting in Wadena next Tuesday. I'm not sure whether or not I will be able to be there, as some of these would-be Farmer-Laborites up here are insisting on their hearing with the union as to whether or not I am entitled to hold my present job. I contacted some of these fellows today and they seemed to pull in their horns, but they are a bunch of double-crossers. The chairman of the grievance com-

mittee who has been raising all the fuss is Erick Ecklund who works for the land and minerals department up here. If he'd go out and work as much for Benson as he does worrying about the eligibility of my holding a job with the state, he'd put up a whirlwind of a campaign for the governor…

[T]he only fellows pushing it are mostly employees of the Railroad and Warehouse Commission who don't like the way I treated Hjalmar…

Willard

On October 14, 1938, Dillon Peterson wrote to Willard regarding the failure of the FL Party machinery to cover northeastern Minnesota appropriately.

Dear Willard:

Member of the Executive Committee of the Party wrote:

"A few Benson placards but nothing extra for being good FL territory on Trunk Highway 53 from Duluth to Virginia.

Virginia to Hibbing pretty good.

From Hibbing to Grand Rapids and thence to Aitkin and on to Brainerd, practically no placards for any of the candidates."

This chap says that the condition is deplorable and asks that something be done about it immediately.

Please advise quick if we should send a trouble-shooting squad in with a car and wide open to travel to help nail up placards, etc…

Give me a brief report on this so can answer the complaint…

Dillon

Munger's response is unknown. But it seems likely that, by the time Dillon Peterson was once again calling Willard Munger on the carpet for dereliction of duty, Munger had little gumption to stretch his already meager finances by gallivanting around the 8th Congressional District in search of Benson road signs.

The issue of political patronage came to the forefront of the campaign when Stassen announced that he would institute merit-based civil service for most state positions. The issue wasn't one that would have resonated deeply with most Minnesotans; they'd heard promises of patronage reform from candidates (including Floyd B. Olson) over the years but the issue always died after the votes were counted. The issue was, however, of vital importance to politicos like Willard Munger who held their positions by partisan fiat. This was also true for Willard's father, District Game Warden Harry Munger, Sr. who, at an advanced age and with only a 4th grade education, was unlikely to find a job paying anywhere near what his position with the Conservation Department paid should Stassen win and "clean house."

Given that 15 – 17,000 workers were employed by the state, Benson sought to galvanize them into action on his behalf.

> Among the many promises being made now by reactionaries in this cam-
> paign, is one to pass a civil service law. For sixty long years, the Republican
> Party had complete control of the government of this state. During those
> sixty years, no effort was ever made to pass such a law. During any one of
> those sixty years a civil service law could have been passed without effort
> because the Republican Party controlled the governor and both branches of
> the legislature.
>
> The record shows reactionary forces have always backed the drive to de-
> stroy our civil service system and pauperize government employees. Reac-
> tionaries in this election are combining to defeat Elmer A. Benson and all
> who fight for a square deal for men and women in government service. I have
> always been interested in your welfare and as evidence of this, the present
> state administration is the first which has permitted state employees to join
> unions of their own choosing...
>
> Remember that every Farmer-Labor vote is a vote to protect your interests
> and the welfare of your family.
>
> Your cooperation is greatly appreciated.
>
> Most sincerely,
>
> Elmer A. Benson
>
> Governor

But the die was cast.

> "Benson lost because he didn't use good judgment—he wasn't very politi-
> cally astute. He was a super dedicated person—there's no question about
> that," Willard remembered. "He wanted to help out the down-and-outers.
> But he lacked the...political savvy that Olson had...He surrounded himself
> with people who were really down-and-out. He surrounded himself not with
> moderates, but with extreme left-wing people. I'm not calling them Com-
> munists because the Republicans did that for me. Benson was not a Commie,
> but they were running the show. They moved into the Farmer-Labor Party.
> They got control of the Farmer-Labor Party and Benson allowed that control
> to come about. I suppose he thought that they were the most articulate, the
> most active, the people he had to have in order to get control of the Farmer-
> Labor convention. After all, he had to compete for endorsement with Hjal-
> mar Petersen, who was more of a right-winger...He knew these left-wingers
> would provide more support and more action and more work to garner the

necessary votes he needed. So I think that's one of the reasons why he leaned that way," Willard continued. "On the other hand, Floyd B. Olson knew he was a sure thing as far as getting the endorsement. He didn't have to worry about that...Olson knew that he didn't have to worry about getting an endorsement from the convention. It was there. All he had to do was win the election. Benson, on the other hand, put all his eggs in one basket for convention votes and forgot about the big votes in the general election. He didn't have them. People became frightened with all the left-wingers who were supporting him and ran out on him...

"So we lost. We lost, I think, by 200,000 votes. Two years before that, we had won by 200,000 votes. It was just a tremendous switch. I came back to Duluth and was broke, with no money. My wife was kind of disappointed. She had always encouraged me about politics. I went back up to the office of the Department of Agriculture and I had a Benson sticker on my car. I had two fellows working for me. This was on my first day back to work and we had some back orders on some inspections. I said, 'Well, let's go down and take care of those inspections.' They always rode with me, see. They came out to the car and said, 'We think we'll walk.'

"'Walk? That's a whole mile almost. How come you want to walk?'

"'We just think we'd like to walk.'

"I didn't know what their problem was.

"Finally they said, 'We're not going to ride in your car with that Benson sticker on it.'

"'Well,' I said, 'then you'll walk because I'm not taking it off.'

"So I drove down and they walked down. I said to them, 'I don't see how I can change my politics that quick and I don't intend to.'

"During the campaign my boss...switched and came out for Stassen. Then after the election, he told me, 'Willard, this is a new ball game. The Republicans are in control and if you want your job, you'll have to play ball. Now I came up to find out whether you want to switch your loyalties to Stassen...'

"I said, 'I'm not a traitor like you are. I can tell you that I don't think I'm going to switch.'

"'I understand your wife is going to have a baby. Why don't you think it over for one week? I'm going to come back up next week to talk to you. You better give this one some real serious thinking because you can stay if you want to switch. We think you're a pretty good supervisor.'

"A week went by, and he came up and said, 'Well, what's your answer?'

"I said, 'The same as it was when you were here before. I'm not switching. I'm not that kind of hypocrite. I'm not going to switch for a lousy job.'

"He said, 'I understand that you're pretty bad off financially.'

"I said, 'You're right. But I'm going to make one request…My wife is going to have a baby in March. Go back and tell the new governor that I would really like to stay on until after she has the baby.'

"This was the first part of January [1939].

"He said, 'I'll go back and see what I can do. I think there's no question about it that they'll let you stay on.'

"A week later, I got a notice that I was done immediately…"

(*Oral History of Willard Munger*, ibid, p. 55, pp. 43 – 46.)

CHAPTER 4

The Gas Station

Stassen's firing of Willard Munger in early 1939 left Munger without the means to provide for his three-year-old daughter and his pregnant wife.

[S]o I went out and started looking around for a job," remembered Willard. "There was no way I could find a job any place…I saw a 'for sale' sign on this white building. A fellow by the name of Wellberg had it. I called him up and asked him how much he wanted for it. He said he wanted $5,000 for it, but I could have it on the basis of thirty dollars a month. So I sold my car for $400.00 and gave him fifty or a hundred dollars for a down payment. I then went to the John Bero Oil Company and made a deal with them. They would deliver 200 gallons at a time because that was all I could pay for. Then I started putting in a few groceries. It was really just an old shack.

Then the steel plant went on strike. I had charged some gas for the steel workers out there, and they didn't have any money to pay me. So Wellberg came out one day about six months after I bought the place with a big handful of cigars. He said, 'Here, Mr. Munger, I'm going to have to give you some cigars. You're way behind on your payments, so you've got to move out.'

I said, 'That's not a very good way to treat me. Ain't you going to give me a chance?'

'Well', he said, 'that's the way I make my money. I sell them and take them back. In these kinds of bad times, that's the only way you can do it. So I'll give you a cigar so we have a good friendship. '

I said, 'That's a hell of a kind of friendship. I'll tell you, Mr. Wellberg, you ain't going to get this place.'

My wife was uptown. I said to Arnold Johnson and George Burr, who were hanging around the station—they didn't have a job either—'Why don't you take care of the gas station and the grocery store? I'm going to walk down to Klearflax [a local rug manufacturer located in West Duluth]…and see if there's a chance to get a job.' This was in the afternoon, see. I was pretty down in the dumps, I'll tell you that.

I got down there and there was a line about a block long of people who wanted to apply for jobs. So I stood in line. I happened to come with my face and hands all full of grease, wearing an old shirt. I'd just been greasing a car. The guy from Klearflax was walking down the line, interviewing everybody, and looking them over. He walked by me and said, 'Hey, you. Where are you from?'

'I'm from Fergus Falls. I just came into town.'

'What did you do in Fergus Falls?'

'I'm a farmer.'

'Come with me.'

[I] knew that they were anti-union so I thought that if I told them I was a farmer, I would have a better chance of getting a job.

He put me to work piling hundred pound bales of flax straw, and I wasn't used to working like that. My hands were so bad I couldn't even close them. I stayed there for about two years. During that time, I had the idea of going to night school up in Duluth in the university's extension program. What do you suppose I was interested in? Ship building…I got forty-three cents an hour working at Klearflax, and I saved my place. Wellberg didn't get it back."

(Oral History of Willard Munger, ibid, pp. 46 – 49.)

One of the individuals Munger befriended at Klearflax was Popular Front activist, Anne Gerlovich. Gerlovich was everything that the supervisors of the plant were trying to avoid; outspoken, radical, and active in union organizing. It was through Gerlovich that Munger became acquainted with political science instructor, Roger Hargrave, another radical who had served in the Communist sponsored "Lincoln Brigade" during the Spanish Civil War. There can be little doubt that Hargrave's service on the Republican side in a war popularized by Hemingway's *For Whom the Bell Tolls* impressed Munger.

As Harry Munger, Jr. recounts, "Willard took a job working for Klearflax as a laborer. He took the job to supplement what he was making at the station and because they had another child. The position was union, which suited Willard's politics. The company made rugs from flax at a factory on 63rd Ave. West in West Duluth. That's where Willard became fast friends with…Roger Hargrave. Hargrave was an old Leftist who, along with George Lund from Duluth, had fought against Franco and the Fascists in Spain," Harry, Jr. remembers. "Roger limped from wounds he received in that war."

The gas station Munger operated at the corner of Grand Avenue and 75th West was located near the Duluth Zoo, a facility built in 1927. But whereas the zoo was a sparkling new brick building, Munger's gas station and grocery store was, at the beginning, something less ostentatious.

"It was a DX gas station," Patsy Munger-Lehr recalls, "with an outside grease pit for greasing cars. It didn't have an indoor garage or bay. We sold cigarettes and candy and a few groceries at first. There was a fire in the old shack; that's what the station really was, a one-level wooden shack. After the fire, Dad decided to move the old station back on the property and build a new cement block building out near Grand Avenue."

Willard Munger recalled that constructing the new gas station at 7502 Grand Avenue in Duluth was a family affair. The cement block version of the station was built while he was working for the Butler Shipyards in Superior during World War II. At the time of his oral interviews with the Minnesota Historical Society, both the original shack and the cement block building were still standing.

> "If you go over and look behind that building [the service station], there's a little shack behind that. That's where my family and I lived," Willard remembered. "One old lady came into the store one day and said, 'Who are those hillbillies who live in that old tar paper shack back there?'
>
> I said, 'I guess that's me, but I'm not a hillbilly.'
>
> I sold my car for $400.00 and bought enough groceries and enough gasoline out of the $300.00 I had left. If you don't think that was a struggle, you've got another thing coming. I've had enough hard knocks but they haven't hurt me. Then I decided to buy a lot of government bonds while I was working in the shipyard, so I was able to build that building you see over there," Willard observed [pointing to the gas station building]. "My wife and I laid every single block in that building—every single one. There wasn't anyone who did any work on that outside of my own family. It took me three years to do it, but I did it..."
>
> (*Oral History of Willard Munger*, ibid, p. 57.)

Will Munger, Jr. recalls that, for a while, the "little shack in the back" didn't even have water or sewer hooked up to it. "One of my first memories of my father is him using a No. 2 shovel to dig a trench from the new gas station back to the shack to bring water and sewer to where we were living," Will, Jr. remembers. "Before he did that, we had to use the washrooms in the gas station. When he built the new station, he salvaged an old heater from a school bus to heat the garage. Both Patsy and I worked there, selling gas, working in the store. But like many things Dad did, something always distracted him before he was finished with a project. He started to paint the outside of the new station white but it never really got done. When the paint that was up started to peel, I suggested we should finish painting it. He never did. It just didn't matter to him."

"Everything we did," Patsy says, "was work. Building the gas station, putting in the electrical for the motel; we did it all ourselves."

Harry Munger, Sr. was also a victim of Stassen's landslide win.

"After Stassen beat Elmer Benson, Dad was transferred to Aitkin as a game warden," Harry, Jr. recalls. "There were petitions circulated with thousands of names to keep Dad in Fergus Falls as the district supervisor but it didn't do any good. Then, the day before civil service took effect, Dad was fired from his job in Aitkin. Dad and Mom both tried to make ends meet by selling Woodman's Insurance again but it didn't work out. The mortgage guy kept coming to the house asking for his money so we sold out and left Fergus Falls.

"We followed Willard to Duluth in 1942. I was in the middle of 10th grade. I went from Washington High School in Fergus to Duluth Denfeld. Dad moved to Duluth first, then came and got us. My parents rented a place on 8th street near Longfellow School. Dad went to work with Willard in the shipyards. Then we moved to a place above Pratt's Rugs, 6032 Raleigh Street."

Harry, Jr. recalls that his older brother was multi-talented.

"Willard was a pretty fair meat cutter. He and Martha had a meat counter, vegetables and other grocery items stocked in the store at the gas station. I worked for him there, when my folks and I came to Duluth from Fergus Falls."

Patsy Munger-Lehr recalls that, once the block building was completed, the station also sold televisions and radios. Will, Jr. remembers the gas station as a family enterprise and, despite constant worries over money, recalls little turmoil between his parents.

"I don't remember Mom and Dad fighting. Their marriage was solid," Will, Jr. recounts. "Dad had great respect for Mom and she was always the driving force, the one pushing him. She made him look good. They were, years ahead of it being fashionable, an equal couple. They worked together at the station, selling soda pop and groceries, pumping gas, cutting meat. Everywhere I went people knew who my parents were. Mom was the president of the PTA. But they were really 'hands off' in terms of their parenting. Sometimes it seemed they were too involved in the 'Big Picture' to know what their two kids were doing."

Patsy Munger-Lehr agrees. "They didn't have the time to be real good parents. As long as we were in school and out of trouble, they didn't give a darn about us. They were too busy with life, with trying to help everyone else. Don't get me wrong, I loved my parents. My mother had the best laugh of anyone I've ever met. She was smart and quick. In addition to being the head of the PTA, she was active in organizing Duluth's Centennial Celebration and charity drives. She wasn't just bright; she was super smart. She was the force behind Dad. I had the utmost respect for both of them, for the 'Munger' name. I remember leaving parties that had liquor at them as a high school girl because I didn't want to get caught and smear that name."

Will, Jr. adds that, "Our parents weren't all warm and fuzzy. But they were kind. They always looked out for the less fortunate. When Grandpa Munger lost his job as a game warden and moved up here, Dad got him a job in the shipyards and then later, in our gas station. Grandpa didn't do much at the station. He liked to listen to baseball on the radio. I'd sit and listen with him. But he wasn't what you'd call ambitious. He'd sell 100 gallons of gas in a day and sort of call it quits. I'd run the station on the weekends and set a goal, 1,000 gallons, and sell it. He was slow and pokey but loveable. Dad and Grandpa Harry were always at odds. They had a volatile relationship. Grandpa died of a heart attack right after he and Dad had a big fight about something. Dad never forgave himself," Will, Jr. remembers. "It was over something trivial and that grated at Dad in the worst way."

Willard Munger, whose father's family had started out Presbyterian and migrated to Norwegian Lutheranism in Otter Tail County, and whose mother remained a Missouri Synod Lutheran even after she and Harry, Sr. came to Duluth, wasn't quick to join a church in Duluth. Martha, despite being raised a Missouri Synod Lutheran, grew to despise the pettiness of the doctrines of the Synod, indicating to Patsy that she chose to leave the church she'd been born into because "they just weren't very nice people." Patsy Munger-Lehr recalls that the family's first church in Duluth was the Norton Park Methodist Church, but in reality, "we didn't go to church that much because we worked at the store most Sundays."

Willard and Martha eventually began attending Our Savior's Lutheran Church (later affiliated with the Evangelical Lutheran Church of America) in West Duluth, mostly because of the pastor, Reverend Pederson. "Mother loved to argue politics and Pastor Pederson didn't disappoint her in that respect," Pat Lehr recalls. "But, like I said, we didn't go to church much as a family. Mom wasn't really that active in the church. She put her efforts into PTA. Dad, he was so bad, he'd hand me his pledge check and tell me to put it in the collection plate for him. I'd tell him, 'No, I'm not going to do that. You need to do it yourself.'"

Though the young family settled in Duluth, a gateway to the great outdoors, Will, Jr. doesn't recall his father being involved in many outdoor activities other than fishing. "He took me fishing quite a bit as a kid. We went to Murphy Lake, Oak Lake. He fished a lot," Will recalls. "I remember him taking out a white gas stove and frying fish in a pan right in the bottom of a wooden boat! But I'd agree with my Uncle Harry that Dad wasn't very organized. We speared in a dark house in the winter for pike. But, as with all Dad's building projects, the dark house he built was overkill. He used angle irons and plywood to build it and then I had to drag the thing onto the ice.

"We also went partridge hunting once or twice but Dad wasn't much of a shot. One time, there was a partridge flying over the road. It hit a power line and fell on the car's windshield. That was about the only way Dad could get a bird," Will, Jr. says with a laugh. "And we didn't camp out often. I remember going up the North Shore. Mom and Dad stayed in a cabin and I slept in a tent. But that was a rare occasion."

Though Willard Munger made a successful adjustment to life outside of partisan politics, other Farmer-Labor politicos weren't as fortunate.

> August 7, 1939
>
> Dear Friend Willard:
>
> Not having heard from you in a coon's age, thought would rattle off a few lines in hopes it would induce you to take time out and let a fellow know how you are making it.
>
> Heard indirectly that you got yourself in the oil station business but no details as to where, how, etc...
>
> Things been pretty tough for me. The folks have been somewhat poorly and I haven't been able to connect on anything. Have ahold of a proposition now that may turn out to be something real. Just starting now, 1st of the month. No income yet.
>
> How are all of the Farmer-Laborites up there? Seems as tho they are getting hopped up again all over the state. Well—I'm off of politics. Don't see any hope for 1940, only a bunch of old spavins running around...

Drop me a line when you can find me so I'll know how you all are.

Sincerely yours,

Dutch Strout

Willard Munger wasn't the type of person to wait for opportunity to find him.

"I stayed there [Klearflax] for about two years. During that time, I had the idea of going to night school up there at Duluth in the university's extension program...I took a lot of courses in ship building and especially ship drafting.

"When the war [WWII] broke out, they found that I had taken all these courses. Robert Butler [the owner of Butler shipyards] had just started up in Superior. He called me up and wanted to interview me."

(*Oral History of Willard Munger*, ibid, p. 48.)

Walter Butler Shipyards was not the first place Munger plied his knowledge of marine drafting. According to a job application Munger submitted a decade later, Munger worked at another Twin Ports shipyard before working for Walter Butler.

Mr. Monger [sic] has been employed by Walter Butler Shipbuilders...for the past twenty-one months as Boat Foreman. During this period, three types of vessels have been constructed, and Mr. Monger was Boat Foreman on the first vessel of each type, with the construction of a total of ten ships coming under his supervision.

Prior to his employment in this yard, Mr. Monger worked for the Zenith Dredge Company...as Shipfitter Leadman on construction of Coast Guard Cutters.

Mr. Monger attended the University of Minnesota and has four credits acquired in three courses of Marine Drafting.

In my association with Mr. Monger, I have found him to be a capable employee and his work has been very satisfactory.

(Letter from Juilus E. Fink, Head Shipyard Inspector
of the United States Maritime Commission.)

The reference to Zenith Dredge is to Willard's having worked on the famed "180s," Coast Guard buoy tenders of approximately 180 feet in length built by Zenith Dredge and by Marine Iron and Shipbuilding of Duluth. In all, some 39 vessels of this class were built, including the *Woodrush* and the *Sundew*, both of which served in Duluth. The *Sundew* is now docked in the Duluth harbor as a floating museum. The *Woodrush* left Duluth for service in Alaska. The last of the 180s, the *Acacia*, was decommissioned by the Coast Guard on June 7, 2006, over fifty years after it was built. (http://www.jacksjoint.com/wagl.htm)

Duluth, Minnesota might seem like an odd location for the building of ocean-going vessels. According to *Minnesota Goes to War* by Dave Kenny (Minnesota Historical Society Press, 2005), Duluth and its Wisconsin neighbor to the east, Superior, had a long and distinguished history of ship building, including the launching of over 100 vessels during WWI. Despite this heritage, no contracts for ships were secured by the shipyards in the Twin Ports from the end of WWI until shortly before the U.S.A. declared war in 1941. That changed when Marine Iron and Shipbuilding in Duluth was awarded a contract to build the first 180s in late 1939. After Pearl Harbor, FDR urged Congress to commit funds for the construction of 18 million dead weight tons of additional shipping. When one considers that the United States' total production of commercial vessels in 1941 was slightly over 1 million tons, it is clear that FDR was calling upon every shipyard in America to gear up for the war effort.

At the war's outbreak, the Duluth city directory listed two shipbuilding concerns in Duluth; Marine Iron and Shipbuilding at 11th Avenue West and the harbor, and Zenith Dredge, South 13th Avenue West and the harbor. By 1942, Barnes Duluth Shipyard was listed as being in operation on Spring Street (in the Riverside location once used by Alexander McDougal to build exotic whaleback boats). Walter Butler then started up in Superior, along with Globe, with Butler acquiring, in 1944, the Riverside works owned by Barnes. In all, according to Mr. Kenny's research, Duluth and Superior produced 191 vessels of all sizes and configurations for the war effort. (*Minnesota Goes to War,* ibid, p. 118.)

Willard Munger's supervisor at the Butler Shipyard considered Munger's work to be exemplary, Saying of Munger, "I consider him an invaluable employee, both from the standpoint of character and ability, leadership and organization...."

The same supervisor indicated that Munger had been in charge of shifts of 100 to 300 men while working as a boat foreman.

Despite the fact Willard Munger was hired to work at Klearflax because the hiring agent assumed Munger would not join the union, Munger had always been a supporter of labor unions. This didn't change when he went to work for Walter Butler.

> August 20, 1945
>
> I have known Willard Munger for three and one-half years. He came to work for the Walter Butler Shipbuilders, Inc. in the early part of 1942 as a

first-class shipfitter. Shortly thereafter, he became a boat foreman and has been such ever since.

He has been a good union member...

I recommend him very highly for the position of supervisor as he has been very well liked by his men and always had their respect.

Holger Modeen, Business Agent

As noted, Munger's later recollection as to how he came to Walter Butler Shipyard is not accurate. He didn't get snapped up by Robert Butler without experience. Munger first acquired basic skills in shipbuilding while working for Zenith and *then* went to work for Butler. Long after the fact, Munger recounted his first interaction with Butler.

"He said, 'Your credentials...are pretty good on the courses that you're taking in ship building. I want you to work for me.'

I said, 'Gee, that's great—that's good. What am I supposed to do?'

'You're supposed to be the foreman,' he said.

I said, 'Foreman! I've never built a boat in my life. I'm not going to take a job like that.'

'Well,' he said, 'you know, I'm going to try you out.'

I said, 'No, you're not. I'm not going to do that because I can't do it.'

He said, 'I'm going to St. Paul and I'll be back Friday. I'm going to leave you here, and you better try and find out whether or not you can do it.'

I said, 'Well, I tell you right now, I'm not going to do it.'

'Well,' he said, 'I'll tell you something. You're going to stay here until I get back next Friday. You see out here on the keel box—there are two underbottoms. The first fellow...got it all screwed up...he got a great big buckle where the two join together. I want you to figure out how you're going to take them apart and re-weld them. I'm going to check you out next Friday and see what kind of job you're doing.'"

(*Oral History of Willard Munger*, ibid, pp. 48 – 49.)

It's clear from this passage that Munger was already working for Walter Butler Shipyard in Superior—that this conversation took place at the shipyard where Munger was working as a shipfitter—when Robert Butler approached Munger and asked him to become a foreman. This conflict between memory and the written record doesn't diminish the fact that, with very little training and only a few months on the job, Munger was being elevated from shipfitter to supervisor.

"If you'd known old man Butler, he was a pretty…persuasive guy," Willard recalled. "So I stayed. The next day I went over to the federal inspectors who had a little office over there. I said, 'Hey, that underbottom out there on the keel block with the big buckle—how do you go about fixing that?'

Now these inspectors were just as new as I was. One of them was a big fat guy. He said, 'Well, why don't you go out and contact the boat foreman and get your advice from him. He'll tell you.'

I said, '[I]'m supposed to be the boat foreman.'

'Well,' he said, 'then you ought to know how to do it.'

That's all the help I got. That made me mad. So I went out and got me a good chipper, a good burner, a good welder. I chipped it apart, put some strong blocks on, and welded it according to the proper sequence. It turned out to be a beautiful job. Now this was the first boat. I went on from there to build sixteen boats."

(*Oral History of Willard Munger*, ibid, pp. 48 – 49.)

The vessels Munger guided through the construction process included transoceanic transports ("Liberty Ships"), smaller coastal transports, and frigates such as the *Dearborn*. At 303 feet in length, the *Dearborn* was originally designated the *Toledo* but was renamed the *Dearborn* prior to its launch in Superior on September 27, 1943. The ship was commissioned for duty on September 10, 1944 and served until it was scrapped in July of 1947. Unlike the unarmed Liberty Ships, which were built to carry troops, supplies and munitions across the Atlantic for the war effort, the *Dearborn* was a fighting ship, boasting guns and depth charge projectors, built to serve as a coastal patrol vessel or as a convoy escort to deter German submarine attacks. (www.navsource.org/archieves/12/08033.htm)

In a lecture given regarding the history of the Butler Shipyards ("Butler Shipyard Legacy" videotape, 1995, Superior Federation of Labor) Willard Munger noted that he and his shipbuilding crew were in some pretty heady company. Famous personalities including Ingrid Bergman, Anne Bancroft and the Dionne Quintuplets visited the shipyards of Duluth and Superior during WWII to promote the sale of war bonds.

"When the Quints came [on May 4, 1943]," Willard remembered, "we had five boats ready to launch on the same day—one for each of the girls. Mine was the last one on the end. The Quints weren't put up in a hotel—they had their own private railroad car which was pulled right up next to my boat. All my crew was lined up on the railing of the boat, waving at the girls, who were waving right back. Robert Butler, the owner of the yard, came walking by and stopped me. 'Munger, get those men back to work,' he said. 'They're like a bunch of blackbirds on a wire.' I said, 'Mr. Butler, you could help me out by moving that train car. Then maybe I could get the boys back to work.'"

Despite being handpicked by Robert Butler to serve as a foreman, Munger wasn't always perfect in his work.

"As the foreman, I was supposed to make sure that the bleeder plugs were secured before the boat was launched," Willard recalled with a smile. "Well, on one boat, I forgot to crawl underneath the hull and inspect the plugs. The boat got launched and it started filling with water. We barely got it into the dry dock. I had to spend four or five days in the FBI office explaining that mistake."

Munger also recalled that one of his best workers was a Communist.

"You'd get guys crowding by the off-ladder near the end of a shift. Sometimes they'd be there 15 – 20 minutes before the shift ended. This guy, he was a real Leftie. He'd say to the crew, 'Men, go back to work until the whistle blows. Mother Russia needs these ships.' You see, it was after the Non-Aggression Pact had been violated by Hitler and we were sending supplies to the U.S.S.R. Well, the FBI heard about this guy and they called me into their office in the yard. 'We hear you've got a Commie working on your boat and we want you to fire him.' I told them, 'Nope, I'm not going to do that. He's one of my best workers.'"

Munger reiterated that he was proud of his membership in the AFL, the union he belonged to while working at Walter Butler, though the union steward, Mr. Modeen, originally questioned Munger's loyalty.

"I worked on, I think, 12 boats as foreman for Butler," Munger recalled. "I was badge #67, so I was one of the first men hired when they started up. Before that, I'd worked over at Zenith. I was the secretary of the union at Zenith, which was a CIO affiliate. Modeen looked at me when I walked in to join the AFL at Butler and he said to me, 'Did you come here to organize for the CIO or did you come here to work?' I said, 'To work. And I'll join the AFL right now.'"

"You know," Willard remarked, "I've always been a supporter of unions. I've run for the legislature 20 times and I've been endorsed by the AFL-CIO 20 times. I was even endorsed by labor in Otter Tail County, in 1934, and I got the hell beat out of me in that election for it!"

Munger had praise for Robert Butler, who, despite taking a shine to Munger, wasn't above getting into heated arguments with his foreman. Walter Butler, Jr., remembered being at the shipyard one day to witness an altercation between his father and Willard.

> "The Butler Shipyards were union friendly," Walter Butler, Jr. recalled. "Our family has always been Democrat and union supporters. Willard is an old friend and the dean of the Minnesota Legislature. He carries great prestige and is one hell of a guy. But," Butler recounted, "he and my dad used to get into it. That's not unusual because I also argued with my father. So did his business associates. But my dad, he had been a heavyweight boxing champion and a football player at the University of Minnesota, and he wasn't one to back down. Despite that, Willard looked right at him one day and said, 'I quit.' Willard stormed across the yard and went into the accounting office to draw his last paycheck. My dad followed him and stopped the accountant from writing out the check. 'You write Munger his last paycheck and you can draw your own as well,' Dad said. He then took Willard aside and said, 'Munger, you can't quit. There's a war going on and our boys need these ships.' Well, there wasn't' much Willard could say to that. So he stayed."
>
> ("Butler Shipyard Legacy," videotape, 1995.)

At the conclusion of World War II, the shipyards were de-activated and Willard Munger and his father found themselves out of work. Harry, Sr. was a man in his late sixties, with no pension to speak of, no financial resources beyond a modest working man's home in the Riverside neighborhood of Duluth, when the shipyard laid him off. Willard gave him a job at the service station. Willard's kindness in such situations seems an odd contrast with the style of parenting adopted by Willard and Martha towards their own children.

"Really, they didn't give a darn about us," Patsy Munger-Lehr recalls. "They were determined that Willy finish college but beyond that, they didn't have the time to be too interested in what we were up to. They were too busy helping everyone else. A good example of this is that Mom was deeply involved with the PTA; she was president of the whole association. But she never once, that I can remember, asked her own daughter about her grades," Pasty recounts with a wistful smile.

On June 2, 1943, Willard Munger suffered the loss of his last surviving grandparent, the erasable Mary Emily Armstrong Munger. Grandma Munger, though a tough and cantankerous old bitty, had an impact upon Willard in a positive way. There's no question that the political discussions Willard participated in with his grandparents helped ready him for the debates he would later be drawn into on the floor of the Minnesota House of Representatives.

Mrs. Munger, Respected Pioneer, Dies

Mrs. L.R. Munger, one of Otter Tail County's highly respected pioneers, died at her home in Friberg, at 5:00 P.M. Wednesday after a long illness. Her health began to fail about 3 years ago, but she was able to be up and about until a week before her death...

Mary Emily Armstrong was born in the town of Sparta, New York, Feb. 23, 1861, and died at the age of 82 years. She was the daughter of John and Margaret Armstrong and the third in a family of 8 children. When she was 4 years old, the family started on their long trek westward to Minnesota. This journey was not made all at once, and it was made for the most part in the typical pioneer covered wagon. They passed through Pennsylvania, Ohio, Indiana, Illinois, Michigan, Wisconsin and Iowa. The family remained in Iowa for a number of years and it was here that Mrs. Munger spent most of her girlhood...coming to Minnesota in 1880, and locating in Buse Township.

In 1883, she was united in marriage to Lyman Robert Munger of Fergus Falls. To this union, three children were born. They were Harry L. Munger, who is now in defense work in Duluth; William, who died at age of 9; and Margaret, now Mrs. Arthur Miller of Friberg. She also leaves three brothers, John H. Armstrong of Aastad; William F. Armstrong of Friberg; and Mark B. Armstrong of Harrison. Arkansas...

(*Fergus Falls Daily Journal,* June 3, 1943.)

The death of Grandma Munger severed Willard Munger's ties to a colorful and distant past; an era of covered wagons, Populist politics, unrestricted logging, and the westward expansion of white settlers onto America's Great Plains. Fully mindful of the work ethic and political leanings of his departed forefathers and foremothers, Willard Munger would put these attributes to good use in his new life in Duluth.

CHAPTER 5

A Valiant Attempt

Duluth's Liberal political scene found itself dominated during the last half of the Great Depression by the Popular Front; the Communist and Socialist influences within the Farmer-Labor Party.

When Willard Munger arrived in Duluth in 1935, he had little practical experience dealing with labor unions. His political associates in northwestern Minnesota were, for the greatest part, non-union workers; farmers and small businessmen; not wage earners affiliated with labor unions. Duluth, as described in great detail in Hudelson and Ross's extensive study of unions, Communism and the Popular Front in Duluth (*By the Ore Docks*, ibid), was a hotbed of extreme Left agitation and political intrigue during the later part of the Great Depression. Willard Munger, having been vetted in politics for the totality of his life, obviously recognized the importance of being affiliated with politicians and union leaders who shared his Liberal orientation. Though Munger explored Communism and Socialism as he acquired his own political philosophy, he never joined either movement. But it must have been an eye-opening experience for the young Pockerbrush politician, having come to Duluth from the relatively staid and tame hinterlands of Liberalism, to the seething pot of radical and Marxist ideals embraced by many of the Popular Front activists working inside the FL Party in Duluth.

> Reflecting the new Comintern policy of seeking unity with all Progressive forces...the Communists continued to reach out to the AFL, seeking cooperation between the AFL and CIO unions and pursuing an eventual restoration of unity in the labor movement. This general orientation of the Communists after 1935 to seek cooperation with all "progressive forces" is known as the policy of the "Popular Front."

> (*By the Ore Docks*, ibid, p. 201.)

For a time, the inclusion of the Communists and Socialists within the FL seemed to work. Benson and the FL Party claimed a massive and significant victory in 1936, earning both United States Senate positions, a majority of Minnesota's Congressional seats, and claiming virtually every state-wide administrative position. But, as Hudelson and Ross point out, that victory was the product of an illusion of unity between the moderate forces in the FL and the Popular Front, a coalition that was doomed to fracture. As war in Europe began in earnest, and after the invasion of Poland by the Germans and the Soviet Union and the unprovoked invasion of Finland by the Soviets, working folks in northeastern Minnesota began to distance themselves from the Far Left. Finns living in and around Duluth and on Minnesota's Iron Range rejected the notion that Soviet intervention in Finland was something to be welcomed. The defection of local Finns from the FL was soon followed by the Poles. This exodus (coming on the heels of Benson's disastrous loss to Stassen) spelled doom for the Farmer-Labor movement in Minnesota.

> The gubernatorial campaign of 1938 was a major confrontation between Benson, supported by the powerful Popular Front...and the enemies of the Popular Front rallying around...Stassen...
>
> (*By the Ore Docks*, ibid, p. 242.)

Benson's insistence that the FL Party embrace the radicalism of the Popular Front was a political miscalculation.

> Benson's forthright and sometimes undiplomatic support of Popular Front politics, and his willingness to use the power of the governor's office to support...labor...angered Conservatives and some of those who had supported him as Floyd B. Olson's successor...
>
> Along with charges of corruption in the patronage system employed by the FL Party, anti-communism played a major role in the campaign to defeat Benson in 1938.
>
> (*By the Ore Docks*, ibid, p. 242.)

Following the election of 1938, the Farmer-Labor movement was, for all intents and purposes, dead. There were isolated successes in terms of re-electing state and federal legislators to a few terms beyond 1938, but, for the largest part, the success of the Party fostered by Floyd B. Olson was not repeated. There came a time when, due to Stassen's mercurial success in Minnesota (a state that President Roosevelt had assumed was safe in terms of presidential politics) FDR decided something had to be done to ensure continued Democratic control of Minnesota's electoral votes.

> Despite unity in support of the nation's war effort, however, political maneuvering continued beneath the surface during the war years. The Farmer-Labor Party never recovered from its defeat in 1938. Behind popular Governor Stassen, the Republican Party successfully redefined its image, embracing the progressive reforms of the New Deal era, and promising to administer them without the inefficiency, corruption and Communist influence charged against former Governor Benson…In the elections of 1940 and 1942, the FLP remained in 2nd place, with the Democrats running a weak 3rd.
>
> Concerned that Minnesota might be lost to the Republicans in the presidential contest of 1944, the Roosevelt Administration wanted to see Farmer-Laborites and Democrats unite…
>
> In the spring of 1944…unity was achieved…While no major gains were won in 1944 or 1945, the new Democratic-Farmer-Labor Party managed to elect a young Hubert Humphrey as mayor of Minneapolis…
>
> The first major test for the newly united DFL in Duluth was the Congressional campaign of 1946. The campaign pitted incumbent Republican William Pittenger against DFL nominee John Blatnik. Blatnik was from Chisholm…He came from a Slovenian family and did not speak English until he entered school…[After receiving a degree in chemistry from Winona State] Blatnik landed a job teaching high school chemistry in Chisholm. He immediately became active in Farmer-Labor politics and was elected to fill the last two years of the Minnesota state senate term left vacant by the death of his good friend, Richard Kelly.
>
> During the war, Blatnik served in the OSS—a precursor to the CIA, parachuting behind enemy lines into Yugoslavia, where he used his knowledge of Slavic languages to establish a…connection with…Tito…
>
> (*By the Ore Docks*, ibid, pp. 252 – 254.)

According to Hudelson and Ross, Pittenger attacked Blatnik personally, alleging that, because of Blatnik's wartime service in Communist Yugoslavia, Blatnik would "take the Communist line." Blatnik fought this smear campaign with a "Vets for Blatnik" network and won the election decidedly. (*By the Ore Docks*, ibid, p. 235.)

Having wrested away a major political office from the Republicans, Blatnik, in conjunction with the efforts of Duluth attorney Gerald Heaney, Minneapolis Mayor Hubert Humphrey, and an assortment of other young DFLers (notably Donald

Fraser, future Congressman and mayor of Minneapolis; Eugene McCarthy, future U.S. Senator and presidential aspirant; and Orville Freeman, future governor and U.S. Secretary of Agriculture) moved to the center and purged the last remaining Popular Front elements from the re-formulated Democratic-Farmer-Labor Party (DFL). By the 1948 elections, the anti-communist wing of the DFL was firmly in control of the state party machinery, including the 8th Congressional District. (*By the Ore Docks*, ibid, p. 270.)

Gerald Heaney (who later became a federal appellate judge) remains vibrant and focused at the age of ninety years old. Heaney candidly recalls those early years of the DFL and his connection to Willard Munger.

"I was born near Red Wing," Judge Heaney recalls. "That's farm country but I was from town. My father owned a meat market and a small grocery store. Neither of my parents was politically active but I got active in my first campaign when I was ten years old."

Heaney's first activity as a young Democrat was to post handbills on telephone poles during the 1928 presidential contest between Herbert Hoover and Al Smith.

"Smith was Catholic," Heaney says with a smile. "And so am I. Irish Catholic on both sides. There was some animosity amongst the folks in our area about that but the thing I remember is the verse the kids teased me with in school: *Sour cats and rotten rats are good enough for Democrats.* That made me so mad, I ended up fighting at school over that verse," Heaney admits.

After graduating from Goodhue High School, Heaney went off to St. Thomas College and then to the University of Minnesota Law School.

"I was a classmate of Orville Freeman's at the U," Judge Heaney remembers. "And he was a good friend of Hubert Humphrey's so I also became Hubert's friend."

After graduating from law school, Heaney worked for the state of Minnesota in the Securities Division. But with America's entry into WWII, Heaney knew that he would be drafted; that his legal career would be put on hold.

"After Pearl Harbor, a friend and I went in on July 5, 1942 and volunteered. I took my basic training with the infantry," Heaney remembers, "and then I was selected for officer's school. I completed that at Fort Benning, Georgia, went with an infantry unit to Columbia, South Carolina, and when they came through asking for volunteers to transfer to the Rangers, I signed up. That got me on the beach on D-Day as a platoon commander. I went with the Rangers all the way, up until the end of the war."

After the war, Heaney remained in Bavaria as a military labor relations expert. The future judge was discharged and he returned home to Minnesota where he married. Heaney then learned of an opening in Duluth with attorney I.K. Lewis working in the area of labor relations law. Heaney joined the firm (which became known as Lewis, Hammer and Heaney) and remained in private practice until his appointment to the 8th Circuit Court of Appeals on December 1, 1966.

During the late 1940s Heaney became heavily involved in DFL politics but disputes that his role in the formation of the new party was as significant as depicted in *By the Ore Docks*.

"The DFL was really put together in 1946 by Elmer Kelm and Humphrey. That was before I was involved. I got involved," the retired judge adds, "in the 1948 campaign, when Humphrey ran for the Senate. Freeman was the chairman of the DFL at the time. Because I was doing so much labor law, it was only natural that I became involved. I think it was during that 1948 campaign that I first met Willard Munger. I got to know Willard and his wife, Martha, from that point on."

Recalling his rise within the DFL (which culminated with Heaney being named National Committeeman from Minnesota), Judge Heaney turns thoughtful.

"I never held any other office in the Party, though I was the Chair of the Duluth DFL Coordinating Committee," Heaney reflects. "That was an umbrella organization that sought to bring together the resources of all three legislative districts involving Duluth. It consisted of the officers from each of the DFL organizations in each district and representatives from labor."

With respect to his relationship with Willard Munger, the judge draws a distinction.

"We were political friends. We didn't travel in the same social circles. But nonetheless," Judge Heaney states, "I had great respect for him. We were on the same side most of the time."

After John Blatnik's election to Congress in 1946, Munger's affiliation with the Congressman enabled Munger to secure a position with the federal government.

"When I was running the grocery store, I got a call from...Heaney that there was going to be an opening in the OPS (Office of Price Stabilization)...That opening required that you had to run a grocery store for five years in order to take the exam. I was the only Democrat who was available to do that except for Clifford Mork, who was mayor (of Duluth) at the time. He became the head of the whole OPS operation for northern Minnesota," Willard recalled. "So I agreed to go down and put an application in for it. I was accepted. That was a good job which gave me $8,500.00 a year. I was given the assignment of chief of the food section for northern Minnesota and part of Wisconsin. I had several people working under me."

(*Oral History of Willard Munger*, ibid, p. 49.)

Munger's records indicate that he was hired for indefinite appointment as the Chief Business Analyst, Food Branch, Office of Price Stabilization, for Region VIII, working out of the Duluth District office. His salary was actually set at $6,400.00 and his hiring was effective May 28, 1951. The job was not a competitive civil service position but was an appointment for a one year trial period. Listed as personal references on Munger's application were: Congressman John A. Blatnik; U.S. Senator Hubert Humphrey (who won a seat in the Senate in 1948); and Earl Bester, International Representative of the CIO.

In his OPS job application, Munger explained the period of absence from his job as the operator of the Standard Oil station in Fergus Falls in 1934. The explanation was surely meant to call Munger's Liberal heritage to the attention of those in charge of hiring for the OPS.

While employed by Standard Oil, Co. I was granted a leave of absence for the following purposes: To represent the farmers of Otter Tail County in Washington, D.C. with regard to the Frazer-Lemke Bill.

(Willard Munger Personal Collection.)

The formation of the OPS was required because of the impact of the Korean War on the American economy.

Price control was necessary to combat runaway inflation generated by the Korean War. When voluntary controls proved ineffective, there was no alternative...

Consumers had $150 billion in liquid assets which they seemed itching to spend. Memories of WWII shortages led to a "buy now" philosophy and sales zoomed. New cars, televisions, refrigerators...it was a salesman's paradise. Consumer credit went up and savings went down. Bond redemptions were considerably ahead of sales...[R]etail prices reached a new all-time high during October...

(Willard Munger Personal Collection.)

The job description for Willard's position (business analyst) was as follows:

> [S]erves as head of the Food Branch and is responsible for the administration of price regulation of groceries and beverages, livestock, meat and fish, poultry and dairy products, agricultural chemicals, fats, oils and soap, wholesale and retail and grocery firms, restaurants, and all other regulations as that may be assigned to the Food Branch.
>
> (Willard Munger Personal Collection.)

Though Munger was never an avid outdoorsman, living in close physical proximity to the St. Louis River helped Munger form a life-long affinity for the river. During the 1940s, Munger's interest in the St. Louis River led him to join the United Northern Sportsmen, a group dedicated to preventing the environmental degradation of Minnesota's lakes, rivers and streams. Despite Munger's later recollections of having formed his environmental ethic as a child, it is far more likely that Munger's interest in conservation arose out of his membership in the United Northern Sportsmen.

> "I'm going to have to go back about thirty-five years," Willard recalled, "when the United Northern Sportsmen said we had to clean up the river. Nobody could fish in it. It stunk so that you could smell it all over West Duluth. You had crud floating on the water. It was a real mess…It was nothing but a really stinky river. That's all it was. Nothing could live in it. What did live in it, you couldn't eat. The walleyes would come out of the big lake and you could probably go out and catch them but you couldn't take them home and eat them. So we organized a group to call for the establishment of a sanitary sewer district to properly take care of the problem."
>
> (*Oral History of Willard Munger*, ibid, p. 80.)

Another major environmental issue brought to Munger's attention through his membership in the United Northern Sportsmen was the planned building of a taconite (low grade iron ore) processing plant on the shores of Lake Superior where the present day city of Silver Bay now stands.

> "The Reserve Mining Company," Munger remembered, "first tried to get a permit in 1947. The group that did the most to fight the dumping of taconite tailings was the United Northern Sportsmen. That was about the only group in the entire state that really tried to fight it. The odds were so great against the group that it was unbelievable. Labor was saying, 'Look at all the jobs it's going to create. Look at all the business it's going to create.'

"They would look at you right straight in the eye and say, 'Munger, do you really believe that you're going to pollute a big lake like Lake Superior with a few tons of taconite tailings in the water? Are you so foolish as to believe that?' They would make you look like you were kind of foolish. They'd point out how big the lake is, how cold it is, and how clear it is.

➤ "People believed you couldn't pollute the lake. People believed that you were a fanatic if you tried to stop it. I think that there is nothing more cruel than to use a person's job as a hostage in order to destroy the environment. You're not only destroying the environment, but in the end, you're destroying the individual…"

(*Oral History of Willard Munger*, ibid, p. 85.)

The Reserve Mining issue was the first environmental cause Willard Munger became involved with. His involvement in that fight was based upon his membership in the United Northern Sportsmen and that group's opposition to the plant from the very beginning. Munger's records include the original state of Minnesota Water Pollution Control Permit issued to Reserve Mining (dated December 16, 1947) as well as the following letter from S.E. Larson of 122 N. 7th Ave. E in Duluth.

The newly proposed taconite plant to be built at Beaver Bay will be dumping 20 million long tons of rock and tailings into Lake Superior per year. Their own engineers estimate that this will be from the size of a pea down to particles finer than flour, and their laboratories admit the finer particles will stand in a bottle of water for ten days before all has settled to the bottom.

This will give you a clear picture of what will happen to our drinking water in Duluth and Superior, to which we have always pointed with such great pride. Just let us have a three day wind from the northeast and see what a wonderful drink we will have from our faucets…

If we allow this one mining operation to start this, there will be many others doing the same thing to our inland lakes and streams over the northern part of the state and robbing us of one of the few luxuries we now have left…

(Willard Munger Personal Collection.)

Willard Munger also became active in civic affairs.

Club to Request City Playground in Norton Park Area
"If our children have to play on the tracks, the city council should at least give us train schedules."

That was the way Willard Munger, West Duluth Businessmen's Club member, summarized his complaint yesterday against city officials for failing to provide a Norton Park playground.

Munger told the club at its meeting in the Tourist Café that he had been promised a playground by Mayor George Johnson for children of the area some time ago. Since then, no action has been taken, he said.

The children were recently ordered away from the Duluth Zoo where they broke a window while playing ball, he said.

"The park superintendent has informed me that no funds are available... However, the children of Norton Park are entitled to a safe place to play... There is a plot of ground at Indian Point which could be developed into a playground with little cost."

(*Duluth News Tribune,* undated.)

In addition, Munger was deeply involved with the fledgling DFL Party.

HHH Benefit Dinner

Fried chicken orders for more than 1,000 guests at the DFL rally Saturday were placed today by the dinner co-chairmen, Willard M. Munger, and Mrs. Margaret Allen, St. Louis County DFL Chairwoman...The dinner...in the Duluth Armory will be a testimonial for U.S. Senator Hubert Humphrey and Congressman John A. Blatnik, Chisholm. Principal speaker will be Congressman Chet Holifield [D-California]. The dinner was originally planned for the Spalding Hotel but later was changed to the Armory because of a large number of reservations.

(*Duluth Herald,* undated.)

Munger's ownership of the grocery store and service station at the corner of 75th and Grand Avenue compelled him to join the West Duluth Businessmen's Club. Patsy Munger-Lehr recalls working at the family business during this period.

"Mom and Dad," Patsy recalls, "had us paint rows of rocks to decorate around the station. The rocks were painted white. They also planted flowers. They did that together. We didn't have a car so when the money from the store needed to be deposited; I took the bus to the bank. And when the new station was built, we rented out the little shack in back for extra money."

Will Munger, Jr. recalls his involvement.

"I used sweeping compound on the floors. I bagged potatoes. I filled bins. I worked with the iceman when he came. Around the holidays," Will remembers, "we had barrels of lutefisk ready for the Norwegians and the Swedes. When I worked the station, I was working for myself. I ran the place on Saturdays. But when Dad was there, it was harder. He was disorganized. I think it was the farmer in him—he saved everything."

Willard Munger's ties to the United Northern Sportsmen deepened during the late 1940s and early 1950s.

United Northern Sportsmen Install New Officers

Newly elected officers of the United Northern Sportsmen were installed Tuesday night at a meeting [Willard was installed as a trustee]...

At the meeting, discussion of Duluth's sewage problems was led by Frank G. Kriedler, chairman of the pollution committee.

"Our group is pledged to work for the conservation of our renewable resources and we are developing a program to make the St. Louis River and harbor suitable for healthful recreational activities," said Kriedler. "There should be no health hazard to people using the river, no disagreeable odors from the water, no accumulation of sludge, oil or other wastes on the banks, or pollution of the water by municipal and industrial establishments," he said.

He urges a city program as follows:

1. A plant or plants to provide a complete treatment of all sewage;

2. Separation of all sanitary and storm sewers;

3. Contract for treatment of sewage with outlying towns or villages;

4. Elimination of all dumping of refuse, garbage, either organic or inorganic along the river or harbor, or where it may enter the river or harbor;

5. Adequate policing and penalties for violations.

(Duluth Budgeteer, undated.)

During the early 1950s, Munger also expanded his involvement in charitable and civic organizations.

Red Cross Drive Now Under Way

The annual Red Cross Campaign for 1951 with the goal set at $94,720 for the Arrowhead Chapter is well underway...

Willard Munger is chairman for the West Duluth business district campaign and has named his workers...

The quota for this section has been set at $1,200 which is over last year's owing to the Korean War which has brought a heavy burden on the Red Cross.

(*Duluth News Tribune*, undated.)

The Red Cross was likely of particular interest to Munger given his anti-war outlook, an outlook fostered by his friendship with Carl Ryan and others over the years. Munger also became more and more vocal about the condition of the St. Louis River.

Club Urges Citywide Study of Pollution Problem

The West Duluth Businessmen's Club this week urged the appointment of a city-wide committee to make a study of the sanitary conditions in the city and harbor...

"The Chamber of Commerce has not lifted a finger to support the many sportsmen's clubs who have been urging a cleanup of St. Louis River," charged Willard Munger. "We must have the active support of every organization if we are to get anywhere with this pollution problem," he said. "Sewage is settling along the lakeshore closer and closer to the intake for Duluth's water supply, but people won't get interested until water from their faucets starts to turn brown!" he stated.

(*Duluth Budgeteer*, May 10, 1951.)

Martha's remonstrations compelled Willard to resign from his position with the federal government.

"That (the OPS job] lasted until I got a telephone call from my wife *telling* me I had to file for the legislature...That was in '52..."

(*Oral History of Willard Munger*, ibid, pp. 49 – 50.)

Ann Glumac, Munger's legislative committee administrator in the late 1980s, supplies additional details.

"The way Willard told me that story is a bit more colorful," Ann relates. "Martha would call him at the Office of Price Stabilization every day to ask, 'Have you filed for the legislature yet?' To which Willard would answer 'No.' The last day for filing, Martha added an ultimatum: 'If you want to sleep on the couch for the rest of your married life, come home without filing.' Willard looked at me, somewhat sheepishly, before continuing, 'What was I supposed to do? I was a young man— only in my forties—and the idea of not sleeping with my wife for the rest of my life was upsetting. So I went down and filed.'"

Willard Munger's second run for the legislature highlighted the issue of conservation. It was a hallmark decision: Munger's campaign emphasized the need to clean up the St. Louis River and protect Lake Superior. Munger's reliance upon pollution remediation as his primary campaign issue was a bold and daring move considering the lack of overall environmental awareness that existed in 1952. Rachel Carson's epic study of the dangers of DDT, *Silent Spring* hadn't been released. The first Earth Day was still two decades away. Willard Munger, by touting conservationism as the key issue in his campaign, was light-years ahead of any other politician; local, state or national, regarding environmental concerns.

Munger's Platform...For Conservation

We are in a period of vast expansion of developing our natural resources and therefore a sound conservation program at this time is necessary that will keep in step with this expansion and assure a water supply free of pollution.

Favors: Legislation to reorganize our conservation department to make it work for the interest of the people instead of special interests.

Favors: Legislation to make it possible to set up a sanitary district for the St. Louis River area.

Favors: Legislation to control pollution in our rivers and streams—now.

Favors: A long-range forestry program administered by the conservation department.

Favors: Legislation to promote our great tourism industry.

Favors: Conservation legislation in line with the present conservation program advocated by conservation clubs and various civic groups to safeguard our natural resources.

(1952 Campaign Brochure, Willard Munger Personal Collection.)

Conservation wasn't Munger's only area of concern. In the same brochure, Willard Munger indicated his full support for the funding of education, farm relief, public benefits for veterans and the aged, and support for small businesses. But it is clear that Munger had learned much regarding the environmental issues of the day and that a significant theme in his first campaign in Duluth was the cleaning up of the St. Louis River.

The primacy of these environmental issues came to the forefront in newspaper interviews with the candidate.

Department Criticized by Candidate by Einer Karlstrand

Reorganization of the Minnesota Conservation Department was called for today by one of the six candidates for the state legislature in the 59the District. Willard M. Munger, a West Duluth grocer and former member of the Office of Price Administration staff here, declared his stand on the conservation issue as campaigning in the district grew more heated.

"We are in a period of vast expansion and development of resources," Munger said. "Therefore, a sound conservation program at this time is necessary that will keep in step with this expansion."

He criticized policies of the state conservation department.

Munger also proposed legislation to make possible establishment of a sanitary district in the St. Louis River area.

(Duluth News Tribune, undated.)

Munger was running against Conservative Dwight Swanstrom, one of two incumbent representatives from the 59th District. Liberal Francis "Frenchie" LaBrosse was the other incumbent in the district. Party labeling in legislative races would not be allowed until 1974 but voters knew that, with nary an exception, the label "Conservative" on the ballot meant Republican and the label 'Liberal" meant DFL. Will Munger, Jr., who was twelve years old in 1952, recalls working on his father's first campaign in Duluth.

"I remember putting up lawn signs during that campaign. That's where Dad started using those 4-foot x 8-foot sheets of plywood for signage. He'd silk screen them himself. He did that until he died. He was a driven man in that election—driven by Mom. She told him, 'Go down and file and don't come home if you aren't running.'"

On the national scene, Adlai Stevenson was running against Dwight D. Eisenhower for president. Minnesota, Wisconsin and Michigan were seen as "swing" states. As indicated, the 59th Legislative District had two state representative seats available. One was occupied by LaBrosse, 44 years old, a public relations director for Blue Cross-Blue Shield. The other seat was held by Swanstrom, 47 years old and the owner of an insurance agency. The two challengers were Munger and Maurice A. Gustafson, a railroad worker.

Organized labor supported Munger's first campaign in Duluth.

Now a word why Dwight Swanstrom must be defeated:

He is undependable. He is a Republican to Republicans; a Democrat to Democrats; and a Progressive to Progressives. Actually, he is only for Swanstrom.

His voting record is bad. In 1947 he voted against good education…In 1949, he voted for a bill allowing railroad companies to hire private strike breakers…He voted for a banker's trust monopoly bill…He voted against an amendment to give adequate funds to mental health. He voted for a bill, the purpose of which was to prevent the publishing of a legislator's voting record. No Wonder!

The 59th has a chance this time to elect two good legislators. Let's get rid of someone who is on all sides of the fence!!!!

Raymond Novack, chairman, AFL-CIO, Railroad Brotherhood Committee for a Liberal Legislature

(*Duluth News Tribune*, November 2, 1952.)

On Election Day, the *Duluth News Tribune* reported that General Eisenhower beat Adlai Stevenson handily. In Minnesota's 59th Legislative District, the tally was:

LaBrosse: 13,130

Swanstrom: 10,445

Munger: 10,035

Gustafson:5,784.

Despite the narrow loss, Munger wasn't one to prolong an unfavorable situation.

Loser Decides Against Recount

One of two St. Louis County candidates for public offices in last Tuesday's election who was considering a request for a vote recount last night changed his mind.

Willard Munger, Duluth grocer, who was put out of the running by 410 votes for a seat in the state House of Representatives from the 59th District, said he thought his chances of overcoming the 410-vote margin were too slim to warrant a recount.

Munger added he was "satisfied" with the election judges' count…

(*Duluth News Tribune*, undated.)

Whether Willard Munger's outspoken stand on environmental issues caused him to lose to Dwight Swanstrom is not clear. What is clear is that, at forty-two years of age, Munger realized he couldn't wait another eighteen years (as he'd done after his loss in Otter Tail County) to run again.

CHAPTER 6

Building a Motel and a Career

Will Munger, Jr. recalls that the issues of a state-wide sales tax and money for K-12 education fueled his father's next campaign. The conservation ethic that had been so prominent in Munger's 1952 run for the legislature was relegated to the bottom of his 1954 platform.

"My Dad was always working to ensure kids had a good education," Will recalls. "And he was dead set against the sales tax."

> Willard Munger, House candidate, said a sales tax "will hurt Duluth business," and pledged opposition to it. He also said he will vote for a Liberal speaker for the House and added, "if we have a Conservative-controlled House, we will have a sales tax."
>
> (*Duluth News Tribune*, October 17, 1954.)

There is little doubt that a strong woman was behind Willard Munger's repeated attempts to win elected office.

"I liked Martha," Judge Gerald Heaney recalls. "She wasn't afraid to speak her mind. She was a strong woman who knew where she stood."

Another person who learned of Martha's persistence, albeit after the fact, is retired State Rep. Dave Battaglia (DFL-Two Harbors).

"I didn't know Martha but Willard talked about her after I was elected to the House in 1976. He talked about how she was the one who promoted him and got him to do things," Battaglia recalls. "When I served with him (1976 – 1994), Willard carried her photograph in his briefcase. He had true affection for Martha. There was no substitute. He talked about her being in the University of Minnesota Hospital, how hard that was. He was a good friend to Frances (Willard's second wife) but it wasn't the same."

The incumbents for the two House seats from the 59th District in 1954 were Liberal Francis "Frenchie" LaBrosse and Conservative Dwight Swanstrom. In his campaign leaflets, Swanstrom touted his experience.

> In the Minnesota Legislature, Dwight Swanstrom holds the following important assignments...
>
> 1. Chairman of the Committee on the University
>
> 2. Appropriations Committee
>
> 3. Committee on Towns and Counties
>
> 4. Commercial Transportation Committee...
>
> His seniority in the legislature is most important to all in this area. Dwight Swanstrom has a host of friends in the House and because of this fact, he is in an advantageous position to further the program in the legislature for Northern Minnesota.
>
> (Swanstrom Brochure, Willard Munger Personal Collection.)

In response, the DFL inserted advertisements in local newspapers attacking Swanstrom's position on the sales tax.

> **Defeat the sales Tax by Voting Against Dwight Swanstrom, Candidate for Representative—59th District**
>
> Dwight Swanstrom stated in the *Budgeteer* on September 2, 1954, that he is against a General Sales Tax.
>
> The record states:
>
> On the 28th day of March, the Conservative leader of the House...introduced the Package Sales Tax Bill...
>
> This is the record of the vote of the legislators from the 8th Congressional District on [the] Package Sales Tax Bill:
>
> For Sales Tax and against consumers: Dwight A. Swanstrom.
>
> Is Dwight Swanstrom's vote on the sales tax right?...Protect your interests! Combat Swanstrom and the Sales Tax! Cut the Conservative control of the legislature!...Vote for men of integrity—Vote for a 100% Liberal Team, a team whom you can depend on to defeat the Sales Tax. Vote for:
>
> Homer Carr, State Senator, 59th District
>
> Willard M. Munger, Representative, 59th District
>
> Francis LaBrosse, Representative, 59th District.
>
> (Unknown Source; Willard Munger Personal Collection.)

In the midst of another political campaign, Willard and Martha Munger embarked upon a new venture in their personal lives.

"I built it (the Duluth Zoo Motel] in 1954," Willard recalled. "I'll tell you how that happened. My wife was running the store…She had sliced off the end of her little finger—just a little bit—and when I came home, she was crying about that little finger.

I said, 'We're going to sell this damn store and build a motel.'

She said, 'Where are you going to build it?'

I said, 'I'm going to pick up some land across the street. That's where I'm going to build it.'

She said, 'You don't have any money.'

I said, 'We'll sell this place [the gas station].' I think I owed about $8,000 on it. So I went down and advertised it with E.B. Erickson, trying to list the place.

He came out and looked at it and said, 'How much do you want for it?'

I said, 'I want $25,000.'

He said, 'I don't want it for $25,000. I'll just look for twenty.'

I said, 'No. I worked too hard on that thing. That's a well-built building.' He wouldn't take it.

A week later, when I came home…my wife said, 'I don't want to stay here anymore. I'm afraid. You know, there was a guy sitting across the street all week, and I don't know why he's sitting over there. He's writing stuff down all the time.'

I said, 'Oh, that's your imagination.'

The next week, the same guy drove into the station and said to me, 'Want to fill my car up?'

My wife said, 'Look out for that guy. That's the same guy sitting across the street.'

He said, 'Do you want to sell this place?'

I told him, 'Yes, I'll sell the place if I can find a sucker who will give me $25,000 for it. I'll say he can have it. I just don't know where you'll find a sucker.'

This guy was with Western Oil and Fuel.

He said, 'Does it have to be a sucker?'

I said, 'Yes, anybody that would buy this place has to be a sucker,' because I had a tough go there. I had to go down to Klearflax to work and make it pay.

A week after that, the guy came in with some papers and a check.

He said, 'I'm the $25,000 sucker. Here's your money.'

So we sold the place and put the money into building the motel. We built it in three different stages and I did all the finishing work on it. All the cabinets I built myself."

(*Oral History of Willard Munger*, ibid, pp. 57 – 58.)

There are discrepancies between Munger's recollection of when the motel was conceived and Munger's financial records. Records confirm that the motel property was purchased on February 20, 1952 and that the first phase of the motel was constructed in 1954.

"I think we bought the original site in 1952. I know it took a few years to get started because when we were practicing baseball for the DX Indians (a team sponsored by Willard Munger's DX gas station) there were piles of cement block over on the motel site for quite a while," Will Munger, Jr. recalls. "And we owned both the motel and the gas station for a period of time. So it makes sense that what Dad is talking about is when he financed and completed the *second phase* of the original motel. The incident with Mom cutting her finger, that wasn't the impetus for the motel being built. We were renting out the little shack in the back to tourists in the summertime and living in an apartment above the gas station. Tourists were always asking Dad where they could find a good motel. So Dad took the hint and built them one. That was how it all started; not with Mom cutting herself.

"Dad hired out most of the work on the motel but acted as the general contractor. He had an architect draw the plans. He was very picky about the construction, making the contractor tear down one whole wall because it wasn't done right, but not so picky about decorating. He would go into the tile and carpet store and buy whatever color vinyl they had on sale. Didn't matter if it matched anything or not. He bought it. I don't know why Mom didn't step in, but she didn't."

Patsy Munger-Lehr recalls that the family didn't move out of the living quarters on the second floor of the gas station until the motel was finished.

"Part of the motel was completed before I graduated from Duluth Denfeld in 1953," Patsy recalls. "We'd be working in the grocery store and have to run across 75th to check in customers at the motel because the motel office wasn't finished. At some point after Western bought the station, my uncle Ernie Winter, his wife, Elsie, and their son, Wesley, came to live in the shack behind the station. The Hargraves family (no relation to Roger) moved in above the gas station and had a café in what had been the grocery store. It didn't do well and eventually Ernie and Elsie turned that space into a convenience store."

Will remembers that the station was leased by Western to the Winter family, who subleased the café to the Hargraves family, sometime around 1957 – 1958. "My Uncle Ernie lost his job working for the Cooperative down in Montevideo, Minnesota. So he and Elsie and their son Wesley came to Duluth. So did Grandma Winter, my mother's mom."

Patsy Munger-Lehr also recalls that the Munger family moved into a housekeeping unit in the basement of the motel.

"There was only a glass block wall separating our unit from Grandma Winter's," Patsy says with a smile. "My mom looked at me one day. You could see Grandma's silhouette through the glass blocks. She was moving around on the other side of the wall. My mom said, 'Patsy, you remember this. This is no way for a married couple to live!'"

In November of 1954, WWII veteran Orville Freeman was elected as Minnesota's first DFL governor, Hubert Humphrey was re-elected to the U.S. Senate, and John Blatnik retained his seat in Congress. Liberal Francis LaBrosse remained in the Minnesota House and was joined by a new Liberal legislator from the 59th Legislative District.

> Willard Munger went all out in campaigning on the DFL and Liberal platform in winning one of Duluth's 59th District seats in the House of Representatives.
>
> His strongest pitch was directed against the passage of a general sales tax...
>
> Munger is the owner of a grocery and motel in Zenith City where he has lived since 1935. He was born and raised on a farm near Fergus Falls and took interest in politics early in life, becoming chairman of the Otter Tail County Farmer-Labor Association when but 24 years old.
>
> He worked in the grain division of the state railroad and warehouse commission for a time and for two years was head of the state agriculture department's northern Minnesota marketing division.
>
> He is a member of various Masonic bodies.
>
> Munger is married and the father of Patricia, 19, and Willard, Jr., 15.
>
> (*Minneapolis Tribune*, undated.)

Willard Munger had finally achieved political office. He had successfully followed the strategy outlined by his paternal grandfather and was in a position to introduce legislation to protect the environment.

CHAPTER 7

Into the Fray

Shortly after Willard Munger's election to the Minnesota House, he was back in Duluth, cutting meat on the weekends. "He was a real good butcher," Harry Munger, Jr. recalls. But it wasn't Willard's skills as a meat cutter or legislator that garnered him his first headline after being sworn in as a state representative.

> *Between Us* by Sünto Wessman
>
> Willard Munger [the state assemblyman]...walked into his West End store and saw a man stretched out behind the counter...as cold as a mackerel...He rushed out for help...got Almon Olsen [he's in tombstones]...and the two gingerly approached the "corpse"...Olsen even took out his handkerchief to shoo the flies off his face while they waited for police and an ambulance...The police came first and summed up the situation in a jiffy...The man wasn't in any particular trouble...that maybe some black coffee and a little less booze wouldn't cure...With prodding, he woke up and looked a bit sheepish...but no more than Munger and Olsen.
>
> (*Duluth News Tribune*, undated.)

To save money while in St. Paul during the 1955 legislative session, Willard took lodging with his brother Harry, Jr., Harry's wife Barbara, and their infant son in the couple's apartment on Grand Avenue. Harry, Jr. was going to night law school at the St. Paul College of Law (now William Mitchell College of Law) and working for an insurance company during the day while his young wife worked as a medical technologist at Miller Hospital. The arrangement allowed Willard to avoid paying for a motel room during the session (there were no per diem payments for lodging expenses incurred by out-state legislators in 1954).

Though the first bill Willard Munger introduced in the Minnesota House involved Lake Superior, it had nothing to do with resource conservation.

Restoring of Package Freight is Asked by **Einar Karlstrand**

A Minnesota legislative committee today recommended for passage a resolution calling upon Congress to restore package freight shipping on the Great Lakes.

The action was taken by the House…committee after Rep. Willard Munger, Duluth went before the group to point out the need for package freight service…

Munger reported that package freight service was taken off the Great Lakes during WWII when the old Poker Fleet was converted to military service. He said that since 1942, there has been no package freight shipping on the lakes…

(*Duluth News Tribune*, January 25, 1955.)

Martha Munger maintained contact with her husband via the telephone and the mail from Duluth.

Duluth Zoo Motel

February 2, 1955

Dear Willard:

Everything is fine. Kids are OK. Butch [Will, Jr.] went to the basketball game and that seemed to make him happy.

The Banquet for Zoo Committee is tonight and I am going. The mayor and his wife are picking me up. I think I should represent the Representative at this affair!

Received your check this morning. Will send it to the bank tomorrow as I can't get away today.

Am sending you some letters. Don't know if they are urgent or not.

Zylinen was out yesterday and one of his next door neighbors—a Mr. Lloyd Berthiaume—4135 W 8th St. is and has been out of work since July. He is a fine worker who can type and take shorthand. Worked at Coolerator [a manufacturer of refrigerators once located in West Duluth] and is about 44 and has 3 kids. He would have been tickled pink to take that steno job.

Another young man about 28 or less is looking for work. Interested in a civil service exam on the highway work area. A DM&IR employee—Engman—also married but no special training, he has been out of work since July.

Marcotte went out on the truck today. Don N. said he was very tickled about it, as his unemployment ran out last month. Those Coolerator employees can't seem to find work. Maybe no company wants them because of their associates.

See you Friday.

Love, Martha

It is obvious from Martha's letter that, despite the elimination of patronage positions in state government, men and women were still looking to Willard Munger to assist them in finding work. How successful Munger's efforts were in each of these individual cases is unknown. But the continued decline of Duluth's manufacturing base, the aging of its industrial infrastructure, is clearly reflected in Martha's correspondence. Coolerator, Klearflax and the sprawling U.S. Steel complex in Gary-New Duluth would all eventually close, ending good paying blue-collar wages for thousands of residents of the Twin Ports. This erosion of industrial and manufacturing jobs continued throughout Munger's service in the legislature, until Duluth's population, gauged at 106,000 in 1960, would barely exceed 85,000 by 1990. This economic reality, the loss of countless good paying jobs over a relatively short period of time, needed to be balanced with Munger's environmental fervor. This would be the greatest challenge for Willard Munger during his career; to enact protective environmental legislation without adversely impacting the working men and women of his district.

Munger's other legislative efforts during 1955 were not limited to conservation concerns.

Area Lawmakers Push School Milk Program Bill

Legislation authorizing Minnesota to establish a school milk program at a cost of $50,000 per year was introduced...in the State House of Representatives. Among the authors are Rep. Willard Munger, Duluth, and Seth Phillips, Pillager.

(*Duluth News Tribune*, March 3, 1955.)

Munger also dealt with the issue of health care during his first legislative session.

State Co-Op Hospital Plan Clears House Committee

Minnesota cooperatives would be allowed to make contracts with hospitals and doctors for their members under a bill which was recommended for passage...

The measure is sponsored by Rep. Sam Franz, Mountain Lake. Rep. Willard Munger, Duluth is a co-author.

Members of the cooperative committee voted for the bill 7-5 after strong opposition to it was presented by medical, hospital and pharmacy leaders.

(*Duluth News Tribune*, March 3, 1955.)

Another example of Munger's involvement in Minnesota's educational system was his support for "Home Rule."

"Home Rule" School Bill Clears Senate by Einar Karlstrand

Duluth's "Home Rule" school bill went to Gov. Orville Freeman for signature...after clearing the senate without opposition.

The measure gives the Board of Education full power to set the maximum tax levy limitation subject to a referendum by a 1,000 name petition...

House authors were Willard Munger and other members of the Duluth delegation...

(*Duluth News Tribune*, March 26, 1955.)

He pushed other educational measures as well.

House Bills to Aid Area Schools Backed

House committees have recommended for passage two bills affecting northern Minnesota schools. They would:

1. Establish a $10,000,000 revolving building fund for distressed school districts; and

2. Authorize the appropriation of $2,000,000 to schools in eight railroad towns.

Rep. Willard Munger, Duluth, an author of the revolving fund...moved for its approval before the education committee. He said the measure is needed to aid districts which do not have the funds to provide for facilities for rising enrollments.

A new formula is established for state refunds to schools in communities unable to tax railroads [through property taxation] because of the gross earnings tax. Affected schools are in Proctor, Two Harbors, Brainerd, Baxter, Waite Park, Breckenridge, Staples and Dilworth...The measure's chief sponsor is Munger...

(*Duluth News Tribune*, April 6, 1955.)

Despite this flurry of work on behalf of K-12 education, Munger didn't forget the environmental emphasis of his failed 1952 campaign.

"Thirty years ago," Willard recalled, "when I was first elected to the legislature...I started talking about a $25,000 bill to study pollution..."

(*Oral History of Willard Munger*, ibid, p. 19.)

Munger's first attempt at conservation legislation was documented in the news media.

Two Northern Minnesota legislators today proposed the creation of an interim commission to study water pollution problems.

Rep. Willard Munger, Duluth, and E.J. Chilgren, Little Fork, introduced a bill in the House setting up an appropriation of $25,000 to conduct the survey. The commission would report January 15, 1957.

It would consider pollution in rivers, streams and lakes and the feasibility of establishing sanitary districts where needed.

The 10-member commission would be expected to write reasonable methods of effective water pollution control.

St. Louis and Rainy Rivers are two of the areas proposed for the study. They are among areas of the State where consideration has been given in the past for sanitary districts.

(*Duluth News Tribune*, April 6, 1955.)

Away from the legislature, Munger continued to work for Liberal causes and candidates.

Stevenson Election Committee

Plans for the appearance of Adlai Stevenson [Democratic candidate for president against Eisenhower] in Duluth October 29 were made at a committee meeting...[attending were] Glenn E. Peterson, Alfred Johnson, general chairman, and Willard Munger, arrangements chair. Stevenson will appear at a Democratic-Farmer-Labor party dinner at the Duluth National Guard Armory.

(*Duluth News Tribune*, undated.)

Munger faced his first re-election challenge in the fall of 1956. During the same election, Munger's choice for president, Adlai Stevenson, was battling President Eisenhower in a repeat of the 1952 national election, and incumbent DFL Governor Orville Freeman was opposed by Republican Archer Nelson.

On November 7, 1956, Eisenhower was proclaimed the winner in the presidential race. Minnesota once again went for Eisenhower though that vote did not transfer to a Republican success at the state or local levels. DFLer Orville Freeman retained the governorship and both LaBrosse and Munger retained their seats in the House from the 59th District, defeating former St. Louis County Agricultural Agent D.T. Grussendorf and steelworker Gilbert Leslie.

That same year, Munger was also elected to a non-political position.

Munger Elected to Head City's New Zoo Board

State Rep. Willard Munger...was elected chairman of Duluth's new zoo board at its organizational meeting...Major action was a move to recommend the hiring of a zoo curator...

At present, zoo operations are handled...by a caretaker...

Mayor George D. Johnson told the group there is "a great need to eliminate the discord in operating the zoo...What we need is a good 'crew pusher,'" Johnson said, referring to the hiring of a curator.

(*Duluth News Tribune*, undated.)

Of the issues that remained important to Willard Munger throughout his legislative career, public funding for the Duluth Zoo (later renamed the Lake Superior Zoo) was always near the top of his agenda. Whether it was the fact that the zoo was a natural draw to Munger's motel and therefore, Munger's initial support for the zoo was self-serving, or his support for the facility was born out of genuine fondness for the place, isn't clear. But what is certain is that the zoo *was* important to Munger. There is no doubt that Munger developed a genuine and profound love for the place and its staff, including Basil Norton and Mike Janis; two directors of the zoo Munger worked closely with during his long legislative career.

Though a newcomer to the legislature, Willard Munger quickly received accolades for his work.

November 1, 1956

Dear Willard:

With election only a few days away, I want to write a few lines to you expressing the hope that you will be in St. Paul for the 1957 Legislative session.

All of the Superintendents of the Gross Earnings Schools appreciate the excellent work that you did in our behalf last session. No single legislator worked as diligently as you did in having a good bill passed for the several schools who have so much of their local property classified as railroad property...

Sincerely,

H.C. Nordgaard

Superintendent

Brainerd Schools

Munger returned to St. Paul in January of 1957 ready to do the work of the people.

City Police Wage Arbitration Plan Clears House Unit by **Einar Karlstrand**

Arbitration panel findings for policemen and firemen in Duluth and St. Paul would be binding upon city councils of the two cities under a bill which cleared a House labor committee...

The measure, which two years ago failed to pass the legislature, was approved by the committee without a dissenting vote.

Reps. Francis LaBrosse and Willard M. Munger, Duluth, told the committee they had been advised of no formal opposition to the bill. The Duluth City Council...unanimously went on record against the bill. The two legislators, explained...they had not been advised of the city council's action...

(*Duluth News Tribune*, February 14, 1957.)

Munger also tackled other issues, including sponsoring a resolution memorializing the legislature's support of national daylight-savings time; co-sponsoring the consolidation of Duluth's Bayview School with the Proctor School District; calling for the defeat of Republican Rep. John Hartle's sales tax plan as "a soak the poor tax"; and formally charging that the State Welfare Department was engaging in a "cold, calculated approach" in dealing with the issue of neglected and delinquent children.

But these were all minor skirmishes in the world of 1950s Minnesota politics. There were three main political "battles" facing Willard Munger and his House colleagues in 1957.

The first major issue that Willard weighed in on during his second term concerned whether or not Minnesota Blue Cross-Blue Shield should be regulated by the Minnesota Insurance Commissioner. It was an issue which affected Rep. LaBrosse in his capacity as an employee of Blue Cross-Blue Shield.

Munger, LaBrosse Clash on Blue Cross Bill Values by **Einar Karlstrand**

State Rep. Willard Munger, Duluth, said today he "could not understand" why the United Steel Workers of America objects to placing non-profit hospitalization and medical plans under the state insurance commissioner. The bill to put Blue Cross-Blue Shield under control of the state insurance department, he said, was given to him to introduce by Robert Hess, St. Paul, vice president of the Minnesota Federation of Labor...

Munger took issue with a statement made recently by Rep. Francis LaBrosse, a member of the Blue Cross staff, in which LaBrosse said his colleague's bill would result in increased costs to subscribers.

"This statement is absolutely misleading and incorrect or it shows a lack of knowledge of the bill and the purpose of the proposed legislation," Munger asserted…"This has absolutely nothing to do with the insurance tax. The purpose and intent of the bill is to protect the policyholder by placing all insurance companies under the direct supervision of the state insurance commissioner."

(*Duluth News Tribune*, March 21, 1957.)

Opposition to a separate bill enacting a tax on insurance premiums collected by insurers was expressed by union leadership.

Steelworkers Rap State Plan to Tax Blue Cross Funds by Einar Karlstrand

The United Steelworkers of America regards as a "sales tax"…Governor Freeman's proposed gross premiums tax on Minnesota non-profit hospitalization and medical service plans…

The measure will be heard today before the Senate Insurance Committee. Area authors are Sen. Homer Carr, Proctor, and Rep. Willard Munger, Duluth…

Freeman followed the recommendation of his interim tax study commission proposing the two percent insurance tax…

Area members of the governor's tax study committee [included]…Nick Krompotich, Coleraine, Steelworkers union staff representative…Earl T. Bester, Duluth, Steelworkers union district director, was an alternative member…

Bester and Krompotich are reported as having fought inclusion of Blue Cross-Blue Shield in the gross premiums insurance tax…

(*Duluth News Tribune*, March 25, 1957.)

Willard Munger was in a "no win" situation. On the one hand, his friend, Earl Bester, was on record opposing the tax bill (a measure the article erroneously ascribed to Munger). On the other hand, the Editorial Board of the *Labor World* questioned Blue Cross-Blue Shield's reluctance to agree to state regulation of its business (the bill Munger was actually sponsoring).

Why Won't Blue Cross Agree to State Supervision?

Duluth's Liberal Representative Willard Munger called attention this week to a new aspect of the controversy over Blue Cross-Blue Shield legislation…

Munger is the co-author of a bill which would place Blue Cross…under the supervision of the Minnesota Insurance Commissioner. This bill has the endorsement of the Minnesota AFL-CIO...but had been bitterly opposed by Blue Cross...

Munger asked why Blue Cross...should insist upon exemption from state supervision when labor is willing to support state supervision of union welfare funds...

Both he and the Liberal Senator Homer Carr of Proctor...have sharply criticized statements in the Duluth daily papers that their bill would increase costs...

(*Labor World,* April 4, 1957.)

The forces opposed to regulating and taxing Blue Cross cleverly tied the two pieces of legislation, the bill by Munger-Carr to regulate Blue Cross *and* the separate bill to tax insurers as recommended by the Tax Study Commission together. Sen. Carr attempted to set the record straight.

To the Editor:

In the issue of the *News Tribune*...an article over the signature of the News Tribune political writer states that Rep. Munger and I are authors of a bill to levy a tax on so-called "non-profit" medical services. This statement is absolutely untrue.

The bill we authored simply places all plans...under the supervision of the Commissioner of Insurance...The bill to tax those companies...is S No. 1423, which carries out the recommendations of the Tax Study Commission that worked for two years studying Minnesota's tax problems....

Homer Carr, Senator, 59th District

(*Duluth News Tribune,* undated.)

Munger's support for the regulatory bill was based upon his perception that, as a "non-profit" unregulated by the state, Blue Cross-Blue Shield was reaping windfall profits which weren't being shared with its policy holders.

Munger Presses Fight to Extend Insurance Laws

"We are informed that the Blue Cross is a non-profit service plan corporation and therefore should not be under the control of the insurance commissioner. Yet they collected over $25 million in gross premiums for the year 1956. It seems indefensible that a corporation should handle this volume of hospitalization contracts without the individuals having the protection of the state insurance laws," Munger said.

(*Duluth News Tribune,* undated.)

The fight to regulate Blue Cross-Blue Shield ultimately went Munger's way but the rift between Munger and LaBrosse would remain for the rest of their shared legislative careers.

Willard Munger also weighed in on a dispute regarding K-12 funding in railroad towns. The issue involved the fact that Minnesota railroads didn't [and still don't] pay real estate taxes on their property holdings but paid [and still pay] a "gross earnings tax" to the state. Thus, schools in towns that have railroad facilities are unable to impose a property tax levy upon railroads akin to that imposed upon ordinary residential and business property. Recalling his own less-than-adequate public education, Munger was sympathetic to the argument that more money needed to be spent on Minnesota's public schools. Thus, he introduced legislation to equalize the taxing discrepancy faced by schools in railroad towns. (*Proctor Journal*, May 2, 1957.)

For many Duluthians, the most important legislative issue of the 1957 session was the funding of infrastructural improvements to the Duluth-Superior harbor. With the advent of the completion of the St. Lawrence Seaway, ocean-going vessels were now able to travel from the Atlantic Ocean all the way through the Great Lakes via the Seaway to Duluth and Superior. The cost of port improvements to handle international shipping was to be shared by three levels of government; the state, the county and the city of Duluth, though support for St. Louis County participation in the scheme proved problematic.

Alarm at St. Paul

One reason Duluth labor called for complete unity among county legislators at St. Paul this year was the need for countywide cooperation on the Duluth port development program. There was a fear the mining industry might try to knife the program.

This week, two Duluth legislators, Rep. Francis LaBrosse, and Rep. Arne Wanvick, attacked the county delegation chairman, Rep. Paul Widstrand of Hibbing...LaBrosse in particular lashed out at Widstrand because Widstrand preferred Rep. Willard Munger instead of Wanvick as the chief author of one of the three port program bills.

Widstrand had good reason for preferring Munger to Wanvick. Both LaBrosse and Wanvick claim to be Liberals but they are a lot closer to Conservative Senator Herbert Rogers of Duluth than they are to their loyal fellow Liberals, Sen. Homer Carr and Rep. Munger. And Sen. Rogers holds an executive job in the very same mining industry which has come out against the port program...

(*Labor World*, undated.)

Northeastern Minnesota Legislators were taken to task for their opposition to the port improvement legislation.

Will Seaport Be Killed in Senate?

Duluth's AFL-CIO Central Body…reaffirmed its support of a 3-bill package to provide $10,000,000 for construction of a major seaport here. Northern Minnesota's mining industry, on the other hand, is trying to defeat any county participation in the port development program.

The whole program was on the ropes late last week after two Duluth legislators angered the Range legislators by publically criticizing the St. Louis County delegation chairman, Rep. Paul Widstrand of Hibbing…[H]owever, Rep. Willard Munger of Duluth succeeded in winning back Range support of the port "package" by agreeing to be the co-author of the county levy bill himself…

So now the mining industry may shift its opposition into the state senate where, by working to kill off the half-mill levy for Hermantown, Floodwood and Lakewood school building needs, it could force legislators with constituents in those districts to oppose any county aid for the Duluth port program…

(*Labor World*, undated.)

With Munger's intervention, the port bill ultimately passed the House.

House Votes $10 Million Port Levies by Einar Karlstrand

Minnesota's House…passed…three bills providing financing for Duluth's $10,000.000 public marine terminal. A threatened fight on the St. Louis County and state fund raising measures failed to materialize…

Rep. Willard Munger, Duluth, chief author of the bill taxing St. Louis County property owners $4,000.000…told the House the three measures are closely related. He explained the county funds were being raised to match a $5,000.000 state-wide levy…The city bill requires a two-thirds vote of the city council and the county measure provides for a five-sevenths vote of the county board…

Munger said the Duluth Port Authority will hereafter be known as a "Seaway Port Authority."

Rep. Lawrence Yetka, Cloquet, chief author of the state bill, declared that "this is not just a project for Duluth. It's a development which will benefit farmers, manufacturers, businessmen and others."

(*Duluth News Tribune*, April 6, 1957.)

Willard Munger would later claim that his most significant contribution to the 1957 legislative session was the passage of the Interim Water Pollution Study Commission bill. When one considers Munger's career as a whole, this claim may well be true because passage of the Interim Study paved the way for the beginning of Munger's environmental stewardship. But the impact of the Interim Study was, as of 1957, two decades away, whereas the passage of the Port Authority bills had an immediate and positive impact upon the economy of northeastern Minnesota. Still, the Interim Study bears significant discussion because it was the forerunner of many other legislative mandates authored by Munger.

Munger Proposes Pollution Study Bill

Creation of an Interim Legislative Commission to study water pollution in Minnesota rivers, lakes and streams, was proposed in a bill introduced by Rep. Willard Munger, Duluth.

The commission would study the feasibility of establishing sanitation districts where needed and recommend methods of controlling water pollution…His measure calls for the appropriation of $25,000 to the commission for the study…

Munger said he introduced the bill because pollution "is becoming our No. 1 problem affecting industry, health and tourist travel…Water supply is the single most important factor in the location of industry," he asserted. "Industry, in the near future, must come to Minnesota because of its adequate water supply. For this reason, we must take steps for a long-range conservation program to cope with future needs…If we are to avail ourselves of federal matching funds as set forth in the pollution bill passed by Congress, we must get our house in order."

Munger noted that the federal program has just allocated funds to the State of Wisconsin for pollution control. The city of Superior is on the preferred list to receive such funds, he said.

(*Duluth News Tribune*, undated.)

As with much of Munger's legislative work, persistence proved to be the key. His second try at passing a funding bill for the Interim Study was approved by the legislature and signed into law by Governor Freeman. What is lost in the above discussion is the genius of Willard Munger's approach to the problem of water pollution.

Steeped not in the environmental activism of say, the Sierra Club or the Nature Conservancy, but with a background as an officer in a sportsman's club, Munger understood that it would take more than environmental zeal to pass the Interim Study legislation. When Munger's earlier effort to pass the bill failed, he revised his message to include reference to the *economic* benefits of clean water; industry needed it, therefore, the study made sense. The overall gist of the bill was the same; that the rivers, lakes and streams of Minnesota needed protection, but protection not only because campers, hikers, fishermen and canoeists wanted pristine waters for their sports. Clean water was a *necessity* in recruiting new jobs to the state. This blend of environmental protectionism and economic advancement would become the hallmark of Willard Munger's legislative career. It was a pragmatic approach which concealed, to some degree, Munger's conservation fervor. Even so, but for a fortuitous event on the Mississippi River, the Interim Study legislation would have likely died another quick death in 1957.

> "You know," Munger recalled, "I told you about my bill in '55...It failed. It would have failed again in '57 if it weren't for a ruptured tank spilling oil in the Mississippi River and killing...ducks. When my bill came up for a vote that day, there was the big story in the newspaper. I didn't have much trouble at all passing the bill because of that crisis...I had some luck from the Good Lord because they had some spills (on) the Mississippi River that got a lot of people excited. So they did pass the $25,000 study. It called for five members from the House and five members from the Senate to act as members of a committee to study the problem."
>
> (*Oral History of Willard Munger*, ibid, p. 19, p. 62, p. 80.)

Munger went on to explain the politics behind the make-up of the commission.

> "Generally, when you author a bill asking for a study, you almost automatically become the chairman. However, the companies and the mining companies were so against any kind of a study...The Speaker of the House was a guy by the name of Ed Chilgren. Ed...came from Little Fork...in the heart of the paper industry—International Falls and so forth. He appointed himself as one of the members of the committee.
>
> The first thing you do when you call the first meeting is elect a chairman. Of course, I ran for chairman because it was my bill. I wanted to direct the study. So he had somebody nominate him as chairman. There was a tie vote so we didn't settle anything at that meeting. He called another meeting, and there was another tie vote. Of course, that's what Ed Chilgren wanted. He wanted to scuttle the committee...So he said, 'Well, I guess there won't be a study commission.'
>
> I said, 'Oh yes there will be, because I'm withdrawing as candidate for chairman and you can be elected chairman.'

He wasn't very enthusiastic about making the study, but we forced him into it. The study went on for quite some time, and there wasn't much happening. I said to Ed...'You know, Ed, sooner or later we have to prepare some kind of a written report. Don't you think we ought to take part of the $25,000 and hire a couple of people to meet with the committee and to write up a report?'

[H]e...agreed with me. In the meantime, I went to the University [Minnesota-Duluth] and had the provost up there suggest two people who would be good at writing a report. One of those people he recommended was Dr. Fred Witzig...Then Chilgren did the same thing.

I said, 'What did you find out about hiring somebody to write the report?'

'Well,' he said, 'the provost gave me a couple of names.'

I said, 'Who were they?'

He said, 'Dr. Witzig, and I can't think of the other guy's name.'

I said, 'Dr. Witzig? I'm absolutely opposed to him.'

He said, 'Why?'

I said, 'Dr. Witzig is too close to the paper companies. I'm absolutely opposed to his appointment.'

The next day, Dr. Witzig had his appointment and he wrote one hell of a good report...The fact is that if I had told Chilgren that Dr. Witzig was a friend of mine...he would've never gotten that appointment."

(*Oral History of Willard Munger*, ibid, p. 82.)

Buried within this discussion is the key to Willard Munger's long-standing legislative success: Munger was capable of keeping his real agenda close to the vest, of playing his legislative cards with keen discretion. No legislator who served with Munger ever alluded to dishonesty as being a tool in Munger's political tool chest. But all who served with him recognized his innate ability to appear home-spun and folksy while, in essence, picking the pocket of his opposition.

Munger's involvement in the Study Commission legislation was noted by the United Northern Sportsmen.

An interim commission consisting of 10 members, five from the Senate and five from the House to study Minnesota's ever-growing water pollution problems was authorized by the state legislature this year.

Willard Munger, Representative from the 59th district, introduced the club sponsored bill in the House and Senator Homer Carr introduced the companion bill in the Senate. The new bill has set up an appropriation of $25,000.00 to make a comprehensive study of the water pollution problems of Minnesota...

Our club has been fighting for years for the protection of our natural waters. This interim commission is probably one of the biggest progressive steps made toward water conservation in Minnesota...

(*Northern Sportsmen's News,* June, 1957.)

The United Northern Sportsmen did more than simply write about Munger's exploits: The group turned out in force to support the bill.

Enforcement of Pollution Laws Demanded by Garth Garamond

Strict enforcement of present and future water pollution control laws was demanded by sportsmen at a legislative commission hearing in Duluth...

The demand came amid charges that taconite plants, oil refineries, and municipalities were contaminating area waters. The legislative commission held a public hearing on pollution problems at the Holland Hotel; the group will make a field study of the St. Louis River and Bay...

Demands for prompt action were voiced by Stanley Larson, Karl McGrath and N.A. Nelson, all of Duluth and members of the United Northern Sportsmen...

"From five to ten acres of the bay are covered in a dozen places every morning by oil wastes," McGrath said. He asserted that wild ducks which alight on the bay are made helpless by oil which coats their feathers, and that children who swim in the bay must scrub for hours to get oil off their bodies...

Anderson also charged that sulphite wastes dumped by a Duluth wood products firm are so strong that odors have forced men in nearby industries to leave their jobs.

Nelson and McGrath attacked what they term inadequate municipal sewage treatment in Duluth. Presence of raw sewage in bay waters, Nelson said, has forced a swimming prohibition at a favorite West Duluth spot.

Carl Lund, acting city utilities director, and Mirko D. Lubratovich, director of public services, said in reply to questions that sewage form city plants west of 70th Avenue West is untreated and that some isolated drainage comes from other points...

Rep. Willard Munger, Duluth, asked Lubratovich if it was true that up to 50% of the city's sewage is untreated. Munger attributed that figure to "the city council president."

Lubratovich replied that about 10 – 15% of the sewage is untreated.

"In other words, the city council president is wrong?" Munger asked.

"He may have been misinformed," Lubratovich...answered.

Munger replied, "Maybe you're misinformed."

Ragnald Svea and Walter Svea, Split Rock; Arnold Jacobson, Little Marais, fishermen; and Arthur Sivertson, fisheries operator, called upon the committee to investigate tailings deposits in Lake Superior...

Walter Svea reported sharp reductions in herring catches after wind or current changes swept in contaminated water.

Richard Hastings, Duluth attorney for the mining industry, and a state pollution control commission engineer pointed out that studies had failed to confirm that the discoloration along the North Shore resulted from the dumping of taconite tailings in the lake...

(*Duluth News Tribune*, September 7, 1957.)

Harry Munger, Jr. recalls that his older brother's protectionist fire was kindled by corporate deception.

"Willard was against industrial pollution in Lake Superior from the get-go," Harry recalls. "I remember being at the 1962 Minnesota State Fair with Willard. He walked up to a booth manned by the mining companies. Reserve Mining was one of the booth sponsors. They had a bottle of clear water with taconite tailings resting on the bottom. Willard walked over and shook the bottle up, and pointed out the suspended tailings in the water to one of the people manning the booth. 'That's what the lake looks like up in Silver Bay after a storm,' he said, before putting the bottle down and walking away. He was against Reserve being granted a permit to dump in the lake from Day One.

"When we moved to Duluth, we lived on Raleigh Street in West Duluth. There were a few times I dove off the boat house at 63rd Avenue West into the St. Louis River to cool off during the summer. There were turds, actual human feces, floating in the water. Billings Park Beach over in Superior was closed down due to kids coming home with a rash from all the stuff in that river.

"Willard was interested, from the moment he got to Duluth, in getting that river cleaned up. The news of the early '50s was full of stories of tar and oil and other waste being dumped directly into the water. The smell of the river was atrocious. There were fish kills and sewer spills. All of that prompted Willard to work to clean up the St. Louis River."

Any success Willard Munger hoped to achieve regarding the establishment of regional sanitary districts depended in large part upon the completion of the Interim Study Commission's investigation and the accessibility of federal funding. While the Interim Commission made slow and steady progress, the fiscal situation in Washington wasn't promising.

John Blatnik's Capitol Chats: Ike Tries to Kill Pollution Plan

Last week hearings were held before my sub-committee on rivers and harbors on legislation to increase Federal grants for construction of municipal waste water treatment plants.

Two years ago, I introduced the new Federal grant program which provides assistance to communities in the construction of needed sewage treatment plants. My original proposal called for a 10-year $100 million a year program. By the time the bill was enacted, this amount had been reduced by half. After a year and a half of experience under the program, it became obvious that $50 million a year is just not adequate...

Construction of sewage treatment facilities increased 40% throughout the country but we are still falling behind in the fight against dirty water...

Less than a week before the scheduled hearings on my bill...the president sent a message to Congress urging the repeal of the treatment plant construction grant program...

[W]e plan on going ahead with my bill to double the program the president wants to repeal.

(Labor World, May 29, 1958.)

The fight to clean up Minnesota's waters rested in the capable hands of Willard Munger in St. Paul and with Congressman John Blatnik in Washington. Munger feared that treating municipal waste (without addressing other sources of pollution) would only be a partial fix. Equally as crucial to Munger's *regional* approach to pollution abatement was the need for the *federal funding* for projects; funding which would supplement the state's financial contribution. As part of its investigation, the Interim Study Commission took testimony from experts.

Dr. Selke Outlines Pollution Problem

At a recent meeting of the Minnesota Pollution Study Commission, Dr. George Selke, Commissioner of Conservation, presented a statement designating a program in which the sportsmen of Minnesota should be interested and in which they should participate...

"Pollution of waters can be defined as the addition of any substances to them that change appreciably their natural quality and reduces their value and potential use for humans and wild animals..."

(Minnesota Out-of-Doors, June, 1958.)

The commission also received petitions from citizens.

Due to the pollution and lack of oxygen in the water of the St. Louis River at Duluth…thousands of walleye pike and northern pike are dying every day. This polluting of rivers is going on all over the state…In order to protect the fish and wildlife of Minnesota, we the undersigned, petition our state representatives to pass effective anti-pollution laws and sanitary districts through the state of Minnesota in the next session…

(Petition in Support of the Interim Study Bill, Willard Munger Personal Collection.)

Munger encouraged an unusual alliance to promote his cause.

"I was after statewide support for the sanitary district, so I went to the steelworkers," Willard remembered. "Of course, the steelworkers like to fish. Labor has never supported the environment very much, but they took this on as a project. They sent out 10,000 letters, some of which I have in my files. They also had petitions asking for the creation of a sanitary district…They took those petitions and went to the state convention and persuaded them to support the creation of a statewide sanitary district as the best way to abate water pollution. They were the first major proposals that I can remember the AFL…really got behind, as far as environmental legislation. Because of their strong support, in 1961, I passed the bill. The Western Lake Superior Sanitary District was patterned after the state-wide legislation. We enacted that into law, and that was a $140 million dollar project."

(*Oral History of Willard Munger*, ibid, p. 82.)

The Interim Commission received petitions in support of Munger's work from; the United Steelworkers of America, District 33; Duluth Central Labor Body, AFL-CIO; AFSCME Local 1125; Amalgamated Meat Cutters Local No. 12; Duluth School Employees Union NO. 956; Head of the Lakes Council of Clerks and Affiliated Trades; NW Bell Telephone Employees Local 4422; Hotel and Restaurant Employees Union Local 84; Wood, Wire and Metal Lathers International Union; and the Bakery and Confectioners Union Local 59.

In June of 1958, an environmental incident occurred which focused public attention on the St. Louis River.

Legislation permitting the establishment of sanitary districts in Minnesota to combat water pollution will be prepared at the next legislative session; two legislators said here yesterday at a hearing into the recent fish kill on the lower St. Louis River.

The hearing, in the Zoo Motel, 7408 Grand Avenue of Rep. Munger, was conducted by a special sub-committee of the State Water Pollution Study Commission. Munger, 59th District, heads the sub-committee...

Munger...said that machinery for establishing a sanitary district program for the state would have to be set up by legislation, but that participation would be left to local option...

Karl McGrath, president of the United Northern Sportsmen, blamed last month's fish kill on water pollution which lowered the oxygen content of the water to a point where fish can't live in it...

McGrath said although the fish kill this year attracted more attention, large numbers of fish also died in the river in past years...

Munger introduced the report of Dr. John Moyle, stating the dissolved oxygen of the water at Fond du Lac was .3 of one part per million, which is below the minimum to sustain fish life...

Ben Gustafson, district fisheries supervisor, said conservation department crews picked up more than 5,000 dead suckers along the shoreline of the river...

Sen. Homer Carr, Proctor, said a sanitary district program is needed but warned that "cleaning up of a river is not something that can be done overnight."

(Duluth Herald, July 16, 1958.)

The Moyle report did not get written without prodding.

June 2, 1958

Dear Mr. Selke:

I am writing this letter to protest the consciously unethical, irreparable statement made in a press release...by Mr. Harry Rogers of the State Water Pollution Control Commission regarding pollution and the recent heavy fish kill in the St. Louis River...

For many years, both Senator Carr and myself have worked with conservation clubs, labor and other civic organizations in this area promoting better conservation laws...It is now apparent that industry, labor and sportsmen agree that the only way to combat water pollution is through establishment of sanitary districts with a long-range program so that industry may stay in our state and flourish...

In reading the May 29th Duluth Tribune, I was greatly surprised to learn that Mr. Rogers came all the way from St. Paul to confer with Mr. LaBrosse about the fish kill in the St. Louis River...

As an active conservationist, author of the bill establishing the Interim Study Committee on water pollution, and a member of the Interim Committee, I am taking exception to the unethical procedure of Mr. Rogers in not conferring with responsible officials or citizens in the area who are genuinely concerned with the welfare of the public and our area.

The morning after the news release, Mr. Rogers telephoned me and stated he would like to discuss the news article with me. I informed him there was much to discuss and his statement had caused irreparable damage to the many years of work that has been done in promoting the sanitary district program. He informed me he was called to Duluth by Rep. LaBrosse and that the only people he conferred with were Northwest Paper Company [a firm located upstream of Duluth in the city of Cloquet which discharged its untreated industrial waste directly into the river] and Mr. LaBrosse…

It is my opinion that Mr. Rogers was brought to Duluth for the sole purpose to obstruct and confuse the people in this area…

These unethical, untimely and misleading statements have caused…damage to the extent that Mr. Rogers can no longer effectively represent the state of Minnesota and he should be requested to submit his resignation immediately…

Your friend,

Willard Munger

Selke dispatched Dr. Moyle to Duluth in an attempt to repair the damage caused by LaBrosse's "end around."

An investigation was made…by Mr. John Hale, District Fisheries Biologist at French River, to determine the extent of the kill and probable cause. The section of Water Pollution Control, Department of Health, was also notified of the situation by this office…Department of Health fieldmen investigated on May 21…

Mr. Hale's report indicated 1,218 suckers and 295 walleye were found dead…and that the lack of oxygen in the water, which may be related to pollution, was the probable direct cause of death…

(*Duluth Herald*, July 16, 1958.)

The fish kill prompted citizens to rally behind Munger's efforts.

Over 2,500 Sign Petitions Asking Water Pollution Control Program

More than 2,500 signatures have been secured on a petition asking the state water pollution interim study commission to recommend legislation setting up a statewide sanitary district program for Minnesota, Representative Willard Munger, Duluth, 59th District said yesterday.

Munger is a member of the commission and author of the 1957 bill which created the commission.

Extensive fish kill due to lack of oxygen in the lower St. Louis River last May increased the interest of residents here in the sanitary district program, Munger said.

"The approach to water pollution control should be made on an orderly, long, range basis," Munger declared. "The 'shotgun approach' under which specific industries are fined for pollution of water is not a proper method; the sanitary district program offers the only real solution of the problem."

Munger said the legislature could set up a statewide sanitary program with a commission to direct it. The plan probably would provide for a district for each of the state's eight main watershed areas. The St. Louis River drainage basin would comprise the Duluth district...

"Minnesota, which ranks second in the U.S. in water supply resources, should have a proper pollution control system both for industry and recreation..."

(*Duluth Herald*, July 16, 1958.)

To understand the work of the Study Commission, a review of minutes from hearings held during the summer of 1958 is illustrative.

July 31, 1958

The commission met in the Hotel Duluth to interview Dr. Fred Witzig and Dr. Robert Owen of UMD as potential commission staff members. The two men were hired at the rate of $750.00 per month for August and September, plus expenses. Subcommittees were set up to explore and investigate pollution problems in the Red River Valley and the Minnesota River valley. Rep. E.J. Chilberg was elected chairman.

August 1, 1958

The commission met in Silver Bay. Many witnesses and people attended the meeting. The reason for the meeting was to discuss Reserve Mining's state-issued permit to dump taconite tailings in Lake Superior. Mr. Montague, the attorney for the mining company, spoke first. The permit was first applied for on January 28, 1947. Hearings were held by the Commissioner of Conservation and the Water Pollution and Control Commission. Permits were issued in December of 1947. In 1956, Reserve was planning an expansion and sought an addendum to its discharge permit. The expansion was approved by the state of Minnesota in 1957. The meeting in Silver Bay included representatives from Reserve, the cities of Babbitt and Silver Bay and Beaver Bay, unions, sportsmen, and commercial fishermen. One of the comments, from Stanley Larson, United Northern Sportsmen, was salient as to whether or not the fine particle discharge into the lake was injurious to the lake.

I am not a chemist but just a common layman but these fishermen must have some reason for doubting some of this evidence. We are not against taconite mining and we don't want to lose any business. But is it right for any industry to have an axe over your head and say, "We're going to move out if you don't do this, or if you don't give in. If you don't cut our taxes, we're going to move out." Do they say anything about that when they go to foreign soil to put up their plants, with the threat that we'll take care of it ourselves instead of sending our boys over to protect them? They do not. It isn't nice that these threats are held over our heads.

November 14, 1958

The commission met at the State Capitol. Profs. Witzig and Owen had finalized their report for review which was discussed by the commission.

Munger then issued a press release regarding the report.

Representative Willard M. Munger stated today that the Water Pollution Control Interim Study Commission held its final meeting…and unanimously adopted a report calling for the establishment of Sanitary Regions in the state…

Rep. Munger will submit a bill embodying the recommendations, to the 1959 legislature for enactment into law…Munger is the author of the legislation establishing the Water Pollution Study Commission. The bill was first introduced and passed the House in 1955 but was defeated in the Senate. In 1957, it passed both Houses with an appropriation of $25,000.00 and provided for five members from the House and five members from the Senate…The commission appointed two UMD faculty members, Dr. Robert Owen, and Dr. Fred Witzig, as assistants in formulating and preparing the report.

(Undated, Willard Munger Personal Collection.)

In 1958, Congressman Eugene McCarthy was campaigning for a U.S. Senate seat. McCarthy, who hoped to join Hubert Humphrey as the second DFL Senator from Minnesota, was running against incumbent Republican Senator Edward J. Thye. Republican George MacKinnon was running against two-term DFL Governor Orville Freeman. The '58 election came on the heels of DFL successes in '54 and '56. In 1954, the Liberals had taken control of the Minnesota House by a single vote. By 1956, 70 of the 131 members were Liberals. Predictions were that as many as 76 of the 131 House seats would be in Liberal hands after Election Day, 1958.

In the 59th Legislative District, the contestants included Incumbent Francis "Frenchie" LaBrosse; Incumbent Willard Munger; Challenger Leo H. Jarvi; and Challenger R.C. Johnson.

Munger sought Senator Carr's endorsement and the older statesman didn't disappoint his protégé.

> Hon. Sen. Homer Carr says: "Any success of a legislator representing his district is due to close cooperation by the district's elected representatives. In my 25 years as Senator from the 59th District, I have never had greater cooperation and team work than I enjoyed in the 1955 session from Rep. Willard Munger, who I am supporting for re-election. I am asking my many friends and supporters to cast their votes for this hard-working legislator who, by his efforts, faithfully represents our district."
>
> (1958 Campaign brochure, Willard Munger Personal Collection.)

A candidate profile touted Munger's ties to labor and his conservation work.

> Willard Munger, who operates a motel and resides at 7408 Grand Ave., is seeking a third term as Representative from the 59th District. He has railroad brotherhood, DFL and AFL-CIO support.
>
> He is vice chairman of the committee on cities of the first and second class, chairman of the education sub-committee on gross earnings, and a member of the labor, employees' compensation, university, education and appropriations committees. He is also a member of the high bridge and pollution commissions.
>
> (*Duluth News Tribune*, July 18, 1958.)

When the ballots were counted, Governor Freeman easily won re-election as did LaBrosse and Munger. And Congressman Eugene McCarthy defeated Senator Thye, returning both Minnesota U.S. Senate seats to Liberal control for the first time since 1938.

As 1958 drew to a close, the Interim Study Commission issued its report.

The commission submits the following recommendations:

Reorganization

1. That sanitary regions be established to coincide as nearly as possible with the several major drainage basins of the state.

2. That the Water Pollution Control Commission consist of the following: the secretary and executive officer of the State Board of Health, the Commissioner of Conservation, the Commissioner of Agriculture, the Secretary and Executive Officer of the State Livestock Sanitary Board, and members representing each sanitary region to be appointed by the governor with the approval of the senate.

3. That the representatives from each sanitary region perform the duties of assisting in the establishment of general policy for the state in matters regarding pollution, of maintaining liaison between the Water Pollution Control Commission and communities, industries, and other persons within their respective regions, and of assisting in programs designed to inform the public of the importance of water pollution control and of methods of achieving that control.

4. That permissive legislation be enacted to encourage and to enable communities and their environs to unite for the purposes of planning and executing those plans to alleviate pollution problems common to their communities.

Changes in the Present Pollution Law

1. That the pollution law be extended to include sub-surface waters.

2. That the state law state that pollution of state waters is prohibited.

3. That the present law be closely examined for ambiguities and statements which lack precision or clarity and which have the effect of limiting the effectiveness of the work of the Water Pollution Control Commission, and that such statements be clarified and where necessary that provisions be strengthened.

4. That specifications of sewage treatment facilities be submitted to the Water Pollution Control Commission and approved before construction of industrial facilities is begun....

(Willard Munger Personal Collection.)

Emboldened by his re-election, Munger would support additional conservation-related legislation during the 1959 session. But developments in Munger's personal life would interfere with his environmental agenda.

CHAPTER 8

Wilting Lady Slipper

By January of 1959, Willard Munger was ready to introduce additional ground-breaking environmental legislation. Working with Dr. Fred Witzig and Dr. Robert Owen of UMD, Munger sought to expand the scope of the Interim Study Commission. First, he argued for the renewal of the commission's legislative charter. Achieving that goal, he pushed for legislation authorizing the establishment of regional sanitary districts. He also sought to include air pollution within the purview of the commission's work and $35,000 in additional funding for the commission.

Munger communicated frequently with Owen and Witzig as he awaited legislative action on his bills in the Minnesota House.

> January 14, 1959
> Dear Mr. Munger:
> Since I saw you last, I have checked the pollution laws of nineteen states and have assembled some information that may be of interest to you. This information relates chiefly to water pollution control agencies.
> Six of the nineteen delegate responsibility of water pollution control to state departments of health. The other thirteen have special pollution control agencies...None of the nineteen has advisory committees of the kind we discussed...Only the California law seems to make adequate provision for contact and communication between the state agency and the respective districts. That may explain why so many of them have dirty water...
> Yours truly,
> Robert Owen

Though Willard Munger continued to work on conservation-related legislation, his mind became preoccupied with a personal matter.

"Mom was having what Dr. Harry Bell, her doctor, called gall bladder problems. This started sometime in late 1958," Patsy Munger-Lehr recalls. "Mom would get deathly ill after eating so Dr. Bell changed her diet. That didn't work."

Will Munger, Jr. adds, "Mom couldn't eat ice cream. Dad would go to Dairy Queen in West Duluth and bring her soft serve because she could eat that but she couldn't eat regular ice cream."

"When Dad came home from the legislature, Mom was in the hospital. Dr. Cook, the surgeon, opened Mom up," Patsy recalls. "She ended up at the University of Minnesota Hospital for quite a while. The thing is, the doctors painted such a rosy picture. When Dr. Cook took out the first bowl obstruction, he said, 'If you have to have cancer, that's the place to have it.' Ultimately, when she was at University Hospital, they diagnosed her with ovarian cancer. Her insides were peppered with it."

Unaware of the true nature and extent of his wife's illness, Willard Munger returned to St. Paul for his third session in the Minnesota House.

> Rep. Willard Munger of Duluth expressed confidence…that a bill authorizing a half mill St. Louis county-wide levy for "distressed" school districts will be approved…
>
> The measure has been recommended for passage by an 8-7 vote of the House Towns and Counties Committee. It is still in committee in the Senate…
>
> (*Duluth News Tribune*, undated.)

Munger also voiced his opposition to the city of Duluth leasing its public gas utility to a private concern. Beginning with his paternal grandfather, Willard Munger's early political mentors had convinced him that utilities were better off being publicly owned than being controlled by private concerns. This philosophy likely influenced his decision to push for government-owned sanitary districts to clean up the state's waterways and also fed his opposition to the gas leasing proposal.

Munger Objects to Plans for City Gas Utility Lease

> State Rep. Willard Munger indicated yesterday he will oppose an attempt by the Duluth City Council to obtain authority to lease its gas utility franchise without the vote of the people. His was the only objection raised among members of the Duluth legislative delegation…
>
> Munger said if the city is going to turn its gas utility over to a private operator, the change should be subject to voter approval…
>
> Munger said he is afraid the cost of gas to consumers would be higher under a private operator…
>
> (*Duluth News Tribune*, January 18, 1959.)

At least one city councilor took exception to Munger's opinion.

Politics Charged in Gas Lease Row

City Councilman John P. Nelson has accused State Rep. Willard Munger of making "political hay" over the council's request for legislation that will authorize them to lease Duluth's gas utility.

Nelson said the Council "has not proposed to turn the gas utility over to a private concern."

Three weeks ago, the council unanimously approved Mayor Eugene R. Lambert's proposal to seek authorization from the state to…lease the utility…

For at least the second time, Munger said…he is opposed to the move… Munger claimed Duluth can have natural gas "efficiently and economically" under municipal operation…

(*Duluth News Tribune*, undated.)

The issue didn't go away.

Candidates Split over Lambert Plan

Duluth's spring election picture can only be described as mixed up after a total of 30 candidates placed their names on the ballot for 7 offices…

But one big issue—whether the city should turn its municipal gas system over to a private operator—may separate Liberals from Conservatives in short order…

At 10:00 A.M. Saturday in the Duluth City Council Chambers…Rep. Willard Munger, chairman of the Duluth delegation, will convene a public hearing on the gas question…

Two candidates for mayor, George D. Johnson and Clifford Mork, already have taken strong stands against the idea…

(*Labor World*, February 12, 1959.)

Munger and Rep. Jack Fena (Liberal-Hibbing) also introduced legislation during the 1959 session to regulate lobbyists. Munger had become acutely aware of the issue during the debate regarding state oversight of Blue Cross-Blue Shield where Rep. LaBrosse, an employee of Blue Cross, worked, in effect, as a lobbyist for his employer while also serving as a legislator.

Two St. Louis County legislators yesterday prepared a bill calling for the registration of lobbyists in the Minnesota Legislature…

Reps. Willard Munger, Duluth, and Jack Fena, Hibbing, said they would introduce the proposal—which includes a section affecting legislators on retainer—today.

Anybody paid a regular salary to lobby would be required to register with the Secretary of State...

Munger and Fena said the bill provides safeguards for groups, such as those representing education or municipalities, who lobby on "behalf of the public." It also exempts church representatives...

(*Duluth News Tribune*, January 23, 1959.)

Presumably, Munger also meant to exempt groups lobbying the legislature regarding conservation matters (Clear Air, Clear Water, Unlimited; United Northern Sportsmen, etc.) from regulation.

Munger's third legislative term also saw him elected to a position of authority.

Munger Heads City Delegation

Rep. Willard Munger was elected chairman of the Duluth legislative delegation...He was nominated by Rep. Jack Peterson...

Munger received 5 out of 7 votes. Peterson and Sen. Homer Carr received one vote apiece...

(*Duluth News Tribune*, January 25, 1959.)

Munger's Interim Study work continued as well.

February 1, 1959

Dear Mr. Munger:

I have examined summaries of the water pollution control laws of the states which were prepared...and have prepared a brief summary of certain aspects of state laws and enforcing agencies...

In 17 states, the Department of Health administers the pollution control program. Most of these states have an advisory council composed of heads of several state departments [conservation, agriculture, forestry, game and fish, attorney general, etc...] 32 states have special pollution control agencies...in 4 states, the boards consist of heads of state departments...and in 3, the board consists of only lay members. The boards of the other 25 consist of both official and lay members...

The closest approach to the plan that you have in mind for Minnesota seems to be several interstate agencies [Ohio River, Delaware River, etc...] In all of those, water supply and use determines the specific control measures, and in every case, the river basin has been divided into regions according to geographical and economic characteristics. Your plan to divide the Mississippi into three regions follows such a plan...

Robert Owen

Munger became involved with the issue of clean water in another context when the Town of Herman (now the city of Hermantown) found itself unable to provide drinking water for its residents.

Bill in Hopper for Hermantown Water Works

Legislation opening the way for installation of a waterworks system in Hermantown has been introduced by Sen. Homer Carr, Proctor.

Carr said he urged speedy enactment of the bill because an "emergency" exists…When the waterworks is constructed; Hermantown would obtain water from Duluth…

Rep. Willard Munger will author the same bill in the House…

(*Duluth News Tribune*, February 19, 1959.)

While this bill is seemingly inconsequential, it is a precursor of more expansive regulatory protections regarding groundwater which Willard Munger would author later in his career.

Munger himself had a small health scare in March of 1959. Stricken with an infection, he spent ten long days in the University of Minnesota Hospital.

House Holds up Fond du Lac Flood Claims

Action on claims made against the state by 13 Fond du Lac residents was held up in the House…

Action was postponed to allow Rep. Willard Munger of Duluth to explain the claims. Munger is hospitalized for a second time because of an infected throat.

(*Duluth News Tribune*, February 24, 1959.)

Released from the hospital, Munger wasted little time getting back into the fray.

Munger Returns to House from Hospital

Liberal State Representative Willard Munger, chairman of the Duluth delegation in the 1959 Legislature, returned to the House this week after 10 days in University Hospital. Munger was stricken with a severe streptoccocic infection that required treatment by University heart and kidney specialists…

(*Labor World*, March 5, 1959.)

Contamination of Minnesota's waterways drew the public's ire.

Pollution Protests Spread by Ed Ahave

Lowest Mississippi River levels in history are touching off new blasts against pollution and the future of fishing in that river and several tributaries…

The latest furor comes from LaCrosse, Wisconsin, where U.S. Fish and Wildlife Service biologist Robert C. Nord stated flatly that pollution originating in the Twin Cities area could affect fishing all the way down to LaCrosse...

At the same time, Clear Air, Clear Water Unlimited said in its report...:

"If a river can die, then rites should be prepared for Old Man Mississippi..."

Nord was quoted in the *LaCrosse Tribune* that new heavy industries in Pine Bend and St. Paul Park have raised havoc with fishing in the Mississippi in recent years.

He also said that rising populations in the Minneapolis-St. Paul metro area has produced more waste that needs treatment and proper disposal.

At the same time, O.L. Kaupanger, Secretary of the Minnesota Emergency Conservation Committee, said that Minneapolis-St. Paul would have to begin secondary treatment of sewage if the river is to be cleaned up. "At present, there is only primary treatment," he said. "This has no effect on oils and phenols..."

(*Minneapolis Journal*, March 8, 1959.)

Legislative foot dragging on the issue made the front pages of Minnesota newspapers.

Water Unit Blasts Stand

Clear Air, Clear Water Unlimited, a state conservation organization, took exception ...to comments made here by Shepperd T. Powell, Baltimore consulting engineer.

Powell, in St. Paul to testify as an industry witness at a hearing on a bill to create state sanitary districts, said in an interview...that industry is entitled to its "rightful" share of river use for waste disposal...

"Mr. Powell's remarks are obviously designed to pour soothing oil on already troubled waters," Warren Bjorklund, organization president said. "His statement that industry is entitled to its rightful share of river use for waste disposal defies logic...Industry must and should have water for its use but it has the same moral and legal obligation as the citizens of this state to protect priceless water supply from pollution...We believe one of Minnesota's greatest industrial attractions is good clean water. The problem is not to see how much dumping streams will tolerate. We believe Minnesotans are best qualified to assess what should be done to protect their water resources..."

(*St. Paul Pioneer Press*, March 12, 1959.)

Education also continued to be a focus of Munger's legislative work.

School District Levy Bill Cleared for House Debate

Enactment of a bill providing for a one-mill levy to assist unorganized St. Louis County school districts was recommended for final passage yesterday.

Rep. Willard Munger, Duluth, said the bill clarifies a law passed in 1957...

(Unknown Source, Willard Munger Personal Collection.)

Harry Munger, Jr. observes that, while his older brother became known almost exclusively as an environmental legislator, Willard's political agenda was never limited to conservation issues.

"He was an early supporter of expanding the campus and programs at the University of Minnesota-Duluth," Harry remembers. "He, along with Homer Carr, was very supportive of the industrial arts and engineering programs. He got a lot of support on this and other educational issues from Martha due to her heavy involvement in PTA. He was also one of the prime movers of bringing a medical school to the Duluth campus."

In 1959, a school aid package sponsored by Munger faced opposition in the form of professional lobbyist Richard Hastings, a Duluth attorney representing the mining industry.

The dispute over whether St. Louis County should levy a half mill for the benefit of four school districts continued yesterday...

Richard Hastings, Duluth mining company attorney...lined up in opposition to the proposal.

On the other side were Rep. Willard Munger, Duluth, and representatives of the Arnold, Floodwood, Hermantown and Lakewood school districts.

Hastings told the subcommittee that school boards have the duty and function of levying taxes in their own districts...

The Duluth legislator said his own taxes would rise because of the half mill. "If I can afford this half mill," he said, "the mining companies can too..."

(*Duluth News Tribune*, April 2, 1959.)

Martha's failing health became Willard's primary focus.

April 6, 1959

My Dearest Martha:

Received your letter this morning and very pleased to know you are feeling better. I think about you all the time.

I count my blessings more now than ever—I am really lucky to have such a fine, beautiful wife. Most men are not this fortunate. After you are well and the legislature is over, you and I are going to spend some time together. Perhaps fishing or some trip that you really can enjoy. You looked so sweet and beautiful Sunday night when I left you that I couldn't help think of how you have been left home to work and slave for the family and business these past 25 years. Of course, we do have a fine family, but we should also have arranged to enjoy life much more by taking time off for a vacation.

I finished my letter to Bob Morris and will mail it tomorrow. It's four pages long. This letter is quite strong but is just what they need.

The legislature has passed most all their bills and are now waiting to see what the senate is going to do. I got my Pollution Interim Study Bill passed Monday and will get the Port Authority passed about Wed. I may try and get the Appropriations Committee to pass out the Educational TV tomorrow.

I sure wish that you were here. Perhaps I would feel better. I know it would help because I get better just thinking of you.

Your Sweetheart,

Willard

P.S. I still have that gold net—it's almost 26 years old and has never tarnished!

This touching letter, the only one from Willard to Martha from the period of her illness that survives, is both a lamentation of time lost and vacations not taken, and a celebration of the work that Willard and Martha accomplished together. As Patsy Munger-Lehr and Will Munger, Jr. alluded to, the marriage between Willard and Martha Munger was truly a partnership. Martha was the one, with full understanding of what the life of a politician's wife entailed, who prodded and pushed her husband to run for office. She cut meat at the family grocery store; sold gas; stocked shelves; ran the motel, and did much of the day-to-day living for the couple while Willard ran for office and later, served his constituents in St. Paul.

But the reality of the situation was that the cancer inside Martha was growing.

May 4, 1959

Dear Willard:

It's Monday afternoon. I feel pretty good—just a few aches and pains. Have been up this morning and part of the afternoon. Didn't sleep too well as I didn't take a sedative. May sleep better today or tonight.

Called Elsie and Pat and everything is fine. Ernest went to the bank too. Maybe Elsie will visit me tomorrow. I don't know how I can stand to stay here until Friday. How did you stay all that time in the University Hospital? It sure must have been lonesome. Will write again tomorrow. My penmanship is very bad but I can't help it.

Love—Your Wife

Martha

Munger suffered his first significant loss of the 1959 Legislative Session when, on the heels of the Interim Study Commission's report being published, he was unable to muster enough votes to enact Sanitary District legislation to implement the goals of the report. The Sanitary District enabling law faced 29 amendments between the introduction of the bill on April 11, 1959 and its passage in the House on April 14, 1959 after which, the proposed legislation died in the Senate.

Despite these professional and personal setbacks, 1959 included at least one positive occasion for Willard and Martha Munger.

Willard and Martha Munger Celebrate 25 Years

Representative and Mrs. Willard Munger of Duluth will hold an open house...celebrating their silver wedding anniversary at the Willard Motel auditorium.

The Mungers have two children, Willard, Jr., a student at UMD, and Mrs. Edwin Carlson, Jr., who resides in Duluth, and one granddaughter, Cynthia Ann Carlson. No invitations have been issued and all friends are cordially invited.

(Unknown source, Willard Munger Personal Collection.)

The year also saw Munger receive further recognition for his work.

October 10, 1959

Dear Rep. Munger:

It is my very great pleasure to inform you of the unanimous vote of the members of Clear Air, Clear Water Unlimited at the third annual meeting... as follows:

"A CAC-WU life-membership for Representative Willard M. Munger of Duluth, Minnesota, in recognition of his outstanding work and efforts towards the control and abatement of water pollution in Minnesota..."

Very cordially yours,

Vera B. Pierson

Secretary, Clear Air, Clear Water Unlimited

That yar, 1959, was in many ways a watershed year for Rep. Munger. He passed a second Interim Study Water Pollution bill. He was re-elected to his third consecutive term in the House. And as the chair of the Duluth Legislative Delegation, he had ascended to modest power within the DFL Party.

Munger outlined his thoughts regarding his role in Liberal politics, and the comparative philosophies of the two major parties in a speech given in 1959 to organized labor.

> Politics is everyone's business—our forefathers fought hard for it in order that you and I might enjoy freedom.
>
> Unless we all take a more active part in political science we may lose this great heritage-our freedom.
>
> The strength of our democracy is as strong as the confidence that you place in it. The confidence and respect is determined by the men and women you elect to public office. You and I have a job to do-you as a voter and I as the candidate. We both have obligations to perform that I shall talk about later in my talk...
>
> As partners in this business of politics, you have the responsibility to acquaint yourself, your friends, and neighbors with the issues in the coming campaign., and also to know your candidates—know his political background-who is supporting him and why! One of the determining factors you should ask yourself—Does the candidate have a code of ethics as recommended by Governor Freeman for all candidates to follow?
>
> I as a candidate seeking re-election have also a responsibility to the people. The candidate must be honest with the people. It is the candidate's obligation to inform the people of his background, his past record and program for the future and most important, who he will align himself with if elected.
>
> The voter has the right to know before he votes which group a candidate will caucus with if elected. Because the vote on Speaker of the House is the determining factor on the type of legislation that will be passed. One of the first votes that you cast as a legislator is the vote on the Speaker—you must either vote Liberal or Conservative-you have no other choice...
>
> Here in Minnesota, we have two strong political parties with two different theories of government.
>
> 1. The conservatives, dominated by the Republican Party, believe that property rights are paramount to that of human rights. They believe business will work out its own problems if left without government interference.

2. On the other side, we have the DFL, people who feel that human rights should be considered before that of property rights-the DFL people also feel that our economic well being is based upon the high purchasing power of the farmer, labor, and small businessmen.

Why did the people of Minnesota lose their faith in the Republican Party and place their confidence in the DFL Party? There are a number of reasons. For this, we shall review the records of both parties.

The Republican Party lost the confidence of the people because it showed a lack of leadership in our state government.

Under the 16 years of Republican leadership, no constructive program was proposed but instead, they gave us:

1. Legislation on behalf of the loan sharks-36% interest;

2. Anti-labor legislation-such as the Minnesota Labor Relations Act, public employees' anti-strike laws and anti-secondary boycott laws.

3. The Republican Party, during its 16 years of rule, has done nothing constructive in behalf of the farmer, labor, small businessman or in the field of education, mental health and conservation.

They have always favored special interest groups at your expense. They attempted several times to shift the burden of taxation from the most able to pay to those with less means.

The accomplishments of the past four years under a DFL administration has been in the best interest of the farmer, labor, education and small businessmen.

We have made more progress in the last four years than any other time in the state's history in the fields of education, labor, higher education, welfare, human rights, agriculture and economic development-especially in this area.

It is true that the last session of the Minnesota Legislature approved the largest appropriation in the state's history. I voted for this appropriation because we must meet our responsibilities as a legislature now.

The Republicans ducked the responsibilities that go with leadership-they ducked their responsibilities of providing appropriations for the state's needs, especially the state's building needs.

The DFL's far-sighted building program will be a great help with respect to instituting a substantial public works program for the purpose of fighting the current depression...

And understand, if you give the Republicans another 16 years, you can expect to see a state sales tax and right to work laws.

(Willard Munger Personal Collection.)

This speech points to Munger's evolution as a politician; from the days of his prairie-formed, farmer-orientated work on behalf of A.C. Townley and the Nonpartisan League, to re-educating himself regarding the issues confronting organized labor. Though Willard Munger followed a distinctly different political path from that of his mentor, Munger didn't forget the Nonpartisan leader.

> "Getting back to Townley…," Munger remembered, "I saw him go downhill. It was a very sad thing to see one powerful person like that disappear. You know, he became very conservative. He became very anti-communist during the time of (Senator Joseph] McCarthy. He could almost see a Communist behind every bush. I don't know how people change like that. I saw a lot of people change that way when they got older, and it's sad, very sad. He had the kind of power in North Dakota where his word was absolute…We didn't have any secretaries or staff people, and on our $500 salary, you didn't have very expensive breakfasts. So when Townley would come in and sit down in the same booth with me in St. Paul, I'd always worry I wasn't going to have enough money to pay for…our breakfasts. So I would duck him a little bit every once in a while."

Munger then explained that Townley's conduct and thinking became strange and other-worldly.

> "I've always had a really deep feeling for the fellow because I think he was a great person," Willard added. "He had an awful lot of influence on my entire life. It was a sad ending to see him disintegrate, to see his mind disintegrate as much as it did. He lost all the philosophy that he used to have…[M]y wife was in the hospital with cancer and he said to me one day, 'I'm going up to the hospital and help your wife.'
>
> I said, 'In what way?'
>
> He said, 'I think I have the power to help heal her. I'm going to put my hands on her and help her.'
>
> That was a sad moment to think he'd declined to that state. I suppose he felt he had had all that power and then it vanished. He would still imagine that he had some power of some kind, and he probably wanted to imagine he still was a powerful individual."

> (*Oral History of Willard Munger*, ibid, pp. 21 – 22.)

Townley died just as Martha's condition was worsening. The *Fergus Falls Daily Journal*, a newspaper that had once carried news of Townley's political exploits in bold headlines on its front page, relegated the former Nonpartisan League leader's obituary to the interior of the paper.

Townley Burial Brings an End to Political Saga

Arthur C. Townley, a political giant who out-lived his brief days of glory by many years, was buried Thursday in a lonely country cemetery.

The founder of the Nonpartisan League, who once made governors and congressmen, was killed in a car accident November 7 in North Dakota...

Townley was killed in his 79th year, nearly 40 years after he quit the League as its once mighty power waned.

No relatives closer than nieces and nephews were among the 40 who attended Methodist services...Mrs. Townley and a daughter died before him. Two brothers could not attend...

For much of his life after his...zenith...Townley lived in sort of political backwash. He often sought political office as an independent but never got more than a handful of votes. He sold insurance, speculated in oil, and practiced faith healing. The man who once espoused State Socialism, was called a Bolshevist, and served a jail sentence for attacking the WWI draft, spent some of his last days making speeches against Communism to anyone who would listen.

(*Fergus Falls Daily Journal*, November 13, 1959.)

Willard's own recollection of Towneley's passing is poignent.

"I couldn't go to the funeral," Willard recalled, "and that bothered me a lot. So I...decided to stop by his grave. I went to the town of Parker's Prairie and looked around there, but I couldn't find it. I went into a restaurant and saw some old people sitting at a table...I sat down and asked them if anyone remembered A.C. Townley.

"'Oh yes,' they said.

"A lady was on a counter stool, and she turned around and said, 'I was at his funeral.'

"I found out from her where he was buried, so I finally found the graveyard in Wrights Town. I stopped to talk to some of the neighbors and they said, 'Townley is buried out in the graveyard, but there's just one big marker for his father...So I went out there, and here was this great big marker that just said 'Townley' on it. No date. No initials or anything. There was no grave markings at all of A.C. Townley. It was kind of sad. Here was this powerful person who was really the father of the Farmer-Labor Party—the party we have right now (the DFL)—and he didn't even have a marker on

his grave! It's kind of sad, you see, how one powerful person fades away
that way."

(*Oral History of Willard Munger*, ibid, pp. 21 – 23.)

An incident involving the motel occurred in December of 1959. The motel's name
had been changed from the "Duluth Zoo Motel" to the "Willard Motel." Will
Munger, Jr. recalls the name change was prompted by the fact that guests were
poking fun at the name by telling friends and relatives they were "staying at the
zoo." The new name was a clever play on the "Willard Hotel," a well-known political hangout in Washington, D.C. that Willard Munger was familiar with from his
1934 sojourn to the nation's capital.

The incident at the Willard Motel, which involved Will Munger, Jr., took place
as follows:

Will was left alone at the motel. His mother was in the hospital and his father
was visiting her. Will was concentrating on his university studies when a city of
Duluth fire inspector entered the motel and confronted him about selling Christmas trees without a license. What happened next is best recounted by Willard's
angry letter to the fire department.

> Mr. John L. Ostman
>> Fire Department
>> City of Duluth
>> February 1, 1960
>> Dear Mr. Ostman:
>
> On Monday, December 21, 1959, I called your office and inquired why a
> member of your department had taken my son to jail on…December 18…
> and forced him to pay $35.00 for a Christmas tree license before releasing
> him. I had already sent a check in to the city clerk and they in turn claim it
> was forwarded to your department…
>
> On December 2, 1959, I took my wife to St. Luke's Hospital…I was in-
> formed by the doctor that her condition was very serious and that they could
> do no more for her. I then decided to take her to the University Hospital…
>
> On December 10…I made out a check on which I noted the check was
> for a Christmas tree license and facts to the disposition of the trees [which I'd
> sold]. I mailed the letter…addressed to the city clerk's office…
>
> On December 18, a member of your department walked into…my mo-
> tel…where my son was studying for an examination, and demanded that my
> son obtain money to pay for a Christmas tree license. My son protested that

he had no right to pay for a license as that was my responsibility...Your man then contacted two police officers who took my son down to headquarters where they obtained $35.00 from him. I had given him this money to buy Christmas presents with. They took him without a warrant and without allowing him to call me...

That same day I had my attorney contact the city clerk's office and ask if they had received a check from Willard Munger for a Christmas tree license. Miss Brown...stated they had forwarded it...to your department...

I wish to offer you the following observations:

In checking the list in your office of Christmas tree licenses, I noticed that 32 were taken out after December 10 and also after they had trees on their lots for sale. I also found that your department had collected directly from the greater number of the licensees. This courtesy...was not extended to me...[I] am the responsible party, not my son. They were not his trees...

It appears that this...cowardly, illegal act in arresting my son, who had no concern with the matter...was motivated by a personal desire to embarrass me. If not for that reason, then I can only attribute the action to lack of training and his disrespect for the integrity of his position and the whole fire department.

In the many years that I have spent as an inspector for the state and federal government, I have always strived to be fair...I have raised a fine family based upon high morals, honesty and integrity and I am telling you here and now that I don't intend to have this questionable character that represents your office come out and deliberately attempt to embarrass my family.

Before your department elevates a man to a position of responsibility, I suggest that you ought to do the same as the state or federal government, to-wit: check into the background of the individual as to his character and temperament. I did a little checking and found facts which certainly raise the issue of whether or not he is qualified to hold a position which requires public contact...

In conclusion, am I correct in assuming that my check was received and deliberately destroyed by someone in your department?...

Unless I receive a satisfactory explanation as to what became of my check...I would suggest you notify the State Public Examiner to make an investigation...

I do feel it is your responsibility, as head of your department, to guard against the possibility that a member of your department would allow his personal or political dislikes to be his rule and guide of action in the exercise of authority...Tyranny has no place in our democratic society...

Very truly yours,
Willard M. Munger

A sworn statement was taken from the secretary by Harry Munger, Jr.

Q: Do you recall…when you received that check from Mr. Munger?

A: Now I don't recall, no…

Q: I called you on Friday, December 18th…

A: Then it was the day before, or two days before.

Q: When I called you, you said "Yes, I remember receiving it?"

A: Yes.

Q: You said, "It was a couple of days ago I sent it over to the fire department?"

A: Yes, it was either the day before or two days before you called…

Q: But do you recall that on top of the check it said for Christmas trees?

A: Christmas tree license.

Q: And at the bottom it said something about disposition of the trees?

A: Yes, it says something like, "Only three trees left," or something, and just something about the trees or where they were, you know…

Q: Signed by Willard Munger?

A: Signed by some Munger…

Q: (W)hat's your normal procedure?

A: I just mark the outside of the envelope for the fire department, and then I put it in the box for delivery to the fire department…

(Willard Munger Personal Collection.)

One can imagine newly-anointed lawyer, Harry Munger, Jr. interrogating Ms. Brown regarding the misplaced check, with his older brother, a state legislator, sitting by his side. Though the matter seems trivial it points out the fact that Willard Munger took his reputation seriously. Even the smallest of attacks upon his character needed to be addressed firmly and with determination.

In addition to dealing with Martha's declining health, the death of Willard's father, Harry Munger, Sr. of a massive heart attack (just a year after Harry, Sr. and Elsie

Munger celebrated their 50th wedding anniversary) devastated the legislator. Willard Munger lamented his father's death, not only because of the sudden and unexpected nature of Harry, Sr.'s passing, but also because Harry, Sr.'s death occurred shortly after a vicious argument between the two men.

H.L. Munger, Veteran State Politician Dies

Harry Munger, Sr. 76, a Minnesota liberal political figure and former district supervisor of game wardens, died yesterday in his residence at 8 Hillcrest Street.

He was the father of State Rep. Willard Munger...

Mr. Munger was one of the original organizers of the Nonpartisan League, the forerunner of the Farmer-Labor Party. He was a close friend of A.C. Townley...and...Gov. Floyd B. Olson.

His family was among the early settlers of western Minnesota.

A native of Fergus Falls, he lived there for 60 years before coming to Duluth...

Last November, Mr. and Mrs. Munger celebrated their golden wedding anniversary. Mr. Munger for years was active in Minnesota and Midwest conservation work.

During World War II, he worked at the Walter Butler shipyards here. He attended the Lutheran Church of Christ the King....

(*Duluth News Tribune*, October 16, 1959.)

One line in the above obituary stands out. "Mr. Munger for years was active in Minnesota and Midwest conservation work..." It seems clear, in this final tribute to Willard's father, that the entirety of Harry, Sr.'s impact upon his son is revealed: Grandpa Lyman wasn't the only Munger who taught Willard Munger about resource conservation.

Martha's battle with ovarian cancer drew Willard away from his work in the Minnesota Legislature.

Beginning with the glowing accounts of his 1934 trip to Washington, D.C., Willard often promised to take his little lady slipper on trips to exotic places; to see sights she'd never seen. But there were no trips during their twenty-five years together; only the day to day grind of running a small business, raising children, and volunteering for various charities to fill Martha's days and nights. Finally, when the news proved to be devastating, with Martha's body wracked by cancer and weakened from radiation treatments, Willard conceived of a trip to

California so that Martha could visit her sister, Helen Trueblood. Mrs. Trueblood recounts the visit.

"When Martha came to visit us in February of 1960," Helen remembers, "she was very sick. Too sick to go see the San Diego Zoo. The picture you have of them on the beach, that's the last one, I think. She was so sick, she couldn't stand another operation. It was so sad. Theirs was a love story for their whole lives. Willard needed Martha. She was extremely supportive of other people, especially Willard. He told me, on that trip, with some sadness, 'I'd be nobody if I didn't have Martha'. I got to see them together, how they were with each other, back in the early 1940s. I lived with them for a while when I worked in Duluth and Superior."

Patsy Munger-Lehr recounts that, once her mother returned from California, Martha never regained her strength.

"She ended up at the University of Minnesota Hospital in Minneapolis. That radiation she was taking," Patsy recalls, "weakened her. She ended up going into St. Luke's Hospital in Duluth in May and she never got out. All those months that she was there, Dad never missed a day. He stayed with her overnight and fed her carrot juice, hoping it would cure the cancer. They even tried a drug that wasn't licensed for use. It came from Illinois. It didn't do any good. There's a terrible picture of Mom in the hospital with Senator Hubert Humphrey visiting her. I hate that picture. It doesn't even look like Mom."

Will Munger, Jr. learned of his mother's condition indirectly.

"I think I heard about it from Patsy," Will recalls. "I just remember no one really ever said anything to me. I went on a fishing trip and when I came back, Mom was sick. Mom's death was a big blow to Dad. And of course, to me too. She had a big influence on me. I think of her a lot. It was really a tragedy. She was someone who you'd want to know what she would have done if she'd lived longer. Though, near the end, when I talked with her, she told me, 'I wouldn't change a minute of my life.' They were always together, working, living daily life. The one thing she never got, that she always wanted, was a house of her own."

Martha's illness interrupted what should have been a high point in Willard Munger's political career. Munger was deeply involved in the 1960 presidential election and DFL politics on a state-wide basis. The following is an excerpt from a speech Munger gave in honor of his friend, Gerald Heaney, when Heaney stepped down as a Democratic National Committeeman from Minnesota. Heaney's departure had not been by choice and Munger selected his words carefully.

In six years as Democratic National Committeeman working closely with Gov. Freeman and legislators, Gerald Heaney made an outstanding contribution to all the people of Minnesota, but more especially, northeastern Minnesota.

Heaney is a powerful, dynamic Liberal leader within the DFL Party. Because of his…leadership, the people of northeastern Minnesota have received more consideration than any similar period of the state's history in the way of increased school aid, road construction, High Bridge, Port Terminal, UMD expansion, etc…

Like all good leaders, Mr. Heaney graciously accepted the will of the majority. Knowing Mr. Heaney as I do, he will continue to serve the people of Minnesota through his activities within the DFL Party…

(June, 1960, Willard Munger Personal Collection.)

Heaney was appreciative of Munger's support.

June 13, 1960

Dear Willard:

I certainly appreciate the sentiment behind the gift that the members of the state legislature from this area presented to me…

During the last three sessions of the legislature, we have accomplished much by working together.

I think I probably realized better than any of you that many of the difficulties we have had were as a result of my Irish temper. I certainly hope, however, that all of you made allowances for this as I am sure that the ends towards which we worked are the same.

I know of no other group of legislators who have accomplished as much for their district than has our group from Duluth and the Iron Range. I certainly hope that we can all continue to work together in the future.

Yours very truly,

Gerry

Though minor in comparison with the personal tragedy unfolding for Willard Munger in a quiet room in St. Luke's Hospital, Munger experienced a major political disappointment as a consequence of Martha's illness. Munger had been selected to attend the 1960 Democratic National Convention as a delegate representing the 8th Congressional District along with Earl Bester, Mary Lushene, and Vladimir Shipka. The "At Large" delegates from the state of Minnesota in 1960 looked like a "who's who" of DFL Founding Fathers and Mothers; Ronald L. Anderson, John A.

Blatnik, Walter Butler, Joseph L. Donovan. Blanche Erkel, Marvin Evenson, Henry Feikema, Clarence Fisher, Donald Fraser, Orville L. Freeman, Clint Haroldson, Gerald Heaney, Ray Hemenway, Hubert H. Humphrey, Ione Hunt, Eugene Mc-Carthy, Geri M. Joseph, Joseph E. Karth, William Kubicek, Miles Lord, George W. Matthews, Walter F. Mondale, Oscar L. Olson, Karl F. Rolvaag, Roy W. Weir, and Donald Wozniak.

Though Willard Munger was unable to attend the convention due to Martha's condition, his younger brother, Harry Munger, Jr. would attend the raucous 1968 Democratic Convention in Chicago as a delegate, an honor which emphasized Harry's own meteoric rise within the DFL.

Munger Elected at DFL Parlay by Richard Jacobs

Party designation of county officers and mineral reservations proposals touched off disputes yesterday at the St. Louis County DFL convention in the Spalding Hotel...

Harry Munger, Duluth, was elected county chairman, succeeding State Rep. Peter Fugina, Virginia, who held the post the past four years.

(*Duluth News Tribune*, April 4, 1960.)

Willard's ability to enjoy his brother's political success was soon eclipsed by personal tragedy.

Mrs. Martha B. Munger, 45, wife of a Duluth state legislator and active in civic affairs, died of a long illness today in a Duluth hospital. She lived at 7408 Grand Avenue with her husband, State Rep. Willard Munger.

Mrs. Munger was president of the Duluth Council of Parent-Teacher Associations from 1957-59 and was also past president of the Fairmont-Norton Park and the Ely-West PTA's and active in Denfeld PTA.

Born in Fergus Falls, Mrs. Munger was a Duluth resident for 25 years. She was a member of Our Savior's Lutheran Church. She and her husband operated the Willard Motel.

Mrs. Munger's interests included the DFL Party, the Community Chest, Women's Institute, Girl Scouts, United Northern Sportsmen, and many fund drives, including the Heart Fund and the March of Dimes...

She was a delegate to the White House Conference in 1955 and a delegate to the Governor's Youth Conference. She was also active in the Duluth Centennial Celebration, a trustee for Duluth Educational Television, a member of the board of directors for the Chisholm Museum, and a solicitor for the

Duluth Symphony Orchestra.

Surviving in addition to her husband are a daughter, Mrs. Patricia Carlson; a son, Willard, Jr.; her mother, Mrs. Martha Winter; a brother, Ernest Winter of Duluth; a sister, Mrs. Helen Trueblood, Reseda, CA; a brother, William Winter, Fergus Falls; and two grandchildren.

(Duluth News Tribune, October 6, 1960.)

Martha's influence on Willard was highlighted in a speech he gave a year after her death. The occasion was a benefit dinner to raise money to help pay Martha's medical bills.

I appreciate this honor very deeply...

Willard, Pat, Ed, and I appreciate this wonderful occasion and we also appreciate the kind and thoughtful consideration given Martha when she was sick. We shall never forget it...

On behalf of Martha and you...I have made a determined effort to pass this [the sanitary district] bill. The passage of this legislation I feel is a dedication to her for all the time and energy she gave to help promote this legislation for the past 15 years. One of her requests in St. Luke's was that I go out and get re-elected and then get this bill enacted into law...

(Willard Munger Personal Collection.)

In November of 1960, Richard Nixon was endorsed by the *Duluth News Tribune* over John F. Kennedy for the presidency. Conservative Elmer L. Andersen was running against Liberal Governor Orville Freeman. Andersen, in a break with his own party, opposed the implementation of a state-wide sales tax.

When the final votes were counted, Willard Munger outpolled Francis LaBrosse in the 59th Legislative District, a small consolation following the personal loss Munger had suffered a month before the election. Both Munger and LaBrosse retained their respective seats. The vote tally was:

Munger: 16,470

LaBrosse: 14,927

Johnson: 7,316

Treviranus: 5,854.

There was an 89.9% voter turnout in Duluth for the 1960 election. In a close race, John F. Kennedy was installed as America's first Roman Catholic president and Elmer L. Andersen defeated Orville Freeman to become governor of the state of Minnesota.

CHAPTER 9

Elmer L. Andersen

Elmer L. Andersen wrestled administrative control of the state of Minnesota away from the DFL with his surprising victory in the 1960 gubernatorial election. Orville Freeman had been a popular three term (the terms remained two years until 1964) chief executive but, in the end, Minnesotans, despite voting for a Democrat for president and returning a Liberal majority to both chambers of the state legislature, put a Republican in charge of the state for the first time since 1954.

Andersen was a moderate Republican and two years older than Willard Munger, having been born in Chicago, Illinois in 1909. He was the son of Scandinavian immigrants and, like Munger, a "self-starter"; working odd jobs at an early age to assist his family. Upon completing his first two years in junior college, Andersen became a traveling salesman, a position which brought him to Minnesota. Once in Minnesota, Andersen furthered his education at the University of Minnesota, obtaining a four-year business degree.

Andersen worked as a salesman for the H.B. Fuller Company, a St. Paul-based industrial supply firm, eventually buying into the company and expanding the company's reach until it became an international supplier of adhesives. He also ran successfully for the state senate as a Conservative from St. Paul in 1949, serving until 1958, when he declined to seek re-election. At the urging of fellow Republicans, Andersen ran for governor in 1960 and won. In an interesting twist, Elmer L. Andersen adopted a position that Liberals had espoused for years.

> I favored taxation based on ability to pay. That's why I opposed proposals to institute a sales tax, unless low-income Minnesotans, senior citizens, and people raising large families could somehow be spared its burden. Many other Republicans preferred a sales tax to the income tax. Freeman spent a lot of campaign time and energy trying to link me to that position. But he could

not make his charge stick. My opposition was one of the reasons that Minnesota had no sales tax until 1967.

(*A Man's Reach*, Elmer L. Andersen, University of Minnesota Press, 2000, p. 187.)

Andersen's victory was by no means a landslide. He won the 1960 gubernatorial election by 22,000 votes, exactly the margin by which Kennedy carried Minnesota. (By way of contrast, Hubert Humphrey won re-election to the U.S. Senate by 200,000 votes). Andersen understood that his victory was, in essence, a referendum against Freeman's quest for another term.

> I may have been tempted to give all the credit for the victory to my Republican team and me. But I knew I had been helped by a number of DFLers who thought Freeman had been governor long enough. He was seeking an unprecedented fourth two-year term in 1960. That bothered some people, even those who liked him. Minnesota was used to frequent turnover in the governor's office. Two-year gubernatorial terms had been the law since statehood was granted, and single-term governors were not uncommon...Some DFLers told me privately that they considered Freeman and his people a bottleneck to the ambitions of younger Democrats. They wanted him to move on...
>
> (*A Man's Reach*, ibid, p. 192.)

Having served on the Senate Conservation Committee in the early 1950s, Andersen had a deep appreciation for Minnesota's natural resources (*A Man's Reach*, ibid, p. 139.) Though their political leanings would, at times, cause friction in their relationship, Willard Munger and Elmer L. Andersen established a life-long admiration and respect for each other that culminated in personal friendship.

> Congratulations on your re-election. I am sure you look forward to again serving the people of your district during the next two years...
>
> [I]f you are in St. Paul before the session begins, please stop by our temporary office, 113 State Capitol. I would certainly welcome a visit.
>
> Cordially,
>
> Elmer L. Andersen
>
> Governor-Elect

Andersen understood, given his narrow victory in 1960, the need to reach out to DFLers.

November 25, 1960

Will you join other 8th District legislators as my guest for supper, Friday, December 2 at 7:00 P.M. in the Spalding Hotel?

In addition to getting acquainted, I would like to obtain your analysis and opinion of the economic situation in Northeastern Minnesota.

Cordially yours,

Elmer L. Andersen

Governor-Elect

Elmer Andersen appreciated the extent of the economic downturn in northeastern Minnesota and used that knowledge to his political advantage.

Then as now, northeastern Minnesota was a DFL bastion. But mindful of the weakness of the mining industry, I campaigned there many times and put forward a series of proposals for stimulating the region's economy. I wanted to assure the mining companies that they would be taxed equitably as they developed the taconite industry. I suggested a job-training program for youth and a retraining program for older workers, coupled with incentives to attract new businesses to the area. One industry I wanted to flourish was tourism. I proposed the establishment of a nonprofit organization that could draw on federal, state and private resources to improve and promote recreational opportunities, and I urged more attention to conservation of natural resources. Before long, the *Minneapolis Star* reported that a "guerilla war" was being waged on my behalf among disenfranchised DFLers on the Iron Range…

(*A Man's Reach*, ibid, p. 188.)

Despite the governor's attempts to reach out to Liberals, there were fences that needed mending before the governor-elect could count on Liberal support.

October 19, 1960

Press Release

The Republican candidate for governor, Elmer L. Andersen, touring the Iron Range area of Northeastern Minnesota, has unleashed an attack upon two Duluth Democrats, Gerald Heaney and Harry Munger.

Speaking to street crowds this morning, Andersen charged that the DFL administration is not concerning itself with the need for jobs on the Range, the need for full work weeks, and the need for business-industry development in Northeastern Minnesota.

"But," Andersen said, "they are concerning themselves with paying off their political henchmen with state funds."

Andersen said there are 150 lawyers in Duluth, "yet only two law firms in the city received funds from the state in 1958 and 1959 for services rendered for highway department searches."

In talks in Grand Rapids, Coleraine and Bovey, Andersen cited figures showing that "Gerald Heaney of Duluth was paid $6,500 in 1958 and 1959 while he was a DFL National Committeeman, and the law firm of Merriman and Munger was paid $23,809 in 1959 for services rendered."

Munger was appointed DFL chairman for St. Louis County in the spring of this year, Andersen said.

"He obviously was well rewarded for his party work. And it appears to me this is an effort by the Highway Department thru a political arm to reward the party faithful."

(Harry Munger Personal Collection.)

Andersen's accusations had drawn an immediate response during the campaign.

October 24, 1960

To the Editor:

On October 19th, the Star published a statement by the Republican candidate for governor that the law firm of Merriman and Munger, of which I am senior partner, received $23,809.00 from the highway department for services rendered. This statement was a distortion of the truth. The fact of the matter is that of the amount our firm received, we paid $11,261.30 to Consolidated Abstract Company of Duluth for abstracting charges...

During the two year period mentioned, our firm rendered opinions...to over 650 separate tracts or parcels of land...on more than 20 highway department projects...The average cost of each title opinion per parcel of land... was less than $23.00 which is below the fee prescribed by the Advisory Fee Schedule of the Minnesota Bar Association...

In conclusion, I believe it would be fair to state that our firm received a reasonable and fair fee for services honestly rendered...

Very truly yours,

Donald Merriman

(*Minneapolis Star*, undated.)

As Willard Munger readied himself for the '61 legislative session, he was constantly reminded of his personal loss.

January 4, 1961

Dear Mr. Munger:

Thank you for the lovely card and the clipping. We're very sorry to hear the bad news about your lovely wife. It was hard to believe that she had to go and suffer like that. She must have been a wonderful person to have such a lovely write-up in the paper like that...

We're proud to have been neighbors to such remarkable people.

Mary and Ben Re

Bell Gardens, California

Despite the affects of Martha's passing, 1961 proved to be a pivotal year for Munger's environmental agenda when the legislature passed, and Governor Andersen signed into law, Sanitary District legislation.

Sanitary Districts

H.F. 492 is a bill dealing with the problem of water pollution and control in our state. It is a bill to carry out the intent and recommendations of the Legislative Interim Water Pollution Study Commission...

I feel there are but two roads to take in dealing with water pollution. First, the establishment of an orderly long-range program as provided for in this Sanitary District Bill, that has proven good in other states; or, secondly, the shot gun approach to the problem, of which would primarily depend upon policing and heavy fines. I do not believe in the second approach, but, if, however, we do not recognize and adopt a sound approach now, we can expect this type of legislation. The public is demanding that this problem be met now...

(Press Release, February 28, 1961; Willard Munger Personal Collection.)

The Sanitary District legislation was not only the culmination of six years of political toil by Munger; it was a piece of major legislation. What had started as a sketchy notion within the United Northern Sportsmen had evolved, over time, into a detailed plan to clean up Minnesota's lakes, rivers and streams. There was really only one man responsible for this transformation. That one man was Willard Munger. Without his dogged determination, the law would have died on the vine in 1955 when Munger's short-sighted legislative colleagues believed that $25,000 was too high a price to pay to study water pollution. But like the German-American characters in a Herbert Krause novel, Willard Marcus Munger was not one to give up.

Commentators across the state expressed support for Munger's vision.

One of the most significant pieces of legislation passed by the recent session of the legislature was the Munger Water Pollution Control Bill which was passed by the House the other day by a vote of 113 to 0 after several amendments offered by the Senate had been approved…

Minnesota is in a unique position. We are not only the birthplace of the "Father of Waters"; we are also the "Mother of Waters." No rivers or streams flow into Minnesota. All of our streams flow out. Thus, if we are polluting waters, there is no one but ourselves to blame…

The Munger bill points the way to the nation to put a stop to water pollution. Its enactment…means that once again our state can become the "Land of Sky Blue Waters." And as our water becomes clean and pure as it flows out of our state, it may be an example for other states to follow so that one day they too can have clean, unpolluted lakes and streams to be used and enjoyed as they were meant to be by our Creator.

(*Delano Eagle*, March 18, 1961.)

Munger was quick to give credit for the passage of the bill to his fallen lady slipper.

June 6, 1961

Dear Curt:

I would like to express my appreciation for the editorial concerning the passage of the Water Pollution Bill which I authored in the past legislative session…

My wife Martha was a zealous proponent of water pollution control and I had promised her my continuing efforts to obtain passage of regulatory laws. It is gratifying to have been able to fulfill this promise…

Willard Munger

(Letter to Curt Miller, Editor, *Labor World.*)

During the 1961 legislative session, Munger was able to count on the support of Governor Andersen for the Sanitary District bill. But Andersen's whole-hearted support of Munger's conservation work didn't insulate the governor from DFL scrutiny.

Harry L. Munger, St. Louis County DFL chairman…charged that Governor Elmer L. Andersen has developed a homing pigeon instinct toward Washington D.C. and federal aid.

Munger's statement was prompted by the contention of Wayne Popham, Fifth District GOP chairman, that three DFL Congressmen are a year behind Governor Andersen in urging a fast tax write-off for the taconite industry…

Munger said [Congressman John] Blatnik procured accelerated tax write-offs for the taconite industry during the Korean War. These, he pointed out, were killed by George Humphrey, a Republican, then Secretary of the Treasury.

(*Duluth News Tribune*, August 10, 1961.)

Other DFLers also criticized the governor.

Ray Hemenway, Democratic national committeeman for Minnesota... charged that Republican Governor Elmer L. Andersen has proved himself to be a puppet of the steel lobby.

"The only leadership Elmer Andersen has shown since becoming governor," said Hemenway, "has been to give the steel lobby a favorable tax position by a constitutional amendment so that the steel interests would have low taxation on taconite and semi-taconite ores for all time to come..."

Hemenway declared, "It is high time that Governor Andersen explains his support of the taconite tax giveaway amendment while the steel industry is paying private landowners one dollar a ton for taconite ore but when mining state-owned land, only pays twelve cents a ton for the same ore to the state of Minnesota. As a matter of fact," said Hemenway, "the first real indication people of this state had that Governor Andersen was thinking of calling a special legislative session again was when they read the full page advertisement in the newspapers of this state some three weeks ago paid for by the steel lobby in an effort to justify the proposed taconite amendment...The only conclusion we can come to," said Hemenway, "is that the steel lobby had advance knowledge of Andersen's plans for a special session..."

(Press Release, August 10, 1961; Harry Munger Personal Collection.)

The extractive nature of northeastern Minnesota's economy was in dire circumstances. A squabble arose over the so-called "Taconite Amendment"; legislation sponsored by the Governor Andersen and legislators from northeastern Minnesota proposing tax breaks for taconite (low-grade iron ore) mining and processing companies.

Eighth District Republicans formally adopted a resolution commending efforts for a taconite amendment—including efforts by its Liberal backers—after hearing a determined speech on the issue by Gov. Elmer L. Andersen in Duluth...

Andersen said that despite efforts to assist the economy of northeastern Minnesota, "there just isn't a substitute for a payroll." And he referred to Democratic-Farmer-Labor Leaders who oppose the amendment as "confoundedly stupid."

He said that DFL discussion of direct reduction is a "smoke screen..."

Before there can be a state-wide vote on the amendment, it must be passed by the legislature. At the 1961 session, the amendment died in the Liberal-controlled House of Representatives Tax Committee...

The governor noted that Democratic Secretary of Commerce Luther Hodges said in Rochester Friday that it appears mining companies need assurances on tax policy before they will invest in taconite plants.

He also noted that Rep. John Blatnik of Chisholm has supported an amendment and State. Rep. Fred A. Cina, Aurora, leader of the House Liberals, was chief author of the measure in the last session.

(*Duluth News Tribune*, October 8, 1961.)

Many residents of northeastern Minnesota believed that, without concessions in the tax structure for mining companies, the wave of new taconite mines and plants that had begun with Reserve Mining was doomed to cessation. Taconite was seen as the economic salvation of the region, though taxation of iron ore and taconite was an issue that Minnesota legislators had wrestled with since the onset of iron mining in the state.

History of Iron Ore Taxation

The first law imposing a tax upon iron mining was passed by the legislature of 1881 which imposed a tonnage tax of one cent for each ton of ore mined and shipped...In 1898, the State Supreme Court...held the tonnage law unconstitutional...

Since the repeal of the tonnage tax law, iron ore mined or unmined has been taxed like any other property on an ad valorem basis...

In 1922, the Minnesota Constitution was amended so as to permit an occupation tax upon the business of mining or producing iron ore.

In 1923, the legislature enacted the royalty tax law which imposes a tax upon all royalties received...

In 1941, the taconite tax law was enacted...The proceeds of the taconite tax [5 cents per gross ton plus]...The proceeds of the taconite tax are apportioned 22% to the city, town or village, 50% to the school district, 22% to the county and 6% to the state...

(Undated, Willard Munger Personal Collection.)

Willard Munger opposed the original version of the taconite amendment because he deemed it "too generous" to the mining companies. He supported tax incentives via legislation: he was not in favor of using a constitutional amendment to revitalize the mining industry. Despite the fact that Munger would eventually come around to supporting a constitutional amendment providing tax breaks for taconite mining firms, his initial reluctance to follow the governor's lead was seen as out of step by other Liberal legislators from northeastern Minnesota.

In the midst of the debate regarding the taconite amendment, Munger faced another, perhaps even more serious disagreement, within the DFL.

DFL Lieutenant Governor Karl Rolvaag, who had successfully held onto his spot even while his running mate, Governor Freeman, was ousted (the Minnesota system allowed, at the time, the governor and lieutenant governor to be from different parties) announced he would run for governor. This announcement put Willard Munger in the awkward position of deciding whether his personal friendship with Elmer L. Andersen or party loyalty would dictate who he would support in the upcoming election.

Rolvaag, like Freeman, was a WWII veteran. After serving as a tank commander in Europe, Rolvaag (son of Norwegian-American author Ole Rolvaag) studied Norway's political system before returning to Minnesota. Rolvaag then became active in the DFL, serving as the party's leader in the early 1950s before running in tandem with Freeman. Rolvaag remained lieutenant governor under Freeman for three terms and served under Andersen for one more term before deciding to run for the top state administrative position in 1962.

When Elmer L. Andersen learned of Rolvaag's decision to run against him, Andersen immediately sought support from his political friends.

> June 20, 1962
>
> Dear Representative Munger:
>
> Representative Peter Fugina has recently announced the formation of a Legislators for Rolvaag for Governor Committee and you are listed as a member.
>
> There are three statements in the letter reading as follows:
>
> "The present governor is obviously a man who cannot even get the cooperation of his own conservative state senate and who obviously has neither the ability nor the desire to work cooperatively with others to solve 8th District problems."
>
> "We believe that the administration of Governor Elmer L. Andersen has been one of hollow, bitter meaninglessness."
>
> "We believe that the Andersen administration has been totally without substance and offers no promise for the future of the people of the 8th District or the State."

I would just like to know from you personally, that this is your considered opinion and a judgment you personally wish to support.

Frankly, as one who has known and worked with you, I would be surprised if you would want to support such a statement. But I would like you to indicate whether you do or do not support such a position.

Sincerely yours,

Elmer L. Andersen

Governor

Receiving no response, Andersen wrote a second time.

July 2, 1962

Dear Representative Munger:

You have not answered my letter of June 20…This I regret.

I can only conclude that the statements quoted in the letter are a correct expression of your position.

It is not possible to preserve a spirit of private friendship and cooperation with people who insult me publicly and indulge in unfounded personal attacks.

I repeat, I don't want it this way, and I deeply regret it. It is your decision—and unless I hear from you I can only conclude that you personally support the statements of the committee referred to in my letter of June 20.

Sincerely yours,

Elmer L. Andersen

Governor

There is no record that Munger responded.

In the midst of the looming battle between Rolvaag and Andersen, Willard Munger continued his work on behalf of the environment by serving on the Great Lakes Commission. The commission is an eight state (Illinois, Indiana, Michigan, Minnesota, New York, Ohio, Pennsylvania, and Wisconsin) organization which was formed in 1955. The commission's stated purpose is to "promote the orderly, integrated and comprehensive development, use and conservation of the water resources of the Great Lakes Basin." Munger advised the commission of the passage of the Sanitary District legislation in Minnesota at a meeting held at the Grand Hotel on Mackinac Island, Michigan. (Notes of Speech dated July 22-24, 1962; Willard Munger Personal Collection.)

Willard also touted his service on the commission in a campaign profile during the 1962 campaign.

> State Rep. Willard Munger, Duluth, filed for re-election to the 59th District House seat…Munger is seeking his fifth term in the House. He is chairman of the Duluth Legislative Delegation and of the House Elections Committee, and is a member of the Appropriations, Education, University and Employees Compensation committees of the House.
>
> He is also a member of the Great Lakes Commission and the Legislative Research Committee's subcommittee on Forestry and Conservation. He is the owner and operator of the Willard Motel, 7408 Grand Ave. in Duluth.
>
> *(Duluth News Tribune,* July 14, 1962.)

The 1962 gubernatorial race proved to be the closest in Minnesota history. The day after the election, Rolvaag held a slim lead of 115 votes with 7 precincts remaining to be counted. After a recount, that margin slipped to 91 votes. But Andersen, always the gentleman, refused to contest the matter in court and Karl Rolvaag succeeded Elmer L. Andersen as governor.

In the 59th Legislative District, where Conservative D.T. Grussendorf was once again running against LaBrosse and Munger, the finally tally was:

Munger: 11,889

LaBrosse: 11,554

Grussendorf: 8,934

Munger and LaBrosse retained their legislative seats, as did fellow 59th District Liberal, Senator Homer Carr (who ran unopposed). But Munger's first-place finish over LaBrosse (for the second election in a row) fostered a sense of ill-conceived political hubris which would prove disastrous.

CHAPTER 10

An Improvident Choice

The following year, 1962, brought changes to Willard Munger's political status.

> Rep. Willard Munger announced today that he plans to step down as chairman of the Duluth delegation to the Minnesota Legislature in January.
>
> The 59th District legislator has been delegation chairman for the last four years. He said the job should be given to another lawmaker…
>
> (*Duluth News Tribune*, November 13, 1962.)

Munger's action did not mean that he was finished accepting leadership roles within the DFL Party.

> Two St. Louis County legislators have been elected to a Liberal steering committee for the 1963 legislative session. Two other area lawmakers are automatically members of the group.
>
> Elected to the committee were Rep. Jack Fena, Hibbing, and Willard Munger, Duluth…Munger said it will be a policy committee along the lines of the House Rules Committee. Conservatives, who will take control of the House from Liberals at the session…will have entire membership of the powerful Rules Committee…Munger said he and Fena were elected from fellow Liberals.
>
> (*Duluth News Tribune*, December 4, 1962.)

One fellow northeastern Minnesota legislator with whom Munger shared a common philosophy was attorney Lawrence Yetka from Cloquet. Though too young to have directly participated in the Farmer-Labor movement, Yetka's father (Frank) served as Insurance Commissioner and Minnesota Fire Marshal under Floyd B. Olson during the 1930s. According to Yetka, one of the most memorable stories his father told took place during Benson's 1938 re-election bid. Benson, who was campaigning in Cloquet, asked Yetka's father how the election looked.

"My father told him, 'Your association with the Communists isn't helping you one bit,'" Larry Yetka recalls, "which prompted the governor to fly into a rage. Benson then asked Willard: 'Is my leftist outlook going to ruin the Party?' To which Willard replied without missing a beat: 'No, Governor, you've already done that.'"

Yetka indicates that, in his view, Benson's ultra-Liberalism was the governor's downfall. According to Yetka, there was also an element of corruption to Benson because he had accumulated a small fortune as the state's Banking Commissioner, a well-known circumstance which didn't bother Benson (whose philosophy seemed to be: "I got where I am playing by the rules that are in place and I won by those rules.")

After graduating from the University of Minnesota Law School, Larry Yetka returned to Cloquet to practice law with his father. The younger Yetka became involved with the DFL Party and attended the 1948 state DFL convention where he met Willard Munger. Both men were then elected to the Minnesota House of Representatives in 1954, '56, and '58. Yetka left the House in 1960 to concentrate on his law practice but remained active in DFL politics.

Larry Yetka recalls Rolvaag's gubernatorial victory as being formulated out of internal struggle within the DFL. There was a question whether Rolvaag or a young legislator from Rochester, A.M. "Sandy" Keith should run against Elmer L. Andersen. Walter Mondale, who was the Attorney General and younger than Rolvaag, was seen by some, including Yetka, as a dynamic alternative to the hard-drinking Rolvaag. But in the end, Rolvaag was the nominee with Keith agreeing to take the lieutenant governor position. Yetka observes that Keith's tenacity in the DFL in-fighting was a foreshadowing of things to come. "Keith would run over his own grandmother to win an election," says Yetka. (Yetka should know: He later served as a justice on the Minnesota Supreme Court during Keith's tenure as chief justice).

After Rolvaag's inauguration in 1963, the internal DFL dispute regarding the taconite amendment became public.

Area Legislators Favor Taconite Amendment

A poll of the St. Louis County legislative delegation shows a 13-2 vote in favor of a constitutional amendment on taconite taxes.

County legislators were less firm, however, when queried about prospects of passing an amendment at a statewide vote...

Rep. Fred Cina, Aurora, said changes should be made in the proposal if they are necessary to gather more support...

In opposition were Reps. Peter Fugina, Virginia, and Willard Munger, Duluth.

Fugina said he is opposed in principle to having the taconite tax issue in the Constitution, but has said he would support a taconite statute...

Munger said he favors a statute...

(*Duluth News Tribune*, February 7, 1963.)

Munger supported *statutory* tax incentives for the mining companies but opposed a constitutional *amendment* giving them favorable treatment.

Taconite Bill Seems Set for Easy Approval by Bob Weber

The taconite amendment introduced Friday in the Minnesota House of Representatives appears headed for a generally favorable reception...

Conservatives, who hold the majority with 79 votes in the 135-member House, appeared fairly solid for passage...

The holdout among Duluth House members is Rep. Willard Munger, Liberal.

"I told the people before the election last Nov. 6 that I opposed the taconite amendment," he said. "I did my own thinking then, and I'm doing it now..."

(*Minneapolis Star*, February 2, 1963.)

Munger also continued to work on conservation-related bills, seeking, for example, to re-introduce moose hunting in Minnesota. Later in his legislative career, Munger would come to blows with other DFLers over his positions relating to the Boundary Waters Canoe Area; Voyageurs National Park; the use of snowmobiles in state and national parks; the trapping of timber wolves; and the hunting of mourning doves, most notably battling State Senator Bob Lessard (DFL-International Falls) on these and many other natural resource issues. Lessard tried to paint Munger as anti-hunting and fishing, which was never the case. Much of what Willard Munger stood for in the conservation arena came from his close association with the United Northern Sportsmen, a group deeply committed to preserving hunting and fishing rights in Minnesota.

Minnesota Moose Season Bill Introduced by Munger

Rep. Willard Munger, Duluth, proposed establishment of a Minnesota moose hunting season in a bill introduced...in the House...

The bill would allow hunting in areas designated by the state conservation commissioner...

The bill proposes a maximum of 2,000 licenses per year with as many as three names on a license...

The last moose season in Minnesota was in 1922, when the "take" was 219.

(*Duluth News Tribune*, February 14, 1963.)

Another conservation issue that surfaced during the 1963 session involved the size of nets and boats used by commercial fisherman in Minnesota.

Lake Fishing Bills on Nets, Fees Approved

Approved 110 – 7 was a bill allowing the use of pound nets in Lake Superior...

Rep. Willard Munger, Duluth, argued that the proposal is a "bad bill," but Rep. William House, Two Harbors, the author, replied that Munger "doesn't know what he's talking about."

Munger contends that the big pound nets would harm the herring and trout populations...

House, however, said Munger is incorrect. Rep. E.J. Chilgren, Littlefork, agreed...saying the use of the nets would help rid the lake of rough fish and would help protect more desirable species...

(*Duluth News Tribune*, March 3, 1963.)

In this brief exchange, one can see the tension between Munger and Chilgren, something Willard recalled when speaking in his oral history about the selection of a chairman for the Interim Study Committee.

Chilgren hailed from the same "neck of the woods" as Senator Bob Lessard where commercial fishing on Lake of the Woods and Rainy Lake was an important economic activity. Munger was always wary of exploitation of Minnesota's natural resources, whether by large multi-national mining and timber companies, or by individuals. His concerns regarding commercial fishing in Minnesota soon brought him in conflict with an old ally.

March 14, 1963

Dear Mr. Munger:

We sincerely hope that you will support H.F. 910 relative to eliminating the 35 foot maximum length of boats that can be used by commercial fishermen in their operations on Lake Superior...

I fail to see where the present law makes much sense. Doesn't it seem more reasonable that on a lake as cold and rough as Lake Superior can get, that if there should be a law limiting the size boat a fisherman could use, it should be as to the minimum size for safety, rather than the maximum…

Sincerely yours,

Sivertson Brothers Fisheries

Stanley S. Sivertson

Stanley Sivertson was a commercial fisherman on Lake Superior who had opposed the discharge of taconite tailings into the lake by Reserve Mining. On the issue of boat sizes allowed for commercial fishing, Sivertson and Munger were clearly at odds.

There is no need to change the present law. The present 35 foot boat restriction protects our industry…Wisconsin licenses 88 boats over 35 feet. Minnesota only has 6 at the 35 foot size. This bill would allow this tug boat fleet to move into our North Shore and destroy our fishing industry…

(Speech to the legislature, Willard Munger Personal Collection.)

Munger also remained concerned with the issue of atomic fallout, an issue he'd raised in previous legislative sessions. Munger's solution was to seek passage of H.F. 1072 (March 13, 1963), which was a non-binding resolution to ask Congress to act nationally on the issue of strontium 90 and radioactive iodine in milk.

In keeping with his Farmer-Labor roots, Munger also tackled the issue of unfair trade during the 1963 session.

Munger Presses Unfair Trade Bill

Rep. Willard Munger, Duluth, said today he may seek a committee hearing next week on his bill against unfair trade practices…

His bill involves sale of items below cost…

Rep. Alfred France, Duluth, an author of the bill with Munger, said that "to the end that this legislation prevents the public from being misled, I think it's very good and very much needed."

(*Duluth Herald*, March 14, 1963.)

Convincing a business advocate like Al France (who lobbied for the iron mining industry after he left legislature) to co-author a law regulating business competition was no small feat. But Willard Munger was able to facilitate such cooperation throughout his legislative career.

An important personal matter occupied Munger's attention during the summer of 1964.

Mrs. Frances Herou, Minneapolis, and State Rep. Willard Munger, 6408 Grand Avenue, were married in an evening ceremony July 2 in Our Savior's Lutheran Church, Duluth. Only the immediate family attended the ceremony, including Munger's daughter and family, Mr. and Mrs. Edward Carlson and children, Cynthia and Cheryl, and his son, Willard Munger, Jr., and his mother, Mrs. Elsie Munger.

After a brief honeymoon on the North Shore, Mr. and Mrs. Munger are residing at 6408 Grand Ave. Both have been widowed since 1960.

(*Duluth News Tribune*, July, 1964.)

Frances Herou had been born Francis Hotch in Minneapolis, Minnesota in 1916. She graduated from Minneapolis Roosevelt High School and received advanced secretarial training before marrying Dr. Ralph Herou, a chiropractor. Frances was a widower when she and Willard Munger began spending time together in 1963. Though Frances would never be a replacement for the intense romantic love that Willard enjoyed with Martha, Willard would remain married to Frances for nearly thirty-three years, longer than he had been with his beloved lady slipper.

"Dad had known Frances for years," Patsy Munger-Lehr recalls. "I think Connie Nelson and his wife fixed them up because they had both lost their spouses. Frances was living in the Cities. They got together for dinner and started seeing each other. Frances wasn't my mother but I liked her a great deal."

"Frances was a good person," Will, Jr. recalls, "and good for my dad. She was the one who really hounded him to do something about DDT. She was the one who suggested Dad push to change the national anthem to 'America the Beautiful' because it was more peaceful. Frances wasn't my mom. Dad loved Mom. I think he married Frances for companionship. She was the one who got him to buy the Airstream trailer (a trailer Willard parked in a St. Paul trailer park during legislative sessions for his lodging)."

"Frances was always worried about what Willard ate," adds State Representative Mike Jaros (DFL-Duluth). "She was always watching him because he loved sweets. He'd even sneak a cigarette or two with his aide, Jackie Rosholt, when Jackie went out for a smoke break. If Frances knew that, she would have killed him!

" I remember driving them to the Cities and stopping for gas. Willard went in to use the restroom and came back with his pockets stuffed with candy. As we're driving down the road, he handed me candy so Frances, who's in the back seat, couldn't see. His mouth was full of candy and she asked 'Willard, are you eating something?' He answered her in a voice so mumbled from all the candy, she couldn't understand him. That was Willard. He was always sneaking cake and pie.

"I think Willard loved Frances but he never got over being married to Martha. Up until the very end, he kept Martha's picture in his wallet. You'd see that picture every time he'd open up his wallet."

That year also brought the completion of the motel. For years, Munger had wanted to have a larger and more private living space, a bigger motel office, a formal lobby, and a coffee shop as part of the complex. When the addition to the motel was completed in 1964, it added a number of rooms, a coffee shop, an office, and a spacious private residence complete with an expansive living room with a fireplace. Though it wasn't the home that Martha had always dreamed of, the new arrangement was clearly a step up from the crowded kitchenette that Willard and Martha had lived in during their last years together.

But the most significant event of 1964 wasn't Munger's second marriage or the completion of the motel expansion; it was his decision to challenge Francis "Frenchie" LaBrosse for the senate seat formerly occupied by Willard's close friend and political mentor, Homer Carr. Carr had passed away, leaving his senate seat vacant. It was Munger's belief that, since he and Carr were fast friends and shared Liberal ideals, he was Carr's logical successor in the Minnesota Senate.

"I was the 8th District chairman at the time," Justice Larry Yetka recalls. "Willard's younger brother, Harry, was the St. Louis County Chair. I knew that both Frenchie and Willard wanted the seat. But Frenchie had served in the House longer. John Blatnik asked me to talk to Willard since we were close friends. So I did. I told Willard, 'Frenchie has a better chance—why not step aside and allow him to run? You can stay in the House and build seniority, and, when the time is right, run for the senate.'

"The thought amongst those in power in the 8th Congressional District was that if they ran against each other, there was a chance we'd lose both House seats in the 59th because they couldn't run for both the House and the Senate in the general election. Willard told me to 'go to hell.' Blatnik thought I could reason with Willard. I couldn't."

Judge Gerald Heaney doesn't recall Blatnik getting involved in the issue.

"But if Larry says Blatnik said that," Heaney concedes, "he probably did. Willard had most of the DFLers," Heaney recounts. "But LaBrosse probably picked up a third of the Democrats and he got all of the Republican votes, which put him over the top. It was a battle royale. The toughest battle I've ever seen. I don't think that Willard saw himself as the successor to Homer Carr. I'd downplay that. I think Willard ran because he felt he was a true Liberal and Frenchie wasn't."

"I worked in Dad's headquarters when he ran against LaBrosse in 1964," Will Munger, Jr. remembers. "Things were going pretty well. They both sailed through the primary. But then, for some reason, Dad thought he needed to debate Frenchie one last time at UMD before the election. I told Dad to get there early so that the crowd could see him first. He refused. He let LaBrosse get there ahead of him and then, when Dad finally got there, he was nervous. He insisted on wearing a bow tie, something he did back then. So LaBrosse had this grand entrance and then my dad shows up with his bow tie falling off. I know Patsy thinks Dad had a mini-stroke due to the pressure of that event. I don't know. But he did limp after that."

"Willard and I talked about whether he should run for Carr's seat," Harry Munger, Jr. recalls. "Willard felt, that, since he was a great friend of Homer Carr's, he should run. I agreed. I went to the precinct caucuses to get him support. I was the County DFL Chair at the time. The Party ended up endorsing Willard instead of LaBrosse. LaBrosse took exception to that and announced he wouldn't abide by the endorsement. They both ran in the primary and Willard won but because there was no party designation back then, both Willard and LaBrosse went on to the general election. But a number of things came up between the primary and the general election that hurt Willard.

"First, the taconite amendment resurfaced. While it was true that Willard opposed the original language of the proposal because it was too open-ended and too favorable to the mining companies, he supported the bill that eventually became law. But his initial reluctance hurt him on the Iron Range and in Proctor.

"Then Humphrey sent a letter to LaBrosse on the eve of the election. The letter became public knowledge. It thanked LaBrosse for his support of Humphrey's health insurance legislation.

"And both Willard and I managed to anger Heaney and Yetka, which meant that none of the powerful DFLers came into the district to help Willard. Blatnik, Heaney and Yetka made it clear, before the convention, that their choice to succeed Homer Carr was LaBrosse. But Willard was determined to replace his friend and mentor and so, we disregarded their advice. Their animosity meant that no one on the state or national level, with the exception of Fritz Mondale and one visit by Sandy Keith, came into the district to support Willard. Fritz Mondale stuck by Willard but it wasn't enough.

Finally, there was the debate at UMD. Willard's trademark bow tie was all messed up and he floundered badly. He wasn't up to snuff and shouldn't have been there.

It was a disaster. After that, Heaney finally came out in support of Willard but it was too late. And LaBrosse had a mole by the name of Annula in our campaign who knew what we were going to do before we did it. They had a leg up on us because of that."

Patsy Munger-Lehr believes that her father did indeed suffer a mini-stroke either before, during or after the ill-fated debate at UMD. There is no medical evidence to support this hypothesis, but anecdotally, Willard developed a slight limp after the debate that plagued him the remainder of his life.

Whatever the physical consequences of running a hotly contested legislative campaign during the same year as entering a new marriage and completing a major remodeling project at the motel, the results at the polls were not as Willard Munger had planned.

> **LaBrosse Whips Munger**
>
> State Representative Frances E. LaBrosse handed the DFL Party a smashing blow by beating State Representative Willard Munger in the 59th District race for state senate...Both were Liberal members of the House seeking the post left vacant by the death of Homer Carr of Proctor. Munger had the endorsement of the DFL and the organization pitched the power of Governor Karl Rolvaag, Lt. Governor A.M [Sandy] Keith, Walter F. Mondale [Minnesota Attorney General] and George Farr, Chair of the State DFL in the race. Keith and Mondale campaigned personally in the district.
>
>   (*Duluth Herald,* undated.)

LaBrosse was the victor with 12,341 votes to Munger's 11,010. Willard Munger lost by a margin of 1,331 votes out of more than 23,000 votes cast. In addition, as had been feared by Heaney, Blatnik and Yetka, the Conservatives won both House seats in the 59th District.

The aftermath of the 1964 election continued long after the votes were counted. Correspondence between Larry Yetka and the Munger brothers confirms the depths of the schism that developed after Willard's defeat.

> January 28, 1965
>
> Dear Willard:
>
> [F]irst, of all, you never should have run for the senate. I told you this in March last year, and I think if you would have followed my advice at the time you would have been the most popular man in the city of Duluth right now, and we would have two House members from the 59th District along with a Senator, as well as being one of the most powerful legislators in the Liberal group.

1. We never seem to learn that when there are two Democrats running in the same primary that to endorse one simply leads to the Republican Party playing mischief and voting for the one who is not endorsed...

2. Your debate with LaBrosse at UMD was a complete fiasco. It should never have been entered into if it was conducted in that manner.

3. Your insisting on drawing in the governor, the lt. governor, and other state officials endorsing your candidacy was exactly a repeat of the same mistakes that were made in the Stevenson's defeat in the presidential primary.

4. I, personally, as 8th District chairman, was bound by Committee action [as it relates to expending funds for races]...I know that your 59th legislative chairman...will verify the fact that I literally begged the Committee for a freer hand in order to help the legislators.

   I have always respected you as a man who has been active in politics for over thirty years, and yet, I was appalled at your making these fundamental errors once again...

   Lawrence Yetka

   Chair, 8th Congressional District DFL

Harry Munger, Jr. wrote a blistering letter to Yetka; only to have Yetka return the diatribe.

> January 29, 1965
>
> Dear Harry:
>
> If being able to turn an adversary's offense into a defense by loud, persistent and overwhelming attack were the sole judge for success in the legal profession, you would be the wealthiest attorney in the Duluth area...
>
> Larry
>
> P.S. Being in an argument with you is like being "dry gulched"—one is hit, hit hard, & then abandoned—left a little hurt, bewildered & alone...

The fight spilled over into the media. Harry, Jr. sought to justify Willard's run in the face of the *Proctor Journal*'s endorsement of LaBrosse, an endorsement that galled the Mungers to no end because it disregarded all the Proctor-related bills Willard had supported.

> **Harry Munger's Petticoats are Showing**
>
> February 11, 1965
>
> Dear Mr. Benson:
>
> Your scandal sheet of Thursday, Jan. 28, 1965 was handed to me...It cer-

tainly would appear that an experienced reporter like yourself would attempt to get all the facts…

1. On January 19, 1965, two meetings were called, both for the same time on January 21st…Patrick McNulty, the duly elected chairman of the coordinating committee, and John Filipovich, the duly elected chairman of the 59th legislative district had called these meetings…It was difficult for me to decide which meeting to go to, as I am a member of both committees, but since the election of officers was on the agenda for the coordinating committee [encompassing the 59th, 60th and 61st Districts] meeting, my choice was to attend that meeting…

2. If you will search your memory and your articles, you will find reference to a quote, following last November's election, attributable to Senator Francis LaBrosse, which stated in essence that he was going to take over the leadership of the DFL Party…

3. While at the coordinating meeting, I saw some faces that I personally didn't recall seeing at the coordinating committee meetings in the past. Two of those faces were those of Roger Hargrave and Glenn Pearson…[M]isters Hargrave and Pearson promptly vacated themselves. They left before any elections were held and it would appear that their true intentions were not for party unity but rather for personal purposes…Neither of these individuals had attended the precinct caucus of the DFL Party last spring and I don't believe that you did either, Mr. Benson…

4. The slate of candidates that was recommended by the nominating committee was not, as you put it, turned down by the "so-called Munger faction." In fact, all of the nominated candidates were elected, except for the position of secretary which was filled by Mary Murphy. Her name was placed in nomination because the 59th District did not have a candidate for any of the offices and it was felt that a district that voted 70% DFL should be entitled to one of the executive officers of the coordinating committee…

May I suggest to you, Editor Benson, that you get on your soap box and start calling for all political parties and all factions thereof to exercise restraint and compassion and to work for better government…

Harry L. Munger

(Proctor Journal, undated.)

Though the acrimony between the Munger brothers and the DFL hierarchy eventually dissipated, Willard Munger never again pursued higher office.

"The reason Willard didn't pursue any higher office after his loss in 1964," Harry, Jr. recalls, "is because he felt he didn't have the education or other qualifications to do so. He wanted to remain in the legislature to mold and pass environmental legislation. And with his seniority (when he returned to the House in 1966) he held the position of Chair of the House Environmental and Natural Resources Committee for much of his career, which gave him a big say in what happened to the environment."

Following his defeat in 1964, Willard hit the road with Frances. The couple toured the southwestern United States and northern Mexico in their battered Ford station wagon and new silver Airstream trailer. The trip was a vacation; not an indication that Willard Munger was through with politics.

Entrepreneur:
A Pictorial

Willard Munger, Ship Foreman (circa 1944).

Willard (right) with co-workers at the Walter Butler Shipyard during winter.

Willard (right) at a ship launching at Walter Butler Shipyards.

Launching of the Dearborn, *September 27, 1943.*
Munger served as foreman of the ship's construction.

The Munger Family, 1950: (Top) Willard Munger, Sr.; Elsie Munger Winter; and Robert Munger. (Bottom) Elsie Zuehlsdorf Munger; Harry Munger, Jr.; and Harry Munger, Sr.

Willard and Martha show off a big catch.

Representative Willard Munger

Willard Munger (second from left) during a 1957 Interim Commission visit to Duluth.

Lyle Brand, United Northern Sportsmen's Club, inspecting pollution in the St. Louis River, 1957.

The Ladyslipper and the Legislator, February, 1960.

Icons of the Minnesota DFL: (from left) Senator McCarthy, Senator Humphrey, Congressman Blatnik; and (standing) Harry Munger, Jr.,

Part Three:

Citizen Legislator

CHAPTER 1

Back to St. Paul

Out of office for the first time since 1954, Willard Munger continued his involvement in the clean-up of the St. Louis River.

> Governor Karl Rolvaag pledged Monday to have a state agency investigate the dumping of ...sewage into the Duluth bay adjacent to the Arena-Auditorium and perhaps demand that the city take emergency measures to solve the problem.
>
> A group of civic leaders brought the pollution problem to Rolvaag's attention during his series of meetings in the county courthouse with Duluthians who wanted to discuss problems with him...
>
> Meeting with the governor were...former State Representative Willard Munger; Glenn Berg, immediate past president of the Arrowhead Civic Club; William Abalan, president of the club; Stanley Allen, chairman of the public health committee of the Duluth Chamber of Commerce; and Joseph Paszak and Curtis Miller representing the Duluth AFL-CIO Central Labor Body.
>
> Rolvaag said he will study the possibility of using a law passed by the legislature in 1963 to get the problem solved. This law would permit the state to order the job done, perhaps do the work itself, and assess the cost against the city. The action would be taken by the state as an emergency measure.
>
> Munger made the suggestion to the governor that this procedure be investigated...
>
> (*Duluth News Tribune*, January 25, 1966.)

Munger also remained active in the DFL Party. As the 1966 elections approached, the DFL found itself embroiled in an internal struggle between Governor Karl Rolvaag and Lieutenant Governor A.M. "Sandy" Keith for the party's gubernatorial endorsement.

59th Seethes After Power Play

The DFL fight in the fitful 59th which began two years ago when the rank and file rebelled against the entrenched party bosses has resumed after a two-year lull...The Munger brothers, Willard and Harry, who imagine they can pattern themselves after the Kennedy brothers, Bob and Teddy, proved for a second time in a month that they have disciplined, personal and tight control of the party machinery...The frontal assault was directed at Proctor in retaliation for its dramatic role in helping elect Sen. Frenchie LaBrosse, the little rebel who refused to be mustered out of politics by the Munger brothers.

They have aligned themselves with Lt. Gov. Sandy Keith against Gov. Karl Rolvaag and are now in position to deliver virtually all of the delegates to Keith...

At the county convention, the Munger contingent, marching in lock-step and on instruction, voted as a block to exclude as delegates those believed to be friendly to the PAC...One militant PAC official professed to be elated with developments...: "They want a fight. We'll give them one. We beat them once and we can do it again. This time we're much stronger and better organized. This time we have influential allies. The Mungerites are losers. They couldn't win the big one when they had everything in their favor. They won't win the one that counts this time either..."

(*Proctor Journal*, April 7, 1966.)

While being anointed "Minnesota's Kennedys" was likely flattering, the Munger brothers were far from wielding the kind of political power the Kennedys claimed in Massachusetts. Still, there was a certain symbiotic chemistry between the dogged and persistent mannerisms of Willard and the fierce competitiveness of his younger brother. The men's contrasting styles complimented what they were about: for Willard, who was seeking a path back to the legislature, a less-confrontational and more conciliatory style allowed him to advocate positions without alienating voters; and for Harry, Jr., his "junk yard dog" demeanor gave him a leg up in the dirty business of back room politics that prevailed in the 8th District DFL. While Harry, Jr. now downplays the role he had in promoting Keith's candidacy, the historical record is clear that *both* brothers were Keith supporters.

No DFL Pick Made in Key 8th District by Roger Skophammer

The Democratic-Farmer-Labor Party will wait until the final round before settling the Rolvaag-Keith fight. Eighth District DFLers, with the key to the party endorsement in their hands, decided at their convention...to draw out the suspense for two more weeks.

They voted, in the day's only major floor fight, to postpone action until a district caucus...There was no other test of strength. The district chairmanship went to Robert Nickoloff, Hibbing, after the endorsements committee deadlocked between Clinton Wyant, Aitkin, and Harry Munger, Duluth.

Wyant and Munger both withdrew in favor of a consolation prize by being named to the important state endorsement committee. A Rolvaag effort to keep him [Munger] off was foiled in a battle behind the closed doors of the district endorsements committee. Munger is a Keith supporter who now counts an 11-4 advantage on the key state convention group...

The no endorsement movement was spearheaded by outgoing district chairman Lawrence Yetka, Cloquet, and Rep. John A. Blatnik, 8th District Congressman...

Gerald Heaney, Duluth, who had been a leader in the push for an endorsement, took the convention floor and said he reluctantly agreed with Yetka and Blatnik...

Keith and Rolvaag both addressed the convention. Keith asserted that he would do a better job of representing the DFL...citing Minnesota Poll figures showing him doing the best of any DFL candidate against Republicans...

Rolvaag indicated he thought DFL leaders...were hasty in their decision that Rolvaag couldn't win...

(*Duluth News Tribune*, June 5, 1966.)

Will Munger, Jr. recalls his own involvement in Keith's campaign.

"In retrospect," Will recalls, "I was used. Keith hired me to work as his campaign manager in the 8th District but, in reality, I now understand he was hiring my dad's name. But I was enamored with Keith. He looked like a Kennedy. He had a perfect wife and family. Compared to Karl Rolvaag, there was no real choice. I went up to the Range to get Rudy Perpich on board. He became a big supporter of Keith's."

Though Keith ultimately won the endorsement, Rolvaag refused to abide by the DFL's decision. Rolvaag defeated Keith in the primary and went on to face Harold LeVander, the Republican nominee, in the general election. The result was a DFL loss, of both the governorship and the legislature. Harry, Jr. recalls the final days of the 1966 campaign in this fashion.

"One of the big reasons Rolvaag lost was because of his drinking. It was well known amongst folks in politics that the governor had a big bottle problem. That wasn't so bad because it was kept under the radar. But during the campaign, Rolvaag was with a group of supporters fishing near International Falls. Rolvaag was sitting in a fishing boat, lit up to the gills, with the boat tied to the dock. No one else was in the boat. He somehow managed to start the outboard and rammed the boat into the dock, hitting a bystander. The guy was hurt and he sued. Because of that, it came out in the papers that Rolvaag was drunk."

Though the DFL took a beating in the 1966 election, losing its majorities in both houses of the legislature and the governorship, Willard Munger ran an effective campaign.

> **LeVander Piles Up 64,357 Vote Lead. Conservative Wave Rolls Over NE Area.**
>
> A Conservative wave rolled across NE Minnesota legislative districts Tuesday. Conservatives won a new seat in the 60th Legislative District of Duluth, won their first Iron Range seat in many years, and made strong showings in usually Liberal districts.
>
> But Liberal Willard Munger bucked the tide in the 59th District, winning back his old seat in the legislature. His victory, offsetting the 60th District loss, kept the Conservative margin in the Duluth legislative delegation at 5 to 3.
>
> (*Duluth Herald*, November 8, 1966.)

The Keith factor badly splintered the DFL, which resulted in the Party's loss of power and eventually led to the passage of a state-wide sales tax amendment, something Willard Munger had opposed since his days in the Farmer-Labor movement. But after a one-term hiatus, Munger was back in the Minnesota House of Representatives.

CHAPTER 2

Voyageurs

The late 1960s were a heady time for those interested in the concept of urban planning. Many public officials believed that rigorous and well-thought out planning could undo the impact of congestion, industrialization and urban blight on cities and return communities back to the pastoral (though romanticized) image of the American past. Willard Munger was not immune to the infectious optimism of the times.

Legislative Report by Willard Munger, Rep. 59B

In my last legislative report, I wrote about proposed legislation relating to Local Consent and Metropolitan Government affecting the Twin Cities seven county area. Several important sub-committees have now been appointed, each to deal with specific legislation such as sewer, open space, mass transit, airport, water and air pollution control, and overall metropolitan government…

It is not a simple matter to reach an agreement that will be acceptable to the great majority of the 319 subdivisions involved…

We in Duluth should learn from the crisis facing the Twin Cities Metro area and not wait for a similar crisis to fall upon us. The federal Government has moved in on the Twin Cities area relative to water and air pollution.

We also have very serious water, air, and health problems facing the people of the Duluth area…

We need an over-all long range plan for metro areas of St. Louis County. We should think and act like a metro area. There is much said about bringing new industry into the area but little is actually done to create the proper governmental environment…

I am working on a bill for St. Louis County which will provide for a joint organization of all subdivisions of government in St. Louis County to study, plan and implement a long range program to deal with problems which are interrelated with metro units of government…

(*Labor World*, March 23, 1967.)

Munger's bill created the Arrowhead Regional Development Commission (ARDC) in 1969. His support of the ARDC (which continues to supply planning expertise to northeastern Minnesota communities) and other forms of cooperative government (such as the Metropolitan Council, which provides planning and pollution control coordination for the Twin Cities metropolitan area) was pragmatic. Munger was aware that, to effectively treat industrial and household wastewater, regional coordination of treatment of that waste would require coordination of diverse governmental units. While regional planning entities would not *control* the operation of sanitary district facilities, they could *assist* the sanitary districts in planning and implementing strategies to bring about the cessation of pollution within their planning districts. Willard Munger was a forward-thinking politician. His vision was never limited to the here and now, but to generations removed from the here and now. He knew that careful management of fiscal resources would allow the environment to get the "biggest bang for the buck."

Conservation issues also continued to occupy Munger's attention.

Munger Raps Commissioners on Land Sale

Rep. Willard Munger, Duluth Liberal, charged Tuesday that members of the St. Louis County Board of Commissioners are "in league" with "timber interests" by pushing ahead with the Kabetogama land sale.

Munger claimed the commissioners who voted to go ahead with the land sale are trying to undercut Agriculture Secretary Orville Freeman's plans to expand outdoor recreation in northern Minnesota…

Members of a group advocating a national park on the Kabetogama peninsula had urged that the land sale be held up.

The group expressed fear that timber companies would buy up land and make it difficult for the federal government to acquire land for a park.

Attorney General Douglas Head eventually voided the sale on the grounds that proper procedures had not been followed…

Munger lauded Freeman's efforts to preserve northern Minnesota's wilderness areas as a "far-sighted program…"

Munger praised Head's "courage" in his decision to void the sale. The Duluth legislator contended that the sale would have obstructed plans for the park.

(*Duluth News Tribune*, April 5, 1967.)

There was more at stake regarding the Kabetogama land sale than first meets the eye. The timber lands involved were located adjacent to the proposed Voyageurs

National Park. Munger had long supported the idea of a national park along the Minnesota-Ontario border.

As recounted by former Governor Elmer L. Andersen in his autobiography, *A Man's Reach*, though the idea for a national park in the International Falls-Kabetogama area was first proposed in the late 1800s, the idea didn't take hold until 1962, when Governor Andersen, who was in the Ely area for the dedication of Bear Head State Park, invited others to tour Kabetogama with him. The tour group included Russ Fridley of the Minnesota Historical Society and noted conservation writer and Ely guide, Sigurd Olson. Never one to put all his eggs in one basket, Governor Andersen also invited Conrad Wirth, the head of the National Park Service (and son of Theodore Wirth, the father of the Minneapolis park system) to accompany the group.

> [The] mission was to help Wirth see the Kabetogama Peninsula as worthy of national park status. We toured the area in the morning, had a delicious fish luncheon at a little place at the end of the peninsula, the Kettle Falls Hotel, and then did a little fishing in the afternoon. Wirth caught a fish. It was perfect, just perfect. He was clearly impressed. In sales terms, we had our foot in the door.
>
> (*A Man's Reach*, ibid, p. 276.)

It was a long and slow journey from Wirth's first visit to Kabetogama to the park becoming a reality. For more than a decade, Gov. Andersen worked with the Minnesota congressional delegation and the Minnesota Legislature on the project.

> It was crucial in 1971, after Congress authorized the park, for the Minnesota Legislature to grant its blessing and direct state officials to take the requisite steps toward the park's establishment, including securing control of the land. Again, happenstance was in our favor. My brother-in-law, Stanley Holmquist of Grove City, was majority leader in the senate that year. He was helpful to us. So were several legislators for the region, including Reps. Irv Anderson from International Falls, and Willard Munger from Duluth...
>
> (*A Man's Reach*, ibid, p. 282.)

Congressman John Blatnik's opposition to Voyageurs was one of the last hurdles Andersen needed to clear. Munger took Blatnik to task publically for his position on the issue, a stand that likely didn't make relations any friendlier between the Congressman and the state representative. Munger's open letter to Blatnik was published as a special supplement to the *Labor World*.

Honorable John A. Blatnik
  Congressman
  House Office Building
  Washington, D.C.
  Dear John:

  I am in favor of the Voyageurs National Park on the Kabetogama Peninsula as recommended by the United States Park Service because we need a National Park in northern Minnesota. The fate of a great natural heritage rests in this decision.

  Many of us may not live to see the full benefits of such a park but it ought to be the purpose of the living to pass on to coming generations, in perpetuity, this scenic grandeur.

  The Great Creator gave us this untamed natural resource, showing in full depth the rugged beauty of his Creation. We have an obligation to humanity to pass on this heritage unspoiled by the greed of private exploitation so that they who follow may witness and more fully understand the works of the Great Architect...

  When this park is established, we will have here in northern Minnesota one of the most unique parks in the United States. The 108,000 acres of land, 58,000 acres of water and 514 miles of shoreline will provide year round diversified types of recreation to millions of people. Some in our area cannot afford to go to Yellowstone or some other National Park. Its wild forest will preserve the wildlife for sight see'ers and biological researchers; its rare rock formations, found nowhere else, will provide special material for geological studies. I am convinced that Kabetogama is so unique that it belongs to the nation!

  We would not want our grandchildren to come to Kabetogama and the Boundary Waters area and read signs "private property, keep off" and we would not want them to point an accusing finger at us and say we allowed special interest to supersede their enjoyment and recreational needs...

  Very truly yours,
  Willard M. Munger
  Representative 59B

(*Labor World,* June 6, 1968.)

The Duluth AFL-CIO Central Labor Body, the Minnesota AFL-CIO Federation of Labor, and Senator Walter F. Mondale joined Munger in endorsing the proposal. But even with such heady support, Munger showed considerable guts by placing Blatnik's lone-wolf stand on the issue in public view.

One can hear the New York inflection of Grandpa Lyman Munger's voice behind the words: "The Great Creator gave us this untamed natural resource, showing in full depth the rugged beauty of his Creation..." There is no doubt that Willard Munger's long walks through the wilds of Pockerbrush country with his grandfather had a significant and lasting impression on Willard. The land ethic instilled upon Willard by his paternal grandfather, coupled with the Socialist ideology imbedded in the Nonpartisan League and the Farmer-Labor Party, created a deep and lasting mistrust in the legislator for corporate promises and intentions, a mistrust that is clear and piercing in Munger's letter to Congressman Blatnik.

Willard Munger's marriage to Frances Herou brought him more than personal happiness and a life-long companion. Frances was an avid organic gardener and health food advocate. It was her role in Willard's life to keep him away from fats, sugar, alcohol, cigarettes and anything remotely deleterious to his health. Frances's watchful eye is likely the reason Willard remained in relative good health for most of his life. When the couple later moved to their new home on Indian Point on the St. Louis River, Frances and Willard would work together in Frances's vegetable garden and Willard, harkening back to his youth in Pockerbrush, would establish honey bee hives. The natural food and honey that came from that small plot of clay-stricken land were clear evidence of Frances's dedication to a simple life-style. In addition, her private advocacy against the use of man-made pesticides was a primary motivator in Willard's crusade to rid Minnesota of DDT.

> In the last 20 years pesticides have been found to cause spectacular mass deaths to fish, insidiously delayed damage to the reproductive capabilities of mammals, fish and birds...
>
> The newly developed pesticides are more dangerous than those in use before WWII. In the period before WWII, insecticides, with a few exceptions...were not persistent. They consisted of organics that were found in nature...The newly developed non-organic insecticides are extremely dangerous because they do not break down-they are persistent and accumulate...
>
> It is necessary that we take a good look at this growing problem...Therefore, I have introduced a bill which would create an Interim Commission to make a study and determine the feasibility of establishing an environmental research center to be operated jointly by the state of Minnesota and the Federal government...All four Conservative authors are able and influential legislators; therefore I feel the bill has a very good chance of passage.
>
> (*Labor World*, "Legislative Report" by Willard Munger, May 4, 1967.)

There was considerable opposition to a state-wide ban on DDT, both because the federal government had not yet banned the compound's use and because Minnesota farmers didn't want to lose the use of a pesticide, which, although dangerous to the environment, was effective against insects.

> Please accept my thanks for your support of legislation aimed at the saving of our whole ecological environmental structure from destruction. I appreciate the editorials and cartoons which have pointed out the dangers of DDT and kindred pesticides, and find your continued publication of stories of DDT contamination a heartening example of fearless journalism...
>
> Minnesota would not be the first state to pass such legislation, as Arizona, Wisconsin, and Michigan have restricted the use of DDT...
>
> The *St. Paul Dispatch* and *Pioneer Press* and their editorial staffs are to be congratulated for an outstanding public service that no other newspaper dared to provide. You have awakened the people of Minnesota to their obligations to this age and to future generations to keep this planet livable...
>
> Very truly yours,
>
> Willard M. Munger
>
> (Letter to the Editor, *St. Paul Pioneer Press*, May 21, 1969.)

"During the debate to outlaw DDT," Willard remembered, "I heard that 'DDT is not a problem. It's just Munger's imagination.' You wouldn't think of anybody even suggesting that we use DDT anymore but the first time around I lost on that bill. Imagine that the farm extension service at the University of Minnesota came in and killed the bill!... They brought in one of their top people to testify against the bill, a Dr. Borlaug, who was a Nobel Prize winner. He made the statement that, 'If Munger passes his bill, how are you going to feed the world? You have to have DDT and pesticides and herbicides in order to grow enough grain.' His final statement was, 'You have to make a choice. What do you want? Birds and bees or people?'"

(*Oral History of Willard Munger*, ibid, p. 20)

Even as Munger was urging a ban on DDT, Minnesota governmental agencies continued to buy and spread the toxin with taxpayer money.

> May 19, 1969
>
> Dear Mr. Munger:
>
> This is in reply to your request of May 2, 1969 for information concerning the amount of DDT and other chlorinated hydrocarbons used by the Conservation Department during the years 1967 – 68.

[T]he Division of Parks and Recreation...reported 120 gallons [of DDT] purchased in 1967 and 498 gallons [of DDT] purchased in 1968...This was applied using ground sprays...

C.B. Buckman,

Deputy Commissioner

Department of Conservation

Munger devoted an entire Legislative Report in the *Labor World* to the issue.

Chemical persistent pesticides could prove to be more dangerous to man than the atomic bomb. We are well on the way of restricting the use of the atomic bomb, but we could destroy our ... natural food chain structure and destroy nature's reproductive processes. We are on the road to no return and this civilization could become prehistoric.

Chemical pesticides are polluters of air, land and water, just as sewage, industrial waste, exhaust fumes, etc...are polluters, but they are extremely more dangerous...

The newly developed pesticides are more dangerous than those used before WWII...

DDT is very cheap to manufacture. That is one of the prime reasons for its widespread use. These newly developed synthetic pesticides are extremely dangerous because they do not break down—they are persistent and accumulative...

In 1963, the President's Science Advisory Committee recommended that we eliminate the use of such chemicals...The Committee did not say "use them with care," it said, "cease their use completely..."

Secretary of the Interior, Stewart Udall, says, "if we do not use thought as a way to wisdom, then our mindless activities are bound to spell finish for the wild creatures who are surely our moral responsibilities—and eventually, perhaps, even for us."

(*Labor World*, February 1, 1969.)

Though Munger was unable to pass a ban on DDT, the DDT fight brought Munger into contact with Governor Harold LeVander with whom Munger worked on other, more successful environmental legislation. LeVander signed into law the Metropolitan Council bill (establishing regional planning for the Twin Cities) and legislation authorizing the formation of the Pollution Control Agency. Gov. LeVander was also, as Elmer L. Andersen had been before him, opposed to a state-wide sales tax, a tax which was passed over LeVander's veto in 1967 by the Repub-

lican-controlled legislature. Additionally, LeVander was a leader in the movement
to ratify the 26th Amendment to the U.S. Constitution—the amendment which
reduced the voting age from 21 to 18. Despite his considerable success as governor,
LeVander chose to serve only one term, returning to the private practice of law in
the Twin Cities after the 1970 election.

There came a point in Munger's legislative career when conservation groups began
to honor Munger for his environmental work.

> Congressman John Blatnik was the speaker for the Saturday noon luncheon
> of the MCF (Minnesota Conservation Federation) assembly. Following his
> discussion of conservation achievements in Congress, he presented an award
> from MCF to State Rep. Willard Munger, of Duluth. Rep. Munger was hon-
> ored for his efforts in the state legislature on pollution control. Rep. Munger
> expressed his thanks and also paid tribute to the United Northern Sportsmen
> of Duluth for the club's efforts in pollution control.
>
> (*Minnesota Out-of-Doors*, October 1967.)

Munger received additional recognition for his efforts.

> Dear Representative Munger:
>   Please accept our congratulations on your being presented with the Legis-
> lative Conservation Award…You have certainly earned this award with your
> many years of effort in the interest of conservation and pollution…
>   Sincerely,
>   Milt Pelletier, President
>   United Northern Sportsmen

The Legislative Conservation Award (sponsored by the Sears-Roebuck Foundation
and the National Wildlife Federation) was presented to Munger at a dinner at
the Ambassador Hotel in Minneapolis where Governor LeVander was the keynote
speaker. According to an article in *Labor World*, Munger was nominated for the
award on the strength of two bills:

Water Pollution Control Study Bill

> Representative Munger authored this bill, which provided for the estab-
> lishment of an Interim Commission to study water pollution in the rivers
> and streams of the state and to determine the feasibility of establishing sani-
> tary districts in the state. Rep. Munger served as the co-chairman of this com-
> mission and he also served as co-chairman of the Sub-committee to study fish
> kills in the St. Louis River…

Sanitary District Water Pollution Control Bill

Munger followed through and authored a bill known as the Sanitary District Water Pollution Control Bill...[and] played an active role in the last session of the legislature as a member of the seven county Metropolitan Sewer Bill sub-committee.

Munger is also a strong advocate for our public forest lands and feels they should remain under the control of State and Federal Governments-to provide for future economic needs of our expanding population.

(*Labor World*, November, 1967.)

Though Munger's legislative initiatives concentrated on conservation, his positions on other issues must be noted to give a clear picture of his political philosophy. Issues addressed by Munger during the 1967 Minnesota Legislature included:

- State-wide fluoridation of municipal drinking water supplies: Munger was opposed to forced fluoridation;

- Bill to license the possession of handguns in public places: Munger opposed the legislation on 2nd Amendment grounds and was appointed to the subcommittee which killed the bill;

- Civil Rights Legislation: Munger supported the bill;

- Funding for Mental Health Agencies through State Grants: Munger supported the bill;

- The Sales Tax: Munger voted against it;

- A bill seeking to control pornography and a bill to establish a horse racing track: Munger opposed both bills. He consistently opposed legalized gambling in the state, an issue that would resurface when he battled to secure funding for the Environmental Trust Fund later in his career.

During the '67 session, a minor political squabble arose regarding Munger's support of LaBrosse as head of the St. Louis County legislative delegation. One would have thought that, given the level of animosity between Munger and LaBrosse, Munger would have supported anyone, even a Conservative, for the position over LaBrosse. Not so.

I voted for Senator LaBrosse because it was a choice between Liberal or Conservative control of the St. Louis County Delegation. The vote was 7-6 in favor of LaBrosse...May I point out that if party loyalty had been forthcoming from certain endorsed candidates during the past elections, you would not now have a Conservative Duluth delegation, nor would we have the situation that now exists within our area poverty programs…

> (1967 Letter to Labor Organizations, Willard Munger Personal Collection.)

During the 1967 Legislature, Willard Munger also dealt with the city of Duluth's attempt to annex neighboring Herman Township. Duluth sought the annexation so as to ensure that its population remained above 100,000 (the required number for classification as a city of the first class).

> The Board of Supervisors of the Town of Herman respectfully requests your assistance in blocking any attempt by the city of Duluth to annex any part of our Town to the City…
> Arthur Fitchner
> Clerk
>
> (January 18, 1967.)

Munger's reply was to the point.

> Please be informed that I firmly believe in home rule and shall support the will of the people of Hermantown…

Munger also continued his legislative work in the area of wildlife conservation. Aghast that the state of Minnesota was paying bounties for the killing of timber wolves (an animal Munger found "majestic") Munger introduced legislation during the 1967 session designating the timber wolf as Minnesota's state animal. Munger's proposal, repeatedly introduced by Munger during his career (never successfully) put him at odds with old friends.

> January, 1967
> Dear Willard:
> Enclosed, you will find the stand that the Sportsmen take on (wolf) boun-
> ties. The alternatives proposed should be given consideration…
> Lyle Brand
> United Northern Sportsmen

Munger delicately laid out his opposition to the Sportsmen's position.

> I am of the opinion that the people supporting wolf bounties are doing it
> more for the sake of pleasing local trappers with the monetary aspect than for
> a sound long range conservation program based upon biological research…
> United Northern Sportsmen during the past 20 years have been in the fore-

front in advocating sound conservation programs, and are so recognized by legislators who have an open mind...I have never forgotten the hard work which your club and its members did in behalf of the Water Pollution Control Sanitary District legislation which passed and became law in 1961...

(Willard Munger Personal Collection.)

Munger spent much of his legislative career advocating wildlife preservation in the face of economic pressure to exploit Minnesota's abundant wild game. His allies in that fight were the Department of Natural Resources (and its forerunner, the Conservation Department) and the Minnesota Pollution Control Agency (which, under Governor LeVander, replaced the Minnesota Department of Health as the state's overall pollution watchdog).

> "The leadership is most important," Willard recalled. "The structure is important but it is the leadership that counts. If it's good, it will keep people on their toes. You know, if a person goes out and doesn't get a deer because a wolf has killed one, he wants Joe Alexander [former DNR chief] fired. If a guy goes fishing and doesn't get his limit, he says there is something wrong with the department... You've got hundreds of those kinds of people. And you've got to work with them. If they don't get a deer, they think that the damn biologists don't know what they're doing. 'I know more than the biologists because I've been hunting deer all my life, and I saw those damn wolves kill the deer.' You know, the Iron Range used to elect their legislators based upon who could promise the most money for bounties on timber wolves...They hate timber wolves. They still hate them up there..."
>
> (*Oral History of Willard Munger*, ibid, p. 64.)

When asked why Grand Marais (which is not an Iron Range town but holds to the same hunting and fishing ethic as the Range) and Ely (an old mining town in the heart of the Vermillion Iron Range) were vying to be the site of the International Wolf Center, Munger responded:

> "[They want the Wolf center] [b]ecause it's an economic benefit. The economic benefits override their hatred of the wolf—but does it really...? I had a bill in the legislature which would make the timber wolf the state animal... My grandson came over to the Capitol to visit me and said:
>
>   'Grandpa, is there anything you want me to do?'
>
>   I said, 'Yes, why don't you take this bill and go into see Joe Begich (DFL-Eveleth). Ask him if he'll sign on your grandpa's bill as co-author.'

In about fifteen minutes, he came back.

He said, 'Grandpa, he doesn't like timber wolves and did he get mad when I came in there with that bill! He didn't sign it.'

I said, 'I knew he wasn't going to sign it, but I was having a little fun with you.'

The feeling was still there. You know, meat hunters are a funny group of people. If they don't get their deer, then somebody has got to be held responsible for it."

(*Oral History of Willard Munger*, ibid, pp. 64 – 65.)

As 1968 came into focus, Munger concentrated his attention on environmental issues.

State Board of Health
July 19, 1968
Dear Dr. Barr:

It has been called to my attention on several occasions that a building housing the Chester Creek Motors…has a drain pipe coming from the building which is dumping waste oil into Chester Creek…

There is no logical reason whatsoever why people should be allowed to pollute our streams with oil. I hope your department will take immediate steps to have this situation corrected at once…

Your friend,
Willard Munger
Representative 59B

The degradation of Duluth's creeks and streams, some of which supported (and still support) spawning populations of native brook trout, was an issue that Willard and his brother Harry, Jr. would confront for the better part of three decades.

Despite Willard Munger's conservation outlook (which often put him at odds with individual union members) Munger generally received "good marks" from the trade unions.

Brotherhood of Railway and Steamship Clerks
August 31, 1968
Dear Willard:

In reference to your filing for re-election to Minnesota House of Representatives in District 59B. As stated at the Hotel Duluth…your record during your 12 years in the state legislature has been most outstanding and warrants the wholehearted support of our Brotherhood…

I feel assured that you will be re-elected Willard and wish to thank you for all the very good work that you have done for our Brotherhood in the past...

Sincerely,

Walter S. Richter, Sec.-Treas.

1968 was an election year. During the state DFL convention, Harry Munger, Jr., was selected as a Humphrey delegate to the Democratic National Convention in Chicago, where supporters of Eugene McCarthy (who was wearing the mantle of peace candidate after the assassination of Bobby Kennedy) pressed for an end the Vietnam War. President Lyndon Johnson had thrown the Democrats into a tizzy by announcing that he would not seek a second term. While Vice President Humphrey enjoyed the support of the party faithful like Harry, Jr., there was a strong and vocal movement amongst the more educated and younger Democrats to nominate McCarthy. But Humphrey was endorsed by the convention and selected Maine Senator Edmund Muskie as his running mate against Richard Nixon and Spiro Agnew. The wild-card was that Alabama Governor George Wallace was also in the race with General Curtis LeMay as third party candidates for president and vice president.

After losing the endorsement, McCarthy remained out of the media spotlight. When he re-emerged from his self-imposed seclusion, McCarthy refused to endorse Humphrey. Locally, Willard Munger was facing a well-known opponent.

> Willard Munger, 57, of 7408 Grand Ave., is a veteran of six terms in the House of Representatives, and is seeking his seventh term. Operator of a Duluth motel, Munger was chairman of the Duluth legislative delegation for two terms and has served as chairman of numerous House committees. He is active in the DFL, West Duluth Businessmen's Club, United Northern Sportsmen, and the Water Pollution Advisory Committee.
>
> Frank (Pug) Puglisi, 62, 9687 Maple Hill Road, Proctor, is making his second bid from District 59B. Puglisi, a school teacher, has coached football, basketball, and track. He has held top coaching positions at the former Duluth Junior College, Duluth Central, and Duluth Denfeld High Schools. He is a graduate of Denfeld, Hibbing Junior College, and the University of Minnesota.
>
> (*Duluth News Tribune*, undated.)

Spiro Agnew appeared at a rally held in Duluth on October 24, 1966 and assailed Humphrey's lack of support for jobs in northern Minnesota. Nixon appeared in

Rochester, Minnesota on October 30, 1968 and hinted that if he won, he might name Minnesota Republican Congressman Al Quie as his "Orville Freeman" (i.e., Secretary of Agriculture).

During the last week of October, Humphrey claimed Nixon's lead was shrinking. Eugene McCarthy announced he would not seek further political office as a Democrat and that he *"was inclined"* to endorse Hubert Humphrey. Nixon warned that there might be a deadlock in the Electoral College based upon the George Wallace factor, Humphrey's late surge, and McCarthy's late endorsement. In what many deemed to be a last-minute political ploy to help his vice president, President Johnson announced a complete halt to all bombing in North Vietnam on November 1, 1968 and informed the American public that the Paris peace talks between the U.S. and North Vietnam would resume.

The *Duluth News Tribune* predicted that 43,000 votes would be cast in Duluth in a very close presidential race (*Duluth News Tribune*, November 3, 1968).

Due to the tightness of the race, Nixon challenged Humphrey to agree that the presidency would go to the person winning the national popular vote. Humphrey declined the offer. Nixon won both the popular and the electoral vote, and Willard Munger beat Frank Puglisi handily to retain his seat.

CHAPTER 3

The Minnesota Miracle

In comparison to the 1968 presidential contest, the 1970 election cycle in Minnesota was relatively staid. Though liberalization of Minnesota's laws regarding abortion became a campaign issue for the first time, the issue had no traction. Hubert Humphrey, who had lost his bid for the presidency in 1968, was running against Clark McGregor for the Senate seat vacated by Eugene McCarthy. Amtrak funding regarding the St. Paul to Duluth North Star train surfaced as an issue, one that Willard Munger would later take up with vigor.

State Senator Francis "Frenchie" LaBrosse faced opposition from Richard "Dick" Palmer, the owner and publisher of Duluth's weekly shopper, the *Budgeteer*. President Nixon was considering Congressman George H.B. Bush of Texas (who was embroiled in a Senate campaign against Senator Lloyd Bentsen) as a replacement for Spiro Agnew as vice president (Agnew had resigned from office after serious ethical breaches were uncovered).

Ex-Olympic hockey star and lawyer Wendell "Wendy" Anderson was running for governor of Minnesota with Iron Ranger Rudy Perpich as his running mate on the DFL ticket against Republican candidates Attorney General Douglas Head and Duluth Mayor Ben Boo. Morgan Park High School teacher Sam Solon appeared on the political scene to run for a House seat in the 60th District as a Liberal.

The major issue in the contest between LaBrosse and Palmer involved Palmer's labeling himself an Independent. LaBrosse claimed that such a label was a ruse: Palmer had publicly stated he would caucus with the majority party and since the Conservatives held that distinction in the Minnesota Senate, LaBrosse argued that Palmer was, in fact, a Conservative.

The *Duluth News Tribune* endorsed LaBrosse and had this to say about Willard Munger's reelection bid:

Among the most envied legislative candidates have been Representative Willard Munger of Duluth in District 59B and Senator Anthony J. Perpich, Eveleth, in the 62nd District, both Liberals, and both, unopposed.

(*Duluth News Tribune*, November 1, 1970.)

Palmer defeated LaBrosse and claimed the Senate seat in the 59th District. Sam Solon won the House seat in the 60th District. Anderson and Perpich bested Head and Boo. And DFL icon Hubert Humphrey returned to the United States Senate as Minnesota's "junior" U.S. Senator (junior to Walter Mondale).

One of the first major acts of incoming DFL Governor Wendy Anderson was the enactment of the so-called "Minnesota Miracle."

Since the beginning of Minnesota's statehood, school districts had relied heavily upon local property taxes to fund K-12 education. That changed with the adoption of the "Minnesota Miracle"; the seminal cornerstone of Wendell Anderson's 1970 run for governor.

Most Republicans (including popular moderate Republican gubernatorial candidate Douglas Head) felt Anderson had committed political suicide when, during the middle of the 1970 campaign, Anderson announced his plan to follow a Citizen League recommendation to reform education by having the state provide the majority of K-12 funding. But the pundits miscalculated voter support for the idea and Anderson ultimately rode his "Minnesota Miracle" proposal to victory.

After serving two terms in the Minnesota House and one in the state senate, Wendy Anderson used his own meager savings and the blessing of his mentor, Hubert Humphrey (Anderson had been Humphrey's Minnesota Campaign Chair in 1968) to win the governor's seat by over 100,000 votes, a landslide by Minnesota standards. Following his election, Anderson sought consensus on his school funding proposal in the state legislature. Within three years, Anderson was able to increase the state's funding of K-12 education to 70% of the total money expended. Using a strategy of cutting property taxes and increasing cigarette, sales and liquor taxes to offset state financial involvement in K-12 education, Anderson attempted to equalize funding for all public schools. But as an article in *Time* magazine was quick to point out, the Minnesota experience under Governor Anderson was much more than simply reforming K-12 education. The ethic of the state's people, a people tied closely to the land, was reflected in their quality of life.

Such an abundance and accessibility of nature has much to do with the Minnesotans' sense of place and roots. More than almost any other Americans, they are outdoor people, and at least 50% of them customarily vacation in their own state. The seasons have their own sporting rhythms. On summer weekends, the traffic moves bumper-to-propeller out of the Twin Cities toward what has been a Minnesotan index of the good life—the lake "up north." The state's license plates advertise it as "Land of 10,000 Lakes," but that is an understatement. Actually, there are 15,291 lakes of ten acres or more, as well as 25,000 miles of rivers, including the Mississippi...

It is a state where a residual American secret still seems to operate. Some of the nation's more agreeable qualities are evident there: courtesy and fairness, honesty, a capacity for innovation, hard work, intellectual adventure and responsibility. The land is large...the population small...Nature is close...and generally well protected...

(*Time*, August 13, 1973.)

This was the state where Willard Munger was born and spent the entirety of his long life. His desire to protect the land, water and sky he'd grown up with was obvious to anyone who had contact with him.

"[I]'m an environmentalist today...because of my background," Willard stated plainly. "I think it's extremely important that we teach good environmental policies in our schools, because you've got to get it when you're young, and that's where I got mine. What you learn in your formative years, you know, generally stays with you. I don't care what it is. Whether it's religion, environment or politics, or whatever, you don't change too much from your formative years...I think it's extremely important that we teach kids the value of the environment."

(*Oral History of Willard Munger*, ibid, p. 19.)

Munger shared a Liberal, populist-based political philosophy with the new governor.

Like the state itself, Anderson can sometimes seem almost too good to be true. The son of a meat packer, he is something of a populist, an anti-elitist and egalitarian...He is uncomfortable with great wealth..."I identify with Truman, Humphrey and Mondale. All of them were poor, close to working people, and came from frugal backgrounds..."

(*Time*, ibid.)

The political egalitarianism of the two men mirrored the philosophy of another northeastern Minnesota politician: Senator Homer Carr.

October 20, 1970

Dear Willard:

I was happy to learn you have no opposition for your re-election to the House…

There must be a good reason for this situation. As you can well remember, I was down to the sessions of the years '55 and '57 and to be sure, I really got an education at the time.

In your case, I observed that you worked hard and were not influenced by the various lobbies and special interests…I believe the most important reason for your not having any opposition is due to the fact of your sincerity and honesty to yourself and the people which you represent. This is to an extent the path that our late Senator Homer Carr, followed…

May we hope that you will continue your actions in the future as you have in the past.

Good health and good luck to you.

Yours truly,

William Swanfield

Munger's continued success as an unabashed Liberal in the largely blue-collar 59th District was a paradox that Munger was often asked to explain.

"I couldn't have gotten elected in any other district but this one," Munger observed. "The people of this district…are a mixture of different nationalities. A lot of them are first and the second generation immigrants. Most people who come over here from across the sea are extremely honest people. I think they forgave me for a lot of my ideas and things that they don't normally agree with because they thought I was completely honest. I think honesty is probably what I consider one of my biggest assets and the reason why I have been re-elected with such big majorities…I have never done anything to make them regret they voted for me…I have never hesitated to tell someone exactly how I feel, whether it means I lose or gain a vote…"

(*Oral History of Willard Munger*, ibid, pp. 59 – 60.)

Munger also observed that the ethnic mix of the 59th was different from other Duluth neighborhoods.

"The difference," Willard stated plainly, "lies in the fact that we had a steel plant here for many, many years that employed a great number of people. That plant brought in people of all different nationalities, especially a lot of first generation people. Those people really stand out. They're unique. It's a tight-knit group. If they're for you, they're for you; if they're against you, they're against you. No question about it. No halfway. Either you're right or you're wrong."

(*Oral History of Willard Munger*, ibid, p. 60.)

As Governor Anderson's "Minnesota Miracle" was debated in the legislature, the city of Duluth found itself in serious economic trouble. United States Steel whose steel, wire bailing and cement plants in Gary-New Duluth had been an economic mainstay of the city for sixty years, announced that it would be ending steel production at the antiquated plant. U.S. Steel's announcement came on the heels of the U.S. Air Force closing its Duluth air base. These announcements created an economic firestorm the likes of which Duluth had never seen.

> Gov. Wendell Anderson asserted his authority on two fronts...to prevent further deterioration in Duluth's sagging economy.
>
> In St. Paul, he struck down a proposal by his own tax commissioner... which would have raised residential and business property taxes throughout Duluth. Then he flew to Duluth and appointed a bi-partisan committee to develop a program to save the city's steel plant, offering to call a special session of the Minnesota Legislature to enact it...
>
> Smelting operations were shut down at the plant in November, greatly damaging the city's economic prospects. Last June, some 800 jobs were lost when the Duluth Air Force Base was phased out...
>
> Efforts by a coalition of Duluth labor, business and government leaders for the last year have centered on the granting of...incentives to persuade U.S. Steel to keep the plant in operation...
>
> The governor's committee includes the DFL lieutenant governor [Rudy Perpich]; Peter Bensoni...Steelworkers Union; Carl D'Aquila, Hibbing businessman; John Dickerson, Duluth banker; Dr. Vernon Harrington, Duluth physician; Dick Kohlbry, Duluth real estate man; John LaForge, Duluth television executive; John McGrath, VP-Minnesota Power; Robert Olson, president of the Steel Workers Local at the plant; Jeno F. Paulucci, chairman of Jeno's, Inc.; Robert Rich, Duluth television executive...; C. Thomas Burke, Duluth Port Authority; DFL State Rep. Willard Munger; and Republican State Rep. Sidney Mason...

(*Minneapolis Star-Tribune*, January, 1971. *Editor's Note: Duluth Mayor Ben Boo and television station owner Frank Befera were appointed as co-chairs of the committee.*)

Against this gloomy backdrop, Willard Munger continued his work on behalf of the environment.

> Duluth DFLer, Representative Willard Munger appeared before a House-Senate Joint Sub-Committee on parks of the Natural Resources Committee on Monday, March 29. Munger spoke in support of his bill...which would authorize the Commissioner of Natural Resources to acquire 120 acres of park land within the city of Duluth and to add that property to the already existing administered Jay Cooke State Park. Munger stated that he is sure of the passage of the bill because of the very favorable reception he received from the committee.
>
> As long ago as 1957, Munger urged that the land lying between Highway 39, Skyline (Mission Creek) Parkway, and the present northern boundary of the state park be transferred to the state through an expansion...Munger noted that the 120 acre parcel includes portions of the historic Grand Portage trail along the St. Louis River, and an Indian cemetery dating back to the time of the Grand Portage. "The Mission Creek area includes the historic route used for centuries by the Indian-and European explorers alike, a route recorded as early as 1680 by the Frenchman, Daniel Greysolon DuLut," emphasized Rep. Munger. "And it deserves to be protected and preserved so future generations may enjoy its magnificent terrain and historic significance in the saga of the early settlement of Minnesota."
>
> (Press Release, March 30, 1971; Willard Munger Personal Collection.)

Sixteen years of persistent political arm-twisting by Munger also resulted in the successful passage of enabling legislation for the Western Lake Superior Sanitary District (WLSSD). The story of *how* Willard Munger brought the WLSSD to fruition is a classic example of Willard's legendary ability to embrace compromise so long as that compromise didn't require Munger to discard his core values.

"When I left the House in 1960," recalls former Justice Larry Yetka, "I didn't run for re-election. We were concerned in Cloquet with industry because we had no clean source for water. The St. Louis River was inundated with tannic acid and a water line from Lake Superior seemed to be the only viable solution. The city obviously didn't have the right of eminent domain outside its boundaries. The industries in Cloquet came to us for assistance. I agreed, started working on the permits, and met with Willard. His response was characteristically Willard.

"'Why should I agree to help you when the people you work for are polluting the St. Louis River?'

"I had a response ready.

"'We can begin to solve the problem by finding a clean source of water.'

"Willard recognized the possibility of using my request to build a collaborative effort on his dream project.

"'If I help you build this water line, then you have to bring Cloquet into the fold and help form a sanitary district to clean up the river.'

"Willard showed immense class in being able to take a risk assisting industry in the face of environmental critics. As soon as the Cloquet water line was completed, planning for the Western Lake Superior Sanitary District (WLSSD), (with Cloquet's full cooperation and participation) began. I even ended up serving as the WLSSD's attorney until I was appointed by Governor Wendy Anderson to the Minnesota Supreme Court in 1973."

Another northeastern Minnesota resident who worked closely with Willard Munger on environmental issues is Dave Zentner, former national president of the Izaak Walton League. Born and raised in Iowa, Zentner was headed for the University of Minnesota in the Twin Cities when his parents moved to Duluth and he followed, graduating from UMD with a degree in business before beginning a career with Banker's Life Insurance.

Zentner's interest in conservation began when he joined the Izaak Walton League in junior high school. An avid fisherman and hunter, Zentner is proud to be known as a "tree hugger" and was a personal friend of the great Minnesota naturalist and writer, Sigurd Olson of Ely. Comparing Olson and Willard Munger, Zentner reflects, "As different as they might have been, they shared a commonality." Zentner lists the three most influential conservationists in his lifetime as Sigurd Olson, Willard Munger and nature writer, Gordon McQuarie of Wisconsin.

Zentner first became friends with Munger during the late 1960s and early 1970s when they were both active in the United Northern Sportsmen. Zentner worked with Milt Pelletier of the organization and Minnesota Pollution Control Agency Regional Director, John Pegors, on the Clean Water Act. But he really became close with Munger during hearings regarding the continuation of Reserve Mining's dumping of tailings into Lake Superior.

"I had a hard time sizing him up. He was a mystery to me. I thought, 'Does this guy really have it together?' But in the end, he convinced me. He could show flashes of brilliance and no one had his impact in environmental and conservation matters in Minnesota. What is sad is, so many folks quoted him after his death, asking, 'What would Willard think?' but they didn't support his ideas then, and they don't support them now."

Zentner adds that he sees Willard Munger in the Progressive vein of Wisconsin's Fighting Bob Lafollette when it comes to politics.

"He was always ready to take care of his constituents and his district before his business or his family. The cause, not power, was the impetus behind his work. To do good, to design a course for good, was his motivation. Art Hawkins, one of the pioneers of waterfowl management, was in the same mold."

With the successful passage of the WLSSD bill, there was ample reason for Munger to "toot his own horn."

> For over 10 years, DFL State Representative Willard Munger worked to gain legislative support for his efforts to set up organized, local sanitary districts throughout the state to combat the serious water pollution threat to our watersheds. Today, Munger's bill, H.F. 1621, creating a sanitary district for the St. Louis River Basin, was approved…by unanimous vote…
>
> When Willard Munger first began his efforts to halt the menacing spread of water pollution, he met with much opposition and disinterest, but he persisted and succeeded in obtaining passage of the Water Pollution Control Act of 1961 an act which became the foundation for Munger's 1971 effort to protect the historic and beautiful St. Louis River Basin…
>
> (Press Release, May 12, 1971, Willard Munger Personal Collection.)

Newspapers were quick to announce Munger's legislative coup.

> Legislation implementing the creation of a lower St. Louis River Sanitary District won unanimous approval Wednesday of the Minnesota House of Representatives. The vote was 133 – 0…
>
> Munger said the measure was needed to "take care of an acute water pollution problem" created by municipalities and industries. "The St. Louis River is polluted and has to be cleaned up," he said. "Since the water flows into Lake Superior, the quality of the water in the river is a great concern, not only to Minnesota, but also to the federal government…"
>
> Rep. Sam Solon, Duluth Liberal, a co-author of the bill, termed the bill, "one of the most significant and far-reaching antipollution measures" ever passed…"I feel very strongly that special recognition should be accorded to Rep. Munger, who has worked for legislation of this type since 1955."
>
> (*Duluth News Tribune*, May 13, 1971.)

And:

> The Minnesota Senate passed and sent to Governor Wendell Anderson for his signature Thursday a House-approved bill creating a lower St. Louis River sanitary district to control water pollution...
>
> In approving the lower St. Louis River sanitary district bill, the Senate concurred with an amendment attached to the measure in the House by Rep. Willard Munger, Duluth Liberal, increasing from seven to nine the number of members on the District's board...
>
> (*Duluth News Tribune*, May 14, 1971.)

Governor Wendy Anderson wasted little time signing the bill.

> Governor Wendell Anderson's office said Friday that he had signed a bill passed by the 1971 Minnesota Legislature creating a lower St. Louis River Basin Sanitary District...
>
> Chief authors were Rep. Willard Munger and Sen. Earl Gustafson, both Duluth Liberals.
>
> The legislation also approved a bill authorizing a $300,000 loan for "start-up" money to be repaid by January 1, 1973. The main authors of this measure were Munger and Sen. Norman Hanson, Cromwell Liberal.
>
> The sanitary district proposal was recommended by the Northeastern Minnesota Development Association to serve the cities of Duluth and Cloquet, the villages of Carlton, Scanlon, Proctor and Wrenshall, and the Townships of Knife Falls, Silver Brook, Thompson, Twin Lakes, Grand Lake, Herman, Duluth Lakewood, Midway, Rice Lake and Solway...
>
> Installation of secondary sewage treatment facilities has been ordered by the Minnesota Pollution Control Agency (MPCA)...
>
> (*Duluth News Tribune*, June 5, 1971.)

Even today, the WLSSD continues to recognize Munger's herculean effort.

Our Roots

Representative Willard Munger's vision was the driving force behind the establishment of the WLSSD. Rep. Munger saw the damage that was being done to the environment for the lack of a regional treatment facility and championed the cause. He worked tirelessly in the legislature to obtain the enabling legislation and, later, the state planning funds for WLSSD's development.

The WLSSD was created by the Minnesota State Legislature in 1971 as a special purpose subdivision of the state to address the problems of water pollution as well as collection and disposal of sewage. Initially, the legislation charged the District with the responsibility of improving and protecting the waters of the St. Louis River and its tributaries. In 1974, the legislature provided the additional responsibility and authority for the Sanitary District to address the problem of solid waste disposal.

The WLSSD covers an area of 500 square miles...

The WLSSD is governed by a nine-member citizen board. Four members are appointed by the city of Duluth, three by the city of Cloquet, one by the Carlton County cities and townships, and one by St. Louis County cities and townships.

(WLSSD Brochure, Willard Munger Personal Collection.)

The WLSSD bill wasn't the only environmental measure Munger authored during the 1971 legislative session.

Duluth DFLer, State Representative Willard Munger today said that he was gratified by House passage yesterday of his bill calling for a ban on the use of DTT and mercury.

Munger, who has worked for numerous major environmental protection measures over the past decade, emphasized that recent studies have demonstrated the extreme ecological dangers resulting from wide-spread use of DDT and noted that his bill would create review procedures to prevent discharge of such poisons...

Munger noted that legislative action on this crucial bill is essential in the face of increasing evidence of the disastrous effects already raising havoc with our environment...

For example, traces of DDT and mercury are found in substantial amounts in every living thing around the world. DDT, with a half-life of 15 years, and mercury, with a 100-year life, remain and accumulate in the environment, spreading their poison to such an extent that whole species of animals have been almost wiped out by the effects of the chemicals...

(Press Release, May 19, 1971, Willard Munger Collection.)

The DDT bill never made it to Governor Anderson's desk. As pugnacious as Munger was in the environmental arena, there were some fights even he couldn't win.

Some argue that Willard Munger's conservation ethic hastened the death of Duluth's steel plant. But U.S. Steel's Duluth works wasn't only faced with increased costs due to heightened pollution standards; it was operating its plant in 1971 with 1910 technology. Even still, the loss of thousands of his constituents' jobs weighed heavily on Munger's mind.

May 25, 1971

Dear Willard:

I'd like to take the opportunity to express my appreciation and the thanks of the Arrowhead Committee for the Environment for all the work you and your colleagues did on behalf of our Duluth Steel Plant bill.

I am confident that had we been successful in the Senate, the House campaign would have proceeded much more smoothly because of the effectiveness of you and our friends displayed. Unfortunately, we did not have that chance...

Sincerely,

John LaForge

Manager

KDAL-TV

The bill referenced in LaForge's letter was killed by Senate Minority Leader Nicholas Coleman of St. Paul.

"I don't believe...the state of Minnesota should be in a position of giving away things to U.S. Steel. I think it's an improper way for the state...to act. The proper way is for the environmental fund that would not only help U.S. Steel but also Reserve Mining and the entire northeastern area of the state..."

(*Duluth News Tribune*, November 1, 1971.)

Senator Coleman argued that legislative inaction had nothing to do with the shut down. "These people are out of work...because U.S. Steel has never kept this facility up..."

Willard Munger was tireless in his support of legislation to fund pollution and technological upgrades for the plant. In doing so, Munger harkened back to the state ownership of essential commercial activities, a doctrine that had been central to both the Nonpartisan League and the Farmer-Labor Party.

Rep. Willard Munger, Duluth DFLer, last Friday introduced a resolution memorializing Congress and the president to "acquire and refit" the United States Steel works at Duluth and the Reserve Mining Facilities in Silver Bay.

Munger emphasized that his resolution called for federal takeover of the Minnesota steel facilities only in the event that the steel company was unable or unwilling to meet its water pollution control obligations as set forth by the PCA and use this as an excuse to close their obsolete plant rather than spend the necessary money to modernize it...

"We cannot tolerate having additional thousands of persons in the Duluth out of work," Munger said. "The Duluth facilities were built in 1915 and have become a way of life for the region. But their operations produce 4,900 tons of air pollution every year and large quantities of untreated sewage." Cost to modernize the facility, including pollution control equipment, would run $50 – 56 million.

According to Munger, company officials have indicated that these anticipated expenditures for pollution controls might cause closing of the steel facilities with the loss of 2,600 jobs and a 25 million dollar annual payroll. There is a further possible job loss impact totaling 17,000 living in the Duluth area.

(*Labor World*, June 17, 1971.)

Governor Anderson was solidly behind the effort to save the steel plant.

Gov. Wendell Anderson gave his support…to new tax incentive legislation which would encourage construction of a modern steel making facility in Duluth.

Thomas Kelm, the governor's executive secretary, disclosed in a letter to Rep. Willard Munger, chairman of the Duluth delegation that Anderson will publicly back the proposal…

Munger, who had announced he would vote against a compromise tax bill, said he'd changed his mind because of the governor's support of the steel plant tax incentive proposal as a separate bill…

(*Duluth News Tribune*, October 18, 1971.)

Kelm wrote to Munger regarding the governor's position.

October 27, 1971

Dear Willard:

Pursuant to your request, I have just finished talking to Governor Anderson and he has authorized me to issue immediately a press release supporting the bill I understand is being authored in the House and Senate as a separate bill for tax relief for the Duluth Steel Plant.

I know you are well aware we have supported this in the past. As participants in the tax conference committee, we tried unsuccessfully to make it a part of the tax bill, and wholeheartedly support this as a separate bill hopefully to be passed by this legislature…

Thomas Kelm

Senator Nick Coleman voiced his opposition to any plan providing tax assistance for the Duluth steel plant. Duluth legislators attacked Coleman for his hypocrisy.

> Rep. Willard Munger, a Liberal and chairman of the Duluth legislative delegation said, at an informal meeting…"I am not going to vote for the state tax bill unless there is a provision in it to encourage construction of a modern steel plant."
>
> Sen. Richard Palmer, Conservative, said, "I refuse to give up on this issue and will assist Sen. Earl Gustafson, the chief senate author in any way possible to get the bill out on the senate floor for action."
>
> Gustafson, a Duluth Liberal, who was not in St. Paul Tuesday, scored fellow Liberal Coleman, saying "I am perplexed at his action. He didn't hesitate to use his position to kill a tax incentive for a Duluth steel plant and yet he apparently approves of a tax incentive to build a taconite plant in Hibbing."
>
> (*Duluth News Tribune*, October 27, 1971.)

Willard Munger was extremely visible in the fight.

> During the regular and special sessions of the legislature, several bills were introduced with bi-partisan support, providing tax credits to U.S. Steel as an incentive to build a new plant or to modernize it in order to make it competitive and keep it in operation…
>
> One of the main reasons for the bills not passing is the simple cold fact that U.S. Steel Corp. showed no evidence in support of either bill. It is difficult to convince a legislative committee to give something to someone who does not wish to accept your offer.
>
> Therefore one must conclude that U.S. Steel fears that the passage of either of the bills would serve as a stumbling block, and consolidate public opinion against them if they should decide to close down the plant, which now seems to be their main consideration.
>
> It is high time we stop placing all of the blame on certain members of the legislature for the failure of passing the bills and place the responsibility where it rightfully belongs-at the doorstep of the steel company who refuses to make any commitments.
>
> As chairman of the Duluth delegation, I called several meetings in behalf of these bills and not once did any representative of U.S. Steel appear in behalf of either bill or give any indication of their position. Rep Mason, the chief author of the bills admitted to our committee many times that he had not received the steel company's support of the bills.

No one of the Duluth Delegation members has a closer relationship than the chief author. Rep. Mason was not able to get a commitment from U.S. Steel. It is unfortunate that the newspaper carried a front page story quoting Rep. Mason as blaming everything on the Liberals. Now his main objective is to build a political smoke screen to protect U.S. Steel Company's action in closing down its operation and refusing to support his own bill. Or was his bill just window dressing?...

I am therefore calling a meeting of the Duluth Delegation, labor leaders, public officials, and U.S. Steel officials to try and get a commitment from U.S. Steel as to their intention relative to the legislation to encourage the continued operation of the plant...

(Press Release, November 10, 1971, Willard Munger Personal Collection.)

The impact of the steel plant issue on Willard's political career cannot be overstated. First, the loss of over 3,000 jobs in a part of the city already reeling from smaller plant closures and cut-backs was, very simply put, an economic catastrophe. Additionally, there was a very real danger, palpable during the Saturday morning breakfast confabs that had started up at the Willard Motel coffee shop between Willard and his constituents, that the steel plant closure would be seen by many as having been caused by Munger's conservation activism, which would likely result in voter backlash against Munger. One can imagine the heated discussions held at the coffee shop regarding this topic, with the mix of folks in attendance representing labor, conservation groups, stalwart DFLers and ordinary Duluthians. Munger was, more than anything else, a listener. He always had his ear to the ground; he was always cognizant of where he stood with the people.

A forum regarding the steel plant was held at Duluth Morgan Park High School. Senator Palmer, Mayor Ben Boo, Rep. Munger, Rep. Solon and Lieutenant Governor Perpich were in attendance to answer questions from students and members of the community. The crowd also heard the position of U.S. Steel as articulated in prepared remarks.

U.S. Steel must continue its careful study of the market situation, including the over-all steel distribution potentials, to insure that no sound, economic, commercial opportunity for plant continuance (including those made available by modernization or new facilities) is overlooked, slighted, or otherwise given improper attention. Only after these studies are completed, and then only in affirmative determination that continuance of operations is prudent, can U.S. Steel look to the potential merit of tax incentives or other legislative assistance…

> (November 16, 1971 address by F.J. Nevers, U.S. Steel,
> Willard Munger Personal Collection.)

Though the students at Morgan Park High School were witnesses to history being made, the forum failed to accomplish anything meaningful. U.S. Steel's position remained firm: the steel plant in Gary-New Duluth would close and no economic or tax incentives would change the corporate decision-making process.

> The full impact of the Duluth steel plant hot side shutdown will not be felt for some time. But community leaders agree to a man that if the facility remains inoperative for an extended period the bite on the Twin Ports' area economy will be severe.
>
> For the 1,300 employees idled by the shutdown, the blow will be cushioned for a time by state and labor contract-negotiated unemployment tax-free benefits….
>
> The Duluth steel plant payroll since 1915 has been of major importance to the Duluth economy…The plant was constructed primarily to meet a regional market demand for certain wire products, namely wire fence and nails…

> (*Duluth News Tribune*, November 21, 1971.)

As angst over the steel plant's demise settled to anger, Munger continued to address the fiscal concerns of his fellow West Duluth businessmen. It must be remembered that, throughout his long career in the House of Representatives (with the exception of the last six years of his tenure (1993 – 1999) Munger was a small businessman, operating a family-owned motel and coffee shop on the thinnest of profit margins. Willard Munger was, in many ways, a fundamental contradiction. He was an ardent and passionate Liberal and yet he was also firmly rooted in the business community, having been a member of the West Duluth Businessmen since opening his gas station in 1939. The dichotomy of these seemingly contrary positions is seen in the following speech given by Munger to the West Duluth Businessmen on December 1, 1971.

> The biggest problem legislatures face in almost every state is that people no longer wish to pay, or can afford to pay, the high taxes required to fund the state services and new programs which they have been demanding from state governments. And too, as taxes go up in a tight economy period, a greater

share of the tax burden is being shifted from big business and industry to the small taxpayer and homeowner.

The governor's bill sought to equalize the tax burden for the small taxpayer and homeowner by a tax reform program based upon the ability to pay. The 1973 Legislature must provide for the taking over of the total cost of state school aids and welfare by the state, if we are to have real meaningful local tax relief, we have started in that direction.

The ever-increasing technological and complicated social environment into which we are moving requires that the economic and social problems created be dealt with by a compassionate and understanding government if democracy is to survive.

One answer would be to get the hell out of Vietnam and use that tax money to take care of social and economic problems here at home...

I know that the legislators who voted for the tax bill are, at the present time, at the bottom of the opinion polls. But we who voted for the tax bill have one consolation-we are so far down on the opinion polls right now, we have only one way to go, and that is up!

May I extend a bit of caution to those who voted against the tax bill? Don't allow the present confusion to push you so high on the opinion polls that you will have to depend on a Republican Safety Net to save you on your way down!...

Many of us in the legislature who voted for this bill recognized that it was a bi-partisan compromise brought about after many previous failures. It was the best bill we could get from this legislature, and far much better than the vetoed bill. It wasn't the bill that I wanted, but the best we could expect with a Conservative controlled House and Senate.

The bill is not all bad. The bill does move Minnesota in the long overdue direction of property tax reform. It concentrates on raising new revenues from non-property tax sources based upon ability to pay.

Major tax reform is evident particularly in the school aid formula, which makes an all out effort to equalize educational opportunities state-wide. We are under pressure to do so by the Supreme Court ruling. The California Supreme Court has held that dependence upon local property taxes creates unequal educational opportunities because it provides for the quality of a child's education based upon the tax base and wealth of the school district. California is not alone. Minnesota's method of financing schools is also being challenged in a suit before the Federal District Court. The case is before Judge Miles Lord and he has delayed his decision pending enactment of

Minnesota's new tax bill...This bill does go in the direction of satisfying the objection of the courts. Under the bill, Minnesota would increase its share of local educational maintenance costs from 43% to 65%...

In conclusion, let me repeat...Republicans frankly wanted workers and ordinary people to foot most of the bill, while the DFL position was bluntly aimed at requiring the rich and upper-income taxpayers to shoulder their fair share of the burden...

The October compromise plan increased the state income tax on a $4,000.00 income family by $14.01 or 53% less than the $29.51 increase under the ...GOP bill. In light of the benefits for this area, it is hard to understand how Senator Palmer can justify his vote against the tax bill, considering there wasn't even the slightest chance for a better one with a Republican controlled House and Senate.

(Willard Munger Personal Collection.)

Munger's business ties were key to many of his relationships. He insisted upon "buying local," trading at the West Duluth paint store (Andren's) and at local hardware stores and lumber yards, rather than shopping at Knox or Menard's.

And though Munger's motel was a marginally profitable proposition, some of Munger's constituents assumed the legislator was getting rich from his years of public service.

"I've got to tell you," Willard recalled, "a good story about my finances. A drunk came over (to the motel coffee shop)...and sat down.

He said, 'Goddamn politicians. They're all crooked.'

I said, 'You ought to make one exception there, buddy, or I'll put you through that window.'

He said, 'Why don't this just prove it. I can remember when you didn't have anything, and now you've got this big, brick motel...'

It just happened that I was two months behind on my payments and the bank had written me a kind of sarcastic letter...I threw it in front of him, and he read it aloud and said, 'Jesus Christ. You've been in the legislature how long? Twenty years and you've still got a mortgage on this place?...You must be awfully stupid...'"

(*Oral History of Willard Munger*, ibid, p. 30.)

The debate over whether Munger was a shrewd or terrible businessman has never been settled.

"My family," Will Munger, Jr. says with a smile, "calls the Willard Munger Inn the 'No-Mo-Money-Motel'. Everyone was convinced (when I took it over in 1993) that it was a loser and a waste of time for me to try to operate. 'It will never make money' was something I heard all the time. You have to understand. My father wasn't a businessman. For him, the motel was a hobby, something to do. For me, it's a challenge and I like to make things work. Making money—that never appealed to Dad. The motel was just an outlet."

Patsy Munger-Lehr takes exception to her brother's remarks.

"If Dad was such a poor businessman, explain how he was able to leave Will a motel nearly free of debt and me a parcel of land and a beautiful brick home right on the St. Louis River," Patsy challenges. "I think Dad was a good businessman."

Whatever one thinks of Willard Munger's business acumen, Will Munger is right: the motel was always secondary to Willard Munger's true love; legislating. But as 1971 gave way to a new year, Willard's political prowess proved no match for corporate stubbornness and economic reality.

> The final decision to close the primary steelmaking facilities was made with great reluctance, Mr. Gott said. "I am pleased that the availability of these alternate employment opportunities within the company will cushion the overall effects of the shutdown," he added…(referring to U.S. Steel positions open in the iron ore mines and in the Lake Shipping operations of the U.S. Steel Fleet)…
>
> "For some time," he said, "finished product output has consumed only 20 per cent of Duluth's steel production. The other 80 per cent of the production has been shipped as semi-finished steel product primarily to other U.S. Steel plants…Our studies have indicated no way by which these semi-finished steels can be furnished from Duluth at costs as low as those which can be attained by other U.S. Steel operations close to the location of such steel consumption…"
>
> (Press Release from U.S. Steel, January 28, 1972.)

U.S. Steel's announcement caused legislators to scramble. The thought was that, if U.S. Steel was pulling out of Duluth, perhaps another steel maker would be willing, with the right economic incentives, to retrofit the plant.

> Gov. Wendell Anderson called for the meeting Thursday after a meeting with three members of a blue-ribbon committee appointed by the governor a month ago…

In the past, Anderson has indicated he would require prior agreement on a tax incentive bill before calling a special legislative session. The situation is complicated by the fact some lawmakers want to tackle reapportionment once again in a special session in an effort to undo the 62-member cut in the size of the legislature ordered by the federal court...

Under the proposed bill, any company building a plant worth $80 million and producing 1,000 jobs could reduce the amount of income, sales and occupation taxes it pays the state...

(*Duluth News Tribune*, February 4, 1972.)

As this book was being written, Ikonics, a small Duluth-based industrial firm, commenced construction of a modest manufacturing plant on the former U.S. Steel site. However, most of the property remains vacant. The state and the city have been largely unsuccessful in their attempts to entice a major industrial concern to relocate to the Gary-New Duluth site.

With the demise of the "hot side" of the U.S. Steel works, the wire bailing operation and cement plant operations soon followed. By 1983, the population of the western half of Duluth had been so depleted by the departure of U.S. Steel and other smaller manufacturing facilities that Morgan Park High School was converted into a middle school and the remaining high school students were transferred to Duluth Denfeld. The departure of blue-collar workers from West Duluth mirrored the exodus of miners and their families from the Mesabi Iron Range when recession hit and the taconite plants went idle. In a short twenty-year span, Duluth lost 20,000 people, going from a city of 106,000 to 86,000 seemingly overnight. What is remarkable is that the folks in the 59th Legislative District who stayed put did not chastise or punish Willard Munger for the area's economic woes.

At the height of the debate concerning the steel plant's demise, Munger purchased a decaying Indian Point resort property on the St. Louis River. The secluded parcel (just a stone's throw from Munger's motel) provided Munger with a sanctuary and with a place to renew a boyhood hobby.

Busy as a Bee More than a Slogan to Munger by Einar Karlstrand

State Rep. Willard M. Munger...uses honey instead of sugar in his coffee. In fact, honey is an important food in his diet.

That accounts for his beekeeping hobby which occupies some of his time between legislative sessions and when he is not on the job operating his West Duluth motel.

Beekeeping ties in with his interest in organic foods which he and his wife grow in their garden and orchard without the use of chemical fertilizers.

From his two bee colonies...Munger expects to harvest 300 pounds of comb honey this year...He uses no sugar.

Keeping bees provides him with a past-time that he has enjoyed since he was a boy on a farm north of Fergus Falls. He regards bees as among nature's most interesting insects...

"Bees need nectar, pollen, propolis and water," Munger said. "They make honey out of the nectar and convert pollen into beebread food for the young bees," he explained. "They use propolis to seal cracks and waterproof their hive. They dilute honey with water before eating it and use water to air-condition the hive..."

He said honeybees can be kept anywhere in Minnesota. The state has 270,000 bee colonies and yearly honey production of 20 – 29 million pounds.

Minnesota has ranked first or second in U.S. honey production for several years.

(*Duluth Herald*, June 26, 1972.)

Irrespective of his devotion to bee keeping, Munger's lifeblood was politics and 1972 was an election year.

Four More File for Legislature

Filing were State Rep. Willard Munger, Duluth Liberal, for re-election to the state House of Representatives from newly created District 7A...Michael Jaros...for election as a State Representative from District 7B...

Munger, who was first elected in 1954, is seeking his ninth term...

Munger, if re-elected, said he expects to be named chairman of either the appropriations or natural resources committee.

Among the problems facing the 1973 Legislature, Munger said in a prepared statement, are economic growth and jobs for Duluth, tax and legislative reform, and legislation to help make Duluth an outstanding educational and medical center of the northern Midwest and southern Canada.

"In a complex society such as ours," he said, "there are many social problems...We can no longer be complacent, ignore necessary reforms, and hide behind tradition."

(*Duluth News Tribune*, July 11, 1972.)

The 1972 presidential election pitted President Nixon against U.S. Senator George McGovern of South Dakota. Duluth millionaire Jeno Paulucci was the national vice chair of the "Democrats and Independents for Nixon." Five hundred American Indians seized the Bureau of Indian Affairs Headquarters in Washington. Eighteen-year-olds were allowed to vote in national elections for the first time. And Watergate was in the news.

> A trinity of top Republican spokesmen…attacked the credibility of the source of recent disclosures about spying and sabotage attempts to disrupt the Democratic presidential campaign. (The trio consisted of) Ron Ziegler, Nixon's Press Secretary, Clark MacGregor, Nixon's Re-Election Chair, and Senator Robert Dole, chairman of the RNC…
>
> (*Duluth News Tribune*, October 26, 1972.)

Munger beat his opponent in a relatively close race, perhaps an indication of some ill-feelings in the district over the steel plant's demise; and political newcomer, Liberal Mike Jaros, upset Conservative Dwight Swanstrom to claim the House seat in 7B for the DFL. Nationally, Nixon trounced McGovern, winning Minnesota and every other state except Massachusetts.

When Munger returned to the House for his tenth non-consecutive term in 1973, he immediately resumed work on conservation-related issues. 1973 was also the year that the Minnesota Legislature went to every year sessions. This intensification of the job duties of "citizen legislators" coincided with 1973 being the most significant environmental session in Minnesota legislative history.

"I came to the legislature in 1969," legislative researcher John Helland recalls, "serving in the House Research Department. I worked first with the Agriculture Committee and later, when the Conservation Committee became the Environment and Natural Resources Committee, I went to work there, where I met Willard. The committee was formed in 1971 – 72 with Representative Wally Gustafson as its chairman. Gustafson was awarded the title, 'Polluter of the Year'. He was a lawyer from Willmar and terrible on conservation issues."

"Willard really cared," John Helland remembers. "He was clearly a Progressive. He cared about people and the natural environment. He wanted to keep it as clean and whole as possible—it was in his heart and his soul. With Willard, it was real—not some political position. He was a true public servant in that way. Gustafson, on the other hand, wasn't interested in environmental issues."

Legislator Shrinks from "Polluter" Award by **Stan Strick**

On the day Rep. Willard Munger took over the House Environmental Preservation Committee, he told members he wasn't going to win the "polluter of the year" award.

The past chairman of the committee, former Rep. Wallace Gustafson, Willmar Conservative, was given the title in 1971 by environmentalists who thought he was their biggest stumbling block to progress.

Munger, a Duluth DFLer, should have ample opportunity to make good on his pledge. Gov. Wendell Anderson's comprehensive environmental message covers everything from land use to mine-land reclamation. In addition, several highly charged issues—like "ban the can" and halting nuclear power plant construction—are back for a second time…

Munger favors Anderson's approach, with a regional program to recycle wastes. The PCA is drafting legislation to include the authority to cut down on materials, such as packaging, which quickly find their way to the garbage can.

The largest controversies ahead concern environmental impact statements and the make-up of the Environmental Quality Board…

In his message, Anderson gave top priority to land use controls. He asked for state power to protect critical environmental areas and scenic rivers, to select power plants and to oversee major land developments…

A number of other issues will surface during the session including:

Increased Tax write offs for installation of pollution control equipment.

Motor vehicle inspection for emissions, noise and safety.

Fees to be charged against industry to pay for the state's pollution checks.

(*Minneapolis Tribune*, February 24, 1973.)

"Willard knew he couldn't carry all the environmental legislation that came up that session," Helland remembers. "So he got Harry Sieben [later Speaker of the House], Bruce Vento [later a U.S. Congressman] and others to carry the bills. Some of the measures that were passed during that year included the Wild and Scenic Rivers Act, the Environmental Quality Council, the Power Plant Siting Act, the requirement for Environmental Impact Statements, the Waste Water Treatment Act and bills regarding air pollution. Willard also pushed for a state-wide, comprehensive planning act modeled on those found in Oregon and Vermont but that never passed."

Another individual who recalls those heady times is long-time Munger aide Jackie Rosholt.

Rosholt, an Iowan by birth, was drawn to Washington, D.C. in the 1960s with hopes of entering the Foreign Service. Unsuccessful in that pursuit, she came to Minnesota in support of Wendy Anderson's 1970 gubernatorial campaign. After Anderson's election, Rosholt worked briefly for the governor but was transferred to the Minnesota Pollution Control Agency to work with PCA Director Grant Merritt. Merritt assigned Rosholt to study the potentiality of state-wide recycling. She presented a report on that issue to the legislature during the 1973 session.

"That's when I met Willard," Rosholt recalls, "and he offered me a job. The DFL was in control. They wanted to hire partisan staff to work with legislators. John Helland was non-partisan. I was hired as a partisan committee administrator for the Environment and Natural Resources Committee by Willard. He felt it was very cutting edge to hire a woman."

Rosholt relates that when Munger came into the House during the 1950s, there was no real professional staff; Munger's only office was his desk on the House floor.

"He had a waste basket, a drawer for filing, and when he wanted to answer mail," Rosholt adds, "he had to go out in the hallway and beg a lobbyist to let him use a secretary from the lobbyist's office. Willard always thought that was wrong—to be beholden to lobbyists. So when the DFL took control, they hired professional staff."

Rosholt's perception of Munger's ethics included a clear understanding that he didn't want to be obligated to anyone.

"DFL committee chairs were required," Rosholt recalls, "to raise something like a thousand dollars for the caucus. They were supposed to ask lobbyists for contributions. Willard wouldn't do it. He'd give the caucus $100 from his own campaign fund but he would never ask for money from lobbyists. The environmental lobbies didn't have money and he wasn't going to take it from the other side."

Rosholt said that her arrangement with Munger was unique.

"I shared his committee chair," Rosholt recounts. "He didn't like the day-to-day job of doing interviews. He'd have me do that and I'd give him the lay of the land. Together we'd come up with a strategy on an issue. The DFL caucus relied upon us to tell them what was on the horizon in terms of environmental matters. This arrangement worked well politically for Willard. When a bill was coming up in committee that he didn't like, he'd tell me 'No way, Rosholt. No way can this pass' and then he'd have me play the bad guy. He'd tell the author, 'You have to talk to Jackie.' That way, he didn't offend the bill's author. He understood the need to keep folks happy, to not ruffle feathers. He could bite his tongue and vote for something if it didn't go against his principles but he never compromised his core beliefs."

Rosholt believes that Munger's legislative tenure had two primary focuses.

"If it was an environmental bill or a bill concerning Duluth," Rosholt adds, "he was committed to the cause. He was on the Higher Education Appropriations Subcommittee and he was always supportive of funding for UMD. But if a bill wasn't about the environment or Duluth, Willard didn't have a lot of interest in the details."

According to Rosholt, Munger's attributes included loyalty.

"He was very loyal. One time, a former legislator-turned-lobbyist, Bob Latz, went in to see the Speaker of the House about me being too partisan. Latz wanted me fired. Willard found out about it and stormed into the Speaker's office. That was the end of it. He saved my job," Rosholt recalls. "But there was a time, right in the beginning, when I nearly quit. During the 1974 session, we had a mandatory deposit bill pending. We had the votes to pass it in the House and it had already passed the Senate. But Wendy [Anderson] and Martin [Sabo] were told by labor that it couldn't pass. The governor couldn't veto it because he had promoted passage of a recycling bill in one of his speeches. So Sabo [who was the Speaker of the House] called Willard and I into his office and told us it couldn't pass out of committee. Now the bill had overwhelming support in committee. Willard held the bill until the time for straight passage from committee to the floor of the House expired. That meant it had to go from the committee to the Rules Committee before it could be debated on the floor. The Rules Committee killed it. I was so mad, I nearly quit."

Ann Glumac, who followed Rosholt as committee administrator, agrees with Rosholt's perceptions.

"Willard liked you to run interference for him. But he backed your decisions. I remember," Glumac recalls, "that there was a bill where both a Republican and a Democrat had introduced competing versions of the bill in our committee. The Republican followed protocol and asked for a hearing so I scheduled one. The Democrat never asked for a hearing and when he found out that I'd set a hearing for the Republican version of the bill, he got mad. He went (all torqued up) to the Speaker's office, wanting me fired. Willard stepped in. He said to the guy, 'You didn't ask for a hearing. What do you expect?' He didn't back down or point fingers at staff. He was very honest and loyal about that."

Grant Merritt, who, after serving as the MPCA Executive Director under Wendy Anderson, returned to the private practice of law, became a close friend of Munger's during the early 1970s.

Merritt, a descendent of the legendary Merritt brothers who discovered the Mesabi Iron Range (only to lose their fortunes to the same Eastern money interests that Willard's early heroes railed against) was born and raised in Duluth. As a Boy Scout (and frequent visitor to Isle Royal National Park on Lake Superior) Merritt became active in the Reserve Mining controversy in the late 1960s because a relative, Milton Mattson, interested him in the issue. Merritt also joined MECCA (Minnesota Environmental Control Citizens Association) which boasted Munger legislative colleague and friend, John Rose (IR-Roseville) amongst its members. Merritt's membership in MECCA and his ties to the Mattson family on Lake Superior's North Shore led to his membership in the Save Lake Superior Association. Merritt also became active in Wendy Anderson's 1970 gubernatorial campaign.

"I was Wendy's de facto environmental advisor," Merritt says. "Then, when Wendy won the election, Dick Moe and Dave Lebedoff twisted my arm to become the head of the MPCA. I didn't want to do it. In fact, I'd turned down a position on the MPCA Citizen's Committee because my law practice was doing so well. But they persisted. So, on March 1, 1971, I became the second Executive Director of the MPCA."

Merritt reiterates the position of John Helland and others regarding the level of cooperation that existed in the early 1970s between the Liberals and the Conservatives on environmental issues.

"Wendy Anderson gave a famous address on the environment. Then we went to work. Wendy had great relationships with the Republicans. They were 'conservative but conservation minded.' One of the primary things that got passed was a Minnesota version of Michigan's 'Sax bill,' which was named after a professor of environmental science from Michigan. The law states that, if pollution or development is shown to have an adverse impact on a natural resource, so long as it isn't *de minimis* (minimal), then the burden of proof shifts to the person promoting the project to show that there is no reasonable alternative. It is a huge thing; one that has been used in litigation many, many times."

Grant Merritt remembers things being distinctly different between the House and the Senate in terms of getting environmental legislation passed.

"When the DFL took over the legislature in 1973, Willard became the head of the House Environment and Natural Resources Committee and you could count on his committee to pass most environmental bills. But in the Senate, for whatever reason, they combined environment and agriculture into one committee, making it much more difficult to pass environmental bills," Merritt says. "I remember Skip Humphrey (son of U.S. Senator Hubert Humphrey) right after he was elected to the State Senate in 1972, trying to find out why a nuclear moratorium bill—one banning the siting of new nuclear power plants in Minnesota—had stalled out in the Senate after passing the House. He came back clueless as to why it hadn't passed. The reason was simple: the farmers in the Senate blocked every piece of environmental legislation they could. They had no interest in being regulated in any way."

When asked to reflect on Munger's personality, Merritt pauses.

"He was sly like a fox," Merritt says. "But you could get him going if you wanted to. A few years after I left the MPCA, I was up at the coffee shop having breakfast. I looked at Willard, who was making pancakes and Heidi (Heidi Lindberg, a longtime motel employee) was standing there, and I said, 'Willard, you didn't have a thing to do with Reserve Mining.' The truth was, much of what he did with respect to the tailings issue was behind the scenes because of his constituents in West Duluth. He didn't want to alienate them. But it wasn't true that he hadn't worked on the issue. He got so mad; Heidi thought he was going to have a heart attack. In truth, because of the nature of being the Executive Director of the MPCA—being an advocate and having the Board function as the policy maker—I was often in hot water and Willard was always there to pull me out of it. Those times I poked fun at Willard, I got him going. In those sessions at the coffee shop, he could really dish it out. But he didn't take it quite as well."

Grant Merritt left the MPCA and became a lobbyist for environmental causes. Merritt recounts a stormy meeting with an Iron Range legislator that took place during his tenure as a lobbyist.

"I wanted to talk to Dave Battaglia (DFL-Two Harbors) about something unrelated to Reserve. I arranged a meeting in Willard's office, which was undergoing repairs at the time. The pipes and wall joists were all exposed. I sat down to talk to Battaglia and he started insulting me. It got my dander up. Finally, I called Battaglia an SOB. He grabbed me and pushed me into the exposed pipes. When Battaglia left, Willard looked at me and said, 'You shouldn't have called him an SOB.' I said, 'I'm going to sue him for assault and battery and you're my witness,' but I never did. About six or seven years later, Battaglia and I were standing next to each other at the dedication of the new Gooseberry State Park visitor's center. I looked up and saw a bald eagle soaring above us. I said to Battaglia, 'Look Dave, an eagle. You would have never seen that if we hadn't gotten rid of those tailings.' Battaglia smiled and I knew we'd be alright."

There were times, according to Merritt, when the fight over environmental legislation became so intense that not only the Republicans, but the DFLers as well, were after him.

"There was a very controversial bill dealing with source reduction and recycling that I was pushing," Merritt remembers. "It got so bad, even the Democrats were against me. And the Republicans, they wanted to bury both the MPCA and the DNR. Willard stepped in and smoothed things over."

Arne Carlson, before seeking and winning the Minnesota state auditor's office in 1978 and the Minnesota governorship in 1990, served as a Conservative and Republican member of the Minnesota House of Representatives from 1970 – 1978.

Carlson was born and raised in New York City but he knew from an early age that his calling in life wasn't the typical New York City boy's dream of working for the city as a firefighter or policeman. The former governor recalls being drawn to politics at an early age, an unusual aspiration which Carlson unknowingly shared with the much older Willard Munger. Both men chose dynamic and inspiring political figures as role models; Carlson's being New York City Mayor Fiorello LaGuardia, Franklin Delano Roosevelt, and Adlai Stevenson; Munger's being A.C. Townley, Floyd B. Olson, and Elmer A. Benson. But unlike Munger, who spent his entire life living and campaigning in the state of his birth, Arne Carlson knew that he didn't want to spend his life in New York.

"I knew I didn't want to live in the city; that I needed a place," Carlson recalls, "with lots of green space. At the first opportunity to leave, when I was able to obtain a scholarship for a preparatory school in Connecticut, I did. Then after I graduated from college, I applied to graduate schools in Michigan, Wisconsin, and Minnesota. I was accepted by the University of Minnesota and that's how I ended up here."

While attending the University of Minnesota, Carlson became involved in Hubert Humphrey's 1960 presidential bid. Despite coming from a political climate where the Democrats were very corrupt, Carlson cast his lot with the DFL in Minnesota until an ugly split in the mid-1960s between Party intellectuals and labor soured him on the Party. Former Governor Elmer L. Andersen then convinced Carlson to join the Conservatives. With Andersen's support, Carlson was elected to the Minneapolis City Council in 1965. A 1967 run for mayor of Minneapolis failed but, in 1970, Carlson was elected as a Conservative member of the Minnesota House, which is where he first came into contact with Willard Munger.

"A little background is needed before we talk about Willard," Carlson says. "I was a pariah in the Republican Party. I was too Liberal. So when the Republicans were in the majority, which they were when I came into the House, I was given the worst committee assignments by the senior Republicans. I was put on committees like the Claims Committee. You see, before the DFL took back control in the 1972 election, even though there were new movements afoot, especially in the areas of environmentalism and consumerism, movements being embraced by the younger legislators and staff people, the senior Conservatives were so tied to business interests that those new ideas, those new movements, weren't given hearings. Then, with Rachel Carson's book and other disclosures, these new tides began to swell. Environmentalism was just in its early stages but it was there."

Carlson reflects that, once the DFL took power and the 1973 Legislative Session began, as a minority member of the House, he was free to choose his committee assignments and he chose to work on environmental issues.

"The DFL recognized these new tides, these new forces of consumerism and environmentalism," the former governor continues. "The committees were very much organized along the lines of the underlying departments but the House Environment and Natural Resources Committee was a bit different. It took broader input than just from the DNR or the PCA—there were all these new groups, just in their infancy, lobbying to do something about the environment after 20-30 years of pro-business thwarting of environmental efforts. You have to understand that the business interests basically funded the Conservative caucuses. Not only funded, but were allowed to participate in the decision making. There had been young, Conservative legislators who supported the new trends in environmentalism and consumerism but they were stifled by the Party. They were forced, by more senior Conservative legislators, to stall and thwart bills relating to these new issues. Most of them lost their positions in the 1972 elections as a result of this.

The Democrats understood the political strength of these new tides and I saw that there was a high degree of talent; in the legislature, in the administration, and in the departments relating to these new issues."

When pressed to describe what set Munger's chairmanship apart from what had gone on before in the Environment and Natural Resources Committee, Governor Carlson is candid.

"As chair, Willard was an interesting fellow. He was, and I don't know a nice way of saying this, older. He was from another generation of legislators. But he was also the first elder in the legislature to allow the younger generation to voice these new ideas. There was a genuine desire, one that was well-founded in my view, that Minnesota needed progressive legislation in both the areas of consumer and environmental protection. Willard's strengths were that he had the respectability of being from that older generation and that he welcomed the activity that came with the new ideas," Carlson says. "I'm not saying that every bill that got passed out of our committee was great, but we were passing laws that should have been dealt with years before. Willard's committee was a magnet for all those bills that had been thwarted for 20-30 years, importantly beginning with water pollution and moving on from there. At every step of the way, there was a battle. On one bill, it might be with the chemical companies. On another, the mining industry. Business was generally opposed to any environmental or consumer legislation."

When asked to describe Munger's treatment of those on his committee (like Carlson) who were from the "loyal opposition," the former governor reflects.

"Willard was cantankerous. But he got along quite well with those of us from across the aisle. Look, everyone has personality traits. Over time, as you work with a person, you figure out how to adapt to the other person's style. For example, Roger Moe (DFL-Erskine; later Senate Majority Leader) never would give you an answer. You'd state your case and he'd listen. But he'd never tell you 'yes' or 'no'. Later on an aide would come by and tell you how Roger was going to vote."

"Willard was fair overall," the former governor says. "Now, understand, the DFL in 1973 is sort of like Obama today, voicing high ideals, ready to change the world. Willard had his own cranky, direct style. There was nothing subtle about him. But, overall, bills flowed through his committee without problem. He was a magnet for all this new idealism. Really, he legitimized environmentalism in Minnesota politics. His was one of the most progressive committees. He ran the committee with an iron hand but it was never unpleasant. It was a great time to be in the legislature. His assistant, Jackie, she was tough. Willard truly enjoyed working with young people, hearing their ideas."

Ann Glumac, Willard's committee administrator during the '87, '88 and '89 sessions, agrees with Governor Carlson's assessment of Munger's leadership style.

"Overall, Willard was very fair," Glumac remembers. "Maybe one or two times while I was committee administrator, there was a bill Willard absolutely hated that didn't get a hearing. But overall, he heard bills that were introduced and it didn't matter from which side of the aisle. He would ask funny questions, keep things light and let folks speak.

There was this one time, when a witness was droning on and on, where Willard, rather than be impolite, started looking at the big wrist watch he wore. Then, because the guy wasn't taking the hint, Willard took the watch off and started swinging it back and forth in the air, sort of like 'tick tock, tick tock'. He didn't have the heart to cut the guy off."

Not every piece of progressive legislation had Arne Carlson's support. The former governor recalls one bill in particular, a bill seeking to have land held by private citizens located in state parks revert to public ownership upon the death of the owner, where he and Munger locked horns.

"We were on the House floor arguing about that one," Carlson remembers. "Willard was pushing for the state to exercise eminent domain over those cabins but I wouldn't give in. Eventually, the rest of the DFL came over to my way of thinking. Willard wasn't too happy about that."

Retired Representative Dave Battaglia (DFL-Two Harbors) agrees that the 1970s were a heady time.

"The Environment and Natural Resources was a very important committee—we went on field trips to Willmar, New Prague and other cities—and we held meetings about lakes, about fish and game issues. We came up to Silver Bay to discuss netting fish in Lake Superior. Willard's committee was very important," Battaglia recounts. "Much of that was due to Willard. He was principled. He was an environmentalist and he was proud of it. And he was respected because of it. But there was more to Willard than just that. He was also very bright politically. Very savvy. For a long time I thought he succeeded by hiring very bright people; by surrounding himself with talent. But in truth, it was Willard. He had the capacity to respect the singular role he was good in—the environment. He had no interest in becoming Speaker of the House.

He also played a major role in the success of UMD. He was a major supporter of building requests and funding in the House for UMD. I think that his love of woodworking and his history in the shipyards made him a natural to support the industrial arts and engineering programs at the university."

John Helland points to the Minnesota Wild and Scenic Rivers Act as an example of how conservation legislation was passed in Minnesota during the early 1970s. Helland indicates that, before Willard contemplated seeking protection for Minnesota waterways, the Minnesota DNR conducted an inventory of the state's rivers. The purpose of the state Wild and Scenic Rivers Act was to protect the shorelines and waters of Minnesota rivers that weren't covered by federal law. Once the DNR's inventory of rivers was completed, a draft bill was created. The language of the bill originated in the House offices, after which the bill was sent to the Revisor of Statutes to ensure that the language was succinct. When the Revisor was through editing the bill, it was introduced onto the floors of the House and Senate. The companion bills were then sent to the appropriate committees where the authors in each legislative body would ask for hearings. If the proposal was a major change to existing law or a major new initiative (such as the Wild and Scenic River law) it would have an introductory hearing followed by other hearings before being referred to a subcommittee. Once the bill was passed out of the subcommittee and was heard by its originating committee, it went to other committees for further hearings regarding tax implications and revenue issues. After all the relevant committees had attached their amendments to the bill, the proposals were passed onto the floor of the House and Senate for discussion and debate, where further amendments took place. Differences in the Senate and House versions of the bill were then sent to a Conference Committee and were ironed out.

Helland recalls that, in the case of the Wild and Scenic Rivers Act of 1973, Roger Moe carried the bill in the Senate and Harry Sieben carried it in the House. Once the Conference Committee approved a final version of the bill, it was sent to both chambers for final passage and then sent to Governor Anderson for signature.

Jackie Rosholt explains the origin of Munger's unique lobbying effort on behalf of the Wild and Scenic Rivers Act.

"The canoe trips around the state didn't start with Willard," Rosholt remembers. "They started with Phyllis Kahn and her subcommittee on parks and recreation. Phyllis suggested that Willard invite farmer-legislators from agricultural parts of the state to canoe some of the rivers the DNR felt were worthy of protection. Even though Willard and Phyllis didn't always see eye to eye, he followed her suggestion and those trips made converts out of legislators who'd never been in a canoe. Willard did the same thing with respect to taking legislators on bike rides. That's how Neil Haugerude (DFL-Preston) became a big supporter of the Root River Trail."

Rosholt credits Munger's ingenuity in another context.

"There was the time when the DNR wanted money for hot showers in some campgrounds," she recalls. "The Conservatives were not too excited about funding an extravagance like hot water. So we went on an overnight camping trip to one of the campgrounds. The DNR set up tents for us and we camped and cooked out. It was a cold night and in the morning, when the legislators had to take cold showers, Willard made his point. The DNR got the funding."

Rosholt's observation about Munger's interaction with Rep. Kahn prompts John Helland to recall Munger's fondness for women.

"Willard always liked women," Helland remembers. "He worked quite a bit with Rep. Sidney Pauly (IR-Eden Prairie). She was on his committee and he was always deferential to her, allowing her to carry legislation regarding the environment. He also battled quite a bit with Rep. Phyllis Kahn. She was feisty. She blocked Willard from being the LCMR chair (in 1989) and took a second term as chair even though she knew Willard really wanted that position."

Jackie Rosholt believes that Munger's relationship with his wife Martha fostered an appreciation for intelligent women.

"The first week I worked for Willard," Rosholt recalls, "he told me about Martha. He said, 'You should've known her, Jackie.' I got the sense that they were deeply in love and mutually committed to politics. It wasn't the same with Frances, his second wife. He cared for her and they had a good time together. But it wasn't the same. I think Willard was in love with Martha until the day he died.

Willard treated women with enormous respect. You can trace that right back to Martha and her intellect. Willard liked bright women and he wasn't threatened by them. He always encouraged me. He was always loyal. He helped a lot of women, legislators and staff, advance by the way he treated them."

John Helland remembers that Munger was able to work effectively on environmental bills with legislators from both sides of the aisle. As an example, Helland recalls that Munger worked closely with Conservative Al France (IR-Duluth) on wastewater issues. According to Helland, France, who was the chairman of the House Finance Committee when the Republicans were in the majority, was helpful in getting Munger's projects funded.

Helland cites the first Earth Day (April 22, 1970) as a seminal moment in Minnesota environmental history.

"Everyone became interested in the environment," Helland relates. "The House created a couple of committees that dealt with those issues and in 1971 created an environmental policy committee…It wasn't as partisan back then. There were a lot of moderate Republicans, for example, who cared about the environment." (www.minnpost.com/markkneuzil/2008/02/04/763/meet_minnesotas_most_p.)

Helland also believes that the election of Wendell Anderson as governor and the ascension of Willard Munger to the chair of the House Environment and Natural Resources Committee launched the "biggest session for environmental legislation in state history [1973]." (www.minnpost.com/markkneuzil/2008/02/04/763/meet_minnesotas_most_p.)

But as forward thinking as Munger was, not every environmental project turned out the way he envisioned.

> Approval was given…to a bill in the Minnesota House authorizing the Western Lake Superior Sanitary District (WLSSD) to regulate solid waste disposal…
>
> Willard Munger (DFL-Duluth), the bill's sponsor, said the new $45 million sewage treatment plant to be built in Duluth by the WLSSD…will burn waste as fuel instead of burying it in the ground.
>
> "I believe the plant will be one of the first of its kind in the nation and I suspect that it will bring visitors from throughout the country," Munger said. "The WLSSD project is one of the things I contemplated last year passing the resource recovery bill. The energy crisis has made the project all the more realistic and feasible…"
>
> (*Duluth News Tribune*, March 8, 1974.)

The WLSSD incinerated garbage for a time, saving landfill disposal space at the Rice Lake landfill north of Duluth. But the plant's incinerator was eventually idled due to the MPCA's concerns over air emissions. Not long thereafter, the Duluth landfill was capped and trash haulers began trucking garbage across state lines for disposal, prompting Munger to promote recycling as an alternative. But even Munger's modest proposal to recycle a portion of the state's solid waste drew criticism.

> "The majority of the county boards have taken action opposing the 15 cents per cubic yard of solid waste deposited in landfills and incinerators," Munger reported. The lawmaker, who is chairman of the House Environmental Protection and Natural Resources Committee, said his compromise bill removing counties with less than 50,000 from the fee provision would be too hard to enforce…

He said he will also propose a one-year study by the MPCA into an alternative way of financing the state solid waste recycling program...

(*Duluth News Tribune*, February 15, 1974.)

A later article confirmed that the user fee was dropped by the House.

As a result of the environmental legislation passed during the early 1970s, Munger received national recognition.

Munger to get Award

State Rep. Willard Munger, DFL-Duluth, has been selected by the US Environmental Protection Agency (EPA) to receive an award...

Frank Corrado...director of EPA's region 5, said Munger would receive an environmental quality award in Minnesota in the elected state government category.

The Duluth legislator was nominated by State Rep. Peter Fugina, DFL-Virginia; Charles Dayton, a Minneapolis environmental protection leader, and the Duluth AFL-CIO Central Labor Body.

Munger is chairman of the Minnesota House Environmental Preservation and Natural Resources Committee...

(*Duluth News Tribune*, September 20, 1974.)

The 1974 elections saw a new perspective brought to state legislative races in Minnesota. For the first time since the early 1900s, party designations were included on the ballot for state House and Senate seats. This change allowed Willard Munger to run as a DFLer for the first time. Another reform removed the separate elections of the governor and the lieutenant governor from the ballot (a tradition which had allowed the election of a governor and a lieutenant governor from opposing parties in past elections). Nationally, Gerald Ford had replaced Nixon as president as a result of the Watergate scandal. Nelson Rockefeller was Ford's vice presidential designate. A trial to preclude commercial logging in the BWCA began. Another trial, the criminal trial of Ohio National Guardsman for allegedly killing four student anti-war protesters at Kent State University, was also set to begin. 8th District Congressman John Blatnik announced his retirement before the 1974 election. Blatnik's longtime assistant, James Oberstar, was running against Republican attorney Jerome Arnold for the seat (a seat that had remained in the hands of the DFL for three decades). The lines for the Duluth legislative districts were re-drawn and the following were races of interest:

7A: Munger (DFL) v. Father Frederick Method (R; Roman Catholic Priest and Right to Life Candidate)

7B: Jaros (DFL) v. Konczak (R)

8A: Gary Doty (DFL; Doty later became a St. Louis County Commissioner and mayor of Duluth for three terms) v. Edward Willie (R).

(The Minnesota Senate in District 7 was not up for election. The Senate switched to four-year terms in 1972.)

Wendell Anderson and Rudy Perpich were re-elected governor and lieutenant governor and Mike Jaros was re-elected to the Minnesota House. Gary Doty won a state House seat from the 8th District. James Oberstar retained the Blatnik seat in Congress for the Democrats. And Willard Munger won his eleventh term in the Minnesota House despite the crushing loss of the U.S. Steel plant, an economic disaster that could well have turned his constituents against him.

Reflecting upon his electoral success, Munger told the following story to highlight the forgiving nature of his constituents.

> "One of the best things that ever happened to me involved a fellow," Willard remembered. "He is a really strong Republican...(N)ever voted for me... One day he came in (to the coffee shop) with a string of fish...and his two grandchildren.
>
> I said, 'John, where'd you get all the fish?'
>
> [H]e said, 'I have a confession to make...I'm going to go over to the polling place and hold my nose and vote for you.'
>
> I said, 'John, that's one heck of a big surprise. What changed your mind?'
>
> 'Well...I took my grandchildren fishing and we got our limit, and every time they got a fish, they hollered their heads off...(I) got such a big kick out of those grandchildren, I was just sitting there thinking, *By golly, if it wasn't for Willard Munger, I wouldn't be out here fishing and having all this fun. So when I get out, I'm going up there and tell him I'm going to vote for him!*"
>
> (*Oral History of Willard Munger*, ibid, pp. 31 – 32.)

CHAPTER 4

Building a Legacy

Munger's 1974 victory elicited this personal note from future vice president-Walter Mondale:

> November 7, 1974
>
> Dear Willard:
>
> Just a note of congratulations on your great victory…What a magnificent day it was for the DFL and your election helped make that possible.
>
> I sense that you're about to participate in the most productive and exciting legislative session in the history of Minnesota. I certainly hope so…
>
> You made us all very proud. Hope to see you soon.
>
> Warmest regards,
>
> Sincerely,
>
> "Fritz"
>
> Walter F. Mondale

Mondale, always an astute political observer, was right on the money. Especially in the area of environmental protection and resource conservation, the mid-1970s would prove to be halcyon days for Democrats in Minnesota.

However, Willard Munger's enjoyment of political success was tempered by personal loss. Willard's older brother Robert (who had lived most of his adult life outside the state of Minnesota) died on November 7, 1974. The brothers had remained close despite the geographical distance between Duluth and Illinois (where Bob spent his final years). Every summer the fisherman in Bob compelled him to spend a week or two in Duluth with his wife (and sometimes his children) at the Willard Motel. By 1975, Willard had experienced the loss of his father, his first wife, and two of his brothers. But, just as he'd done after Martha's untimely death, Willard kept his nose to the grindstone and continued his work in the Minnesota Legislature.

February 12, 1975

Dear Representative Munger:

Thanks for your letter of February 5 requesting comments on a draft bill relating to land use policy and regulation.

It appears that this bill is similar or identical to HF 3344 which you introduced during the 1974 session. It is also similar to a draft bill prepared at the request of Sen. Purfeerst which was the subject of testimony before a subcommittee to the Senate Natural Resources and Agriculture Committee in January. At that subcommittee hearing, it was evident that there is strong and widespread opposition to major new legislation dealing with land use regulation in Minnesota at this time. Since your draft bill is even stronger in the regulatory area than the one considered at the senate subcommittee hearing, I must presume that your draft bill would receive even greater and broader opposition…

Sincerely,

James T. Shields

Minnesota Association of Commerce and Industry

A business group's opposition to a law proposed by Representative Munger was never the bell-weather by which he gauged the possible success of a bill. Instead, Munger uniformly relied upon the positions of conservation-minded citizen groups for advice.

> "If it weren't for the people from the Izaak Walton League, the United Northern Sportsmen, the Sierra Club, and those other environmental groups," Willard observed, "we would still be in the Dark Ages in the environmental field…They are the ones who brought about our awareness that there had to be something done. It sure didn't come from industry. It didn't come from labor…"

> (*Oral History of Willard Munger*, ibid, p. 95)

Following the progress of the land use bill through its early stages of development, one can see how differing viewpoints are received by a legislator, evaluated, and acted upon.

February 14, 1975

Dear Rep. Munger:

Thank you very much for giving me the opportunity to comment on the draft of the bill relating to land use planning…

The League of Minnesota Municipalities does not have any formal position at the present time on any particular state land use bill and I do not
expect our board of directors to endorse or oppose any particular land use
policy. The direction I have been given is to review all proposed land use
policy bills for consistency with League legislative policy as outlined...

Sincerely,

Mentor C. Addicks, Jr.

Legislative Counsel

With numerous agencies, individuals and groups weighing in on his land use planning bill, Munger agreed to participate in a land use forum on the campus of the
University of Minnesota-Duluth.

March 3, 1975

Dear Mr. Munger:

Let me take this opportunity to thank you for agreeing to participate in
our Land Use Forum. We are certainly fortunate to have a person of your
position as a participant. As you know, the title of the forum is, "Land Use:
Private Rights and Public Interests..."

There are four things we would like to have you do as part of the program.
First, we would like you to participate along with five other panel members in
presenting your views regarding the important issues related to private rights,
public interests, and land use...Second, as part of the same presentation, we
would like your comments as to Dr. Freilich's speech...The third task relates
to group discussions regarding the problem of "sprawl." The afternoon portion of the forum will focus on group discussions related to the problem of
extension or sprawl of residential and commercial developments into open
areas. Your only task in relation to the group discussions is to serve as a resource person along with other panel members and planning staff...

UMD Department of Sociology and Anthropology

During the early 1970s, Munger once again became embroiled in controversy involving Reserve Mining. The matter came to a head when lawsuits were brought
challenging Reserve's authority to dump taconite tailings in Lake Superior. The
litigation sought to eliminate Reserve's waste water discharge permits, permits that
had been in existence since 1947. United States District Court Judge Miles Lord
(attorney general of Minnesota under Orville Freeman) handled the case.

"Lord had to be kind of partial," Willard remembered, "in order to offset the
lack of impartiality on the part of the polluters. They weren't very impartial

in their positions. I'll tell you that. So in order to compensate for that, he had
to be the other way a little bit."

(Oral History of Willard Munger, ibid, p. 92.)

Munger had always opposed dumping taconite tailings in Lake Superior. As the case
in federal court unfolded, health concerns over the asbestos-like nature of the tailings
fibers (which some experts suspected made the tailings carcinogenic) caused the city
of Duluth and other cities using Lake Superior water to ban the consumption of mu-
nicipally supplied water. Truck after truck carrying filtered water in cardboard cartons
roared into the Arrowhead Region. Northlanders, who had always relied upon the
clean, cold water of Lake Superior to flow unimpeded from lake to tap, began to filter
their drinking water before using it or stocked up on cartoned water.

> "The Reserve Mining Company," Willard recalled, "first tried to get a permit
> in 1947. The group that did the most to fight the dumping of taconite tail-
> ings was the United Northern Sportsmen...Labor was saying: 'Look at all
> the jobs it's going to create. Look at all the business it's going to create.' They
> would look you right straight in the eye and say, 'Munger, do you really be-
> lieve that you're going to pollute a big lake like Lake Superior with a few tons
> of taconite tailings...?' People believed you couldn't pollute the lake. People
> believed you were a fanatic if you tried to stop it...
>
> Some of the leaders of labor weren't too sympathetic [to my position], but the
> average person was pretty understanding, otherwise, I wouldn't have been re-
> elected...The union people from Silver Bay came down [for a DFL convention
> in Duluth] and they had a large mobile home in the parking lot [of the Duluth
> Arena complex]. Their purpose was to bring out different people together and
> get them to pass resolutions condemning [Judge] Miles Lord. Wendy [Gover-
> nor Anderson] didn't go out to them because they were...unruly. I said, 'I'm
> going to go out and talk to them.' Some of the people said, 'No, you're not.
> You're not going out there. You'll start a riot...' I...went out anyway...They
> were drinking beer and the first thing I said to them was, 'Hey, you got a bottle
> of beer for me?' They said, 'Hell no...' So I stayed and talked...and they were
> giving me a pretty rough time...I...struck up a conversation with some of the
> guys inside the mobile home...I reached in the cooler and grabbed a bottle of
> beer and started drinking it. I sat down, and I didn't leave. Then everybody
> started laughing...Somebody asked me if I would support Miles Lord if he
> [closed the plant]...I said, 'If the company refuses to change...of course I will
> support him.' It got pretty rough. [But] nobody did any harm to me..."

Oral History of Willard Munger, ibid, pp. 85 – 86.)

But Munger didn't escape from the Reserve controversy wholly unscathed.

> "I got a little note in the mail," Willard recalled, "a couple of days later that
> said, 'If you're going to take our jobs away from us, then we'll take care of
> you.' I didn't pay much attention to it…When I was down in St. Paul, a
> truck parked in front of my coffee shop and two guys got out. One of them
> started from this end and the other started from this one, and they went
> around and knocked out every window (with hammers)…I can't prove it
> was over the Reserve issue but it was a pretty strong coincidence. You'd better
> believe it, because the note I received referred to my position on taking their
> jobs away. That cost me $1,400 bucks—I had no insurance. I have never
> been a very wealthy person, so it took me about a month and a half before I
> got enough money to replace the windows. Everybody came by, wanting to
> know what happened. It really didn't hurt me any, because I think everybody
> kind of sympathized with me…It hurt my pocketbook, but it didn't hurt me
> otherwise."

> (*Oral History of Willard Munger*, ibid, pp. 86 – 87.)

A key group involved in the Reserve Mining litigation was the Save Lake Superior
Association. Munger's fierce opposition to continued disposal of Reserve's tailings
in the lake brought him into contact with the Association. It was in this context
that Munger met two life-long friends; Arlene Lehto and her brother, Alden Lind.

"My father was a member of the IWW (International Workers of the World),
Arlene Lehto recalls. "He fled to Canada during the Pinkerton raids in WWI. He
fell in love and got married, eventually moving back to the States. He came back as
the editor of the Finnish language paper, the *Industrialisti*. My father and Willard
became friends because they shared a common background in Socialism. Eventually my folks saved up their money and moved up on the North Shore. They built
a family-style resort and motel at Milepost 42, between Gooseberry Falls and Split
Rock Lighthouse. I went to UMD and was approached, due to my folks' interest
in keeping the lake clean, about forming a new conservation group, the Save Lake
Superior Association. I was its first president. My brother Alden (who was a college
professor) moved back to Minnesota in 1974. He took over as president and was
followed by Arnold Overby."

Lehto's environmentalism led to her involvement with the DFL Party.

"I hadn't been politically active, but when I found out that Jack LaVoy, a
Duluth Democrat, wasn't going to seek re-election, I decided to run," she recalls. "I
lost in the primary to Gary Doty. But that's how I met Willard. I was at the motel,

in the basement conference room where he always had his victory parties. I got to talk to him in depth. I'd met him at picnics, particularly at the Labor Day Picnic at the zoo, but I never really talked to him until that night in the basement of the motel. It was 1974."

Lehto, a young, dark haired, Finnish-American beauty, soon became a favorite of the elder statesman from West Duluth. When Gary Doty decided against a second term in the House, Munger urged her to run in District 8A. She won and, shortly after being elected, the Reserve issue heated up. The folks in support of continued dumping decided to hold, as Lehto recalls, a "dog and pony show" regarding the issue. Other major environmental and conservation issues of the time (1977) included the opening and management of Voyageurs National Park and the controversy surrounding further restrictions of motorized traffic in the Boundary Waters Canoe Area.

"Ed Fride [an attorney], one of the hired guns for Reserve," Lehto remembers, "got up in front of the group and was spreading half-truths and misinformation. I stood up and said, 'Fride, that's a bunch of bullshit and you know it.' I think I shocked everyone in the room with one exception. Afterwards, Willard took me aside and praised me for standing up to Fride."

It was in the legislature that Lehto really came to know Willard Munger. Because the Democrats had taken control of the legislature in 1972, Munger's seniority installed him as the chairman of the Environment and Natural Resources Committee and he appointed Lehto to Fish and Game Subcommittee. When Lehto, never a shrinking violet, pointed out to Munger that it was the only subcommittee without a vice chair, Munger made her vice chair as a freshman legislator, something that was totally unheard of, especially for a woman. The real reason behind the appointment was something only Munger knew.

"Glen Sherwood, the chair of the subcommittee, was a Democrat who later bolted the party and became a Republican. Somehow, I think Willard suspected Sherwood's defection before it happened. When it did, because Sherwood was no longer in the majority party, I became the chair. I always believed Willard had a premonition about that," Lehto recalls.

Lehto, along with her brother, Alden Lind, and EPA scientist Gary Glass (Duluth Water Quality Lab), John Pegors of the MPCA (Duluth office), Steve Balach (one of Munger's Republican friends) and others met regularly every Saturday morning at the Willard Motel Coffee Shop to discuss politics. The topics, which were debated vigorously over breakfast prepared by Munger himself, ranged from what was taking place in St. Paul to what was taking place in Washington, D.C.

Both Lehto and Munger were honored by the EPA for their work on the Reserve Mining issue.

Arlene Lehto Honored by EPA

Mrs. Arlene Lehto, chairperson of the Save Lake Superior Assn., has been honored by the EPA in its first Environmental Quality Awards competition for Minnesota.

Mrs. Lehto was chosen in the citizen activist category. Rep. Willard Munger, DFL-Duluth, received similar recognition in the government category.

(*Duluth News Tribune*, undated.)

Lehto observes that her brother Alden Lind and Willard Munger shared an intense friendship.

"They were exact opposites," Lehto says. "Willard was a street savvy politician. Alden was an intellectual. Willard always had his finger on the pulse of the people, the working class. Alden thought he had the same insight but he didn't. He wasn't practical and he wasn't one to sit down and negotiate. He was too adamant in his beliefs to be effective. But they both loved verbal combat, the give and take of ideas."

Lehto pauses as she reflects on the "Odd Couple" nature of the men's friendship.

"Alden had no sense of humor. He was always serious. Sometimes, I got tossed into that same category. Folks said I was too serious, just like Alden. I didn't see it that way. But maybe they have a point…Willard was more practical. He could put environmental issues into a non-political context and work well with the Republicans on his committee. But he always had a funny relationship with the Iron Range Democrats. He never really trusted Irv Anderson (DFL-International Falls)."

Jackie Rosholt, Willard Munger's longtime committee administrator, disagrees: Rosholt doesn't believe that the rift between Munger and Irv Anderson was personal.

"Willard liked Irv," Rosholt recalls. "They just didn't agree on conservation and environmental issues."

According to Arlene Lehto, Munger possessed many positive attributes as a legislator.

"He was the best vote counter I've ever met," Lehto recalls. "And when things got heated and words got said that probably shouldn't have, he'd quietly take the combatants aside and sort it out privately. He had an uncanny sense about how to bring people together."

In terms of Munger's negatives, Lehto offered a mild criticism.

"He usually sat way in the back on the House floor. He had this mumbling style of speech. He was hard to understand at times. But that could also be a positive. Sometimes, when he was being critical of someone's position, he'd let his voice drop intentionally, so they couldn't hear what he was saying about them…And he was very quiet about how he did things. When Majority Leader (later Congressman) Martin Sabo wanted someone to speak on the floor of the House about Hubert Humphrey's death, Sabo approached me to do it. I knew, without being told, that Willard was behind the request. Willard had been the person who introduced me to Humphrey. You can contrast Willard's quiet, behind-the-scenes style, with that of Eveleth DFLer, Joe Begich. Whereas Begich would pound his fist or shoe on his desk for attention, Willard wouldn't. Willard was like the tortoise in the old fable; slow and steady. Begich had the flash and the temper. Begich was the hare. And we all know who won the race."

Though it was clear to Lehto that Munger enjoyed being around attractive women, he was from a generation where manners mattered.

"I never saw him inappropriate with female staff or colleagues and he certainly would never use physical force or threats in arguing with a woman. He could be combative and he did have a temper but it was never personal or physical," she remembers.

According to Lehto, you never knew what to expect when working on legislation with Munger.

"We were working on a bill dealing with sharing acid rain information with Ontario. I was the lead on the bill. My senate counterpart backed off the bill. I was upset. I went to Willard for advice. He said, 'Go onto the floor of the Senate yourself and argue for the bill.' Now, I was in the House. That was unheard of. I said, 'I can't do that. It's against Senate rules.' Willard said, 'If you want the bill to be heard, you have to do it.' So I went, spoke on the Senate floor (the first and only time I think that's ever been done). The bill got passed and became law, no thanks to my Senate sponsor."

Another person who became deeply involved with Munger's environmental efforts during the mid-1970s was Environmental Protection Agency scientist and coffee klatch regular, Gary Glass.

"I was born in Duluth," Glass remembers, "down on Park Point (a sand spit separating the St. Louis River from Lake Superior) when only poor people lived on

Park Point. We lived on the lake side and I had friends who lived on the bay side. The lake side was clean but the bay side was brackish and scummy—you didn't dare swim in it."

Dr. Glass, who obtained his PhD in chemistry from the University of Minnesota and did post-graduate work at the University of Wisconsin, was torn between teaching and working for industry when he learned that Congressman John Blatnik had procured funding for a water quality laboratory to be built in Duluth.

"In 1968, I went to work as a research chemist for what was then known as the Federal Water Pollution Control Agency. That became the Environmental Protection Agency (EPA) in 1970. We were charged with examining the impact of industrial and municipal discharges into fresh water and maintaining standards for fresh water applicable across the country. There were two labs; ours dealt with fresh water and there was one in Rhode Island that dealt with salt water. We were to 'make the water fit for fish.' That was our charge. We were not to investigate the human element of the discharges.

"When officials from the federal government toured the Great Lakes by air, they found that the largest discharge of pollutants in any of the Great Lakes was from Reserve Mining. They set up what were called 'enforcement conferences' between the State Water Commissioner and Reserve to try and get the company to cease its discharge. That didn't work so the matter went into state court in Two Harbors in front of Judge C. Luther Eckman. I spent an entire summer in Two Harbors assisting the state's attorneys. I was the front guy for the director, Don Mount. He was supportive of my work to a point but in the end, when we didn't win in state court, he said 'I don't want to hear any more about the issue.'"

The Reserve Mining saga didn't end with Judge Eckman's decision in state court.

"The EPA brought an action in federal court in front of Judge Miles Lord," Glass recalls. "And when the attorneys visited the EPA lab in Duluth, there I was; the guy with the knowledge literally hidden in a closet by Mount. We didn't know at that point that the tailings contained asbestosform particles which are carcinogenic; that came later, as the case was in process. When we determined that the currents and winds were bringing the discharge from Reserve into Wisconsin waters, the attorneys' eyes lit up. Now we had interstate impact that made it a federal issue."

Glass remembers meeting Willard Munger for the first time.

"It was 1975 and I was involved in the federal case. Mount wasn't happy with me. He'd back me a ways and then, on some key issues, he wouldn't. In 1975, they dissolved my team and re-assigned the technicians who were working with me. I was labeled a "senior researcher" but I only had one tech to work with. I began to look outside the lab for support and that's how I came to meet Willard.

"We'd discovered the asbestosform nature of the tailings and had issued a recommendation that residents of the area shouldn't drink unfiltered water from Lake Superior. Part of the problem I was having was that Blatnik's edict, when the place was built, was that we were supposed to stay out of 'local issues.' Of course, my involvement in the Reserve cases violated that edict.

"My first impression of Willard was that he didn't look like a guy who had a lot of power. He looked like a regular guy. He'd cook you pancakes in the motel coffee shop. He wasn't full of himself. He was supportive but suspicious—Willard always had a sort of a chip on his shoulder when it came to PhDs, especially university PhDs. I think it went back to University of Minnesota scientists telling him how wonderful DDT was. But he liked me, thought I was one of the 'good guys', because he knew my work on Reserve."

Glass recounts that his involvement with the famous coffee klatches began in the early 1980s.

"When the EPA wouldn't give me anything substantive to work on, Willard was happy to listen to my ideas and those of Alden Lind and John Pegors. We were the three primary members of the group that got together with Willard nearly every Saturday morning beginning in the early 1980s.

"Willard was happy to have me work on LCMR-funded projects. George "Rip" Rapp, a geologist from the University of Minnesota-Duluth and I worked on mercury and acid rain problems under LCMR grants that Willard procured for us. I had up and down cycles with the agency. Willard was very interested in getting the mercury from coal-fired power plants out of fish. This was in line with my post-doctoral work in chemistry so it was a natural for me to work on the mercury problem. Willard understood that the way you limit mercury in water and fish is to limit its discharge into the air but the MPCA kept backing off that and the federal Clean Air and Clean Water statutes didn't recognize the interplay between air and water; the hydrologic cycle of water. There was a gap there."

Glass recalls very little other than the environment being discussed by the coffee klatch trio.

"There would be other people at the coffee shop," Glass remembers. "We'd show up, Pegors, Lind and I. Willard was expecting us. It really took off when Reagan got elected and I was told that my acid rain research was done; that my funding was gone and that I had to wrap my research up in three years. Willard wasn't too happy at the time about what was going on at the WLSSD. So he talked me into seeking appointment to the WLSSD board. I was appointed by Mayor John Fedo and served from 1985 – 1995. The EPA tried to forbid my appointment. I told them, 'to hell with you.' I never saw myself as running for political office—I'm not a politician. But Willard was an inspiration in that sense. I saw what he did and now I'm on the Duluth School Board.

"Sometimes, when I tried to get into political fights, like opposing the siting of a new landfill for Duluth, Willard would look at me and say, 'Glass, keep your nose out of that. What the hell do you know about landfills?'"

Dr. Glass smiles as he recounts the discussion.

"It was almost always a big breakfast when we were there at the coffee shop. He wouldn't take any money for it. He'd make eggs, bacon and pancakes. If he had Canadian bacon, he'd fry that up. Alden and he loved that. They both knew they shouldn't be eating it but they did anyway. And when Frances would come by, Willard would hide his full plate of food under an empty plate so she wouldn't see what he was eating.

"Constituents would stop in and talk to Willard about their problems. He'd talk to everyone. If he didn't have the time, he'd make the time."

"Willard looked to Alden and me as experts on environmental issues," Glass asserts. "I was the science guy. He didn't want me to get fired. 'I need you to keep your job,' he'd tell me. He wrote letters supporting the work I was doing under the LCMR grants. He was tenacious. And so was Alden. That's probably why Willard liked Alden so much. They shared that trait. He and I shared something too. It was a credo, 'You're never defeated unless you give up. '

"I testified at hearings before his committee. I remember being there to talk about the work we were doing on acid rain. Willard left the hearing to go to the bathroom. While he was gone, someone got something changed, something important regarding our funding. When Willard came back, a staffer told him what had happened. Willard got angry and said, "Goddamn it you sneaky bastards, this is my project!' He got the funding put back to where it had been before he left the room."

The land use bill that Munger introduced in the 1975 Legislature session continued to generate debate. Munger used the bully pulpit of his committee chairmanship to explain his support for the bill.

The purpose of this meeting of the Environment and Natural Resources Committee is to get an overview from people in out-state Minnesota as to their thinking about whether or not the legislature should or needs to adopt a comprehensive land resource management policy for the state of Minnesota...

Land and water is our greatest natural resource-everything we do indirectly or directly is related to land use. The future of this civilization may well depend upon the way we use our land resources. The danger signals indicate we had better do something about land resources before it is too late.

Minnesota, like many other states, does not have a single or specific land use policy, nor does it give the local units of government the proper tools and guidelines to work with for good sound land use management. Instead, we have a great collection of policy statements relating to areas of land use problems.

The question before us, I suppose, is "Do we need such a land use resource management policy to:

a. Protect your prime agricultural land form urban sprawl;

b. Minimize erosion;

c. Protect groundwater recharge areas;

d. Eliminate unnecessary reduction of forests;

e. Protect areas containing unique or endangered species by providing proper habitat for wildlife;

f. Provide and plan for areas best suited for parks and open spaces;

g. Preserve areas of cultural, esthetic or historic importance;

h. What is going to be our long range policy of copper-nickel mining in Minnesota?...

A good example of what happens with no land use planning is allowing Reserve Mining Company to build their taconite plant on the shores of Lake Superior and allow dumping of 67,000 tons of tailings into the lake and destroying the water supply for thousands of people. This not only affects the health and welfare of people but in the end, it's going to cost Minnesota hundreds of thousands of your tax dollars.

Minnesota cannot afford a second major mistake as this, that indirectly or directly affects all the people of Minnesota.

(Comments before the House Environment and Natural Resources Committee, Willard Munger Personal Collection.)

Munger's support was not enough to see the land use bill through to fruition. The law never passed.

1975 also saw the advent of the United States' first serious energy crisis since the end of WWII. Munger took a leadership role in creating the Minnesota Energy Agency.

> "I think we were at one time well prepared (for another energy crisis)," Willard recalled, "because we passed a lot of legislation establishing an energy agency. It was one of the first in the nation, and I was the chief author of the bill. I was chief author of all the energy conservation bills from 1973-1978, and (as of 1987-1988) most of those conservation energy bills have been discarded. We forget sometimes about what has happened in the past, and we're not too concerned about the future. We take everything for granted—that tomorrow will be like today. But it isn't."
>
> (*Oral History of Willard Munger*, ibid, p. 61.)

Munger's successful shepherding of the 1975 Energy Bill through the legislative process points to one of Munger's primary attributes as a legislator: competiveness.

"I remember," Arlene Lehto recalls, citing an example of that trait, "we were canoeing the upper St. Louis River on one of the early visits of the Environment and Natural Resources Committee to various rivers around the state. Willard was working on the Minnesota Wild and Scenic Rivers Act. Anyway, I was in a canoe with a tall blond guy. Willard was determined to lead the group down the river to the landing but my canoe came in first. It ticked Willard off that someone else got to the landing ahead of him. In his mind, the chair of the committee should be the one the reporters saw coming into the landing."

John Helland offers his own observations as to Munger's personal attributes.

"Willard could be headstrong and stubborn," Helland remembers. "But he was a good listener. He always asked for help, from colleagues, from the staff, to get his thoughts together and to marshal support for his projects. He was, as I indicated before, very good at working with folks from both sides of the aisle. He would start out the first year of a biennium, the budget year, by asking all the members of the Environment and Natural Resources Committee to tell the others on the committee what it was about the environment that drove them to seek a seat on the committee. He'd ask each member, 'What is it that you really care about?' In this way, he could gauge how sincere a person was about conservation. He was also very shrewd. He knew the process and how to get things done, that you needed to start with a strong bill, so that you could end up with a bill through compromise that you could support. He wouldn't, however, compromise his fundamental principles. He wasn't above sending a bill elsewhere if that meant there was a chance to keep it alive. Through it all, he was always polite to the witnesses who appeared in front of his committee."

In terms of Munger's oratory skills, Helland smiles as he recalls Munger's addresses on the floor of the House.

"As he got older, he got confused a bit. But he'd surprise you. He'd give a bad speech on the floor but then turn around and be dynamic and articulate the next time. He never spoke on the floor unprepared. He knew he wasn't the best public speaker and he worked hard on that."

As Munger's political career continued, he became more involved in the work of legislative committees. As a member of the Legislative Commission on Minnesota Resources (LCMR; now the Legislative-Citizen Commission on Minnesota Resources [LCCMR]) and as chairman of the House Environment and Natural Resources Committee, Munger traveled to places distant and exotic.

Dr. Erkki Kivinen, Pres. Int'l Peat Society

August 22, 1975

Dear Dr. Kivinen:

As you probably have heard, a group of Minnesota people including four legislators from the state are planning a technical study trip to Europe to assess the use of peat for fuel. We shall attend the I.P. S. Symposium in Kuopio September 23-26th…

The Minnesota group includes the following persons:

State Legislators:

Rep. Irvin Anderson, International Falls

Rep. Willard Munger, Duluth

Senator Norbert Arnold, Pengilly

Senator Roger Moe, Ada

Others:

Robert Herbst, Commissioner, Minnesota DNR

Mr. and Mrs. Roy Larson, Engineer, Midwest Research Institute

Dr. and Mrs. Rouse S. Farnham, University of Minnesota, Department of Soil Science.

Sincerely,

Dr. Farnham

Détente between the United States and the Soviet Union was in its infancy when Dr. Farnham proposed a tour of European peat facilities to the LCMR. Imagine Munger's anticipation at the prospect of visiting the strange and mysterious birthplace of the Communist revolution, a country he had heard both praised and denigrated during his Farmer-Labor days. There can be no doubt that it was a seminal moment for Willard Munger to be selected for the trip. But before the group from Minnesota was dispatched to the hinterlands of Finland and the Soviet Union, another less exotic journey awaited Willard Munger and his colleagues.

CHAPTER 5

Travels for the Environment

As Minnesota considered copper-nickel mining, longtime *St. Paul Pioneer Press* columnist Don Boxmeyer described the copper-nickel mining industry already in place in Canada.

9/3/75

[T]hompson, Manitoba. This is a city of concrete curbs and gutters in muskeg; of purple and white condominiums, super markets, drug stores, hungry timber wolves, and wild ravens…You're either in town or in the bush, 400 miles north of Winnipeg on the endless, monotonous muskeg that stretches northward…

Thompson is a town of startling, unsettling contrasts…a frontier town that has successfully outgrown its boom years as INCO developed a massive copper-nickel mine and smelter 22 miles outside of town. Or more accurately, the town was developed 22 miles outside the mine…

A reality also is the fact that INCO operates with virtually no…environmental restrictions…The smelting of 22,000 tons of ore daily results in 1,200 tons of sulfur dioxide (SO_2)…a toxic pollutant being unloaded on the countryside through INCO's tall smokestack. The Canadian Forestry Service has reported that dispersion of the SO_2 and other particulates has resulted in the decline in the growth of forest over a 50 square mile area…

9/4/75

Shebandowan, Ontario. Shebandowan Lake is like something out of a Hamm's beer commercial… [with an] active copper-nickel mine churning several hundred feet below…

The mine produces 10,000 tons of high-grade copper and nickel ore each week. One of the most visible and environmentally damaging aspects of mining-smelting-is not done at Shebandowan…: the ore is shipped 652 miles to INCO's Sudbury plant for refining…

The Minnesota visitors to the mine were outfitted in coveralls, rubber boots, hard hats, battery-powered lamps, gloves and safety glasses…

Later, the visitors toured an underground mine at Sudbury and went deeper than 4,000 feet…Underground mining, to the Minnesotans, is more acceptable than the open-pit mining for obvious environmental reasons. But it is more expensive, and INCO says the break-even-point- at which underground mining cannot be profitably done-is about 1 percent combined copper-nickel ore. The ore along the BWCA of Minnesota that INCO wants to mine by the open-pit method, however, is less than 1 per cent in richness…

Rep. Willard Munger…said he intends to introduce legislation to outlaw open-pit mining in the vicinity of the BWCA.

9/5/75

Sudbury, Ontario…Sudbury. The name has become synonymous with environmental blight…The Sudbury region, with its 13 mines, now produces 60 per cent of the non-Communist world's nickel, and is the fourth largest North American producer of copper. But the region also produces sulfur dioxide…a harmful pollutant…INCO and other mining companies moved their fires indoors, but the SO_2 was not contained, merely dispersed to the atmosphere through tall smokestacks. The tallest of those is now "Superstack" a 1,250 foot chimney from which up to 5,200 tons of SO_2 has poured daily. Superstack, the world's tallest chimney, is Sudbury's omnipresent symbol…Sudburians can recall when they left their storm windows on, tightly sealed, all year long. When the SO_2 pt blistered paint off their homes, burned the leaves off the trees and yellowed the tombstones on the hill. Now Superstack emits 3,600 tons of SO_2 daily, and some Sudburians seem satisfied that as long as the prevailing winds drag the plume far downwind, there is no problem.

One resident, a college professor, rationalized: "I know it's not good, but as long as it's not good for someone else, it's not bad for me."…

After touring…the Minnesotans were disturbed at the relative flexibility in provincial environmental standards…

In addition to controlling air emissions, the Minnesotans can expect to be more concerned than the Canadians over controlling seepage from tailings ponds. Reclamation also will be a problem; growing hay is one thing; replacing Minnesota timberland is quite another.

Some legislators have talked of prohibiting open-pit mining near the BWCA…

(*St. Paul Pioneer Press and Dispatch*, by Don Boxmeyer, September 3 – 5, 1975.)

The possibility of copper-nickel smelters being located next to the BWCA and Voyageurs National Park sent a chill down the spines of dedicated environmentalists. The prospect drew a different reaction from Iron Range legislators. With the taconite industry in decline, Rangers were desperate to find a singular industry to put people back to work. Copper-nickel mining seemed like a very real alternative to the vanishing iron mining industry; an economic "home run" for northeast Minnesota.

But the ugly specter of Sudbury and its legacy of sulfur dioxide pollution were omnipresent as proposals for copper-nickel exploration in northeastern Minnesota were discussed. Willard Munger wasn't shy about his position on the issue: He was vehemently opposed to any open-pit mining or smelting of minerals within a protected zone around the BWCA.

"There will be no 1,200 foot super stacks to solve problems of air pollution or any other kind of problems in Minnesota," Munger said, following a tour by 26 Minnesotans of three INCO operations in Canada. "We do not put up big smokestacks to keep from polluting one area only to pollute another further away."…

The BWCA appears to be a major obstacle…confronting INCO's proposed open pit mine south of Ely. Environmentalists contend a 1,000 foot deep open pit would not be compatible within one mile of the federally protected BWCA. They contend it would be a source of water pollution to BWCA watersheds…

Munger, chairman of the Minnesota House Environmental and Natural Resources Committee, believes the solution is underground mining. He concedes, however, that some dozen legislators on the tour feel that a shaft and concentrated buildings also would be undesirable in the area…

The copper-nickel question, Munger notes, also goes beyond environmental considerations. Social and economic questions, including what may someday be national need, abound. Yet it is Sudbury's "Super Stack" or the environmental questions that appeared to stick most in many of the tour's minds.

As Munger says, it's great that sulfur dioxide from the stack doesn't land in Sudbury. But for somebody, somewhere, it's not great.

(*Duluth News Tribune*, September 7, 1975.)

As the issues relating to copper-nickel mining fermented, Munger's planned trip to Europe took shape.

> September 18, 1975
>
> Dear Willard:
>
> The Minnesota DNR recently received a grant...for a twelve-month program to perform a preliminary technology assessment and environmental evaluation of a large-scale peat development effort in Minnesota...An important aspect of the overall program will be the participation of an Advisory Committee, representing the broad spectrum of technological disciplines and regulatory actions that will be involved...
>
> I would like to invite you and the other legislative members who are accompanying us on the Study Tour of peat technology and use in Europe, to serve as ad hoc members of this Advisory Committee...
>
> It is expected that the next meeting of the Advisory Committee will be held later this fall after the European study tour has been concluded.
>
> Yours very truly,
>
> Robert Herbst
>
> Director
>
> Minnesota DNR

Much of Minnesota, including the northeast, the north central and the northwest regions of the state contains thousands of square miles of peat bogs. These environmentally sensitive filters of ground water remain largely untouched. Minnesota, despite its vast peat deposits, had never explored nor developed peat as a resource before the early 1970s. As the energy crisis of that era spawned scientific inquiry into alternative fuels, some looked upon Minnesota's peat bogs as viable alternative sources of energy. The journey that Munger and his cohorts were about to take to Europe was an exploration of that idea; the commercial exploitation of peat as well as an inspection of Finland's copper-nickel mining and processing facilities.

Munger's notes from that trip illustrate the thinking process he engaged in when researching environmental and energy issues.

> 9/19/75
>
> Left Mpls. 1:45. Arrived in Milwaukee. Left Milwaukee. Arrived in NY at Kennedy airport 4:40 P.M. The fog was bad and we had a "hold pattern" for more than 1 hr. Attempted to land by instrument but had to "gun" plane into air just as it was about to clear the runway because a small plane was on the runway. 400 foot ceiling. Left NY 6:00 P.M. on SAS 912 nonstop to

Copenhagen. Arrived 7:20 9/20/75 (time change). Left Copenhagen 8:15 on SAS 42. Arrived in Helsinki at 10:50 A.M. Nonstop. Bus $3.00. Taxi $5.00. Luggage $1.00 Lunch $6.00. Dinner $14.00.

9/21/75 in Helsinki.

Weather is beautiful. Rested. Visited depot and took pictures of people on train. Breakfast $3.00. Lunch $4.25. Dinner $13.50. Hotel $29.00.

9/22/75

Left Helsinki Hotel 9:30 A.M. by taxi and went to one of Finland's technical research centers on peat research to a town outside of Helsinki called, I believe, Kapiola. We were treated to a wonderful lunch…research on peat-1,300 people. We were given a good review of their peat operation by Prof Erik Eckman and Verkko T. Rauhala. Taxi fare to research center was 15 Finnish Marks ($2.75). They went all out to explain their research. Left Helsinki airport on FinnAir 536 at 3:00 P.M. for Kuopio…

9/23/75

Hotel Kustaa. 9:00 A.M. City Hall, Kuopio attend international peat society symposium of Commission II. More than 140 representatives from all leading peat resource countries of the world. Sponsored dinner for big wigs from countries. Break-no cost. Lunch-guest of city.

9/24/75

Break at hotel-no cost. Lunch @ copper mine-no cost. Dinner-banquet-no cost. Copper-nickel…Left Kustaa Hotel for Outokumpu Mine-underground. Returned from mine back to motel and went to banquet for members of peat delegation.

9/25/75

All day tour of power plants and peat bogs. Inspected peat bog operations. Breakfast-no charge. Lunch-no charge. Dinner at Tampere-no charge (at power station). Dinner-We had another wonderful dinner at which time a presentation was made relative to a new power plant.

Left for copper-nickel smelter and refinery at 8:30 P.M. Arrived 11:00 P.M. (approx.)

9/26/75

We had breakfast at the guest house at 8:30 A.M. Lunch-no charge. We inspected the copper-nickel smelter and had a good briefing from the plant Mgr., Mr. Esko. The company employs about 9,000 people for all operations. They have SO_2 recovery of 95 – 96%—a loss of 2% up the stack and

3% in slag or about 2,000 tons per year. (SO_2 loss of about 500-1,000 tons per year).

The plant produces: 60,000 tons of copper; 6,500 tons of nickel; 100,000 tons of sulfur. Included in the 60,000 tons of copper is 18,000 tons of recycled scrap copper. They also produce $2,500,000.00 of gold; silver. 85% of the heat generated is recovered for power. 200 foot stack. 6% of net sales goes to research. The old plant destroyed most of the vegetation and the company had to pay a lot of money for damages. The new plant or remodeled plant is about 20 years old under the new operators. No loss paid to farmers any more since new operators. New trees and other vegetation was planted and is now back to normal. Land is farmed within 1.6 miles of plant and no damages have been paid for many years. The trees and vegetation look very healthy and shows no sign of damage from plant operations as pics will show. I'm really surprised at how good everything looks right next to plant. Top personnel can retire at 52 with 1/2 salary for 25 years. Workers can retire at 57 with 1/2 salary. 25 years service—50%. 30 years service—60%.

Left host house at 2:45 P.M. for Helsinki to catch plane for Leningrad. Leave Helsinki—6:45pm. Arrived Leningrad—8:30 P.M. Snack at Leningrad—$5.00.

9/27/75

Left Leningrad Hotel to visit All-Union Scientific Research Center for Peat Industry. Taxi—$6.50. Breakfast—no charge. Lunch—$7.00. Dinner—$15.00. Peat electrical power plant. They use 1,400,000 tons of peat per year. They store 100,000 tons for winter use. No coal or other fuels used. No problems with stack emissions—98% recovery of ash. There is danger of peat dust. Cost comparisons were provided between peat, coal and oil. Lunch at the hotel was 6 rubles. An unbelievably huge power plant. Russians went out the way to please delegation and were most cooperative on giving information.

9/28/75

Leningrad. Raining. Bus tour of city and pack up. Leave Leningrad on FinnAir. Arrived in Helsinki. Arrived Copenhagen on FinnAir. Taken to Hotel Ascot at 9:30 P.M. Taxi—$15.00. Breakfast—no charge. Lunch—$5.25. Dinner snack—$3.00.

9/29/75

Copenhagen. Breakfast—$6.00 extra. Lunch—$4.50. Dinner—$10.00. Taxi—15.00. Luggage—$1.00. Left Copenhagen. Arrived Frankfurt. Transferred. Arrived Cologne—10:30 A.M. Drove to Bonn by taxi (Hotel Birgischehot).

9/30/75

Break with room—no charge. Lunch—no charge. Dinner on plane-no charge. We went to inspect the brown coal operation at? Germany, one of the largest open pit mines in Europe. Coal from this mine supplies energy for largest thermo power plant in Europe and supplies electricity to many countries. This mine will supply coal for the next 50 years. Energy ratio is 2 1/2 to 4. The mine produced 35 million tons last year. Can produce 50 million strict tons. In order to open mine, company must get agreement from 59 different agencies. Reclamation: I believe their reclamation program is one of the best in the world. The company takes credit for it but in checking I find out that the government is real strict in land use. I must admit that the company has accepted its responsibility and has gone all out in a reclamation program. The mined out area is back-filled with huge machines which can move 200 tons per minute. It's [the overburden] loaded into train cars and dumped in the backfill and leveled off for farm land. It takes only ten minutes to dump one train load…

10/1/75

Arrived Edinburgh, Scotland 11:00 P.M. Hotel Roxburgh. Taxi—$4.00. In Scotland, we drove out to the gasification pilot plant about 30 miles from Edinburgh. The plant no longer produces gas from peat for commercial use because of the new discovery of offshore gas. About 15 American companies are financing an experimental project on gasification of peat. All gas utilities are owned and operated by the government (establishment of a governmental authority). The Mgr. of the authority gave little encouragement to American gasification of a high btu gas-when in operation, they used a low btu gas. Not much impressed with Scotland visit. Breakfast-no charge. Lunch—guest, no charge. Dinner—$8.00.

10/2/75

At Edinburgh airport at 1:00 P.M.

10/3/75.

Arrived Dublin—2:00 A.M. Hotel Hibernian Royal. Taxi—no charge. Luggage—$.80. Lunch—$4.00. Dinner—$6.00. Ireland also has a bough peat operation both in the field operations and energy producing end. Ireland also has its peat resources owned and operated by the government. A board of directors comprised of seven members appointed by the government runs the entire peat operations of the country-they are appointed for 4 years and are given wide power in land use programs. For instance, if land owner is not making proper use of land, the land can be taken away. He must be given proper compensation under proper procedure. This board or authority "Bord Du Mona" got started after WWII. The board has a capital outlay of over 28 million pounds for the machinery and land purchases. Ireland is a poor country. Ireland has always been a poor country. In the past, people who were evicted from their property were forced into the peat bogs and the sterile land grew little food. Breakfast—? Lunch—guest. Dinner—no charge. Peat is the salvation of Ireland. 1/7 of the land area is peat. Peat in the big bog we visited runs to an average depth of 20 feet from 10 feet up to 30 feet deep. Peat now employs more people than any other industry providing necessary energy. Ireland is like Minnesota. It has a rainfall...30 – 35 inches in median part, average of about 25 – 30 inches. Population is 4.5 million compared to Minn. 3.8 million. Northern Ireland 1.5 million. South 3.0 million. Total 4.5 million...At turn of the century, Ireland had a population of over 8 million people. It has been cut in half. They have at present time over 100,000 unemployed.

Harvest of Peat:

The peat is harvested with many, many large machines. They have on this one large bog over 620 small tractors. When we were there all the machines were in for repair-they have a large repair shop that provides work during the off season...They harvest the peat lands 24 times in a season...

Briquette Plant:

They produce at the plant we were at 1400 tons of briquettes per day-most is used for home consumption...

The peat now produced saves the country over 50 million pounds in energy cost-over $120 million. About 300,000 tons of briquettes go for domestic per year. Peat provides 25% fuel for power plants. They have an 80 megawatt power plant burning peat...

Land Use:

The reclamation of land after peat has been harvested is mostly used for grass lands-they have provided very fine grass lands. We also saw some lands used for agriculture. There is quite a division of opinion as to what peat should be used for...How land is used: 11 million acres in grass; 1.5 million under cultivation; 3 million acres in bog...

(Willard Munger Personal Collection. *Editor's Note: Munger would return to Scandinavia in 1977 when another environmental issue, the storage of hazardous waste, became a hot-button topic in Minnesota.*).

Munger's experience in Europe, coupled with what he observed in Ontario, caused him to formulate a firm and unyielding position regarding copper-nickel mining in northeastern Minnesota, a position which he announced openly in a speech given at UMD in October of 1975 after visiting other copper-nickel operations in Texas.

I agree with Mr. Ritchie that copper-nickel mining and smelting in NE Minn. is one of the most important issues to be decided by Minn. during our generation because of its environmental and economic-social impact it will have on the area.

$2 Billion Resource

It is estimated that copper-nickel resources in NE Minn. has a potential wealth of $2 billion-this alone should alert us to magnitude involved and the need for some long range carefully thought out policies dealing with all facets of copper-nickel mining.

We Will Have Mining in Minnesota

It is my opinion that we will have both mining and smelting in this area, but only after we have been satisfied they can be clean operations that will enhance the social-economic structure of the area and will not destroy our water, forest and recreation values that we now enjoy.

Minn. Cannot Afford the 2nd Mistake

The first mistake was when the state granted the permit allowing 67,000 tons of taconite tailings to be dumped into Lake Superior. Minn. cannot afford a second mistake. Nor will we allow it to happen. Minn. has a past history of allowing the exploiters of our natural resources to write the rules and regulations. They no longer have a captive legislature-those days are gone.

To really understand where we are going, let's look back to an era in our history when the natural resources in our state were turned over to private exploiters by a captive legislature with its cruel results. Our once beautiful forests were stripped of virgin pine, leaving only ugly cut over, deserted brushland to remain a distressed area for a lifetime. The destruction of our forests was really the 1st great mistake. It really should not be called a mistake but rather a crime against society.

A New Alertness with the New Generation

A new generation has arrived. This new generation in the legislature, both Republicans and DFLers, will not allow these crimes against society and the state to ever be repeated. They are concerned and believe we must go in the direction of protecting the total environmental structure and protecting the state's economic interest. Yes, because of their concern, we will act more wisely on the remainder of the state's natural resources; our forest, minerals, land, water and air quality.

There are More Questions than Environmental

Copper-nickel mining raises more questions than that of the environmental impact. We will have to consider the questions of:

1. Taxation

2. The social-economic impact

3. Effects on the state's other natural resources such as timber and marginal agricultural lands

4. Boom and bust operations

5. Location of smelter

6. Whether or not it is in the best interest of all concerned that the state own and operate the smelter

I feel the best interest of the state would be served by it having one smelter owned and operated by the state. We perhaps would have 8-10 companies mining ore. If several smelters were built we would have complete environmental chaos. If the state were to own and operate the smelter it would be in partner with private industry such as our port authority, Amtrak, etc…

South Dakota Cement Plant

This is not without precedent. South Dakota owns and operates its own cement plant very successfully…

Much Involved

A two billion dollar mining operation in the heart of one of the nation's top recreational areas cannot be taken lightly, nor should the prerogatives of final decision making rest solely with department heads and staff. We are dealing with Minnesota's future. The legislature, after broad government and private input, will establish a land use and mining policy which must protect the future of Minnesota's environmental quality and the state's economic interests.

The Environment and Natural Resources Committee

The Environment and Natural Resources Committee, of which I am chairman, is deeply interested in copper-nickel mining. Last month, eight members from our committee and staff were authorized and made a tour of copper-nickel operations in El Paso, Texas and Inspiration, Arizona to give committee members a first-hand look at copper-nickel mining and smelting.

The full committee was authorized to attend the symposium here at UMD. Most of the members are here in attendance.

The only way we will have a safe, clean operation of copper-nickel mining and smelting is to do what we are doing here today: discuss the many problems and look for solutions. You don't solve these problems by name calling. It is my opinion we will have copper-nickel mining. I have much confidence in the MPCA, the DNR and the state legislature to do the job.

(Willard Munger Personal Collection.)

Raised in the heritage of the Farmer-Labor Party, where it was not heresy to promote governmental ownership of grain mills, banks, electrical systems, telephone networks and mines, Munger was proposing that the state of Minnesota, not some exploitive corporation, own any copper-nickel processing facility built in Minnesota. It was a radical, and indeed, a politically dangerous position to announce. But Willard Munger didn't blink when the critics charged him with disguising Socialism, or worse, Communism, as environmental protection.

There will always be a debate as to whether Willard Munger was a Socialist. Willard's younger brother, Harry Munger, Jr. has this take on Willard's political philosophy.

"Willard wasn't a Socialist," Harry says thoughtfully. "But he was close. I'd say he was a Liberal, with a capital 'L'. He wasn't a Progressive. That label, today, to me, is too limited, too 'Green'. Willard's key issues went beyond environmentalism. The Duluth Zoo. Education. Fair taxes. Human rights. Maybe, after all, he was a Socialist. Socialism seeks change through the democratic process rather than through force. Maybe that does fit Willard."

One of Munger's closest colleagues in the Minnesota House was Michael Jaros (DFL-Duluth). Jaros spent his youth in Germany and Yugoslavia, coming to Minnesota in 1960. Upon arriving in Duluth, Jaros enrolled in a preparatory school with the goal of becoming a Roman Catholic priest but eventually determined that the priesthood wasn't his calling. After deciding to pursue a secular vocation, Jaros attended the University of Minnesota and obtained a degree.

Jaros's interest in American politics was tweaked when he accompanied his brother Carl (a photographer for the *Duluth News Tribune*) as Carl covered a campaign stop in Duluth during the 1960 presidential election by John F. Kennedy. Jaros (who was unable to speak English) was introduced by his brother to Congressman John Blatnik with whom Mike could converse in Serbo-Croatian. Blatnik in turn introduced Jaros to Walter Mondale (who was running for Minnesota Attorney General) and Kennedy.

"After I met Kennedy," Mike Jaros recounts, "I was awestruck. I couldn't sleep. I don't think we've had a real president since Kennedy."

Jaros obtained his U.S. citizenship in 1966, voted for the first time in 1967, and sought to become a DFL State Convention Delegate from St. Paul (where he was living) in 1968.

"I liked Rockefeller, but, because of the Vietnam War, I switched to McCarthy. Ultimately, I left McCarthy and supported Humphrey," Jaros remembers. "I was working as a teacher ten blocks from the State Capitol. I watched the legislature whenever I could and witnessed the votes on the 'Minnesota Miracle'. Both Dwight Swanstrom and Dick Palmer from Duluth voted against Wendy Anderson's tax reforms and that angered me."

After moving to Duluth's West End (now Lincoln Park) neighborhood, Jaros concluded that Swanstrom was vulnerable.

"My main focus," Jaros recounts, "was always, and still is today, on economic and social justice. I was very happy with Anderson's 'Minnesota Miracle' and was displeased with Swanstrom's votes against tax reform and his stand on social issues. When I decided to run, I went to his insurance office in the West End and asked him, 'Mr. Swanstrom, why did you vote against the tax bill?' He got mad at me and shouted, 'Wendy don't know nothing about taxes. He's nothing but a hockey playing punk!' I told him to go to hell. Because Judge Heaney saved two slots in the re-formed 7th District [after reapportionment], I ran for 7B. That covered most of Piedmont Heights and Duluth Heights and the West End from 6th Avenue West to 39th Avenue West."

Jaros shared a Liberal philosophy and outlook with Willard Munger and Munger became the young immigrant's political mentor.

"I met Willard at the convention in the old 59th District," Jaros remembers. "He was wearing a suit. I called him 'Mr. Munger'. To me, an immigrant who had trouble speaking English, Willard was a big man. When I met him during the 1972 campaign, he was suspicious of me. Being a German Lutheran, he was naturally suspicious of Catholics. This was an issue because I was supporting state aid to parochial schools, something Willard was always against. In fact, Willard once told me, 'It took the Catholic Church 500 years to figure out that Luther was right.'

"Another issue that was a thorn between us was the decision in *Roe v. Wade*. I'm against abortion but, because I support the rule of law, I had a tough time with that one. There was an amendment brought in the House by Tad Jude, a 'Right to Life' bill supporting a constitutional amendment in Minnesota to ban abortions. What is interesting is that the Republican Party at that time was against the amendment. I ultimately voted against it because I decided I was there to vote for my conscience, not for my church. Turns out that Willard and I in the House and Jim Ulland (IR-Duluth) in the Senate were the only local votes against it. What's really sad is that Jack LaVoy (DFL-Duluth) actually switched my vote. I'd voted against it, turned my back to talk to someone, and LaVoy flipped my voting switch over to a 'yes' vote without me knowing it. Willard was mad about it but the Speaker, Martin Sabo, said there was nothing that could be done.

"As a young politician, I learned so much from Willard. He was more Liberal than folks half his age. He was 61 years old when I met him and he was light-years ahead of all the young punks that viewed him as an old man. He was philosophically sound on everything. Though his love was the environment, he was good for labor and on economic and social justice issues…I don't know if Willard was a Socialist. I can say this. I am not a Socialist but I'd say my philosophy is in line with the Christian Socialist parties in Europe. I'm a Christian Socialist Democrat. Willard was a truly amazing person."

Willard Munger's work on conservation issues was nearly always ahead of its time. Long before lakeshore property in Minnesota was selling for hundreds of dollars a front-foot, Munger was troubled by the state's leasing of state-owned lakeshore property (including school trust parcels) to private citizens. These leases generated small annual payments to the state and allowed the leaseholders to build modest cabins, all of which troubled Munger's sense of what public ownership of lake and river frontage should be about. For Munger, it was about preserving access *for the public*: since the state owned the land, it should not be reserved for the benefit of a few private leaseholders.

A study conducted by the DNR in 1970 revealed that St. Louis County had the largest concentration of state-owned lakeshore, 256 miles, of which 21.6 miles was leased to residents. The issue of leasing state-owned lakeshore to private citizens would resurface in the 1990s when Munger would support DNR efforts to eliminate the program.

As Munger's environmental reputation grew, folks outside the state of Minnesota took notice.

October 4, 1976
> Dear Rep. Munger:
>
> I would like to congratulate you on your legislative work on mining and I would be interested in seeing your bills and information concerning safer and more ecological concern in extracting natural resources...
>
> Sincerely,
>
> Perry Bullard
>
> Michigan State Representative
>
> 53rd District
>
> P. S. Keep up the fight!

Rep. Bullard enclosed an article from the *Pick and Axe*, a newspaper published in Bessemer, Michigan.

> It was good to see that Willard Munger of Duluth made it without any real problems through another primary election. Munger has spent several decades in the Minnesota Legislature and has been one of Reserve Mining's toughest critics for nearly thirty years...
>
> But alas, all is not rosy with Munger. He recently took issue with Reserve's plan to try to dump at Milepost 7. He was quoted on Twin Ports television, and within several hours of the telecast, two heavies turned up in a pick-up truck, withdrew ball-peen hammers, and proceeded to beat the bejeebers out of the huge picture windows in the front of Munger's little coffee shop...
>
> Well, maybe that's the price you have to pay for greatness. We would do well to have a Munger of our own, here in Michigan.
>
> (*Pick and Axe*, undated.)

The Minnesota press explored Munger's legislative prowess in detail.

> **Profile of Willard Munger**
>
> Environmental laws not only don't mean loss of jobs, they can mean more jobs, in the view of Willard Munger.
>
> Munger, 65, has served in the legislature as representative...since 1955, and by merit of seniority now chairs the House Environment and Natural Resources Committee.
>
> In that post, he has written and passed several bills which might be called "environmental" that have statewide impact, he said...
>
> There is, Munger said, "a need to provide the right kind of a climate to increase jobs in this area, to provide an atmosphere of diversified economy. And I think we are doing that," he said. "I might point out that the WLSSD...will

cost $103 million, plus another $7 million which I got for starting a recycling…which will save the taxpayers of this area about $250,000 per year…"

"Superwood was down at the legislature fighting for the sanitary district bill because if we didn't get the sanitary district bill, they were boxed in. They had no alternative to dispose of their waste…"

One project Munger said he would work on during the 1977 session is a comprehensive state copper-nickel mining policy which would let prospective mining companies know in advance what standards they will have to meet.

"I think we're going to have copper-nickel mining in the area, and what we want is a good state policy that's going to guarantee a safe operation," he said. "I don't think the people of Minnesota are going to accept the kind of copper-nickel operation they have in other parts of the United States."

Other goals for the upcoming session include a comprehensive land use planning policy …and guidelines for developing the periphery of Voyageurs National Park.

"And another piece of important legislation that we're going to consider is that dealing with energy…And I think the most important piece is a good, comprehensive bill on energy conservation. I feel there is an energy crisis just around the corner and it's up to us to move now before we have a crisis."

On another environmental matter, Munger said he supports Gov. Wendell Anderson's plan to make Milepost 20 economically feasible to Reserve Mining Company as a tailings disposal basin site…

Munger said he also favors the plan of Department of Natural Resources Commissioner Robert Herbst for "zoning" the BWCA over that of Rep. James Oberstar.

The two plans differ primarily in the size and shape of inner and outer zones, the inner to be preserved as a primary wilderness area, the outer to be open to less restricted use…

"One of the things that I'm a little reluctant to go along with Oberstar on is that he seems to want to open it up for logging and I think we ought to take care of our timber outside the BWCA before we get too excited about the timber within the BWCA," he said. "What's wrong with having a little bank there in the future when we really need it?"…

(*Duluth News Tribune*, October 26, 1976.)

CHAPTER 6

DFL Meltdown

Willard Munger never lost sight of building personal relationships. Munger had many friends from "across the aisle" including Conservative Representative Rod Searle of Owatonna.

Beginning as a youth in Pockerbrush, Munger had an affinity for woodworking and carpentry. This desire to create spilled over into his adult life in Duluth when he built the DX service station and supervised the construction of the Willard Motel. After completing the motel, Munger installed a sophisticated woodworking shop in the motel's basement. Stored in the rafters of that workshop was Munger's pride and joy; black walnut lumber supplied by Rod Searle. Searle's walnut was often crafted by Munger into lamp bases, picture frames, toy trucks and cars, and, on occasion, gavel sets given as retirement gifts to Munger's brother and sister legislators.

> January 22, 1977
>
> Dear Willard:
>
> I wish I could convey to you my appreciation for the gift of the beautiful walnut gavel set you created and crafted from Rod's walnut reserve. Ten years of working closely in our committee helped me understand the contribution you make by continuing to give your best effort year in and year out…I issue you a standing invitation to stop in with or without warning any time, visit us, and break bread…and have a good time. We are right on Highway 210 just one mile west of Deerwood…
>
> Good luck in the 1977 session…they are giving you an important but tough one in the power line controversy!
>
> Wendy didn't want to solve All the problems…
>
> Kindest personal regards,
>
> Howard E. Smith
>
> Crosby, Minnesota

Rod Searle was born in Camden, New Jersey in 1920. In 1947, after working as a salesman for Johnson and Johnson, Searle and his wife decided to make a change.

"I didn't grow up on a farm," Searle advises. "But we thought we'd give it a go. My wife only had two stipulations for the move: One; that the house had to have central heating; and two, that it had to have running water. So wouldn't you know, when we arrived on the farm in Waseca, in the middle of the spring thaw with mud everywhere, my first job was to dig a septic system!"

Searle loved farming.

"We had a typical family farm," Searle remembers. "A small herd of milk cows, a couple of chickens, some hogs. This was all at a time before the advent of large farm machinery."

When asked how he became involved in Conservative politics, Searle reflects.

"I used to make the run into Waseca with our milk. I'd stop in and talk to the city attorney. Folks were lamenting about finding someone to run against Hubert Humphrey. I said, 'I'll run,' half in jest. This was in 1954," Searle remembers. "So they came to me just before filings closed and asked me to run; not for the U.S. Senate, but for the state legislature. I was going to school at Mankato State part-time and farming full-time. I ran and lost by nine votes. I ran again in 1956 and got elected."

Searle wasn't an environmentalist when he started farming but, as his involvement with the land increased, Searle became interested in conservation issues. He met Willard Munger during the 1957 session when both served on the House Education Appropriations Subcommittee.

"Working with Willard," Searle remembers, "I learned about the way UMD was treated like a second-class citizen by the regents. The regents were arrogant. They wanted everything for the Minneapolis campus and to hell with Duluth. I worked with Willard and others to get a special appropriation for Duluth to make the faculty salaries to be on par with the University of Minnesota. The regents didn't like that too much."

Rep. Searle and Rep. Munger also worked on other educational issues.

"Willard was," Searle recalls, "a great supporter of the UMD medical school and the setting up of family practice as a specialty. The committee we were on was chaired by Dick Fitzsimmons of Argyle. The notion of a specialty in family practice was his idea but Willard wholeheartedly supported it, as did I."

By 1961, the Searle farm was no longer a working farm.

"I got out of farming when the big machinery was coming in," Rod Searle remembers. "I figured out that I was better off renting the land out than farming it myself. We did that on shares; in good years, we did well; in bad years, we shared the loss. It was a cooperative effort. As a trout fisherman, I was interested in conservation. So we turned the land into a tree farm. We built duck ponds. We were one of the first farms to plant contour strips to prevent erosion. Today, all you see on our place is grass, trees and pheasants. In 1978, our 280 acres was named 'Outstanding Minnesota Tree Farm.'"

One of the more memorable episodes Searle recalls regarding Munger as chairman of the Environment Committee (Searle served on the committee) took place during discussions concerning Voyageurs National Park.

"Irv Anderson wanted to get $30,000 for the project," Searle recounts. "He came before Willard's committee. Because it involved appropriations, I made the motion that the request be referred to the Appropriations Committee. Irv got a little miffed and started using inappropriate language. I guess he thought he deserved different treatment because he was the House Majority Leader. Willard didn't raise his voice. He simply looked at Irv and said, 'Mr. Majority Leader, that's not how we run this committee and that's not language we use.' Irv got so mad, he walked out. But Willard was like that; calm and deliberate even when dealing with people of power."

Searle shared Willard Munger's concern and love for public education. He served on the Education Committee under Peter Popovich (DFL-Hibbing; later, Chief Justice of the Minnesota Supreme Court) where Searle also had considerable contact with Gerald Heaney, who appeared before the legislature as a lobbyist for teachers.

Searle recounts how he came to be Speaker of the House. During the 1978 election, one of the Republican candidates, Robert Pavlak of Hastings, was accused of unfair campaign practices. The matter went to court, which meant that Pavlak wasn't seated, leaving the House divided 67 to 67.

"Gerry Heaney had a hand in that," Searle recalls. "After reapportionment by the 8th Circuit, when someone asked, 'What do we do if the House is tied?' the court [on which Heaney sat] said: 'That'll never happen in a 100 years.' Then, six years later, it happened. So Pavlak's case went to court. Everyone thought it was a cinch that the judge [who was a Democrat and was involved in the 1962 Rolvaag recount] would side with the DFL. I was elected Speaker as a compromise in the evenly divided House. Then the judge ruled the other way and Pavlak ended up being seated, which gave the Republicans the majority. That didn't last because the Minnesota Supreme Court overturned the decision and Pavlak lost his seat, which threw things into a cocked hat. Irv Anderson wanted me to resign. I looked over the rules with the clerk, and I said, 'The rules say that the Speaker is elected. So if you want me out, you're going to have to un-elect me.'"

Searle served out the remainder of the session as Speaker and in 1979, when the DFL was split between those who wanted Irv Anderson as Speaker, and those who didn't (including Willard Munger, Arlene Lehto and others), another compromise was reached which made Fred Norton (DFL-St. Paul) the Speaker for the 1980 session. (For a far more detailed discussion of this unique era in Minnesota legislative politics, the reader is directed to Rep. Searle's fine book on the topic, *Minnesota Standoff*, Alton Press, 1990).

With respect to whether or not Willard was a supporter of Irv Anderson's bid to be Speaker, Searle says he never was sure of the relationship between the two men. But he clearly remembers an incident involving another Iron Range legislator, Rep. Joe Begich (DFL-Eveleth).

"Begich went on a rant, a tirade, against me. It got personal," Searle remembers. "He called me an SOB. Willard knew how to use the gavel. He didn't use it often, but when he used it, you knew he meant it. He threw down the gavel on Begich in a committee meeting and ruled that Begich's loud, abusive and inappropriate language was out of order."

The end of Rod Searle's long legislative career came in 1980.

"I got out because of the politics of the times," Searle relates. "The right wing of my own party didn't understand the need to talk to and compromise with the DFL. I said to my party, 'How are you ever going to get anything done if you won't talk to those who don't agree with you?' And DFLers like Irv Anderson didn't help. I'd go into Irv's office and he'd greet me with: 'Here comes the enemy.' I saw that it was time to get out."

Regarding the black walnut trees that still grow near Munger's Indian Point home, Rod Searle is quick to refute the notion that the trees started from stock he gave Munger.

"I had some pictures in my office framed in black walnut. That impressed Willard. So he invited me up to his place on Indian Point and took me down to where he'd planted a grove of black walnut trees. The trees were doing well," Rod remembers. "I asked him how he was able to get them to grow in Duluth. He said, 'Two things. One, they're protected here from the weather and two, I use elephant manure from the zoo.' Then he showed me his workshop in the basement of the motel. I was very impressed. Willard was a craftsman. He asked if I had any black walnut. I told him I did and that's how he started getting dried black walnut from me. He repaid me by framing two original watercolors I owned with walnut I gave him. Those frames are really built."

Rod Searle saw first-hand the traits of craftsmanship and originality that were the hallmark of Munger's youth in Pockerbrush.

"What impressed me more than anything," Rod recounts, "was the big framing device he'd invented and put together in his workshop to ensure that the joints of the picture frames were flush and tight."

Searle also recalls the legislative fact-finding trip to Sudbury, Ontario.

"All of us on the Environment and Natural Resources Committee came back from that trip with a real fear that opening up areas near the BWCA to copper mining would expose the wilderness to pollution," Searle remembers. "I'd been up there [to the BWCA] on a few occasions and, as a member of the Committee and the LCMR, I didn't want to see northeastern Minnesota end up looking like Sudbury."

Ann Glumac, Willard Munger's committee administrator in the late 1980s, says that the relationship between Munger and Searle wasn't unusual.

"Willard didn't choose close friendships based upon party affiliation," Glumac observes. "One of his closest friends in the legislature was John Rose, a Republican from Roseville. John was a conservationist and on that score, he and Willard were alike. But on other issues, they didn't have much in common," Glumac remembers. "Willard also had a close friendship with Elton Redalen, a Republican farmer from Fountain. They fought tooth and nail over the plastic milk bottle bill but Elton had us to his home for dinner and they were able to agree on many other conservation-related bills."

Returning to Representative Smith's short "thank you" to Munger regarding the gavel set Munger crafted for the former legislator, one passage in the letter stands out. At the time Smith penned his message, west-central Minnesota farmers were opposing a 430-mile electrical distribution line being built over their land. The protest against the power line was led by Carlton College professor Paul Wellstone. While Smith's throw-away reference to the power line dispute doesn't discuss the matter in detail, the fact that Smith called the brewing tempest to Munger's attention in a casual letter of thanks indicates how public the debate had become. It is also historically significant that Wellstone and Munger first made each other's acquaintance during the power line controversy.

At first blush, it might appear that there was little in common between Professor Wellstone and the craggy-faced DFLer from Duluth. But the men shared two traits. One was their love for the common man. Not some false or forced accommodation with farmers, factory workers, housewives and miners to gain votes; but a true understanding and affinity for the daily lives of ordinary citizens. Their second shared characteristic was their political backgrounds. Both men had been raised in households dominated by politics of the Left.

> The power line struggle marks an important period in Wellstone's development as a politician. While he had already demonstrated a gift for inspiring his students…it was not until he arrived in the harsh environment of western Minnesota that his leadership capacity stood out. Wellstone was working in a deeply conservative area of the state, where strangers are viewed suspiciously. He was a short, Jewish college professor with an Afro haircut and no background in farming or agriculture. Yet the local farmers accepted and even embraced him…
>
> He was also learning to speak eloquently. Always articulate and personable, Wellstone was developing a persuasive speaking style that recalled the great progressive orators of the early 20th century. Like former presidential candidate Eugene V. Debs, whom his mother went to see as a small child in New York City, Wellstone had a particular talent for using cadence to build a speech…He moved audiences with a preacher-in-the-pulpit style that Minnesotans had not seen since Hubert H. Humphrey.
>
> (*Paul Wellstone*, Bill Lofy, The University of Michigan Press, 2005, p. 43.)

Munger did not, however, share Wellstone's gift for oratory. Munger was at his best in small groups or working the political machinery of back-room politics, using personal relationships and friendship to convince others of the moral rightness of his position. Wellstone, while equally as principled, used his great speaking ability to inspire crowds; two very different approaches to accomplish similar political ends. But whatever their differences, from the time Wellstone met Munger, the younger man expressed his admiration for the older politician.

Long after the power line issue had died down and Wellstone had run unsuccessfully for the position of State Auditor, and then, in a brazen and seemingly impossible political quest, won a seat in the United States Senate (beating Republican incumbent Rudy Boschwitz in 1990—the only challenger to unseat a sitting Senator that year) the story of Wellstone's miraculous rise from obscurity was put into print. Soon after its release, Senator Wellstone sent a copy of *Professor Wellstone Goes to Washington* (Dennis McGrath and Dane Smith, University of Minnesota Press, 1995) to Munger. The personal inscription from the new Senator to his mentor written inside Munger's copy of the book is revealing:

Willard,

　Eleanor Roosevelt

　Dr. Martin Luther King, Jr.

　Robert Kennedy

　Willard Munger

　These are my heroes in American history. Thanks for all your friendship and support—

　Paul

　Senator Paul Wellstone

(Willard Munger Personal Collection.)

The two men forged a personal friendship which lasted all of Munger's life and Munger used his considerable political clout to assist Wellstone during Wellstone's campaigns. Just after page 150 in *Professor Wellstone Goes to Washington*, a photograph appears showing the two men, arms raised and standing on the rear platform of Wellstone's beloved Green Bus on Superior Street in downtown Duluth. Wellstone's handwritten comment is scrawled across the photograph in Munger's copy of the book:

　Willard—I love this picture!

　Paul

(Willard Munger Personal Collection.)

The 1976 presidential race saw Georgia Governor Jimmy Carter and Minnesotan Walter Mondale running against President Gerald Ford and Kansas Senator Bob Dole. Hubert Humphrey (who had run for and lost the Democratic nomination for president in 1972 to George McGovern) remained in the U.S. Senate but had been diagnosed with cancer and had undergone surgery in New York City. Another Minnesotan, Eugene McCarthy was seeking the presidency as an Independent. A political newcomer, school teacher and DFLer, Mary Murphy, was running against Henry Larson for a House seat in District 14B (Hermantown). The other races of interest were:

　7A: Munger (DFL) v. Floyd R. Samways (IR)

　7B : Jaros (DFL) v. Harry Welty, Jr. (IR)

　7th District Senate: Sam Solon (DFL) v. Mike Konczak (IR)

　　(*Editor's Note: In an attempt to distance itself from the National Republican Party following the Watergate scandal, the Republican Party of Minnesota added "Independent" to its name and became the Independent Republican Party of Minnesota. This nomenclature existed from 1975 until September 23, 1995 when the term "Independent" was dropped from the party's name.* En.wikipedia.org/wiki/Republican_Party_of_Minnesota.)

Despite his illness, Humphrey easily won re-election, becoming (with Mondale's election as vice president) once again the "senior" U.S. Senator from Minnesota. Carter-Mondale garnered 51% of the popular vote to Ford-Dole's 48%. McCarthy drew 1% of the vote. Munger beat Samways 6,625 to 3,410 and Mary Murphy won her race easily.

But the real story of the 1976 election was not an answer, but a question: What would happen to Mondale's U.S. Senate seat once Mondale was sworn in as vice president?

Governor Wendell Anderson and Lieutenant Governor Rudy Perpich went into seclusion to discuss the Mondale Senate seat. What came out of those meetings set the stage for a DFL disaster. Apparently no one in the Anderson Administration was a student of Minnesota history. In 1936, when Floyd B. Olson had the chance to resign as governor and have Hjalmar Petersen (the lieutenant governor who would become governor upon Olson's resignation) appoint Olson to a vacant U.S. Senate seat, Olson declined to exercise that option. Instead, Olson appointed popular FL Banking Commissioner Elmer Benson to the Senate post. The political hay that an opposing party could make out of the ego-driven appointment of one's self to the U.S. Senate was obvious to Floyd B. Olson. Why this lesson wasn't apparent to Governor Anderson is anybody's guess.

What transpired was predictable. Anderson resigned as governor based upon a back-room promise that, once Perpich was sworn in as governor, Perpich would appoint Anderson to fill Mondale's vacant U.S. Senate seat. The deal was struck. Anderson resigned. Perpich ascended the throne and promptly executed his duty.

House Environment and Natural Resources committee administrator Jackie Rosholt recalls that when the idea of Anderson's resignation and Perpich's elevation to the governorship first surfaced, it was universally seen as a bad idea in DFL circles.

"But Willard really liked Rudy," Jackie continues. "He was close to Rudy and wasn't about to make waves."

In 1978, Senator Wendell Anderson faced a contested race against Republican millionaire Rudy Boschwitz. The "senior" seat (once occupied by Hubert Humphrey) was also open due to the reluctance of Muriel Humphrey (Humphrey's widow who'd been appointed to fill out the term after her husband's death) to remain in the Senate. Businessman Bob Short—who beat Congressman Don Fraser, the endorsed candidate, in the DFL Primary largely because of Fraser's support of the BWCA—was running against Republican attorney Dave Durenberger for the Humphrey seat.

Shortly before the 1978 election, a compromise bill banning logging and mining in the BWCA was sent to President Carter for his signature. The bill was sponsored by Senator Anderson and Congressman Bruce Vento of St. Paul. Congressman James Oberstar was the only Minnesota member of Congress to cast a vote against the compromise. On October 17, 1978, protesters disrupted a campaign stop by Senators Wendy Anderson and Ted Kennedy at the Eveleth Holiday Inn where cries of "Judas, Judas" rang out regarding Anderson's support of the BWCA bill. Both Oberstar and Bob Short urged Carter to veto the bill. President Carter refused the suggestion and the BWCA bill became law, though Carter attempted to undo the damage to Anderson's senatorial bid by visiting Minnesota on Anderson's behalf.

The local races for House in District 7 were a replay of 1976:

7A: Munger (DFL) v. Samways (IR)

7B: Jaros (DFL) v. Welty (IR)

Munger touted his experience as the major reason for voters to support his re-election.

Munger's re-election means more for Northeastern Minnesota because:

- Munger is a Legislative Chairperson

- Munger's effectiveness has been proven.

- Munger is a chief author of major legislation.

Munger worked for:

- Legislation creating the Minn. Energy Agency and every major Energy Bill passed to date including the omnibus Energy Bills of 1974-1977 and 1978;

- The $108 million Lake Superior Sanitary District;

- Minnesota Resource Recovery Act of 1973;

- Prohibited the use of non-returnable plastic milk bottles;

- Restoring AMTRAK passenger train service;

- Prohibiting the sale and use of PCBs.

Munger can do more for this area:

As a member of the Education Division of Appropriations, he was instrumental in obtaining:

- Expansion of the UMD building programs;

- The French River Fish Hatchery;

- New State Office building in Duluth;

- UMD Medical School;

- Area educational needs.

The Future is bright:

Munger's energy legislation in the long run and WLSSD will do more to bring in new industry and boost the area economy than all the other efforts combined providing for a sound diversified industrial and business growth picture and the St. Louis River will be returned to multiple use. We will have industry, fishing and recreation on the same river, and will be able to eat the fish!

(*Duluth Budgeteer*, November 1, 1978.)

On election eve, Walter Mondale announced that Anderson was leading Boschwitz. Boschwitz's own poll had the challenger ten points ahead and the Minnesota Poll had Boschwitz leading 49-46. Bitter over his primary loss, Don Fraser refused to endorse Bob Short in the other Senate race. President Carter came back to Minnesota on November 3, 1978, visiting Duluth the Friday before election day in hopes of turning the tide. But Durenberger won his race against Short nearly 2 – 1; Boschwitz beat Anderson; and Al Quie beat Perpich to reclaim the governorship for the IR. However, despite Willard Munger's support of the BWCA compromise bill and the establishment of Voyageurs National Park, issues that hurt other Democrats in northeastern Minnesota, Munger beat Samways 4,767 to 2,682 in West Duluth where the voters apparently were more interested in continuity and principles than single issue politics.

Victorious Munger calls DFL Beating a Disaster

Willard M. Munger, dean of Duluth members of the Minnesota Legislature, scanned Tuesday's election results today and commented, "It was a disaster for the DFL." Although he won re-election in District 7A handily, it appeared the DFL would lose control of the House, where he had served since 1954...as well as the governorship and two U.S. Senate seats. Asked who he thought might be able to put the Party together again, Munger said; "I don't know, but it needs to be one hell of a good carpenter."

(*Duluth Herald*, November 8, 1978.)

Chapter 7

Battles Major and Minor

Amtrak, the federal entity providing passenger rail service to Duluth, was suffering. Unable to make ends meet through fares, the state of Minnesota provided an annual subsidy to keep the North Star train running. Though service was not formally discontinued until 1985, there were signs in the late 1970s that passenger rail service to Duluth was in jeopardy.

> July 31, 1978
>
> Dear Rep. Munger:
>
> Please be advised that the Department of Economic Development in conjunction with the Minnesota Department of Transportation have mutually agreed upon the firm of National Biocentric of St. Paul to undertake a feasibility study of Amtrak service between the cities of St. Paul and Duluth...
>
> If we do not hear from you by the 7th we will assume that the specifications which are outlined within sections 3 and 8 are satisfactory...
>
> Sharon L. Wemlinger
>
> Assistant Commissioner
>
> Department of Economic Development

Munger had his committee administrator, Jackie Rosholt, respond to Wemlinger.

> August 3, 1978
>
> Your letter states that if you do not hear from Rep. Munger by August 7, you will assume that the specifications outlined are satisfactory. This letter is to inform you that you may not make that assumption. Rep. Munger's comments, if he chooses to make any, will be forwarded to you at the earliest opportunity...
>
> Jacqueline Burke Rosholt

There were multiple reasons behind Willard Munger's push to keep passenger trains running.

First, Munger relied upon passenger train service for transportation as a young man. There was an egalitarian motive at work behind Munger's support for Amtrak: Munger understood that not everyone can afford to own an automobile.

Additionally, Munger recognized that trains are more energy efficient than automobiles in moving masses of people from one location to another.

Though the majority of the folks Munger represented approved of his pro-conservation positions, there were always naysayers, particularly in the labor community, who sought to detract from his success. Labor's disaffection with Munger's environmental fervor escalated during the late 1970s.

> It's time for laboring men and women to take a hard look at where jobs will be coming from in the future…and work together to make sure today's jobs are protected…and our kids will have a good chance at a good life…
>
> For instance, some small businesses in Ely and Grand Marais are going to have rough time because of the BWCA legislation just passed. So what's a few jobs? What if it was yours?…
>
> The environmentalists never bother to put a price tag…or point out that working people will be paying the bill.
>
> Look at Minnesota. How many jobs will be created with the lock up of the million acres in the BWCA? Already…one logger is closing down operations and laying off about 20 employees. The people in the area will be lucky if they can hold their own…
>
> Voyageurs Park was touted as a real boon to the International Falls area. How many new jobs have been created since those 200 thousand acres were removed from logging—and resorts forced out of business?…
>
> How many jobs are going to be created when the State takes over 66 thousand acres on the St. Louis or Cloquet Rivers…or more thousands of acres along the Minnesota River and the Cannon River and the Kettle River and the Rum River—just to name a few of those being considered for Wild and Scenic River designation?…
>
> Then there's the wolf zone in Northern Minnesota…When are the environmentalists and bureaucrats going to put as much energy into ensuring the long range survival of working people?…
>
> The land grabs that are either happening or on the drawing boards are more than a northern Minnesota problem…they affect every taxpayer in this state. The long range effects of these land grabs may look like a drop in the

bucket…But remember how those rings spread out—it's called the ripple effect—unless we get together and put a stop to it—it's going to swamp us all.

Local No. 294—Electrical Workers

Hibbing, MN.

(*Labor World*, November 9, 1978.)

Labor's dissatisfaction with Munger likely cost him a position on the Legislative Commission on Minnesota Resources (LCMR).

Munger Loses Job on Resources Commission by Janet Burns

A difference of environmental philosophies was blamed…by Rep. Willard Munger…for not being reappointed to the Legislative Commission on Minnesota Resources by Rep. Irvin N. Anderson, DFL-International Falls.

Munger, a strong environmental proponent, said…he was disappointed at Anderson's action. But, he added, he is still head of the House Environmental and Natural Resources Committee…

Munger said Phyllis Kahn, Minneapolis, and Fred Norton, St. Paul, also environmental supporters, were not reappointed.

Munger has served since 1973 on the commission which evaluates programs proposed to preserve, develop and maintain the state's natural resources. It then recommends to the legislature appropriations and closely monitors those programs.

Munger said the reason for his being removed from the commission may have been political.

He claimed he has always been in favor of the BWCA, scenic rivers, Voyageurs National Park and an open space program.

"I'm a strong advocate," he said, "and I don't believe Anderson is. He's more likely to listen to anti-environmental organizations and he's been under pressure to remove me. It's easy to paddle downstream but I've always paddled upstream…."

Carol Lee…Executive Director of the North Star Chapter of the Sierra Club, said; "I think it was unfortunate Munger was not reappointed. The natural resources chairman should be on that commission…"

Larry Forbes, Duluth, who heads the Northern Lights Group of the Sierra Club, said he had heard speculation that Munger had not been renamed…

"I think Munger has been very good on the commission. I am disappointed, but I'm not surprised."

(*Duluth News Tribune*, June 14, 1978.)

But at the same time Munger was being politically penalized for his environmental positions, he wielded considerable power within the DFL.

> A close vote is expected today when House DFLers choose between a southern Minnesota farmer and a northern Minnesota mill worker for their top leadership post in 1979.
>
> Rep. Irv Anderson of International Falls, House Majority Leader the past six years, and Rep. Carl Johnson of St. Peter, head of the Education Committee since 1973, are seeking the No. 1 post. About six DFLers were said to be wavering between the two camps and how they divide could determine the winner. Or, the race could be close enough so that Rep. Willard Munger of Duluth could cast the tie-breaking vote.
>
> With Munger undecided, one count showed a 33-33 deadlock.
>
> "I'm genuinely undecided," he told a reporter. "They both have their pluses and their minuses. I'm going to wait and see what they have to say."
>
> (*Duluth News Tribune*, November 18, 1978.)

As related previously, the House was split evenly in 1979 between Democrats and Republicans (67 to 67) which resulted in the election of moderate Republican Rod Searle of Waseca as the Speaker. By the 1980 session, when Irv Anderson resumed his quest for that office, the DFL held a slim 68-66 majority in the House. According to Arlene Lehto (who served in the House for three terms) the DFL's narrow majority made for interesting politics.

"There were five of us who decided not to support Irv for Speaker," Lehto recalls. "Willard was always wary of Irv. We ended up supporting a legislator from the Twin Cities (Fred Norton, later a member of the Minnesota Court of Appeals) over Irv, mostly because of Willard."

(*Editor's Note: Anderson wouldn't get another chance to serve as Speaker of the House until the 1993 session, when he gained Munger's support and was finally elected to the post.*)

During the late 1970s and early 1980s, one of Willard Munger's favorite activities was ballroom dancing. One of the people Munger often selected as his dancing partner was a woman who lived in the trailer park where Munger rented a space for his road-weary Airstream travel trailer during legislative sessions. Her name was Barbara. Though Barbara's last name is a casualty of time and faded memories, Mike Jaros remembers her clearly.

"Willard didn't have a telephone in his trailer in St. Paul. The trailer park where he stayed was north of the Capitol in the White Bear area." Jaros remembers. "I heard stories from the House staff that Willard would come in late because the waterline to his trailer froze. It was winter so living in a trailer wasn't the most convenient. The bed he slept on was small and uncomfortable; just a big single. I know Frances stayed with him in the trailer every once in a while but mostly, he was on his own and Frances stayed in Duluth to run the motel. It was a pretty lonely existence. Barbara and her little boy lived right across the road from Willard. I had dinner with Willard, Barbara, and her son at her trailer. Willard seemed genuinely fond of the boy. I know Willard used her shower from time to time when his wasn't working. She was considerably younger and nice looking, divorced, I believe. I never went dancing with them—that was something he did with Arlene Lehto and others. I'm not sure whether Willard's connection with Barbara was more than mere friendship. It may have been but I don't know. All I know is that it was a lonely existence, him in that trailer all by himself.

"When I came back to the legislature, Willard took a room near mine at the Travel Lodge. Later, at the Kelly Inn, we shared a room. He didn't use the trailer anymore because we were getting per diems."

Patsy Munger-Lehr doesn't recall her father dancing much with her mother, though she does remember Willard and Frances dancing for exercise.

"Dad really liked women," Patsy remembers, "so it wouldn't surprise me if he went out dancing. He always said after mom died that he wouldn't marry a woman with kids. That's another reason I think Frances appealed to him—she didn't have children. My girls still talk about coming back from St. Paul with Dad and Arlene. Dad stopped the car at Tobie's Supper Club in Hinckley where there was a band playing so he and Arlene could dance. My girls weren't too happy about that."

Lehto verifies the dancing incident in Hinckley, chuckling as she remembers Patsy's girls being upset with Willard and her for stopping in the middle of nowhere to dance.

Mike Jaros left the legislature in 1978.

"Al Quie wanted to destroy the 'Minnesota Miracle,'" Jaros recalls. "He took away tax indexing, cut income taxes for the wealthy and put more pressure on regressive taxes like sales and property taxes to fund state obligations. I was disheartened by it. I was 35 years old and I decided to change what I was doing."

Jaros was convinced by others to run for county commissioner against Gary Doty, one of two Doty brothers who served in the Minnesota Legislature. Jaros recalls little love between Willard Munger and the Dotys during their service together in the legislature.

"There was an agreement between Rod Searle and Willard," Jaros remembers, "regarding the Waseca campus of the University. Because of low enrollment, that campus was always in danger of closing. But Rod and Willard had a deal where Willard would push the Duluth delegation to support keeping Waseca open and, in return, whenever UMD needed funding, such as for the medical school and the like, Rod would see to it that we got the money. Well, Ralph Doty served in the senate. He'd promised to support the Waseca campus, promised Willard he'd do that. And then he didn't. That set Willard off. Willard's position was, 'I promised Searle and Doty promised me.' Willard called a meeting of all the local legislators and went right after Doty. Doty looked incredulous. 'What?' Willard said, 'You're nothing but a goddamned double-crossing liar.' Ralph Doty, who along with his brother Gary prides himself as being religious, took offense. 'Representative Munger, we don't use language like that where I was raised.' Willard got angrier and spewed, 'Well then, you're nothing but a horse's ass. Is that better?'"

Jaros recalls a similar incident between Munger and Ralph Doty's brother, Gary, who, before becoming a St. Louis County Commissioner and three-term mayor of the city of Duluth, served one term in the Minnesota House.

Jaros was talking to Gary Doty about an issue when a very irate Willard Munger approached. Munger was nearly seventy years old; a rumpled-appearing, older gentlemen in a suit. Doty was a former college football player and an avid marathon runner. The difference in the men's physiques didn't seem to bother Munger.

"Willard marched right up to Gary," Mike Jaros recalls. "I have no idea what he was mad about. But when Doty tried to deflect Willard's anger by saying, 'You know what Willard? I think you've been in the legislature too long,' Willard grabbed the lapels of Doty's sport jacket and stammered, 'You, you, you...' He pulled so hard he ripped the lapels right off Doty's jacket! Gary Doty put his tail between his legs and ran," Jaros recounts with a smile.

One would think that, with the animosity shown by Munger towards the Doty brothers, Munger would have encouraged Jaros to run against Gary Doty for the county commissioner post. That was not the case.

"Willard wasn't happy that I was leaving the legislature," Jaros recalls. "And when I lost the election to Gary Doty, I was without a job. I went to Washington, D.C. and went through a program with the Foreign Service. I spent a year out there before I resigned and came back to Duluth. Ben Gustafson had replaced me as a DFLer in the House from my district. Ann Glumac, who later worked for Willard in the House, was a reporter with the *News Tribune*. Ann asked me if I'd heard that Ben wasn't going to run for re-election. I hadn't but I filed and ended up running against Mark Steen, a very conservative Republican, in 1984. I won and, once I got back to the legislature, I worked with Willard on many local bills, especially those involving the expansion of the Duluth Entertainment and Convention Center (DECC), any bill involving the Duluth Zoo, anything involving UMD and the conversion of Lake Superior College (LSC) from a technical school into a real college. Willard and I always sympathized with LSC's plight—UMD always got the money, it was the Taj Mahal. I also supported Willard in his quest to keep Amtrak running, which we managed to do with a million dollar subsidy every two years for about a ten year period until Gerry Willet (DFL-Park Rapids) killed it in 1985."

As the 1970s drew to a close, mineral exploration in northeastern Minnesota once again became headline news.

> ### Mineral Exploration Firms Say Regulatory Bill too Strict
>
> Mining industry leaders said Tuesday that a bill putting mineral exploration under state licensing and regulation is stricter than necessary and would jeopardize investments of their companies...
>
> Rep. Willard Munger, DFL-Duluth, who chairs the House Environment and Natural Resources Committee...said the state should spell out a policy for uranium exploration and development in the same manner as it did for copper-nickel a few years ago.
>
> "It should have been done a long time ago," Munger told reporters. He said additional public testimony will be taken...and his committee will vote on the bill...
>
> The bill says the commissioner of health and the natural resources commissioner shall have the power to inspect exploratory borings or drillings... Mining company officials objected to a provision which says the firms must turn over to the state core samples of all drillings...
>
> (*Duluth News Tribune*, April 4, 1979.)

The same issue of the newspaper included an article about the Three Mile Island disaster.

> Federal officials said...a troublesome gas bubble no longer poses any significant danger of explosion at the Three Mile Island nuclear plant...

"I would say there is no more bubble at the top of the core…We no longer consider a hydrogen explosion a significant problem" [Harold Denton of the Nuclear Regulatory Commission] said. "The site remains stable…the bubble poses no further significant safety problem"…

Robert Bernaro, a federal decontamination expert, arrived to assess ways of eventually cleaning up the radiation in the facility—a task he said would take "many, many months, maybe a year or two."

(*Duluth News Tribune*, April 4, 1979.)

Munger's perennial attempt to reign in Minnesota's solid waste problems was also re-visited during the 1979 legislative session.

79 Gutless Lawmen

This a fitting description for 79 members of the Minnesota House who have avoided voting on a critical state issue by sending a bill, in effect, to legislative limbo.

The bill would have placed mandatory deposits on all beverage containers sold in the state. The deposit would have been ten cents. This was a new form of the "ban the can" legislation that has been kicked around the Capitol for the past ten years.

The objectives of the bill were honorable and there is no question that the bill would have been effective, as made evident by the lobbying effort put up by the state's bottle and can manufacturers to kill the legislation…

The bill was approved by the House Committee on Environment and Natural Resources…by a vote of 14 to 9. But when the bill came up for a full House vote…a majority of representatives chose to side-step the issue…Instead of voting the bill up or down, they took the gutless route by sending the bill to the House Labor Committee for further review. Considering that labor interests are among the main opponents to this kind of legislation, that action amounted to sending the bill to its death without a fair trial…

As a result, Minnesota will continue to waste natural resources and pay higher prices for beverages—all because 79 legislators don't have the guts…

(*Duluth News Tribune* Editorial, April 16, 1979.)

The "ban the can" legislation wasn't Willard Munger's first rodeo when it came to dealing with solid waste reduction.

"I used to think my greatest achievement was the passage of the first packaging and recycling bill in the United States," Munger recalled. "It banned the nonreturnable plastic milk bottle, and the legislation was thrown out by the state supreme court. The court case went to the United States Supreme Court, which upheld the law as constitutional. Then our legislature threw out the bill…"

(*Oral History of Willard Munger*, ibid, p. 83.)

The Quie Administration began in 1979. The House of Representatives was evenly divided between the Republicans and the Democrats and the Democrats controlled the Senate. Attempts to weaken some of the environmental legislation passed during the "Minnesota Miracle" years came to the attention of the media.

Minnesota Rivers Need Protection

We hope Rep. Willard Munger holds to his word. The chairman of the House Environment and Natural Resources Committee says no bill likely to weaken the state's Wild and Scenic Rivers law will get out of his committee.

Rivers mean a lot to Minnesotans—something the legislature recognized in 1973 when it passed the law, designed to protect rivers like the Kettle, Crow and Rum from unsightly development. Yet some people would gut the law by removing the power of the Natural Resources Department to designate which rivers to preserve; that would leave protection to the whims of local landowners and officials…

Some criticism leveled at the DNR is deserved…But much of the criticism is uninformed and misconceived. Opponents—sometimes the same people who battled the banning of motorboats in the BWCA Wilderness—claim that the law is a "land grab" that "it's taking of property without compensation…"

The law sets up some minimal zoning standards but does not permit the DNR to force the sale of riverfront land…

"The great majority of our river frontage remains unspoiled, and our options on its use are still mainly open," says University of Minnesota Prof. Thomas Waters, a leading river specialist. "But time is running out and interest grows in the economic gain to be had by high-density development…The year 1979 may be a key year. It could very well determine whether future Minnesotans can look back to a foresighted citizenry and legislature for preservation of our state's river treasures." We agree.

(*Minneapolis Tribune* Editorial, April 22, 1979.)

The *Duluth News Tribune* didn't agree.

Scenic River Buck Stops Here

A scenic river designation bill now before the Minnesota Senate offers our state government a new opportunity for openness by placing decisions on a sensitive statewide issue where they belong—up front with Minnesota's top elected officials.

Minnesota's scenic river program, established by the legislature in 1973, is designed to keep selected sections of state rivers in an undeveloped condition to preserve some riverbanks in their natural condition. Under the current statute, the Commissioner of the DNR can, after holding public hearings, designate a river or section of river "scenic" and thus put into effect zoning procedures to bar further development along that river. To date, about 340 miles of five Minnesota rivers have been so designated. Six other rivers, including the St. Louis and Cloquet in NE Minnesota, are being considered for inclusion in the program.

But river property owners…have objected to some provisions of the program, claiming its zoning restrictions deprive them of some of their rights as landowners…Other opponents contend designation…should not be left to just one person, especially to an appointed official…

The legislature has received several proposals to ease some of the inequities…The bill now before the senate is a just compromise of that issue. The revised law would transfer final authority on…designation…to the State Executive Council. That six-member panel is made up of Minnesota's top elected officials…

This bill should find fast and firm support in the Senate…However, should it clear the Senate, it faces a potentially undemocratic hurdle in the Minnesota House. DFL Rep. Willard Munger of Duluth, who heads the powerful Environment and Natural Resources Committee is a strong advocate of the current scenic river law. He has expressed reluctance to allow any law which would alter that law be heard in his committee. Munger could, in effect, kill the proposed scenic river legislation through inaction.

Such inaction would further abrogate Minnesota's democratic process…If this bill clears the Senate, Munger should allow it, indeed, should encourage it, to pass through his committee for consideration by the full House…

(*Duluth News Tribune* Editorial, April 22, 1979.)

The *St. Paul Pioneer Press* ran a retrospective of Representative Munger's service.

Environmentalist is not Distracted by Gary Dawson

He strikes terror into the hearts of those who are riding the political backlash against increased acquisition and zoning of lands for wilderness and recreation.

Neither governors, majority leaders nor an alarmed public have shaken this stubborn environmental protectionist from his self-appointed duty of "preserving what we have for our grandchildren."

To his political foes, especially northern Minnesota legislators threatened with wholesale holocaust over the hot land use issue, he is simply known as "Ol' Willard."

"Ol' Willard"…is DFL state Rep. Willard M. Munger, the powerful chairman of the House Environment and Natural Resources Committee. The 68-year-old Munger, approaching 24 years of service in the House, is standing as a rock in the face of a public onslaught against increased governmental controls and restrictions on private and public land in the name of environmental protection.

And that is causing problems for politicians, many of whom suffered defeat over land use issues in the 1978 election…Lawmakers from agricultural areas want to stop state acquisition of abandoned railroads for trails and turn the land back to farmers. Legislators from northern areas and other regions want to take away DNR's authority to designate and manage streams as "wild and scenic rivers…"

"It's a backlash from Voyageurs National Park and the BWCA," Munger observed…" Frankly, these people scare the hell out of me. They're opposed to anything that will benefit people in the future—our children and grandchildren. If we had the same philosophy 75 or 100 years ago, we wouldn't have a state park in the state…"

To northern Minnesotans upset about increased recreational and development restrictions, Munger says they would be more upset if all the land had been acquired by private interests and citizens would be facing one large sign saying, "Private Property, Keep Out!"

Munger is under attack this legislative session for his stands in favor of eliminating state funding for the Voyageurs Park Citizens Advisory Committee and opposition to the creation of a BWCA Citizens Advisory Committee. He has also not scheduled a hearing on the wild and scenic legislation and will not hear any legislation allowing counties or the legislature veto power over designations. But he says he might allow a hearing shifting final wild and scenic authority to the State Executive Council…

Munger, who cut his teeth on the populist politics of former Farmer-Labor Gov. Floyd B. Olson in the Fergus Falls area, likes to tell the story of his last election in his district, which includes a portion of the St. Louis River.

"I told them I was for Voyageurs National Park, for the BWCA, for wild and scenic rivers, for Coastal Zone Management, and that I supported expansion and development of state parks. They told me, 'Well, you're beat.'

The fact is because I stuck with my convictions, I wound up with more votes than any other time I ran!"…

What are his thoughts about two popular northern Minnesota legislators who are leading the backlash…Sens. Bob Lessard, DFL-International Falls, and Douglas J. Johnson, DFL-Cook?

"They are like throwing a piece of wood in the water. They drift in the stream, drift with the tide of public opinion, and it doesn't take any effort to do that…"

Munger regularly knocks heads with House DFL Caucus Leader Irv Anderson…who says Munger ought to "take into consideration rights of local citizens…"

Lessard sees a greater danger in Munger's…philosophy:

"If Willard Munger had his way, everything north of Brainerd would be a wilderness open only to backpackers and an occasional skier…"

"I'm not worried about what people say about me," says Munger, who claims he has the "best political background of any legislator here." He adds, "I never once considered when I vote on a bill how it's going to affect my re-election. People respect the fact I fight for my convictions…"

The *International Falls Daily Journal* suggested editorially that Anderson should not have allowed Munger to be chairman of the committee.

But Anderson rejects that idea, saying, "It would have caused too much disruption in the caucus and wouldn't be fair."

(*St. Paul Pioneer Press*, April 29, 1979.)

The proposed BWCA legislation authorized a citizen's advisory committee but Munger wasn't keen on that provision.

February 2, 1979

Dear Jerry:

Your letter…asks for my comments on the operation and effectiveness of the Voyageurs Citizens' Advisory Committee in light of the fact that you are considering creation of a similar committee for the BWCA…

When Rep. Irv Anderson first proposed the Voyageurs Committee, I supported the legislation [and ended up on the Citizens' Committee with former Governor Elmer L. Andersen]…Since serving on the committee, I have changed my opinion.

The committee membership is extremely unbalanced geographically… More than once, I have referred to the group as the "Voyageurs Park Harassment Committee"…Some, like former Governor Elmer L. Andersen, have resigned in frustration…

I cannot support the creation of another committee…without assurances that its makeup will be balanced.

Sincerely,

Willard M. Munger

The frustration Munger experienced regarding the BWCA and Voyageurs National Park bills was based partly on Munger's inability to sway Iron Range DFLers to support conservation legislation. But sometimes Munger's dedication to task managed to turn an Iron Range foe into a lifelong friend.

"I was born and raised in Buhl," Dave Battaglia (DFL-Two Harbors) recalls, "attending Hughes High School there before moving on to junior college in Virginia (Minnesota) and then St. Cloud State. I graduated and got a job teaching in Two Harbors beginning in 1953."

"I was only in Two Harbors four years before I decided to run for mayor," Dave remembers. "But I'd been involved in Buhl politics as a kid. The candidates hired me to count votes at the polls during the primary, to see where the votes were coming from, where they needed to put in extra effort. I got involved in the Community Health Center here (in Two Harbors) which was controversial because some thought it was socialistic medicine—it was the first HMO in the country. That connection generated friendships and got me to run against the mayor who'd been in office for many years in Two Harbors. I won and served 18 years as mayor. That's where I had some contact with Willard. He and Gordon Butler (Conservative Senator-Duluth) worked hard for us on the gross earnings issues regarding railroads and school taxes. In that context, I got to know Willard a bit. When his first wife passed away, I sent him a resolution of condolence passed by the city council. When I showed up in the House 16 years later, Willard shocked me because he remembered that gesture from all those years before."

Battaglia ran unsuccessfully against Conservative Representative Jim Ulland before defeating Norman Kine from Ely for the House seat from District 6A in 1976.

"At first, it wasn't harmonious between us," the former teacher remembers. "This was during the height of the Reserve Mining issue. I was concerned about jobs, the jobs of my friends and relatives working in Silver Bay and in Two Harbors. Willard just didn't seem to have any similar concerns. In the beginning, we weren't even cordial towards one another. But as Willard got a feel for me, and I got a feel for him, things came together. The real telling point was when he made me the chair of the Fish and Game Subcommittee. That floored me but it really upset his good friend Arlene Lehto. What I need to say is that my affection, and I mean this sincerely, was immense for the man. He never did anything for spite and he sincerely believed in what he was doing."

Battaglia noted other connections between the two men.

"Look, I come from a railroad town. I was there with Willard on Amtrak. My guys are all railroaders. And what happened was that, instead of fighting against state parks and national parks as I'd set out to do, I started authoring those bills! That's the impact Willard had on me. We'd ride down for LCMR meetings together with Frances in the car and when Willard was gone, she'd tell me, 'You know, David, Willard thinks a lot of you. He thinks you're one of the better legislators.' Now whether she was saying that to make me feel good or not, it meant a lot to me."

The newspapers of the times coincide with Battaglia's memory.

> State Reps. Willard Munger of Duluth and David Battaglia of Two Harbors are waging war against… [Governor] Quie over public access to two lakes near the Twin Cities.
>
> Quie recently prohibited the state [DNR] from buying public access on Lake Minnetonka…and on Bass Lake…
>
> If Quie's representatives testify…that the public access shouldn't be bought because the lakes are so overcrowded, Battaglia said he'll offer amendments that would limit the size of the motors allowed on the two lakes…
>
> "The people in the metropolitan area gave an inordinate amount of help to our people up north…(imposing) restrictions such as eliminating the use of motors on some of the BWCA lakes…"
>
> "What's good for the goose is good for the gander," Battaglia said.
>
> (*Duluth Herald,* February 2, 1982.)

Battaglia is quick to point out that Munger's friendship went beyond politics.

"I'll never forget this. I was in a terrible airplane accident. A Cessna went down trying to fly to Doug Johnson's (DFL-Cook) cabin," the former representative reflects. "Joe Puzel, one of the other guys with me, got killed in that crash and I was all banged up and in intensive care. Willard came to visit me in the hospital…He came into my room and held my hand. Then he went out and told my wife, 'Jean, he's going to be alright. He gave me a strong grip so I know he's going to make it.' And when I heard that from Jean, I thought, *this guy must know something, he must really know what's going on."*

When asked to assess Munger's relationship with Iron Range legislators, Battaglia smiles.

"He'd always ask Joe Begich, 'Rep. Begich, aren't I a fair chairman?' sort of trying to bait Begich. And Begich would always answer, 'Yes, Mr. Chairman, you're fair. But you could be a hell of a lot fairer.' The Range legislators feared Willard—feared his environmental capacity. With them, job loss was always the number one concern. They always thought Willard was out to cost jobs. The first few years, I spent a lot of time with the Range delegation. But that changed as my relationship with Willard grew stronger."

The retired teacher pauses when asked to comment about Munger's legendary struggles with Senator Bob Lessard from International Falls.

"I never could understand," Battaglia says, "why folks were so loyal to Lessard. He was one of the poorest legislators in terms of performance. I remember being at the governor's mansion in St. Paul and Rudy [Perpich] was thanking all of us for our help. He went around the room, specifically indicating what we'd each worked on that deserved his thanks. When he got to Lessard, Rudy looked at him and said, 'Bob, why don't you try to help out a little bit?' Lessard tried to say that he didn't have any budget for his committee. But every committee has a budget. The difference between Lessard and Munger was simple. Willard had a reason behind whatever he did. Bob was a hunter and a fisherman and nothing else. He fought for bills related to those interests but little more. Willard, on the other hand, had a broad scope. He was interested in parks, forestry, waters; the environment. He was a prime supporter of my bill to get nets out of Lake of the Woods; to stop the commercial netting of walleyes. He gave the issue to me and gave me all the support I needed to carry the bill. Every day, I see more evidence of Willard delivering what needed to be delivered in terms of conservation and the environment."

Battaglia echoes Rod Searle's sentiments about the decline of bipartisanship in Minnesota politics.

"You could get along with the other side," Battaglia remembers. "Many of my best friends in the legislature were Republicans, like Dave Bishop and Rod Searle. That changed as time went on."

When asked about the flack that Willard created by supporting Republican Rod Searle over DFLer Irv Anderson for Speaker of the House in 1978, Battaglia smiles.

"Irv didn't get along with the Speaker, Marty Sabo. Irv always wanted to be Speaker. He did some good things but I remember taking him apart in our caucus. This had to do with Indian Treaty issues, about hunting and fishing. Irv had promised to support my bill regarding payments to Mille Lacs (an Ojibwe band) but in the face of some heavy opposition, including lobbying by Bud Grant (outdoorsman and former coach of the Minnesota Vikings), Irv backed off. I went after him because he didn't follow through like he said he would. I don't recall there being any big disagreements between Willard and Irv. Irv simply wasn't Willard's kind of guy."

Minnesotans from across the state wrote to Munger expressing their appreciation for his steadfast refusal to buckle under to the pro-development mentality of the Quie era.

> April 29, 1979
>
> Dear Rep. Munger:
>
> A person should not need a reminder, such as Gary Dawson's piece on you in this morning's Pioneer Press, to express appreciation of a legislator who takes the long range view of our dwindling natural resources and who seeks to preserve for our children the little we have left...
>
> When I come up to Duluth in mid-September to watch the hawk migration, or whenever as a family we drive slowly up old 61 along Lake Superior, we are grateful for what has been saved from "development" in favor of beauty, beauty for which we should be stewards.
>
> Again, let me thank you most sincerely for your dedicated work.
>
> Sincerely yours,
>
> Gerhard T. Alexis

Not every fight Willard Munger took up was based upon high moral principles. In the early 1970s, the Miller Hill Mall was constructed adjacent to Miller Creek in Duluth's Piedmont Heights' neighborhood. Miller Creek had once served as an open sewer for the Duluth air base until a sewer line was constructed to carry the waste from the base to Duluth's sewer treatment facilities. This single act cleaned up the stream and allowed native brook trout to flourish. Even with the advent of the Miller Mall on the banks of the creek in the early 1970s, the stream held its own. But the attractiveness of the Miller Trunk (U.S. Highway 53) corridor was too great. Other retail stores sought to develop in the creek's flood plain with little regard to the consequences.

Harry Munger, Jr. was one of the first Duluthians to question the wisdom of unlimited development along the creek. With the stream running through his backyard, Harry had a somewhat selfish reason for protecting the stream; his children fished in, swam in, and skated on Miller Creek. It wasn't long before Harry enlisted the assistance of his legislator brother to fight further intrusion into the creek's watershed. One reason cited by Harry for seeking state intervention was that commercial development adjacent to Miller Creek had caused catastrophic flooding in the downstream neighborhoods of Duluth.

Wetlands Fill-In Makes Rains Lethal by Doug Smith

For years, wetlands were considered worthless hindrances…Developers filled them in and built upon them as cheap alternatives to expensive…city land.

In Duluth and Hermantown, development mushroomed along Miller Trunk Highway, gobbling the wetlands that once soaked up excess rain…

But then came the rains. Water once retained in the spongy wetlands ran wild over acres of concrete and asphalt parking lots. Streams swelled to overflowing and homes and businesses were inundated…

[R]esidents in the area also attest to the developing problems.

"I've been watching it [Miller Creek] long before the controversy arose between Hermantown and Duluth," said Harry Munger…"With each little development, you see more and more water flowing down the creek," he said—adding that the once-clear creek is muddied with sediment washed into it from paved-over wetlands. Munger said he had no flooding problems at his home until the last two years. And he cites the filled-in wetlands as the reason…

Munger is angry at Duluth and Hermantown for not controlling wetlands development. He said he was disappointed the U.S. Army Corps of Engineers withdrew controls over the area. He said there should be no more development…

Hermantown officials say development can be done without adding to the flood problems…

"Anything that is built here will have sophisticated retention facilities that will gradually release water into Miller Creek," Hermantown Mayor Helmer Ruth said…

Hermantown officials say Duluth has caused its own flood problems with Miller Hill Mall and Airpark Industrial Park development…

(*Duluth News Tribune*, August 12, 1979.)

Though floods *did* impact the Miller Creek basin in 1972, the real impetus behind the public discussion concerning development within the creek's watershed was something far removed from environmental concern: The city of Duluth was determined to stop a retail shopping development in neighboring Hermantown. Without divulging its true intentions, the city of Duluth enlisted Harry Munger, Jr. as a plaintiff in a lawsuit against Hermantown. Harry, in turn, enlisted his brother's support.

> "About six years ago a group of businessmen came to my office in St. Paul," Willard recalled. "They said, 'Willard, you've got to help us preserve the wetlands in Hermantown'—that's out of the city limits—'because they're going to expand the mall in Hermantown and they're going to destroy those wetlands.'
>
> "Of course, it was true that they would be destroying the wetlands they have up there. I looked at the group and not one of them looked like an environmentalist to me but I went before the PCA and gave them some strong arguments...As soon as they (the city of Duluth) got the Hermantown project stopped, they turned around and wanted to do the same project on the Duluth side...I really laced into them and told them what a bunch of hypocrites they are. They really suckered me in on that deal. They'll never do it again."

(Oral History of Willard Munger, ibid, p. 70.)

Harry Munger, Jr. was adamant that neither Duluth nor Hermantown should develop the Miller Hill corridor without making significant concessions to preserve Miller Creek's brook trout fishery. Unfortunately for the children of Hermantown, Piedmont Heights and Lincoln Park, no one listened. The Miller Hill Mall eventually added a Sears store and other retail shops in the 1980s, expanding the mall's size and further infringing upon the creek. Kohl's, Wal-Mart, Best Buy and other franchise stores opened up in Duluth and Hermantown, intruding further and further into the wetlands, paving precious marsh and swamp, the essential filtering mechanisms of the creek's watershed. Efforts by the Miller Creek Task Force, a group formed to rehabilitate the creek, proved fruitless. Today, few brook trout remain in Miller Creek, their spawning beds destroyed by sand infiltration; the creek's water warmed far beyond the tolerances of trout.

The irony of Miller Creek's demise is that, as powerful as Representative Willard Munger was, he couldn't use his political power to save the creek flowing through his brother's backyard.

CHAPTER 8

For the Grandchildren

Willard Munger always had an unorthodox alliance with the labor movement. Perhaps this came from Munger's place of origin: Northwestern Minnesota was virtually devoid of organized labor during the Great Depression, the time frame when Munger cut his political teeth. But despite Munger's agrarian roots, his lifetime voting record was nearly 100% labor-approved, with some minor exceptions. But those minor exceptions, including the fight regarding deposits on beverage containers, were loud and, at times, ugly.

"I can't understand why people are afraid to oppose labor," Willard recalled. "I've opposed labor in every session on their position on the deposit bill...I don't think labor is a one-issue organization. They will oppose the deposit bill. But they're not going to throw you out of office because you oppose them on this one issue. However, labor had enough influence that some of the legislators counted votes instead of issues and took the position they did. I never—I have never given up my philosophy for a vote and never will. And I haven't lost the election because of it, either. I think people have more respect for you if you fight for what you believe in—if you have a philosophy, if you dedicate yourself to that philosophy, and if you fight for it. Nobody respects somebody who is wishy-washy and weak...

"I've been very candid in talking to people in my coffee shop, and I'll never be able to force them to understand how I vote. I argue with them because I want them to see it my way, and sometimes I win, sometimes I don't. I don't think I've lost votes because of the strong positions I've taken. I think I've gained respect...When you pass major legislation, you bring about a change. Anytime you bring about change, you have opposition. You can't have a major change without some opposition. I think opposition brings about good government..."

(*Oral History of Willard Munger*, ibid, pp. 83 – 84.)

One of the hallmarks of Munger's outlook was his vision. Whether it was trying to improve the higher education facilities at UMD or Lake Superior College, improving tourism opportunities in Duluth, upgrading the Duluth (now Lake Superior) Zoo, or passing environmental legislation, Willard Munger looked towards the future.

"He never went with the tide, he knew what needed to be done and he did it," Rep. Jean Wagnenius, DFL-Minneapolis said…" He was not of his generation. That's not where I saw him…He was looking out for generations that were coming up…" (www.legal-ledger.com/archive/713mung1.htm.)

Another of his DFL colleagues, Rep. Alice Hausman, St. Paul, agreed.

"He was like a Native American chief: When we make decisions, we should consider the seventh generation…That's never popular to do." (www.legal-ledger. com/archive/713mung1.htm.)

But as 1980 began, Willard Munger found himself inexorably linked to his political past. Munger sought assignment by Speaker of the House Fred Norton on the legislative conference committee establishing the Hubert Humphrey Institute of Public Affairs at the University of Minnesota (Minneapolis). As an early convert from the FL to the DFL, it was fitting that Munger sought to serve on a committee charged with honoring Humphrey's life of public service.

> March 17, 1980
>
> Dear Willard:
>
> I appreciate the fact that you will ask to be on the Conference Committee with respect to the Humphrey Institute. We need your support on that Committee.
>
> The most recent reports that I receive on Mike Sieben are that he is for the Institute but would like to have it built on the West Bank. Unfortunately, this simply won't work…The plan is to have a conference center and motel in connection with the Institute, both of which will be built with private funds…Unfortunately, there isn't room for an entire complex on the West Bank…
>
> In any event, you have been a real source of strength in the endeavor and all of us who honor the memory are thankful to you.
>
> Sincerely,
>
> Gerald W. Heaney

Mike Sieben (DFL-Hastings; one of numerous Siebens who've served in the Minnesota Legislature) apparently had more "pull" as they say: the Humphrey Institute was built on the West Bank near Mondale Hall and the Elmer L. Andersen Library.

During the 1980s, proposals to mine copper-nickel in northeastern Minnesota once again stirred debate.

Environment Like Munger's Middle Name by Ann Schimpf

State Rep. Willard Munger is a one-man environmental dynamo. As chairman of the Environmental Preservation and Natural Resources Committee...the Duluth DFLer has been directly or indirectly responsible for the creation of the WLSSD, creation of the state Environmental Quality Board, the solid waste recycling act, a power plant siting bill, the Wild and Scenic Rivers Act, the creation of the Minnesota Energy Agency, and the recently passed uranium exploration bill.

One of Munger's greatest rewards has been seeing the St. Louis River cleaned up...

But now that some environmental battles have been won, he's ready for others.

"Mostly we'll be fighting to protect the tremendous gains that were made in the '70s," said Munger. "But I see the regulation of our untapped natural resources such as uranium, copper-nickel and peat as our main priorities."

"We're sitting on 15% of the world's supply of copper. We are also either No. 1 or No. 2 in the U.S. in peat resources...To stick our heads in the sand and say we won't develop them is foolish. I'll do everything I can to see that development does not harm our delicate environment."

(*Duluth News Tribune*, April 20, 1980.)

Munger's philosophy; that environmental protection and commercial development can be accomplished simultaneously, was formed when he joined the United Northern Sportsmen *and* the West Duluth Businessmen's Club in the 1940s.

"I think the environment will do more to enhance business in Minnesota than any other program that we might want to embark on," Willard remembered. "I'm going to give you an example. Like I told you earlier, when the paper mill (Lake Superior Paper) came to Duluth, they had a meeting at the Moose Hall. I just couldn't resist going up there during the meeting and asking the people who wanted to build a paper mill, 'Why are you coming to Duluth?...'

"The president of the group—I think his name was Kelly—said, 'We're considering moving to Duluth with our paper mill for two reasons—you've got clean water, and you now have a plant that will take care of our waste. That's why we're coming here.'

"If it hadn't been for the cleanup of Lake Superior and for the building of a wastewater plant big enough to take care of them, there wouldn't be a paper mill here...

"If it weren't also for the strong position that environmentalists have taken in protecting our forest lands and using reforestation techniques to provide for raw materials, the paper mill wouldn't be here. The position that environmentalists are taking in protecting the forests from acid rain indicates that they are concerned about the future. The people interested in paper are interested in the forest, or they wouldn't have any raw materials. They know that the attitude of people in Minnesota is to protect those forest lands, and that will make them more interested in coming to a place where they know their future products will be secure.

"You can go on and on and on and find that the environmentalists have done more to create jobs than anyone else. For instance, the environmentalists' position on hazardous waste. We think that Minnesota should build and operate our own hazardous waste plant to save industries the cost of shipping it out. It's a hell of a big inducement to bring new industry to the state of Minnesota. 'Come to Minnesota. We'll take care of your hazardous waste...'

"Also, the quality of life means something to the people. People want to come to Minnesota to work and to live. If we don't have a good quality of life, they'd probably go someplace else. That goes for the executive staff as well as for the skilled workers.

"I don't take a back seat when it comes to taking some credit for helping industry. When I first was elected to the legislature, environmentalists were considered to be more or less kooks. They were the people who took jobs away from people. They were the people driving industry out of the state. 'Industry won't come into the state because of the environmental policies—because we make them clean up their smokestacks and their dumping of pollutants into the rivers and streams.' Those days are over...."

(*Oral History of Willard Munger*, ibid, pp. 87 – 88.)

Indeed, industry, while not always enthusiastic about the details of Munger's environmental legislation, had, by the early 1980s, become supportive of Munger's overall position.

April 25, 1980
Dear Mr. Munger:

On behalf of 3M…I would like to express our appreciation for the support you gave in bringing about the passage of the Minnesota Waste Management Act of 1980.

Both the public and private sectors…will benefit from having a coordinated method for handling the disposal of solid and hazardous waste…

Sincerely,

L.W. Lehr

Vice Chairman of the Board, 3M

Environmental groups also continued to express their appreciation.

May 5, 1980

Dear Rep. Munger:

On behalf of the Tettegouche Park Task Force, I would like to extend our sincere appreciation to you for taking off from your busy schedule to meet with us concerning the future of Tettegouche State Park.

For me, it was a good feeling to "mend fences."

Sincerely yours,

Ruth Ericson

President

Northeastern Minnesota Environmental-Economic Council

Munger's work on behalf of state parks and wildlife areas is something that many Minnesotans don't appreciate.

"I've been on the Parks and Trails Council for years," former MPCA Director Grant Merritt reflects. "And it's very clear to me that one of the things Willard worked hard on and doesn't receive a lot of recognition for is the work he did on behalf of state parks. Bill Morrissey, who just retired as the DNR's Deputy Commissioner of Parks, verifies that Willard had a hand in many, many projects involving our state parks. Our current governor [Tim Pawlenty] is wrong when he states that there hasn't been a new state park dedicated in Minnesota in thirty years. Willard worked on Glendalough State Park out near where he grew up, land which had been part of a hunting estate owned by the Cowles family. They donated the land to the state and Willard worked hard to get it dedicated as a park. This was in 1992. Willard took Bill Morrissey out there and explained that one of the six lakes in the proposed park was a lake he'd fished as a kid."

Merritt also believes that Munger's involvement in Tettegouche and Grand Portage State parks was critical to their creation and development.

The battle to create Tettegouche State Park was one of the early disagreements between Willard Munger and Dave Battaglia. The proposal to create a new state park on the North Shore of Lake Superior (on the heels of the creation of the BWCA and Voyageurs National Park) didn't sit well with North Shore residents.

> *Tettegouche: A Jewel Riding on a Pendulum* by **Greg Breining**
>
> Time is running out on Tettegouche. Tettegouche, a 3,400 acre expanse of hills, valleys, spring fed lakes, creeks, cliffs and outcrops on the North Shore is an area where...the [DNR] has long wished to make a state park. Moreover, the state, using federal grants, could perhaps buy the [parcel]...for as little as $60 per acre.
>
> "It's a tremendous buy," said State Rep. Willard Munger..."It would be a tragedy and a shame if Minnesota let it slip away. It would haunt me for the rest of my life."
>
> But Tettegouche is as controversial as it is beautiful.
>
> "Anyone who wants to think about getting a park is going to have a big fight on their hands," said Jeanette Durkee, Silver Bay..."We just feel we have enough state parks, and we don't want any more land in state parks..."
>
> Opponents to a Tettegouche state park, state forest, or state anything else say the land should not be removed from Lake County tax rolls....
>
> A former St. Paul bank official...who owns the property, has given the Nature Conservancy an option to buy the land. The Conservancy will buy the land if the state, in turn, agrees to buy it...
>
> The forest has not been cut since 1911...[And it is] the kind of property that encourages superlatives...
>
> "It's beautiful," Munger said. "There isn't another area in Minnesota so beautiful."
>
> "I am very much opposed to it [public ownership]," [Rep.] Dave Battaglia said. "I suggest they sell it to any private individual. I don't care what they do with it..."
>
> (*Duluth News Tribune*, February 11, 1979.)

A compromise between the state of Minnesota and North Shore residents was eventually reached and Tettegouche was added to the state park system.

In May of 1980, Willard Munger's sister, Elsie Winter, suffered the loss of her husband, Ernest. It should be recalled that Ernest Winter was the brother of Willard's first wife and that the two couples grew up together in Fergus Falls. When Willard and Martha sold their service station in West Duluth to Western Oil, Ernest, Elsie and their son, Wesley, moved to Duluth to manage the station. The Winter family continued in the service station and convenience store trade until early 1980, when Ernest and Elsie retired and moved into a house in Morgan Park. Their time together in retirement was short: Ernest passed away on May 18, 1980. (*Duluth News Tribune*, May 19, 1980.)

As 1980 drew to a close, the public's attention was drawn to the presidential race between President Jimmy Carter and former California Governor Ronald Reagan. America was in the throes of a deep recession and Carter was having difficulty mustering any semblance of a campaign. To make matters worse for the embattled president, the Iranian hostage situation was front page news. Locally, Voyageurs National Park remained a subject of controversy in northeastern Minnesota.

Willard Munger was running against Conley for the House seat in District 7A and Munger won that contest, 6,690 to 4,236. But Ronald Reagan overwhelmed Jimmy Carter, bringing an era of "trickle down" economics and widespread deregulation of government, including the deregulation of federal environmental protection, to Washington.

The importance of the interaction between state and federal environmental legislation cannot be overstated. Beginning with John Blatnik's sponsorship of water treatment legislation in the 1950s, the primary funding source for major environmental projects came from the federal purse. The impetus behind the extensive state environmental legislation authored by Willard Munger during the early 1970s came on the heels of Congress passing (and President Nixon signing into law) the federal Clean Water Act, Clean Air Act, and the federal Wild and Scenic Rivers Act.

But the uncertainty of federal funding for environmental projects, occasioned by the "hands off" approach of the Reagan (and subsequently, the Bush) administrations made the issue of continued money for environmental projects a concern for environmentalists in Minnesota. It was thought that a dedicated source of *state money* was needed to fund environmental and conservation-related projects in Minnesota. Thus the concept of an Environmental Trust Fund, perhaps Willard Munger's greatest legislative triumph, was born.

"I think the idea for a trust fund may have come from Judge Heaney," John Helland recalls. "I know I drafted the bill and that Ann Glumac was also involved. I guess I never knew for certain where the idea came from but, for some reason, I think Heaney was the one either who came up with it or pushed it once he and Willard talked about it. The problem was that relying on the general fund wasn't working. Willard thought the way to earmark money was to allocate a percent of the state sales tax to a trust fund. This was based upon some history; the fact that the LCMR received dedicated funding of two cents per pack of cigarettes from the cigarette tax. Given that there was a recession on at the time, funding for the environment was hard to come by and Willard thought this would prevent his programs from being given short shrift."

In the midst of legislative discussions regarding the creation of an environmental trust fund, Willard's mother died.

> **Elsie E. Munger, Pioneer in DFL**
>
> Elsie E. Munger, 93, formerly of 7408 Grand, died…
>
> The mother of State Rep. Willard M. Munger, she had been active in the DFL party during its formation and prior to that was active in its forerunner organizations, the Nonpartisan League and the Farmer-Labor Party.
>
> She was born…near Fergus Falls and lived in Duluth since 1942. She was a member of the Lutheran Church of Christ the King.…
>
> (*Duluth News Tribune*, March 25, 1982.)

As indicated in Elsie Munger's obituary, she had lived at the Willard Motel for a period of time. Upon Mrs. Munger's transfer to a local nursing home shortly before her death, her daughter, Elsie Winter (and son Wesley) moved into the motel unit that Mrs. Munger had occupied. Elsie and Wesley Winter lived in the unit until Elsie Winter's own death on April 4, 1983 due to complications from diabetes. Willard, while not necessarily an avid church-goer, followed the admonitions of the Carpenter by taking care of his brothers and sisters; by making his motel available to family members less fortunate than himself with little thought to profit. Munger had, in succession, taken in his mother-in-law, his mother, and his sister and his nephew to ensure they had a clean, safe, affordable place to live.

In 1982, DFLer Rudy Perpich (who had returned to Minnesota after serving as Special Consul to the Balkans) was running for governor against IR businessman Wheelock Whitney. Twin Cities DFL millionaire Mark Dayton was challenging incumbent Republican U.S. Senator Dave Durenberger. And amendments to the Minnesota State Constitution on the ballot included:

- The establishment of an intermediate Court of Appeals; and

- The allowance of pari-mutuel horse racing (Canterbury Downs).

Willard Munger was opposed by IR candidate Archie Wilcox for the House seat in 7A, and a DFL newcomer by the name of Paul Wellstone was running against former IR state legislator Arne Carlson for the position of state auditor.

Rudy Perpich won the 1982 gubernatorial election. Durenberger held onto his U.S. Senate seat (despite having been outspent by Dayton $7 million to $3.5 million; one of the most expensive Senate campaigns in history). Carlson bested Wellstone. Willard Munger retained his seat in District 7A, beating Wilcox 8,156 to 2,617. And the DFL retained its majorities in the House and Senate, which meant that Munger retained his leadership role.

In his position as chair of the House Environment and Natural Resources Committee, Willard Munger continued to work with and listen to Republicans.

> May 26, 1983
>
> Dear Chairman Munger:
>
> I want to thank you for your leadership on the Environment and Natural Resources Committee this session. It was both pleasant and educational to serve under you.
>
> I was particularly impressed by your even-handedness in spite of the charged nature of some of the issues with which we dealt. Your conduct in committee is something all members would do well to emulate.
>
> My hope is that your summer is a relaxing one. Duluth is a great place to be in the summer and I have to admit, I'm a little envious of you…
>
> Best regards,
>
> Craig Shaver
>
> Wayzata
>
> *(Editor's Note: Shaver was a three-term member of the House who served as an IR member of the House Committee on Environment and Natural Resources.)*

Munger also continued to be recognized for his environmental stewardship.

Munger Named Committee Vice Chairman

Rep. Willard Munger, DFL-Duluth, was elected vice chairman of the Legislative Committee on Minnesota Resources. (LCMR)…The commission was "created in 1963 to provide the legislature with background necessary to evaluate natural resources programs and to preserve, develop, and maintain the natural resources of the state," Munger said.

(Duluth News Tribune, June 22, 1983.)

In 1989, Munger started sponsoring an annual canoe trip on the St. Louis River (or one of its major tributaries) as part of his involvement with the LCMR.

"I think the idea started with Rudy [Perpich]. He had a canoe trip that Willard went on and Willard decided it was a good thing to do," legislative researcher John Helland recalls. "Willard did it to recognize his supporters and those who helped him. We canoed all of the parts of the St. Louis River watershed; the upper St. Louis, the lower St. Louis, the Cloquet, and the Whiteface. Then we'd return to Willard and Frances's place on Indian Point for a picnic."

Longtime Munger friends Steve Balach and Stanley Glumac would barbeque lamb and pork and former Duluth Chief of Police Eli Miletich and Harry Munger, Jr. would carve meat for the guests and the events enjoyed much coordination and support from Munger's legislative staff and his daughter, Patsy Munger-Lehr.

The election of Rudy Perpich to his first full term as governor was a distinct advantage for Willard Munger's environmental programs. Not only were the two men political allies; they were sincere friends, which gave Willard Munger unfettered access to the governor.

Former committee administrator Jackie Rosholt recalls an incident which illustrates the legislator's relationship with the governor.

"We were working on an energy bill. I don't remember which one," Rosholt says, "but the senate wasn't coming around. We were deadlocked in conference committee and it was late. I went home, got into bed and at 3:00 A.M., the phone rang. 'Jackie, you need to come back to the Capitol.' I said, 'Who is this?' 'Rudy. Rudy Perpich.' I didn't believe him," Rosholt recounts. "He said, 'It's really me. You need to come back because we have an agreement and we need you to draft the final legislation.' I still didn't believe him. 'See, Willard, I told you she wouldn't believe me,' is what I heard in the background. Willard got on the phone and convinced me to get dressed and come back. I got dressed and went back to the Capitol. Willard and Rudy were alone, eating pizza in the governor's office. I drafted the revisions, the bill was passed, and I got home about five in the morning. I'm not sure my husband believed me when he woke up and saw me coming in the door and I explained where I'd been."

Rosholt continues the story.

"Turns out, Willard was so afraid of waking me up, he had the governor call. The governor promised me a steak dinner, a common ploy that Willard used to get folks to do something. Willard bought me plenty of lunches and steak dinners but I never collected from the governor!"

In 1984, Minnesota favorite son and former Vice president Walter F. Mondale and Congresswoman Geraldine Ferraro challenged incumbents Ronald Reagan and George H.W. Bush for the presidency and vice presidency. Indian gaming made its debut in Duluth with the announcement that the Fond du Lac Ojibwe Band had entered into a development agreement with the city of Duluth involving the old Sears and Roebuck building on Superior Street. The Bong Bridge, named in honor of Poplar, Wisconsin World War II ace and Medal of Honor winner, Richard I. Bong, opened (replacing the old Arrowhead toll bridge linking West Duluth and Superior). And Willard Munger ran unopposed for his 15th non-consecutive term in the Minnesota House of Representatives.

Former DFL Governor Karl Rolvaag endorsed Mondale for president. Mondale came to Duluth on October 30 to campaign. Reagan was pushing for wins in all fifty states. He won 49 of them; all but Minnesota.

Duluth City Councilor Mark Steen, a religious conservative, ran against DFLer Mike Jaros. Jaros had left politics and DFL Rep. Ben Gustafson had held the 7B seat in Jaros's stead but declined to run for re-election. Jaros won back his old seat, beating Steen 5,693-2,708. Steen's candidacy was based primarily on moral issues: He had led the fight to defeat a proposed city ordinance precluding discrimination based upon sexual preference. Steen was also very open in his opposition to the United States Supreme Court's decision in *Roe v. Wade.*

Despite running unopposed, the 1984 election was a political disappointment for Munger. The Republicans regained majority status in the Minnesota House, which cost Munger his committee chairmanship (a position he had held since 1973). The Republican victory, and with it, the selection of arch-conservative Rep. Dave Jennings from Truman as the Speaker of the House, was a bitter pill for Munger to swallow.

Chapter 9

Last of the Old Guard

By 1985 Willard Munger was, in a very real sense, the last of a vanishing breed, a reality that was driven home by the death of former Governor Elmer Benson on March 13, 1985 at the age of 89. Benson had remained politically active for a short time after his loss to Harold Stassen in 1938, running unsuccessfully against Henrik Shipstead (who had left the FL Party for the Republican Party) for the U.S. Senate and serving as the Minnesota campaign manager for Progressive Party candidate Henry Wallace's failed presidential bid against Harry Truman in 1948. After Wallace's defeat, Benson returned home to Appleton, Minnesota, where he lived until his death.

Munger had missed the funerals of A.C. Townley and Senator Homer Carr, which likely prompted his decision to attend Benson's memorial where he delivered a stirring eulogy.

In Memory of Elmer Benson

There are not too many of us left who had the privilege and honor to personally know former U.S. Senator and Governor Elmer Benson who rose and towered high among the great liberal leaders of the Nonpartisan League and Farmer-Labor party—A.C. Townley and Floyd B. Olson, respectively.

I knew them all. As chairman of the Ottertail County Farmer-Labor Party and Farmer-Labor campaign supervisor for the Eighth and Ninth Congressional Districts in 1936 and 1938, I was there among them, working to change an out-dated, decayed socio-economic system that brought about turmoil, suffering, and with it, the Great Depression.

As a young activist, I once introduced Benson at a Farmer-Labor meeting in Fergus Falls during the time he was Banking Commissioner, suggesting that some day he would be governor of Minnesota. The prediction became a reality, and with it, brought hope for peace on earth, hope for the forgotten, the unfortunate, the unemployed, the farmers driven from their homesteads by a ruthless unregulated socio-economic system.

Benson's unflagging courage and dedication in fighting for the rights of humanity, civil liberties, peace, and his efforts in uplifting the lives of the unfortunate, the forgotten, and victims of the Great Depression, brought forth new faith in democratic government.

Benson championed causes not for their popularity but for their benefits to society. Benson had a purpose in government and it was to serve people instead of the special privileged few. Benson's greatest asset was that he had a philosophy and purpose in life and dedicated his efforts to uphold and fight for those ideals.

Yes, Benson was a radical and hated by the special privileged, but he brought about social and economic changes in his time: social security, taxes based upon the ability to pay, unemployment and workers compensation insurance, socio-economic benefits, and conservation of our natural resources and environmental protection we now enjoy and accept as good and necessary government policy.

It pleases me to know that the definition of a present day conservative is one who worships the works and efforts of dead radicals who brought about change that we today cherish and accept.

Willard M. Munger

State Representative

(Willard Munger Personal Collection.)

It must have been illuminating for Munger to realize that, as he rose to speak in honor of Elmer Benson, he was the sole survivor of a nearly-extinct breed; the political equivalent of the last passenger pigeon. Indeed, Munger's age was beginning to become a subject of media interviews and articles.

Munger's 75th Year Off to Favorite Kind of Start

It was 5:30 P.M. Tuesday and Minnesota House DFLers were filing out of a long, heated caucus…After most representatives had left, Rep. Willard Munger of Duluth was still inside talking politics…It was clear from the drained faces that not everything in the DFL Party meeting had been agreeable.

"I liked what you said, Willard," a representative called as Munger left the conference room.

By the time he'd reached his office, another colleague stepped in.

"Thank you," she said as if Munger had just taken the heat for everyone else.

"Well, I always say, when you take shot at somebody, hit 'em hard or keep your mouth shut," Munger responded…

He's the oldest lawmaker in the House and Senate…

"Nobody's even close," he said.

Munger…said he plans to run again in this year's election, but it may be his last term.

"When you're 75 years old, you've got a lot of people waiting…"

But that doesn't mean he's tired.

"I never get tired of politics," he said. "I love politics. Always have, always will…."

(*Duluth News Tribune*, February 5, 1986.)

To honor Munger's thirty years of legislative service, his friends and supporters planned a celebration at the Duluth Entertainment and Convention Center (DECC). The event drew hundreds of politicians, union officials, environmentalists, legislative staff, family and friends to the DECC on October 18, 1986. The speakers at the celebration offered different perspectives of Munger's legacy.

"Willard is old fashioned in that he values honesty…which is something we need," Meg Bye, Duluth councilwoman and DFL activist said during her short address. "He has never followed the polls—he looks to the long term…He takes a long term view."

Mike Jaros considered his friend in an unusual light; that of teacher.

"We served together for eight years [from 1972 – 1980] and I figured out he was the best teacher in the state…in the nation, when it came to instilling what it takes to be a true public servant. And folks listen to him. When UMD came to us asking for $2 million, Willard didn't think that was enough. He got $7 million for them!"

Sandra Gardebring (former MPCA Commissioner and later, Justice of the Minnesota Supreme Court) recounted her first meeting with Munger after she became the head of the MPCA.

"I was 29 years old, a lawyer, with no administrative experience and I suddenly had 250 people working for me. I thought, *Well, I might as well go to the mountaintop…to the person most respected regarding environmental issues.* I stopped in to talk to Willard. At first, he was a little suspicious but then he warmed to me…"

Conservationist Dave Zentner smiled as he tried to communicate Munger's enigmatic nature.

"He can get madder than hell…and sometimes, I can't figure out what he is up to. But then I sit back and let him go to work."

Dick Palmer, Conservative legislator and long-time Munger friend, was a bit sheepish about being on the rostrum with all the DFLers.

"I feel like a chicken in a fox cage here tonight. But I'm here because Willard is a genuine, real person. He raises bees. He cans peaches. He took care of Fred Sowl [a Duluth police detective] when Fred was a kid. He not only gave Fred a job and paid him, he knew Fred liked bananas. He'd always send some bananas home with Fred after Fred was done working… This guy represents us from his heart. He's a man of the future… Duluth's future is bright because of his foresight."

State Rep. Mary Murphy recounted her long connection to Munger.

"I'd sit down in the motel basement and address a stack of sample ballots. Willard would walk by and tell us what a good job we were doing. But just as we were finishing, he'd come by again and say, 'You know, I think I have a few more of those you can do,' and out would come another stack. Everyone had to have a sample ballot," Mary recalled. "Ronald Reagan said when he became president that he'd restore pride in America; that he'd bring heroes back. But he didn't know about Willard Munger. Willard is a Minnesota hero and Ronald Reagan should hear about him."

DNR Commissioner Joe Alexander lauded Munger's work on behalf of non-game wildlife.

"The 'chickadee check-off,' which is something that Willard backed, giving funding to the smaller animals that don't get the support pheasants and deer do, is every bit as important as his other work…And because Willard came from a game warden's family, I knew, when I first met him, we'd work things out," Alexander said through a smile. "There are already monuments to Representative Munger—there are rivers that flow clear, wetlands that won't be drained, and forests…that can be harvested."

Sam Solon, 7th District State Senator, noted that there was a lot of affection being shown by those in attendance towards Munger. Solon hoped that there was "enough of that love to spill over for the rest of us."

Governor Rudy Perpich also spoke.

"I cut everything short [in St. Paul]," the governor said, "so I could be here. I've been looking forward to this for quite some time. Willard's been a participant in the political process in Minnesota for over 50 years. He worked with one of our greatest governors, Floyd B. Olson. But if you want to know who Willard's people are, just stop by his coffee shop…

He's very partisan but he knows he must work with both sides...Willard's a man who keeps his word...He never blasts me in public or in front of other legislators; he waits until we're alone, in my office, to do that.

When I mentioned him in my State of the State Address, the first legislator ever mentioned in a State of the State Address, I was hoping folks would catch that and, in the future, that they'd research the name and find out why he was mentioned. Willard, folks will remember you...and that's why I've declared today 'Willard Munger Day' in Minnesota."

Munger didn't disappoint the crowd when it was his turn to speak.

"You know," Munger began, "a legislator is no better than the back-up support he receives...During the period from 1973 to 1983, the Environmental and Natural Resources Committee received and passed 120 environmental bills, of which 60 are said to have had national impact. Minnesota is No. 1 in the United States because of this. And that's in large part to Governor Perpich. You see, when folks don't support my bills, they get called into Rudy's office. I don't know what he tells them in there but when they come out, I have their vote."

Noting that Dick Palmer and his brother Harry were in attendance, Willard quipped, "I have two political advisors. I have my brother Harry, who, because he's an attorney, thinks he knows more than I do. He's on the radical side. So I go to the *Budgeteer* and listen to Palmer, my Conservative friend. So you see, I have a bipartisan advisory committee."

Willard also shared a story about Governor Perpich.

"One Sunday morning, someone was knocking on the door to the coffee shop. I got up in my underwear and said through the door, 'Who's there?' 'It's Rudy, Rudy Perpich.' I said, 'Sure, and I'm Jimmy Carter. Now who are you and what do you want?' He said, 'Come on, Willard, it's Rudy. Get up and make me some pancakes.' It was 7:00 A.M. and he'd driven himself all the way up to Duluth. That's the kind of governor we've got." (30th Anniversary Celebration Videotape)

In 1986 newcomer Becky Lourey, a DFLer from Pine County, challenged long-time IR Representative Doug Carlson in 14B. Pro-life candidate Michael Hughes got the IR nod to challenge Munger in District 7A. Though Lourey lost her bid for a legislative seat, Munger won re-election handily despite being vehemently pro-choice in a predominantly pro-life district. And with the Democrats back in power in the Minnesota House, Munger reclaimed his chairmanship.

Munger Heading for New Term

Willard Munger appears to have kept the tradition going. Minnesota's senior lawmaker took an early lead in the District 7A race…over IR challenger Michael Hughes…Munger, 75, a DFLer, has represented the West Duluth district for 30 of the last 32 years—from 1954 – 1964 and from 1966 – 1986…

Munger said he appreciated Hughes' clean campaign tactics.

"I'd say everything went well and I want Hughes to know I appreciate him running a good, clean campaign," he said.

(*Duluth News Tribune*, November 5, 1986.)

Unfortunately, Republican control of the Minnesota House during the previous session had caused irreparable damage to one of Munger's pet projects.

"I don't think," Willard recounted, "that…Amtrak…really had much to do with my getting votes. Amtrak was one of my issues in the legislature. It was not my chief concern as a member…It was one of the side issues that developed. I am a strong believer that if you're going to have clean air and preserve enough land to feed people, then we have to cut down on building roads. Cars create more pollution than trains do. Cars use more energy than trains do. If the energy crisis had continued, Amtrak would still be running. We lost the election (in 1984) and the Republicans took over. I couldn't get a hearing on it. They wouldn't even give me a hearing on it…The Republicans, when they got into control, passed a budget resolution. This budget resolution said that any bill that was introduced without being approved by the budget commission would not be considered by a committee. Mine required quite an appropriation, so they wouldn't give me a hearing on it. Not even a hearing, which is I think most undemocratic. I think Amtrak is going to come back. I think our future energy crises will dictate that we change our mode of transportation from what it is now…The future will dictate the return of rail service."

(*Oral History of Willard Munger*, ibid, pp. 60 – 61.)

Former DFL State Senator Ralph Doty recently revisited the issue of passenger train service from the Twin Cities to the Twin Ports.

On Passenger Rail Service's Return, Munger was a Prophet by **Ralph Doty**

If Duluth State Rep. Willard Munger were with us today, he'd have every right to say "I told you so."

When he died in 1999 at the age of 88, Munger was both the longest-serving member of the Minnesota House of Representatives and the oldest person to ever serve in that body. His reputation was that of a fierce fighter for a clean environment...But it is less known that Munger was also an impassioned advocate for passenger rail service...For years, Munger fought...to keep passenger rail service operating to and from Duluth...Eventually, Willard Munger's luck in sustaining the rail passenger service ran out. In 1985, when gasoline was selling for a little more than a dollar a gallon, his detractors argued that passenger rail service...was unnecessary...

Later...Munger predicted that when gasoline prices got to $3 a gallon-a preposterous thought in those days-passenger trains would come back to Duluth. Now...Ken Buehler, Executive Director of the St. Louis County Heritage and Arts Center...[is] leading a push for the return of train service to the Northland...If the Twin Ports gets rail service again, then the visionary Willard Munger will have been proven correct.

(*Budgeteer News*, June 11, 2006.)

John Helland recounts Willard's prowess at hiding Amtrak funding in bills unrelated to transportation.

"He hid the money part of Amtrak in bills that folks thought were going to die," John remembers. "But he had a way of making sure the bills survived and that the appropriation for the train did as well."

Munger made many impassioned pleas to keep passenger train service operating.

The United States is one of the few countries in the world where railroads are privately owned and operated, and the only major country where the railroad transpiration system is not owned and operated by the government...

(Willard Munger Collection, Minnesota State Historical Society, Box 148.F.6.5B.)

Munger also rebutted Senator Jim Ulland's (IR-Duluth) assertion that Munger's political maneuvering on the issue was counterproductive.

Amtrak's North Star Run is Worth Fighting for by **Willard Munger**

Recent news releases by Sen. James Ulland relative to Amtrak legislation require that his politically inspired fiction be separated from the facts.

In my 26 years in the legislature, I have developed my own...record without politically downgrading the efforts of [another]...Jim should take the advice of my grandfather who once told me "you seldom hitchhike to success for long on the backs of the energetic..."

> Ulland was quoted as saying I was "simple and unrealistic" in my pro-
> posals…
>
> Simple or not, the North Star runs despite Sen. Ulland and the governor
> [Al Quie]…"

(Duluth News Tribune, June 7, 1981.)

On a related topic, John Helland discounts the notion that Munger was the origi-
nator of the Minnesota "Rails to Trails" program, a state measure which duplicates
a federal initiative to purchase abandoned railroad rights-of-way for use as recreational trails.

"We did that piecemeal," Helland recalls. "I was with Joe Louis, Jr., the son of
the boxer, on a trip where he talked about his involvement with the national group
promoting the idea. It started out East, then moved into Wisconsin. Minnesota
farmers were worried about bringing riders out from the cities. They thought crime
would soar. But those fears were unfounded."

It is Helland's recollection that once Rudy Perpich dedicated the former Minnesota-Wisconsin Trail in Munger's honor (it's now known as the "Willard Munger
State Trail"), Munger began bicycling for his health. That was the point, Helland
argues, when Munger fully appreciated the benefits of the "Rails to Trails" program.
Helland's memory may or may not be correct. Before the State of Minnesota developed the Willard Munger Trail, Munger *was* involved in the creation of another
recreational trail in Duluth.

The Western Waterfront Trail hugs the shoreline of the St. Louis River in West
Duluth and passes within a stone's throw of the home Willard and Frances Munger
built on Indian Point.

> "There are a lot of things that are unpopular at the time," Willard recalled, "but
> after it's all done with the people change their mind. For instance, just to give
> you a small example, I got some cigarette money from the LCMR for a water-
> front trail…When the neighbors first heard about it—that was during an elec-
> tion year—they had a meeting down here at the Point. They were all against the
> waterfront trail. I was passing out my literature, and somebody tore it in half
> and threw it at me and said, 'You're going to bring…hoodlums into the com-
> munity. I don't want you around. I don't want nothing to do with you.'
>
> "I said, 'You know what I'm doing? I'm giving my entire point of land
> that I've got to the city so that their trail can go right in front of my house.
> I don't want hoodlums going around my place either, but I don't think there
> will be any.'

"Do you know that every single person down on that point now brags about the trail, walks the trail, and thinks the trail is the greatest thing that ever happened? But when it was established, it was the worst thing that ever happened, see?"

(*Oral History of Willard Munger*, ibid, p. 32.)

Some of Munger's critics were difficult to convince.

"The other day...the retirees [from the steel plant] had a big mass meeting in the Moose Hall," Willard remembered. "They had this Willard Anderson from the Range come down. He just raised hell with the elected officials and criticized everybody. 'Everybody is up there hanging out, and they're not doing anything for the retirees.' He went on and on for about an hour. I got so damn mad at what he was saying. He said, 'They're spending all the money on parks. They're spending all the money on Spirit Mountain [a ski hill owned by the city of Duluth]. They're spending all the money on the waterfront trail. That money could be saved and you retirees could get a better pension.' That's just a damn bunch of B.S., you know. He went on and on.

So they asked me to speak, and I said, 'Willard, you might have the same first name as I do, but I want to tell you something: you're nothing but a cheap demagogue.' There were about 300 people there...I thought I'd be kicked out right there, but I wasn't. I went on to tell them a few things— about how important these fishing piers [for the disabled] and parks are to retirees. Ninety percent of those facilities are used by retirees, and that's what they're there for...I could have done like other guys up there—just said nothing and whitewashed everything and said a few words and sat down, but I didn't."

(*Oral History of Willard Munger*, ibid, p. 33.)

At an age where many of his contemporaries were retired (or dead), Munger introduced the bill which many observers consider to be his greatest environmental legacy; the Minnesota Environmental Trust Fund.

Munger Wants State Fund Established for Conservation by Jim Ragsdale

Rep. Willard Munger, back in charge of the House Environment and Natural Resources Committee after a two-year hiatus, said...he will propose the establishment of a new state fund for a wide range of environmental and conservation projects.

Munger, DFL-Duluth, said he believes such a fund, if it could be established by a constitutional amendment...would help "get away from the

Band-Aid approach" to protecting the environment and provide a stable source of funds…

Munger said he will propose that the fund be established by amending the state Constitution, which would require approval by Minnesota's voters, and that a small share of state tax revenue be dedicated to the fund…

(*Duluth News Tribune*, January 16, 1987.)

Though Governor Perpich was in support of Munger's trust fund idea, the two men didn't see eye to eye on every issue.

Munger Angered by Plan for Environmental Board

State Rep. Willard Munger…has complained about a plan to study disbanding or modifying the Minnesota Environmental Quality Board. "If the governor's plan is to abolish the EQB, then I'm 100% opposed…"

Gov. Rudy Perpich…named State Planning Agency Director Tom Triplett to head the board and to conduct a study on whether the board is needed. The board, comprising seven state agency heads and five citizen appointees, was created in 1973 to coordinate environmental activities and policies among state agencies.

Steve Chapman, executive director of Clear Air, Clear Water, Inc., a Minnesota environmental group, said: "It would be a tragic mistake to discontinue the EQB…"

Triplett aide Jack Ditmore was named to direct the agency staff while the study takes place.

Munger said he was perturbed that Perpich didn't consult with him…

The Duluth DFLer said he was asked during the 1984 legislative session for suggestions on a replacement for Tom Kalitowski. Kalitowski has been named executive director of the MPCA.

"I told them Ditmore would make a good choice…Now I find out they're planning a study on whether to abolish the board. I'm burned."

Triplett said changes in state laws have relieved the agency of most of its responsibility…

The board hasn't met in two months and may no longer have enough work to justify its existence, he said.

(*Duluth News Tribune*, May 10, 1987.)

The EQB was one of the successes Munger and his legislative cohorts achieved during Wendy Anderson's "Minnesota Miracle" administration, a period, as John Helland recounts, of unheard of environmental legislation and success. For Munger, as forward thinking as he was, to have to confront the unwinding of any of the threads of environmental protection he had created was unthinkable. But Munger's successful sponsorship of the trust fund bill proved to be more important, in the long run, than minor skirmishing over the EQB.

> "One of the highlights," Willard recalled, "of my legislative career…was the passage of the environmental and natural resources trust fund. One of my biggest disappointments was the fact that the senate refused to permanently dedicate its funds through constitutional amendment. I have to blame Senator (Roger) Moe for that particular disappointment. Rather than the funds being dedicated through a constitutional amendment, half the money from the lottery will flow into the trust fund for five years. But after five years, then what…?
>
> "[On] the other hand, I'm extremely happy we did get a trust fund that is to be permanently established through a constitutional amendment. Once the money gets into a trust fund, it can never be taken out…You know, I talked about a trust fund ten years ago, but nobody paid much attention. I think what helped passage of the trust fund more than anything else is the news media and public education. Every week you have a television program showing how we're destroying the environment…When we know that ninety percent of the people use underground water for drinking and the experts tell us that now forty-two percent of all our wells show some signs of pollution, people start thinking. They start thinking even more when they read that our research people at the university tell us that ninety percent of cancer is caused by environmental pollution.
>
> "We're talking about the individual now. We're talking about you, and we're talking about me…Of course people are concerned. Everybody wants to live. Nobody wants to get cancer—everybody is afraid of it. I just got a letter yesterday from the Cancer Society that says one out of every three people is going to have a bout with cancer of some kind sometime in his or her life. So it's pretty damn serious, isn't it? When you trace it back to pollution in the environment, you become concerned…I'm affected and you're affected."
>
> (*Oral History of Willard Munger*, ibid, pp. 73 – 75.)

The issue of cancer and its environmental causes was a serious concern for Munger. He lost his lady slipper to an excruciating death due to ovarian cancer. He had witnessed the demise of his mentor and hero, Floyd B. Olson to the dreaded disease. He had watched his daughter Patsy's husband, Ed Carlson, die from Leukemia.

Munger's older brother Robert succumbed to lung cancer a few short years after his retirement from a lifetime of employment with Montgomery Wards. Longtime DFL stalwart Hubert Humphrey fought a similar battle with cancer and lost. Cancer had touched Munger in very personal and real ways and would also claim the life of Willard's colleague and friend, Governor Rudy Perpich in 1995. Even after Willard's own death from liver cancer in July of 1999, the disease continued to wreak havoc upon those who had been important figures in Munger's life. In October of 2000, Willard's environmental cohort, Congressman Bruce Vento passed away due to environmentally-caused lung cancer. And in December of 2001, the state senator who had shared District 7 with Munger for over two decades, Sam Solon, died of liver cancer less than two years after Munger's passing. Cancer was an issue that loomed large in Willard Munger's life and his dedication to curb the disease through pollution abatement was a priority.

Munger's committee administrator from 1987 – 1989, Ann Glumac, remembers the topic of cancer research being a sensitive subject for her boss.

"There was a group lobbying Willard on legislation," Ann recalls, "that would have prevented using animals in laboratory experiments. They were very earnest and thought they had an ally in Willard. Willard politely heard them out but explained that his first wife, Martha, had died of cancer and that the doctors tried experimental treatments on her. 'What makes you think a dog's life is more valuable than my wife's?' he asked tersely. That ended their visit."

Though Munger wasn't particularly pleased with the final version of the Environmental and Natural Resources Trust Fund, he supported passage of the law.

> "I think the money will be spent very wisely," Willard reflected. "I think the bill itself spells out that the money should be spent on long-range programs and that this will not support ongoing programs such as the DNR and the PCA. It specifically spells out that it will not be used for such projects as the super fund and wastewater treatment...I've always felt, and the records show, that Minnesota has led the way on protecting the environment. Minnesota has to lead the way again...So I think a tremendous, tremendous amount of work will be accomplished through this environmental trust fund. I hope that fifteen years from now, $100 million could be spent from the interest."
>
> (*Oral History of Willard Munger*, ibid, pp. 75 – 78.)

John Helland recalls that Willard Munger wasn't enthusiastic about enacting a state lottery or using proceeds from state-sponsored gambling to finance the trust fund.

Munger's original concept was to use a portion of the state-wide sales tax as the source of environmental funding, an idea that was unacceptable to Governor Perpich. In the end, the voters of Minnesota were asked to approve both a lottery *and* the trust fund.

As was usually the case, Munger was able to accept a compromise to his original proposal if the principle behind his idea remained intact. When his proposal to finance the trust fund with tax money was opposed by both Governor Perpich and Senator Moe, Munger recognized he was in a battle he couldn't win.

> "I think we've structured it in a very good way," Munger recalled, "by having two issues on the ballot—the trust fund proposal being separate from the lottery. I think that's an excellent way of doing it. I was opposed to putting them both together for the simple reason that there are a lot of environmentalists who don't like the lottery. The same environmentalists know that the trust fund isn't very useful if there isn't a lot of money there. So an environmentalist will go in and pull the lever for the trust fund, and right underneath will be the lottery. That will provide the funding for what he just voted for. I know what he's going to do. He's going to hold his nose and pull the lottery lever...
>
> "I was extremely disappointed [that the lottery was going to be used to fund the trust fund]...This is what I told the Rules Committee. They asked me whether I was disappointed. I said, 'Of course I'm disappointed. But you know, there were two ladies talking across a fence on a farm. Mrs. Olson says to Mrs. Peterson...'I understand your daughter is getting married next Sunday.' 'Yes, yes, she's getting married.' Mrs. Olson said, 'Who is she going to marry?' 'Well, I'll tell you,' Mrs. Peterson says, 'she's not marrying the man she wants. She's marrying the man she could get.'
>
> "And that's the real way it is with the trust fund. It's the only thing I could get to fund it. On the original bill, I had funding coming from a percentage of the income, sales and cigarette taxes, but Senator Moe said, 'Absolutely, no...' so I had to take what I could get...
>
> "Perpich did an awful lot in support of the...trust fund. He had eight or nine meetings around the state, pushing the fund. Of course, he might have been doing it as a way to pass the lottery bill. No, I think he is sincere about the environment and natural resources trust fund. He did an awful lot to generate support. I owe him a lot for what he did. He's been a strong supporter of environmental legislation, very strong."

(*Oral History of Willard Munger*, ibid, pp. 77 – 80.)

Perhaps the most prestigious honor Willard Munger ever received was awarded during the trust fund debate.

Munger Cited for Conservation Work

State Rep. Willard Munger…received the highest award accorded by the Izaak Walton League of America for his lifetime achievements in environmental and conservation legislation.

Munger, DFL-Duluth, is serving his 16th term in the Minnesota Legislature…

The "54 Founders Award" given to Munger at the 65th Annual National Convention of the League…is "in recognition of a lifetime of contributions to the conservation of America's renewable natural resources."

Previous recipients of the award have included environmentalist author Rachel Carson in 1963, former Secretary of the Interior Stewart Udall in 1964, Lady Bird Johnson in 1966 and conservationist and author Sigurd Olson in 1969.

"I felt a little out of place with all those biggies," Munger said. "I'm only a little guy in the works. But it's nice…"

Munger's latest project is an Environmental Trust Fund. Under the plan, two-thirds of the money appropriated each year by the legislature for environmental projects would be put into a trust fund. After the fund reaches $1 billion, the interest would be spent on the environment.

(*Duluth News Tribune*, July 17, 1987.)

When Willard Munger began his crusade to clean up the St. Louis River in 1952, no one knew who Rachel Carson was. By the time Munger was named an Izaak Walton '54 Founders Award honoree in 1987, Carson's book, *Silent Spring*, had become a bestseller and, along with the writings of Aldo Leopold and Sigurd Olson, required reading for those interested in the environment.

As observed earlier, Willard Munger's credentials as an outdoorsman were meager at best. One of Minnesota's premier outdoor writers, Ron Schara of the *Minneapolis Star*-Tribune mused over this seemingly contradictory man; a conservationist who rarely canoed, virtually never hunted or fished, and who biked only after a trail was constructed next to his home.

Munger's Mission-Clean Up State's Act by Ron Schara

Do you really know why it's not nice to fool Mother Nature? You'll get on the wrong side of Willard Munger.

They're close, Willard Munger and Mother Nature. Munger's political enemies say they were born the same year. But that's not true. Munger is only 77…

Today if you cross Munger, you may have to start cleaning up your environmental act. He'll make it the law…Munger didn't jump on the environmental bandwagon; he helped build it. And he made it roll. Sometimes ahead, sometimes back, but mostly forward…

Munger is gearing up for the Environmental and Natural Resources Trust Fund. It's his idea. "The trust fund is the most important bill concerning natural resources in the last fifty years," Munger said…"The trust fund will be written into the State Constitution…so no governor, no legislator will ever be able to take away the natural resources money that belongs to you."

Who is this driven man with the rocky face, who actually believes Minnesotans will vote to stash $1 billion into an environmental trust and spend the interest to secure, protect and rehabilitate the state's resources?

Indeed, Willard M. Munger might appear, at first glance—in a state with hordes of wilderness buffs, river paddlers and deer hunters to be an unlikely general of Minnesota's environmental frontlines.

His outdoor credentials are limited to the pursuit of ruffed grouse and a good crappie fishing hole…

Munger's list of environmental victories is long and impressive, including support for the Reinvest in Minnesota Program…

"(T)he legislature would pass good environmental laws, good resource laws but never appropriate the money…Or when they needed extra money, they always take them from resource funds. That's why I came up with the trust fund idea…"

Munger can be a little stubborn.

For years, he has refused to support legislative attempts to allow the hunting of mourning doves…

"I know my position is a little far-fetched and a little inconsistent…But the dove to me is a bird of peace. I hear them cooing outside the motel."

The doves, of course, aren't squawking about the chairman's stance.

(*Minneapolis Star-Tribune*, January 31, 1988.)

Mourning doves are no longer safe in Minnesota but the birds can't blame Willard Munger. Munger was able to block a hunting season on doves for the entirety of his legislative career: it wasn't until five years after Munger's death that mourning doves became legal prey for Minnesota hunters.

Schara's article also mentions one of Munger's seminal legislative achievements on behalf of wildlife conservation. In 1986, the Reinvest in Minnesota (RIM) program was enacted with Munger's full support. The program, which has been instrumental in allowing Minnesota to continue a viable hunting season for pheasants, as well as the preservation of habitat for other game and non-game wildlife, authorizes the Commissioner of Agriculture to select marginal agricultural land for inclusion in an easement program establishing conservation reserves for wildlife and waterfowl production.

Governor Rudy Perpich began calling Willard Munger "Mr. Environment" during the trust fund debate.

> ### Trail to be Named in Munger's Honor
>
> Minnesota's Mr. Environment, Rep. Willard Munger of Duluth, was honored with yet another testimonial dinner…
>
> Munger…was honored by more than 300 legislators, environmentalists and sportsmen.
>
> In his honor, Department of Natural Resources officials announced they will name a section of the Minnesota-Wisconsin Boundary Trail—running from Carlton to Duluth—for Munger…
>
> Munger was said to have tears in his eyes at the event, where he gave a moving, impromptu speech on his environmental efforts…
>
> (*Duluth News Tribune*, February 15, 1988.)

John Helland remembers that the event was planned by Glen Anderson and Fred Norton. The two men were worried that Munger, who was suffering from serious health concerns at the time, might not be around much longer. It was suggested to Governor Perpich that, rather than wait until the summer to announce the re-naming of the Minnesota-Wisconsin Border Trail as the "Willard Munger State Trail," it should be done sooner than later. Perpich agreed and made the announcement at the dinner, though the formal ceremony dedicating the trail wasn't held until the following summer. John Helland reflects that Munger was likely "the first Minnesota politician to have something named after him while still alive."

Ann Glumac recalls that Munger was suffering from a respiratory infection at the time and that it was her job to drive Willard and Frances Munger to the surprise event.

"I told Willard and Frances we were going to see Rudy at the governor's mansion," Ann remembers with a smile. "When I made turns that didn't make sense, Willard started questioning me. I told him there was a water main break and we needed to take another route."

Glumac also recalls that the next summer, when the LCMR visited the newly named Munger Trail and rode bicycles from Carlton to Duluth, Munger had a grand time. "He was in his seventies and he beat all of us into Duluth, even Gene Merriam (DFL Senator-Coon Rapids) who was considerably younger…Willard sure got a kick out of that."

Glumac, the second of three committee administrators Willard Munger employed during his tenure in the House, knew Munger before taking the position.

"I worked as a legislative page during high school," she recalls, "and since I was from Morgan Park High School in Willard's district, I got to know him."

Glumac went to Gustavus Adolphus College in St. Peter following high school before completing her studies in English Literature at the University of Minnesota. She interned for the *Duluth News Tribune*, where she covered the legislature, eventually landing a job as a legislative reporter for the *Tribune*. She remembers stories her mother and grandmother told about Willard and Martha Munger's grocery store.

"My grandmother was in the store one day," Glumac remembers, "and there was another woman there who made the comment that, in all her years of marriage, she and her husband had never had one cross word. My grandmother looked at the woman and said, 'Well then, that must be one spineless man you're married to.' Willard loved that story and told it often."

The comments made by Will Munger, Jr. about his father's lack of organization are echoed by Glumac.

"After I left the newspaper," Glumac recalls, "I went to work for Rudy Perpich as Deputy Communications Director. The Republicans were in control of the House. When the Democrats came back into power in 1987, Willard offered me the position of committee administrator and I accepted. He always liked to say he stole me from the governor. One of the first things I did was try and organize Willard's files. There was a big stack of photographs of his first wife. He told me about Martha, how he called her his lady slipper. It's why he had a framed poster of a lady slipper flower on the wall in his House office."

Glumac continues.

"I asked him if I shouldn't organize the pictures so he could take them home. He didn't want to do that because it would upset Frances."

Ann smiles when she thinks of the relationship between Willard and Frances.

"You know, in the years I worked with Willard, I think I only saw Frances in the building ([the State Office Building] three times. She'd wait out in the car, in the parking lot, her own little silent protest, I guess."

"Willard liked strong women," Ann reflects. "And he was a very special person. He had incredible integrity. He had a vision and he was wise enough to know that you can achieve your vision incrementally. This wasn't just with respect to his environmental causes, but with everything he did. He knew that half a loaf wasn't always a compromise. And he had such energy—he was just like the energizer bunny! But I differ with Walter Mondale on Willard's speaking ability. Yes, he was a mumbler. But he spoke the oratory of the 1930s. He had that cadence, like Floyd B. Olson, and he spoke in high minded rhetoric—and I mean that in a good way—something you don't hear very often. The other thing was that Willard worked very, very hard to prepare for presenting a bill. He would write copious notes in his beautiful penmanship, slaving over his desk for hours. He didn't take speaking on the House floor for granted, even if it was a relatively easy bill."

"And he was so conscious of his role as a public servant," Glumac observes. "I remember him explaining that a legislator shouldn't have an answering machine. It was alright to not be there to take a call; a constituent would understand that and call back. But if you had an answering machine, the voters wouldn't believe that you'd ever call back."

"This concern," Glumac adds, "for other people wasn't an act. There was a bill about gay rights introduced in the House by Karen Clark (DFL-Minneapolis) who was a lesbian member of the House. She gave a good speech in support of the bill but it went down in flames. She was so disheartened. I watched Willard, this man in his seventies, shamble his way down the House floor to her desk. He came up to her and put his hand on her shoulder. He did this right after the vote, in front of the entire House. He sent a message to the others in that chamber that 'this is a person I care about.' Here's this guy from West Duluth doing this. And trust me, gay rights was not high on his constituents' needs list. I made note of what he did that day."

Bills that Glumac worked on with Munger included the Trust Fund bill, the Reinvest Minnesota concept, and sweeping groundwater protection legislation where, according to Ann Glumac, Munger showed his legislative acumen.

"On the groundwater bill," Glumac recalls, "Willard was very cagey. He did something I don't think had ever been done before. He divided the bill into five pieces, five separate sections. He had four co-authors, two from each party, and himself as chief author. Each co-author introduced and spoke on a section. So you had two Republicans, Dave Bishop (IR-Rochester) and Elton Redalen (IR-Fountain) from southern Minnesota farm country, supporting the bill. The bill was introduced in this way as being something that more than just Willard Munger supported."

"There are some other things that come to mind about Willard," Glumac remembers. "Like the fact that he had these big hands and yet, he was very adept at using chopsticks. He also had a way of dealing with people that was his very own. Sometimes, he'd set traps for people. I remember a guy who wanted to be on Willard's committee. He stopped by to talk to Willard. Willard looked him over and said, 'You know, it's all well and good, this environmental stuff, but I really do think that we're getting carried away with these wetlands laws. There are just too many regulations. A farmer can't even drain a swamp anymore to get a crop. Wouldn't you agree?'" Glumac smiles as she recalls the story. "I watched that poor guy walk right into it. I cringed. I wanted to tell him, '*Don't do it buddy.*' But I didn't. Of course, he agreed with Willard, who got cross and said, 'Well, I don't think we'll be needing you on my committee.' Willard would much rather have you openly disagree with him than feed him a line. He didn't like folks who agreed with him simply to get along."

While Willard's brother Harry, Jr. discounts Willard's fishing abilities, Ann Glumac recalls there was a time when Willard's innate fishing ability shone.

"We were out fishing on Willard's pontoon boat in the St. Louis River with Gene Merriam from the MPCA and a guy from the DNR. Gene and the DNR guy were using syringes to inject air into their worms to keep them off the bottom. Very sophisticated. Willard was driving the boat so he wasn't really fishing. He had a dried up worm on his hook from a day before. The worm was trailing in the water behind the boat. Wouldn't you know it, Merriam and the DNR guy didn't catch a fish and Willard landed a beautiful tiger muskie with that dead worm!"

Ann Glumac eventually left the legislature to become assistant director of the MPCA before returning to Duluth as the executive director of the Great Lakes Aquarium. Though the aquarium didn't open until after Willard Munger's death, Glumac sought the legislator's support for the facility during its' planning stage.

"I never heard Willard call it "the Republican Fish Tank," but I heard Arend Sandbulte from Minnesota Power say that's what Willard called it," Ann remembers. "Willard was always concerned that the aquarium would take funding away from the zoo. I never confronted Willard about this perception and in the end, his criticism of how the aquarium was built, not getting a broad base of community support, was justified."

When asked to recall other anecdotes from her time working with Willard Munger, Ann Glumac nods her head and laughs.

"Well, he and Tommy Rukavina (DFL-Virginia) both have great senses of humor. They didn't often agree but they loved each other. There was a time when, by accident, the two of them wore identical sport coats on the floor of the House. They switched jackets. Because Tom is so short, he looked like a little kid wearing his dad's jacket. And Willard was so tall, he looked like he was wearing a strait jacket. Tommy was only a couple of doors down from Willard's office so they'd go back and forth quite a bit. You'd hear them raising their voices, getting really angry. And then there would be laughter. Willard got along well with Tom. He didn't do well with folks who weren't up front about their positions. You could disagree with Willard so long as you were up front about it.

I can remember one big argument he and I had about conservation officers and their authority to search...Willard thought they should be able to search a boat with no probable cause. I told him that what he was supporting was something that police officers looking for a dead body in a freezer didn't even have. It got heated. He said, 'You always win,' and he walked away. Then he came back, sort of like poking his finger in the cage of a tiger, and started in again. I got madder. He said, 'I can't win an argument with you, can I?' I said, 'Apparently not.' That's how it was with Willard. You could disagree and, a few minutes later, you were back to being friends."

Ann Glumac's observation, that Willard Munger had a terrific sense of humor, is verified by others. When tempers flared during committee meetings, Munger had a tool chest of anecdotes, including his celebrated, "whiskey frog story" available to lighten the mood.

Willard Munger's Celebrated Annual Whiskey Frog Story

A long with his feistiness, his generosity and his mumbling speech, Willard Munger will be remembered for his frog story...

Once, when Munger was just a boy, he was out fishing with his grandfather. But the two forgot to bring bait. So they went looking for a frog to put on their hooks. It was an unsuccessful search, until they spied a snake with a frog in his mouth.

The snake, however, didn't want to give up his feast.

Luckily, the senior Munger had a bottle of whiskey, and he dropped a bit of the alcohol into the snake's mouth. More interested in the whiskey, the snake dropped the frog.

Later, as they fished, Munger's grandfather felt something on his arm. He looked down to find the same snake, only this time, the snake had *two* frogs in his mouth!

(www.legal-ledger.com/archive/713mung2.htm.)

David Bishop (IR-Rochester) often referred to as one of Munger's "Republican Friends," was a successful lawyer from Rochester, Minnesota when he came into the legislature in 1983. As Rep. Bishop remembers the situation, he became involved in the trust fund legislation purely by accident.

"I'd been somewhat involved," Dave Bishop recalls, "with energy policy during the Perpich years. I went with on the trips to Sweden, Norway and Ireland to inspect peat...But I hadn't worked much with Willard. One day (in 1987) I saw Willard and Wayne Simoneau (DFL-Fridley) at the coffee pot. I could hear Willard going on about something. 'Those bastards,' he said. You could tell he was upset. I came up to him and asked, 'Willard, what bastards are those?' 'My damn caucus,' he said. I asked, 'What's the problem?' Willard turned to me and explained. 'They won't let the trust fund bill get to the floor. Won't let it get out of the Rules Committee.' Simoneau nodded his head. 'They turned him down.'"

"Well," Bishop continues, "in 1987, the Democrats controlled the legislature. The Rules Committee was dominated by the DFL. I asked Willard, 'Why not? It's a good bill.' He said, 'They don't like it.' Simoneau chimed in. 'They don't want Willard to get all the lottery money.' I looked them both over and said, 'Well, I've got some folks on there (the Rules Committee) that I can talk to.' Willard looked at me and shook his head. 'You're just a minority member. What can you do?' But I went and talked to Ann Wynia (DFL-St. Paul), Bob Vanesek (DFL-New Prague) and others on the Rules Committee. I asked them, 'What's the matter with Willard's bill?' Wynia was dead-set against the lottery. She believed that it would cause the underprivileged to spend too much money on gambling. I asked, 'What about a different source of funding...or what if Willard took less from the lottery proceeds?' Wynia seemed agreeable to thinking about options.

"I went back to Willard and explained that the members of the Rules Committee thought the bill took too much from the lottery for the environment. 'They're wrong,' Willard said. I asked, 'Could you take half?' Willard looked at me and said, 'Bishop (he always called me 'Bishop'), if all I can get is half, I guess I'll take half.' Now at the same time, Rudy Perpich was pushing the Greater Minnesota Fund. The thought occurred to me that, if part of the lottery proceeds was designated for the

Greater Minnesota Fund, part for the General Fund, and part for the Environmental Trust Fund, then maybe the idea could make it out of Rules. I came up with the idea to split the proceeds from the lottery three ways and went back to Wynia with the idea and she agreed with it. I picked up some other support and went back to Willard."

"'OK Willard,' I said. 'I've got three votes if you'll agree to share the money.' He agreed to it and I drew up an amendment to his bill. After he read it, he said, 'This amendment; I want you to present it to the Rules Committee. You persuaded them to hear it so you should present it.' In twenty years in the House, I think it was the only time," Dave Bishop recalls, "I appeared before the Rules Committee on something controversial. I presented it, it went through, and it made it out onto the House floor. What was unique was that, Willard was in the background. I'd been the one to come up with the compromise so he had me explain it and push it in the House. He wanted the person who deserved the credit to get the recognition. The bill went to Conference Committee," Bishop remembers, "and I think it ultimately came out as 60% of the lottery to the General Fund and 40% for the Environmental Trust Fund."

"But that isn't the end of the story," Dave Bishop recalls. "I was up at my cabin in northern Wisconsin and Willard called. 'Perpich is coming up to Duluth to sign the bill.' I said, 'That's great.' He said, 'And I want you here. You had a hand in getting the trust fund passed so you should be here.' I drove up to Duluth and I was surrounded by DFlers; Sam Solon, the mayor, Mary Murphy, and a bunch of city councilors. When Willard spoke, he took me by surprise. 'This is a good piece of legislation,' he said. 'But there's someone here I want to have talk. This bill wouldn't have passed without him. He's a Republican from Rochester and I want him to say a few words.'"

"I was," Rep. Bishop reflects, "unprepared to speak. There were all these DFLers in attendance and Willard ignored them and called upon me, a Republican, to speak. I got up and reminded the crowd that, while the governor had signed the bill into law, there was more to do. The voters still needed to approve the idea by voting for a constitutional amendment, which they did.'"

Rep. Bishop also recalls the unique method Munger used to pass the Groundwater Protection Act.

"My involvement in the bill came about because one of the county commissioners in Olmstead County came to me about the status of our county landfill. Because we have karst geology in our area, we are drinking water that's only 30 years old. Our landfill was failing, causing contamination of the groundwater. I said, 'I know who to call.' I called Willard. I said, 'Willard, we have a heck of a problem down here in Olmstead County with our landfill.' Willard said, 'I know you do, Bishop. And I'm working on it right now. I have a bill that Ann Glumac is working on. It's a comprehensive groundwater bill. I'm going to have you work on it during the next session [1989].' Then he called a meeting. Ann was there and so were Elton Redalen (IR-Fountain), Len Price (DFL-Woodbury) and Henry Kalis (DFL-Wells). Willard said, 'Ann's worked the bill up. It's in five parts. Each of you will research and carry one part of the bill. Bishop, you're going to have wells and abandoned wells. Kalis and Redalen will take agriculture; non-point source pollution of groundwater. Price, you'll have the cities because St. Paul has its own water problems. And I'll be in charge.' And that's what he did. He divided it up like that. The fact that there were two Democrats and two Republicans wasn't done for politics. We weren't co-authors for window dressing. We came together and passed the bill into law. Today, you can't transfer a piece of property in the state of Minnesota without disclosing whether the property has any abandoned wells. The legislation became a model law for the country. And all five of us, not just Willard as the chief author, were honored by a national think-tank for the bill. It was a fantastic piece of scripting. It was unique."

Dave Bishop reflects before continuing.

"He let others take credit for their work instead of seeking the honor for himself. He talked about the five of us as a group, as all of us deserving credit for the passage of the law. That's not something you see very often in the legislature."

Not every environmental bill Munger pushed had Rep. Bishop's support.

"I remember him becoming very upset," Bishop offers, "over a packaging reduction bill that was stuck in the Commerce Committee. I was on the Committee. The chair of that Committee, John Sarna (DFL-Minneapolis) had been around awhile. Willard's proposal was for a two-cent tax on every item that came in a package, whether it was chewing gum or a television. He brought that idea to Sarna and Sarna just sort of rolled his eyes. Sarna decided to deal with it by having Jim Farrell (DFL-St. Paul) and I form a subcommittee to study the proposal. 'You two are in charge,' Sarna said. 'I'm putting the bill on the table for more study.'

Willard wasn't very happy that it had been referred to a subcommittee. But what he didn't know was that Sarna took me aside and told me, 'Bishop, don't bring that bill back. You keep it in subcommittee and don't ever bring it back.' And with that, Willard's bill was dead. As much as I loved Willard," Bishop reflects, "I thought that idea was a little over the top."

Munger, Dave Bishop recalls, wasn't only a tough environmental advocate. "He was also a lion when it came to issues regarding Duluth," the former legislator relates. "I remember. There was a conference committee regarding a bonding bill. It was made of ten legislators, five from the Senate and five from the House. Mike Freeman was the chair. It also included Roger Moe, Sam Solon and Dennis Fredrickson from the Senate. There was Willard, Kalis, Lynn Carlson, and a Democrat from western Minnesota I can't recall, and myself from the House. There was an announcement as to the make-up of the conference committee and then nothing happened for a while. Finally, Freeman called a meeting but Solon and Munger weren't there. Freeman addressed us and said, 'I've called this meeting and I didn't tell Munger or Solon because I wanted to make it clear that not one of you is going to support Duluth until the end. I'm tired of being nit-picked by those two on every project just so they can get money for Duluth. We do all the other projects and then we'll deal with Duluth. They will be last, not first.' The point of the story is that even in his own party, they considered him so cagey, so good, he had this reputation even the leaders of the DFL were scared of."

Dave Bishop concludes his thoughts regarding his service in the Minnesota House.

"There are few legislators who you can say, 'they are loved.' But Willard was. I have a strong admiration for him. Even now," Bishop confesses, "as we're talking about him, I find myself smiling."

Despite Munger's bout with illness, he wasn't about to consider retirement as the 1988 session wound to a close.

Munger, Burger Eschew Retirement Plans

There will be no retirement talk in 1988 for the two oldest members of the Minnesota Legislature...

"I'm in perfect health," said Rep. Willard Munger, DFL-Duluth, the oldest member of the legislature, who plans to seek a 17th two-year term in the House this fall.

Munger, who operates a motel in Duluth when not at the Capitol, is 77 and three weeks older than President Reagan.

Rep. John Burger, IR-Long Lake, is only 72 and said he waited too long to get to the legislature to think about retirement after only three terms. He first ran for the House in 1968 but was defeated...I'm not going beyond 100," said Burger. "I have 28 more years, good years..."

Munger has served 32 years and if he's re-elected and serves another term, he will match the record. Two Republicans who served from 1941 – 1975, Augie Mueller…and former Speaker Aubrey Diriam…, and DFLer Joe Prifel…who served from 1939 – 1973, also served 34 years in the House.

The overall longevity record is apparently held by the late Don Wright of Minneapolis, who served eight years in the House and 34 years in the Senate before he was defeated in 1970…

Despite his age, Munger's stamina is legendary. He was a member of a conference committee in 1987 which was locked in an all-night bargaining session over what projects to include in a $470 million bonding bill.

One conferee and other members dozed off and awoke to find Munger and Sen. Sam Solon, DFL-Duluth, negotiating the Duluth projects.

"I held my own…," Munger recalled. "We got what we wanted. But we didn't get it until 5 o'clock in the morning."

*(Duluth News Tribune, May 10, 1988. **Editor's note: The longevity record for combined service in the Minnesota Legislature [House and Senate] is not 42 years but actually 44 years.**)*

Munger proceeded to run for his seventeenth term in office against IR candidate Rilla Opelt. During the 1988 election cycle, Duluth Mayor John Fedo was indicted on a 22 count complaint alleging corruption and bribery. The matter went to the jury and Fedo was acquitted of all charges. In the presidential race, Vice President George Bush was running against Massachusetts Governor Michael Dukakis. DFL State Senator Hubert "Skip" Humphrey III was running against U.S. Senator Dave Durenberger. And Gov. Rudy Perpich was challenged by Minnesota businessman Cal Ludeman.

Perpich won a second full term, partially on the strength of his work in support of the Environmental Trust Fund. George H.W. Bush won the presidency in a landslide. And Willard Munger easily won his legislative race against Rilla Opelt: 9,125 to 2,079 votes.

The successful passage of the trust fund amendment in 1988 and the lottery amendment in 1990 (which allocated 40% of net lottery proceeds to the environmental trust fund) were, in many ways, Willard Munger's crowning legislative achievements. Environmental projects totaling $80 million were financed by the fund between 1991 and 2001. The market value of the trust fund by 2001, the year that an additional authorizing amendment was passed by Minnesota voters, was over a *quarter of a billion dollars!* ("Environment and Natural Resources Trust

Fund Revenue" by John Helland, Minnesota House of Representatives Research Department, August, 1998.)

The question of Willard's retirement from public life was revisited during the summer of 1989.

Munger Will Run for 18th Term

Rep. Willard Munger of Duluth, the dean of the Minnesota Legislature, has decided to seek re-election in 1990—probably for the last time.

The 78-year-old Munger, who is...older than former President Reagan, has earned a reputation as an unbending defender of the environment during his 33 years in the Minnesota House. Gov. Rudy Perpich calls him "Mr. Environment"...

He wants to set the record for longevity in the House..."I'm tied right now...I'll break the record if I go one more time."

Former Speaker Aubrey Diriam of Redwood Falls and former Rep. Augie Mueller of Arlington, both Republicans, served 17 terms from 1941 – 1975. And former Rep. Joe Prifel, DFL-St. Paul, also served 34 years from 1939 – 1973.

Even If he serves another term, Munger will be far short of the overall record...set by Sen. Donald O. Wright...He served 44 years in the legislature, including 8 in the House and 36 in the Senate...

A second factor which could prompt a Munger retirement in 1992 is reapportionment. The Duluth area is losing population and because of that, Munger said it's likely he will find himself in a district with another incumbent...

"The chances are 90 percent, or 80 percent," that he will step down after one more term, Munger said...

Munger was chief author of the ground water protection bill signed into law...He is also chief author of the other major environmental bill in 1989, a $37.5 million recycling bill that died when it ran into a filibuster...

"I may be 78 but I'll tell you something," he said. "I did a helluva lot better job carrying those two than I did 20 years ago..."

He has already introduced a $25 million bonding bill for the 1990 Legislature to consider, which would help finance the cost of capping abandoned wells suspected of polluting the state's ground water supplies...

He's pleased that some of the unpopular causes he championed decades ago—such as a DDT ban—are now state law...

When he first showed up at the Capitol in 1955 as part of the first DFL majority in the House, he was regarded as somewhat of an environmental kook.

"I still might be a kook, but I'm a respectable kook now," he quipped…

"I'm 78 years old now, and I don't color my hair either…A lot of people think I do, but I don't. There's nothing wrong with people coloring their hair, don't get me wrong."

(*Duluth News Tribune,* June 6, 1989.)

Despite Munger's success in passing the solid waste recycling bill in 1989 and the heady praise he received for enacting the trust fund amendment, Willard Munger was not immune to disappointment. Munger dearly wanted to be named chairman of the LCMR. In 1990, he finally got his chance to run for the post. And he lost.

Kahn Beats Munger for Environment Fund Post

State Rep. Willard Munger of Duluth, credited with initiating a state environmental trust fund authorized by voters last fall, won't be the leader of the legislative commission that determines where money from that fund is spent.

By a one-vote margin…Rep. Phyllis Kahn of Minneapolis beat out Munger to head the Legislative Commission on Minnesota Resources…

Until (Munger's) defeat by Kahn, Munger had considered his biggest political disappointment was losing an election for the Minnesota Senate…

"This hurts worse," he said…

Because the House and Senate alternate members every two years in the leadership position…Munger wouldn't become the chairman even if he serves another two-year term as he hopes to do…

Munger was a leading figure in establishing the environmental fund…He is chairman of the House Environment and Natural Resources Committee and has been a member of the legislative commission for many years but has never headed it…

Kahn claims she "didn't run against anyone—I ran because I think I have the best background to do it." She believes that Munger will still be "Mr. Environment" to legislators…

"This job requires a different kind of skill than just being the person who is the best champion of the environment of the state," Kahn said…

(*Duluth News Tribune,* June 13, 1989.)

"Phyllis and Willard had their battles while she was on his committee," John Helland recalls. "It wasn't that Willard didn't like opinionated women—that wasn't the issue. It was that she never could admit she was wrong. When she stayed on for another term as the head of the LCMR, that was a blow. I know Willard felt badly about that."

Ann Glumac recalls another story involving Rep. Kahn.

"We were sitting in Senator Gene Merriam's office discussing some legislation. Gene had dozed off the day before during the conference committee. Phyllis had an amendment that was a bit untoward," Glumac reflects, "and it passed even though both Merriam and Willard opposed it. The next day when we were sitting in Gene's office, Gene was incredulous that Phyllis had slipped one by him. Willard sat in a chair, at first smiling, then quietly chuckling, and then laughing out loud. Finally, he said, 'I thought I was the only one to get schnookered by Phyllis. I don't feel so bad now because she got Gene too, and he's a senator!'"

Despite Munger's issues with Rep. Kahn, there is no indication that Willard Munger was misogynistic. The women who were interviewed for this biography indicated they were always treated with the utmost respect and that their opinions were given full deference by Munger. Kahn's being female wasn't the issue. But to be rejected by your peers, by men and women who recognized you as "Mr. Environment" but wouldn't honor that recognition with what Munger believed to be a suitable allocation of power, was a blow.

Longtime Willard Motel employee Heidi Lindberg agrees with the assessment that Munger had an abiding respect for women.

"I couldn't have had a better boss," Lindberg says. "I never saw Mr. Munger treat a woman with disrespect."

Though she worked for Munger for essentially minimum wage, Lindberg understood the constraints on Munger's finances.

"Rooms rented for $18 – $20 a night," Lindberg recalls. "So he couldn't really afford to pay me more. But he did other things for me. Like when Christmas gifts were dropped off by lobbyists or friends, gifts of food and sweets. He would send them home with me for my family and kids. When he would go to the grocery store, he would buy an extra ham or roast and drop it off at my house. He knew my husband was out of work and that every little bit helped."

Lindberg relates that her first contact with Munger was as a constituent.

"My husband lost his job at the steel plant," she remembers, "and there was an issue that came up in Bayview Heights involving Charlie Bell [Duluth businessman and Conservative politician] buying land along Skyline Parkway from the city of Duluth and having a water line extended to it so he could build a new house. Our house was left off that water line and I was mad about that so I went to see Willard. I pounded my fist on the counter of the coffee shop when explaining the situation.

Willard listened. Then I looked around and asked, 'Are you looking for someone to work here?' Willard said, 'Are you serious?' I said 'Yes'. 'What can you do?' he asked. 'Anything,' I said. He called me the next day. 'Can you come to work?' 'When?' I asked. 'Now,' he said. So I went to work for him."

Lindberg remembers that when she showed up for work, Munger had a surprise for her.

"He said, 'You sure you can do anything?' I said 'Yes'. He said, 'Well, I have a little problem in one of the rooms. See if you can fix it.' I went to the room and the toilet was plugged. It was nasty. Willard showed up. He stood behind me laughing. 'No, you don't really have to deal with that. I'll do it. I was just seeing how badly you wanted the job,' he said. Willard had great fun retelling that story over the years, how he tried to call my bluff, but how I called his."

By the time Lindberg started working at the motel in 1978, the coffee shop was rarely open for paying customers.

"But I helped him cook and serve breakfast to politicians," Lindberg remembers. "I cleaned, painted, did laundry, made up rooms. Pretty much anything I was asked to do."

Lindberg's assessment of Willard Munger is broad in scope.

"The most important thing," she reflects, "is what kind of politician he was. He was a people's man. He was for the working class. There wasn't anyone he wouldn't listen to and try to help. "

To illustrate her point, Lindberg reels off a number of anecdotes.

"Lots of folks said he didn't know how to run a business," she asserts. "Even his family thought that. They were upset he gave food away to his friends on Saturday mornings. But there was another side to him doing that. I remember two women with four kids coming into the motel and renting Room 215. That room had a single bed. Six people and one bed! When they came into the coffee shop the next morning, they ordered coffee and toast for themselves and their kids. Willard was cooking. He stacked plates full of pancakes, sausage and bacon. 'Bring this to them,' he said, pointing to the women. 'But Willard,' I said, 'they only ordered toast and coffee.' 'I don't care. Bring it to them.' He kept insisting until I finally did what I was told. You see, he knew they had no money. A couple of weeks later, he received a letter from those women. They were from North Dakota and in town for a vacation. Their car had broken down and it cost almost all their trip money to fix it. They sent Willard a check for their breakfast but he tore it up. He told me, 'You know Heidi, if I walked into the Tappa Keg (a local tavern) and bought a round for everyone, I'd be a big man. But give a family a plate of food, and they call you an idiot.'"

Munger's charity extended to being a mentor for neophyte politicians.

"There was a young man, brand new in the legislature from the Twin Cities," Lindberg recalls, "who stopped into the coffee shop for advice. He asked Willard, 'What do I need to know?' Willard said, 'Don't take nothing from nobody. That way, you don't owe anyone anything. And then, when you make a mistake, it's your mistake and you can deal with it. You won't be beholden to anyone.' A few months later, the same guy came back. He'd made a terrible mistake on a vote. It was so bad, it gave him nightmares. And it was a vote against one of Willard's bills. Willard told him not to worry about it. So long as it was his vote, and not a vote he took on behalf of someone else, Willard could live with it."

Lindberg and Munger didn't always see eye to eye. But, like his legendary standoffs and arguments with Tom Rukavina and his own brother, Harry, most disagreements between the boss and his employee blew over with time.

"I remember," Lindberg says with a smile, "Governor Perpich showed up with his staff. They took over the whole coffee shop. There was no room for other customers. Willard was excited to make Rudy breakfast. They were great friends. Willard was cooking, making regular pancakes, and got the idea that the governor should have crepes, special pancakes, instead of the usual recipe. I told him, 'Willard, he's no better than anyone else. He's a guy from Chisholm and your regular pancakes are good enough for him.' Willard got mad at me. 'I'll make him special pancakes.' He finished an order of his regular cakes, which I was supposed to give to Rudy's staff. But I gave them to Rudy instead. Then Willard made the crepes and handed them to me. 'These are for Rudy,' he said. I told him, 'Rudy's already been fed.' 'What?' 'I gave him the first pancakes you made. He's eating them already.' 'Goddamn you sonofabitch, do what you're told!' Willard yelled. I got so upset I walked out of the coffee shop. Rudy came outside to talk to me. I said, 'See what you did, governor? You're no different than anyone else but because Willard wanted to make you special pancakes and I gave you regular pancakes, you cost me my job.' From that day on, Rudy called me 'Little Shit'. Later, when I was in the hospital, Rudy sent me flowers that said, 'To Little Shit, from Governor Perpich.'"

Mrs. Lindberg was also able to observe Munger's interactions with other politicians, including Duluth Mayor John Fedo and Senator Paul Wellstone, in her position at the motel.

"I remember Fedo stopping by one Saturday morning for coffee with Mike Jaros and the others," she recalls. "Willard wasn't too happy with the mayor. Willard had found some money for the zoo which the city used someplace else. 'Fedo,' he said, 'when my parents gave me lunch money for school, they expected me to buy lunch, not cookies. How can I go back next session and ask for the same money I already asked for because you spent it on something you weren't supposed to?'"

Lindberg recalls that Paul Wellstone stopped in to visit Munger at the beginning of his 1990 run for the U.S. Senate. It was just Wellstone and his campaign manager sitting in the coffee shop with Munger, trying to get the political lay of the land in Duluth.

"Wellstone and Willard were very much alike. They both had a passion for the common man. And success never went to Wellstone's head," Lindberg observes. "When he came in, I really fell in love with him as a politician. He and his manager were asking if Willard couldn't provide a couple of free rooms for the night because the campaign was low on money. Willard looked at Wellstone and said, 'You got no chance, Wellstone, if you can't even afford a room at the Willard Motel.' I looked at Willard and then at Wellstone. '205 and 206 are empty,' I said. 'They can stay in those rooms.' Willard and I argued about it but I insisted that Wellstone could win. Willard didn't think so. I said, 'Sure he can, Willard. If he goes coffee shop to coffee shop, all around the state, he can win.' That's exactly what Wellstone did and he won. So when he came back to Duluth for the Labor Day picnic at the zoo a year later, I was standing with Willard near the stage. Wellstone saw me and came down from the stage to talk to me. He remembered my name and he thanked me, right there, for believing in him. He looked at Willard and said, 'Willard, Heidi was right about those coffee shops.' And Willard smiled and said, 'Isn't she always?'"

State Representative Tom Rukavina believes that there was a deep and abiding connection between Paul Wellstone and Willard Munger. Rep. Rukavina's voice catches when asked to discuss the relationship between the two men. Paul Wellstone perished, along with his wife, daughter and others, in an airplane crash near Eveleth, Minnesota on October 25, 2002 enroute to the funeral for Rep. Rukavina's father.

"I knew both of them very well," Rukavina relates. "And it seems to me that there are three things that they shared, three things that I think made them extraordinary politicians. First, they both were brutally honest. You could argue and disagree with Wellstone but you knew where he stood. Same thing with Willard. Second, both men had tremendous respect for working people, which, I think, came from their backgrounds. And third, both men were strong environmentalists."

Not everyone who walked through the doors of the coffee shop received the same warm welcome that Paul Wellstone and Munger's other political friends received.

"There was this guy from Minnesota Power," Heidi Lindberg recalls, "who pulled up in a company car in front of the coffee shop windows. Willard and I were sitting down, drinking coffee. Willard knew who the guy was. He said, 'Look, he's putting on his big shot suit jacket. Who's he trying to impress?' The guy came into the lobby of the motel. Willard got up and went over to talk to him. Now Willard had just come up from his shop in the basement. He was covered in sawdust. His clothes were all rumpled and dirty. His hands were dirty. He asked the guy, 'Can I help you?' The guy said, real important like, 'I'm here to see Representative Munger.' 'Speaking.' The guy eyed Willard and wouldn't believe him. 'No, I need to talk to Representative Munger.' 'You are,' Willard said. The guy thought Willard was playing a trick on him, got mad, and left. Well, he went back to Minnesota Power and apparently found out his mistake. He came back an hour or so later and sat down to talk to Willard. Willard listened but then told the guy, 'Look, I don't trust you. You need to leave. You came in here, took one look at how I was dressed, and made up your mind I wasn't someone worth talking to. So now, I don't trust you. And I've decided that you're not someone worth talking to.' Arend Sandbulte, the president of Minnesota Power, ended up coming out later that day to talk to Willard."

Recalling how Willard hid his vices from Frances brings a smile to Heidi Lindberg's face.

"When I was outside having a cigarette, Willard would come out and join me," she remembers. "We'd be out there, smoking, and Frances would come outside. Willard would hand me his cigarette so I'd have two of them, one in each hand. Once, he shoved his cigarette in my mouth, filter out, and I had to try to hold it in my lips without burning the inside of my mouth. 'That woman is strange,' was all Frances said when she saw me standing there with my cheeks all puffed out.

"Then there were the times when we were sitting at a table in the coffee shop having breakfast. I'd have to sit next to Willard so that, when Frances came in, he could shove his food onto my plate. One time, Willard was sitting at the counter and said, 'Frances, I'd like a piece of bread and an egg.' So she brought him a piece of toast and an egg, which he thought was hardboiled. He thought he'd be funny and crack the egg on his head. Turns out, she'd given him a raw egg and he splattered egg all over his hair!"

The coffee klatch had its regular cast of characters.

"Mike Jaros was Willard's best friend," Heidi Lindberg recalls. "Mike drove him back and forth to the legislature and was always out at the motel. He also liked John Pegors an awful lot. And Alden Lind. Gary Glass was someone he respected but never quite trusted. And his Republican friends included Steve Balach and Harry Newby, Sr. from Cloquet. He also thought a lot of Grant Merritt and Mike Janis, from the zoo."

Lindberg remembers Munger's involvement in the construction of his new home on Indian Point.

"My son-in-law Denny and Willard," she recalls, "laid every tile in that house. Willard was 74 years old and there he was, showing Denny how to lay tile! Willard's grandson Jeff built the stairway leading from the house down to the river. Jeff was so proud of that project. When Willard saw Jeff's work, he smiled and said, 'That's a Munger!'"

Ann Glumac relates another humorous story about gender and working with Munger.

"The House required mandatory anti-sexual harassment training," Glumac remembers. "Willard was very proud that he was exempted from attending. He argued successfully that he was too old to present a problem for anyone. Shortly after the training, we were having a meeting in my office and because we were often loud, I had the door closed. Part-way through the meeting, because it was only the two of us in the room, I got up to open the door. When Willard asked why I opened the door, I told him it was because I didn't want anyone spreading rumors about us. He giggled and giggled at that."

Rep. Munger would serve an additional ten years in the House but after being bested by Rep. Kahn, he never attained the coveted chairmanship of the LCMR. Truly, Willard Munger was the last of his era and in some ways, as the 1990s began, time seemed to be passing him by.

CHAPTER 10

The Battle Rages On

The relationship between Willard Munger and his DFL partner in the senate, State Senator Sam Solon from West Duluth, is challenging to define.

"Willard always thought that Sam was a patsy of the businessmen, the special interests," Mike Jaros recalls. "They never got along all that well."

"Sam and Willard were never pals," Harry Munger, Jr. agrees. "They respected each other but Sam was too business-oriented for Willard and Sam took the shine off Willard's star with respect to UMD. That was one of Willard's biggest achievements; bringing UMD into the forefront as a university by getting the school adequate funding. So it irked Willard that Sam got attention for UMD and other issues Willard had worked on long before Sam was elected."

Though the two men weren't personally close, it is highly unlikely their political differences ever led to blows. Still, the possibility of two statesmen brawling over an issue had a certain Wild West flare to it that the media found irresistible.

Duking Out Issues? By John Myers

The rumor spread like wildfire through the Capitol...

In one of the their numerous arguments over who was the strongest supporter of state funds for the Lake Superior Zoo expansion, Senator Sam Solon, DFL-Duluth, 58, hauled off and slugged Rep. Willard Munger, DFL-Duluth, 79, in the nose.

That's the rumor.

But the two combatants and another Duluth lawmaker at the scene say it's not true. Yet city of Duluth lobbyist Rory Strange insists physical contact was made...

Munger and Solon deny any punches were thrown...

Rep. Mike Jaros, DFL–Duluth, was supposed to have been a witness. He was there but laughs at the suggestion a punch was thrown...

"Yeah, it took us two hours to revive him," Jaros joked. "It was nothing…just pointing fingers and loud…"

Strange said Jaros witnessed the incident…

"I have a hard time wondering why people are denying this," Strange said. "I can't deny it. I was standing there."

"It didn't happen," Solon said. "We argued. We always argue. But we don't hit each other. What are they trying to prove?"

(*Duluth News Tribune*, April 28, 1990.)

Mike Jaros doesn't recall the incident. He *does* recall an incident from the 1970s where Munger confronted Senator Jim Ulland (IR- Duluth). According to Jaros, Munger, who was visibly upset with the young Republican, reportedly exclaimed "Jim, if you weren't a senator, I'd knock you on your little ass."

Ann Glumac covered the altercation between Munger and Ulland as a reporter for the *Duluth News Tribune*.

"Willard called up and was mad that I had written the piece," Glumac reflects. "The impetus behind Willard getting angry was a disagreement over how to continue funding for Amtrak. Jim wanted a compromise bill; to get what he could. Willard wanted the whole subsidy. It got pretty intense and words were said between the two of them in committee. So when Jim told Willard, outside the meeting, 'Congratulations Willard, you just killed Amtrak,' Willard got mad and he said what I quoted. But that wasn't the end of it. When I married Bill (Jim Ulland's brother) Willard missed the reception. He felt bad about that. He just forgot. But I teased him anyway. I said, 'Willard, the reason you missed my reception was because you didn't want to see Jim Ulland again.'"

With respect to the Solon incident, John Helland recalls something happening, though he believes it involved the grabbing of lapels, perhaps some pushing and shoving, but no punches being thrown. Whatever took place, the two legislators apparently settled their differences in quick fashion.

Still Friends

State Sen. Sam Solon…and Rep. Willard Munger posed at Lake Superior Zoo with zookeeper Scott Wisherd and Bonnie, a pot-bellied Vietnamese pig. The DFL legislators from Duluth asked to have their picture taken together because they were angered by a rumor spread by Rory Strange that Solon hit Munger…after arguing over zoo funding. Solon and Munger vehemently deny there was any physical contact…

(*Duluth News Tribune*, April 30, 1990.)

If there was any lingering animosity between Munger and Solon, they managed to "bury the hatchet" by the summer of 1990.

> ### DFL Legislators Unify Political Campaigns by John Myers
>
> Duluth's veteran DFL lawmakers joined forces...to announce their joint campaign for re-election...
>
> Rep. Mike Jaros, Rep. Willard Munger and Sen. Sam Solon said they are running as a team, stressing their seniority and cooperative relationship along with their records...
>
> (*Duluth News Tribune*, June 22, 1990.)

Munger continued to pile up accolades from various organizations for a "job well done." Though Senator Bob Lessard and Representative Irv Anderson remained skeptical regarding Munger's dedication to fishing and hunting rights (a wariness shared by most other Iron Range legislators) Munger's background, as a member and an officer of the United Northern Sportsmen, and as chair of the House Environment and Natural Resources Committee, made him a formidable figure in the area of wildlife management.

> ### Munger Receives Award from Fishing Congress
>
> The Minnesota Sportfishing Congress has presented Rep. Willard Munger, DFL-Duluth, with its Presidential Award for his leadership in passage of the Environment and Natural Resources Act.
>
> A portion of the act allows for voters to decide in November whether 40% of the state's lottery proceeds should be constitutionally dedicated for the next ten years to the Environmental Trust Fund.
>
> The Minnesota Sportfishing Congress is a non-profit organization with more than 48,000 members...
>
> (*Duluth News Tribune*, September 23, 1990.)

1990 was not only the year that Minnesota voters approved the lottery and the allocation of 40% of the lottery's proceeds to the Environmental and Natural Resources Trust Fund; it was also a re-election year for Willard Munger and a year of significant political intrigue. Paul Wellstone left his position at Carlton College in Northfield, Minnesota to run against two-term U.S. Senator Rudy Boschwitz. But the biggest story of the campaign season was the controversy which arose over IR gubernatorial candidate John Grunseth's antics in a backyard swimming pool.

Following the disclosure that Grunseth swam nude in his pool with his teenage daughter and her girlfriends, Grunseth was urged to quit the race. The IR desperately wanted someone else to take on Governor Rudy Perpich during the final weeks of the 1990 campaign. Minnesota State Auditor Arne Carlson, a moderate Republican (who had lost the IR endorsement to the more conservative Grunseth) was urged to run as a write-in. On October 23, Carlson announced he would run but Grunseth refused to drop out. Another news story surfaced involving Grunseth and a woman who had been Grunseth's mistress through the candidate's two marriages. Grunseth admitted the affair and quit the campaign. Arne Carlson replaced Grunseth as the IR gubernatorial candidate but Sharon Clark, Grunseth's running mate, refused to step down in favor of Joanne Drystad as the IR candidate for lieutenant governor. The Minnesota Supreme Court eventually ruled Clark could be removed from the ballot in favor of Drystad.

A major environmental story surfaced during the last days of a very confusing campaign. Metal barrels deposited in Lake Superior by defense contractor Honeywell in the 1960s became the subject of an effort to determine whether they were leaking hazardous materials into the lake.

President George H.W. Bush visited Minnesota on November 2 to boost Boschwitz's and Carlson's chances but the *Duluth News Tribune* endorsed Wellstone and Perpich.

Paul Wellstone defeated Rudy Boschwitz. A major factor in Wellstone's upset victory was a letter sent to Jewish voters by Boschwitz's campaign the weekend before the election. The backlash from the voters, both Jews and non-Jews, cost Boschwitz his seat. However, Munger's close friend, Governor Rudy Perpich, lost his race to Arne Carlson and retired from public life.

Offsetting Munger's disappointment over Perpich's defeat, lottery funding for the Environmental Trust Fund passed as a constitutional amendment, 81-19%. Munger protégé and DFLer Becky Lourey succeeded in her third attempt to defeat IR veteran legislator, Doug Carlson, for a seat in the Minnesota House. And Willard Munger won re-election to his 18th non-consecutive term.

Munger also turned 80 years old the following January and a birthday party was held in Munger's honor at the Good Fellowship Hall in Morgan Park. Unable to attend, Munger's sister-in-law Helen Trueblood (Martha Munger's sister) sent her birthday wishes via the mail.

January 18, 1991

Happy 80th, Willard! Over 60 years since those high school days when you went steady with my sister, Martha—and how we discussed you—and the romance went on for life…Sometimes you would tease my mother…you surprised her when you put your arm around her. You surprised her another time with your environmental project when you built her a "rock garden" in her yard and a pool for goldfish. You put those one-inch creatures in the pool and in a couple of months; they were 6-8 inches long!

I recall a trip you made up north with Dad and Nils Nealson. One dark night…you guys found a "nice spot" to sleep under the stars. In the middle of the night, the three of you were awakened by earthshaking and rumbling, jumping out of your sleeping bags with your adrenalin reaching those stars as you felt the breeze from the train…roaring past…

Willard, may you have continued success and happiness for another 20 years at least.

Love, Helen

Back in St. Paul, Munger faced opposition to his conservation agenda.

Munger Staves Off Territorial Challenge by John Myers

Rep. Willard Munger appears to have successfully fought off an effort to end-run his authority over legislation dealing with fish and game issues.

Munger, DFL-Duluth, was livid last week when he learned of the creation of a new game and fish subcommittee under the House Commerce Chair.

Munger is chairman of the Environment and Natural Resources Committee which already has a fish and game subcommittee. He saw the effort as a way to circumvent environmental concerns to cater to the tourist industry…

The new subcommittee would be headed by Rep. Anthony Kinkel, DFL-Park Rapids. According to witnesses, Munger spotted Kinkel in the House Chamber and pointed his finger at him and said "You're a cheap little SOB…"

Munger was especially angry at House Speaker Robert Vanesek, who gave tacit approval to the new…subcommittee. Vanesek apparently had been convinced by some lawmakers that Munger was short-shrifting fishing and hunting concerns…

Munger, a 34-year veteran of the House, called Vanesek's consideration of the proposal the worst insult he'd received in his legislative career…

Vanesek said Munger was overreacting because no decision had been made on which committee would get first control of fish and game bills…

Vanesek appeared to be backpedalling. Indications are that the environmental fish and game subcommittee will keep control over hunting and fishing legislation...

(*Duluth News Tribune*, February 5, 1991.)

Munger retained control over hunting and fishing issues in the House. He also managed to pass the conservation bill that would define the final decade of his political career. Cobbling together a coalition of rural Republicans and a diverse group of Democrats, Munger convinced Governor Carlson to sign into law the most progressive wetlands law in the country. John Helland recalls the origins of the Minnesota wetlands bill.

"It came from two sources," John Helland recalls. "Marcus Marsh (IR-St. Cloud) tried to carry a similar bill in 1989 but, because the Democrats were in control, it went nowhere. On the national level, President George H.W. Bush was also pushing for a federal wetlands conservation bill. When Rep. Marsh couldn't get his bill passed, Willard agreed to take it over. It wasn't passed until 1991 and it took many, many hours of committee hearings and conference committee hearings to get it through."

Munger received his fair share of praise from conservation groups after the passage of the Wetlands Preservation Act.

Willard Munger: 'You said we didn't need it.'

The first piece of legislation introduced this session in the House—the wetlands protection bill—was given final approval in the House on a 116-13 vote. The approval comes after hundreds of hours of public hearings and dozens of compromise measures aimed at getting support from farmers whose wetlands would be controlled by the DNR.

HF1 sponsor Rep. Willard Munger (DFL-Duluth) urged legislators to vote for the wetlands bill, something he says he has been working on for 20 years.

Minnesota's original 12 million acres of wetlands have diminished to 3 million, Munger told legislators, and those that remain are essential to purify groundwater, prevent flooding and runoff, and recharge underground aquifers...

Although some legislators argued that the bill isn't needed, Munger begged to differ.

"When we wanted legislation to ban DDT, you said we didn't need it. When we wanted to regulate mercury, you said we didn't need it. Today we have mercury in Minnesota lakes because a few years ago, you said we didn't need to regulate mercury. Now," says Munger, "the DNR says you can catch the walleyes, but don't eat them."

(Minnesota Session Weekly, May 17, 1991.)

Governor Carlson heralded Munger's effort.

Munger Praised for Wetlands Work

Gov. Arne Carlson…hailed the $17.1 million wetlands preservation bill as the best example of what can be accomplished when there's bipartisan cooperation in the Minnesota Legislature.

The IR governor signed the bill into law…and staged a symbolic bill-signing ceremony…at the Minnesota Valley Wildlife Refuge overlooking the Minnesota River.

Carlson praised the chief House sponsors, Rep. Willard Munger, DFL-Duluth, and Marcus Marsh, IR-Sauk Rapids, for steering the bill through five major House committees and to eventual passage.

The governor said Munger, 80, the dean of the legislature, is known as "'Mr. Environment' for all the right reasons…"

Munger said he wanted to thank Carlson for making passage of a wetlands bill a high priority even though that might get him into trouble with fellow DFLers who have been quarrelling with the governor over a series of votes.

(Duluth News Tribune, June 6, 1991.)

Arne Carlson's views on the wetlands bill haven't changed.

"In my first State of the State speech [1992], I paid tribute to Willard, mentioning him personally in the speech for his work on wetlands, sustainable development and the expansion of our state parks," Carlson remembers. "That wetlands bill, I don't recall how specifically Willard was involved but I know that we didn't have any major problems with it in the House. It was the first in the nation to develop a no-net-loss scenario. There was, however, a bloody fight in the Senate. Dallas Sams (DFL-Staples) was courageous. He showed lots of guts. He came from an area with many farmers and whenever you are trying to put restrictions on land, there's going to be a farm fight. The fact that the fight in the Senate was so bloody but the bill passed the House with ease is a credit to Willard."

Carlson, who now spends winters in Florida, reflects on the importance of the bill.

"You know, we have the same problems in Florida," the former governor laments. "There is this natural conflict between developers, who'd pave everything over if they could, and the environment. We need the wetlands to purify and absorb water—to prevent flooding. Look at all the terrible floods we're having today as a result of past decisions. Frankly, America has done a poor job of protecting our wetlands. You need the Mungers of the world, who look at these things with an open mind, who understand that it isn't jobs *or* the environment but that you can have both."

Munger's philosophy with respect to the environment and the economy never wavered. From the very beginning, when he joined United Northern Sportsmen in the late 1940s and began his crusade to clean up the St. Louis River, Willard Munger did not want to pit jobs against conservation. But he also realized that the 100 year history of northeastern Minnesota inevitably meant environmental degradation unless strong legislation was in place to protect the forests, waters and skies of the area. He was never anti-development but he was always pro-environment.

> "I think the Duluth economy," Willard said, "lies in a couple of fields. I think that northeastern Minnesota will become a great medical center and educational center not only for this area, but for North Dakota, South Dakota, Wisconsin, and Canada. In my estimation, that's what's going to happen. Secondly, I think we've got to depend a lot on renewable resources such as timber. I look to the day when the forest industry is going to become the number one industry in the state of Minnesota and farming will be second.
>
> "I expect to see mining in northeastern Minnesota. I think that the environmentalists insisting that we have a comprehensive study on copper-nickel mining was a more positive approach...I think industry wants to know in advance what the state is going to expect of them...the only reason that they [industry] haven't gone to work and expanded on the copper-nickel activities in northeastern Minnesota is because copper's price is at a low point. It's fifty cents, I think, a pound. It's not feasible to mine until it gets up above a dollar...Industry doesn't like to put scrubbers in smokestacks, but industry knows that if they don't put scrubbers in the smokestacks and don't spend the money to combat air pollution, that they aren't going to have any forest[s]...left fifty years from now. Without forest[s]...this town will close down. They know that, but they don't like to be pushed into a position to do something...
>
> "They [the timber and mining industries] have had a background of exploitation in northeastern Minnesota—moving into virgin forests and ex-

ploiting them without any concern for the future…There was exploitation of the iron mines without any regard to the residue or the tailings they leave. That's an example of a 'let's get all we can get and get out' policy. Those days are over."

(Oral History of Willard Munger, ibid, pp. 89 – 90.)

Willard Munger's undying dedication to preserve Minnesota's natural resources was not a "one man band." Throughout his career, Munger relied heavily upon his partisan committee administrators Betty Goihl, Ann Glumac and Jackie Rosholt, and non-partisan researchers such as John Helland, as well as legislators from diverse backgrounds to promote his environmental agenda. In addition, environmentalists, both citizen-lobbyists and paid lobbyists, were instrumental in bending the ears of recalcitrant politicians and getting the message out.

Betty Goihl, Munger's last committee administrator, began her work in the legislature in 1977 as Martin Sabo's legislative assistant. Goihl was raised in Lake City, Minnesota, attended college in Iowa and ended up teaching art for a time in Australia before she landed the job with Speaker Sabo. Goihl returned to Australia for a vacation. When she returned to Minnesota, Goihl learned she'd lost her position with Sabo.

"There had been an election and because of that, I'd lost my job. Willard was looking for a new legislative assistant. Mike Jaros talked him into hiring me without an interview. Jackie Rosholt was his committee administrator at the time and when she decided to leave, Ann Glumac came in for a time. But then she left and Willard was without an administrator. Ann told Willard, 'Why don't you just make Betty your administrator?' So he did. It was 1989 and I stayed with him until he died."

Goihl continues the story.

"When he made me the committee administrator, he needed to hire a new secretary, a legislative assistant, to replace me. What he told everyone he interviewed was that he had to go to Australia to hire me and that I would jump for him like a kangaroo. Well, Marge, who replaced me as his secretary, said, 'I'll take the job but I'm not jumping like a kangaroo for anyone!'"

Goihl reflects on her relationship with Munger.

"It was 1989 and so it was just at the end of Rudy's term. Willard would take me along to meet with Rudy and Roger Moe. He brought me to the governor's mansion to discuss bills. It made me feel so important. He taught me a lot. He allowed me to stretch myself. I wrote most of his letters. I reviewed all the bills. I thought up agendas for committee meetings when there weren't any bills pending, like discussions of the deformed frogs that kids had found or discussions of the NSP (Northern States Power) cask issue.

"He really turned over the reins of the day-to-day management of the committee to me. He was extremely trusting and confident in a person's abilities. I really value his generosity that way and I try to practice it myself. When he was talking with someone, he always let them tell him something even if he already knew what they were saying. It made them feel good that they were imparting information to the committee chair. It made them feel important."

Goihl continues.

"He was one of the few chairs who would let a member of the opposing party take over the chair in his absence. It might be the senior Republican on the committee or someone else. He just liked giving people the opportunity."

But, according to Goihl, Munger could use his gavel when necessary.

"If a bill was really controversial and there were too many amendments being proposed, he'd slam the gavel down and say, 'We're adjourned.' That was it, the meeting was over. It may have angered some members but they respected him for that as well."

As Munger aged, his staff became more important.

"John Helland and I sat on either side of him and we made sure he was organized," Goihl reflects, "especially in the later years. We'd keep him on track. He got slower. He had a corneal transplant. He had his eyelids tightened. He wore a hearing aid—not that he wanted to—but at least he wore it. There was a definite slowing down as he grew older. He always wanted to walk to the chamber. He'd use the walls to support himself, to guide him to his seat. There were a couple of times when he got off the elevator with Mike Jaros that he stumbled and Mike caught him."

"And on the floor, though he always mumbled," Goihl says through a laugh, "it got much worse. It became very hard to understand him. In the end, he wasn't debating much on the floor, only presenting his bills. But he was, to the very end, pretty alert for a man in his eighties. I think that came from staying busy."

When asked about Munger's proclivity for sweets, Betty Goihl laughs again.

"Oh yes, he loved his sweets," she recalls. "He loved Serlin's pies and caramel rolls from Tobie's. He brought fresh rolls from Tobie's into the office every Monday morning. Then he started adding chocolates and candy to that. And when freshmen legislators had their first bill up for a vote in his committee, he made sure they brought cookies. You weren't supposed to eat during the meetings but that wasn't a problem so long as you brought cookies.

Willard was, as I said, very generous. He took me to so many lunches at Serlin's—always insisting that we get the luncheon special. I used to pick him up at the Kelly Inn in the morning and, if he didn't have an evening meeting, drop him off there at night. There were times in the morning when I'd have to go in and get him because he was so wrapped up in talking with other legislators over breakfast. He loved living there at the Kelly Inn, having breakfast with other lawmakers, going into the bar after work to talk politics."

Ann Glumac reiterates her bosses' legendary sweet tooth.

"When I worked for Willard [1987 – 1990], he had just started getting his social security checks. He wasn't real eager to get those but they were more or less forced on him. He would take me out for pie at Serlin's. He called his social security checks his 'mad money,'" Glumac remembers. "When we were in Duluth, both before and after I worked for him, he'd take me to Gallagher's restaurant in Hermantown because they had good pie. When he took me to Serlin's for lunch, he'd bring me back to the kitchen with Irv Serlin, the owner, and Irv would show me where they made the pies. Then Irv would sit in our booth with us as we ate our pie."

When discussing the famous LCMR canoe trips and picnics that Munger sponsored at his home on Indian Point, Betty Goihl grows lighthearted.

"I spent a lot of time organizing those," she recalls. "In the beginning, both Frances and Willard canoed. Frances stopped canoeing and then later on, Willard did too. But on every trip, someone had to fall in the water. I remember John Helland and I were in a canoe together one year and we hit a rock and went in. Willard brought that story up endlessly, so much so, it began to irritate John."

When asked to describe Munger's working relationships with other politicians, Betty Goihl pauses before answering.

"Well, it seemed he was always at odds with Irv Anderson and Tom Bakk, all the Iron Rangers. Though with Tommy Rukavina, he had a funny relationship. They'd scream at each other on the floor. Tom would get so angry at Willard, he'd storm out. Then Willard would go to Tom's office; they'd shake hands and make up. Tom would say, 'I love you Willard, you're just like my grandpa,' and they'd be back to being friends. He had the same kind of relationship with Dave Battaglia. Now with Irv Anderson, there was a bill that Irv wanted heard in Willard's committee that he sent down with someone else. Every day the guy, Mike Charboneau, would show up—Willard called Charboneau 'Old Stonewall' because he never smiled—and tell Willard, 'The Speaker would like you to hear this bill.' And every day, Willard would tell Old Stonewall, 'No, not today.' That bill never got heard. I don't even remember what it was about. But it never got heard."

According to Goihl, Munger's relationship with Rudy Perpich was unique.

"I think he got along with Arne Carlson, but with Rudy, there was something special. With Rudy, they were such good friends. He didn't need to make an appointment to see the governor. Willard would just grab me and we'd show up at the office. Rudy always made time to see Willard."

Goihl recalls the relationships Munger had with female staff and legislators.

"Now with Phyllis Kahn, well, she knew everything. She wanted things her way and that caused some friction. Especially over the LCMR, when she became chair and Willard didn't. That really hurt him. He liked Mary Murphy a great deal. In fact, the legislature had a dance where they were crowned king and queen. Alice Hausman and Dee Long were favorites. And he spent a great deal of time with Arlene Lehto. He liked Republican Sidney Pauly a lot as well. He was the kind of boss who treated you fairly. He wasn't someone who'd order you to do something. He trusted you to do it right and never treated you as inferior. I felt he was my friend, that he appreciated me."

One of the key players in much of Munger's environmental work was John Pegors, an employee of the MPCA's Duluth office. Pegors was also one of the "regulars" at the coffee klatches held at the motel coffee shop every Saturday morning. Those klatches, as others have related, were a sounding board for many environmental and political ideas.

> "Pegors," Willard remembered, "is a very, very highly respected friend of mine. I respect him because John Pegors does have a philosophy…He is dedicated. He believes in strong environmental legislation. He fights for what he believes in, even though he's not very tactful sometimes in doing it…I had a bill to outlaw DDT, and John was one of my hardest workers. John was a free-lance lobbyist. What I mean by 'free lance…' is that he wasn't getting a paycheck. We were making a little headway on the bill, but we had a few setbacks. We had to develop some strategy. The Republicans were in control, and it was an awful problem to get it passed. So I got Thomas Newcome to be the chief author, and I was listed as the second author. And it worked. Of course, John was my right-hand in all this lobbying.

"I remember one time when Newcome was in the Speaker's chair. Lloyd Duxbury was the Speaker of the House [1963 – 1969] at the time, and Newcome was just sitting in for a short time as Speaker while Duxbury was doing something else. I had this bill before my committee to outlaw DDT and John was sitting up in the balcony folding his hands, praying for me. Somebody got up and asked if my bill had gone through the governmental operations committee, because that's the committee it had to go through.

"Well, it hadn't gone through the governmental operations committee. If I said it hadn't, then the Speaker would have ruled that the bill was out of order and that it had to go back to the committee. So I hesitated, and I didn't come out with a clear-cut answer…I kind of hesitated to even answer the question. A couple of times I looked up and…Pegors was shaking his head 'no' to say that it hadn't gone through the operations committee. I said I didn't know if it had…

"'You don't know? You ought to know that,' Newcome said…So Newcome said, 'Well, why don't you just lay this bill over for an hour or so and see if you can't get together…and see if you can't work out something.'

You know, by golly, we passed the bill. I'll never forget John up there…I think the world of John. John has gotten himself in some trouble once in a while because he's something like I am, I guess. Sometimes he says things he shouldn't say at the wrong place and at the wrong time."

(*Oral History of Willard Munger*, ibid, pp. 90 – 92.)

1992 saw Munger firmly entrenched in the Minnesota House for his 18th non-consecutive term. How he survived the election challenges thrown at him over the years was discussed in an article in the *Duluth News Tribune*.

Munger Bucks Big Money Trend

Some Minnesota legislators have bucked the trend toward high-priced campaigns for what they believe is greater independence.

Among them is Rep. Willard Munger, DFL-Duluth. He raised $6,993 and spent only $3,187 to win election to his 18th term in the legislature—the longest tenure among anyone now in the Senate or House.

When he first stepped into his House office 38 years ago, Munger was a darling of special interests. By the end of his freshman session, he was the goat.

"Toward the end of the session, I didn't have many invitations on my spindle because they didn't like the way I was voting," he says. "They didn't want to waste their money."

Munger…isn't a purist. He takes contributions from political action committees. He just doesn't take many…

"I would like to see completely public financed campaigns," he says. "Any individual has to be naïve if he thinks contributions in large sums from special interests don't have an influence…They don't give money because they are your friends."

(*Duluth News Tribune*, April 16, 1992.)

Even though the Democrats controlled the legislature, Munger wasn't happy with the environmental bills that came out of the 1992 session.

Package Reduction Bill Dies but Munger Fight Hasn't

Rep. Willard Munger had high hopes for the 1992 legislative session. But he—and the state's environment—took a bit of a beating.

Munger, DFL-Duluth…planned to take the initiative from major environmental strides in recent years to pass yet another major environmental bill…

The bill would have required a 10-cent deposit on all non-returnable containers, a move likely to double recycling rates from 40 to 90 percent, as happened in Oregon.

The bill also would have taxed most toxic chemicals used in retail products and packaging, and it would have required the amount of packaging around our products be cut by 25% within four years…

"The second half of this [two-year] session was the worst I've ever seen," for environmental protection, Munger said. "We didn't do anything we should have…"

Despite their tough sessions…both Munger and the state's environment are expected to recover…

"I'm going to come back next year and pass a bill with the packaging, toxic chemicals and deposit bills all in one," Munger said. "It usually takes me a couple of years to get what I want. That's why I've been here so long."

(*Duluth News Tribune*, April 17, 1992.)

Munger continually battled his friends in the labor movement over "ban the can" legislation. The law was seen as contradictory to labor's interests in that passage of it would have reduced the demand for new beverage containers. The bill never passed, though Munger made other inroads in the solid waste piling up in Minnesota's landfills by sponsoring initiatives to fund recycling sheds for rural areas and recycling pick-up in urban areas throughout the state. These measures continue to account for the recycling of over 40% of Minnesota's solid waste.

Alan Netland, president of AFCSME Local 66 for over twenty-five years, and president of the Duluth Central Labor Body Council 96 for more than a decade, worked closely with Willard Munger.

"I left Grand Marais after high school and came to Duluth in 1971," Netland recalls, "to attend UMD. I graduated with a double major in sociology/psychology. My first involvement with the DFL was in 1972 when I caucused for McGovern. I learned very quickly how the system worked. I was hired as a social worker by St. Louis County and became active in the union, Local 66. In 1982, the union was about to endorse Arne Carlson over Paul Wellstone for State Auditor. That didn't make any sense to me. So I tried to find someone to run for union president but no one wanted to buck the leadership. I ended up running myself and winning by 3 votes. It was in the context of the union that I came into contact with Willard."

Unlike many of his union counterparts, Netland supported Munger on "ban the can."

"We became friends in the mid-1980s," Netland remembers. "Over the years, because of his stand on the 'ban the can' legislation, many labor leaders sort of abandoned Willard. I supported that bill. I liked his 'no compromise' style. I learned that, if you wanted to keep up on what was going on in Duluth politics, you needed to go out to the coffee shop on Saturday mornings. There was Willard, making bacon and eggs, pouring coffee. He wouldn't sit down until everyone had food. Then the stories would start. He'd have a table of local Republicans, like Jerome Blasevic, sitting off to one side, so there wouldn't be any arguments. He'd say, 'I need to get a Republican view on this', and then go over to them. There were people like Dan Hoffman, Proctor City Administrator, Ray Critchley-Mayor Fedo's right hand man, and others there as well."

Netland reflects further.

"Willard Munger was a guy you wanted to know," he remembers. "Sam Solon was a guy you worked with. They had distinctly different styles. Sam was a compromiser, the ultimate deal maker. That's why he was the head of the Commerce Committee in the senate. Willard didn't make deals. He didn't compromise. Sam saw that as a weakness, as unrealistic. But I agreed with Willard's approach. 'If it's not controversial, if someone's not mad about the bill, then it's not worth a damn' was something he said often. And I agreed with him on that. Proposed legislation, in Willard's eyes, was only meaningful if it riled someone up. "

Netland watched the legislative sessions of the early and mid-1980s and learned how Munger approached the art of politics.

"He was extremely loyal. And he demanded loyalty from others. He had a very long memory and if you didn't return his loyalty, well, then you were done," Netland observes. "His wish list wasn't big. Some money for the train. Some money for the zoo. And the environment. And if the state AFL-CIO wouldn't support him on these things, then he'd say, 'forget it.' The Central Labor Body was one of the only unions that consistently gave Willard money. It wasn't much, maybe five hundred bucks, but he was always appreciative. He'd say, 'Thanks, now I can print some brochures.' Even though Willard voted with organized labor 95% of the time, that 5% got him in trouble with some union leaders. Why, I don't really know. He was always strong for the working men and women of his district. He was strong on workers' compensation, on pensions, on every issue related to organized labor. He was there to support collective bargaining for governmental employees when the law passed in 1973. And even though Sam Solon was on the wrong side of the workers' compensation issue in 1986, it was Willard who had trouble with union leadership over 'ban the can.'"

An incident took place in the rural Douglas County, Wisconsin on June 30, 1992 which spurred Munger into action. On that date, a Burlington Northern freight train suffered the derailment of a tanker car full of benzene. The car at issue toppled from a bridge crossing the Nemadji River, dumping 34,000 gallons of the hazardous chemical into the river. The benzene and water combined to form a poisonous cloud which threatened the health and safety of nearly 150,000 residents of the Duluth-Superior area. 50 – 60,000 people directly in the path of the gas cloud were evacuated. No one died from exposure to the plume, though claims of injury and property damage (including lost livestock) prevail to this day. Biologists estimate that thousands of fish died as a direct consequence of the accident. Munger brought his Environment and Natural Resources Committee to Duluth to hold hearings regarding the transportation of hazardous materials. The hearings (held in the Duluth City Council chambers) featured Munger asking tough questions of railroad officials. The disaster, and Munger's response to it, made national news, including an interview of Munger on PBS's "McNeil-Lehrer Report."

"Having 50 – 60,000 people evacuated caused me," Munger related during the PBS interview, "to do some serious thinking. It's pretty clear to me that the accident was a result of the deregulation of the railroads."

Advocates for tighter regulation of tanker cars, including Lawrence Mann, a lawyer representing railroad workers, pressed Munger to take action. Railroad officials pointed out that it was the chemical companies themselves, not the railroads, who owned and maintained the tanker cars, setting up a situation of the "fox guarding the henhouse." It became clear to Munger that the enactment and enforcement of stricter tanker standards was a federal, not a state, function. Still, Munger vowed to find a solution to prevent similar accidents.

"I had a bill to ban DDT," Munger related towards the end of the McNeil interview, "that I tried to pass in Minnesota. It was killed in committee the first time I introduced it. The next time, there'd been a spraying of DDT in the Twin Cities, which killed all the robins. When the bill came up that second time, someone carried in a basket of dead robins during the hearing and dumped them on the table. The bill passed," Munger related, enforcing the notion for viewers of the McNeil-Lehrer show that Munger wouldn't let a paltry concept like federal pre-emption deter him from protecting the environment.

At 81 years old, Munger decided to retire from the day-to-day operation of the motel. Willard and Frances deeded the motel property to Will, Jr. and his wife, Sally on September 14, 1992. Willard, who had owned and operated the motel for nearly four decades, decided that it was time to move into the new home he and Frances were building on Indian Point.

The Indian Point property was purchased by Willard and Frances in 1971. Harry Munger, Jr. recalls that the price for the property (which included twenty-plus lots overlooking the St. Louis River) was less than $15,000.00. Harry also recalls that he had to insist that Willard buy the property, calling his older brother "crazy" if he passed up the opportunity.

When Willard and Frances deeded the motel to Will and Sally, they also entered into a Quit Claim Deed transferring the house on Indian Point to Willard's daughter Patsy, subject to a life estate which allowed Willard and Frances to remain in the home until their deaths.

Like everything Willard Munger constructed, the house on Indian Point was "built to last." Willard asked his daughter Patsy's second husband (Harvey Lehr, a contractor from the Twin Cities) to draw up blueprints for the home. When Harvey questioned why anyone in their right mind would use steel I-beams to support a wooden patio deck, Munger just smiled and told Harvey to "let me worry about that."

Another puzzling aspect of the project was the large hole that Munger insisted be dug when the basement was excavated. Munger planned to install an indoor swimming pool ("for exercise" he said) in the hole. The pool was never installed and, in the end, "The Pit," as Patsy Munger-Lehr and others came to affectionately call the concrete block-lined chamber, was converted into storage space.

1992 was another election year and Munger was seeking his 19th non-consecutive term in the Minnesota House. Munger was once again opposed by IR candidate, Rilla Opelt, whose major focus was Munger's age. Opelt was also a pro-life Catholic who made no bones about her opposition to *Roe v. Wade*. The *Duluth News Tribune*, which had been largely supportive of Munger's environmental efforts, endorsed Opelt, citing Munger's advanced age as a concern.

There was also a hotly contested presidential race between President George H.W. Bush, former Arkansas Governor Bill Clinton and millionaire Ross Perot. Though polls proclaimed the race between Bush and Clinton to be "a dead heat," Clinton won a convincing victory (43% -39%) over President Bush. (Perot claimed 18% of the popular vote, which worked in Clinton's favor). Voters ignored the *News Tribune's* endorsement and elected Munger to a 19th term in the House by a margin of 9,871 to 5,117 over Opelt.

Shortly after his re-election, Willard Munger addressed the issue of environmental stewardship in the *Duluth News Tribune*.

> *Nature's Health Will Determine Industry's Survival* by **Willard Munger**
>
> This year I celebrated my 82nd birthday…
>
> I have experienced firsthand a very important part of our American history that no one will ever again witness.
>
> I saw the evolution from the horse and buggy to the airplane…I also witnessed the destruction of our forests, atmosphere, soils and other critical ecosystems. Some of us have taken more than we need. No creature on the earth does this.
>
> The key to our economic expansion has been mass consumption. The American economy's purpose was to produce more consumer goods—more was better. Nature was our machinery and we were at the controls, using enormous inputs of energy, chemicals, metals and paper at the expense of the earth.
>
> Now our economy is threatened…Our culture has aged much like I have. First, a needy, hungry child, then a somewhat self-absorbed adolescent, and now, hopefully, a mature, reflective adult.

"Jobs versus owls" is no longer the debate. We can have all the jobs and production in the world, but if we end up with a lot of non-useable waste, we will be burying ourselves in a sea of garbage...

We in the North Country have a connectedness with the cycles of nature. We live very close to the seasons.

The critical process on which the whole of nature is based is more familiar to us who enjoy the great outdoors than those who spend their time in shopping malls...

"Closing the loop" requires a responsibility on our part for the fate of the items we buy, sell and consume, not only yard waste, but cardboard, newspaper, office paper, glass, but also other materials, such as plastic and packaging...

A change in society's throw away mentality will help enhance a sustainable environment...

This change will not come by recycling alone...Reduction in our use of daily essentials such as energy, water, food and housing is just as important. Less costly alternatives to non-renewable coal, gas and oil fuels are crucial. We must develop an attitude of efficiency...

In addition...local entrepreneurs can be encouraged to develop their dreams as we launch the age of information, ideas and service...

Now I am 82 years old. I went through the growing pains and made mistakes, becoming wiser in the process. I wish the great North Country a similar development so that all of us together can pass onto future generations what we know, love and cherish...

(*Duluth News Tribune*, March 24, 1993.)

For more than two decades, Munger sought to address the issue of product packaging through legislation. But persistence alone could not overcome the objections raised by business and labor to Munger's position. No packaging reduction bill was ever signed into law in Minnesota despite Munger's eloquent and heart-felt pleas. But Munger's stubborn resolve did, in the end, create its share of success stories. Perhaps no battle has been more chronicled with respect to Willard Munger's ability to dodge, weave, take a punch and come back for more, than the fight over Northern States Power's (NSP's) storage of nuclear waste on Prairie Island.

When NSP was about to run out of above-ground storage for the waste generated by its nuclear reactor on Prairie Island, an island sitting in the middle of the Mississippi River southeast of the Twin Cities, Munger vigorously opposed NSP's plan to increase the number of storage casks on the island.

His Horse Trading's Good for Environment by John Myers

Just before the first House-Senate meeting on the emotional nuclear storage legislation, Sen. Steve Novak tried to crack a joke.

"Here comes Willard Munger," Novak said, "the guy who wants to close Northern States Power Co.'s Prairie Island nuclear power plant and put 500 workers on the street...."

"You quit saying that," Munger snapped in a crowded committee room. "I may be 83 but I can still kick your ass."

Munger then invited Novak, 44, to go outside to settle the issue.

Fur never did fly. But it was clear that Rep. Willard Munger, DFL-Duluth, the state's oldest and longest-serving lawmaker, was ready for battle...

Mr. Environment is at it again. "I love it," Munger said..."I love to sit across from them and go to it."

At 83, when a lot of men worry about fishing or card games or their grandchildren, Willard Munger has been trying to draft the state's most comprehensive energy policy ever.

It's not that he doesn't worry about his grandchildren. Just the opposite, Munger said. They're the reason he's working so hard.

"When I'm done with this legislation, Minnesota will have the most comprehensive renewable energy policy of any state in the country," Munger said. "I may have to give in on nuclear storage to get it, but you have to give some to get some..."

There has been immense pressure on Munger and his House allies to give in to a Senate plan to allow NSP to store spent nuclear fuel rods in metal casks outside the Red Wing power plant along the Mississippi River and near a small Sioux Indian band...NSP and the Senate wanted 17 casks with few other strings attached. The House offered no casks and lots of strings.

A compromise was expected to include four or five casks and numerous conditions...

If the bill passed, Munger appeared...to be successful in ordering NSP to create at least 500 megawatts of wind-generated electricity and another 100 megawatts of biomass (clean-burning wood, crops and other natural items) generated electricity by 2003.

That's double the renewable energy requirements in the Senate bill. And even Novak agreed it would be the greatest commitment to wind energy of any state in the nation except California...

Munger wasn't always a player in the nuclear storage issue. He had little to do with the bill halfway through the 1994 legislative session...

But when a newspaper reporter asked Munger…what his alternative plan was, Munger was speechless.

"I went home…and couldn't sleep," Munger said. "It wasn't enough to say I opposed nuclear waste along the river. I had to come up with an alternative…"

He came back to the Capitol armed with a plan…Now, much of his plan could be adopted as law. And while Munger was about to give in and allow some temporary storage of nuclear waste outside the plant, he insists he won big for Minnesota's environment and renewable energy.

"Our energy policy will be to phase out nuclear and phase in renewable," Munger said. "If we pass this, I will get a lot of hell for allowing the casks. But we will have something even Bill Clinton doesn't have. An energy policy…"

(*Duluth News Tribune*, May 6, 1994.)

The windmills constructed because of the Prairie Island compromise were the beginning of the state's search for cheap, clean, renewable energy.

1994 saw Munger running for his twentieth term in office. Once again, he was opposed by Republican Rilla Opelt. Once again, Opelt made Munger's age the major issue of her campaign but Munger's campaign literature turned his age into an attribute: experience.

Endorsed by the Farmer-Labor party in Ottertail County, Munger has been a consistent and dedicated Liberal for over 60 years. He has fought hard to uphold his convictions and principals. Munger's thinking on issues on environment, social and economic reform are as young and sound today as they were when he was chair of the Farmer-Labor party of Ottertail County in 1934…

The *Congressional Record*, dated 4/27/35…reads:

"Willard Munger, secretary of the Fergus Falls unit of the Farmer-Labor Assn. of Minnesota praying for the passage of the Workers' Unemployment and Old-age Insurance which provides for establishment of unemployment, old-age and social insurance…"

Munger is a friend of education:

During 25 years as a member of the Education Division of Appropriations, Munger was instrumental in obtaining funds for UMD Building expansion.

Munger supports increased Foundation Aid Funding for Public Education K-12.

Opposed to vouchers for funding education.

Opposed to increase in student tuition.

In the 1994 session the storage of nuclear waste was hotly contested. The Environment and Natural Resources Committee did pass, and the full House…approved, a good, far reaching comprehensive alternative, renewable energy phase-in program, which he authored…The sad part is that the Final Conference Report provided for nuclear waste storage at Prairie Island. Because of the senate position at the conference committee and weak-kneed legislators, Minnesota will now become the first state in the nation to officially approve and become a depository for high level nuclear waste…Munger voted "No!"

(1994 Campaign Brochure, Willard Munger Personal Collection.)

In 1994, DFL State Senator John Marty was running for governor against incumbent Arne Carlson. Vice president Al Gore came to Minnesota on November 1st to stump for State Senator Ann Wynia against broadcaster Rod Grams for a seat in the United States Senate, followed by President Clinton who stopped in Duluth two days later for the same purpose. When the votes were tallied, the Democrats lost majorities in both the U.S. House and the U.S. Senate to the GOP. The national Republican tidal wave allowed Arne Carlson to easily beat John Marty and Rod Grams beat Ann Wynia as well, making the two United States Senators from Minnesota distinctly at odds in terms of their politics; Grams being ultra Conservative and Paul Wellstone being ultra Liberal. And Willard Munger once again bested Rilla Opelt 7,414 to 4,247 in Opelt's last attempt to unseat Munger.

As the 1995 legislative session began, Willard Munger was nearing his eighty-fourth birthday. At an age when many Minnesota-born octogenarians live out the twilight of their lives in Arizona, Texas or Florida, Munger was contemplating his past, his future and what was left to be done to safeguard the planet he loved. He was not at all interested in playing golf (it is doubtful he ever swung a club) or fishing (he was a disinterested angler at best) or card playing: he was interested in legislating.

CHAPTER 11

A Last Stand

Dave Zentner cites the Buffalo Ridge-NSP compromise as an example of Willard Munger's political savvy.

"He was so pragmatic," Zentner recalls. "During those Saturday morning coffee klatches at the coffee shop, he'd listen to diverse voices, such as myself, Alden Lind, John Pegors, Gary Glass, and Steve Balach. Steve was the group's token Republican though Willard always suspected me of being a covert Republican. I'm not, but Willard thought I was. Anyway, Willard enjoyed soaking up the idealism and then he'd bring us back to reality by asking, 'How do we get it done?' He never made apologies for his positions and was a master of assigning tasks to people he knew could get things done. He hated the idea of increasing the storage of nuclear waste at Prairie Island. He was ready to fight tooth and nail to stop it, even bringing in the Native Americans to oppose storing the waste adjacent to their reservation. But when he knew he couldn't stop it, he dug in his heels until he got NSP to commit considerable resources to the wind farm project. Buffalo Ridge is now touted as an international success, a hallmark of wind generation. Willard lost the battle but proved his point.

He did the same thing in 1991 with the Wetlands Conservation Act. He wanted to preserve all wetlands five acres or more but knew he couldn't pass it. He ended up compromising with the northern legislators to get it passed."

Willard and Frances Munger reveled in their new life on Indian Point where Frances maintained her organic garden and Willard tended his grove of black walnut trees, pruned his apple orchard, and took care of his bee hives. Theirs was an idyllic existence, one that Willard had wanted for himself and Martha when they moved to Duluth in the 1930s but one that he ended up enjoying with his second wife nearly sixty years later. Sometimes Willard's hobbies, not his environmental fervor, made news.

What's that Buzzing?

Excuse State Rep. Willard Munger…if he's a little impatient that the 1995 Minnesota Legislature couldn't get its job done on time.

Munger is in a hurry to get home…Munger raises bees…and he recently got a call from the Duluth Post Office saying that a package for him with three pounds of honey bees is waiting to be picked up.

The last time his bees arrived at the post office, a postal worker poked a hole in the packaging and some of the bees got out…

(*Duluth News Tribune,* May 24, 1995.)

Will Munger, Jr. recalls that, as wonderful as the house and grounds on Indian Point turned out to be, he wasn't an early supporter of buying the place.

"I wasn't someone who supported Dad buying the Point," Will remembers. "I'd been away from Duluth and didn't realize the river was in the process of being cleaned up. I said, 'Dad, why do you want to buy that piece of trash located next to a sewer?' I was wrong about that, but I was remembering how it looked when I went down to the resort that was there as a kid. I didn't think that the river would ever amount to anything."

Willard Munger continued to sponsor environmental legislation. When his efforts to stop commercial expansion along the Miller Trunk Highway failed, he teamed up with his brother Harry and Dave Zentner to secure funding to restore the Miller Creek watershed.

"One smaller project he and I worked on," Dave Zentner recalls, "was creating and obtaining funding for a Joint Powers Board between Duluth and Hermantown to oversee the restoration of Miller Creek. Willard tried to get a watershed district formed to control development in the two cities but that didn't fly. So we obtained grant financing to attempt shore land restoration and control of the run-off into the trout stream. We got the Joint Powers Agreement signed and worked on that project for quite a while but the agreement expired and the effort died. Not every fight Willard picked was a winner."

Dave Zentner also observed that while Willard worked well with moderate Republicans like Governor Arne Carlson and Jim Gustafson of Duluth, working with the new, arch-conservative face of the Republican Party was a different story. According to Zentner, the right-wing Republicans never appreciated where Munger was coming from.

"They didn't understand him because he wasn't grammatically brilliant," Zentner observes. "Willard appeared to them to be a befuddled old man, a plodder. It was a hell of a disguise!"

Well into his ninth decade of life, Munger's advanced age had certain benefits.

Happy Birthday

Rep. Willard Munger [blew] out 85 candles on his cake at a birthday salute for the veteran Duluth DFLer…Actually, he blew out…49 of the candles; Lt. Gov. Joanne Benson gave him a hand blowing out the final 36. Dignitaries praised the Duluth DFLer, who has served in the House for nearly 40 years, for his staunch defense of environmental protection…

Gov. Arne Carlson proclaimed it "Willard Munger Day."

(*Duluth News Tribune*, January 19, 1996.)

Munger's 85th birthday party took place after the legislature's business had been concluded for the day. The event was emceed by Diane Jensen, Midwest Coordinator for Clean Water Action.

Speaker of the House Irv Anderson made it clear that, while he and Munger didn't always agree on environmental legislation, they were indeed friends.

"Willard's a politician," Anderson quipped, "who doesn't believe in term limits. He was here, in the House, before many of you in attendance were born."

The Speaker continued.

"I've known Willard for an awfully long time," Anderson reminisced. "I first became aware of him in 1964 when he and Frenchie LaBrosse were involved in a huge debate. The Taconite Amendment was the issue. LaBrosse was for it and Willard was against it. I watched those debates on television because I was running for my first term. I won. Willard didn't. So my first term here was without Willard. But after that, as long as I've been here, Willard's been here."

Anderson sought to dispel rumors that the two men didn't get along.

"We've seen eye to-eye-on some things and gone toe-to-toe on others. But when you can have a colleague like Willard, you know that democracy works."

Senate Majority Leader Roger Moe roasted Munger.

'You know," Moe said, "this really is a sad story. Since Willard's been around, *Titanic* sunk; we've had two world wars; we had the Great Depression; Watergate; the Soviet invasion of Afghanistan; a bombing of the World Trade Center [the first bombing in 1993]; Love Canal; Chernobyl; Three Mile Island; *Exxon Valdez*; the enlargement of the hole in the Earth's ozone layer; and fires and a blow down in the BWCA. Willard, you have a lot to answer for," Moe deadpanned.

Senator Moe's remarks turned serious.

"Willard's greatest asset is his humor and his wit; not just his longevity; not just his commitment and long history of public service; not just his celebrated steward-ship of our natural resources. We love you and admire you as a person. I've enjoyed working with you."

Senate Minority Leader Dean Johnson (Johnson was an IR Senator at the time, changing party affiliations to the DFL and winning re-election in 2000 as a DFLer) challenged those in attendance to have breakfast with Munger.

"I saw Willard eating by himself at the Kelly Inn," Johnson revealed. "He spot-ted me and said, 'I know you're a Republican, Johnson, but sit down and have something to eat.' I did and we proceeded to talk. As we ate, he said, 'Let me tell you something. Not many Republicans are supportive of what I'm trying to do. You need to change some votes…' Then he proceeded to relate to me the history of the legislature and the governors he's served with.

I wish each of you would sit down and talk with Willard and hear the history of the state. You see, I was curious. When he came into the legislature, I was seven years old. People were building bomb shelters in their backyards. We were in con-stant fear of nuclear attack.

Willard, you've taken us a long, long way. For a servant of your stature, a pas-sage from the Bible seems appropriate (Johnson is a Lutheran pastor). That passage is, 'Well done, my good and faithful servant.' From you Willard, I've learned that it's not how we cast our votes while we're here, but how our colleagues respect us."

Munger received a number of awards during the celebration including the Eagle Feather Award from the Minnesota Raptor Center for his work on behalf of the bald eagle and other birds of prey.

U.S. Senator Paul Wellstone reflected upon an early visit with Munger.

"I was new to the political game. So I went to see Willard. We were at his house overlooking the river. He said, 'Wellstone, I want you to remember this. I take stands not everyone in my district like. Yet election after election, I get 80% of the vote.' I said, 'Representative Munger, I'd like to know how you do that.' He pointed to a group of fishermen bobbing in the river in their boats. 'See those fishermen?' I said, 'Yep.' Willard didn't take his eyes off the boats. 'Well, every time they catch a fish, they think of Willard Munger.' What Willard was saying to me is that all politics is local."

Wellstone went on to present Munger a copy of Vice President Al Gore's book, *Earth in the Balance*, personally inscribed by the author.

Congressman Bruce Vento reminded the audience that he served six years in the Minnesota House with Munger, including time on Munger's Environment and Natural Resources Committee. Vento couldn't resist taking a humorous poke at one of Munger's non-environmental positions.

"Willard," Vento said, "I'm glad you lost funding for Amtrak. Since the train stopped, I've really enjoyed biking on the Munger Trail."

Vento went on to describe Munger as "a Minnesota natural resource, a Minnesota original."

House Minority Leader Steve Sviggum related a story involving Munger's roots.

"Most folks here don't know that Willard ran unsuccessfully in 1934 for the House in Otter Tail County," Sviggum said. "The LCMR was touring near where he'd been born, out in northwest Minnesota, and Willard explained that this was where he first ran for office. Senator Gene Merriam asked: 'Willard, just what is it that makes the voters in Otter Tail County so much smarter than the voters in Duluth?'"

Sviggum then noted Munger's legendary tenacity.

"You are as immoveable as the oaks you seek to protect; as strong as the eagles that now fly over Minnesota; but you are as warm as my father. You've accomplished what you have by being fair and with great integrity."

State Rep. Mike Jaros quipped that "Representative Munger is like a father to me. Of course, I sometimes didn't listen to my father and I sometimes don't listen to Representative Munger either," Jaros said through a smile. "Willard doesn't base his decisions on polls but on what is right. I admire that. It says a lot about him. He's not only a leader in the environment, but on social justice and human rights. I hope, Representative Munger that you can serve until 2010; when your 30 year mortgage is up!"

Ben Gustafson (DFL-Duluth), recalled being at a candidate forum with Munger where Munger's Republican opponent was making light of the legislator's age.

"Willard, in a calm, deadpan voice, asked 'Are you supporting anyone for president?' 'Yes.' 'Who are you supporting?' 'Governor Reagan.' Now that question had two purposes. One, Willard wanted to pin the guy down as a Republican in a very Democratic district. And two, he wanted to deal with the age factor. 'So you don't have any problem with Reagan's mental faculties?' 'No, I don't.' The point had been made. 'And of course you know,' Willard said smiling, 'that Ronald Reagan is older than I am.'" (*Author's Note: In fact, Willard was fudging a wee bit. Ronald Reagan was born on February 6, 1911, making him* younger *than Munger by about two weeks.*)

Lieutenant Governor Joanne Benson attended the party on behalf of Governor Carlson and announced that Willard's 85th birthday had been declared "Willard Munger Day" by the governor. She also announced that the Minnesota Natural Resources Foundation, a private charity, had named its new award (to be given to the environmentalist of the year) the "Willard Munger Award."

When Munger took the microphone, he noted that his longevity was due to his wife Frances.

"She's always after me," Willard said. "She's always telling me, 'Don't you eat any pie. Don't you eat any candy.' When I get back to Duluth, she's always asking, 'Did you eat any pie? Did you eat any candy?' And of course, I always say, 'No.' At 85 years old, you can lie a little bit."

Munger was quick to deflect all the praise heaped upon him.

"You don't pass a bill until you have 68 votes up on that board," Willard said, pointing to the voting board in the House chambers. "It's because of bipartisanship that these laws, some pretty good environmental laws, got passed.

When I look out at my good friend Bishop who's done so much, I feel a little bit guilty hearing this. But let me tell you something. I like it," he said quietly.

Reiterating observations that had already been made, Munger concluded his remarks.

"We do a lot of squabbling here, but when it comes down to what's best for Minnesota, we can join hands. I don't care what side of the aisle they're from. They're here for the very same reason—to work for the betterment of the state of Minnesota." (House TV, January 18, 1996.)

In the fall of 1996, Willard Munger found himself in a bitter electoral contest for the first time since 1964.

Munger Faces Test by **Norm Levey**

Sunday morning at the Willard Munger Inn...begins with a discussion of deformed frogs and deforestation. West Duluth's legendary legislator is holding court, as he does every weekend morning, at his favorite spot—his own coffee shop.

Willard Munger, 85, has got himself elected to the Minnesota House 20 times by sticking to one message—protect Minnesota's environment. That message has been so successful, he doesn't usually have to sweat on Election Day.

This year...Brad Bennett could change that.

Bennett is no stranger to the people of his district. He is a Duluth School Board member and a longtime community activist...

Munger is an old-style Democrat whose progressive roots go back to fighting farm foreclosures during the Depression.

Bennett, 50, is an unapologetic Conservative who has earned himself a reputation as a fiscal hawk...Bennett has a history of supporting Republican causes but he is running as an Independent.

Munger has seemed content to put his campaign signs around the district and rely on his name...

Bennett is campaigning with the enthusiasm of a promising freshman trying out for the varsity team...(H)e has hit the pavement, congenially, and sometimes a little nervously, knocking on doors...

In 40 years in the legislature, Munger has deservedly earned the title "Mr. Environment." He was instrumental in getting money to clean up the St. Louis River...He has led the fight to impose tougher restrictions on industries that dump toxic chemicals...

And just last year, he focused the state's attention on a disturbing number of deformed frogs appearing in Minnesota...

"Willard is leading the charge"...says Gary Glass, a chemist with the EPA who is researching mercury deposits in water...

Munger talks passionately in his gravelly voice about protecting the shorelines of Minnesota lakes from development...

Bennett says Munger's environmental record is all well and good, but what about the other issues?

As a School Board member, Bennett has earned a reputation for being tight with the district's money...As the district's labor negotiator; he tried to negotiate very tough contracts with teachers...

In 1988, Bennett was at the center of a major controversy when he used a school district car for nine months for his own personal use...Only after the abuse was made public did Bennett agree to pay the district...for the use of the car.

Bennett says now he deeply regrets using the car...

There are no Republicans running against Munger this year...Bennett gathered more than 600 signatures to get on the ballot as an Independent...Bennett has accepted $500 from Republican Senate Minority Leader Steve Sviggum.

Munger is hammering away at Bennett for lying…"Honesty in government begins at the campaign level," Munger has said.

(*Duluth News Tribune*, October 14, 1996.)

It irked Willard Munger that Bennett knew he couldn't win in Munger's district as a Republican so Bennett claimed to be an "Independent." Bennett's declaration of political neutrality, after accepting campaign funds from Republican Minority Leader Steve Sviggum, offended Munger's sense of ethics.

With Willard's brother Harry digging up evidence of less than honorable conduct by Bennett (with respect to Bennett's divorce proceedings and financial abuses) Bennett's character—not Munger's age—became the major focus of the campaign. Bennett's wrongful use of a school district vehicle also reinforced the notion that Bennett was not trustworthy.

The 1996 election season included Kansas Senator Bob Dole challenging President Bill Clinton. DFLer Becky Lourey (who had served several terms in the House) ran for the 8th District State Senate Seat formerly held by DFLer Florien Chmielewski. Republican challenger Rudy Boschwitz sought to reclaim his U.S. Senate seat from Paul Wellstone. President Clinton visited Minnesota on Wellstone's behalf and drew a standing-room-only crowd to the UMD gymnasium, the locale for John F. Kennedy's last speech in Minnesota.

Howie Hanson, editor of the Duluth monthly, *Twin Ports People*, recounted a crucial debate between Munger and Bennett during the 1996 campaign.

Willard Remains Sharp as a Tack at Tender Age of 85 by Howie Hanson

Legendary, forty-year Rep. Willard Munger (DFL) 85, danced circles around several rookie politician types [while attending] a candidate forum hosted by Lincoln Park businessmen…

All the political wannabees were there…

[Gary] Eckenberg, who chairs the…Lincoln Park Neighbors Coalition, asked Munger and his opponents if they would sponsor a property tax reform bill…

"It will be one of the main issues in the legislature, to shift the cost of K-12 education to the state, and that should make a big difference," Willard answered. "We might not reach the 100% mark, but we'll go another 10 – 15% in that direction…We'll have a more uniform educational system throughout the state and the rich districts and the poor districts will finally be treated the same. It goes beyond the tax benefits—it's good for kids."

> Brad Bennett [replied]... "I'm more inclined to see a system that does away with the entire current funding mechanism and changing it to a more direct aid—whether it be funded through a property tax or a sales tax combination, a straight sales tax or a straight income tax..."
>
> Willard [had] the last word..."I'm happy to hear Bennett say he wants to do away with local aid from the state and shift the tax onto the backs of the homeowner. I hope he repeats that real often..."
>
> (*Twin Ports People*, November 1996.)

The morning after the election, the *Duluth News Tribune* proclaimed, "Clinton Keeps His Job." Independent Ross Perot was again a factor in the presidential race, pulling in 8% of the popular vote. Clinton won re-election with 49% and Dole finished second with 41%. Becky Lourey won her bid for the Minnesota Senate. And in a three-way race for the House seat in District 7A, Munger convincingly retained his legislative seat. The popular vote showed that negative campaigning by Bennett caused a considerable backlash against the would-be politician:

Munger: 8,398 (57%)

Bennett: 5,469 (37%)

Bushey: 983 (3%)

Munger thanked his supporters during an appearance at the Labor Temple in Duluth in the company of a special friend.

Tireless Wellstone Returns November 6 to Say Thanks

The front door of the Labor Temple opened at about 2:30 P.M. on Wednesday, November 6, the day after a huge general election and through it came newly re-elected Sen. Paul Wellstone and his wife, Sheila. No handlers, no staff, just two people who drove up to Duluth to say thanks to some of their friends who had helped them in their campaign...

Among those who came to the Labor Temple...was Rep. Willard Munger, who was recently re-elected for the 21st time and will now be the longest serving legislator in Minnesota history.

Munger expressed the feelings of many Minnesotans [towards Wellstone]... "I've seen a lot of them come and go and I'll tell you why I admire you the most—you have a philosophy, you let people know it, you fight for it and are dedicated to it, and you don't run and hide when people call you a Liberal..."

(*Labor World*, November 20, 1996.)

Given that Munger never shied away from his Liberal roots, it wasn't a surprise that he was named "Progressive Politician of the Year" for 1996.

Munger Honored as Progressive Legislator

Rep. Willard Munger received Minnesota Alliance for Progressive Action's 1996 elected official award at its seventh annual dinner and celebration in Minneapolis. The honor recognizes "outstanding leadership in building a progressive movement…"

MAPA's membership includes AFSCME, Clean Water Action Alliance, Minnesota Americans for Democratic Action, Minnesota Community Action Assn., Minnesota National Organization for Women, Minnesota Senior Federation, United Auto Workers, United Transportation Union, United Steel Workers of America, and Women Against Military Madness.

Senator Paul Wellstone received the elected official award at the 1995 MAPA ceremony.

(*Duluth Budgeteer News*, December 15, 1996.)

Being inexorably linked to the likes of Paul Wellstone was part of a political continuum that stretched back to Eugene Debs, Lyman Munger, A.C. Townley, Norman Thomas, Floyd B. Olson, and Elmer Benson. Over his lengthy legislative career, Willard Munger never refuted his connection to the Socialism, Progressivism, and Liberalism of his youth. If anything, as Mike Jaros observes, Willard Munger became *more* progressive as he grew older.

"He was more Liberal," Jaros observes, "than most folks half his age. He was good philosophically on everything; though his love was the environment…He was always to the Left, way to the Left of those young punks in their shiny new suits who thought they knew what it meant to be a Liberal."

Even in the later stages of his career, Munger's vision was directed towards the future.

"Some of the legislation that was pending before my committee," Willard recalled, "didn't get a hearing. There was a bill regarding the selling off of some state-owned lakeshore property. I'm strictly opposed to the state selling any state-owned lakeshore property. I think that should be held for public use. If you don't watch that very closely, your developers will be moving in slowly, and you won't have any public lakeshores left.

"I was down in one of the southern states, and I went all the way along the shore of one of the big lakes down there. I was trying to find a place to have my lunch and I got run off every single place I stopped. I must have spent a half a day trying to find a place. I wouldn't want that to see anything like that happen in Minnesota...

"The leaseholders [of public lakeshore in Minnesota] all got together and organized an association for the sole purpose of having a bill introduced to force the state to sell that land to them. That was two years ago...when I wasn't chairman of the Environment and Natural Resources Committee. Then the legislature approved the sale...It wasn't that the state wanted to sell....It was the local pressures from the local people and the local legislators up north that convinced the legislature. The DNR was opposed to it. If I had been chairman at the time [in 1985 when the Republicans controlled the House] that bill would have never passed...It's a foot in the door and the establishment of a precedent. The developers will be moving in now full force. They will use that as an example. They will tell us that they're going to bring in new business, that they're going to increase the population..."

(*Oral History of Willard Munger*, ibid, pp. 68 – 69.)

Munger's objection to the sale of state-owned lakeshore reflected his egalitarian roots: everyone, every man, woman and child in Minnesota should be guaranteed access to the state's lakes, rivers and streams.

"The fact is that if the developers do finally succeed, they will have established precedent that has never happened in the past seventy years," Willard continued. "Once you establish that precedent, your case is weakened a hell of a lot..."

(*Oral History of Willard Munger*, ibid, pp. 71 – 73).

The lakeshore lease issue was one that brought Munger into conflict with other DFL legislators. Tom Rukavina (DFL-Virginia) has been in the Minnesota Legislature since 1986 and served for six years as a member of Munger's Environment and Natural Resources Committee. Born in Virginia, Rukavina grew up on the city's north side ("It makes a difference," Rukavina notes. "I grew up in a neighborhood surrounded by first generation immigrants"), attending Mesabi Community College and the University of Minnesota-Duluth, obtaining his degree in political science, before returning to Virginia to work at Minntac. Rukavina won a seat on the Virginia School Board, becoming, as he notes, "the youngest person and the first Roman Catholic to ever attain a seat on the board." A run for the legislature followed but, after losing that race, he went to work as a tour guide at Iron World in Chisholm.

"That's where I met Willard," Rukavina recalls. "There was a bus full of legislators touring the place. Of course, I knew who he was. But I hadn't met him. After I gave my talk, Willard came up to me and said 'I know who you are and I like you. You've got a golden tongue. Someday, you're gonna be in the legislature with me.'"

After winning a House seat in the 1986 election, Rukavina settled into his office in the State Office Building in St. Paul. Willard Munger officed just down the hall from the new legislator. The office between Munger and Rukavina was occupied by legendary Iron Range DFLer Joe Begich from Eveleth.

"I've really come full circle," Rep. Rukavina says during a telephone interview. "I'm sitting here in Joe Begich's old office, which is now my office, talking to you. Willard would pass by Begich and stop in to see me nearly every morning. He'd come in for a piece of candy and always lay a quarter or a dime or whatever he had down to pay for what he took. I'd look at him and say, 'Willard, take that money with you. Don't insult Iron Range hospitality by trying to pay for candy.'"

On the subject of how Munger got along with Iron Range DFLers, Rukavina is more kind than critical.

"He and Joe Begich tangled; they differed on things. But they were always the best of friends. Willard didn't hold a grudge. He never let a vote on a bill impact a friendship. He never really got upset. I think that's because he believed in the democratic process, the give and take of positions."

Regarding the oft-related rift between Munger and Irv Anderson, Rukavina downplays the conflict.

"I know Willard wasn't happy about the changes in the Wetlands Act, changing the ratio of replacing wetlands from two to one to one to one. That was Irv's doing and Willard wasn't happy about it. But he supported Irv, I believe, the second time Irv wanted to become Speaker."

Though Rukavina considered Munger to be a mentor, there were times when their differing outlooks on resource management issues placed them in conflict.

"School trust lands were given to the state by the federal government for use as school property," Rep. Rukavina recounts. "Willard was dead set against folks owning those lake lots. Ron Sando of the DNR began a lawsuit over the issue. My position was that my friends and neighbors were going to lose their cabins, cabins that, in some cases, they'd enjoyed for years. Sando's lawsuit ended up forcing these people to put their lakeshore leases up for auction and buy them back from the state. Mrs. Griggs, whose children were friends of mine, had a place on Crane Lake that she lost at auction. There were another 500 – 600 leaseholders that were about to lose their leases. They were afraid, after seeing what happened to Mrs. Griggs, to bid at auction. Willard and those damn environmentalists wanted to preserve the lakeshore but I'd grown up on the Range and I didn't like what was happening. I knew that there were only three ways you could deal with trust fund land: auction it; replace it with other public land of equal value; or condemn it as was done for Voyageurs National Park.

Willard and I were on opposite sides of the issue. I proposed that we trade county tax forfeit land for the leased lakeshore land. The county could then sell the lots to the leaseholders and the proceeds would be used as sort of a mini-environmental trust fund. Willard didn't like my solution. So I had to take him on and beat him twice over the same issue; once in Dee Long's Tax Committee and once on the floor of the House. I saw him before the floor vote and I said, 'Willard, Sando's wrong and you're wrong. I'm going to beat you on the floor. I'd suggest you don't say anything.' He didn't take that too kindly. 'Goddamn you Rukavina,' he said, 'don't you treat me any different than anyone else. Treat me the same asshole-way you treat everyone.'"

Tom Rukavina went on to win that fight but, as he'd previously indicated, the battle never became personal.

"Betty is right," Rep. Rukavina observes, referring to Munger's committee administrator at the time, Betty Goihl. "I did tell Willard that he was the grandfather I'd never had. Of course we disagreed. But Willard was a man ahead of his time. And he never backed down from his beliefs, whether it was on his 'ban the can' deposit bills, the BWCA, or whatever. He never compromised his beliefs but he never held a political disagreement against a person."

Despite the fact that Rukavina is Roman Catholic and Munger was Lutheran, religion wasn't an issue of concern between the men.

"I had lots of discussions with Willard, including discussions about the old FL days, about John Bernard, stories that I can't repeat here. But we didn't talk much about religion or ethnicity, though I got the sense that Willard was fascinated by the ethnic mix of West Duluth. It was something different from his own background and that intrigued him. And he got his fill of Iron Range ethnicity because at one time, all three of us, Begich, Battaglia and I were on his committee together!"

Rukavina echoes what others have said about Munger in two other contexts: Munger's ability to bring home bonding money from St. Paul for Duluth projects and his strong positions on labor issues.

"As much as Willard was an environmentalist," Tom Rukavina says, "he was a strong labor person. Other than the 'ban the can' dispute with labor, he was always on the same side of issues related to working men and women. His belief in the working person was as strong as any of us in the legislature.

And he was a master of bringing bonding money home to his district. I called Sam Solon and Willard the 'Porkers' for the way they always managed to get money for Duluth. The only Duluth project I ever heard him denigrate was the aquarium. He called it the 'goddamn Republican fish tank.' But other than that, he and Sam were always on the bonding committee. It was miraculous how, year after year, Duluth's projects seemed to make it through but Range projects didn't. They'd fight over their priorities—Sam would be looking for money for his projects and Willard would be looking for money for the zoo. But they managed to get what they wanted for Duluth. That changed in 1998 when Rep. Loren Solberg (DFL-Bovey) and Sen. Jerry Janezich (DFL-Chisholm) were on the conference committee. That year, Duluth *and* the Range got all their projects funded."

In keeping with his efforts to preserve the school trust lakeshore lands for public use, Munger also sought to include the upper St. Louis River and its major tributaries, the Cloquet and the Whiteface, in the Minnesota Wild and Scenic River program.

"Willard was truly a man of vision," Dave Zentner recalls. "A good example of this is how, eventually others, even those opposed to his position on an issue, would come to agree with him. That's what happened in Brevator Township. There was an attempt to designate parts of the Cloquet, St. Louis and Whiteface Rivers in St. Louis County wild and scenic. That proposal, one dear to Willard and my hearts, went nowhere. Much of the frontage on these rivers, including the St. Louis River (which flows through Brevator Township northwest of Duluth) was owned by Minnesota Power (MP) and was already open to public use with no cost to the public. Folks living near the river didn't see any reason to add another layer of governmental control to protect something they were already using for free. But then, in the early 1990s, when that same river frontage was posted "for sale" by MP, rumors began to circulate that a developer from the Twin Cities was going to put up condos all up and down the banks of the St. Louis River.

Willard, Alden Lind and I ended up appearing at a packed Brevator Town Hall. The town supervisors sheepishly admitted, 'We thought you guys were ridiculous when you proposed designating the St. Louis River as wild and scenic...Now we see we were wrong.' Willard didn't gloat over this turn-around, but went to work, meeting with MP CEO, Arend "Sandy" Sandbulte to see if MP was interested in selling the land to the state. An agreement was reached and the land was purchased by the state to be held for public use in perpetuity."

Zentner ranks the Minnesota Power land sale as one of the three top achievements of Willard's legislative career, along with the creation of the WLSSD and his efforts to promote recycling and the reduction of solid waste in Minnesota.

John Helland notes that the 22,000 acres of land purchased in the Minnesota Power shoreline preservation deal is the largest real estate transaction ever engaged in by the state of Minnesota. The completion of that agreement was celebrated at Munger's Indian Point home in grand style.

Munger, a Champion for the Environment by Joan Farnham

A celebration marking the successful conclusion of a decades-old fight to protect the St. Louis River ended with a picnic on St. Louis Bay and a cameo appearance by Senator Paul Wellstone…

Willard Munger was the host of the picnic, attended by more than 150 in the backyard of his bayside home. Politicians, judges, bureaucrats, environmentalists, family, friends and lobbyists—all gathered to enjoy each other and Munger's company…Many at the picnic said the celebration marked a milestone for the 86-year-old popular politician whose career spans more than four decades…

"Ever since Willard arrived in Duluth…he's worked to clean up the St. Louis River and protect it," said John Helland…"So yes, I'd say it's a milestone in his career."

But Munger has no intention of sitting back on his laurels and relaxing.

In fact, the man who now holds the record for the longest serving member of the House, is already fighting to do the same thing for northern lakes as he's done for the St. Louis, Cloquet and Whiteface Rivers—keep their shorelines wild.

"I have a bill in the legislature to do that," he said. "On public forest lands in northern Minnesota, there are hundreds of lakes. We should put a public access of 200 feet around those lakes so they can't be developed. They can build back from that if they want…"

Munger might very well win this fight, as he's won so many in the past, through judicious coalition building and legislative savvy.

Munger calls it being bipartisan.

"The only time I'm political is election time…As soon as that's finished, I become bipartisan."

Even during elections, he's willing to let Republicans help out, if they want to, he said, grinning.

Some do. Jerry Anderson, a staunch Republican, worked so hard on Munger's last re-election campaign that Munger refers to him as his campaign manager...

"I've known Willard for years," Anderson said. "He's a humanist. He's personable. He's easy to get along with. There are so many Republicans who can live with his liberal ideas..."

(*Duluth Budgeteer News*, September 14, 1997.)

But the real story of 1997 was that Willard Munger was once again alone. Frances, his wife of thirty-three years, passed away in St. Paul on November 20, 1997 after suffering a stroke. It was another major loss for the old man. And though the connection Willard shared with Frances appeared to be less passionate than the love he openly displayed for Martha, Willard and Frances Munger shared a life of mutual respect that remained strong throughout the three decades they were together.

"Frances's death was hard on Dad," Patsy Munger-Lehr recalls. "Frances was a very smart woman. She was always there for my father. After she had the stroke, she lingered on. Dad had to make the decision to pull the plug. It was the hardest thing he ever did in his life. She never had children but loved and treated my children as her own grandchildren. I know my dad felt guilty about her death. Frances had walked Dad to work at the legislature that morning. Then she went back to their motel room and had a stroke. It was terrible."

Will Munger remembers that, back when he was working in the Twin Cities after college, Frances invited both he and his father to dinner.

"I still remember that night," Will says. "My dad was getting in the car after dinner. Frances was standing at the front door. My dad said 'Oh, I forgot to say goodbye to Frances.' He walked back and I guess he thought I couldn't see him kiss her. But I did. That's when I knew, from that kiss, that there was more than just dinner going on.

"Frances wasn't my mother but she was a good person and good for my dad. Dad loved women. He was in love with my mom. He was married to Frances, I think, for companionship. Still, they got along well and she was always there for him."

Left alone in the big house on Indian Point, 1998 brought with it yet another legislative session for Willard Munger. The new year also provided Will, Jr. an opportunity to highlight his ownership of the Willard Munger Inn.

"I had the motel up for sale and the newspaper guy was supposed to be doing a piece on the motel to help get it sold. That's what I thought was going to happen," Will recalls. "Then the guy asked if Dad could sit in and give some history on the building of the place. Well, you know what happened. My story became Dad's story. The article didn't do a thing to help sell the motel. It ended up being all about Dad!"

Built to Last by Daniel Bernard

The Willard Munger Inn provided Willard Munger, Sr. with a living while he launched a record-long career as a state legislator. Constituents would stop by the Inn's coffee shop on Saturday mornings to talk politics with the elder Munger. In recent years, son Willard Munger, Jr. has run the Inn. Now, the family has put it up for sale.

In 1954, while he was running his first successful campaign for the Minnesota Legislature, Willard Munger also oversaw construction of the motel …

He dug the trenches for the foundation a little too wide for the taste of the city inspector who visited one day. The man looked at how much concrete Munger was pouring into the ground, at the steel rods he intended to lay in as reinforcement. *Extravagance*, he thought…

"Get a contractor," the inspector advised…"He'll save you money."

"I don't care," Munger replied. "I don't want it to settle…I want a strong foundation."

"I've felt that way about everything in life," Munger said…"If you don't have a strong foundation, you're not gonna be successful."

Munger clearly enjoys telling the story. Granted, critics of the DFLer's… liberal politics might view the anecdote as evidence of…tax and spendaholism.

Then again, the Willard Munger Inn is still standing…The same philosophy of durability could make Munger's political career outlast the family business…

Munger's wife of 33 years, Frances, died…Though Munger campaigned in 1996 on the assumption that his current term would be his last, he said last week he couldn't picture himself staying at home.

"I had some problems there with my wife dying," Munger said…"I'm not gonna sit around here. I might as well be in the legislature…rather than sit around and be sad…"

The children once played baseball on the land. The inn … gave the family a living. And its coffee shop became a mini-town hall where Munger's constituents would drop in on Saturday mornings…

"It's sadder'n hell, because my whole life is in this motel, and the store," Munger said, referring to the grocery store-gas station that preceded the motel...

When Munger, Jr. took over for his father, he wanted to rename the business the Willard Munger Trail Inn...The elder Munger vetoed that, saying he was leery of seeming to capitalize on a state-funded resource...

"My dad is a great politician, humanitarian and environmentalist," said Munger..."But I'm the entrepreneur..."

In recent months, the younger Munger removed the coffee counter and turned the space into a lounge...The elder Munger's gaggle of unpaid political consultants has taken to meeting at his house...instead.

The motel's future is anyone's guess...

"There is a little competition, but it has great potential," said the younger Munger. "The population of the Twin Cities keeps growing. There's more and more demand on tourism up here. I think the prognosis of the Inn is good."

(*Duluth News Tribune*, January 5, 1998.)

Willard Munger insisted that any notoriety he attained as a conservationist was achieved with help from others. In 1998, four men who worked together in the Minnesota environmental movement were honored in Duluth. The gathering of Alden Lind, Willard Munger, Gary Glass and John Pegors was providential because, within the span of a few years, all of the men save Glass would pass away.

Four Environmental Pioneers Reminisce by Joan Farnam

Environmental war stories kept everyone engaged at Peace Church... Laughter, chuckles, open mouth amazement, as well as applause...greeted the four environmental pioneers who were honored...Organized by the Lake Superior Alliance...the event featured Rep. Willard Munger...who has been called the father of the environmental movement in Minnesota; Save Lake Superior Association's Alden Lind; internationally-recognized mercury researcher Gary Glass; and former MPCA official John Pegors.

"I remember pulling acid rain stickers off my briefcase when I went to Washington during the Reagan administration," said Glass...Glass was one of the pioneers who got in on the ground floor of water quality research at the EPA..."I took the stickers off so I wouldn't be labeled an environmentalist..."

Lind, who moved to the Northland in the late 1960s, said working on the Reserve Mining case was his first real environmental activist role..."When I got to Duluth, there was already a good healthy effort underway," Lind said. "Once you dip your toe into that kind of activity, you just keep going."

Pegors said that as regional director of the MPCA in Duluth, he was one of the people who led the search for the source of asbestos in Reserve's mine tailings...

Munger said his environmental advocacy began at his grandfather's knee...He has been a strong advocate for a number of environmental issues over the years, but one of his proudest victories is the establishment of statewide sanitary sewer district systems, including the WLSSD...

> "When I got to Duluth [from Fergus Falls in 1935], the first thing I wanted to do was go fishing," he said. "I was told you can't go fishing in the river. It's too polluted. I didn't believe it until I saw it. This is one of the reasons I became active..."
>
> (*Duluth Budgeteer News*, September 31, 1998.)

As Willard Munger indicated in the "Built to Last" interview, the death of Frances caused him to re-think his retirement plans. After months of contemplation, Munger decided to file for what would turn out to be his last election.

CHAPTER 12

Elegy

The 1998 state-wide elections involved startling upsets and changes in the balance of power in Minnesota. Former Democrat and St. Paul Mayor Norm Coleman ran for governor as a Republican against his one-time mentor and boss, DFL Attorney General Hubert "Skip" Humphrey, III. Professional wrestler and actor Jesse "The Body" Ventura (whose sole previous foray into politics had been as a part-time suburban mayor) also threw his hat in the gubernatorial ring as the Reform Party candidate.

Willard Munger was challenged by Republican Alan Kehr in District 7A. Despite Willard's age (he was nearly 88 years old) the *Duluth News Tribune* endorsed Munger for a twenty-second term in the Minnesota House.

On November 4, 1998, the day after Election Day, the *Duluth News Tribune* headline read: BODY SLAM. VENTURA: 'WE SHOCKED THE WORLD.' Norm Coleman finished a distant second to Jesse Ventura. But unlike Skip Humphrey, whose political career ended with his third-place finish in the 1998 governor's race, Norm Coleman would resurface four years later to challenge Senator Paul Wellstone for Wellstone's seat in the U.S. Senate.

Though Munger handled Kehr's challenge with little difficulty (Munger, 7,952 or 67%; Kehr, 3,893 or 33%), the 1999 legislative session was disappointing for Munger and the DFL. For the first time since 1985, the Republicans were in control of the Minnesota House of Representatives. Conservative control meant that Munger, the House member with the most seniority, was no longer chairman of the House Environment and Natural Resources Committee. With the Republicans in control of the House, the Democrats in control of the Senate, and the governor's chair occupied by a Reform Party adherent, the triangulation of Minnesota governance spelled doom for any important environmental legislation. This major change in the way Minnesota was governed was compounded, in terms of environmental and conservation legislation, by the onset of the dehabilitating illness which afflicted Munger in February of 1999.

Mike Jaros recalls that immediately after the election Munger seemed out-of-sorts.

"I chalked it up to a winter cold and the fact that we were both extremely depressed that we'd lost control of the House," Mike recalls. "By the time the session started, Willard seemed his old self—the cold was gone. But then, when we were living next door to each other in the Kelly Inn in St. Paul, I noticed he was feeling poorly. I think he didn't want to go to the doctor because he was afraid of what he was going to find out."

"I think," Will Munger, Jr. reflects, "that Dad knew what was going on even before he was diagnosed. I remember him leaving the toilet unflushed. He was trying to tell me something wasn't right. It's disgusting to say this, but it's true. But I didn't take the hint, didn't know what the black stools meant. And he was in such pain when he walked. I had to literally push him up stairs. But, as proud a man as he was, he never said anything."

Patsy Munger-Lehr remembers watching her father's health decline.

"I was driving him down to the Twin Cities," Patsy recalls, "to House sessions. My husband Harvey had died. I started coming back home, staying with Dad on Indian Point. He started looking real tired, real bad the weekend before he had his episode in the legislature."

John Helland recalls that Munger hid his health problems from his staff.

"I didn't realize how sick he was," Helland recounts, "until he collapsed."

Harry Munger, Jr., doesn't recall how he found out that his brother was ill.

"He wasn't one to go to doctors much," Harry observes. "Patsy would make him go when he needed to."

Despite Willard Munger's failing health, Munger remained interested in environmental issues. As a member of the House Environment and Natural resources Committee, Munger was active in scrutinizing the proposed expansion of Northshore Mining in Silver Bay. The old Reserve Mining plant, which had gone through bankruptcy and re-emerged under new ownership, was seeking to directly reduce taconite ore into pig iron. This proposal alarmed Munger's environmentalist friends.

> January 25, 1999
>
> Dear Brett:
>
> I have been slowly acquiring the sense that I'm not getting very far very fast
> on the North Shore Mining matter. Let me, therefore, pick up the pace...

[I] believe the potential effects of DRI pig iron production on the region are such as to require a full-fledged EIS [Environmental Impact Statement]...Take careful note of Section 303...of the Clean Water Act. We are rapidly approaching the day when we will need to consider rationing the right to emit and/or discharge pollutants into the air, soil and waters of the planet. It would be well for Minnesota to be in the forefront in considering that prospect.

Yours truly,

Alden Lind

CC: Willard Munger

Munger also remained dedicated to educating children about the environment. Munger's Personal Collection contains a proposal for the construction of an environmental learning center at Stowe Elementary School in the Gary-New Duluth neighborhood of Duluth. Stowe was already providing after-school environmental learning opportunities, and had, in 1997, won the Governor's Award for Excellence in Pollution Prevention. The school sits on a 40-acre parcel which Munger believed would easily accommodate an environmental learning center. The project, a favorite of Munger's, was supported by community members and educators and appears to be one of the last initiatives the legislator was working on before his death. It seems a perfect legacy, this work on behalf of an environmental learning center, a concept which combines two of Willard Munger's most passionate issues; public education and environmental stewardship.

In late February, the public learned that Willard Munger was seriously ill.

Munger Taken to Hospital

State Rep. Willard Munger...was hospitalized and reported in good condition after briefly losing his ability to speak. The 88-year-old was held overnight for evaluation at Regions Hospital in St. Paul...

The concern that rippled through the political community was a reflection of both Munger's advanced age and of his stature as the most influential architect of the state's environmental policies.

Munger...had complained of fatigue in recent weeks during his daily walks from his office to the nearby capitol. Wednesday, while interviewing with two researchers from the Minnesota History Center, he became unable to speak...

(*Duluth News Tribune*, February 11, 1999.)

The prognosis wasn't good.

"When the bad news came," Mike Jaros remembers, "I went to the hospital. I was there to watch the surgery on closed circuit television with Will, Patsy and other family members. It was a long operation that started in the morning and didn't end until eight at night. I thought the doctor said, 'The operation went well,' meaning, they'd gotten all the cancer. Turns out, I didn't hear the doctor right. I guess there was more."

"We knew," Patsy Munger-Lehr recalls, "right then, after the colon surgery that it had spread to the liver. But Dad didn't want anyone to know. It was apparent what was going to happen. Dad was realistic about it. I was trying to talk him into building a garage down on Indian Point. He said to me, in the middle of all of his medical turmoil, 'Patsy, we're not building a garage. Only Republicans have garages.'"

"I was so proud of him," Patsy continues, breaking down into tears. "Here he is, 88 years old, and he knew what was happening but he took the chemotherapy anyway. He took the chemo and went back to work in the House on his little electric cart. The doctor had me work with him on exercises after the surgery. Dad did everything I asked of him. He did all he could to beat it. But he couldn't."

Mike Jaros marveled that, throughout the chemotherapy sessions, Munger maintained his pride.

"He never lost his hair," Jaros says through a smile. "That was always a mystery to me; Willard's hair. Even when we shared a hotel room together during sessions, I couldn't break him. He vehemently denied that he colored his hair. But I was suspicious. I mean, he had different shades of black that he'd use. It was a little, harmless fib, the 'I don't dye my hair' line. But I never broke him," Jaros says with a laugh, "and I never caught him red-handed either. His hair color was a private thing, something he didn't want the public to know.

"Willard returned to the House after surgery and remained at work while undergoing chemo. He made the general floor sessions, though I don't think he made any committee meetings. He worked in his office. He managed to spend time in the House and at his office until the end of the session. He was living with Patsy. We didn't talk about the progress of his illness. I had this feeling that he'd beat the thing; that he'd survive. Even though I had been through seminary, we didn't talk about the religious aspects of his situation."

Jaros recounts that, over the years, he and Munger had discussed Munger's irregular church attendance.

"Mostly what he and I talked about on our rides from Duluth to St. Paul and back were the old days. But once in a while we'd get more serious and talk religion.

He was always frank and admitted he didn't have much use for established religion. He sort of apologized, felt it was a failing. He'd say, 'I haven't gone to church much…' And I'd respond, 'Willard, you really don't have to. Your actions speak for you. Remember what Jesus said, 'they'll know you by what you've done.'"

The extent of Munger's illness was not immediately revealed to the public.

Munger Stable After Surgery by Daniel Bernard

State Rep. Willard Munger was in stable condition Wednesday evening after surgeons successfully removed a cancerous growth from his colon. Doctors believe they removed all cancerous tissue and predicted the 88-year-old DFLer from Duluth would recover fully and return to work in the legislature…

"It was very localized. They think he's going to do well," said Pat Motherway, spokesman for Regions Hospital…

Munger's daughter, Pat Lehr, said the rest depends on his legendary tenacity…Lehr was part of a crowd of Munger's relatives that waited at the hospital during surgery, including grandchildren, brother Harry Munger, son Will Munger, and their spouses…

The growth was small, but the colonectomy procedure…called for removing a relatively large section of the intestine containing the diseased portion and then reconnecting the two healthy parts of the intestine.

Before surgery, Munger was strong but cranky because surgeons hadn't allowed him to eat or drink since Tuesday.

"He said he'd give half of Minnesota for a glass of good water," [Betty] Goihl [his committee administrator] said.

(*Duluth News Tribune*, February 18, 1999.)

In some ways, Willard Munger's last days mirrored those of his hero, Floyd B. Olson. The major difference in the two situations was that, while Olson may have *suspected* his cancer was terminal, he was never *told* the true extent of his illness. In Munger's case, no one sugar-coated the truth. While both men exhibited raw defiance and courage in the way they met their fates, Munger knew much more about the intricacies of the disease that was taking his life. Despite this knowledge, Munger kept up appearances.

Munger Back to Work in Mid-March

Optimism abounded Thursday as…Rep. Willard Munger…continued to recover from surgery Wednesday evening that removed a cancerous tumor from his large intestine.

Munger's family expects him to be back in action in the legislature by mid-March and Munger was booking fishing trips. While he rested in the intensive care unit of Regions Hospital…Munger invited the surgeon, anesthetist and oncologist to come fishing with him in northern Minnesota when he recovers.

"The anesthetist said he thought [Munger] was a tough old bird," said Betty Goihl, Munger's legislative assistant.

(*Duluth News Tribune*, February 1999.)

Willard Munger also refused to concede that his 22nd term would be his last.

"Those same punks, the ones who thought Willard too old to hold office," Mike Jaros remembers, "were always threatening to run against the 'old man.' I kept them away—'this old man is more Liberal, more progressive than any of you young guys'—I meant that. Willard stayed current—he had old fashioned values and ways of doing things—but he accepted change. I saw him in the office learning to use a computer when they came in during the early 1990s—when I was refusing to learn how to use one!"

Despite Mike Jaros running point for the old man, potential replacements for Munger began to surface.

Would-be successors to the District 7A House seat representing West Duluth have been waiting for years for Munger to retire. His statements…indicated he will keep them guessing. The aspirant closest to running is former Superior Mayor Herb Bergson. Bergson formed a campaign fund-raising committee in late January with $100 of his own money but said he ceased fund raising after Munger was hospitalized….

"Under no circumstances would I run against Willard. I respect him too much," Bergson said. "I need to start raising money in case Willard decides to retire and I do run…But if he decides not to retire, maybe it'll be for 2002, or 2004."

(*Duluth News Tribune*, February 27, 1999.)

Bergson stood by his promise and did not seek Munger's seat. (*Editor's Note: The former mayor of Superior would run for mayor of Duluth, losing to incumbent Mayor Gary Doty. Bergson would then win a seat on the Duluth City Council. He later defeated businessman Charlie Bell in the 2003 mayor's race, becoming the first man in history to be elected mayor of both Superior, Wisconsin and Duluth, Minnesota.*)

Despite his dire situation, Munger never lost his legendary sense of humor.

It's Only Natural Munger is Upset with the Law by **Doug Grow**

Father Nature was not in a good mood.

"It's going to be like going back to the robin's nest after the crows have eaten the eggs," he muttered.

Father Nature, also known as Rep. Willard Munger...has been recuperating at his daughter's home...

On Feb. 12, Munger...was visiting in his office with a couple of people from Norway. Suddenly, he was unable to speak. The words would form in his brain, but when he moved his lips, nothing would happen. He was rushed to a St. Paul hospital...

Munger blames himself...He'd been getting weaker over the past six months, he said, but he kept putting off seeing a doctor. He tried to keep his increasing weakness from himself, his friends, and his legislative colleagues.

"I'd walk from the Capitol to the State Office Building," he said. "One day a Republican caught up with me and said, 'Willard, I'll walk with you.' He went slow, but I couldn't keep up and I'd say, 'You go ahead. I have to stop here and wait for somebody.' Stupid. Can you find anybody—Democrat or Republican—who is so stupid they'll put their job ahead of their own health?..."

These days, his daughter insists that Munger use a walker, which he despises...

His daughter sees no problem with the walker. Father does.

"I'm not using this," he grumped...

"He wants to use a stick," said [his daughter] Pat.

"I want a walking stick that's about a foot higher than my head," Father Nature said.

"I think he wants to be Moses," Pat said.

Both laughed.

But the one thing that's certain is that Munger wants to get back as soon as possible. He fears that his life's work is continuing to be undone...

"I've got to get back before they give the state away..."

(*Minneapolis Star*-Tribune, March 8, 1999.)

With Libertarian Jesse Ventura in the governor's seat, Munger wasn't optimistic he had the strength (or the votes) to defeat the "property rights" movement, a movement that had been growing in strength since the Reagan years of federal deregulation. Even still, Willard Munger did have an ally within the Ventura camp.

Munger Working on Ventura's Team by Daniel Bernard

Gov. Jesse Ventura, who loves to say how much he despises...career politicians, would seem to have little in common with someone like State Rep.
Willard Munger...

Yet it's a little known fact in the state Capitol that Ventura and Munger are
working on the same team.

Julie Munger, that is.

Munger, the 23-year-old granddaughter of the Duluth legislator, works
on Ventura's communications staff. She's one of five people who respond to
citizens who write or call the governor...

Munger said her left-leaning ideology was a source of amusement for the
governor when they met at a staff meeting last week.

After giving his stands on the issues, Ventura turned the tables and asked
his staff whether cities should be able to hold gun makers liable in court...

Only Munger said cities should be able to sue...

"He said, 'Oh Jeez, Rachel [Wobschall, Munger's boss], you've got a tough
job ahead of you. You've got a bleeding heart working for me,'" Ventura
said...

Rep. Willard Munger says he's not disturbed to see Julie working for a
Reform Party member. The legislature's oldest member notes he first ran on
the Farmer-Labor ticket before the third party was absorbed by the Democrats...

(*Duluth News Tribune*, March 11, 1999.)

Shortly after this glib piece appeared, the public was made aware of the true extent
of Willard Munger's illness.

Munger's Cancer Spreads to Liver **by Daniel Bernard**

State Rep. Willard Munger's cancer has spread to his liver...and the...leg-
islator has decided to begin chemotherapy treatment March 22.

His family was deeply shaken by the news, but Munger reacted with determination.

"'When can I start chemotherapy?' is the first thing he said," his daughter,
Pat Munger-Lehr said. "My dad is not going to give up that easily. He said, 'I
have one choice,' and he said, 'that's to take chemotherapy...'"

Doctors told the family that the cancer could prove to be slow-growing,
allowing Munger several years of life...

"[R]ight now, this is hard," said Munger-Lehr, who has been caring for her
father at her Minnetonka home...

"With his age and life expectancy, the doctors said chances are he would die of some natural cause before the cancer would ever kill him," said son Will Munger, Jr. "But anytime you have cancer, you worry about it...Some people will say 'Why even take chemotherapy?' He wants to do that," Will Munger said. "I think he thinks he's got a long time to be here yet..."

Even on Friday, Munger-Lehr would not rule out the possibility of her father running for another two-year term in fall 2000...

"Right now, Dad is not feeling top-notch," Munger-Lehr said. "He's tired. He's had reporters visiting. He's 88 years old..."

Although it may not prove practical, Munger wants to consider dropping into the Capitol for a few hours late next week, aided by a wooden cane made for him by Rep. Harry Mares (IR-White Bear Lake).

"You know what he said to the oncologist today? 'I'll see you at my canoe party in June,'" Munger-Lehr said. "I'm optimistic that he will do well with the chemo," she said of her father. "I know he's going to fight hard. He's a fighter."

(*Duluth News Tribune*, March 13, 1999.)

Munger's recovery from surgery took longer than expected.

Others to Fill in for Munger on Panels

State Rep. Willard Munger...still has high hopes of returning to work soon after beginning chemotherapy treatments for liver cancer...but the 88-year-old legislator has asked fellow Democrats to fill in for him on a temporary basis on his legislative committees...

Munger said he hopes to attend sessions of the full House as soon as next week...

"I feel real good. I'm not going to wrestle with you, but I think it's remarkable the way I've shot back," Munger said...

(*Duluth News Tribune*, March 26, 1999.)

Though Willard Munger never returned to his beloved Environment and Natural Resources Committee, he found his way, "big stick" and all, back onto the floor of the Minnesota House of Representatives.

Munger Returns to House Floor

As Rep. Willard Munger returned Monday to the legislative chamber...the political legend was revealed to be a mere mortal.

The 88-year-old...DFLer moved slowly with the help of a walking stick and his children's arms. Although he sassed the whole House in his brief address...his voice was occasionally raspy and faint.

"I've been watching you people on TV for a month. That's long enough," Munger teased…

His colleagues cheered the return of a figure who has become the institution's wise-man and mascot.

"In 16 years, I've never known anyone that's shown more guts…and—what's the word that begins with C?—chutzpah," said Rep. Dave Bishop, R-Rochester. "I've got so many things to say about Willard Munger that I'm blocked…"

[M]unger hopes to attend sessions of the full House as soon and as often as possible…

"We'll see what the chemotherapy does," Munger told a reporter. "If chemo doesn't work, I'll have to consider what I'll have to do with my seat…"

Despite warm words from both sides of the aisle, Monday's session was less than comforting…While Munger sat silently, a strong majority voted to repeal the Twin Cities' vehicle emissions testing program.

"It does discourage me but it doesn't discourage me to the point where I'm gonna give up," Munger said…

Munger said that until he dies, "I want to keep on going the same direction I've been going for the last sixty years. I don't intend to change now…"

(*Duluth News Tribune*, March 30, 1999.)

Speaker of the House Steve Sviggum expressed admiration for the chamber's oldest legislator.

Munger Gets a Hearty Welcome

[A]lmost seven weeks after being hospitalized…Rep. Willard Munger returned to the state House…Aided by a walking stick; Munger was the first representative to arrive and took his place in the seat at the back of the House…

"It's beautiful," the Duluth DFLer said. "It feels great. It isn't any fun staying at home…"

"It's great to have you with us," House Speaker Steve Sviggum said, greeting Munger at his desk. "This is where you belong."

(*St. Paul Pioneer Press*, March 30, 1999.)

Betty Goihl acknowledges that Munger's stubbornness met its limit in fighting cancer.

"I drove out to see him at Patsy's with Alice Hausman. Patsy told me that she was sleeping in the same bed with him to make sure he slept through the night and got up when he needed to. She made sure he was dressed well, so that when he made it back to the House sessions, he was in a suit and tie. He also told me," Goihl remembers, "that he'd never use one of those electric carts. He ended up having to use one but he didn't want folks to know. So he had me take it down the elevator for him. Then he'd ride it to the House but he insisted upon walking to his desk through the side entrance. It worried me because even over that small distance, he wasn't very stable. People could tell he was suffering and it was very difficult to watch."

Even in the throes of a fatal illness, Munger took the time to educate the new governor about conservation issues.

> April 12, 1999
>
> Dear Governor Ventura:
>
> There is an important issue before us on which I'd like to comment.
>
> In 1930, 1931 and 1933, the people of Minnesota bailed out a few northwestern Minnesota counties who invested in huge peat wetland drainage projects. The people of Minnesota paid millions of dollars to assume the ditch bonds of five northwestern Minnesota counties...
>
> Because these consolidated conservation lands ("con-con" lands) were paid for by all the people of Minnesota, they became the property of all the people...The con-con lands were managed by the...DNR...
>
> When I was elected to the legislature in 1954, the state was paying off these ditch bonds. Years later, I remember flying over the same area and still being able to see the many, many ditches criss-crossing the land.
>
> In 1991, former DNR Commissioner Joe Alexander dedicated 104,000 acres of the con-con lands as wildlife management area to be managed by the DNR's Fish and Wildlife Divisions...
>
> At the end of his tenure this past January, former DNR Commissioner Rod Sando had the courage...to issue a commissioner's order to designate the remaining 175,000 acres of con-con land for public use and wildlife habitat...
>
> Shortly after...Sando left...Acting Commissioner Ray Hitchcock put a six-month hold on the Order...Commissioner Garber has now arranged for meetings to discuss the future of these con-con lands.
>
> In the meantime, the five counties want a more direct solution. They want to buy it back... [T]hey have visions of privatization—exclusive hunting preserves, ATV recreation areas and other enterprises—without regard for flood prevention, water table stability, plant and wildlife protection and natural resource management.

Rep. Irv Anderson has introduced H.F. 1412 which would rescind the commissioner's order...

As you know, I've been ill and recovering at a distance...Here I have been able to take a broader view of matters and can see the property rights movement take hold. I am amused at the flip flops that members advocate for first, state control, then, local control, and then back to state control...

For the past 70 years, I have consistently supported education, social and economic justice and protection of the state's natural resources for the good of the whole.

I view HF 1412...to be an affront to all that I have worked for over the years. I would respectfully request that you veto these proposals in whatever form they appear before you.

Sincerely,

Willard Munger

(Willard Munger Personal Collection.)

Journalists sought Munger out for retrospective interviews.

Willard Munger's Long Walk by Daniel Bernard

Willard Munger walks haltingly to his seat in the Minnesota House of Representatives... carrying an 88-year-old body that has been drained by cancer...He lowers himself into his seat, too tired to speak even when his own amendment is under attack...

At 43, he entered the legislature and began to fulfill his grandfather's marching orders to protect both the environment and the state's working people. His ideas were consistently ahead of the environmental awareness of the nation...

"He is one of the only visionaries we have ever had," said Rep. Bob Milbert, DFL-So. St. Paul. "He was looking a generation ahead-not five years or ten years..."

Munger...was one of a few northern lawmakers to support federal control of land in the region, such as the Boundary Waters and Voyageurs National Park. Munger wanted even more, such as federal protections for more rivers, but northern politicians blocked those efforts. Rep. Irv Anderson (DFL-International Falls) says Munger's faith in federal control of wilderness was long out of step with most northern Minnesotans...

Rep. Tom Osthoff, DFL-St. Paul, said Munger's longtime strategy was to introduce an extreme bill and hold his tongue as the bill was watered down...But during the conference committee at the end of the process, he would call in his markers to get the bill restored…"It took people a while to figure out that Willard didn't care what you did to his bill as long as you kept it alive," Osthoff said…

And Munger remained and remained. He would sometimes co-opt a potential election challenger by telling the person he was grooming him as his hand-picked successor-then years would pass, said Randy Asunma, a former Munger campaigner who said he got that line himself…

In January, Republicans took over the House and began undoing a passel of environmental regulations Munger had helped install. The next month, Munger experienced a series of health problems that reduced him to watching House proceedings on cable television…He says he would rather struggle to the House floor than relax at home. "I wasn't built that way. I couldn't pull myself away from what I've been doing for 70 years. Not gonna change after 70 years…When I leave here, I want to leave the environmental structure and the economic and social structure as good as I had it for future generations…"

Ann Glumac, Munger's committee administrator in the late '80s, said some politicians have given Munger short shrift in his old age…"I see people underestimate Willard…," Glumac said. "But I also think that they're fools. He kind of goes along in his own steady way and he gets pretty much what he wants."

"He is in this for all the right reasons," Rep. Osthoff said. "He brings dignity to all of us."

(*Duluth News Tribune*, May 2, 1999.)

The *News Tribune* also profiled Munger's achievements. Much was left out in that the listing didn't include Munger's work on behalf of Minnesota's K-12 school children, the University of Minnesota-Duluth, the Lake Superior Zoo, the Port of Duluth and many other non-environmental causes Munger championed over his 43 years in the House. Still, the list is impressive.

Munger Synonymous with Environmental Protection

Willard Munger's advocates say that it isn't how long the legislator served or how old he was…but what he accomplished while he was in office…

DDT

[M]unger, later calling it his toughest fight ever in the House, successfully passed a DDT ban. But the bill died in the Senate…

Sewage

"Before the WLSSD, you could walk across [the St. Louis River in Duluth]. Now you can swim across it..." The river, although still in the process of cleaning itself, is considered to have made a remarkable recovery. It's now a prime fishing spot in the region...

Wild and Scenic Rivers Act

Patterned after a 1968 federal initiative, this law....allowed the DNR to restrict or prohibit development on sections of streams to prevent ecological damage...

Bicycle Trails

[T]he idea of the state building long-distance bike trails was resisted. Munger pushed hard...The trails are now considered an integral tourism element and an important recreational opportunity...

Environmental and Natural Resources Trust Fund

When Minnesota voters legalized a lottery in 1988, it was in part because they knew some of the profits would go to clean up the environment. In 1990, Munger...won...approval...to require a profit split for environmental projects. The trust fund gets 40% of lottery profits...When the lottery flow...was set to end...Munger pushed for a second...referendum...[in the fall of 1998] that renewed the arrangement for another 27 years. Among 46 lotteries in North America, only Colorado puts such a priority on the environment and outdoors projects.

Minnesota Power Plant Siting Act

This act...require(s) the state to certify the need and the company to suggest alternative [power plant] sites, with the state holding public hearings in each case, and the state picking the ultimate plant location...

Minnesota Energy Conservation Act

Munger's...legislation require(s) energy-efficiency labels on appliances sold in Minnesota, prefiguring a federal requirement...

Groundwater Protection Act

This...law restrict(s) the use of some pesticides and fertilizers to prevent the contamination of underground drinking-water sources...The bill also looked to find and close old wells that allowed contaminants to flow freely into the aquifer...

Recycling

[The]...act subsidize(s) recycling programs by imposing a fee on garbage collection...The...act helped push recycling into everyday life, allowing most

Minnesotans access to curbside or nearby recycling services and creating an industry for recycled products...

Wetlands Protection

Munger was the impetus behind one of the most comprehensive wetlands protection laws in the nation...(F)armers, developers and rural lawmakers... worked to relax the law to allow more development...The crux of the bill remains intact...and Munger's effort is ...saving wetlands from being drained and filled for subdivisions and corn...

St. Louis River Land Purchase

Munger joined a host of local officials to celebrate the ...purchase of 22,600 acres of land along the St. Louis, Whiteface and Cloquet Rivers...In its largest single land purchase ever, the state got 150 miles of pristine shoreline for about $4.2 million from Minnesota Power. The utility had decided to sell it to developers. Munger pushed to have the state buy the land to keep it undeveloped.

(*Duluth News Tribune*, May 2, 1999.)

Old friends also contacted the ailing legislator.

May 5, 1999

Dear Willard-Greetings.

How are you doing? We know you have been hospitalized in and out. The *Journal* kept tabs on you so we know–but now I don't. Are you OK now? I trust you are back on you cherished job...

I imagine you know Harvey died 5 years ago...I lived on by the lake for 2 years. Then I sold out and came to Fergus. I live in an apartment here with 100 others about my age. I'm 85. So we get along great. Old people can be quite wonderful...

I came across this letter from 1981—from you! What an interesting letter!...Also in the same package was pages out of my memory book...This large page was marked off so 4 friends wrote on each side. I suppose you remember them...Everyone in our Social Science class remarked about "the politician" who argued. Everyone...remarked about "they would never forget" the famous Social Studies class and the debates! I don't remember too much of what was said but I remember "Munger stood his ground." And like you say in your letter..."Mr. Wilson gave us the liberty to express our beliefs..."

Are you the only Munger boy left? I really appreciated the 1981 letter, Willard. I hope you enjoy reading it again.

Old Friend,

Myrtle [Kenyon]

The following is Munger's earlier letter to Mrs. Kenyon.

May 18, 1981

Dear Myrtle:

I am amazed at the keen insight you still have in recalling our political activities which happened some 50 years ago. But it is more important to know that our political philosophy has stood the test of time and that most of the social and political changes we fought for have now become a reality.

Our purpose, back some 50 years ago, to uplift the economic, social status of the poor and forgotten, has not been in vain. We are making progress, but not altogether satisfactory in the environmental field. We are more aware of the problems but we have much work left…

We have lived in a very special time…No one in the…future will ever again witness the radical changes from horse and buggy to high technology…

With the change comes the responsibility to preserve and protect this old earth's fragile environment made not with the hands of man but developed by a greater power in the universe…

It's often frustrating to find those in church on Sunday thanking God for all these blessings bestowed upon us and then find these same people the rest of the week condemning environmentalists…

We were fortunate to grow up in a diversified area such as found in Friberg Township—one half "hill billy" country of forest, lakes and streams, and the southern half with its prime agricultural land…My grandfather homesteaded the land and was an average family-type farmer with 160 acres but he sure loved his woods and outdoors more than farming. He was a great philosopher, a naturalist and liberal in his political thinking…

It's Environmental Awareness Day, April 23, 1981, and I'm at my desk in the House… where I have served the last twenty-five and one-half years…As I write this letter, I recall your brother Marvin and the good people of Friberg Township who were always in support of those ideals…At this time, I'm not quite sure how successful those efforts have been…

The problem we face in the legislature is that too many members lack the convictions, courage and dedicated commitment needed to enhance those ideals for which you, the people of Friberg Township and my grandfather so strongly believed is necessary…

The changing world is now so complex that we can no longer afford to have the environmental and economic policies of this nation determined by those possessed with a horse and buggy…mentality…

I was so pleased with your interesting letter regarding our high school years that I have placed it in a walnut frame which hangs in my office…(By the way, I made the walnut frame myself!)…

Your friend,

Willard M. Munger

(Willard Munger Personal Collection.)

Munger's last address to the House was delivered on May 11, 1999.

I was less than ten years old when my friends and I opened the door to the inner sanctum of a beautiful tamarack swamp…Walking across the foot-thick, spongy moss carpet, we seated ourselves on a soft moss-cushioned log. We sat there in total silence under the lofty ceiling of the tamarack trees.

Even though the floor was covered with exotic wild flowers, tall ferns and pitcher plants, the beautiful lady slipper out shined them all. The birds singing back and forth, the sun's rays peeking through the dense green foliage, and the pink lady slippers all around, created an enclosure that looked like a ballroom-Nature's own ballroom.

The Great Architect of the Universe drafted this earthly paradise. The environment's delicate, fragile life-supporting ecosystem gave us this natural ballroom. I shall never forget the experience.

Several years later, after graduating from high school, I returned to look at my pink lady slippers.

As I approached, I heard a crow calling from his perch atop a dead tamarack tree. The crow seemed to be warning me: "The ballroom and its dancing pink lady slippers are gone…forever." The swamp had been drained.

One of the greatest disappointments of my life has been the disregard I've observed of our natural resources. There's been overuse and abuse of our land, air, water, forests, and wetlands. Short-term goals have often won out over long-term sustainable policies…

We cut our forests…

We have polluted our own nest—the environment, with wastes and toxic chemicals.

We have drained 90% of our wetlands, including the disastrous missteps in tiling hundreds of acres of northwestern Minnesota…

Environmental progress has been made over the years. Through legislation, we've created sanitary districts…We've attempted to reduce packaging and …ban DDT…We've adopted numerous pollution control remedies and prevention measures. We passed the Groundwater Protection Act, the Environment and Natural Resources Trust Fund, solid waste recycling…and the Wetland Conservation Act.

But this year, we're backsliding. Rep. Betty McCollum and I introduced an amendment…to fund research so that the study of deformed frogs…could continue. It was defeated by the Republican Majority. This is a good indication of just what the 1999 legislative session has been like for the environment. It's a losing battle when we don't care about why there are deformed frogs, the best indicators of how well our fragile, delicate, life-supporting ecosystem is doing…

For more than 70 years, my philosophy has not changed. Sustainable use of our natural resources creates social and economic benefits. Short-term, selfish motives reap their own social, economic and environmental rewards.

Far from being out of touch, this philosophy has only become more relevant as we march toward the new millennium.

We may be replaceable, but our great natural heritage, handed down to us for all to use and enjoy, must be protected and preserved for future generations…

(Willard Munger Personal Collection.)

Munger's final message to his colleagues may be the purest expression of what Willard Munger knew, experienced and stood for. In many respects, the words form an elegy to Munger and to his life's work. Despite desperate health, Munger made nearly all the floor votes during the 1999 session. And though he was unable to vote on the 1999 tax bill, his parting "shot" to House members supporting the tax bill was vintage Willard.

Long-time Legislator Leaves Before Tax Vote

Despite colon cancer surgery, despite liver cancer, despite chemotherapy, 88-year-old Willard Munger was able to complete his 43rd session as representative…though he left during the evening recess…

Until the tax bill was tabled before the recess, Munger had planned to end his session by voting against it.

"I think the tax bill is very attractive to the average legislator because it's a two-year endowment on re-election…"

(*Duluth News Tribune*, May 18, 1999.)

Munger's vagueness as to his political plans didn't deter the "young punks" from announcing their intentions.

Swapinski to Run for House Seat

Amid expectations that ailing legislator Willard Munger will not seek re-election in 2000...Duluth City Councilor Dale Swapinski says he is prepared to step in.

"If the opportunity arises where Willard decides he can no longer serve...I am going to run," Swapinski said... "I don't care who else files."

Meanwhile, former Superior Mayor Herb Bergson, Jr., said...he decided against running ...Citing a desire to remain near his sons, ages 10 and 12, Bergson...said he may instead run for an at-large seat on the City Council this fall.

Brad Bennett...a former Duluth School Board member has considered running in 2000 since he lost to Munger as an Independent in 1996.

(*Duluth News Tribune*, May 14, 1999.)

As the political vultures gathered, Munger was confronted by reality.

Munger Suffers Setback, Returns to Hospital by Daniel Bernard

Fatigue and a high fever sent State Rep. Willard Munger back to the hospital early Monday in what doctors called a complication of his chemotherapy...But the stubborn legislator is expected to be released today and was determined to return to duty in the House...

Weakened by a round of chemotherapy...the 88-year-old legislator nevertheless attended the seven House floor sessions since April 6. Munger rode a motorized cart to the House floor and stayed for an average of four hours each time...

"I probably over did it," Munger said.

Munger was susceptible to infection because of a drop in white blood cells that is common during chemotherapy...Late Sunday, with Munger running a fever of 102 degrees at his daughter's Minnetonka home, she called an ambulance that took him to Abbott [Northwestern Hospital]...

Munger's white blood cell count was recovering with medication, said his daughter, Pat Munger-Lehr. His doctor advised that he should return to the House if he feels up to it, Munger-Lehr said.

"That's what we're going to strive for," she said.

During his appearances on the House floor...Munger's fatigue was apparent. After briefly presenting a minor bill to the body on April 6, he remained seated and silent, his eyes occasionally drooping.

Munger-Lehr, who has acted as Munger's caretaker...said she feels obligated to respect her father's wish to return to duty even if it could sap his strength.

"Dad is such a strong person. He wants to continue to do his job in the worst way...Here's his daughter trying to keep him healthy (but) all this man wants to do is work. If he does wear himself out, that's his choice," she added. "If he wants to do it, my car is ready and raring to go."

(*Duluth News Tribune*, May 27, 1999.)

By Memorial Day, the news was public. Willard Munger was dying.

Munger's Cancer Not in Remission by Daniel Bernard

Chemotherapy has stabilized Rep. Willard Munger's liver cancer but has not reversed it, the Duluth legislator and his family learned Friday.

Now, Munger must decide whether to continue the treatments—which have so fatigued him that he was admitted to a Minneapolis hospital Thursday night—or let the cancer run its fatal course.

Munger, 88, was to spend Memorial Day weekend in Abbot Northwestern Hospital... making that decision. He had already made up his mind about one thing: He's coming home.

"He wants to go back to Duluth because that's his favorite place to be in the whole world," said his son, Will Munger, Jr.

The results from CT scan tests were revealed Friday. They showed the cancerous portion of Munger's liver was about the same size as measured in mid-February...

Fatigue and other side effects of chemotherapy sent Munger to Abbott on April 19. That happened again late Thursday, when Munger's home health aide was concerned about his fatigue and a high white-blood-cell-count...

Will Munger said his father was receiving antibiotics...The family hoped he would be released Monday or Tuesday and would return home...

"He hasn't made up his mind what he's going to do now," Will Munger said. "He's doing as well as can be expected for somebody that's 88-years-old and who's got cancer."

(*Duluth News Tribune*, May 29, 1999.)

One gets the sense that Will Munger, Jr. was slowly realizing that his father wasn't going to be miraculously healed. Before the setback on Memorial Day, Will had maintained (at least publically) a cheerful optimism about his father's situation. That cheerfulness was replaced by acceptance, acceptance that there were some things even Willard Munger's innate doggedness could not change.

Munger Leaves Hospital, Returns to Duluth

State Rep. Willard Munger has returned to his West Duluth home...The legendary ...legislator was met by friends, family members and the sight of the St. Louis River...

Munger spent part of Thursday contemplating Clough Island as geese flapped by his kitchen window. But as he rests, a difficult decision will press on him: whether to continue the enervating chemotherapy that kept his liver cancer from advancing. His son is betting Munger will keep fighting...

"If I know my dad, he wants to make it through that next session of the legislature, and he thinks he can get back there," Will Munger, Jr. said. "He wants to live through that next session. I think that's what's keeping him alive..."

His son said Munger remains weakened but entertained a group of about 10 well-wishers who greeted him at his home on Indian Point. They included friends from politics and environmentalism, among them activist Alden Lind and Lake Superior Zoo Director Mike Janis...

(*Duluth News Tribune*, June 5, 1999.)

The accolades continued.

Wellstone Accepts National Wetlands Award for Munger by John Myers

U.S. Senator Paul Wellstone...accepted a prestigious national environmental award, only it wasn't his to keep. Wellstone was filling in for state Rep. Willard Munger, who is battling cancer at his home in Duluth.

As reported here in April, Munger was this year's winner of the Environmental Law Institute's "Outstanding Wetlands Program Development Award" for his work to protect Minnesota's dwindling wetlands.

Wellstone accepted the award on behalf of Munger, whom the Senator has befriended over the years...

"I've been saying this for years...I have four heroes in American politics," Wellstone told the *News-Tribune* in a telephone interview..."One of them is Eleanor Roosevelt. One is Dr. Martin Luther King. One is Bobby Kennedy. And one of them is Willard. I'm honored to receive this award on his behalf. For Willard, environmentalism is not some cause he advocates because it's trendy. He's been doing it a long time. He's imbued deeply with a connection to the land. He knows we're just stewards on this Earth. He's helped give form and give voice to this ethic in Minnesota more so than anybody in the state and more so than anybody in the country."

(*Duluth News Tribune*, June 20, 1999.)

Lake Superior Zoo Director Mike Janis and others also gathered to honor Munger's fifty years of legislative activism on behalf of the zoo.

Zoo Addition Named in Honor of Munger by **Ron Brochu**

Duluth's senior state legislator was honored...for his longtime support of the Duluth Zoo. Its new animal care center was named in honor of Rep. Willard Munger, who convinced legislators to fund the $1.3 million facility.

"This zoo would not be what it is today were it not for Willard Munger," said Duluth Mayor Gary Doty. "He had the vision to see that this could be more than a neighborhood zoo, but one that serves the whole region."

Munger, who is hospitalized...was represented at the ceremony by...his son, Will, and a daughter, Pat...Sen. Sam Solon, DFL-Duluth, said his long-time colleague and friend appreciates the honor.

"'He knows what's going on here today and he has that grin on his face... When you say the name Willard Munger, it is recognized anywhere in the country as far as the environment is concerned...'"

(*Budgeteer News*, June 27, 1999.)

As the end drew near, Munger seemed content to watch the slow progression of summer from the windows of his home overlooking the St. Louis River. It was likely of comfort to him, as he contemplated the waterway he'd saved, that old friends hadn't forgotten him.

June 30, 1999

Dear Willard:

I greatly admire your strength of will, attending the legislative session while undergoing treatment. You and Rudy are so much alike, not allowing illness to interfere with your duty to the people.

You have such an extraordinary record of accomplishment. Rudy always spoke of how honored he was to serve with you.

Please accept my sincere gratitude for your friendship and my best wishes to you and your family.

Most sincerely,

Lola Perpich

(Willard Munger Personal Collection.)

Mike Jaros describes his last visit with Munger.

"I saw him in St. Mary's hospice," Jaros recalls. "He was lying in bed with an oxygen tube in his nose. I asked, 'Willard, are you in pain?' He said, 'No.' I had to go to Washington for something. It was the last time I saw him. I didn't go to the memorial service. I didn't want to see Willard in a coffin. I didn't want to remember him like that. But I did go to the funeral."

Ann Glumac remembers visiting Munger at his Indian Point home near the end.

"He was in his bedroom. You know how it is visiting someone who's sick? His face was waxy and yellow. I was crying as I sat next to him. I asked, 'How are you doing?'" Glumac relates through tears. "He said, 'People keep telling me about Ann Glumac and how great she is.' Then he explained how he'd had Patsy order extra meat for the annual LCMR picnic because there was going to be a big crowd that year. I held his hand and I remember being struck by how elegantly tapered his fingers were. That's what I remember about my last visit with Willard."

A gathering of family and friends took place at Munger's home on Indian Point on the 4th of July. Munger was unable to leave his bed but he made an attempt to speak with and acknowledge everyone who stopped in.

Within days, Willard Munger returned to the hospice unit of St. Mary's Hospital in Duluth. He passed away on July 11, 1999, comforted by his son, his daughter and other family members.

CHAPTER 13

Epilogue

Governor Ventura announced that a special election would be held to replace Willard Munger in the Minnesota House. The primary was set for September 14.

Munger Jr. Making Bid for Father's House Seat

Twelve days after Rep. Willard Munger Sr.'s death, Willard 'Will' Munger, Jr. announced Friday he will run for the seat his dad held…Gov. Jesse Ventura…declared a special election to be held…for the seat.

Munger, 60, said people began encouraging him to run soon after his father died… Munger, Sr. was one election away from being the longest-serving lawmaker in any house in the state's 142 year history…

[Will] Munger said…he will attempt to carry on his father's legacy but has no delusions of ever being able to fill his shoes. "It would be a little presumptuous of me to go to St. Paul and say 'I'm the environmentalist…'"

(*Duluth News Tribune*, July 24, 1999.)

Others also filed for the office.

Six Candidates File to fill Munger Seat

The filing deadline passed Tuesday for District 7A seat for western Duluth, offering a couple of surprise non-candidates and the possibility of heated party races…Two prominent DFLers will compete for the party nomination in the primary, City Councilor Dale Swapinski, and Will Munger, Jr. son of the late lawmaker. Three candidates filed as Reform Party members…the Republicans enter the race unified behind an already-endorsed candidate…Allan Kehr…

DFL party leadership has decided to skip the endorsing process and let the primary decide its candidate. Swapinski…fired the first…salvo. "There may be those who look upon this race as a birthright. I do not…I look at this election as an opportunity to offer new ideas-ideas that reflect what all of you care about most: education, the economy and the environment."

Munger...runs the family's West Duluth motel...His campaign will focus on creating good-paying jobs, increasing health-care access to senior citizens and improving the public school system...

Two well-known possible candidates decided against filing...At-large City Councilor Yvonne Prettner Solon said she could not run because her health would not allow it. She was diagnosed this winter with breast cancer...Brad Bennett's decision not to run...came as a surprise...Bennett is involved in too many volunteer activities to run, he said...

(*Duluth News Tribune*, August 4, 1999.)

Will Munger, Jr.'s campaign proved problematic.

"Dave Bishop talked to me about it," Will recalls. "Even Judge Heaney called and offered his support. And Dad always told me, 'Someday, I want you to take my seat.' But I made a misjudgment. I hadn't been living back here (in West Duluth) long enough to run for office. I should have known that."

Mike Jaros agrees.

"Will didn't seek me out," Jaros recalls. "But I got together with him just before I went on a trip to Bosnia. I took him out to lunch and I told him, 'Don't do it just because folks expect you to.' But I shared with him a poll that showed that the numbers looked good for him. I tried to get Dale (Swapinski) not to run but he wouldn't listen to me. Somebody found out Will wasn't registered to vote in Duluth. They also found out his drivers' license listed his home address as being in Minneapolis. I don't know why you'd do that; run without changing your address. But Will did. Then he made it worse by trying to explain the address snafu in a letter he mailed out to voters. The letter only reinforced the negatives. It wasn't a very good idea."

The result was predictable. Will Munger lost in the DFL primary to Duluth City Councilor Dale Swapinski and Swapinski went on to win the general election. But that is not quite the end of the story.

In 2000, the boundaries of District 7B (Jaros' district) and 7A (Swapinski's district) were redrawn, merging 7A with Rep. Tom Huntley's district (6B in East Duluth). With the 2002 election looming, Jaros approached Swapinski about whether or not Swapinski was going to challenge the veteran DFLer.

"Dale told me he wouldn't do it," Jaros recalls. "He told me that I was his mentor and he wouldn't challenge me. I'd known him a long time. Willard and I helped get him elected to the city council."

Despite Swapinski's assurances, Jaros wasn't convinced.

"Dale said, a couple of times, 'You know, Mike, most of the new district is mine,'" Jaros recalls. "I sensed he wanted to run. So I told him, 'You come to the convention at Denfeld (the high school in West Duluth where the district DFL convention was held). If you win, I'll support you. If I win, you support me. He shook my hand. It meant that whoever was endorsed, that was the end of it. I got the endorsement. Then, just before filings closed, I learned that Dale had filed. When I confronted him about going back on his word, he claimed he was running as an 'Independent.' He said he'd been talked into it by 'Jesse's people.'

"I'm glad he ran as an Independent. Marcia Hales ran as a Republican. I won with fifty-five percent of the vote. Dale got twenty-five percent because he was attacking me, using misinformation. He said I wasn't a Progressive. I showed our debate audiences the high marks I'd gotten from the Sierra Club and other progressive groups. I got an 'A.' Swapinski got a 'D-plus.' He forgot the lesson that Willard had lived: a man's word is all he has."

"Jaros and Willard were really, really close," DFL Rep. Tom Rukavina notes. "You have to realize that I've sat next to Mike Jaros for every day of my political career. And because he speaks Croatian and I'm half Croatian, I've picked up a few swear words from him along the way," Rukavina says through a laugh. "Mike's the smartest guy in the Minnesota House and one of the kindest people I've ever known. He and Willard lived together in that tiny motel room at the Economy Lodge. That should tell you something."

In the end, Willard Munger's friend and protégé of many years succeeded Munger in office. And though Mike Jaros isn't Willard Munger's biological son, he is most assuredly Willard's political offspring. Jaros is but one of many elected officials who learned about honor, dignity and integrity from Willard Munger during the old man's legendary career.

Ann Glumac called Willard Munger "a great man." Labor leader Bernie Brommer hailed Munger as "an extraordinary ordinary Minnesotan." Others wrote and spoke platitudes about Willard Munger after his death. Some of those well-meaning commentators distorted Munger's legacy, examining his life through lenses clouded by their own agendas.

The truth is that Willard Munger was a man who had a penchant for mumbling; a man of unimposing physical stature whose loose jowls and craggy face clearly showed the wear of years; a man whose manner of dress harkened back to another era; a man of limited formal education. But he was determined, stubbornly so, and he was dedicated to principles that he'd been taught at a young age. He never lost sight of who he was or where he'd come from. He was a boy from Pockerbrush who listened to his grandfather's admonitions. His lifetime of public service was based upon the premise that a man or woman of ordinary intellect and means can make a difference. But as important as Willard Munger's legislative legacy may be, it is Munger's personal integrity, his willingness to reach across the aisle to work with political opponents, and his undefeatable belief in representative democracy which should be remembered and celebrated.

Citizen Legislator:
A Pictorial

Congressman Blatnik presents Munger with the 1967 Minnesota Conservation Award.

Signing state legislation regarding Voyageur's National Park.

Rep. Dave Battaglia and Willard.

Sen. Bob Lessard and Willard.

Arlene Lehto and Willard campaigning "Duluth style."

Speaker of the House Harry "Tex" Sieben being dressed down by Chairman Munger (also present: John Helland, Joe Begich, Dave Battaglia, and Shelly Polanski seated at the table).

Bill signing with Gov. Rudy Perpich (Munger is second from the left.
Future Congressman Bill Luther is second from the right).

Gov. Al Quie signs the 1979 Energy Bill.

Willard explaining the legislative process to Duluth school kids touring the Capitol.

Another Munger campaign.

Willard working the floor (Rep. Ted Winter seated).

Willard and Judge Gerald Heaney.

Willard pours coffee at the motel coffee shop.

John Herman, Willard, and Chuck Dayton.

The annual LCMR Picnic at Willard's Indian Point Home.

Dedication of the Willard Munger State Trail
(Willard and Gov. Perpich holding the sign).

Cong. Bruce Vento and Willard speaking at the Minnesota State Capitol on Earth Day, 1990.

Bill signing with Gov. Perpich (standing from left: Duluth Mayor John Fedo, Rep. Mike Jaros, Sen. Jim Gustafson, Willard, Sen. Sam Solon. seated: Frances Munger and Gov. Perpich).

Willard,
 Eleanor Roosevelt
 Dr. Martin Luther King Jr.
 Robert Kennedy
 Willard Munger

 These are my heroes
 in American history.
 Thanks for all your
 friendship and support—
              Paul
 Senator Paul Wellstone

Wellstone inscription inside Willard's copy of Professor Wellstone Goes to Washington.

Willard examins Miller Creek.

The Bee Keeper.

Frances and Willard Munger, Indian Point.

Willard's 80th birthday party.

Willard speaking out regarding the Prairie Island Nuclear Power Controversy.

Willard, Patsy Munger-Lehr, and Senator Paul Wellstone, Indian Point, LCMR Picnic.

Reps. Willard Munger, Tom Huntley, and Mike Jaros, Duluth's "DFL Team."

Willard and House Pages (Grandson Jeff Munger on right).

Willard and Gov. Elmer L. Andersen. Andersen has just received the 1998 Willard Munger Environmentalist of the Year Award.

The 1998 LCMR Canoe Trip (canoe in background is piloted by three of Willard's grandchildren; Martha Carlson, Julie Munger and David Lehr).

Willard relaxing at his Indian Point home on the St. Louis River.

Willard's return to the House after cancer surgery (left to right: John Munger, Julie Munger, Patsy Munger-Lehr, Will Munger, Jr. and Willard).

Sen. Paul Wellstone accepts the National Wetlands Award on behalf of Willard in Washington, D.C., in June 1999. Also in attendance from left to right; Betty Goihl, Patsy Munger-Lehr, and Cong. James Oberstar).

Appendix

Minnesota State Representative Willard Marcus Munger 1911 – 1999.

Remembering Willard

His eyes were blue. The blue of Minnesota lakes. The blue of a cloudless Minnesota sky. That's what one noticed immediately about Willard Marcus Munger. It was as if the Great Architect had created the legislator in the image of the Minnesota waters that sustained him; spiritually, physically and politically, for nine decades of life. That Willard lived to be an old man who accomplished much is a given. But he always insisted that there was more to do, and in the end, perhaps that's what allowed the cancer to take him. His tireless efforts to protect Minnesota's waters, soil, sky and natural habitats drained him to the point where he could fight no more.

> Obituary: Longest Serving State Legislator
>
> State Rep. Willard M. Munger, 88, of South 70th Ave. W., died Sunday, July 11, 1999, in St. Mary's Hospice...
>
> Munger served in the Minnesota House of Representatives from 1954 until his death.
>
> During his legislative tenure...Munger chaired the Environmental and Natural Resources Committee. One of the lasting legacies of his years as chair of that committee was the establishment of the Environmental Trust Fund. Additionally, Rep. Munger was a strong supporter of public education and human rights...
>
> (*Duluth News Tribune*, July 12, 1999.)

As the *Duluth News Tribune* noted in announcing the legislator's death, when one considers the length, depth and breadth of Willard Munger's public service, it's difficult to make comparisons.

> Most times when people say, "They don't make 'em like that anymore," the expression seems tired or overstated or somehow inappropriate. But it seems merely fitting when applied to Willard Munger...
>
> (*Duluth News Tribune*, July 12, 1999.)

Munger's legendary dry wit was in evidence, through the retelling of favorite "Willardisms" at his memorial and funeral. According to reports carried statewide by the *Duluth News Tribune*, Willard's wry humor had clearly left an impression.

> Two out-of-season election signs of trademark orange sat on the lawn of a West Duluth church…marking the location of the visitation for the late Rep. Willard Munger. "Experience works for Duluth" states the familiar political slogan of the 88-year-old DFLer, who was Minnesota's oldest sitting lawmaker…
>
> (*Duluth News Tribune*, July 13, 1999.)

During the funeral service the next day, Willard's son, Will Munger, Jr., called the signs to the attention of Pastor John Hanson, the presiding minister at Our Savior's ELCA Lutheran Church where the visitation and funeral were held.

"He's been a member of this church for 40-some years now and this is the first time a Lutheran minister allowed him to put a lawn sign on the front yard," Will Munger quipped.

The *News Tribune* also quoted Rep. Steve Trimble (DFL-St. Paul) recounting one of Trimble's favorite "Willardisms" during the visitation-memorial.

> A University of Minnesota researcher approached (Willard) requesting $100,000 to genetically alter fish to make it larger…Munger asked how big a fish they could get if she was given $200,000. A bit bigger, the woman replied. Then how about with $500,000, he asked. "How big a fish do you want?" the woman responded. "I want a fish so big I can use Republicans for bait," Munger said.
>
> (*Duluth News Tribune*, July 13, 1999.)

But Willard Munger was also a cagey politician who knew how to work the legislative system. When money for the Lake Superior Zoo, a favorite beneficiary of Munger's largesse, was tied up in a conference committee dispute at the end of a legislative session, Munger didn't yield to the strong will of the head of the committee, Mike Freeman, son of former governor and DFL icon, Orville Freeman.

"Mike…was loath to include the money. Munger told Mike: 'If you don't put in the money for the zoo, I'm going to turn you father's picture to the wall,'" recalled Judge Gerald Heaney. (Minneapolis Tribune, July 19, 1999)

Much of Munger's success came from simple persistence. When Munger was elected to the Minnesota House in 1954, one of the first bills he introduced was legislation to fund a study commission to evaluate the problem of water pollution. The bill failed to pass even though Munger was seeking only $25,000 towards the study. The matter was back for consideration again in 1957. That bill passed but it took nearly two decades before the legislature would fully adopt Munger's vision for regional treatment of sewage and solid waste.

> "He would start with the smallest step, be willing to take as many years as necessary to get what he wanted," said Rep. Tom Huntley, DFL-Duluth. "Most politicians think about next November. Willard was always looking a generation or two down the line…Once the bald eagle was near extinction, largely because of DDT," Huntley said. "Willard lived to see it taken off the endangered species list. He did it all with a high school education, but he was a visionary, ahead of his time…
>
> (*Minneapolis Star Tribune*, July 15, 1999.)

This work ethic, something Munger learned as a boy growing up in the hardscrabble world of family farming in Friberg Township near Fergus Falls in northwestern Minnesota, was the undergirding of his much-respected success over a political career that stretched from the Great Depression to the cusp of the New Millennium. Munger accomplished what he accomplished, not by dazzling oratory or political chicanery, but by invoking fundamental values learned as a Lutheran farm boy growing up in rural Minnesota.

> "He had a very practical streak," said Rep. Peggy Leppik (R-Golden Valley). "He was willing to work on legislation for a long time, work it over, listen to the opposition."
>
> (*Minneapolis Star Tribune*, July 15, 1999.)

Willard Munger's passing in 1999 received more attention from journalists than the death of any other state representative in Minnesota history.

Colleagues Remember Munger's Passion, Zeal, Humor
by Jim Snyder and Christopher Sprung

"[H]e never went with the tide, he knew what he needed to be done and he did it," Rep. Jean Wagenius, DFL-Minneapolis, said…"He was not of his generation. That's not where I saw him…He was looking out for the generations that were coming up…"

"He was like a Native American chief: When we make decisions, we should consider the seventh generation," said Rep. Alice Hausman, DFL-St. Paul. "That's never popular to do."

Rep. Betty McCollum (now Congresswoman McCollum), DFL-North St. Paul, equated Munger's fierceness to that of a "mother bear protecting her cubs."

"If he could out-vote you, out connive you or out muscle you, he'd do whatever he had to do to win. He was so devoted to the cause," said Sen. Sam Solon DFL-Duluth...

McCollum, who served on Munger's committee since 1993, observed: "He knew how to take baby steps so he could walk away with something."

Those baby steps led Munger to national recognition as one of the most successful defenders of environment in the nation...

But Hausman said Munger didn't dwell on the accomplishments of his 43 years in the legislature. "He never spent too much time talking about the successes of the past. The biggest issue for Willard was always the issue he hadn't dealt with."

Many colleagues said that Munger's loss will leave a void that won't easily be filled... "His legacy is obviously going to be very difficult to live up to...," said Rep. Dennis Ozment, a Rosemount Republican who took over Munger's committee chairmanship last session.

"We lost a piece of history going into the next millennium," McCollum said.

(www.legal-ledger.com/archive/713mung1.htm.)

The *Duluth News Tribune* provided in-depth coverage of Munger's death.

State Loses Devoted Environmentalist by Matt Nelson

[S]tate Sen. Sam Solon of Duluth recalled Munger—a colleague of 29 years—as a stalwart defender of his district and the environment.

"You've lost, in my opinion, the most devoted, dedicated man of conviction in one area, the environment," Solon said..."He had so much courage and conviction...Willard had a calling. I don't know who is going to carry the ball continuing the work..."

Neither does Dave Zentner, a Duluthian who served as National Director of the Izaak Walton League.

"There's not anybody in sight," Zentner said. "Hopefully all the environmental education that has happened since [the first] Earth Day will make more Willard Mungers, but right now it is bleak."

Longtime friend... Alden Lind of Duluth, agreed that finding a replacement for Munger will be hard. "He could ...see through nonsense in the blink of an eye," Lind said.

(*Duluth News Tribune*, July 12, 1999.)

The Twin Cities media didn't forget Munger at the time of his death.

State Legislator Willard Munger, Environmental Activist, Dies
by Larry Oakes and Terry Fledler

"He was an ardent environmentalist before there was Earth Day," said former state Sen. Gene Merriam. "He was quite courageous and visionary..."

"If you're going to pick the most influential person in terms of environmental protection in Minnesota over the past 50 years, his name would certainly come to mind," said Minneapolis lawyer Charles Dayton...

"People come and go from the legislature and burn out, but Willard never does," Mike Jaros, a fellow DFL legislator from Duluth said earlier this year. "He keeps going because he believes in what he's doing. He's a true statesman who has always worried more about others than himself..."

"He went through that whole Depression, Nonpartisan League, farmer unrest stuff," said Craig Grau, a political science professor at the University of Minnesota-Duluth...

"I was sent to the Capitol as a green activist thinking I knew something...and when I got there, I found out Willard had invented it," said Diane Jensen, who worked around Munger for 13 years as a lobbyist for Clean Water Action...

"The guy's got a mind that never stops," Alden Lind, well-known conservationist said...

"Willard has left a mark," Prof Grau said. "He's left the place much better than how he found it."

(*Minneapolis Star-Tribune*, July 12, 1999.)

Other articles reflected upon Munger's dignity.

'The Dean': An Eternal Legacy by Patrick Sweeney and Jim Caple

"[W]e all came to know him as the dean, or the father, of the legislature," said Rep. Loren Jennings, DFL-Harris, who sat next to Munger..."I listened when he talked...He told me to always respect the place...He said it's alright to disagree, but always keep your word and fight extremely hard for what you believe in..."

Jennings said that Munger, as chairman of the House Environment and Natural Resources Committee, was a stickler for decorum...Jennings, who seldom wears a necktie, recalled an incident almost 10 years ago when he went tieless to present a bill before Munger's committee.

"He said 'In my committee, men wear ties. We'll hear your bill next week when you dress properly,'" Jennings recalled. "It was a nice way; it was very fatherly..."

(*St. Paul Pioneer Press*, July 12, 1999.)

Family members from Otter Tail County added their recollections.

Relatives Remember Munger's Days of Youth

Local relatives remembered him as a man who loved to build things and respected the environment. His greatest quality was his honesty, says cousin and Friberg native Mary Holo.

"I always admired what he did in politics, but even more so for his honesty, which got him in trouble sometimes," she said. "You don't get politicians anymore who put honesty above popularity…"

Cousin Kenneth Clamby remembered Munger taking care of him as a boy…"He'd talk to me about a lot of political stuff, which I wasn't very interested in because I was too young to know about politics," Clamby said. "But then I'd always be able to go fishing with him. He was always thinking of other people…"

(*Fergus Falls Daily Journal,* July 12, 1999.)

The *Budgeteer News* also had its say.

Friends Recall Many Munger Stories by Dick Palmer

"He was always suspicious of PhD's," said Alden Lind, a college professor [with a PhD]…"He'd look at me and wonder whether I was authentic or not…We finally discovered we were pretty much on the same wave length…I think he knew I was arrogant as hell but that didn't bother him."

"One of the things I admired about Willard is that he had a true vision, and that I could trust him, and that's not something you can say about most politicians these days," said Debbie Ortman, an environmental activist and Hermantown city councilor…

Rep. Mary Murphy, DFL-Hermantown, said Munger was rarely critical of others…

While many people remember his work for the environment, [Murphy] remembers how much he did on behalf of UMD…He served on the Higher Education and Appropriations committees…and helped get the funding for a number of buildings at UMD…

State Sen. Bob Lessard, DFL-International Falls, often had disagreements with Munger when the two were each chairing their chamber's environmental committee. Lessard remembers …discussing…deformed frogs. Lessard told Munger how to hypnotize a frog…"I gave that demonstration to Willard one day…and Willard replied: 'Sen. Lessard, that's the only thing that I think you can give me lessons on that I don't already know.'"

(*Duluth Budgeteer News,* July 14, 1999)

Friend and long-time motel employee Heidi Lindberg has a more personal take on what Willard Munger stood for.

"I've never seen such an honest and compassionate man," Lindberg stresses. "People came to see him and he never turned anyone, regardless of their station in life, away. There was this older couple who lived out in Morgan Park (a Duluth neighborhood). They had used all their life savings to put their daughter's husband through medical school. Then when their daughter and the doctor needed a place to live, they deeded their duplex to them. The couple was supposed to have a life estate in the upstairs, a place to live until they died. But the doctor and their daughter divorced and the doctor stayed in the downstairs of the duplex. Because it had been deeded over to the doctor and the paperwork didn't specify their rights, the doctor started eviction proceedings against his former in-laws. They came to see Willard. He got the attorney general, Skip Humphrey, involved. But I saw the tears in Willard's eyes when he had to tell the people there was nothing that could be done for them. It just broke his heart."

Articles reporting the funeral service made it clear that the final celebration of Willard Munger's life was a major event.

Mourners Fondly Remember Willard Munger

Nearly 600 people gathered together at a small, spare, Lutheran church... to remember State Rep. Willard Munger...

The Duluth DFLer began his legislative career in 1954, and from the start made the environment his signature issue.

Over the years, he sponsored landmark legislation that would change the face of the state... He proposed legislation that launched the state's now-extensive system of bicycle trails, cleaned up the St. Louis River, created the program that protects the state's wild and scenic rivers...and established the Environmental and Natural Resources Trust Fund...

(Pat Lehr, Willard's daughter) said she realized the scope of her father's work when his illness became known..."He went for an MRI and the woman came up to me and said 'Thank Willard for the clean air and water...'"

His life in politics never brought him much material wealth, Harry Munger said. Upon being elected, Munger moved into Harry's Twin Cities home during legislative sessions...to save money. "The hours were too long and the salary too poor, but he wanted to be a legislator..."

(*Minneapolis Star-Tribune,* July 15, 1999.)

The *Duluth News Tribune* was not about to be outdone by its larger Twin Cities rivals.

Packed Church Pays Tribute to Munger by **John Myers**

The lunch served at Our Savior's Lutheran Church in West Duluth after Willard Munger's funeral…would have made the longtime legislator smile…

[I])t was served on hard china with real silverware.

"This is a Styrofoam-free environment," quipped Pastor John Hanson, during the service…

Munger, the long-time chairman of the House Environment and Natural Resources Committee, helped push curbside recycling, cleaner landfills and natural resource conservation…He also pushed for years to encourage less packaging and to eliminate containers that couldn't be reused or recycled…

Munger's brother Harry, noted in recollections during the service that the family was proud to be considered environmentalists—even if the label brought indignation from…others who favored progress at the expense of a diminished environment.

"Willard has left us physically, but his spirit reminds us that such things are wrong," Harry Munger said. "His spirit will tell us that we often don't realize what we have until it's gone. Look into the mirror…And say, 'I believe we should keep our air and water clean for myself and my children.' Say 'I'm an environmentalist'. It feels good to be an environmentalist. Say that and you'll see Willard's reflection winking back at you in the mirror."

Willard's daughter, Pat Lehr, noted her father had a sense for the environment…Once, when she had ordered a crew to cut down an ailing basswood tree from her father's yard while he was away, he came home and scolded her.

"He said, 'Pasty, I never thought you'd do that to me,'" Lehr said.

So, to make up for it, the Munger family passed out tree seedlings during Wednesday's funeral…

"Maybe 571 white pine seedlings will make up for one old basswood," Pat Lehr said.

The service ended with a teary-eyed rendition of "American the Beautiful". It's the song Munger fought for in the legislature to replace "The Star Spangled Banner", which Munger considered too warlike…

The service, which filled the church to capacity, was attended by many of the lawmakers and state officials with whom Munger helped shape the state's most important environmental legislation—including former Governor Elmer L. Andersen, whom Munger often praised as a visionary environmentalist…

Also attending were DFL Party heads and other politicians who worked with Munger or courted his support…including former Vice President Walter Mondale, former Hennepin County Attorney Mike Freeman, and former state Attorney General Warren Spannus.

> (*Duluth News Tribune* July 15, 1999. *Editor's Note: For an article regarding Willard's proposal to adopt "America the Beautiful" as the National Anthem, see the* Duluth News Tribune *dated April 8, 1983, p.1.*)

Betty Goihl, Munger's last committee administrator, remembers being asked to obtain the white pine seedlings handed out to mourners during the service.

"That was fitting," Goihl recalls, "since Willard always worked to preserve the white pine. It was his favorite tree."

Goihl also shares her personal view of Munger's contributions.

"He wasn't one to be on an ego trip," Goihl says, "like some of them. We heard a lot of Republican bills—he'd listen to the author and, if he thought the bill had merit, we'd hear it. That's not the way it's done anymore. Today, they don't reach across the aisle like that, like Willard did."

Jackie Rosholt, another of Munger's committee administrators, believes that Munger's major strength as a legislator was his ability to build support for compelling bills.

"He would support minor bills authored by others even when he really didn't like the bills. But he did it so as to count those authors as supporters when he needed them to pass legislation he felt strongly about."

"He was also very well liked," Rosholt adds. "And he was also a good actor. He rarely lost his temper but when he did, I always got the sense that it was to make a point, that it wasn't real."

Minnesota Governor Jesse Ventura wasn't in attendance at Munger's funeral service and his absence was duly noted.

Match to Munger!

On page 1B of the July 14 *Star Tribune*, I noticed a funeral of Willard Munger. In reading the accompanying article, I see that Munger was a "career politician." A quote in the article states: "His life in public office never brought him material wealth."

I scanned the photo to see if I could see the governor, who surely would attend the funeral of someone who gave so much of himself to the state of Minnesota. After all, the flags were flying at half mast at the governor's order.

Then I remembered…While Rep. Munger was being laid to rest, Jesse—

wearing rhinestone sunglasses and a feather boa—was prancing on stage next to a scantily clad woman and preparing to line his pockets with an undisclosed amount of cash. Isn't Jesse the one who is always accusing career politicians of lining their pockets? Match goes to Munger! Ventura counted out of the ring.

Gregory J. Roehl, Dayton

(*Minneapolis Star-Tribune*, July 19, 1999.)

Another citizen recalled his one and only "up close and personal" contact with Munger.

Remembering Mr. Environment

As a young reporter in the mid-1970s, I interviewed Rep. Willard Munger at his home on the St. Louis River. Munger, who died last week did the interview, and then spent 20 minutes talking about his pride and joy—several black walnut trees that he grew from seed, 150 miles north of where they should grow at all. He touched them and treated them like his children. It was the type of "hands on" care he exerted for the environment…

Those walnut trees are still here…Would that Willard were. Fortunately, he is a trunk from which many roots have sprouted, and will keep growing, well into the next century.

In Jean Giono's book, *The Man Who Planted Trees*, it says, "When I reflect that one man, armed only with his own physical and moral resources was able to cause this land of Canaan to spring from the wasteland, I am convinced that in spite of everything, humanity is admirable."

Willard Munger was evidence of that admirability.

Alan Searle, Vancouver, WA

(*Minneapolis Star-Tribune*, July 18, 1999. *Editor's Note: Alan Searle is the youngest son of Munger friend and legislative colleague, former Speaker of the House, Rod Searle.*)

Minneapolis Tribune Reporter Nick Coleman also profiled the public's reaction to Munger's passing.

For Generations to Come by Nick Coleman

[A]t a Tuesday evening "sharing"…his legislative secretary, Betty Goihl, proudly showed off a T-shirt with Munger's likeness that read: "Environmental Kook."

"He may have seemed an environmental kook, but he learned the environment better than anybody else and he knew what we should do," said State Rep. David Bishop of Rochester, who calls himself "Willard's

Republican friend." Pointing to Munger's ...years of service in the legislature, Bishop called Munger a "classic example of why term limits is a dumb idea..."

"He was an extraordinary ordinary Minnesotan," Bernie Brommer, president of the Minnesota AFL-CIO said...

(*Minneapolis Star-Tribune,* July 15, 1999.)

Congressman Bill Luther (DFL- Minneapolis) made certain that folks outside the state of Minnesota understood the impact of Munger's work.

In Memory of the Late Willard Munger

Mr. Luther:

Mr. Speaker although cancer took him from us at age 88, Willard Munger will not merely go down in history as the longest-serving member of the Minnesota House...Far more importantly, he will be remembered as "Mr. Environment."

In 1954, Willard Munger began his career in the Minnesota House where he remained a leading contributor to Minnesota's environmental legislation for four decades...Willard Munger truly exemplified what it means to be a public servant...

It was Willard Munger's vision of ensuring a pristine environment for future generations that fueled his passion. His legacy will endure for years to come, especially for those of us who have the opportunity to travel the almost 70 miles of biking trails stretching from Duluth to Hinckley, Minnesota, aptly named the "Willard Munger Trail."

As a friend and mentor to me and others, Willard...will be missed, but he will never be forgotten. His accomplishments are far too great. His life reminds all of us of the simple truth that anything is possible when one truly stands up for one's beliefs. Thank you, Mr. Environment, for making the world a better place...

Congressman Bill Luther

(*Congressional Record,* July 22, 1999)

Labor leader Alan Netland highlighted Munger's humility.

I recall driving him and Frances [Munger's second wife] to a banquet in Minneapolis...About 600 people were gathered for the Minnesota Alliance for Progressive Action's annual banquet to honor Willard...Willard talked about those who had inspired him and the work that still needed to be done. On the way back, he said he "didn't realize it was going to be such a big deal."

> That's the way Willard was. He plugged away at his work, never trying to
> make it into a big deal…
>
> *(Duluth News Tribune,* July 28, 1999.)

Retired 8th Circuit Court of Appeals Judge Gerald Heaney divides Willard Mung-er's historical significance into two areas: Munger's local political influence and his state-wide environmental impact.

"First, Willard was a man of immense integrity," the judge offers quietly. "Willard was tenacious. He had, above all else, an innate desire to help working people and the less fortunate. He wasn't always the most politic when trying to get things done. But that was Willard.

"In terms of his legacy, what Willard did was end decades upon decades of Conservative rule in the western part of Duluth. Before Willard, the Conservatives had controlled the 59th District for years. He ended that and it hasn't been in Republican hands since. Willard's impact upon the Liberal movement and his development of Farmer-Labor and DFL ideals need to be remembered.

"On a state-wide basis, his legacy is clearly the environmental legislation that he authored and passed."

EPA scientist Gary Glass considers Munger's treatment of people to be the legislator's most significant attribute.

"Alden Lind and I always considered Willard a good friend. Could have been better friends but Alden and I are PhDs and that put up some barriers to a stronger relationship with Willard. You lost ten points with Willard right off the bat if you were a PhD. But he was always," Glass recounts, "free with his time. I never saw him turn anyone down who needed to talk to him or who needed help. The way Willard saw it, every person had value. Willard truly believed he was there, in the House, to serve people. That's how he was all the time. And I saw him in some very intense situations."

Dr. Glass doesn't discount, however, Munger's work on behalf of the environment.

"All the environmental laws we have in Minnesota, most especially the Trust Fund, are his legacy. The Trust Fund is still there, to finance conservation and education and research. And then there is the state trail system. That's another long-lasting tribute to Willard's work."

Though Willard Munger's voice is no longer heard, the results of his actions live on. For ten years, Munger sponsored an annual canoe trip and picnic under the auspices of the Legislative Commission on Minnesota Resources (LCMR). The event did not disappear immediately upon his death.

Friends Remember Willard Munger on Annual Canoe Trip by Joan Farnam

A glorious day and a river with secrets capped the celebration of Rep. Willard Munger's life last weekend.

"We just had a wonderful time," said Patsy Munger-Lehr…as she talked about the 10th Annual Canoe Trip and Picnic that was held on the St. Louis River in honor of her father…

Every year for the past ten years, legislators, lobbyists, environmentalists, community members, and Munger's family and friends have clambered aboard canoes to spend the morning on the St. Louis River or one of its estuaries enjoying the fruits of Munger's clean-up efforts…

When Munger died…13 days before the canoe trip was scheduled, everyone wondered if it would be canceled…

"It was just a fitting thing to have the memorial canoe trip…" Lehr said…

"My feeling on the river was, 'Boy, the river looks healthy,'" said Debbie Ortman, an environmentalist…"But I think about the contaminated sediments on the bottom of the river. We all know that even though it looks clean, there's still a lot of toxic chemicals at the bottom…Willard is responsible for getting it to this point. Now the community and all of us that use and enjoy the river need to continue to fight…"

At one end of the yard, Steve Balach and Stanley Glumac were barbecuing lamb…

"We're doing this in memory of Willard," Glumac said. "We are bound and determined to do a good job."

Harry Munger and Eli Miletich did the honors of slicing meat for the guests…

It was a day of mixed emotions—joy to be outdoors with family and friends, sadness at losing a man deeply loved…

"When I left the house this morning, I was feeling misty-eyed," said Dave Zentner, former national president of the Izaak Walton League. "There was a lot of emotion."

For Lehr, who remembers her mother telling her… not to swim in the river…it was especially touching.

"It was so much fun to watch the canoes leave and then watch them come in here…it was fitting for that to be Dad's memorial canoe trip."

And will there be another next year?

"Who knows what they might do...It would be nice to continue it," she said. "If we do that, I'll be there, helping."

(*Duluth Budgeteer News*, July 28, 1999.)

Al Netland observes that Munger's picnics were more than mere political gatherings.

"I never canoed on one of those trips," Netland reflects, "but I made it out to a few of the parties after the trips at Willard's place on Indian Point. The gatherings were a reflection of a lifetime of work. There were not only DFLers there; you ran into state officials, local folks, politicians from both sides of the aisle, just a lot of different people who came together to celebrate Willard's work. And you could see, from his beautiful spot on the river, the evidence of his work. The clean river. The canoes coming in. The gatherings were a real symbol of how he dealt with people. Everyone who walked in the door of the coffee shop was equal. Big shot or not, he'd cook you the same breakfast. He'd ask, 'What's on your mind?' and it didn't matter if you were someone important or not. He listened to your views."

Netland also laments the loss of Munger's leadership.

"Bipartisanship has been destroyed," Netland observes. "Look what happened (in 2007) with the governor. Six Republicans who dared disagree with Pawlenty lost their leadership positions and are all likely to lose their elections next time around. All because they did what they thought was right. There are very few statesmen, at any level, left. Willard was that. He was a statesman."

Netland smiles when discussing Munger's longevity.

"Never," Netland asserts, "in a DFL convention did the issue of Willard's retirement ever get any serious discussion. You knew he was going to die in office. When asked about retirement, he'd always say, 'I just took out a thirty year mortgage (at the age of 74, to build his house on Indian Point). I have to work. I've got a lot of payments to make.'"

When asked to comment on Munger's strengths, weaknesses and his legacy, Alan Netland grows thoughtful.

"He was principled. He didn't compromise. He wasn't a hustler or a smoozer. He was also very compassionate. He understood people very well. And," Netland adds, "like I said before, he was loyal. You could disagree with Willard on a bill but agree on other things. He didn't discard friends easily. On the other hand, he really didn't give a damn what people thought of him. He might have got more done if he'd been more flexible, but that was Willard. He played hardball. That was his role."

Legislative committee administrator Ann Glumac shared her perceptions of Willard Munger in the *Senior Reporter.*

He Knew What He Believed in and Lived Accordingly by Ann Glumac

Willard Munger died a very lucky man…He loved well, was well-loved, by a large, close-knit family and a diverse—some would say odd—collection of friends. He was respected for his tireless public service…

In my opinion, however, Willard's greatest reward wasn't his environmental ethic; our natural world was in many respects simply the most obvious beneficiary of his commitment to principles and his dogged determination to fight for what he believed in…

Willard was a great man because his principles were as integral to his being as his backbone…he was successful because he pursued those principles with a mixture of humor, kindness and a keen insight into human behavior…

He and I didn't always agree… At those times, he said I reminded him of his grandmother because she was opinionated too and he liked strong women.

Though an unrepentant Liberal, he wasn't afraid to walk on common ground with Conservatives. The state's landmark ground water legislation was shepherded through the process by a team that included Willard, two other Democrats and two Republicans…They were farmers and city dwellers, diverse in their thinking on most issues, but they came together to protect the groundwater…Willard knew their beliefs weren't based upon party ideology or geographic concerns. He knew them by their commitment…

He knew the legislative process…and regularly surprised hot-shot strategists who thought they had the old guy licked. He rarely lost an issue in his committee; he could count votes better than anyone I've ever seen because he studied people's motivations and gauged their degree of support for their principles.

In the 20 years that I knew Willard, I loved him for his humanity, his humor, his high-pitched laugh, his stories and his dedication to family and friends. I also envied him for his steadfastness in fighting for principles in a world where black and white almost always blend to gray. I've been privileged to meet or work with many leaders and public figures, but Willard Munger is the only great man I have ever known.

(*Senior Reporter*, August, 1999.)

Former Minnesota Governor Arne Carlson's assessment of Munger's place in history is similarly succinct.

"His is a legacy of environmental care and protection," Carlson says. "He ze-roed in on one aspect of human endeavor, the environment, and broke ranks, not only with his own DFL caucus, which often wanted to use a 'go slow' approach, but also with his generation. He broke ranks to push for environmental protection. He unleashed the notion that the legislature could listen to and use new ideas in the areas of the environment and conservation. Minnesota had always had this heritage and image as being a place of vast resources available for commercial use. Willard's far-sighted legislative career put that in a new light by making Minnesota a leader, a state with high appeal because of its clean waters, natural beauty, and clean air. He gave the young voices their day in the sun and when I served with him (during the 1970s) it was a great time to be in government."

Retired State Representative Dave Battaglia (DFL-Two Harbors) recalls Munger's steadfastness.

"Everyone," Battaglia says, "(Minnesota Governors) Rudy Perpich, Al Quie—they all had tremendous respect for Willard. You know, he didn't have ordinary scraps—he was so pure in his opinions—they all knew if Willard was behind it, it was an honest bill. He was an exceptional legislator, that's no baloney. He took some tough stands but, because he was Willard Munger, he got away with them."

Works Cited

Print and Electronic Media:

Andersen, Elmer L. *A Man's Reach*. Edited by Lori Sturdevant. Minneapolis: University of Minnesota Press, 2000.

"Butler Shipyard Legacy." (videotape) Superior, Wisc.: Superior Federation of Labor, 1995.

Gieske, Millard L. *Minnesota Farmer Laborism: The Third-Party Alternative*. Minneapolis: University of Minnesota Press, 1979.

Haynes, John Earl. *Dubious Alliance: The Making of Minnesota's DFL Party*. Minneapolis: University of Minnesota Press, 1984.

Hudelson, Richard and Carl Ross. *By the Ore Docks: A Working People's History of Duluth*. Minneapolis: University of Minnesota Press, 2006.

"Interview with John Helland (2/4/2008)." MinnPost Web site. www.minnpost.com/mark-kneuzil/2008/02/04/763/meet_minnesotas_most_p (Accessed March 1, 2008.)

Keillor, Steven J. *Hjalmar Petersen of Minnesota: The Politics of Provincial Independence*. St. Paul: Minnesota Historical Society Press, 1967.

Kenny, Dave. *Minnesota Goes to War*. St. Paul: Minnesota Historical Society Press, 2005

Krause, Herbert. *Wind Without Rain*. City Unknown: The Bobbs-Merrill Company, 1939.

— — . *The Thresher*. City Unknown: The Bobbs-Merrill Company, 1946.

Lein, Linda Frances. *Hannah Kempfer: An Immigrant Girl*. Fergus Falls: Minnesota: Annika Publications, 2002.

Lofy, Bill. *Paul Wellstone: The Life of a Passionate Progressive*. Ann Arbor: University of Michigan Press, 2005.

Mayer, George. *The Political Career of Floyd B. Olson*. Minneapolis: University of Minnesota Press, 1951.

McGrath, Dennis J. and Dane Smith. *Professor Wellstone Goes to Washington*. Minneapolis: University of Minnesota Press, 1995.

McGrath, John S. and James J. Delmont. *Floyd B. Olson: Minnesota's Greatest Liberal Governor*. City and publisher unknown,1937.

Mitau, G. Theodore. *Politics in Minnesota*. Minneapolis: University of Minnesota Press, Second Edition, 1970.

"Minnesota Republican Party." Wikipedia en.wikipedia.org/wiki/Minnesota_Republican_Party (Accessed June 2, 2007.)

Munger, Mrs. R.L. (Transcribed interview of November 14, 1939) Fergus Falls, Minn.: The Otter Tail County Historical Society, 1939.

"Remembering Willard Munger." St. Paul Legal Ledger Capitol Report Web site. www.legal-ledger.com/archive/713mung1.htm (Accessed June 24, 2008.)

Robertson, Margaret. "Oral History of Willard Munger." Audio tape recorded November 23 and 24, 1987, and June 10, 1988. St. Paul: Minnesota Historical Society, 1988.

Searle, Rod. *Minnesota Standoff: The Politics of Deadlock.* Waseca: Alton Press, 1990.

"Thirtieth Anniversary Celebration." (videotape) City and producer unkown, 1984.

Weimer, Ray and Tom Bourne. "Workhorses of the Fleet." JacksJoint Web site from www.jacksjoint.com/wagl.htm (accessed March 1, 2007.)

Wellstone, Paul. *The Conscience of a Liberal: Reclaiming the Compassionate Agenda.* Minneapolis: University of Minnesota Press, 2001.

"Willard Munger 85th Birthday Celebration." (videotape) St. Paul, Minn.: House TV, 1996.

Yarnall, Paul. "The *Dearborn.*" NavSource Naval History Web site. www.navsource.org/archieves/12/08033.htm (Accessed April 20, 2007.)

Other materials, including campaign literature and unattributed newspaper clippings, from them private collections of Harry Munger, Sr., and Willard Munger.

Newspapers & Magazines:

American Guardian
Askov American
Congressional Record
County Press
Delano Eagle
Duluth Budgeteer
Duluth Budgeteer News
Duluth Herald
Duluth News Tribune
Farm-Labor Leader
Farmer-Labor Progressive
Farmer's Union Herald
Fergus Falls Daily Journal
International Falls Daily Journal
Labor World
Minneapolis Journal
Minneapolis Star

Minneapolis Star Tribune
Minnesota Leader
Minnesota Out-of-Doors
Minnesota Session Weekly
Minnesota Voice
Northern Minnesota Leader
Northern Sportsmen's News
Pelican Rapids Press
Pick and Axe
Proctor Journal
Senior Reporter
Session Weekly
St. Paul Dispatch
St. Paul Pioneer Press
Time Magazine
Twin Ports People

About the Author

Mark Munger is a lifelong resident of northeastern Minnesota. Mark, his wife René, and their four sons live on the banks of the wild and scenic Cloquet River north of Duluth. When not writing, Mark enjoys hunting, fishing, skiing, chasing kids, and working as a District Court Judge.

*The author on the shoreline of Brule Lake in the BWCA—
the wilderness Willard Munger fought to protect.*

Other Works by the Author from Cloquet River Press

The Legacy (2nd Edition)
Set against the backdrops of WWII Yugoslavia and present-day Minnesota, this debut novel combines elements of military history, romance, thriller, and mystery. Rated 3 1/2 daggers out of 4 by The Mystery Review Quarterly.
Trade Paperback • ISBN: 0972005080 • $20.00 USA • $25.00 CAN

River Stories (Sorry—out of print!)
A collection of essays describing life in northern Minnesota, with a strong emphasis on the out-of-doors, the rearing of children and the environment. A mixture of humor and thought–provoking prose gleaned from the author's columns in The Hermantown Star.
Trade Paperback • ISBN: 0972005013 • $15.00 USA • $20.00 CAN

Ordinary Lives (2nd Edition)
Creative fiction from one of northern Minnesota's newest writers, these stories touch upon all the elements of the human condition and leave the reader asking for more.
Trade Paperback • ISBN: 9780979217517 • $20.00 USA • $25.00 CAN

Pigs: a Trial Lawyer's Story
A story of a young trial attorney, a giant corporation, marital infidelity, moral conflict and choices made, *Pigs* takes place against the backdrop of western Minnesota's beautiful Smoky Hills. Reviewers compare this tale with Grisham's best.
Trade Paperback • ISBN: 097200503X • $20.00 USA • $25.00 CAN

Doc the Bunny and Other Short Tales
A sequel to *River Stories*, this book is packed with over three dozen humorous, touching essays about life lived large in northeastern Minnesota. Munger demonstrates once again why he is fast becoming recognized as a regional writer of finely crafted fiction and creative non-fiction.
Trade Paperback • ISBN: 0972005072 • $15.00 USA • $20.00 CAN

Suomalaiset: People of the Marsh
A dockworker is found hanging from a rope in a city park. How is his death tied to the turbulence of the times? A masterful novel of compelling history and emotion, Suomalaiset has been hailed by reviewers as a "must read."
Trade Paperback • ISBN: 0972005064 • $20.00 USA • $25.00 CAN

Esther's Race
A story of an African American registered nurse who confronts race, religion, and tragedy in her quest for love, this novel is set against the stark and vivid beauty of Wisconsin's Apostle Islands, the pastoral landscape of Central Iowa, and the steel and glass of Minneapolis. A great read soon to be a favorite of book clubs across America.
Trade Paperback • ISBN: 9780972005098 • $20.00 USA • $25.00 CAN

Other Books from Cloquet River Press

Back of Beyond: A Memoir from the North Woods
The debut effort from Minnesota author Susanne Kobe Schuler, this memoir of building and working at a family style Minnesota resort during the 1940s is a sure-fire winner. Come, meet the Kobe family, their friends, their relatives, the guests of the resort and join them for a trip back into a kinder, gentler time set in the deep woods of northeastern Minnesota.
Trade Paperback • ISBN: 9780979217500 • $15.00 USA • $25.00 CAN

Visit us on the web at: www.cloquetriverpress.com